The Essential Piece

Living Out Luke 14:26 in Everyday Life

The Essential Piece

Living Out Luke 14:26 in Everyday Life

Timothy Williams

Printed in the United States of America.

Packaged by WinePress Publishing, PO Box 428, Enumclaw, WA 98022. The views expressed or implied in this work do not necessarily reflect those of WinePress Publishing. Ultimate design, content, and editorial accuracy of this work is the responsibility of the author.

ISBN 1-57921-293-X
Library of Congress Catalog Card Number: 00-101323

Dedicated to those willing to embrace a Christianity with a curse.

If anyone does not love the Lord—a curse be on him. Come, O Lord! (1 Cor. 16:22)

I certainly feel different . . . wonderfully different. For me this anointed teaching on the cross and dying to self has put everything in its place. It's like I've had a jigsaw puzzle, unfinished on the floor, missing one piece. This basic, central, foundational message was missing from my life. I had made mental assent to this theology but had no revelation of its hidden power. I finally feel like I'm on the right road, that there is hope for me to change.

I knew I needed changing (as did most of my friends . . . !), but I did not know how . . . I tried to change myself, prayed to God about it, had various Bible reading plans, was serious about daily devotions, etc., but none of that changed me.

But this message has had the power to change me . . . ! Through it, God revealed to me the purpose of the cross . . . it is an instrument that He wants to use in my life to annihilate self, pride, justification, self-righteousness, the need to be right, or even to have rights. Now as I read the Bible, it seems that this message is screaming out from every page . . . !

—N.S. from Japan

Contents

FOREWORD

It might seem a little unusual for a wife to write the foreword to her husband's book. I feel, however, the reader must understand that the words written here are real and have brought life to our marriage of twenty-five years. By sharing my side of the story first, I hope to open your heart to the miracle of hating our lives for Christ.

Married at nineteen and eighteen, Tim and I had a shaky beginning. "Nine out of ten marriages resulting from an unwanted pregnancy end within the first year," announced newscaster Walter Cronkite. We heard those words during the first week of our marriage. At the time I knew we had no guarantees that we would not end up becoming a statistic.

Having been raised in the church, I felt the shame of getting pregnant out of wedlock. I knew the biblical commitment of marriage and set out in my own effort to fulfill it. Yet as the pressures mounted—bills, college, and a new baby—the love we thought we had for each other grew into bitterness and hatred.

Determined to make our marriage work, I read every book on becoming the "total woman." Fortunately Tim's search for answers led him to study the Bible, and we started attending the college campus church. Our personal relationships with God grew steadily, and I found myself clinging to my husband more. I became content with the new life we had found in Christ.

That contentment was soon shaken by Tim's questioning, "Did you know that the Bible says that I am to hate you?"

"Hate me? Just when you are beginning to act like you love me?" I demanded. Tim gently read Luke 14:26, "If anyone comes to me and does not hate his father and mother, his wife and children, his brothers and sisters—yes, even his own life—he cannot be my disciple."

That day I saw a love for God in my husband I knew I did not have. And I have to admit, it took me a while to understand and accept what Tim was trying to teach me. From that moment, however, Tim and I made a commitment to live out Luke 14:26. Any love we would have for each other or our children would come from God, the source of perfect love. Any other love would be self-seeking and motivated by human emotions, and we would ask God to purify such love.

As Tim and I strived to keep this vow, we discovered the one essential element that was missing in our lives—the cross of Christ. Jesus said, "*If anyone would come after me, he must deny himself and take up his cross and follow me* (Mark 8:34). The only way we could possibly learn to hate each other in a biblical sense was to deny ourselves and take up the cross that God had planned for us. The word hate is offensive, and very few understand what Jesus meant by using this term. But Paul refused to remove the offense of the cross, and many were offended by Jesus. So the more Tim and I surrendered to the cross in our lives and did not shy from its offense, the deeper our love for God and each other grew.

Our marriage had many obstacles to overcome. Setting priorities of God first and family second was not enough. Making promises we could not keep only left us feeling guilty and frustrated. When Tim and I quit trying to improve our marriage and set out to hate each other according to Luke 14:26, we discovered our love growing deeper each day. Realizing and accepting that God is, indeed, a jealous god who demands all our devotion freed us to allow His love to flow through us.

As you read this book, I challenge you to allow Jesus' words to penetrate your heart. Yes, Jesus meant it when He said we were to hate. He was serious when He said we must love God with *all* our heart, soul, and mind. How can there be room for anything else?

Jesus spoke the truth when He said we will face many sufferings as we pick up His cross. This book is a result of Tim allowing that cross to crucify self in his life and learning to hate all other loves. As you read, it is our hope that you will begin to understand the depth of God's love and find that you too cannot settle for anything less. We pray that you, too, will discover the joy of finding the essential piece.

Carla Williams

1

THE TERM *Hate*

The man who loves his life will lose it, while the man who hates his life in this world will keep it for eternal life. (John 12:25)

A man must hate where he lives that he might settle in heaven.

A man must hate where he walks that he might be guided by God.

A man must hate his recreation that he might enjoy God's Sabbath rest.

A man must hate his comfort that he might labor for God.

A man must hate his love for his wife to have holy power to love her as Jesus loves the church.

A man must hate his children that he might give them up as a gift to God.

A man must hate his father and mother that we all might be brothers.

A man must hate his words that he might have the bread of life.

A man must hate his doctrine that he might gain the living Truth.

A man must hate his thoughts that he might have the mind of Christ.
A man must hate his opinions that he might speak words of wisdom.
A man must hate his idea of right and wrong that he might do God's will.
A man must hate money that he might make others rich.
A man must hate his strength that he might be empowered by the Holy Spirit.
A man must hate his kindness to know how and when to love.
A man must hate his righteousness that he might grow in the holiness of God.
A man must hate his own life that he might receive the mystery of God.

Mentioned Only Once

Hating for Jesus is *not* a matter of going up to someone and slapping him in the face. Hating for Jesus is *not* the worldly kind of hate in which you seek to destroy someone else. No, it is something much more difficult to live. Hating for Jesus stands at the very heart of Jesus' teaching and carries with it just as much power as when God said, "Let there be light."

> And God said, "Let there be light," and there was light. (Gen. 1:3)

We read "Let there be light" only once in Scripture, but what power lies behind those words! The darkness was displaced, and man can see the handiwork of God's might. "Jesus wept" is written in the Bible only one time, and yet the shortest sentence in Scripture moves everyone who reads those words. Jews gathered around the tomb of Lazarus were moved to say, "See how he loved him!" For Jesus' dead friend, the words, "Lazarus, come out!" meant the difference between life and death and the difference between a mere body rotting in a tomb and God glorified. Written only once in

Scripture, those words brought Lazarus to life and caused his enemies to seek to kill him again.

Just because Scripture mentions a concept only once does not mean the importance of the teaching is diminished. A hinge on a door, though small, allows the entire door to swing open freely. The same is true with Jesus' use of the word "hate" in John 12:25 and Luke 14:26. Once the Holy Spirit gains enough access to our hearts to enlighten us about this type of hating, a door will swing open to something large and grand. A whole new room filled with the treasures of God will open up to us. Your name is written only once in the *Book of Life*. Do you really want to stick with the idea that things seldom mentioned in Scripture are unimportant?

Let no man exclude himself with the excuse, "It is mentioned only once in Scripture" from what Jesus had to say. Jesus comes to each of us, like He came to Lazarus, and calls us by name to come and "hate" for His sake. For each of us, godly hatred is the difference between rotting in the tomb or removing the grave clothes from our lives. Most things that hinder our walk with Jesus can be traced right back to our failure to live Luke 14:26.

What will it be for us? A universe filled with darkness or the light of God displacing the darkness in our lives? Jesus calls us out of the noisy crowd of "Christians" to come and hate in Him.

> Large crowds were traveling with Jesus, and turning to them he said: "If anyone comes to me and does not hate his father and mother, his wife and children, his brothers and sisters—yes, even his own life—he cannot be my disciple." (Luke 14:25–26)

Hating for Jesus *is* a salvation issue. It separates the sheep from the goats and the foolish virgins from the wise. Jesus clearly states that those who will not hate their lives in this world forfeit eternal life. If a man does not have this hate, he is not a Christian and is hell bound for damnation.

> The man who loves his life will lose it, while the man who hates his life in this world will keep it for eternal life. (John 12:25)

Ashamed of the Word

> If anyone is ashamed of me and my words, the Son of Man will be ashamed of him when he comes in his glory and in the glory of the Father and of the holy angels. (Luke 9:26)

One never sees "Hating for Jesus" T-shirts in Christian bookstores. You can't buy a sweatshirt that has printed on the front, "I hate my mother . . .", then on the back, ". . . and my father, brothers, and sisters for Jesus." The church is too embarrassed and ashamed of the cross today to wear such an item. Indeed when was the last time you heard two brothers in your church discussing how much they hated each other in Christ? No doubt you would have been horrified at such a conversation and embarrassed that they discussed such a thing in front of immature believers or unbelievers.

Over many years of preaching, I have encountered person after person who could not even believe that Jesus said we must hate. Although they claim to have been Christians for many years, they have never heard of such a thing. I recall sharing Luke 14:26 with an elderly woman. She quickly flipped to the front of her Bible to make sure it was the "Holy Bible." How is it possible a passage that speaks to the very heart of what it means to be a Christian is so rejected? How is it possible a passage that every person should consider before he or she becomes a Christian is skimmed over? How is the salvation call of Jesus so easily overlooked? The church has come to worship its steps to salvation rather than God's plan. We reduce the salvation call to a short tract rather than make contact with a living God. We are idolaters of our altar calls because we refuse to hate our wisdom and understanding of Scripture.

The reason for this idolatry is that men have become increasingly ashamed of the cross of Christ, the essential piece of the gospel. All the worldly preaching about the cross has emptied it of power.[1] The majority of current hymns, books, and music are self-centered and lifeless because we no longer treasure hating for Jesus. Old books and publications have been sanitized to avoid the rough edges of the cross. I know of one church that physically covers the cross in the church building they rent so as not to offend Jewish visitors.[2] Such is the low state of the church. Indeed commentary after commentary writes off these passages as shallow and inoffensive. We are told to interpret them to mean only that by comparison to other loves, our love for God must be the greatest. The offense of the cross has been removed and quickly explained away. Some theologians claim that Jesus chose the wrong word, that He should have never said *hate*.

Consider well that Jesus did not do what we are doing in this book now. He never explained to the crowds what He meant. They had no choice but to take Christ literally because He never explained Himself. Just picture yourself walking along with Jesus, enjoying the miracles and free food, talking about loving God and your neighbor, and then, out of the blue, He says that you must hate, and He just keeps on walking. To say that you would become uncomfortable about this man Jesus would be an understatement.

When was the last time your pastor or your church left folks hanging on this issue? When was the last time you shared the gospel with someone and left them in their confusion to wrestle it out before God? See what I mean? We do not want to be misunderstood. We are concerned about only ourselves and, therefore, remove the offense of the cross from our messages and lives. We want Jesus to be easy on our flesh, so we make it easy for others to accept Christ. We have been idolaters of the worst kind; we have made Jesus into our own image. All because we reject what Jesus had to say about hating. Yet, like the birth of light in a dark universe, the word *hate* bursts forth to challenge all darkness.

Make no mistake about it; the Bible uses the word *hate*. It is the Greek word *miseo,* which is also used in Matt. 10:22, 24:10, and other passages. Matt. 10:22 speaks of the whole world hating Christians, while Matt. 24:10 warns of Christians who fall away and hate each other. The Greek word used in those passages is the same one used in Luke 14:26 and John 12:25. The literal meaning of the word is *to hate or detest* in the fullest sense. It is a very strong and old verb that speaks with much emotion. Even the commentaries speak of not watering it down "till the point is gone." In other words, *hate* is such a strong word that one naturally recoils from its demands and seeks to weaken it, but not too much, the commentaries warn. Yet it is the same word used when Jesus talks about loving those who hate you, your enemies.

Because men feel uncomfortable with the word *hate*, they resort to explanations or qualifications. We do not desire to get stuck in the quicksand of what the Greek says. Our purpose is to run to the cross so we might understand why Jesus used the word. How ironic that the Greeks look for wisdom, and we run to the Greek to avoid the pain of the cross.

> Jews demand miraculous signs and Greeks look for wisdom, but we preach Christ crucified: a stumbling block to Jews and foolishness to Gentiles, but to those whom God has called, both Jews and Greeks, Christ the power of God and the wisdom of God. (1 Cor. 1:22–24)

Let us run to the cross where Jesus is crucified, leaving behind miracles and the Greek, so that we might partake of the power and wisdom of God. Let us first meditate on God's law before looking at His miracles.[3] After all, the vast majority has either looked to miracles or to definitions of the Greek, rather than to the living God. Let us take hold of a cross with the power to crucify us—a cross that feels uncomfortable and accepts the unsettling words of Jesus.

The word *hate* is in the most accurate of Bible translations. Personally, I like the Spanish Bible, which translates *hate* in Luke 14:26 as *utterly abhor*. It drives home the emphasis of Jesus' words. For those still in doubt and wanting a way out, below is a small sampling of some translations, including the Greek.

> If anyone comes to me and does not utterly abhor his father and mother, wife and children, brothers and sisters, even his own life, he cannot be a disciple of mine. (Luke 14:26 SPANISH)

> If anyone comes to me and does not hate his father and mother, his wife and children, his brothers and sisters—yes, even his own life—he cannot be my disciple. (Luke 14:26 NIV)

If any man come to me, and hate not his father, and mother, and wife, and children, and brethren, and sisters, yea, and his own life also, he cannot be my disciple. (Luke 14:26 KJV)

If anyone comes to Me and does not hate his father and mother, wife and children, brothers and sisters, yes, and his own life also, he cannot be My disciple. (Luke 14:26 NKJV)

Whoever comes to me and does not hate father and mother, wife and children, brothers and sisters, yes, and even life itself, cannot be my disciple. (Luke 14:26 NRSV)

If anyone comes to Me, and does not hate his own father and mother and wife and children and brothers and sisters, yes, and even his own life, he cannot be My disciple. (Luke 14:26 NASB)

ei:G1487 ei_tis:G1536 . erchomai:G2064 . . . miseo:G3404 . . pater:G3962 . meter:G3384 . gune:G1135 . teknon:G5043 . adelphos:G80 . adelphe:G79 eti:G2089 . . heautou:G1438 psuche:G5590 kai:G2532 . ou:G3756 - dunamai:G1410 . . mathetes:G3101. (Luke 14:26 HG)

If anyone comes to Me, and does not hate his own father and mother and wife and children and brothers and sisters, yes, and even his own life, he cannot be My disciple. (Luke 14:26 NNAS)

If any man come to me, and shall not hate his own father and mother, and wife, and children, and brothers, and sisters, yea, and his own life too, he cannot be my disciple. (Luke 14:26 DNT)

If any one doth come unto me, and doth not hate his own father, and mother, and wife, and children, and brothers, and sisters, and yet even his own life, he is not able to be my disciple. (Luke 14:26 YLT)

When determining the worthiness and accuracy of one of the many new translations hitting the market each year, use this passage as a test. If the translator(s) are willing to fudge on this

Greek word, they are willing to change anything that does not suit their flesh. That is how powerful and clear this word *hate* is in the Greek.

Any translation that does not live up to this definition is not worthy of your attention. After all, the concept of hating one's own life can be seen throughout the pages of Scripture from Genesis to Revelation. From Adam, who did not hate his wife and listened to her words; to Cain, who did not hate his righteousness; to Noah, who hated his own life and worked many years on the ark; to Abraham, who hated his own nation and people; all the way to the last saints mentioned in Revelation, who do not shrink from death, the idea of hating your own life resounds. Those who say that Jesus mentioned hating only once do not understand the slightest thing about the cross of Christ or what the Bible is about—avoid them.

> I urge you, brothers, to watch out for those who cause divisions and put obstacles in your way that are contrary to the teaching you have learned. Keep away from them. (Rom. 16:17)

Hate That We Might Love

Jesus said the greatest commandment is this:

> Love the Lord your God with all your heart and with all your soul and with all your mind and with all your strength. (Mark 12:30)

We must love God with *all. All* means 100 percent! However, to those who say that Luke 14:26 and John 12:25 mean only that we love God more than all other things, *all* means only 51 percent. They love God more than all other loves; therefore, they allow a small majority to suffice. It does not matter to them that worshipping God while still having other loves constitutes idolatry. Indeed this is why Scripture says, "Do not make any gods to be alongside me" (Exod. 20:23a). Those who love God only more than other loves have many gods alongside Him. God directly warned against idolatry throughout the Old Testament and the message continues in the New Testament: "Dear children, keep yourselves from idols" (1 John 5:21).

The greatest commandment does not read, "Love the Lord your God with a majority of your mind, strength, and soul." The commandment says *all,* which means 100 percent, not 51 percent. Only in the church is 51 percent considered 100 percent. In no way

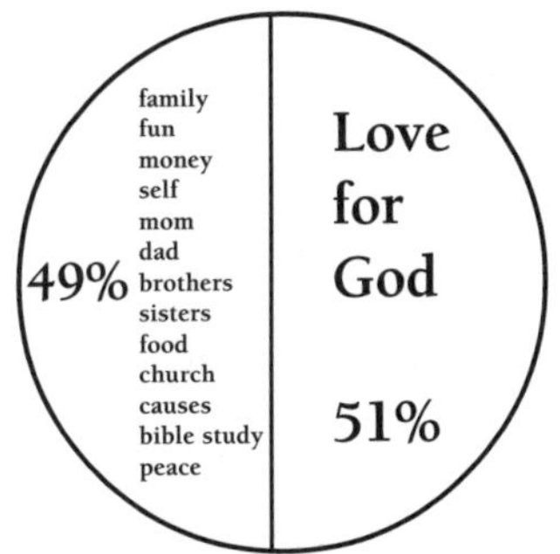

does the commandment imply that we should love God merely more than half or more in comparison with other loves.

The circle above represents our life filled with many loves. In order for us to grow to love God with all, we must push out every other love. Otherwise we cannot possibly come to a place where we can say that we love God as He commands.

Luke 14 and John 12 are merely the *how to* of the greatest commandment. Jesus has told us how we can grow in our love for God and other men. He has given us the key that will allow the Holy Spirit to work the greatest of all commandments in us.

A man or woman unwilling to grow in this hatred will never know how to love God or his "neighbor as himself" by the power of the Holy Spirit. If you want to be filled with God's love, then all other loves must go. Yet the only way we can possibly let go of our loves is to learn to hate them.

Love

God's love manifested through us.

Think of it this way: God is love, pure love, holy love, and the source of love. God's love is the only real love in the universe. When man separated himself from God, he lost the ability to love. Once someone returns to God with a surrendered heart, then God will begin to pour His love through that person, "for love comes from God."

> Dear friends, let us love one another, for love comes from God. Everyone who loves has been born of God and knows God. (1 John 4:7)

When we continue to allow sin and self to remain in us, we cannot really love others. Though we might be in the church doing good deeds, if we do not hate, then we are unable to love. It might appear to others to be love, but it is not God's love in us; it is our prideful self doing its deceitful work. God is the only source of the river of love that wells up in us to eternal life.[4] There is no better way a man can love than to love another with God's love. There is no greater holy worship than to love God with the love He pours in us. We are to love as Jesus loved, and Jesus loved others only with the love God willed and worked through Him.[5]

My wife discovered this concept while working with physically and mentally handicapped children. She seemed to have a God-given gift to love these people. Yet as her walk with the Lord grew deeper, she realized the shallowness of her love. She gave out hugs to these kids in order to feel special herself. Once she died to her selfish motives, God could pour out tremendous amounts of love through her.

When John writes that he knows and relies on God's love, he means more than just resting in the fact that God loves him. John also means that he has God's love in him and he *knows* God's love. John knew that daily he needed to rely on God's love rather than his own ability and wisdom to love others.

> And so we know and rely on the love God has for us. God is love. Whoever lives in love lives in God, and God in him. (1 John 4:16)

Think of a prism. It cannot produce light, but when light passes through it, we see a rainbow. In the same way, when God's love passes through us, everyone can see His love. The cleaner the prism, the better the rainbow shines. If the prism is cloudy or has faults in it, the effect is not as strong. The Bible says that God is pure light, an "unapproachable light, whom no one has seen or can see."[6] Pure light in the universe cannot be seen; no scientist has ever seen pure light. Indeed when you look out in the morning you are not looking at sunlight. When you look at the tree in your front yard you see what the light reveals, but not the light itself. If the tree were not there, you would not see light. In fact without the tree everything would be complete blackness. Astronauts traveling in space are amazed at the blackness and darkness because there is so little in space to reflect the light. In the same way, if we do not let God's light shine through us, men cannot see His love. If He had said, "Let there be light," before creating the heaven and the earth, the darkness would have remained.

Jesus said that "apart from" Him we could do "nothing." That means we cannot even love others or God without Him giving us the power. This is why John said that those who rely on God's love live in God and God in them. Those who have hated their loves in the fullest sense of the word have room for God to fill them with Himself and thus His love. To have God in us is to have love, for "God is love" (1 John 4:16). Don't believe this? Then just look at the world's attempt to love.

The reason for godly hatred is both logical and reasonable. Our love, even at its best, is tainted with self and sin. Scripture says our love is "worthless."

> All have turned away, they have together become worthless; there is no one who does good, not even one. (Rom. 3:12)

Until we see with spiritual eyes just how true it is that Grandma is equal to a mass murderer, we will never understand this teaching. Love apart from the power of Jesus is a vile and contemptuous thing. No man is able to show love apart from God. The kindest act performed by Grandma or anyone else, if not done in God's power, is one of cruelty.

> A righteous man cares for the needs of his animal, but the kindest acts of the wicked are cruel. (Prov. 12:10)

Unfortunately, we view acts of love by men with sinful, darkened eyes. In our minds, our actions appear full of wisdom, kindness, and love. Until we see how corrupt our love really is, we will never be willing to hate our acts of kindness. Oh, for a church that would have hate in their fellowship. Rather than simply socializing, they might come to really love one another according to God's will.

Again, our love is totally corrupt, for we love others with selfish motives and darkened wisdom. We have children because it makes us happy and fulfilled. We discipline our children because we want them to look good to others or ourselves. A wife will tell her husband she loves him so she can hear the words back. We give to the poor, sing hymns, serve, or help others because it makes us feel better. We give ourselves to a cause because it makes us feel spiritual and righteous. In everything we do, in every way we love, it always comes back to us and our selfishness. God's love is the only totally selfless love. We must rely on it if we dare hope to become pure enough to see God.

> Blessed are the pure in heart, for they will see God. (Matt. 5:8)

If you desire this purity and love, then you must prepare yourself to be taught by God to hate. For only those who hate, reject, utterly abhor, and push aside their love(s) as Jesus commands will have room for God's pure love. Like empty branches connected to the vine, the more empty you become, the more fruit you produce.[7] If you are unwilling to hate your own life, then you will be "thrown away" and left to slowly "wither" spiritually.

> Remain in me, and I will remain in you. No branch can bear fruit by itself; it must remain in the vine. Neither can you bear fruit unless you remain in me. I am the vine; you are the branches. If a man remains in me and I in him, he will bear much fruit; apart from me you can do nothing. If anyone does not remain in me, he is like a branch that is thrown away and withers; such branches are picked up, thrown into the fire and burned. (John 15:4–6)

If you remain in Jesus and He remains in you, then you will be filled with the fruit of God's love. Only those who find it a joy to hate remain empty enough to be filled with the life of God. They become empty enough because they willfully push out everything in the circle of their little lives, including themselves, so that God might be all in them. He who is willing to hate will be given power to love God with all his heart, mind, and strength.

Hate: A Quick Definition

Taking all scriptures into account, a crude and quick definition of what Jesus said can be put this way:

> *Hate*: To put forth all the energy a man has to oppose, reject, abhor, ignore, and refuse that which stands in the way of God's will and power. To do so to the point that only God's love and life remain. To empty one's self to the point that all that remains in the person is God.

We know when Jesus said we must hate that He did not mean *by comparison*. Such definitions make no sense. When you state that you hate chocolate ice cream, does that mean only when compared to vanilla? No. When we say that we hate chocolate ice cream, there is no comparison. If you hate your neighbor, does this mean that you just love him less compared to how much you love your friends? No. It means that even if you did not have any friends, you would still hate him.

Think back to when you were in school. When you hated someone, you really hated that person. You went out of your way to slander him, to avoid him, to rejoice when harm came to him. If any of your friends dared to say anything good about that person, you were quick to refute it. *Hate* is an absolute word that implies a great deal of energy, power, and effort. If Jesus had meant *by comparison*, He would have said, "dislike," not "hate."

Just try a comparison love with your wife. Tell her that compared to other women she is the one you love more. Try telling her that she has the majority of your love. Likewise, try telling Jesus that by comparison you will give Him the majority of your love. Just try telling Jesus that compared to all other husbands you could choose, He won out. In fact, tell Jesus that someone was a close second and see how He feels about marrying you. You have been promised to Jesus and He does not want anyone who fluctuates between a 49 percent and a 51 percent love for Him. In fact, Jesus only wants those who love Him, not with a 99.9 percent depth of love, but with a 100 percent love. Jesus is not interested in mere virgins; He wants only "*pure* virgin[s]" (emphasis added). There is a big difference between the two.[8]

> I am jealous for you with a godly jealousy. I promised you to one husband, to Christ, so that I might present you as a pure virgin to him. (2 Cor. 11:2)

Now do you understand why Jesus used the word *hate*? We are to be a people going out of our way to abolish any other loves and affections. After all, our God is a jealous God.

> For the Lord your God is a consuming fire, a jealous God. (Deut. 4:24)

God is not selfish; He is worthy. Nothing else is like God. No one else is worthy of even a fraction of our love or affection. He is above all else worthy of all of our love.

> Whenever the living creatures give glory, honor and thanks to him who sits on the throne and who lives for ever and ever, the twenty-four elders fall down before him who sits on the throne, and worship him who lives for ever and ever. They lay their crowns before the throne and say: "You are worthy, our Lord and God, to receive glory and honor and power, for you created all things, and by your will they were created and have their being." (Rev. 4:9–11)

Because Christians (true Christians) are the only ones who know He is worthy, they are willing to hate for Jesus. They do not have to be convinced to hate, no more than the man who finds a treasure in a field must be convinced to sell all in order to get the treasure. Such Christians know and grow in the knowledge that

God is worthy and can see both the wisdom and the need to grow in hating for Jesus. Indeed it is their joy! Let us, with God's permission, begin to look at this joy in Jesus. If all of this is confusing and hard to understand, then plead with God to soften your heart and open your mind. A hard heart and dull mind will keep you from understanding this teaching.

> . . . for they had not understood about the loaves; their hearts were hardened. (Mark 6:52)

> Then he opened their minds so they could understand the Scriptures. (Luke 24:45)

2

Large Crowds

Let us begin where Jesus did. He began with the large crowds traveling with him. Travelers next to Jesus heard His voice, fellowshipped with Him, experienced His miracles, and even gave up much to follow Him. They were travelers, like so many in the church today, who could swear that Jesus was very close to them. However, they were only unsaved travelers, and Jesus warned them about it. The difference between a traveler and someone saved is hate.

> Large crowds were traveling with Jesus, and turning to them he said . . . (Luke 14:25)

Today in churches everywhere, large crowds claim to be Christians; however, they are merely travelers on the road with Jesus. It was to such travelers that Jesus turned to say something very important. He spelled out exactly what it meant to be saved. Today, Jesus stops and turns to whole churches and individuals traveling with Him to explain what it means to claim Christianity. What wicked times we live in when so many church leaders and Christians no longer turn to those seeking Jesus and tell them they must hate. Instead they promote sloppy salvation altar calls and easy one, two, three, ask-Jesus-in-your-heart salvation prayers. If we dare to hope in the salvation of Jesus, we must pass from being a mere traveler and, I quote, become a "disciple."

Tower and Terms

The transition from a traveler among the crowd to a saved disciple must not be taken lightly. Jesus says you must first "sit down" and "estimate the cost." You must consider if you are honestly willing to go on to the finish because only completed deeds are acceptable in His sight.[1] In fact, Jesus will tell this group of travelers twice that they must "sit down" and "count the cost." Jesus made it clear that in the same way we must consider well our decision before accepting Him as Lord and Savior.

In each biblical account of someone accepting Jesus as Savior, the process of counting the cost took place. Even the noble thief on the cross next to Jesus saw and understood what the cost would be for him. Whenever we decide to build something, we estimate the cost to see if we can finish. How much more should this be true when it comes to matters of Christ?

> Suppose one of you wants to build a tower. Will he not first sit down and estimate the cost to see if he has enough money to complete it? For if he lays the foundation and is not able to finish it, everyone who sees it will ridicule him, saying, "This fellow began to build and was not able to finish." (Luke 14:28-30)

Again, this is not an idle or minor concept. Let every man be fearful to say he understands and agrees with this teaching, since to truly understand drives one to sit down and count the cost. I know plenty who did sit down to estimate the cost but later quit building anyway.

When you share the gospel with others, do you quickly try to save them? Or do you, as Jesus directs, tell them to consider very carefully their decision? Do you explain to them in great detail and show by your life that they must hate for Jesus' sake, or do you offer the peace of Jesus without first explaining the terms of that peace?

> Or suppose a king is about to go to war against another king. Will he not first sit down and consider whether he is able with ten thousand men to oppose the one coming against him with twenty thousand? If he is not able, he will send a delegation while the other is still a long way off and will ask for terms of peace. (Luke 14:31–32)

While they remain a long way off from being saved, do you get others to ask about the terms of peace? Every person must examine if they are humble and willing to give up all. For Jesus will take and demand all, make no mistake about that!

When I first began following the Lord, no one told me I must give up everything. Yet, I felt God urging me to drop out of college. Don't misunderstand me. God may call someone to go to college. For me, however, the calling was clear. At the time, my wife and I were active in a campus ministry. You can imagine the reaction of our leaders. It took me over a year and a half to finally let go. In fact, I went to the admissions office one day, but chickened out and went home. The next day I became determined to obey God's call and dropped out. The admissions attendant said, "Too bad you didn't do this yesterday—you would have received a full refund." While the money was unimportant, God has ways of making His point clear. In fact, by the time God finally got through to me, I needed only a very small number of credits to graduate.

How utterly wicked not to explain and teach others how to hate. How unloving it is not to explain to a searching person the cost of following Jesus. We become false teachers when we do not specifically tell someone that before they begin to follow Christ they must "give up everything."

> In the same way, any of you who does not give up everything he has cannot be my disciple. (Luke 14:33)

Anyone who has not given up everything cannot rightly claim to belong to Jesus. The twelve apostles, when first called, left all to follow, and we must do the same. Please, please understand this is not the goal of the Christian life—this *is* the starting point. Everything that we have been looking at must happen *before* we become disciples of Jesus. To obey the call of Jesus means we must immediately leave everything and follow Him.

> So they pulled their boats up on shore, left everything and followed him. (Luke 5:11)

In Scripture, those willing to give up all for Christ readily acknowledged this to be true.

> Peter said to him, "We have left everything to follow you!" (Mark 10:28)

This is no abstract, futuristic kind of idea, but the starting point of the Christian life. No wonder a man must sit down and estimate the cost before claiming salvation. I had one man tell me that among all the Christians he knew, not one had given up everything. I was so dumbfounded I could not reply. For how does one convince another that not only is it possible to give up all, it should be the norm among Christians? Most just sneer and say, "Well, *you* own things," not realizing that one can still give up all and be given tools by Jesus for His work.[2] Of course at this point, many falsely claim they gave up all, yet the cross cannot be found. Such people are merely mockers of the truth—an abominable group.

> They claim to know God, but by their actions they deny him. They are detestable, disobedient and unfit for doing anything good. (Titus 1:16)

Without this kind of deep conviction from God, our gospel calls and offers of salvation remain less than worthless.[3]

Sadly the shallow conviction adopted today demonstrates the vast majority of gospel calls. Even in the back of many Bibles is a form to sign for salvation with no mention of counting the cost. We cannot even begin to count the churches where salvation is a matter of just saying a simple prayer. No one is sent home to first count the cost. At the first sign of conviction, we lead others to the altar. Remember, the travelers had been with Jesus for some time, watching, listening, and contemplating. Yet Jesus told them to sit down and count the cost.

Sunday after Sunday, pastors ask anyone desiring salvation to come forward. Over time the gospel calls have been made easier and easier. Little doubt this is part of what Jesus meant when He predicted that the "love of most would grow cold."[4] In Jesus' day one had to count the cost, but through the ages it has been reduced to a bowed head and programmed prayer. In Jesus' day believers had to think carefully about becoming a disciple. Now we tell searching people the words to say and save them on the spot. We never tell anyone to stay in his or her seat or go home and consider this decision. Even those who do say, "Consider what you are about to do," remain powerless because they never mention hating for Jesus. The offense of the cross has been removed and therefore emptied of its power. Oh, let each church come before the Lord and hate their salvation calls. Let each Christian hear what the Spirit has to say about all this teaching and they will no longer offer cheap grace and prefab salvation calls.

> Salt is good, but if it loses its saltiness, how can it be made salty again? It is fit neither for the soil nor for the manure pile; it is thrown out. He who has ears to hear, let him hear. (Luke 14:34–35)

How many salvation messages could be "thrown out" because hating for Jesus is considered a minor thing, a matter of comparison? Again, without this issue of hating for Jesus presented clearly, our salvation calls are not "fit" for the "soil" or the "manure pile."

We are fast approaching a time when many will lose their saltiness through the current false revival taking place. If we expect to survive, then we must increase our saltiness and learn to hate in

Jesus before it is too late. If we refuse to be taught by the Holy Spirit in this matter, then it will be impossible for us to be made salty again. If you are willing to be taught by the Spirit, do not let go. You get only one shot at it. Many will oppose you and tell you to tone it down. If you give way to them, you become as corrupt as those you preached against. Remember well that only those who hate their lives will find eternal life. Those who hate are the only ones saved in Jesus, for they have passed from being mere travelers to being disciples.

> The man who loves his life will lose it, while the man who hates his life in this world will keep it for eternal life. (John 12:25)

Void Factor

Many people, when confronted with an uncomfortable Scripture, resort to using the void factor. Satan appealed to Jesus in this way and hoped that Jesus would use such a tactic. The void factor goes something like this: someone quotes a Scripture you do not agree with, so you retort with one that voids the original verse. As a result, no agreement can be reached and no Scripture obeyed. In other words, it gets the person who disagreed off the hook.

For instance, someone quotes Luke 14:26 emphasizing that one must "hate his father and mother," so the other person reaches for the void Scripture. They might say, "But the Bible says that we are to *honor* our father and mother." Therefore they have voided out the first passage in question. It is a classic pharisaic move to nullify the uncomfortable scriptures that go against our ideas and beliefs. In other words, they remove the offense of the cross from Scripture. Jesus put it this way:

> Thus you nullify the word of God by your tradition that you have handed down. (Mark 7:13)

We nullify what Jesus says about hating father and mother for the sake of family traditions, our flesh, and own peace. The solution is not to get a balanced view of Scripture, but to obtain the mind of Christ. In other words, we must let God work His wisdom and will in us with *all* Scripture, not just the ones we like. This requires much fear and trembling to make sure we hate enough so God's will might be worked in our lives. Where you do not find this "fear and trembling," you will not find God's will being worked in a Christian's life. It is that simple.

> Therefore, my dear friends, as you have always obeyed—not only in my presence, but now much more in my absence—continue to work out your salvation with fear and trembling, for it is God who works in you to will and to act according to his good purpose. (Phil. 2:12–13)

When we walk in fear and trembling, the Holy Spirit can then work both the hating of your father and mother and the honoring of them. If you follow Jesus, you will be led to both hate and honor your parents at the same time and obey all Scripture by the power of His Spirit. This is one of the mysteries of the cross in a man's life.

> To them God has chosen to make known among the Gentiles the glorious riches of this mystery, which is Christ in you, the hope of glory. (Col. 1:27)

3

Following Jesus

Joy Set Before Us

> . . . and follow me cannot be my disciple. (Luke 14:27)

If we seek to apply this teaching without following Jesus, we will end up in utter deception. For it is only as we follow Jesus that self can be exposed. At one meal we may be eating "heads of grain" while at the next meal we may be sitting down at a banquet.[1] We may be sleeping in our bed one night and the very next night, resting our heads on a rock. All of these inconveniences to the flesh bring out who we really are and how far we have to grow in the Lord.

While being considered for my first pastoral position, my wife and I were required to spend a night or two at several members' homes. At one place we were given a thin mattress that was flat on the floor. The home was a trailer on a Midwest pig farm. It was a hot, humid midsummer night, and the flies swarmed around. Needless to say, it was not comfortable. We spent other evenings in different surroundings and never knew what to expect. Indeed over many years of following Jesus, we have slept in many different places and under many different conditions. Some we could rejoice in; others revealed our sin.

To this day the running joke around our house is what sleeping schedule I am on. Sometimes for months at a time God will have me working all night long, while at other times I am up during the day. Yet many times it is a combination of the two. God puts me on the schedule necessary to complete whatever work needs to be done. Many situations have arisen, and God's timing always amazes us. The important thing is that in following Jesus as to when I sleep I must "beat my body" and "make it my slave."[2] You can imagine how much self and sin has come out in following Jesus in this.

We must let God guide us in all things, even down to what address to go to.

> The Lord told him, "Go to the house of Judas on Straight Street" (Acts 9:11)

So many times I run ahead of what the Lord wants to do. I try to push the Lord along to make Him move a bit faster. As I have sought to stay in step with Jesus this sin has been made clear many times.[3] One incident I remember well happened while traveling through Kansas. When I drive, I keep on going no matter what the weather is like. Such an attitude makes me useless to the Lord. In extremely flat Kansas, you can see rain or snow from many miles away. Though I saw a tremendous rainstorm ahead, I was still going to drive through, even with five children with me. We stopped at a fast food place to eat and a man walked up behind me and very firmly said, "Do not go on." I turned, told my wife, and then turned back around to thank the man, but he was gone. We knew God was telling us to stop, and we ended up getting the last motel room in town. While the next time God may want me to press on through the storm, the lesson was in place. I must listen and wait for God in all things.

If we seek to follow Jesus without hating our own lives, we will inherit despair and self-pity. If we just pick up a cross without following Him, we will become self-righteous, thinking we have endured much for God. A Christian must deny all areas of his life if he is to be a disciple. Therefore, we turn our attention to Jesus, the only one who can perfect this kind of faith. Let us "fix our eyes on Jesus" as the Scripture below says to do, so we may see how He lived all of this.

> Let us fix our eyes on Jesus, the author and perfecter of our faith, who for the joy set before him endured the cross, scorning its shame, and sat down at the right hand of the throne of God. (Heb. 12:2)

Before we proceed we must pause and notice that the joy of the crucified life is *before* us just as it was with Jesus. This is not to say that God does not give us joy. He gave Jesus joy.[4] But so much of the joy we hope for is before us—not here and now. Consider the rock from which you are being cut.[5] We must endure the cross if we want the resurrected life. Crucifixion is a slow process and demands much suffering before we get a taste of the joy. Just like Jesus, we must wait for days for God to resurrect us from our sin. We must be thoroughly convinced of our weakness and sin of self. The body must wait in helplessness in the tomb for God's power to give it new life. When it is dark in the tomb and you think there is no power to this message, just wait; He will come to you. He will do what you are powerless to do. He will give you the power to be obedient and to say, "Thy will be done," with joy abounding in your heart. It is the waiting on God that puts us to the test, but as Peter promises, in "due time" God will bless us.

> Humble yourselves, therefore, under God's mighty hand, that he may lift you up in due time. (1 Pet. 5:6)

Do not become discouraged, and do not seek out a softer message. Just understand that God has much joy waiting for you.

This is why Jesus warned us that we would have "trouble" in this world, but to "take heart" in the fact that He overcame the world.[6] He has overcome our sin, so let us then press on toward the cross to die to self.

How Jesus Lived

There is no better way to bring all of this together than to look at how Jesus lived while on earth. We will now examine how He lived the Christian life and how this hating was revealed in Him. We will in our own lives see how Jesus could always say, "Thy will be done."

> He went away again a second time and prayed, saying, "My Father, if this cannot pass away unless I drink it, Thy will be done." (Matt. 26:42 NASB)

Jesus did not come just to deliver us from hell, nor did He come to start the Christian religion. Jesus came to do much, much more. He came to bring the good news that we can deny ourselves and gain the resurrected life. Jesus died on the cross to deliver us from the self that sends us to hell. Because He lived a crucified life, Jesus could secure the means by which we might be saved. Now we too can crucify our sinful selves and put them to death by His power. Once self is put to death and we no longer live, Jesus can give us Himself to live in us so that we might have rich fellowship with God.

Everything we will examine here is the rest in God that we are warned not to miss in Hebrews.[7] Jesus walked always in the rest of God, and we too are to enter that rest if we desire salvation. Indeed it is "in repentance and rest" we find salvation.[8] Resting means we surrender in all things to "Thy will be done" and are dependent on only His strength, righteousness, and obedience. We are to rest in what God has done, in His provision for obedience and forgiveness. Salvation is just this: saying and living "Thy will be done" in everything. Unless we find it our joy and freedom to live just as Jesus did, in total surrender to the will of the Father, we have no part in His salvation. Jesus is clear on this, and this is what He came to bring.

> Whoever claims to live in him must walk as Jesus did. (1 John 2:6)

We will be looking at exactly how Jesus walked and how we should also walk with God. In doing so, we will also see how each of us must walk if we are to be saved. Walking as Jesus did determines whether you are a sheep or a goat. Either you live the Christian life, or God lives the Christian life through you. In other words, a goat lives the Christian life while a sheep allows God to live it through him. The sad fact, however, is that most are mockers who have learned well to confuse the two. We live in a time when false preachers teach others how to look, talk and act like sheep, while all along they are really goats. Notice the key words Jesus used in the following passage:

> Not everyone who says to me, "Lord, Lord," will enter the kingdom of heaven, but only he who does the will of my Father *who is in heaven*. Many will say to me on that day, "Lord, Lord, did we not prophesy in your name, and in your name drive out demons and perform many miracles?" Then I will tell them plainly, "I never knew you. Away from me, you evildoers!" (Matt. 7:21–23, emphasis added)

Notice that in verse 21 it all comes down to true fellowship with God and to which voice you listen to. Jesus tells us plainly that only those who do the "will of the Father *who is in heaven*" will be saved (emphasis added). Watch out for preachers who talk of "godly principles," for there is no such thing. There is only God who gives life to all things. We are not to just obey the Bible with its ink on pages. Rather just as Jesus received direct fellowship from heaven every hour of every day, so must we. Certainly everything should be in line with the Bible, but this requires surrender and giving up of one's life that most will not tolerate. Paul states clearly that his ministry was not one of principles, but of the living God.

> You show that you are a letter from Christ, the result of our ministry, written not with ink but with the Spirit of the living God, not on tablets of stone but on tablets of human hearts. (2 Cor. 3:3)

Most people live a Christian life, with all of its morals, good deeds, and acts of worship, but fail to surrender all to God. They don't really love the good news. Oh, they will boast that they drive out demons, prophesy, and do all kinds of ministry work for the Lord; however, they have no real fellowship with God. It is not the voice of the Lord they hear, but the mocker's voice that mimics spiritual things. They merely tack on the name *Jesus* to their activities, morals, and emotions. This is a tough one because such a deceived person is unaware of his condition. In order to avoid this you need to pray diligently until you surrender. Jesus proved this when He prayed again and again—to the point of sweating blood. Jesus wrestled in prayer until it was His joy to say, "Thy will be done." A joy that would lead only to a cross filled with pain. Is this what you pray and surrender to?

That is why Jesus says in Matthew 7:23 that one day He will tell false Christians "plainly" that they are not saved. Such people will fall into this condition because they hate the good news that calls for the total loss of one's self. They refuse to lose the self with all its pleasures, wants, desires, church dogma, comforts, goals, morals, ideals, hopes, and dreams. Jesus will tell them plainly, "I did not live in you."

The Mount of Olives

> Then Jesus went with his disciples to a place called Gethsemane, and he said to them, "Sit here while I go over there and pray." (Matt. 26:36)

Let us go with Jesus into this garden of decision and sit there with Him. For there we also wrestle with the choice of following our will or His. On the Mount of Olives we decide to live for God or to allow God to live through us.

Now, bear in mind that Jesus could only succeed at this point because every day of His life He had entered this garden in small ways. Let no believer ever think that they gave all to God on the day they found salvation. To give all of your life to God means a lifetime vow, not a one-time surrender.

Jesus was baptized and began His walk with God, but it was in the garden that all of His surrendering bore fruit. If Jesus had not been walking hourly with an attitude of "Thy will be done" reigning in His life, He would have failed at this moment. Likewise, the day you became a Christian was only the beginning. Like Jesus, you must often go to the garden of self-denial, so that when the day of reckoning comes you will bear fruit for God.[9] Remember that those who do not produce fruit are cut off and thrown into the fires of hell.[10] Indeed you must pick up a cross and deny self "daily" in order to gain victory[11] on that day Jesus brings salvation.[12] This is why the Scripture says:

> Therefore, my brothers, be all the more eager to make your calling and election sure. For if you do these things, you will never fall, and you will receive a rich welcome into the eternal kingdom of our Lord and Savior Jesus Christ. (2 Pet. 1:10–11)

What fruit grows on your Mount of Olives? What has your struggling produced? Have you wrestled unto joyful submission or wrestled against the will of God? Have you confused the kicking against the "goads" with battling unto submission?[13] Are you deceived like Saul, before he became *Paul*, that you are doing God's will, but in reality you are fighting against Jesus? Do you just agree with the things of God without any obedience or transformation? After all, God does not need your agreement; He needs your surrender. For everyone in hell agrees that they are guilty but are unable to submit to God's will. Even if they were let out of hell, though they might now agree with God, they would never be able to joyfully surrender to God's heavenly plan for them. They would never submit to the crucifying of self and the losing of their life for God. Do not let the nobility of your ministry or work deceive you—self must be put to death.

> All a man's ways seem right to him, but the Lord weighs the heart. (Prov. 21:2)

What is in your garden? Is it the rotten fruit of self-will, self-planning, and selfishness or the sweetness of a life lost in the will of God? Don't be taken in by your own fruit, which you have concluded is good for *you*, because you think you understand the gospel. The fruit Eve saw in the garden—the fruit of self-will and desire—caused sin to enter into the world. The fruit was good for food and desirable for gaining wisdom but was really the fruit of sin. Likewise our churches seem to have an abundance of wisdom that appears to be good fruit but in reality is the fruit of rebellion. The bottom line is if the fruit appears good for you, it is sin. This is why Paul says that whatever benefited him he considered loss. For whenever we benefit, we lose a little more of Jesus. My constant prayer before the Lord is not that He give me what I want, no matter how much I ask, but that His heart be my heart. For I know that whatever is to my profit is garbage and keeps me from deeper fellowship with Him whom I love.

> But whatever was to my profit I now consider loss for the sake of Christ. What is more, I consider everything a loss compared to the surpassing greatness of knowing Christ Jesus my Lord, for whose sake I have lost all things. I consider them rubbish, that I may gain Christ. (Phil. 3:7–8)

For Jesus came to kill whatever is personally good for you that you might have His life. When Adam and Eve ate of the fruit that was good for them, pleasing to them, they died. We must decide which garden to go into each day, the Garden of Eden or the Garden of Gethsemane. Both gardens have good fruit, but one is good for *you* and the other is the good fruit of God.

> When the woman saw that the fruit of the tree was good for food and pleasing to the eye, and also desirable for gaining wisdom, she took some and ate it. She also gave some to her husband, who was with her, and he ate it. (Gen. 3:6)

Enter your garden to see what sprouts there, and do not judge it good unless God has so instructed you. Let us, with the help of God, see what we have planted. We will do that, as God leads, by watching how Jesus walked. For if Jesus had to pray to the point of sweating blood and being overwhelmed to death, why should we think we will escape turmoil? If He who perfectly surrendered in everything, had to be comforted with a visitation from an angel, how can we rest assured of our Christian walk and surrender to God? Therefore, prepare your heart and soul for some fear and trembling.

> Serve the Lord with fear and rejoice with trembling. (Ps. 2:11)

Through God

Most individuals labeling themselves *Christian* hate the light of God. They do not like its searching and revealing powers. If they allowed the light a brief moment to search their lives, it would show that their religious acts were not of God, but only in the *name* of God. All of their prayers, ministry works, answered prayers, teaching, serving, and Bible study would be shown as self-effort and sin. In short, they do all of these things in their own power, by their own wisdom, and for themselves. It was for benefit of self that they served God. As a result, they hate the light of God because it reveals that their religious works were not done *through* God but *for* God.

> Everyone who does evil hates the light, and will not come into the light for fear that his deeds will be exposed. But whoever lives by the truth comes into the light, so that it may be seen plainly that what he has done has been done through God. (John 3:20–21)

The good news is that you can do nothing that God does not show you to do. This is not Christianity of your own design, but one where the living God works all things in you. This surrender of all, minute by minute, is true salvation. Giving up your life and allowing Jesus to live through you shows you are a true child of God.

> This is how God showed his love among us: He sent his one and only Son into the world that we might live through him. (1 John 4:9)

It is not enough that you live your life saying, "OK, it's done in Jesus' name." In truth, you have no life, no personal time, nothing of your own power that allows you to live for Jesus. Jesus will not give His throne to another. No man, no matter how religious, can have Jesus and himself on the throne at the same time. No wonder so many hate the light.

This revelation shocks the system, but those who have good and noble hearts accept its truth and humble themselves. They persevere and endure the pain of the Garden of Gethsemane and the cross until they get a portion of the resurrected life. Others hate the light and turn away in anger and often persecute those who lead lives of self-denial. This is living in the truth; this is sound doctrine—the coming to God to lose all of self, so as we die then Jesus can live in us.

We need to have the heart of Jesus that doesn't avoid the cross that leads to death. We must tell God it is for this very reason we come to Him—to be put to death on the cross. Notice below that Jesus says those who choose to serve Him must "follow" where He goes. And where did Jesus go? He went to a place of trouble, a place where the cross would deal with the sin and flesh of man. Let us tell the Lord that we want to be a "kernel of wheat" that "falls to the ground and dies." Pray and tell the Lord this, and He will begin the work in you. Let us, however, fully realize that when God begins to do this it will "trouble" us a great deal. No one goes easily to the cross to die. Even Peter at the end of his life would be led to a place he "did not want to go."[14]

> Jesus replied, "The hour has come for the Son of Man to be glorified. I tell you the truth, unless a kernel of wheat falls to the ground and dies, it remains only a single seed. But if it dies, it produces many seeds. The man who loves his life will lose it, while the man who hates his life in this world will keep it for eternal life. Whoever serves me must follow me; and where I am, my servant also will be. My Father will honor the one who serves me. Now my heart is troubled, and what shall I say? 'Father, save me from this hour'? No, it was for this very reason I came to this hour." (John 12:23–27)

A dead man has no plans, hopes, or desires, and this should be true with Christians. Only when we die can we be saved, and only to the degree we have died can we say we are alive in Christ. You would not go up to a dead body laying in a casket and ask, "Say, what do you think about this?" or "Hey, any idea what this Scripture means and how we should live it?" If you saw a person talking to a corpse for spiritual counsel, you would think they were crazy. Rightly so. No sane person talks to a dead man. You too must die and seek nothing from that dead old man. In short, stop giving yourself good advice, and make sure anyone offering advice does not talk from his or her dead sinful self. Self is so totally wicked, selfish, and vile that it cannot live the Christian life. We must die and Jesus must live in us.

However, what usually happens is that most people try to let Jesus live in them as they remain alive. In other words, they try to jointly rule with Jesus. Or worse yet, they try to get the sinful self to agree with God. They always secretly hope Jesus agrees with them and will grant them what they want. Many sermons reflect this attempt. You must become as dead as a corpse in a casket, and this death must come by the slow process of crucifixion. No thoughts of your own must live. No energy or strength to do anything for God, no power to fold your hands and pray, no wisdom to explain what Scripture means, no movement of the mouth to share the good news must remain alive. In fact, you become so dependent on God that you don't raise your head off your pillow except by God's powerful grace.[15] Certainly no concern for money, retirement, or anything else of a worldly nature must live in you. In short, a dead man is just that, dead to all things. Are you dead and dying in Christ? To gain a life like this you must hate your life. You must hate all of it.

Painful Stuff

> Now my heart is troubled, and what shall I say? "Father, save me from this hour"? No, it was for this very reason I came to this hour. (John 12:27)

By now, you realize that the cross which crucifies you is painful. Notice above in verse 27 that Jesus is "troubled" concerning His cross. If the message troubled Jesus, it will trouble you greatly. Though on a daily basis Jesus experienced the pain of a crucified life,[16] it distressed Him to consider the fullness of the cross. Likewise, if you stop to consider the cost of the cross in your life, it will trouble you. You have no hope of salvation in your life without the daily pain of the cross. Yet, the false teachers tell us it was all finished when Jesus died on the cross. They say that Jesus did it all for us and there is nothing more to do. Of course, this is the half-truth false prophets love to proclaim and the people like to hear.

Are you prepared to allow this suffering in your life? Please understand that we do not mean suffering because of sins you have committed, but suffering because you die to self and say "No" to sinful acts which please your flesh. Do you suffer because you no longer do what you want to and your body cannot stand it?[17] When a heroin addict comes off the drug, his body cries out for more. In the same way as we begin to say "No" to sin, our flesh will cry out to be fulfilled. Jeremiah saw this same reaction in the people of Israel. Even though everything Jeremiah had said came true and they were now in captivity, they tell Jeremiah, as God offered them mercy:

> We will certainly do everything we said we would: We will burn incense to the Queen of Heaven and will pour out drink offerings to her just as we and our fathers, our kings and our officials did in

> the towns of Judah and in the streets of Jerusalem. At that time we had plenty of food and were well off and suffered no harm. But ever since we stopped burning incense to the Queen of Heaven and pouring out drink offerings to her, we have had nothing and have been perishing by sword and famine. (Jer. 44:17–18)

In today's church this means that individuals complain that when they began to live the message of the cross everything went bad. As long as they worshipped in the old church way, everything went fine and they felt blessed. However, when they began to consider this message, everything bad seemed to happen. Of course everything does seem fine spiritually when self is not disturbed by the cross of Christ. A spoiled brat is a good child, as long as he gets what he wants. But let a parent start to lay down a few rules, then watch how good their child remains. In fact, this was one complaint Jeremiah voiced toward God. He asked God why everything went well for the people, but he was judged.[18]

The difference between these two attitudes is the difference between heaven and hell. If you want the joy of Jesus, then prepare yourself now for hourly suffering with Him.

This ought to be simple to understand. Without death on the cross there can be no resurrected life. If Jesus had not died on the cross, there would have been no resurrection. He had to die according to God's plan and in the way God set down, or we would have no hope of salvation. Unless we share in His sufferings and fall to the ground to die in helplessness and humility, we will not bear fruit. In fact, those who do not share in this suffering are not children of God. We have no inheritance waiting for us in the kingdom of heaven unless we share in the sufferings of Christ. A seed that falls to the ground must wait for God to provide all the nutrients necessary for life. Like the seed, our old self must rot away so that the new life might spring forth.

Right and Wrong

> For God knows that when you eat of it your eyes will be opened, and you will be like God, knowing good and evil. (Gen. 3:5)

Jesus' actions were never an issue of right and wrong. When man and woman fell in the Garden of Eden, everything became an issue of right and wrong. Good and evil became more important than fellowship with God. Man's judgment of right and wrong overshadowed a relationship with God. We wanted God only to fulfill our whims or to make us happy when something didn't go right.

In the following example, we will see how Jesus never decided between good and bad. Nor was the issue a matter of what the "Bible says." Jesus' main concern was that God always worked through Him. Our Christianity reflects not the Mount of Olives, but the Garden of Eden. We, like Adam and Eve, decide good and evil by choosing how and when to apply Scripture. We live out biblical teachings rather than allowing Jesus to live it through us. Truly we have become gods in the name of Christianity.

We fill our churches with an abundance of Bible studies, outlines, and commentaries. Every member brags that his or her church preaches the truth and is scriptural. How diligently we seem to know the Bible and try to live it out, but our studies and applications are in vain. Indeed such things only get in the way of Jesus because we become puffed up and self-righteous in our beliefs and actions. We never die to our wisdom and knowledge of good and evil; therefore, Jesus does not live in us. Instead, we live a lie. All of our diligent study of the Bible gains us nothing. Indeed it only hinders Jesus from saving us. How often Jesus comes to crucify us and we quote Scripture back at Him. Think about it. Bible study can actually keep someone from being saved!

> And the Father who sent me has himself testified concerning me. You have never heard his voice nor seen his form, nor does his word dwell in you, for you do not believe the one he sent. You diligently study the Scriptures because you think that by them you possess eternal life. These are the Scriptures that testify about me, yet you refuse to come to me to have life. (John 5:37–40)

The people in this passage were a so-called biblical people who diligently studied Scripture. They, like many Christians, thought they were going to heaven and possessed eternal life because the Bible told them so. They claimed all the promises of salvation, but the very Scriptures they knew so well judged them as false believers. They refused to come to Jesus to die to self. Again, they denied themselves in some areas—all men do that—but would not come to Christ to die. Jesus says in verse 40 they refused to come to Him to have life. In short, they loved the message about God's salvation, but didn't like God's delivery. Like many today, they accepted any message of peace that pleased self, but they loathed and rejected ones that called for a crucified self.[19]

In John 6 we see the great pleasing of self found in our churches today. This exists even among those who talk about self-denial. Scripture says that in the last times churches will be "lovers of pleasure" and self rather than lovers of God.[20]

To be dead to self means that we have no thought of salvation, heaven, peace, rest, miracles, blessings, joy, or wishes. Remember that self is dead, and dead men have no thoughts. In other words, many churches talk of dying to self only to gain something for themselves. This is a very sinister form of darkness, which most Christians call light.[21] In John 6 we see a great crowd following Jesus, but they only followed to take from Jesus.

> Some time after this, Jesus crossed to the far shore of the Sea of Galilee (that is, the Sea of Tiberias), and a great crowd of people followed him because they saw the miraculous signs he had performed on the sick. (John 6:1–2)

As we move on in the passage we see Jesus leading them to a rather startling discovery of what salvation really means. In our churches today we would have seen these zealous followers as strong believers. Indeed they often hold positions of leadership. They seemed so eager to find Jesus. They prayed so much and served so well. They worshipped and rejoiced so deeply and talked much of Jesus. They went to great lengths to evangelize. However,

Jesus knew they did not understand what salvation really meant. Indeed they didn't have the slightest clue as to what the good news is all about. Just look at their eagerness to find Jesus.

> The next day the crowd that had stayed on the opposite shore of the lake realized that only one boat had been there, and that Jesus had not entered it with his disciples, but that they had gone away alone. Then some boats from Tiberias landed near the place where the people had eaten the bread after the Lord had given thanks. Once the crowd realized that neither Jesus nor his disciples were there, they got into the boats and went to Capernaum in search of Jesus. When they found him on the other side of the lake, they asked him, "Rabbi, when did you get here?" Jesus answered, "I tell you the truth, you are looking for me, not because you saw miraculous signs but because you ate the loaves and had your fill." (John 6:22–26)

Truthfully these people followed Jesus for the free food and basic spiritual needs. They desired the peace, love, and happiness they thought He could provide. They sought hard for Him, yet their motives were selfish. Jesus fed their bellies and they loved it. Our false pastors feed our flesh with false promises of peace and salvation. Churches overflow with members because the messages satisfy self. Great works and searches to do God's will are done because bellies are fed in the name of Jesus. Like the unrepentant thief hanging on the cross next to Jesus, we cry out for salvation, but salvation *from* the pain of the cross. Listen to what this thief asked of Jesus:

> One of the criminals who hung there hurled insults at him: "Aren't you the Christ? Save yourself and us!" (Luke 23:39)

The thief demanded salvation. He wanted relief from what would be called today the hard, narrow, not loving, and legalistic message. Yet, he hated a Jesus who came with a cross. The thief desired Jesus for selfish reasons, just like Christians today who want a message without the cross. In fact, some of the most popular preachers, writers, and speakers proclaim denial of self but do not understand it.

Which thief hanging next to Jesus are you? They both cried for salvation. Yet one submits to the will of God and finds salvation, while the other is angry with God for such a hard gospel. Most want salvation, but they want a salvation from the narrow message. Sure, most churches have a cross in their messages but a false cross that leaves self alive. Think about it: though crucified next to Jesus and enduring all that pain, the thief still went to hell. How sad that so many today endure crosses next to Jesus but never lose their lives.

Many Christians have accepted the disciplines of God and His grace in vain.[22] In fact, they deceive themselves into thinking they are fine in the Lord just because He tries to crucify them. Nothing could be further from the truth. We must all die to self and then wait in a grave for God to lift us up in His timing. To merely hang on the cross will profit us nothing. We must eventually go on to victory and the resurrected life. Many have left the Lord because they wearied of the real cross. In short, they would say, "I just can't live like that." They tired because they would not die, and, therefore, forfeited the joy and power that could have been theirs. When they say, "There is no joy in that message," they speak truthfully for themselves because they refused to die. But those who love God find the cross to be the power and joy of God. For example, when one person left the church she went around spreading the rumor, "Love and truth are there, but there is something wrong that I can't put my finger on." When this got back to us it made the obvious point that Jesus said it was the love and the truth that would show which groups really belonged to Him.[23] The thing she could not put her finger on and did not like was that the cross produced the love and the truth. Now the slander has changed because she found out this rumor worked to our favor. The rumor now is that we don't have the truth or any love. Such is the way of the cross. Many live as enemies of its blessed power. Until we too can warn others "with tears" that "many live as enemies of the cross," we do not understand the power of God.

> For, as I have often told you before and now say again even with tears, many live as enemies of the cross of Christ. (Phil. 3:18)

Jesus soon straightened these folks out, and a lot of straightening out needs to happen today in our Sunday schools, seminars, churches, and projects! Jesus told those following Him that they must live the way He does, and it totally shocked them.

> Jesus said to them, "I tell you the truth, unless you eat the flesh of the Son of Man and drink his blood, you have no life in you. Whoever eats my flesh and drinks my blood has eternal life, and I will raise him up at the last day. For my flesh is real food and my blood is real drink. Whoever eats my flesh and drinks my blood remains in me, and I in him. Just as the living Father sent me and I live because of the Father, so the one who feeds on me will live because of me. (John 6:53–57)

At first these people thought Jesus talked about eating His physical body, but they realized that He meant something much tougher. Once Jesus said these are "spiritual words" it dawned on them that they had to walk as He did.[24] They had to walk in fellowship and obedience to God just as He did. Eating the flesh of Jesus means you must surrender your flesh, just as He did, to be obedient to God. To drink His blood means all that gives you life is the life of Jesus in you. Most people wouldn't notice a difference if Jesus left them, since He never lived in them to begin with. If God had removed Himself from Jesus, He would have been dead instantly. This is not so with us. We are gods knowing good from evil and producing within ourselves the peace and thoughts of salvation. Our Christianity is one unto ourselves—not a death unto self.

Just as we have seen countless times, Jesus finally got through to them what it means to be saved. When they understood what He really meant, all they could do was cry out, "This is a hard teaching. Who can accept it?"[25] When they fully realized the true good news, they decided they really did not want it. They realized this so deeply that many who were not just travelers, but disciples left Jesus. If there is one thing you can be sure of, it is that Jesus first caused the travelers to leave and then caused many who had become disciples to drop out. I have watched firsthand many a traveler stop walking and many a disciple turn "back and no longer follow." Notice the subtle hint God gives us when the verse number is 666.

> From this time many of his disciples turned back and no longer followed him. (John 6:66)

They leave to go on their merry spiritual way. No doubt they went to find a church they felt comfortable in. For you can be sure, they didn't stop praying and going to church. Few are ever honest enough to admit they are going to hell and want nothing to do with God. Let us with soberness realize that these were *disciples* that turned back. They were, as we would say today, "saved" individuals, but they turned back because Jesus had shown them that they too must hate self and go to a cross. For them the good news was not good news at all. They saw no hope or joy in ridding themselves of a totally wicked self. They did not find enough joy in just fellowshipping with God. They found no joy in what Jesus said and lived. Indeed for those perishing, the message of the cross holds no joy or power.

> For the message of the cross is foolishness to those who are perishing, but to us who are being saved it is the power of God. (1 Cor. 1:18)

Being Made Well

So many are like the invalid in the following passage waiting on God to be healed. They long for Jesus to come their way and make them well, to bless them in some way, to fulfill some prayer and hope they have. They love to listen to the preachers who say God wants to fulfill their every desire. How they long to be made well and how they await with eager expectation for Jesus to come their way. But they receive the grace of God in vain, and once made well, begin to please themselves. They begin to live for themselves, all in the name of Jesus. Watch this happen in John 5:

> Some time later, Jesus went up to Jerusalem for a feast of the Jews. Now there is in Jerusalem near the Sheep Gate a pool, which in Aramaic is called Bethesda and which is surrounded by five covered colonnades. Here a great number of disabled people used to lie—the blind, the lame, the paralyzed. One who was there had been an invalid for thirty-eight years. When Jesus saw him lying there and learned that he had been in this condition for a long time, he asked him, "Do you want to get well?" "Sir," the invalid replied, "I have no one to help me into the pool when the water is stirred. While I am trying to get in, someone else goes down ahead of me." Then Jesus said to him, "Get up! Pick up your mat and walk." At once the man was cured; he picked up his mat and walked. (John 5:1–9)

Like He asks so many of us, Jesus asked the man if he wanted to be made well. As in John 5:7, we whine with excuses as to why we have not changed. The church overflows with people who make excuses. They enjoy the blame game too much to give up their sickness of sin. They love their sin and don't really want to be healed. This is obvious because right after Jesus blesses them, they join a church, speak of God's power, yet begin to sin mightily.

> Later Jesus found him at the temple and said to him, "See, you are well again. Stop sinning or something worse may happen to you." (John 5:14)

How could something worse happen? Something worse than being paralyzed for a long time? What could it possibly be? Hell, of course! This man used the blessings of God to go to church, the temple, and began to live his life of sin. Who in the world does this sound like to you? Have we not spurned the cross of Christ in our lives? Do we not worship where we find it convenient? Do we not decide what we consider to be right and wrong in the Lord? Isn't it true that we make plans and do our own spiritual thing while trying to pray down blessings upon ourselves? Is it not we who live and Christ who is dead to us? The time has come for us to "stop sinning" in the "temple" before something worse happens. The time has come to let God be all in our lives. Let us stop playing the spiritual word game and start letting the Holy Spirit crucify all of self.

For the few who give themselves fully to God, the cross and hatred of self become sources of deep joy. Truly, they only wish it could be theirs in more abundance. How they weep daily because the flesh remains so strong and hinders the blessing of being dead on the cross. For them every tear over sin is a tear of life. Every humiliation, shame, and sense of guilt brings a peace that passes all understanding. They embrace with heartfelt power everything that produces weakness.

> If I must boast, I will boast of the things that show my weakness. (2 Cor. 11:30)

Your reaction to all this reveals your spiritual condition. If you think this message is foreign to the good news, then you are alienated from Christ. If you feel hostile, then grace is hostile to filling your soul with its life. If on the other hand, you rejoice without self-righteousness, then the cross will work its power of life in you.

Will you eat the flesh of the Son of Man? Will you drink His blood? Let us go joyfully with a thankful heart and tell Jesus that we will let go of all so that He might be Lord of our lives.

What Sin Really Is

Sin is not a matter of missing the mark or a matter of right and wrong. Sin does not allow God's will to work through you. This is what Scripture means when it speaks of "anything that does not come from faith is sin."[26] Faith is a total surrender to God's will and a complete dependence upon His power. Faith trusts God enough to let Him have His way, both in terms of will and in terms of the power to live it. The legalist and the liberal both reduce God's will down to "what the Bible says" or whether something is OK to do or not. Why do you think God requires faith? Because in order for a man to have faith he must come out of himself. He must place his trust fully in someone else. Faith embraces someone or something other than one's self.

It might be OK to watch a certain television program, but it might not be God's will. It may even be proper to eat something right now, but it may not be God's will. Jesus did not come to show us right from wrong. We got that in the Garden of Eden. He came to give us fellowship with God. Those who have reduced Christianity down to right and wrong are true legalists. Therefore, everyone who takes the Bible and comes up with a formula for what is or isn't OK, deserves the label *legalist*. For you see, doing what is best in the Lord, not what appears lawful, is all that matters.

> And this is my prayer: that your love may abound more and more in knowledge and depth of insight, so that you may be able to discern what is best and may be pure and blameless until the day of Christ, filled with the fruit of righteousness that comes through Jesus Christ—to the glory and praise of God. (Phil. 1:9–11)

Only as the cross crucifies your self will you have a pure enough love for God to be able to discern what is best. This, as verse 11 says, will produce the "righteousness that comes through Jesus" in our lives. Then we can become "blameless" and "pure" by knowing what is "best" and not what is lawful. You can bet you will feel a lot of trembling when discerning whether or not something is God's will. Each day and each moment, a lover of God finds himself consumed with the thought, "Am I in God's will?" The great fear being that we might use Scripture to justify selfish ends. Yet so many allow Satan to lift them, just as he tried to lift Jesus, and then quote Scriptures of God's love to them.

Satan quotes Scripture to Christians to persuade them to please themselves in the name of God. So many worship the Bible and not the living God. Their own thoughts have become the word of the Lord.[27] They respond to Satan quoting Scripture, and they jump off the temple, thinking God will save them. As we read Matthew 4:6, notice that it was a salvation proclamation and testimony about

God's love that Satan preached. Today also, Satan lifts folks up in the church, takes them to the "highest point," and talks about how much God loves them. It is the ultimate salvation call by the evil one. For he speaks of God's love and assures them they will be saved. He says they can disobey or ignore certain Scriptures and remain in God's grace. Satan even quotes Ps. 91:11–12 in context. How many there are who jump off while quoting Scripture in all its proper context!

> Then the devil took him to the holy city and had him stand on the highest point of the temple. "If you are the Son of God," he said, "throw yourself down. For it is written: 'He will command his angels concerning you, and they will lift you up in their hands, so that you will not strike your foot against a stone.'" (Matt. 4:5–6)

This frustration and fear is all part of the glory of the cross in one's life, yet there is no other way. Lovers of God are consumed about whether or not something is God's will and whether or not His presence is in it. Indeed they do not want one promise if God will not go with them. In the following passage, although God promises "rest" to the Israelites, Moses wants only God Himself. Many are content just to take some rest and peace from God, but are not really interested in God Himself.

> The Lord replied, "My Presence will go with you, and I will give you rest." Then Moses said to him, "If your Presence does not go with us, do not send us up from here." (Exod. 33:14–15)

These true lovers of God are concerned whether or not their conversations and actions flow from the Holy Spirit, not whether or not something looks spiritual. This fear and trembling allows God to work His will in us. For when we feel extremely afraid of our own will, we can open our hearts to the will of God.

> Therefore, my dear friends, as you have always obeyed—not only in my presence, but now much more in my absence—continue

> to work out your salvation with fear and trembling, for it is God who works in you to will and to act according to his good purpose. (Phil. 2:12–13)

God can "will . . . to act" according to His good purpose only when we have a "fear and trembling" from the cross of Jesus in our lives. It is God we trust for all, both the will to act and the power to act. Let us hate so that it might be "according to his good purpose."

Anything that comes from the power of the flesh is sin. You can pray one hundred times by the power of the flesh, and it will profit you nothing. The flesh and what you can do for God counts as nothing. A million prayers in the flesh still equal zero.

> The Spirit gives life; the flesh counts for nothing. The words I have spoken to you are spirit and they are life. (John 6:63)

You can decide a million times to serve God better, but if it is not God's will acting in you, then you will gain no victory over sin. A man or woman who does not have this fear and trembling does not walk with God. Indeed they cannot know the will of God or hear His voice. So, from now on, we should have no concern over whether or not something is OK to do. Our only question in everything must be: "Is this the will of God right now, and is it being done by His power?"

Going to Dinner

Five minutes count when it comes to doing God's will. A Christian should never do anything apart from God or His timing. Saying "Thy will be done" means you don't walk out your front door unless God moves you to do so. Indeed one does not go to work, school, or the store unless it is the express will of God. Don't even assume you should go to work every day; wait and listen for God's will. He just might have something else in mind.

Not only did Jesus have contentment in not doing anything apart from the will of God, but also He waited moment by moment to know that will. Jesus was also not moved by any obligation or situation. The same should be true of us. No social or religious obligation should compel us to do anything. No situation should gain control over our actions or decisions. A spirit-filled Christian always finds himself above and beyond such things. We might conform to those things in order to "not offend." Then again, God might have us offend someone.

> But so that we may not offend them, go to the lake and throw out your line. Take the first fish you catch; open its mouth and you will find a four-drachma coin. Take it and give it to them for my tax and yours. (Matt. 17:27)

> Then the disciples came to him and asked, "Do you know that the Pharisees were offended when they heard this?" (Matt. 15:12)

Jesus did not care if He offended someone. But this is not so with us. We have our plans and timetables. We always have our good reasons for going somewhere and doing something. Like Jesus' brothers did, we give our recommendations and make them sound godly and noble. As they did, we tell God what to do. We don't want to wait for God's will because we want some desire of our flesh fulfilled. If we do wait, it is in the hope that God might give us what we want. Oh, we cloud our words with holy-sounding promises and our sermons with sweet songs of false submission, yet we tell God what to do. Like Jesus' brothers did, we put pressure on Jesus to conform to our plans and ideas. We slander God by accusing him of being secretive and aloof.

> Jesus' brothers said to him, "You ought to leave here and go to Judea, so that your disciples may see the miracles you do. No one who wants to become a public figure acts in secret. Since you are doing these things, show yourself to the world." (John 7:3–4)

Jesus surrendered His opinions, knowing that God had told Him not to go. Likewise, we should surrender to God's will to the point we do not go on a trip, or to the movies, the grocery store, or the bank unless He has shown us. Only what the Father does should we do. For most of us, any time seems right. We truly are gods, and we know how best to serve the Lord. We have all the justifications; we know the course to plot and to take. We appear spirit-filled and ready to go. We just hope God blesses our plans and that nothing bad happens to us. It is not from a position of the cross that we cry "Thy will be done." Rather, from a position of self we cry, "Bless my spiritual plans," or "Lord be with me." Listen carefully to the rebuke "for you any time is right."

> Therefore Jesus told them, "The right time for me has not yet come; for you any time is right." (John 7:6)

Jesus knew—either because He hated His own plans or because he had no clue of God's will for the next minute—that the Father did not desire for Him to go to the feast at that moment. Whatever the case, Jesus waited for God to make clear what He should do next.

> "You go to the Feast. I am not yet going up to this Feast, because for me the right time has not yet come." Having said this, he stayed in Galilee. (John 7:8–9)

However, five minutes later Jesus leaves for the feast. Or maybe it was twenty minutes later. Who knows the exact time? The important thing is that shortly after, Jesus knew the time had come to go to the feast. He knew when the time was right and the manner in which He should arrive. Jesus understood He must go in secret this time. At other times Jesus marched out in the open. It all depended on God's will for the moment.

Jesus knew God's will moment by moment because He surrendered His own opinions. God has had to hit me over the head sometimes to teach me this lesson.

One time when my wife and I were traveling, we stopped at a hamburger place to grab a quick lunch. Carla stayed in the car as I ran in to buy our carryout meal. She then decided to follow me and naturally locked the car, not realizing that I had left the keys behind. Tired and hungry, I was furious and took my meal to sulk in my sin at the back of the restaurant, leaving my wife to solve the problem. God immediately showed me why this had happened. About a dozen Mormon missionaries came in, sat down, and surrounded me. They were all fired up about their long-lost Mormon brother returning to their religion.

I set my anger aside because I saw God's will. A conversation erupted, and we began firing questions back and forth. The Spirit led me to ask questions that raised doubts in the one young man who had just returned to the Mormon church. Fear and frustration rose in the other men, who kept asking me where I came from and who I was. Apparently they thought I was an anti-Mormon crusader of some kind because they were being boxed in left and right. After comparing their beliefs with Satan's Garden of Eden deception of becoming like God, the young convert admitted that he followed a fallen religion based on a lie. At that point the other missionaries quickly swept their friend out of the building. We could see them patting him on the back and trying to convince him of the validity of their church.

I had to admit that God wanted me there for a reason. If Carla had not locked the car, we would have missed the moment. Our conversation, no doubt, set that particular young man on a deeper search for truth. This was a classic case of five minutes making a total difference in the will of God.

Not only does God tell us when it is His will for us to go somewhere, but also He tells us how we should go: whether or not to take the bus, which car to drive, when to go to dinner, whether or not to go home to dad's funeral, or even to enjoy your own honeymoon.[28] This is not being a robot but being a ship moved along by the wind. The ship has a crew with life on it, and there is much for them to do. But it is the wind that gives power and direction. Jesus said those born of the Spirit are like the wind. You never know which way they are going to go or how they are going to act, but you know it is the wind moving them along.[29]

Everything is surrendered to God's will: vacations, skiing, what home to buy, pizza parties . . . everything! Yet, by looking at church bulletins, you can tell Jesus has had nothing to do with our plans, for we love pleasure rather than God.[30] Every time we refuse to lose our lives, we leave Jesus behind, even when going to a religious feast. How many people leave Jesus behind when going to church?

> However, after his brothers had left for the Feast, he went also, not publicly, but in secret. (John 7:10)

Did Jesus lie? Was Jesus playing word games? Did He knowingly lie to His brothers by saying the time was not right for Him, then following soon after they left? Would we not accuse Jesus and those who walk in the Spirit of being deceivers? The answer is obvious. Jesus waited moment by moment for God to work His will.

How about us? Is it not true we move and act in a Christian manner for God? We want to know His plans immediately. Jesus, however, learned to wait each second for God to communicate His will. This, believe it or not, truly brings a life of peace. Such peace rests in knowing that God gives life to everything—even our minds and thoughts. Unfortunately, most of us do not want to surrender, and we, therefore, use our own thoughts to conjure up feelings of peace. The Spirit must gain control of our minds and thoughts, and this only happens as we learn to hate and die.

> The mind of sinful man is death, but the mind controlled by the Spirit is life and peace. (Rom. 8:6)

The more we hang onto our own thoughts, the more unrest and lack of peace we have. Only as we let go, rather hate, our own thoughts can the Holy Spirit control our minds. Are we willing to let the Spirit control what we think? It is merely holy brainwashing taking place. God is cleaning up our minds.

How little of the cross and surrender remain in the house of God. We set out to evangelize; we form our committees, reach out to our neighbors, do our good deeds, and treasure the latest gimmick for sharing the gospel. When God seeks to stop us in order to show us how to surrender, we blame it on the devil. How we pray and cry out to God for success not realizing that we are praying against the Lord. For it is never our plans the Lord blesses. Never! God never blesses our desires. Rather, He blesses His desires for us, through us. Though the goal be noble, if it is not through Him and started by Him, it is not of Him. Paul learned this while trying to preach the gospel.

> Paul and his companions traveled throughout the region of Phrygia and Galatia, having been kept by the Holy Spirit from preaching the word in the province of Asia. When they came to the border of Mysia, they tried to enter Bithynia, but the Spirit of Jesus would not allow them to. So they passed by Mysia and went down to Troas. During the night Paul had a vision of a man of Macedonia standing and begging him, "Come over to Macedonia and help us." After Paul had seen the vision, we got ready at once to leave for Macedonia, concluding that God had called us to preach the gospel to them. (Acts 16:6–10)

No doubt, Paul felt he should preach in the region of Phrygia and Galatia, but he was wrong. Undoubtedly, Paul thought he would give Mysia a try, but he was wrong. Only after a vision did Paul conclude where to go. No warm fuzzy feelings. No well-laid plans. Just a conclusion that God wanted him to go to Macedonia.

When was the last time the Holy Spirit told you not to share the gospel? When was the last time your church had a project to preach the gospel and then discovered God would not allow it? For that matter, when was the last time you even asked God if everyone should come together for church? Maybe each person needs to stay home and spend some extra time alone with God. Ah, but we couldn't hear that. It would take away our plans for Sunday and deprive the church of some badly needed revenue. Not to mention how bored everyone would be sitting at home waiting on the Lord. The Lord has had me, as a pastor, cancel worship many times. However, that is a dangerous thing to do because we are likely to just start eating and drinking and then playing in the name of the Lord. And if self is not dead and waiting on God, playing can be sinful and deadly.

> And do not be idolaters as some of them were; as it is written, "the people sat down to eat and drink, and stood up to play." (1 Cor. 10:7 NASB)

Waiting on God produces genuine faith. All other kinds of faith seen in the church today are hype and self-delusion. Only those who give up their plans and really hate their faith will be given a pure faith that comes from heaven. Are we willing to be taught?

> Don't you believe that I am in the Father, and that the Father is in me? The words I say to you are not just my own. Rather, it is the Father, living in me, *who is doing his work*. Believe me when I say that I am in the Father and the Father is in me; or at least believe on the evidence of the miracles themselves. I tell you the truth, anyone who has *faith in me will do what I have been doing*. He will do even greater things than these, because I am going to the Father. (John 14:10–12, emphasis added)

The Father in Jesus does the work, and it should be the Father in us doing the same thing. But unfortunately, we are all too alive in our work for God. The miracles we say we believe in are supposed to show us the need for the emptied life and our powerlessness, but they do not. Instead, we want more miracles, entertainment, and happy sermons. Just listen to the jokes coming from the pulpit. What sin! Especially considering that Scripture says in our preaching we should witness "seriousness" and preach the Word, not tell stories.

> In everything set them an example by doing what is good. In your teaching show integrity, seriousness and soundness of speech that cannot be condemned, so that those who oppose you may be ashamed because they have nothing bad to say about us. (Titus 2:7–8)

Instead, we want our seminars to be exciting and filled with play. We want preaching *about* the Word, not preaching *of* the Word. How "corrupt" we have become in the name of the Lord.

> Then the Lord said to Moses, "Go down, because your people, whom you brought up out of Egypt, have become corrupt." (Exod. 32:7)

This is precisely why so many miracles today are not of Jesus. When Jesus healed ten lepers, only one came back to thank Jesus. Based on such statistics, only 10 percent of those touched powerfully by Jesus ever come back to Him. The faith found in our churches does not spring from God doing His work in a crucified life. It is merely the hype and dancing of fools. Only those emptied of self will do greater things; it will not be them, but God, doing it.

True faith waits upon God for power rather than promoting healings and miracles. Contrast today with how Jesus surrendered and totally depended on the Father. Today's evangelists promise miraculous, spirit-filled, awe-inspiring good times in the Lord. Jesus, however, could not do any miracles except in God's timing. Jesus could not predict that on a certain date or at a specific meeting He would perform miracles. In other words, sometimes Jesus did not have the power to heal. If Jesus walked over to someone lying in a casket and in self-effort He said, "Arise," it would not have worked, and He would have been in sin. As the Scripture below tells us, Jesus was dependent upon God for His power to heal.

> One day as he was teaching, Pharisees and teachers of the law, who had come from every village of Galilee and from Judea and Jerusalem, were sitting there. *And the power of the Lord was present* for him to heal the sick. (Luke 5:17, emphasis added)

"And the power of the Lord was present for him to heal the sick" is the attitude we all must learn to wait for. If that power is not there, we must not force a healing. I can remember very early in my Christian walk going into a bedroom to pray for a handicapped individual to be made well. Just as I entered the room, God made it very clear it was not His will or timing. Like Elijah, I was not being sent there.[31] If I had forced the issue, it would have been presumptuous sin and would have caused much pain. If the voice that told me not to heal had been blamed on the devil, then I would have come close to committing the unpardonable sin.

Claiming anything in Jesus means nothing and usually is the act of a selfish follower of God. We seek to claim the promises of God to force Him to do something, thus setting the promises above God. We hold God's Word over Him and the ink on pages becomes God. My wife and I were once at a large conference and the preacher kept on preaching and talking about the gift of tongues. He was not going to stop until a tongue was spoken. Finally, after a long period of time, someone spoke in tongues. Since my wife has the gift of interpretation, she was quickly able to discern that the tongue was not of God. If the preacher had not tried to force God's hand, but had simply asked God if a tongue should be spoken, he would not have opened himself up to such a situation.

Jesus had a relationship with the Father and understood when to wait for God to heal.[32] Certainly every promise is "yes" for those who honestly love God with a love that waits upon Him and lives only to say, "Thy will be done."

> For no matter how many promises God has made, they are "Yes" in Christ. And so through him the "Amen" is spoken by us to the glory of God. (2 Cor. 1:20)

So why can certain ministries predict a miracle time? How can your church know for certain that revival will happen on a specific date and with a particular preacher? Easy: the odds of such predictions are not of God nor by the power of His Holy Spirit. When Scripture says, "For in him we live and move and have our being,"[33] it means we should realize the need to surrender to Him in all things. Acts of self-will and self-determination caused angels to become demons.[34] Self-will must be judged, for it is the opposite of love. This is the lesson King Saul never learned.

Saul, who had been given a charge in the Lord, failed to have God's heart. True, Saul seemed at first to have obeyed the Lord and even protested that he did.[35] Isn't this the response of most Christians today? They protest that they really do obey and love God.

Later, of course, Saul does admit to sinning and even asks for forgiveness,[36] but it was too late. His heart had been revealed. Saul obeyed the general principles of God but cared nothing for the voice of the Lord moment by moment.

If you say you care more about the voice of the Lord than the written code, then you will begin to walk in the kind of surrender Jesus had. Anything less is rebellion against God, and you practice divination, or as divination is defined, you try at an *inspired guess*. We believe that because we place the name of Jesus in front of our wild predictions that God will bless us, or that if we back something up enough with Scripture, then it must be correct. Of course nothing could be further from the truth. It takes a crucified heart to hear the voice of the Lord and a hatred for one's life to wait for that voice. Those who practice divination try to find just the right words and feelings to justify their religious life in the Lord. But God cares about fellowship only—fellowship with Him. He desires a fellowship so close that we let Him live through us. We must listen to His voice at all times. But *must* is too strong of a word. For those with good and noble hearts, His is the only voice they *want* to hear.

> But Samuel replied: "Does the Lord delight in burnt offerings and sacrifices as much as in obeying the voice of the Lord? To obey is better than sacrifice, and to heed is better than the fat of rams. For rebellion is like the sin of divination, and arrogance like the evil of idolatry. Because you have rejected the word of the Lord, he has rejected you as king." (1 Sam. 15:22–23)

Can you see now that rejecting the voice of the Lord means more than simply rejecting the Bible? Rejecting the voice of the Lord means rejecting God Himself. After all, the whole Bible points to a relationship beyond mere ink. Otherwise, it would be like someone saying that the love letters he carries around from his wife *are* his wife. It would be like telling your wife that letters ought to be good enough for her; you don't have to live in the same house.

Either through rebelling against the voice of God or mocking His voice, we avoid Him who crucifies our flesh. Like the Israelites in the wilderness, we want a god that feeds our flesh. And, like them, we do it all in the name of the Lord. We find pastors who justify us or make us feel uncomfortable just enough to feel a false sense of righteousness.

> When Aaron saw this, he built an altar in front of the calf and announced, "Tomorrow there will be *a festival to the Lord*." (Exod. 32:5, emphasis added)

Ministry

We see that only as we draw close to the cross by the power of the Holy Spirit will we understand how to truly hear the Lord's voice. Only as the Holy Spirit portrays Jesus clearly crucified will this message become good news to us.

> "Who are you?" they asked. "Just what I have been claiming all along," Jesus replied. "I have much to say in judgment of you. But he who sent me is reliable, and what I have heard from him I tell the world." They did not understand that he was telling them about his Father. So Jesus said, "When you have lifted up the Son of Man, then you will know that I am the one I claim to be and that I do nothing on my own but speak just what the Father has taught me. The one who sent me is with me; he has not left me alone, for I always do what pleases him." Even as he spoke, many put their faith in him. (John 8:25–30)

As verse 30 declares, pleasing the Father means to put your faith in Him. The disciples did not understand that Jesus was nothing and that they too had to be nothing. They did not yet trust Jesus enough to be dead to self. Jesus did not expect them to become mindless robots but to find life in God when they surrendered self. Jesus explained that He only repeated what He heard from God (verse 26 says, ". . . and what I have heard from him I tell the world"). As you obey verse 28 in your own life and lift up the Son of Man, you too will finally understand the salvation of

God. That salvation demonstrates that Jesus did "nothing" on His own, and you too can do "nothing."

When God can enlighten us about the cross and the crucified life and when the Son of Man has been lifted up in our hearts, then we will understand why we must hate our own lives. At the cross we see the futility of acting for God and we understand that Jesus did nothing on His own but was totally dependent on God for everything. When Jesus is "clearly portrayed as crucified"[37] in our preaching, men will see the truth in all of this.

> Jesus said to them, "If God were your Father, you would love me, for I came from God and now am here. *I have not come on my own*; but he sent me." (John 8:42, emphasis added)

God does not bless our plans; dead people have no plans. Besides, our plans come from a darkened and sinful soul, especially when they are "godly" plans. Even Jesus did not say to God, "Hey, I have this great ministry idea. Why don't I go to earth and show them your love, do some miracles, feed some folks, and give them the Holy Spirit?" Jesus said that He did not come on His own. In other words, it was God's idea and instigation that sent Jesus to earth. God already has work for us to do; we do not need to come up with any ministry ideas or invent some new way of sharing the gospel. His plans are perfect, and those who hate their own lives also hate their own ideas for God. Look at the freedom we have in Christ in the next Scripture. We don't have to bother ourselves coming up with ideas about how to work for the Lord. We are free to spend our time loving God and others. What a Sabbath rest it is when no particular cause for Christ becomes more important than fellowship.

Consider how Paul walked away from an open revival door simply because of one thing. He could not find Titus, so he said "goodbye" to an open door in the Lord. If you are in a church where the pastor brags that he is a project person rather than a people person, you need to strongly encourage him to repent. He does not have the heart of God, which is first, and only, a heart for people. Consider that the whole project called the *universe* was made for one reason—fellowship. God made the world to give man a little space in which to fellowship with Him. Fellowship meant more to Paul than an open door did—a door the Lord had opened. How many fail the test of an "open door" from "the Lord" because they do not realize the goal of the cross.

> Now when I went to Troas to preach the gospel of Christ and found that the Lord had opened a door for me, I still had no peace of mind, because I did not find my brother Titus there. So I said good-by to them and went on to Macedonia. (2 Cor. 2:12–13)

Remember, the second greatest command is like the first: to "love your neighbor as yourself."[38] The two commands go hand in hand. He who fulfills the greatest commandment by hating for Jesus will also live the second greatest command. There is no need to worry about a ministry or a work in the Lord. Love is the work He "prepared in advance" long before the earth was formed. Let us be found hating our work so much that we will live for His work. His work is our bread for the day that gives us strength to live.

> For we are God's workmanship, created in Christ Jesus to do good works, which God prepared in advance for us to do. (Eph. 2:10)

Many cannot understand the message of the cross because of whom they listen to. The cross does not make any sense to someone who wants to do his or her own thing, no matter how noble.

> Why is my language not clear to you? Because you are unable to hear what I say. You belong to your father, the devil, and you want to carry out your father's desire. He was a murderer from the beginning, not holding to the truth, for there is no truth in him. When he lies, he speaks his native language, for he is a liar and the father of lies. (John 8:43–44)

When we do not understand the cross, we begin to trust in things like tongues, water baptism, biblical preaching, uplifted feelings, being slain in the Spirit, numbers, inward speculations, and all manner of outward works. God allows only those willing to endure the pain of the cross in their lives to walk with Jesus. Truly, Jesus will show them the way. Take warning, however, Jesus will never bless your plans and will never lead you in a way you want to go. We must go where He leads us and wait there for Him.

> Whoever serves me must follow me; and where I am, my servant also will be. My Father will honor the one who serves me. (John 12:26)

4

BIBLE KNOWLEDGE

Doctrine and Learning

We go to church to learn the Bible. We send preachers to seminary to learn the truth. We read books by famous authors to glean insight into the Word of God. We cherish books, magazines, and tapes that talk of morality and returning to God. We read and re-read things to motivate us unto morally good behavior, yet remain dead in our Bible studies because we will not die unto Christ. Our learning and understanding are merely the thoughts of man trying to comprehend ink on pages. Until we learn to hate our truth, we never have His truth in our inmost place.

> Surely you desire truth in the inner parts; you teach me wisdom in the inmost place. (Ps. 51:6)

God can no longer get through to us what His Word means; we have become a nation that worships the Bible. We idolize that which was supposed to lead us to the living God and a surrendered life. Like the Israelites in the Old Testament, we make our religious things into idols and worship them. Indeed we have a Bible that is suited to everyone's tastes and desires. We have as many idols as we do towns, with one designed specifically to please each person. How sad that there are nations without Bibles, and we in the United States have trouble deciding which version we want to buy.

> You have as many gods as you have towns, O Judah; and the altars you have set up to burn incense to that shameful god Baal are as many as the streets of Jerusalem. (Jer. 11:13)

How sad to see that many have made the cross, and even the Bible, a thing of idol worship. The "bronze snake"—the idol of the Israelites—of the Old Testament is the cross of the New Testament. The only things that keep the Bible, church, or cross from becoming idols are death to self and hating. If this death to self is not there, then these things become just a means to an end. In other words, we use such things to receive blessings from the Lord.

> He removed the high places, smashed the sacred stones and cut down the Asherah poles. He broke into pieces the bronze snake Moses had made, for up to that time the Israelites had been burning incense to it. (It was called Nehushtan.) (2 Kings 18:4)

Let us turn from the Bibles we have idolized and look to a living Jesus. He then will lead us to study the Bible version of His choosing and in the way He directs. When this happens, then we find the following passage working in our lives.

> The Jews were amazed and asked, "How did this man get such learning without having studied?" Jesus answered, "My teaching is not my own. It comes from him who sent me." (John 7:15–16)

Jesus demonstrated the way for us to study to show ourselves approved unto God.[1] We must receive our teaching directly from God even when it comes through the teachers He sends. Jesus proved that total surrender grants a man wisdom to understand the Word. Years of Bible study mean nothing and hours of prayer profit nothing if self has not been put to death. Tape series, Bible outlines, and massive amounts of books about the Bible become meaningless without death to self. Jesus' teaching came directly from the Father, without Jesus "having studied." Indeed, in the next verse Jesus tells us that those who love God will experience this or "find out" that it is true.

> Jesus answered, "My teaching is not my own. It comes from him who sent me. If anyone chooses to do God's will, *he will find out* whether my teaching comes from God or whether I speak on my own." (John 7:16–17, emphasis added)

Do you see it? We speak on our "own" from our "own" Bible study and classes we have taken. However, if we choose to do the will of God, we will find out that Jesus' teaching did not come from years of study. We will discover this because we too will be taught directly by God, just as Jesus was. The promise we find in Hebrews tells us that each man will know the Lord, and God will teach each man about Himself. How could it be otherwise? If you fellowship with someone, you begin to know them very well. Those who die to self have fellowship with God and thus have knowledge of the Most High God.

> No longer will a man teach his neighbor, or a man his brother, saying, "Know the Lord," because they will all know me, from the least of them to the greatest. (Heb. 8:11)

While men today speak on their own, Jesus never did. Jesus did not borrow words from a sermon outline or other preachers; that would be to commit the sin of Jeremiah 23:30. Nor did He repeat the three steps on how to be saved that are taught in Sunday school and assume, because the words were correct, that it was the Word of God. His teaching did not come from man; rather, He let God apply Scripture through Him. Yes, God gives us teachers, but they often leave out the most important matter. Ephesians says that teachers should point us to the Head, Jesus Christ.

Teachers expound their thoughts about the Bible instead of pointing us to the living God, who puts us to death so that we can have rich fellowship with Him. It is so much easier to hear from a man than to suffer on the cross. This explains why Paul celebrates the fact that he will fill up in his flesh (or feel) the sufferings of Christ. The question for each of us is are we rejoicing in receiving the sufferings of Christ in our lives, sufferings that produce a selfless love and total concern for others?

> Now I rejoice in what was suffered for you, and I fill up in my flesh what is still lacking in regard to Christ's afflictions, for the sake of his body, which is the church. (Col. 1:24)

To put this another way, all teaching should point us to where we must suffer in Christ to have fellowship with God. Remember that this is what makes a disciple: that we counted the cost and are willing to pay the price to have fellowship with God. If this cross resonates from a man's teaching, then you can be sure, if you have a good heart, that you will "grow up into him who is the Head, that is, Christ."

> It was he who gave some to be apostles, some to be prophets, some to be evangelists, and some to be pastors and teachers, to prepare God's people for works of service, so that the body of Christ may be built up until we all reach unity in the faith and in the knowledge of the Son of God and become mature, attaining to the whole measure of the fullness of Christ. Then we will no longer be infants, tossed back and forth by the waves, and blown here and there by every wind of teaching and by the cunning and craftiness of men in their deceitful scheming. Instead, speaking the truth in love, we will in all things grow up into him who is the Head, that is, Christ. (Eph. 4:11–15)

How many worry about being caught in a cult because they do not want to follow a man. Yet any church that does not have the kind of cross we have been looking at does just that—they follow men just like a cult. The crucified life brings us into unity with God and keeps us from following just an idea or a man.

> Discretion will protect you, and understanding will guard you. Wisdom will save you from the ways of wicked men, from men whose words are perverse. (Prov. 2:11–12)

The cross keeps us from cults and the deception of dead churches and false brothers. It is not logic that keeps a man from a cult or deadly opinion but the fact that he allows Jesus to crucify his flesh. What gives the lies and the dead churches power? They can appeal to our flesh. This was the only way Satan could tempt Eve. He appealed to her flesh with strong logic. Indeed many mainline churches are like cults; they just appeal to the flesh in a different way. Some prefer the codes of a cult, while others might enjoy the entertainment and social atmosphere of a particular church.

If we hope to escape every trap, then we must ask God to make the cross real to us, and we must resolve in every situation to know only the cross of Christ. Again, this takes much resolve on your part. Every day and in every situation we must commit ourselves to staying with the most basic and powerful thing God wants to work in our lives: the cross. For example, a new trend of revival is sweeping the church today. To escape its trap, we must remind ourselves that all we need is the cross in our lives. We must plead with God to make this a reality so that we are not taken in by every wind of teaching that moves over the church.

> For I resolved to know nothing while I was with you except Jesus Christ and him crucified. (1 Cor. 2:2)

In our counsel we must resolve to stay at the cross and not to be taken in by all kinds of fancy ideas.[2] This cross does not come with fanfare and flamboyant preaching.

> I came to you in weakness and fear, and with much trembling. My message and my preaching were not with wise and persuasive

> words, but with a demonstration of the Spirit's power, so that your faith might not rest on men's wisdom, but on God's power. (1 Cor. 2:3–5)

So much faith in the church today comes from the power of man and his preaching. We refuse to know a powerful cross in our lives and are, therefore, drawn to the flash of the video presentation, the liveliness of worship, or the intrigue of a Christian novel. How much of our buying of Christian things could be rejected if we knew the power of the cross? We must come to know that we need nothing but the cross of Christ. I once heard of a woman who said that she could not survive without her morning walks with the Lord. How sad that morning walks were her god or at least an idol. For each of us needs nothing but Jesus in our lives by way of His cross. If we knew this power, how much more work would get done for the Lord than gets done while we spin our wheels with counselors, speakers, seminars, and books? The church is so busy at being busy, rather than busy at doing the work of God because we refuse to resolve.

To understand the Bible, you must surrender your life and be consumed with "Thy will be done." In order to have that kind of heart, you must spend time with Jesus, for, as we will see in a moment, this makes men wise. We must let Him deal with our sin powerfully for years. We must be willing to be rebuked over and over again; we must long for God to humble and break us.[3] Take a look at the twelve disciples who spent years being rebuked by Jesus. There was not a thing they could do right, and every day it got harder and harder to follow Him as the cross and the crucifixion drew closer and closer. Only after the cross pressed deeply into their lives were the disciples ready for the Holy Spirit, and all who saw them took note of the fact that the cross had done its work.

> When they saw the courage of Peter and John and realized that they were *unschooled, ordinary men*, they were astonished and they took note that these men *had been with Jesus*. (Acts 4:13, emphasis added)

"Unschooled, ordinary men" who had spent time with Jesus and being crucified to themselves—that is what is needed today. Very often, and I do mean very often, individuals will want to know what my qualifications are for preaching. When I simply tell them that I have been spending time with Jesus, their reactions are always, "So?" Those who do not understand the cross find no power in such a statement. Indeed, to them, the speaker appears only as a self-righteous fool. After all, how many churches looking for a pastor would be impressed with a résumé that simply said, "I have spent time with Jesus"?

If we want true doctrinal unity in the church, then let each man go to God and be crucified. Let God deal with sin as we surrender our pet doctrines to Him. Look at the Scripture below.

> The man who thinks he knows something does not yet know as he ought to know. But the man who loves God is known by God. (1 Cor. 8:2–3)

Before we head out into deeper waters, do you see it is not what a man knows but whether God knows Him or not? For a man who is loved by God will be given knowledge about all Scripture. Again, men know all sorts of things about the Bible; some men can fathom the Greek and Hebrew, others can speak quite eloquently of the traditions surrounding the times of Jesus, but they do not know as they ought to know. For only the broken man, crucified to himself, is known by God.

Authority

Jesus spoke with power and authority because He spoke the very words of God. We speak with no real power and authority because we use our own biblical words. We talk like the Pharisees, voicing one opinion and thought about God after another. We debate, discuss, and clamor about God but cannot speak with any real authority.[4] Indeed we reject men who can speak with authority by the Holy Spirit as being self-righteous and legalistic. Now do not confuse the hype you see in churches today with speaking with authority. What we are talking about here is not the foolishness we see happening today that brings in the most people during pack-the-pew week. This is the authority to forgive or not forgive someone of his or her sins. Read how Jesus gives such authority to men.

> On the evening of that first day of the week, when the disciples were together, with the doors locked for fear of the Jews, Jesus came and stood among them and said, "Peace be with you!" After he said this, he showed them his hands and side. The disciples were overjoyed when they saw the Lord. Again Jesus said, "Peace be with you! As the Father has sent me, I am sending you." And with that he breathed on them and said, "Receive the Holy Spirit. *If you forgive anyone his sins, they are forgiven; if you do not forgive them, they are not forgiven.*" (John 20:19–23, emphasis added)

Jesus appeared to His disciples after the crucifixion. Don't let that be a minor point; the disciples had undergone the baptism of crucifixion Jesus had promised them. God had finally gotten through to them on a deeper level than just an intellectual one and had shattered so much self that they were ready for a greater work. These men had finally been broken and were now ready to live a life of a deeper daily brokenness. Therefore, Jesus could breathe the Holy Spirit on them. But notice verse 21; it is very important: "As the Father has sent me, I am sending you." As they now went out with the same surrender of self that Jesus had, they too could forgive or not forgive sins. It would not be they who would forgive sins; rather, it would be the Father speaking through them. So little power fills the church today; hearts are not revealed like Jesus exposed hearts. Men are not told they are not really Christians; no one is told they are headed for hell; Christians do not judge their brothers and sisters nor refuse to eat lunch with them.[5]

We judge and tell others they are forgiven when we have not been given authority by God to do so. We think that because they jumped through all of our religious hoops, then they are saved, but God has not told us that is true. Like the Israelites, they presume they are saved and can go into the promised land. After all, they have confessed their sin and repented, and, therefore, assume God must have forgiven them. Often we do this in our own walks with the Lord. We become convicted of sin, we weep about it, we confess it as sin, we say and do all the correct things, and then we assume God has forgiven us. We claim the promises that we are forgiven because we feel the guilt in our lives. We get up early in the morning to get a really good quiet time because we know we have been lax in the Lord, and we think that because of our repentance God has forgiven us.

> When Moses reported this to all the Israelites, they mourned bitterly. Early the next morning they went up toward the high hill country. "We have sinned," they said. "We will go up to the place the Lord promised." (Num. 14:39–40)

But all of our claiming of the forgiveness of God does not mean He truly has forgiven us. We cannot force God to do anything, and we must learn to wait on the cross until death has done its work in our lives. Since we do not wait for God to finish the work, we keep failing in our Christian walks. We are defeated every time because we will not hang on the cross and wait for God to put us in the tomb. Then, we will not wait in the tomb until He raises us from the dead. We do this because it is far less painful to claim a promise in our own timing than it is to suffer on the cross. Let us pray and ask God to put more people like Moses in our churches who will warn us when we are only presuming the presence of God in lives.

> But Moses said, "Why are you disobeying the Lord's command? This will not succeed! Do not go up, because the Lord is not with you. You will be defeated by your enemies." (Num. 14:41–42)

We judge and condemn others when we have no wisdom from heaven and, therefore, no authority to speak. We are like the twelve apostles, before they were broken, who thought that anyone not with them was not part of Jesus.[6] No wonder Jesus said that we would be judged for every careless word we proclaim.

> But I tell you that men will have to give account on the day of judgment for every careless word they have spoken. (Matt. 12:36)

The ultimate in careless words lies in quoting Scripture. It shows that we think we are like God, knowing good and evil. Quoting Scripture apart from the death of self and the power of the Holy Spirit is the deepest form of arrogance. Even with all the talk of power and authority in the church today, we do not see the true power of God but merely the babbling of insane men preaching from the pulpit.[7] With books on morality and the need for spiritual renewal, we do not see the death of self. Indeed surrender of self has become the means by which we get things from God. It is selfishness disguised in sheep's clothing. It is the ultimate in deception. The world and men walk all over Christians because we will not die, and the power we think we have is a lie.

> Woe to you, because you are like unmarked graves, which men walk over without knowing it. (Luke 11:44)

He who created the universe with a word longs to speak through you. But again, you must be put to death on a cross. You must come to see the worthlessness of your words. The cross with its long, slow, and painful process must do its work. This is not death by firing squad. Rather, it is a trial before men that tests your patience and trust in God and rids you of any defense of self. It allows your faith to be mocked and your life to be flogged. Afterwards begins the real pain of walking through town with your cross and slowly being drained of your life. Please read the next Scripture carefully.

> For I did not speak of my own accord, but the Father who sent me commanded me *what to say* and *how to say it. I know that his*

> *command leads to eternal life.* So whatever I say is just what the Father has told me to say. . . . (John 12:49–50, emphasis added)

Do you understand that this "command leads to eternal life?" In this command God tells us not only "what to say" but also "how to say it." Look at this again. God gives His words to speak and shows us how to say those words. After all, who knows how or when to rebuke a Pharisee or when to gently speak to the woman at the well?[8] Which of us knows the proper time to crack the whip in the church or to speak gently?[9] This is why Paul prays, in Eph. 6:19–20, that words and courage be "given" him from God. Paul knew that his spiritual words carried no power and that only God's words in him had the power of life. Paul knew that if he quoted God in the way he thought was best, it would end in folly. Paul was totally dependent on God not only for the words, but also for how those words should be spoken.

Those surrendered enough to speak just the words God gives them and in the manner He directs truly offer others eternal life. Think about it . . . do you have the power to offer someone eternal life? How dare we think we know how to declare the Word of God! Only God knows how to declare His word.[10] How arrogant of us to think we have the power and knowledge to be able to offer the Christian life to others. Yet to look at the church fellowship around us, it appears that everyone thinks they have this knowledge and power. Even in church fellowship God is clear about how we should be quoting Scripture. When you fellowship, do not quote Scripture in the strength of your own power. This is why the Bible tells us to shut up and be quiet when we go to church. [11] Yet how often we hear, "Well, I think this . . .," and "They ought to . . .," and "Tell me more." We are minigods playing God; we are not empty servants quoting the very words of God.

Peter says that if we speak, we should speak as if declaring "the very words of God" with the "strength God provides." We all have strength in ourselves to act out the Christian life and to quote Scripture. We are called to hate and deny our strength and to rely on God's strength only. The trouble is most of us cannot tell when

God's strength does the work or when we do the work for God in our own strength.

> If anyone speaks, he should do it as one speaking *the very words of God.* If anyone serves, he should do it with the *strength God provides*, so that in all things God may be praised through Jesus Christ. To him be the glory and the power for ever and ever. Amen. (1 Pet. 4:11, emphasis added)

If you want to speak before men about the gospel, then practice death to self. Let God wrestle self out of you until only His words and strength remain. In this way when you offer eternal life to someone it will be with God's words and in the manner God wants. And if the Holy Spirit is in it, there is indeed a leading to eternal life. Otherwise, we are merely Pharisees traveling over "land and sea" to win our converts.[12] Let us all make sure that when we strive to save souls it is not just we who are planting the seedlings; let us make sure God has planted it through us.[13] Remember that every plant God has not planted will be pulled up by the roots. Nothing will remain of our labor.

Unity with God

> I have brought you glory on earth by completing the work you gave me to do. (John 17:4)

It cannot be said enough that Jesus' ministry did not come from Himself. Jesus did not instigate the work of God but surrendered and waited on the Father continually. Jesus came to bring this kind of surrender and brokenness. Anything less than this will send us straight to hell, for in that case the salvation of God is salvation from self. True salvation is saying second by second, "Thy will be done." Doing nothing, buying nothing, eating nothing, speaking nothing that the Holy Spirit has not worked. We have already seen this is a hard teaching, but it is nevertheless the salvation of God, which few want and few find.

Look carefully at what Jesus came to bring, for the sanctification that He brought means death to you.

> For them I sanctify myself, that they too may be truly sanctified. My prayer is not for them alone. I pray also for those who will believe in me through their message, that all of them *may be one*, Father, *just as you are in me and I am in you*. May they also be in us so that the world may believe that you have sent me. I have given them the glory that you gave me, that they may be one as we are one: I in them and you in me. May they be brought to *complete unity* to let the world know that you sent me and have loved them even as you have loved me. Father, I want those you have given me to be with me where I am, and to see my glory, the glory you have given me because you loved me before the creation of the world. Righteous Father, though the world does not know you, I know you, and they know that you have sent me. I have made you known to them, and will continue to make you known in order that the love you have for me may be in them and that I myself may be in them. (John 17:19–26, emphasis added)

Remember that Jesus was an empty jar drained of self-will, self-determination, and self-thought. He came to bring this kind of unity. In John 17:21 He says, "that all of them may be one, Father, just as you are in me and I am in you," and we have seen how Jesus was one. Again, in verse 22 He repeats, "they may be one as we are one." Only with this kind of unity will the world honestly see Jesus. Verse 21 says, "May they also be in us so that the world may believe that you have sent me." Do you want people to see Jesus in your church? Then go and die; go and hate.

The unity Jesus prayed for has nothing to do with all churches agreeing. In fact, Jesus came to cause division. The only kind of unity Jesus meant was one where you would die so He could live in you, that you and He would be one as He and the Father were one. Verse 26 says, "and that I myself may be in them." Also in verse 26, Jesus talks about knowing that the love of the Father "will continue to make you known in order that the love you have for me may be in them." Without death to self, no one can experience the love of God in his or her life. It does not matter how many answered prayers you can count or how many consequences you can point to, or in what ways you have felt the movement of the Spirit. Goodness, Jesus fed and healed multitudes who never received this unity.

Don't you understand that all such acts of God were sent to persuade us to allow Him to crucify us? Let us not rebel when God has done so much good among us. For to be sure, God probably has answered many of our prayers, guided us in many ways, and spoken kindly to us, but is self being crucified? Do we continue to rebel even as He shows us His kindness? These warnings were written down for us that we might not do what they did.[14]

> He did miracles in the sight of their fathers in the land of Egypt, in the region of Zoan. He divided the sea and led them through; he made the water stand firm like a wall. He guided them with the cloud by day and with light from the fire all night. He split the rocks in the desert and gave them water as abundant as the seas; he brought streams out of a rocky crag and made water flow down like rivers. But they continued to sin against him, rebelling in the desert against the Most High. (Ps. 78:12–17)

When Jesus said in John 17:26, "I myself may be in them," He meant that we must die so He can place a new self in us. Paul showed that he understood this in his letter to the Galatians.

> I have been crucified with Christ and I no longer live, but Christ lives in me. The life I live in the body, I live by faith in the Son of God, who loved me and gave himself for me. (Gal. 2:20)

True lovers of God can talk as if the crucified life is completed even though they know the "finish" must be made real. In the same way, we are saved, are being saved, and will be saved.[15]

> Not that I have already obtained all this, or have already been made perfect, but I press on to take hold of that for which Christ Jesus took hold of me. (Phil. 3:12)

On the cross Jesus said, "It is finished," because the victory had been won, and a way has been made open for us to enter the Holy of Holies, to be able to cry "Abba" or "Da Da." So why not give ourselves over fully to the victory? Let God have His way to crucify our flesh; let God purify the church as He sees fit. Having finished does not mean God will not deal with things in our lives. Rather, He will be patient knowing that the finished work of Jesus will be made complete in us as we surrender more each day.[16] Let us be willing to be made one with Jesus.

> Or do you show contempt for the riches of his kindness, tolerance and patience, not realizing that God's kindness leads you toward repentance? But because of your stubbornness and your unrepentant heart, you are storing up wrath against yourself for the day of God's wrath, when his righteous judgment will be revealed. (Rom. 2:4–5)

5

Power, Grace, and Love

Not Oppressive

> The thief comes only to steal and kill and destroy; I have come that they may have life, and have it to the full. (John 10:10)

Many people feel this teaching sounds oppressive and hard, and I have to agree it is impossible to live. Indeed if you can live what your pastor preaches, you are not hearing the gospel of Jesus. No man can fully live this unless the Lord enables him to go on to the heights of obedience. Indeed our feet must be transformed for us to live and endure the cross. For when the cross does its work and we become barren, pruned back, and empty of any fruit for God, despairing totally of who we are in the Lord and how much we have failed Him, then we can rejoice. Praise God that He makes our feet like the "feet of a deer," and it is He who will "enable" us to "stand on the heights."

> He makes my feet like the feet of a deer; he enables me to stand on the heights. (Ps. 18:33)

Unfortunately, men do not want the gospel of Jesus, so they water it down to make it possible to live. In short, we do not like what Jesus has to say, so we change what He means. But for the few who press on to let God be God, hopelessness will be their friend. For only in hopelessness will we find hope—hope to obey God and walk like Jesus walked. We say we want God and are tired of all our sin, yet we refuse to go to Jesus on His terms. Until we begin to say, "No one can live this," and "This is hopeless," we will never be ready for the power of God in our lives. We will never be ready for mercy until this despair enters our lives daily from the cross of Christ.

> You were wearied by all your ways, but you would not say, "It is hopeless." You found renewal of your strength, and so you did not faint. (Isa. 57:10)

Instead of saying it is "hopeless," we want false preachers who tell us just to have hope and be of good cheer. He who humbles himself and says it is hopeless will find the cross to be the pathway to the resurrected life. Drink deep of the hopelessness that God wants to work in your life, and you will be blessed.

See how Paul praises God for this hopelessness? See how God pronounced a death sentence in Paul's life so that He could give him more of the resurrected life? No tear is wasted, and those who mourn are promised blessings.[1] God placed Paul in a situation that was "far beyond" his "ability to endure" so that he could die more to self and gain more of Christ. He felt the sentence of death, not in an abstract book study way but from the cross pronouncing a death sentence in his life. Let us be willing to endure this also that we might be dependent on God.

> We do not want you to be uninformed, brothers, about the hardships we suffered in the province of Asia. We were under great pressure, far beyond our ability to endure, so that we despaired even of life. Indeed, in our hearts we felt the sentence of death. But this happened that we might not rely on ourselves but on God, who raises the dead. (2 Cor. 1:8–9)

Again do not run from the hopelessness that God tries to work in your life. Remember that Jesus hung on the cross and wondered why God had left Him. Likewise, there will be times when God deals with your pride, for instance, and though you think you have repented, it will feel like God has forsaken you. This is where faith becomes faith, where we say with Job, "Though the Lord slay me I will trust Him."[2] For indeed, God will slay you, and you must cling to faith that everything is in His hands. Then, when prideful self has been broken, you will be blessed in Jesus.

We only rob ourselves of a closer walk with Christ when we refuse to let God crucify us. I remember as a young Christian finding every day full of pain, confusion, weakness, and conviction. It was as if God showed me pride and self every second of every day. My bones literally ached.[3] This went on for years, and just when I thought it was over, another wave of discipline came pounding over my head.[4] It would be one dreadful, deep experience after another showing me who I really was.

Often, others told me just to focus on the forgiveness of God. I tried hard to do so, but it was in vain. No one said such things were normal and to praise God for His work. Therefore, I often complained, "If this is the good news, I don't want to tell anyone about it." Of course after God had done that first major work, I understood what was happening; God had given me His cross for my life. And once I had a very small taste of the resurrected life I wanted more. Although the flesh hates it and I often recoil, I am filled with more joy than words can express. No smiles, indeed I may have tears, can express this inexpressible joy that God works by way of the cross. For the cross achieves my goal, "the salvation of my soul."[5]

Again, we must carry the death of Jesus and not the cross we choose, not a cross we pick out with its timeline for when and how to deal with sin. It cannot be a death from a false humility or an on-and-off type of crucifixion. Indeed nothing hurts worse then to get on and off the cross. I have watched as many go through the double pain of getting back on the cross to allow God to start the process over again. Much of the suffering they experience results from their folly of getting down off the cross. This is what Paul meant when he said that he was "again in the pains of childbirth" until Christ was formed in his brothers and sisters.[6] If you will not suffer on the cross, then others who are more spiritual must suffer for you.

Paul knew that only in weakness was he made strong.[7] This is true, utter weakness and despair of self. It is not the phrase we try to use as magic, "Oh, I know I need God, but I'm not perfect." All pride, excuses, reasons, and justifications for not obeying God must be killed. We must remain on the cross until we feel naked and exposed before God and men. We must let God break us until we admit all the secret rebellion and self-interest that live in us. We must grovel in our sin as long as God wills it, so that the blood may cleanse us. We must writhe in pain at what and who we are if we want the power to obey God. When God works this in our lives we will say with David, "I am a worm and not a man."

> But I am a worm and not a man, scorned by men and despised by the people. (Ps. 22:6)

We must let all human joy be removed from us so that when the work is done it will be His joy in us—the joy of heaven. After all, isn't this what the cross produced in Jesus? For God gives the power to live the true Christian life only to those with broken hearts and the knowledge of how to remain broken on a daily basis. Only those who put self to death by the Spirit find the joy that comes from God instead of the Church's hype machine. There is no other way. Notice in John 15:4-5 how obedience and emptiness intertwine. Only those who allow themselves to become nothing "bear much fruit."

> Remain in me, and I will remain in you. No branch can bear fruit by itself; it must remain in the vine. Neither can you bear fruit unless you remain in me. I am the vine; you are the branches. If a man remains in me and I in him, *he will bear much fruit*; apart from me you can do *nothing*. (John 15:4–5, emphasis added)

Unless we have experienced in Christ His brokenness, surrender, and obedience, we have been living the false Christian life that any man can live by his own power. We might have allowed God to clean up our lives once, but then went right back to all of our self-will and effort.[8] We count on God's grace, forgetting that His grace gives us the power to walk like Jesus in total surrender.

> For the grace of God that brings salvation has appeared to all men. It teaches us to say "No" to ungodliness and worldly passions, and to live self-controlled, upright and godly lives in this present age. (Titus 2:11–12)

The grace we have been taught is not really God's grace but merely man's attempt to make the good news into his own image. Truly we become "detestable, disobedient and unfit for doing anything good." Until this hits us with great tears and pain, we have not received the grace of God into our lives as we should. Nor can we count ourselves as a disciple of Jesus, for our life of disobedience proves we do not belong to Him.

> They claim to know God, but by their actions they deny him. They are detestable, disobedient and unfit for doing anything good. (Titus 1:16)

If we want the power to live the Christian life, we must let go of a self-centered heart. It does not matter that we "claim to know God." Our actions deny Him. We must go to the cross of Christ if we want to have the power to live the impossible. If we desire the joy and peace of Jesus, if we want the abundant life, then we must receive from God this kind of faith. It is a faith that was like Jesus', a faith totally dependent and surrendered to God, a faith lost in loving God with no concern for self. To those not willing to shrink back from death and from death to self, this is what it means to die in the Lord and *for* the Lord.

> They overcame him by the blood of the Lamb and by the word of their testimony; they did not love their lives so much as to shrink from death. (Rev. 12:11)

We have established that we must walk as Jesus walked, surrendering all to the Father. Let us now look at how we can hate specifically as He commanded in Luke 14:26. Remember that large crowds were following Jesus. It is easy to fool ourselves into thinking we follow Him. Hating separates the followers from the disciples.

> If anyone comes to me and does not hate his father and mother, his wife and children, his brothers and sisters—yes, even his own life—he cannot be my disciple. (Luke 14:26)

6

Hating Your Mother and Father

Hating Your Mother

Since Jesus hated His mother, utterly abhorred His human love for her, He could allow God to direct how to honor her. When Jesus did this, it looked on the surface of things like He used her as a sermon prop. Here, a loving mom comes to see her son out of concern for His health. She comes with good motives. In fact, she gets the whole family together to help Jesus.

> When his family heard about this, they went to take charge of him, for they said, "He is out of his mind." (Mark 3:21)

Jesus' mother showed up because of some rumors, and Jesus responded with the rudest of remarks. He told a whole crowd that Mary was not really His mother. Jesus renounced His mother in no uncertain terms. If you had been there, would you have rebuked Jesus and told Him that the Bible says we are to honor our fathers and mothers? Would you have quoted Scripture to Him who is Scripture? We would have told Jesus to be a little kinder and to use a softer approach so those listening would continue to pay attention to Him. Just look at how unlovingly Jesus responded to His mother:

> Then Jesus' mother and brothers arrived. Standing outside, they sent someone in to call him. A crowd was sitting around him, and they told him, "Your mother and brothers are outside looking for you." "Who are my mother and my brothers?" he asked. Then he looked at those seated in a circle around him and said, "Here are my mother and my brothers! Whoever does God's will is my brother and sister and mother." (Mark 3:31–35)

First, Jesus left Mom "standing outside," and if there is one thing moms do not like, it is not getting the attention they think is due them. Jesus would not even take a moment for the mother who loved Him all those years. "What ingratitude and lack of love Jesus demonstrated," we would exclaim. This is because our ways of love are so different from God's. Indeed God says that as "the heavens are higher than the earth, so are my ways higher than your ways and my thoughts than your thoughts."[1]

Secondly, the whole crowd testified that Jesus' mother waited outside to talk to Him. Instead of Jesus responding kindly to a mother's concern, He rebuked her in front of everyone. And it was not just any rebuke. He told the crowd that they were His mother because they were doing God's will. How thoroughly embarrassed Mary must have felt. Jesus thought more of the crowd than of His own mother.

Did you catch that? Jesus called His mother an ungodly woman. He told a whole crowd of people that His mom was in sin and could not understand the will of God. When was the last time the Holy Spirit led you to use your mother as a sermon prop? See, you do not even hate your mother enough to know how to honor her in the Lord. Instead, most of us have a sinful human love for our mothers that shows favoritism rather than a pure love flowing from the throne of God. If we were willing to hate our love for our mothers, God would be able to fill us with His pure love, but instead we compromise the message. We would be able to do the most loving and best things toward our mothers, no matter how it looked to them. Instead, we use God's Word to justify our fleshly desire to please our mothers. We obey our mothers to keep peace in the family, not to make peace between them and God.[2]

Your only goal with Mom must be to get her to the cross of Christ. If she is a Christian, then it is to keep her at the cross. If she refuses to draw near to the cross to understand, so be it. May a curse be on her. Does the curse trouble you? See how far we have to go in our love for God? We think God will show Mom a little more grace and mercy because she *is* our Mom. However, Paul says that if anyone, including Mom, will not love the Lord, then (and I quote) "a curse" be on her. Plus, to top it off Paul points out that he writes "this greeting" in his "own hand." Can you imagine you writing this in a Mother's Day card and being proud of the fact that you wrote it?

> I, Paul, write this greeting in my own hand. If anyone does not love the Lord—a curse be on him. Come, O Lord! (1 Cor. 16:21–22)

Jesus, however, had a mother who really loved God and who, years later, understood her son's words. She would understand all Jesus' apparent lack of love when she drew near to the cross. How sad that many a mom will never realize this kind of love because they will not let self be crucified at the cross. They forfeit hearing Jesus say, "Dear woman." Oh, the rich love of God—that just before everything is to be completed on the cross, Jesus takes care of His mother. Of course, many a mother would complain that Jesus thought of them last. Would your mother be indignant with you that you did not think of her first and foremost before going to the cross? As always, the response to the cross reveals a man's heart.

Are you willing to suffer the wrath of your mom for years in hopes that she might hear God say to her, "Dear woman"? It takes a man with the ability to hate in the Lord to display this kind of love.

> When Jesus saw his mother there, and the disciple whom he loved standing nearby, he said to his mother, "Dear woman, here is your son," and to the disciple, "Here is your mother." From that time on, this disciple took her into his home. (John 19:26-27)

Remember that Jesus did not come to His mother later in the day and explain things about rejecting her. He knew that the best way to honor her was to let her pride be wounded; she needed desperately to see her sin.[3] She needed to go home and pray before God about what her son had said. It was the most loving thing Jesus could have done. Jesus did not make the cross easy for her like we would have. He did not come to her and say, "Gee, Mom, I love you, and I know this is hard for you to understand, but I am really OK. Now do you want to accept Me as your personal Lord and Savior?"

Jesus was not concerned about His own feelings or His mother's understanding. His only desire was that she get right before God. He possessed a selfless love. God wants to work this kind of pure love in all of us, but we must hate our fleshly love for our mothers in order for it to happen. Of course, not everyone who is rude to his or her mother loves her. It is enough to say that if you want to love your mom with God's love, then hate your love for her. Only then will you be given wisdom and knowledge as to how you can honor your mother.

It should be noted that some find it terribly hard to love their mothers. Such people must hate their bad feelings and allow the Holy Spirit to work an attitude of servanthood in them. In their serving they must not allow themselves to be manipulated or swayed from the will of God. While this sounds simple, I have witnessed many forsake the Lord because they could not get this down. Either way, the key to loving and honoring a mother must be guided and empowered by the Holy Spirit, and the only way to make room for that power is to hate in Jesus.

Hating Your Father

With the hating of your father we come back to the void Scripture dilemma. Jesus said this:

> And do not call anyone on earth "father," for you have one Father, and he is in heaven. (Matt. 23:9)

The void Scripture comes into play when we quote Paul, who seems to disobey Jesus when he himself tells the Corinthian church that he is a "father" to them. Paul goes even further in this when he refers to Timothy as his "son."

> Even though you have ten thousand guardians in Christ, you do not have many fathers, for in Christ Jesus I became your father through the gospel. Therefore I urge you to imitate me. For this reason I am sending to you Timothy, my son whom I love, who is faithful in the Lord. He will remind you of my way of life in Christ Jesus, which agrees with what I teach everywhere in every church. (1 Cor. 4:15-17)

How do we put all these scriptures together? Should we nullify one Scripture by quoting another? Never! We shall elevate them both up to heaven and obey them. We shall not bring one down by lifting up another and thus disobey one over the other. They both are of equal value in God's sight.

This shows us that we must hate the human nature in us, which gives ungodly allegiance to another man. We must vomit out of our hearts this love for man so that we might gain from God a pure and honest love—a love from heaven that hears from God as to whom we can call "Father." Choosing in ourselves whom we can call "Father" is total sin and will only end in idolatry. Where God is *all*, giving us His love for another man, He remains on the throne, and no idolatry takes place. Where this hatred is present we can honor godly men.[4] Yet without this hate, honor turns into flattery and idolatry.

God has given us each a human father to honor. Yet, we cannot know how to do so until we come to hate our human love for the men we call "Father." Until we purify our hearts and see all men as brothers, we can never really love as we should. A simple test of this is the *rejoicing measurement*. If someone rejoices more when a family member comes to the Lord than they do when someone in China repents, they are full of idolatry. Just because someone has our family DNA does not make them more worthy of our concern and love. Truthfully we all come from the same DNA of Adam and Eve. If someone you know puts more effort into praying for a family member than he or she does for the neighbor up the street, something is astray in his or her heart. We are all brothers, and God rejoices just as much when someone who is not related to us comes to Him as He does in the salvation of our family members. To be filled with God's love means to have an equal amount of love and concern for everyone. In the same way, I am no more distressed when a family member falls away from the Lord as I am when someone falls away whom I do not know well.

This concept of hating one's father will come out in some very harsh and real ways when compared to the world's love for family members. Even when you honor your father by calling him "Father," everyone will sense something different. They will be able to sense the lack of idolatry, and if your father is an unbeliever, most likely he will resent it. Remember that when we fell in the Garden of Eden, we chose to become "like god." Men, especially fathers, want respect and honor as though they were minigods. They want their advice and talk of life to be accepted as wisdom. They want to be looked up to for the men they think they are.

When you allow God to remove such idolatry of human love from your heart, you cannot hide it from others. Everyone will see how you serve and honor your father, but it will be based on truth with God as your Father. Everyone will sense it just as one might smell perfume in a room. Some will think the "fragrance" smells like "life," while others will say it smells like "death." You simply will not be able to stop everyone from seeing and sensing something different when you call Pop, "Father."

> To the one we are the smell of death; to the other, the fragrance of life. And who is equal to such a task? (2 Cor. 2:16)

For some, God might forbid them to call their dads, "Father." For others, God might see fit to give them permission to honor their human fathers in this way. God will work and allow whatever is best for His glory and your father's heart. Do not begin, however, to say that you know what God's will is in this matter until you hate your own desires. It takes some real wrestling before God's throne each day to know His will with your human father. Whatever the particulars concerning this issue, know that God will remove any earthly attachment to a man you call "Father." By the time you finish your walk with God on earth, you should honestly be able to say, "I have no father but God." In fact many who give all to God find their parents do not want anything to do with them. They do not mind their children being religious—that looks good to everyone. But they do not want their children to give all to God.

At your father's funeral, you can tell others that your Father still lives. Those who cannot function after their fathers die need to see their idolatry—not a therapist. In fact, it is very possible that it may not be God's will for you to attend your father's funeral.

> He said to another man, "Follow me." But the man replied, "Lord, first let me go and bury my father." Jesus said to him, "Let the dead bury their own dead, but you go and proclaim the kingdom of God." (Luke 9:59–60)

If Jesus said this once in a literal way, then He is very likely to say it again. Why is it that we are so quick to claim all the "good" passages about God's peace, love, and forgiveness literally but are not willing to do so with the painful passages? How is it that when Jesus speaks literally about dying for our sins we fully accept His words, but when He speaks of our sin we reject that? Let us accept all Scriptures and allow the Holy Spirit to give life to them. The quality of a man's Christianity is tested by his acceptance and obedience to the scriptures he does not like.

In fact, since we have it written that we must remain busy serving Jesus, we should assume that we should not even take time to attend our fathers' funerals. After all, our "fathers" are only those who do God's will, and if our human fathers do not follow God, then they are no longer our fathers and deserve no special recognition. If Jesus told this to a man who was just beginning to seek God's will, how much more can those in the middle of doing God's will find this to be true? Let us start by taking Jesus at all of His Word just as we do with the comfortable Scriptures. We should be surprised if God does send us to our fathers' funerals rather than if He does not. Yet how many are surprised even at the thought of such a possibility? I remember visiting with a Christian whose father was in the hospital. We began to discuss the cross and came around to the hypothetical situation that God may have him do something else while his father died in the hospital. Such a thought was abhorrent to him, and he turned his back on God. If it is hard for us to even discuss these things, what does this say about our relationship with God?

If your father does God's will, then he is your brother, and you will soon see him in heaven. Therefore, there is no need to stop your work for the Lord and go to his funeral. In the scope of things, the death of a godly father is merely a short separation. In fact, I pray that my sons are so busy doing God's will that they skip my funeral and keep on working. I will see them soon enough. So if you want to assume God's will about your father's funeral, then assume not to attend. In summary, it would be very unusual for God to call someone to go to a funeral according to what we read in the Bible.

However, since we do not worship or follow ink, we must seek God on what to do when our human fathers die. If it is to God's glory, He will send you to the funeral. If it is not to His glory, you will not be allowed to go. Just be found hating your father so that you will know whether to go or not and how to conduct yourself. This happened to a sister in the Lord. Her father was a church hypocrite. So, in obedience to the Spirit, she obeyed 1 Cor. 5:11–13 and would not associate with him. When her grandmother died both she and her father, whom she had not seen in years, attended the funeral. Because she loved the Lord, she did not waver from her love for her Father and refused to talk with her earthly father.

As if to drive the point home, while she was still in town, her other grandmother died. The temptation to remain and comfort her earthly father tugged at her heart. This woman knew, however, that God desired for her not to attend the second funeral and, therefore, left town. Jesus' words "let the dead bury the dead" became a reality in her life.

A Word About Family

If you have hated your father and mother in the Lord and God does not send you to their funerals, you will not only obey but also approve of His decision. If God does send you, know that you will make some enemies in the Lord; for God longs to divide families. See why you must hate father and mother in order to hear what God wants to work? You must hate your parents because Jesus is "distressed" until He can begin to divide families. We must feel that same distress in our hearts. Before our evangelism will truly be effective, we must have the heart of Jesus, including His distress.

> I have come to bring fire on the earth, and how I wish it were already kindled! But I have a baptism to undergo, and how distressed I am until it is completed! Do you think I came to bring peace on earth? No, I tell you, but division. From now on there will be five in one family divided against each other, three against two and two against three. They will be divided, father against son and son against father, mother against daughter and daughter against mother, mother-in-law against daughter-in-law and daughter-in-law against mother-in-law. (Luke 12:49–53)

Have you hated your family enough that you have the heart of Jesus? Are you burning with this type of "fire"? Do you feel you cannot wait until His Spirit begins to shake up your family? Jesus came to bring division and those who love Him rejoice in that fact. Why do we think about peace in a family when Jesus said He came to bring just the opposite? True Christians love to see families torn apart by Jesus because that means some will come to Him and others will take their place of destruction. While we desire that no one perish, isn't our joy to be the same as Jesus, to see the "rising and falling of many"?[5]

I always laugh when someone says something against another group like, "That group is a cult because they divide families." Such statements tell me everything about their Christianity: that they do not have a clue as to what Jesus taught. It takes some real godly hatred to eagerly desire this division. So whether you call someone "Father" or not, whether you go to a funeral or not, you must determine to become so dead to your family ties that you are distressed until the fire of division "kindles" in your family.

How much godly hatred we must pray for before we can claim to hear God's voice concerning honoring our father and mothers! If you do not long for division and do not want to be the source of it, you have not yet learned to hate your father and mother. You are not even ready to become a disciple, let alone to be called a *Christian*. For this is what Jesus wishes; it is what He came to bring.

All this takes place with respect, gentleness, and kindness—but the effect remains the same. Remember: if you are led of the Spirit, you can break bones with gentleness, and the gentleness of Christ can divide families.[6] If they crucified Jesus because of the love of God in His life, how much more will they crucify those of us who are weak and frail? Jesus warned that our enemies will be members of our own households. Let us begin to hate those ties now so that the fire can be kindled. For the very last thing a Christian is concerned with is human genealogy. Our family is not of this world.

These are just a few examples of the hundred different ways in which the Holy Spirit might lead us in this matter of hatred. Without hating our fathers and mothers, we will focus in on the family to the point of idolatry. We will claim to keep the promises of God for our families while we idolize them and in the end find ourselves without God and hope of salvation. Then it will be revealed that we were mere travelers on the Christian road with Jesus, taking all the blessings but refusing to die to self.

Saying Goodbye

Even the simplest of things must be surrendered before the cross of Christ before we can ever claim that we know God's will concerning our families. Even the simple act of saying "goodbye" must be surrendered and crucified on the cross.

> Still another said, "I will follow you, Lord; but first let me go back and say good-by to my family." (Luke 9:61)

This man wanted only a quick goodbye, and he promised to return and follow Jesus. Yet this was not God's will, and that phone call on Mother's Day may not be His will either. Those flowers you sent to Mom on Mother's Day may have been sin and may have entrapped your mother further in her sin. On the other hand, flowers sent to your mother may help save her soul. You will never know what is best until you hate your desire to please her on Mother's Day. Indeed God may want you to send the flowers the day *after* Mother's Day, who knows? Remember that a simple thing like saying "goodbye" may be sin.

> Still another said, "I will follow you, Lord; but first let me go back and say good-by to my family." Jesus replied, "No one who puts his hand to the plow and looks back is fit for service in the kingdom of God." (Luke 9:61–62)

There is work to be done for Christ which does not include the niceties of family obligations. A gift to our fathers on their birthday may not be God's will. Let me remind you that it is not up to us to decide how to best honor our fathers and mothers.[7] Our decisions would be tainted with sin no matter how much Scripture we quote. God, who is love, knows what is best and will work that love in us. Of course it may be God's will to say "goodbye," buy a gift, or make a phone call, but we will never know until we hate every family obligation. We will never be the salt and light in those situations until we learn to hate scripturally. For a man must be dead to his feelings on what to say and how to say it so that Jesus might speak through him. We must be dead to our parents' whims, demands, and manipulations. No firm guideline, principle, or law can be set down; this is a heart issue and will be seen in how the Holy Spirit leads us. Whatever the case, know that our parents will sense that we hate them in Jesus. Jesus does not light a lamp and then hide it under a bushel. Following Jesus in this matter will come out in ways our parents like and dislike. For example, a group of college students, young in the Lord, went home on breaks with a real servant attitude. Mothers would often tell us, "I couldn't get them to do dishes at home, but now they come home and do them without complaining!" The parents were happy until other deeper spiritual issues began to arise; then our ministry was their worst enemy.

No longer will you pay any heed to your parents just because they are your parents. God, however, might tell you to obey your mother and father as He told Moses to obey his father-in-law. Yet, all obedience must pass by Him first. Notice in verse 23 how Jethro and Moses sought the Lord's will together. No advice should be taken, no matter how noble sounding, until it meets with God's will.

> Jethro, Moses' father-in-law, together with Moses' sons and wife, came to him in the desert, where he was camped near the mountain of God. Jethro had sent word to him, "I, your father-in-law Jethro, am coming to you with your wife and her two sons." So Moses went out to meet his father-in-law and bowed down and kissed him. They greeted each other and then went into the tent. Moses told his father-in-law about everything the Lord had done to Pharaoh and the Egyptians for Israel's sake and about all the hardships they had met along the way and how the Lord had saved them. Jethro was delighted to hear about all the good things the Lord had done for Israel in rescuing them from the hand of the Egyptians. He said, "Praise be to the Lord, who rescued you from the hand of the Egyptians and of Pharaoh, and who rescued the people from the hand of the Egyptians. Now I know that the Lord is greater than all other

> gods, for he did this to those who had treated Israel arrogantly." Then Jethro, Moses' father-in-law, brought a burnt offering and other sacrifices to God, and Aaron came with all the elders of Israel to eat bread with Moses' father-in-law in the presence of God. The next day Moses took his seat to serve as judge for the people, and they stood around him from morning till evening. When his father-in-law saw all that Moses was doing for the people, he said, "What is this you are doing for the people? Why do you alone sit as judge, while all these people stand around you from morning till evening?" Moses answered him, "Because the people come to me to seek God's will. Whenever they have a dispute, it is brought to me, and I decide between the parties and inform them of God's decrees and laws." Moses' father-in-law replied, "What you are doing is not good. You and these people who come to you will only wear yourselves out. The work is too heavy for you; you cannot handle it alone. Listen now to me and I will give you some advice, and may God be with you. You must be the people's representative before God and bring their disputes to him. Teach them the decrees and laws, and show them the way to live and the duties they are to perform. But select capable men from all the people—men who fear God, trustworthy men who hate dishonest gain—and appoint them as officials over thousands, hundreds, fifties and tens. Have them serve as judges for the people at all times, but have them bring every difficult case to you; the simple cases they can decide themselves. That will make your load lighter, because they will share it with you. If you do this *and God so commands*, you will be able to stand the strain, and all these people will go home satisfied." Moses listened to his father-in-law and did everything he said. (Exod. 18:5–24, emphasis added)

If you do anything just to please your parents, unless God has willed it, then you remain in sin. If God leads you to please them, then it is not you, but Christ living in you. Remember, you are supposed to be dead in Christ. Does a dead man have a desire to please his mother or father? Yet how quickly we try to please Mom and Dad in even the simple things like inviting them over for dinner.

Didn't Jesus already command us not to invite our family over to dinner? Didn't Jesus say, "Do not invite"?

> Then Jesus said to his host, "When you give a luncheon or dinner, do not invite your friends, your brothers or relatives, or your rich neighbors; if you do, they may invite you back and so you will be repaid. But when you give a banquet, invite the poor, the crippled, the lame, the blind, and you will be blessed. Although they cannot repay you, you will be repaid at the resurrection of the righteous." (Luke 14:12–14)

Of course, if your family members are "blind," "poor," "crippled," or "lame" physically and spiritually, invite them as the Spirit leads. Honor them, however, by revealing their blindness and offer them life. Treat them as you would any stranger in the Lord, showing the same love and the same concern shown to all men. After all, if there is one thing certain about the love of God, it shows no favoritism. This is why Paul charges Timothy "in the sight of God and Christ Jesus and the elect angels" to do "nothing out of favoritism."

> I charge you, in the sight of God and Christ Jesus and the elect angels, to keep these instructions without partiality, and to do nothing out of favoritism. (1 Tim. 5:21)

Stop all the socializing and wasting of time and get on with the work of Jesus. Stop doing the family thing of going over to Mom and Dad's for dinner and then repaying them by inviting them back over to your house. Get on with the real work of Jesus by serving those who cannot serve you back. Hate your worldly obligations so that when an obligation must be filled it is done by the Spirit. If you have this hatred, then Jesus might, if it is His will, have you invite Mom and Dad to dinner. Let your motto be that the days are evil and the workers are few, therefore, so much for Christmas dinners and family reunions! Indeed to a Christian, a family reunion is a forest of dry timber ready for the match. It is an opportunity for the Spirit to start the fire Jesus wished and longed for.

God will give rich wisdom and knowledge to those who desire to do His will. What joy will be given to those who make God Lord of every situation, even to the saying of "goodbye." They will be given power to honor their father and mother. They will feel the deepest and purest of love in themselves for their parents. I know I do.

7

Hating Your Wife

As If You Did Not Have a Wife

Before we get started with this verse it must be pointed out that Jesus does not say anything about hating one's husband. One of the primary reasons is that Jesus is addressing men who must be the spiritual leaders. The other reason is that Christians are engaged to be married to Jesus. Jesus is our husband, and there is no need for us to hate Him.

When Adam fell in the Garden of Eden, all men became worshippers of women; therefore God judged man for listening to his wife. As a result, all men turned their backs from God for just a moment and listened to another voice. Men gave up their position of leadership and accepted advice that agreed with the flesh. Therefore, men must learn to test all advice and listen to God only if they hope to become the spiritual leaders in the home. This testing requires that men learn, from the Holy Spirit, how to hate their wives. I know many a man who turned his back on God because of his wife.

> To Adam he said, "*Because you listened to your wife* and ate from the tree about which I commanded you, 'You must not eat of it,' Cursed is the ground because of you; through painful toil you will eat of it all the days of your life." (Gen. 3:17, emphasis added)

As we will see, marriage is a worldly affair, and anyone seeking to serve God must fully realize this. Therefore, the husband must set the example in the Lord demonstrating how to hate for Jesus. Paul puts the command for a man to hate his wife this way:

> What I mean, brothers, is that the time is short. From now on those who have wives should live as if they had none. (1 Cor. 7:29)

Each married Christian man must live his daily life as if he were not married. In other words, a married man should live as if he did not have a wife. Of course marriage is not forbidden, and it certainly has the blessing of God.[1] Yet in order for a marriage to be godly, each person must live properly in the Lord. Jesus' instruction to hate a wife deals directly with this issue of a godly marriage. Jesus' words are the how-to of a godly marriage and an honest worship of God.

These comments by Jesus and Paul were meant to describe marriage as the beautiful arrangement God planned. God does not seek to restrict married couples by laying down hard rules. We have to overcome, however, the idolatry that comes naturally in a marriage.

> I am saying this for your own good, not to restrict you, but that you may live in a right way in undivided devotion to the Lord. (1 Cor. 7:35)

Hating your wife is for your "own good." Unfortunately, because of the Fall, the very arrangement of marriage makes us worldly. This worldliness must be purged in order to have a godly marriage. The worldliness comes in when we seek to do one thing—to please our mate. A man who gets up every day and sets out to please his wife makes himself a worldly man. Instead, he must hate his wife and live as though he did not have one. A husband should get up in the morning, look at the woman next to him, and ask, "Who are you?" Again, the "affairs of this world" in a marriage happen when a man seeks to "please his wife." A man who seeks to please his wife, to make her happy, is a worldly man. He is not Spirit-filled in the pleasing unless he hates her in a godly way.

> I would like you to be free from concern. An unmarried man is concerned about the Lord's affairs—how he can please the Lord. But a married man is concerned about the affairs of this world—how he can please his wife. (1 Cor. 7:32–33)

A husband should only have one concern each day, and it is not the wishes of his wife. It does not matter what the day's agenda is (taking out the trash, mowing the yard, fixing certain items, or just going shopping). He must hate the demand of such things so he can hear the will of God. Sometimes it might be God's will to do those things, but we will never know until these things do not nag us. A husband must hate his desire to be with his wife. His only desire is to be with God. Out of that everything else will come in due time and in a holy way.

Please do not commit the void factor sin at this point. We will explore soon enough how a husband is to love his wife "like Christ loved the church." Certainly God works an eternal love in a marriage given over fully to Him. Unfortunately, very few willfully give their marriages completely over to God. Men remain unwilling to hate their wives and to live as if they "had none." Therefore, God cannot create godly marriages, and couples turn to all kinds of self-help books and worthless seminars. If a wife wants a godly marriage, then she should act as if she were not married. If a wife wants a strong spiritual husband, she should pray for him to live as though she were not there.

This requires that she hate her own life, for what woman willingly asks her husband to pretend she is not there? Of course, God will work a deep love and affection in a godly marriage, but in His timing and way. Remember what happened to Adam when he gave Eve some attention at the wrong time? Just a moment of the wrong kind of attention and he fell into disobedience and idolatry. A moment's attention in the wrong direction[2] and the gates of hell swung open to receive him.

Because of the Fall, women were listened to, and they want to be worshipped. They demand that their husbands listen to them and meet their needs, feelings, and concerns. Adam "listened" to his wife once, and we husbands continue to do the same thing to this day. This is one reason, out of many, why women are not permitted by God to be preachers or to have authority over a man.[3]

To hate your wife means that you eagerly reject her demands, requests, and opinions. How different things would have been if Adam would have hated his wife's opinion on the very small matter of fruit. If he had checked with God first, sin would not have entered into the world.

How different the cross is from the world.[4] Counselors and seminars tell men that they do not give enough attention to their wives, and the Bible says they should live as if they were not married.

Every day I get up as a married man, and I set out to hate my wife's demands and schedules for me. In short, I tune her out so that I might tune into God. Once I do this, then God can communicate to me His will. His will might include meeting some of the demands of my wife, and it might not. In other words, she is not god, and it is to God I must turn for direction and inspiration. Many days God leads me to meet almost every demand and schedule that my wife sets down. On the other hand, there have been plenty of days I did not do one thing she wanted. My goal is to hate my plans to please or not please my wife and to hear God only. For a Christian, the statement, "Behind every good man is a good woman," should not hold true. What should be true is that behind any good person is God only.

Many days God requires my wife to drop her plans and give her full attention to my concerns. After all, God created her to be my helpmate. All of this of course goes against the flesh, for we want to be served rather than to serve. Plus, whether or not a wife's needs are met, most women resent not being the center of attention. Remember, in the garden woman first chose to become a god. The desire for this worship and attention remains deep-seated in a woman, just as it is within man to go along with the woman and not be the leader God meant him to be. The man who hates will be given a proper holy love that was in him before the Fall in the garden. For example, one time when my wife attended a conference for several days, I sent her flowers. Now, before you jump on the bandwagon saying, "See, you pleased your wife," let me tell you what I wrote on the card. I wrote, "Remember who you are engaged to." I wanted to remind her not to get caught up in all the fanfare of the conference and to remember she is really promised to Jesus. I wanted her to know that I am merely her brother in the Lord and someday I must present her to Jesus ready for marriage to Him.

Have I ever sent my wife flowers or given her gifts to remind her of the love God has put in my heart for her? You bet. When I hate my wife God pours His love through me in many different ways, and He always gets all the glory.

Master

Hating returns a man's soul and heart to the position of leadership God meant for him. The husband should have a wall of activity and zeal to reject all demands but God's in his life. The wife senses, and others can tell, that the husband really is in charge. Many a woman in the church would find marriage to a true godly man intolerable. For everyone knows that no leadership/submissive game is being played. Such leadership is straightforward, and everyone knows who is in charge, just as everyone knows that Jesus is in charge. Nor does a wife live a lie by telling everyone that her husband is in charge while she really holds control. For everyone can see how he lives his life and conducts himself and that he walks with authority and leadership in the home. Of course, the world and the worldly resent this, but it leads the way to the storehouse of love God has for a marriage.

Married couples refusing to live like this have a divided love for God, which is idolatry. 1 Cor. 7:34 is clear. Those who seek to please their wives are divided in their interests and concerned with worldly affairs. One part of them wants to please the Lord, and the other part wants to please their spouse. However, two gods cannot possibly sit on the same throne. A man will destroy himself if he tries to please both. He will be pulled in two different directions until he is torn apart and suffers from spiritual burnout. No matter how many promises he makes to be a good family man, he is bound to fail, at least in God's sight. God must have all of our attention if there is to be life in a marriage. Fellowship with Him only must lead to all other fellowship. Ever tried to listen to two people talking at the same time? It is an impossible situation, especially if they both are trying to say something important. Your wife has something important to say and so does God. The question is who gets all your attention?

How sad to watch a man try to grow spiritually in the Lord under circumstances where the wife drips on him.[5] Many women destroy the efforts of the Holy Spirit when their husbands really start becoming the man of the house. These "religious" women have their ideas of what constitutes a godly man and on what timetable it should happen. They were the first to play god, and until Jesus transforms a woman, that desire remains in her. Thus, when the Holy Spirit begins to work something contrary to their ideas, they stop the work of God. I have seen many a religious woman tear down her own house with her own hands[6] all because she did not like the way God worked in her husband. Let us turn our attention to the following Scripture:

> But a married man is concerned about the affairs of this world—how he can please his wife—and his interests are divided. An unmarried woman or virgin is concerned about the Lord's affairs: Her aim is to be devoted to the Lord in both body and spirit. But a married woman is concerned about the affairs of this world—how she can please her husband. (1 Cor. 7:33–34)

Those choosing to remain single have an easier spiritual walk than those who are married. Therefore, singles are the very last group needing a special ministry. The singles in a church should remind the married how to live in the Lord. Yet, since marriage has become an idol in the church today, we feel sorry for singles and give them extra attention. We are completely backwards in our worship of God, and a cross-carrying, godly home is indeed rare. Religious homes can be found, but *hating* homes cannot.

Although my love for my wife grows deeper each day, many times I wish I were single. If I were unmarried, then I would have more freedom to serve the Lord, and I could focus more on the needs of Christ. It takes real work, hatred, for married couples to remain devoted to the Lord, not only in body but also in spirit. Let us look at Ephesians 5:25, the passage most people resort to for their void passage.

> Husbands, love your wives, just as Christ loved the church and gave himself up for her. (Eph. 5:25)

So how did Christ love the church? Does Jesus give into the wishes, demands, and opinions of the church? No. Jesus served His wife by being a real leader. Jesus ignores her whims and shows the course to follow every day. Jesus "gave Himself up" and sought not to please Himself or to do what He wanted each day. Instead, He denied His desires and plans and those of His bride that He might hear from God how best to serve and love her. Jesus lets God mature the church through Him, and husbands are to be the same instrument of blessing. This is exactly how love grows in a godly marriage.

Consider for a moment, do you as Jesus' bride tell Jesus what to do each day? A man should lead his wife in the same way the church obeys Jesus. In the same way that Jesus leads the church, man must lead his home. To be sure, the leadership is done in the deepest of love, but it is done with the greatest of authority and power. Most women want spiritual men full of gentleness and love but will not tolerate any real authority and leading.

> Wives, submit to your husbands as to the Lord. For the husband is the head of the wife as Christ is the head of the church,

> his body, of which he is the Savior. Now as the church submits to Christ, so also wives should submit to their husbands in everything. (Eph. 5:22–24)

Just as the church submits to Jesus in everything, "wives should submit to their husbands in everything." A man will have to hate his desire to let things run themselves. A woman will have to hate her desire to do her own thing, and she must submit as God wants her to. I could care less what my wife demands, just as Jesus could care less about what I want. Only when I submit to the needs and plans of Jesus will I find happiness. In the same way, as a family submits to the plans that God inspires in a husband, then everyone will find happiness, love, and joy.

In order to hear God's perfect daily plan for his family, a husband must hate every demand placed on him. He must be willing to lead without having to explain every step. The responsibility must be fully a husband's for the spiritual condition of his family and wife. Even though the wife must have everything explained to her because of the Fall, a husband must push forward with those things God wants to work. No more than Jesus has to explain everything to His bride should a husband have to explain his reasons for doing something in God. In fact, he may not know exactly what God is working and could not explain it even if he wanted to. Indeed God may not let him know every step. Like Abraham, a husband may not know where he is going.[7] Just like Jesus demonstrated, there are some things for which we just have to trust in God.[8]

Sometimes a husband might not know God's plans but must step out in obedience anyway. I learned this many years ago when I felt the Lord calling me to move our ministry. Like Abraham, I had no idea where we would end up. We did, however, feel led to visit a town out West three times. The first trip included our entire family and a brother from the church. We had no idea why we were there, but knew it was a time of testing and searching God's will. During that visit, the brother and I attended a Christian meeting. There we engaged in a fifteen-minute conversation that we did not realize would play a vital role in discovering God's will for our ministry.

On the second trip out, we actually packed up all our possessions and family and moved to this town. Even though it looked foolish, my wife and I felt that if we did not do this we would be in disobedience. As ridiculous as it seemed, we felt led to return home after a week. The only problem was that we did not have a home. We had allowed some friends from our church to move into our house. We felt abandoned and had no idea where God wanted us. We did, however, know that God was emptying us of self and testing to see if we would obey no matter what happened. And even though the questions raged and we saw much sin, we waited on God to show His will.

A sister in the church offered us a one-room apartment for the summer. During this time, Carla and I traveled back to the western town to wait for God's instruction. Our children stayed behind wondering where they might go to school in the fall and where we would live. We spent two weeks at our motel room and a local park, praying and waiting on God. We never received a clear call as to where our ministry would be; all we heard was a direction to wait. Questions and doubts filled our hearts and minds as we wrestled with self and sin. God showed us in many different ways that our focus cannot be on our ministry but on Him totally. We knew how Joshua must have felt marching around Jericho, not knowing why or what the outcome might be. It looked stupid to everyone else, but soon the walls would come tumbling down.

After returning, we received a phone call two months later from the people I had spoken to during the first trip at the fifteen-minute meeting. This phone call opened the doors for our ministry. We would have never thought that a casual meeting would later lead us to discover God's will. But He had to take us the long way around, deal with our sin, and empty us out to get us to the place He wanted us in.

Like Jesus, a husband must wash his wife in the Word by the power of the Holy Spirit. This is not as easy as it might sound, nor will the wife find it always a pleasurable thing. In Bible times, washing clothes was done by laying the clothing on a rock in the stream and then beating it with a club to remove the dirt. This is what David meant when he said in Psalms 51:7, "wash me." Certainly we are not talking about wife beating here but the tremendous responsibility of using the Word of God to make someone "radiant" in Christ. We are talking about being very active in making permanent changes in someone. There are days when I am worn out by washing the whole family with the Word.

As any woman will tell you, laundry is a tough chore. It is no cutesy, mushy kind of thing to love a wife enough to "make her holy, cleansing her by the washing with water through the word," that will leave her "without stain or wrinkle" in Christ. Remember, Scripture says that she is the weaker one who allowed sin to come in and that among a thousand women not one righteous woman could be found.[9] Does the cross sting a little here?

> Husbands, love your wives, just as Christ loved the church and gave himself up for her to make her holy, cleansing her by the washing with water through the word, and to present her to himself as a radiant church, without stain or wrinkle or any other blemish, but holy and blameless. (Eph. 5:25–27)

However, most men do not really want this leadership and responsibility any more than the women really want to submit. As a result, they often reach a religious compromise. A woman will act as if the man is in charge while the man will let the woman take care of directing the home.

Many years ago, I was preaching on submission and leadership in the family. We were looking at how Sarah called Abraham "Master." Everyone gave a hearty "Amen" to the Scriptures in the sermon. I was a very popular preacher until I said that for the next month every wife was to call her husband "Master." I explained we practice all kinds of other scriptures, so why not practice 1 Peter 3:6 and call husbands "Master" instead of by their real names? This meant that no matter where they were—in the store, at the in-laws' house, at home—they were to address their husbands as "Master."

The amazing thing was not the fact that the women in the church found this very hard, but that the men did not want it to happen either. Their covers had been blown, and they did not want the responsibility that comes with leadership. It revealed to the women that their levels of submission were not what they thought they were. The things that happened that month would fill a whole chapter.

As we saw earlier, God will direct in His timing how to meet the needs of a family. One of the greatest freedoms in Christ is to not worry any more about quality family time. I no longer have to schedule quality family time. Certainly when we were first married I tried in vain to schedule such time, but the Lord's will always got in the way. When I learned to enter the Sabbath rest of God, I found abundant life.[10] I now know that I need to give my full attention to God, and He directs my steps.[11] My only burden is seeking God, and what a glorious freedom that brings. What a blessing this is for everyone else in the home. For how can others not be blessed when the husband seeks only God? This is the glorious freedom and power of the cross. We do not need all the marriage books on how to be better husbands. All we need is to allow God to crucify us; then we will have selfless love for our wives. We will be made into what Jesus wants us to be. Those who know this power will understand it. Everyone else has to run to the gimmicks in the church to put their marriage together. Begin to hate your wife and look only to the Lord, and God will change you into the man that He, not your wife, wants you to be.

Don't worry if you don't get quality family time for a month. God has everything in control. He will work when and how your family comes together. For one thing, if God's love fills a family, whether together or apart, they will feel love for one another. Isn't this the same love you feel for the body of Christ around the world? Although you cannot be physically with a brother or sister in China, can't you still feel one with them? Isn't this the kind of love that the Holy Spirit has worked in you?

What an amazing thing to watch God work this love in a family who does not focus on their family. For when every member looks only to God, He can work and will in a perfect way. One time our family had not had much time together for a while. We had been busy working for the Lord and had not seen each other much. The Lord led us to go the mountains and spend some time in a cabin together. As we prepared to leave, I felt an urgency to get out of our house by 9:00 A.M. We rushed around, and I hurried everyone out the door. Sure enough, around 10:00 A.M. a friend staying at our house heard a knock at the door. Some enemies showed up demanding their sinful desires be fulfilled. We, of course, were long gone, and by the time we returned, they had left town. How wonderful is God's timing in all things. He was able to hide us in the shadow of His wings and at the same time give us quality family time. Had I resorted to plans and book ideas on what makes a good family, we would have missed seeing the power of God work in our family.

Let each couple preparing for marriage vow to live as though they were not married. Let each couple write in their wedding invitations that they promise to hate each other in Christ. And let all who are married ask the Holy Spirit to write in their hearts the Scripture below.

> That you may live in a right way in undivided devotion to the Lord. (1 Cor. 7:35)

Listening to Your Wife

We do not have the time here to look at all the dynamics of a godly marriage. However, I want to emphasize that those who hate their own wives will know when and how to love them properly in the Lord. In fact, hating our wives' opinions and thoughts will allow us to hear from God when it is time to listen to her. Let us take a brief look at the perfect godly marriage, Abraham and Sarah's.

Abraham over the years had learned to listen to God alone. However this does not mean that God will not use a wife to speak to a husband. Indeed she is a helpmate and God will move in her life to bless a husband. So do not be surprised if God blesses you by giving your wife spiritual wisdom and insight. Just make sure you do what Abraham did. He sought God and heard directly from Him to "Listen to whatever Sarah tells you." To discern when your wife speaks on her own and when she speaks the wisdom of God, you must first learn to hate her.

> The matter distressed Abraham greatly because it concerned his son. But God said to him, "Do not be so distressed about the boy and your maidservant. Listen to whatever Sarah tells you, because it is through Isaac that your offspring will be reckoned." (Gen. 21:11–12)

For husbands to know how to wash their wives in the Word and to know how to make them radiant means they will often be led to admonish in ways that their wives will not like. If a man worries about pleasing his wife, this purification cannot happen. Blessed is the man who can hate his wife enough to love her and present her radiant, clean, and holy in the Lord. Blessed even more is the man seeking only God's will every hour of every day and shows, by his example, what everyone must do in the household. Blessed is the man who hates his wife enough to follow only Jesus in *all* things.

8

Hating Your Children

> And he will go on before the Lord, in the spirit and power of Elijah, to turn the hearts of the fathers to their children and the disobedient to the wisdom of the righteous—to make ready a people prepared for the Lord. (Luke 1:17)

Jesus came "to turn the hearts of the fathers" back to "their children," and I have felt that power work mightily in my life. Let's look at how God turns hearts back—by way of the cross and man hating his own life enough to surrender his children to God.

Hating our children means parents get out of the way of the Lord's will. As simple as that sounds, I know many who left the Lord over this very thing. In America, where things come easy, we become opinionated about and possessive of our children, and we will not allow God to work in their lives. We compound this by striving to always make our children happy and safe rather than doing what is best for them in the Lord. Jesus said that we need to hate our feelings, ideas, and concepts concerning our children.

Years ago, I studied the Bible with a man, in the hope of leading him to Christ. When his wife did not like this idea, she laid down the law. Since the marriage was rotting, the only thing that kept the man in the marriage was his daughter. His wife made threats that he would never see his daughter again, which caused him to stop following Jesus.

Sometimes it does not even take that much of a threat in a man's life to get him to stop following Jesus. Once while I was preaching in Germany, a man came to set me straight on my doctrine. He was highly angry about all this "stuff" as he called it. As I gently explained everything he came to understand, accept, and see what Scripture teaches. We continued to talk late into the evening until we got around to discussing Russia. He was in the U.S. military and had done some work in Russia after the fall of the Berlin Wall. He described the conditions, and stated that he would never take his family there. I casually made the statement, "Unless of course it was God's will." That reality, that God could, if it were His will, send them all to Russia, was enough to send him huffing out the door. He never did come back to hear any more of the gospel, and as far as I know, he stopped serving the Lord.

What we have looked at so far clearly shows that we must utterly reject anyone's pressure to live the Christian life in a certain way. Our attitude as Christians should be that if someone does not like what God works, then too bad. If a marriage fails because of Jesus, the partners must trust God and move on. Let my wife leave, let everyone forsake me, let me be barred from seeing those I love—it will not matter. Our fleshly desire to see others, that is, to be with those we love, must be fought against so that we might follow the Truth and love Jesus. Like the saints of old, our faith and trust must shine forth.

> Who through faith conquered kingdoms, administered justice, and gained what was promised; who shut the mouths of lions, quenched the fury of the flames, and escaped the edge of the sword; whose weakness was turned to strength; and who became powerful in battle and routed foreign armies. Women received back their dead, raised to life again. Others were tortured and refused to be released, so that they might gain a better

> resurrection. Some faced jeers and flogging, while still others were chained and put in prison. They were stoned; they were sawed in two; they were put to death by the sword. They went about in sheepskins and goatskins, destitute, persecuted and mistreated—the world was not worthy of them. They wandered in deserts and mountains, and in caves and holes in the ground. These were all commended for their faith. (Heb. 11:33–39)

Many people have children for their own pleasure or to give their lives meaning. These people do not hate their desires but go on with their own plans to have as many children as they want. Or, when given children by the Lord, they enjoy them for themselves. The worship of family remains most important to them, and it would be impossible for them to hate their children in the Lord. They love family outings, barbecues, sporting events, and what most call **family things** more than they love the Lord. They will always want to please their children for their own pleasure and therefore fail miserably to prepare them for a loving God. These individuals will find little use for the message of hating for Jesus.

When our first son was four years old, my wife and I began to hear God's call to have more children. You need to realize that we had just spent three years as houseparents for mentally handicapped men and had no desire for any more responsibility. We wanted a break. We knew, however, that we had better find out what God wanted. It took almost a week of praying and fasting for us to finally surrender to His will. As a result, we had two more birthsons and have taken in numerous temporary-custody children. Our lives have been filled with joy, but according to God's plan, not ours.

Abraham and Isaac

Our concern lies with the deeper matters of faith and with the very difficult idea of sacrificing our sons and daughters to the Lord. This is not a sacrifice in a physical sense, like those who worship idols or self believe, but a sacrifice in which those of faith give God everything to do with their children as He wills. We need to look no further than our father of faith, Abraham, for an example. We step into the scene where God had stopped Abraham at the last moment from actually killing his son. Let us be found cooperating to the fullest with His plan and will.

> "Do not lay a hand on the boy," he said. "Do not do anything to him. Now I know that you fear God, because you have not withheld from me your son, your only son." Abraham looked up and there in a thicket he saw a ram caught by its horns. He went over and took the ram and sacrificed it as a burnt offering instead of his son. So Abraham called that place The Lord Will Provide. And to this day it is said, "On the mountain of the Lord it will be provided." The angel of the Lord called to Abraham from heaven a second time and said, "I swear by myself, declares the Lord, that because you have done this and have not withheld your son, your only son, I will surely bless you and make your descendants as numerous as the stars in the sky and as the sand on the seashore. Your descendants will take possession of the cities of their enemies, and through your offspring all nations on earth will be blessed, because you have obeyed me." (Gen. 22:12–18)

Because Abraham had "not withheld" his son, his "only son," God told Abraham that he was blessed in Him. How many parents withhold their sons and daughters from the hand of the Lord? They refuse to lift the knife and to carry the fire of faith. Lifting the knife will come out in many small and large ways every day. It is a constant giving of the lives of our children over to God's loving will. To slay their vanity, selfishness, and talents as He directs takes a changed heart in a man willing to do that for his children.

For example, every teenager looks forward to driving, but in our house the Father reigns supreme. Therefore I went to everyone's Father and asked God if and when it might be God's will for our children to start driving. For our son, Joshua, that day did not come until he was seventeen, but what a grand time it was getting his license in the Lord. He learned to wait on the Lord and wrestle with the flesh and face those who laughed at him. In short, more spiritual growth took place than we could have imagined. Of course with our other son, God may want him to drive as soon as he legally can. God the Father knows what is best for any and all children; my only goal is to keep lifting them up to the Lord.

To lift the knife as he did, Abraham certainly had to hate his feelings for his son. He had to hate his son's desires in order to offer him up to God. Just look at how submissively Abraham's son reacted to the will of God. Abraham must have really hated his son on a daily basis in order to prepare him for such a day. Notice that Isaac did not struggle or fight against what happened. Isaac did not even offer one word of objection. What a deep, trusting, loving relationship they must have had. There is little doubt that Isaac had been taught to "do everything without complaining or arguing" from birth.[1] Since Isaac did not complain about taking out the trash, he could offer his whole life to God with complete trust. How did Isaac and Abraham get to this point of complete trust in God?

> When they reached the place God had told him about, Abraham built an altar there and arranged the wood on it. He bound his son Isaac and laid him on the altar, on top of the wood. Then he reached out his hand and took the knife to slay his son. (Gen. 22:9–10)

Abraham, like any good father, had hopes and dreams for his son. He had to hate those hopes and dreams so that God could form the child into what He wanted. Through Hannah, who entrusted God with her child, the world was given a Samuel. Her trust in God was not in vain. Although Hannah's son was raised under a man who totally failed at raising his own sons, Samuel was still protected by God. God can always raise up godly children no matter what the circumstances.[2]

God gave me a taste of this when our youngest son was thirteen—about the same age I imagine Isaac was on the altar. I had planned and scheduled a seminar on the very subject of hating for Christ. The night before the seminar, we found out that our son, Josiah, would need to undergo emergency brain surgery. I contemplated canceling the seminar but knew that would not be

God's will. I left the hospital knowing I may never see my son alive again.

All children have wants and desires that they expect their parents to fulfill. A godly father must hate those desires and sacrifice them to the Lord so that he can raise his children in a holy way, separated unto the will of God and purified for His work. Abraham had done this, and Isaac reaped the fruit of a surrendered spirit that could love and trust God. What unity and love they had in the Lord, both son and father united in the same zeal for God. How rare this is today. Even among children planning to become missionaries, there still remains so much self that God's work is often hindered—all because the fathers are not men of hate.

My wife stood by me at the Hating Seminar only to be called away to sign the permission papers for surgery. When Carla arrived she noticed piles of tissues on Josiah's bed and knew he had been crying. The doctors had told Josiah, without our presence, that he would probably die. Carla's motherly claws immediately extended. Josiah, however, reassured her, "It's OK. I had a long talk with God and told Him I'm ready." What a grand joy it was to see him filled with God's peace and presence. What a blessed way to start one's walk with the Lord. As I taught about hating for Jesus, my family was learning it firsthand.

In passing, notice Sarah is not with Abraham and Isaac. Abraham had to hate his wife's opinion about this matter and lead the family in God's will. In addition, she had to submit to Abraham while trusting God to protect them both. She had not heard God's voice about this issue. At best God gave her a peace that everything would be all right. But don't think for a moment that Sarah could not read on Abraham's face that something troubled him and that it concerned her only son. She could have whined, "You hardly listened to me when I told you to send Ishmael away, and now you don't want my opinion at all on this." But she did not; she remained silent, trusting God. This is why wives are told not to give way to "fear" when God works in ways they cannot understand.[3] Therefore, her husband and son grew in the holiness of

God. How many wives today, if they would just shut up, could allow God to work some good in their home?[4]

A parent's longing for their children to conform to their opinions, beliefs, and desires is very strong. Even Jesus' mother wrestled with this, and as we saw earlier, Jesus dealt with her in a strong way. At the age of twelve, Jesus' mother's demands got in the way of God's will. Mary and Joseph could not find Jesus on their way home from Jerusalem and so, like any parent would, they became upset and worried. However, when they finally found Jesus at the temple, all they cared about was that Jesus had treated them so badly. Their personal feelings overshadowed their understanding of what God wanted to work. Their irritation hindered the voice of wisdom from heaven. Many times I have seen parents hinder a moment God arranged by enforcing their rules, regulations, and religious ideas. How sad to see God seeking to reveal Himself to a child, yet parents getting in the way by either scolding or spoiling.

> When his parents saw him, they were astonished. His mother said to him, "Son, why have you treated us like this? Your father and I have been anxiously searching for you." "Why were you searching for me?" he asked. "Didn't you know I had to be in my Father's house?" But they did not understand what he was saying to them. Then he went down to Nazareth with them and was obedient to them. But his mother treasured all these things in her heart. (Luke 2:48–51)

Let every mother and father "treasure" in their hearts what they do not yet fully understand. To Mary's credit, she always treasured in her heart the mysterious things God did with her children. Doing so allowed her to kneel one day at the foot of the cross, gaining complete understanding of the mercies of God. As a result, God permitted her to see the glory of God work in her son's life. See how she "treasured" the working of God in her son's life from the moment Jesus was born.

> So they hurried off and found Mary and Joseph, and the baby, who was lying in the manger. When they had seen him, they

> spread the word concerning what had been told them about this child, and all who heard it were amazed at what the shepherds said to them. But Mary treasured up all these things and pondered them in her heart. (Luke 2:16–19)

Again, treasuring up the things of God in her heart allowed her to endure the sufferings of Christ. Likewise, every parent has to realize that they cannot protect their sons and daughters from the sufferings of Christ. Indeed—and this is tough—we should want them to endure as much as they can for the sake of the gospel. It takes some real hatred of our children to rejoice when God works suffering in their lives. This suffering caused Mary to come and take charge of Him. How much more difficult will it be to us who have not had angels announce the birth of our children? These sufferings of Jesus will happen to anyone who claims to be a Christian.[5] Watching our children suffer is probably one of the toughest battles we will face. It was tough watching Josiah suffer during his illness. But now, after his recovery, we can see the lessons God taught him. Paul wanted to spare those desiring to marry from this pain.[6] Watching God discipline and train our children is even harder.

For those who have been taught some sloppy theology, let me remind you that "if indeed we share in" the "sufferings" of Jesus, we will be allowed to hope in His salvation.

> Now if we are children, then we are heirs—heirs of God and coheirs with Christ, if indeed we share in his sufferings in order that we may also share in his glory. (Rom. 8:17, emphasis added)

Let me give a very small example of this. After much prayer, we knew God wanted our children to go to public school. Certainly in our flesh we would have rather not have them face the trials of public school and we would have homeschooled them. However, as we watch them mature in faith and dependence on God, hating our instincts to totally protect them, we can praise God for what He has done over the years. We knew that Moses went to public school and that God could protect our children.[7]

Many times we wanted to step in, but our sons would say, "No; I want to work through my fear and stand up for the Lord."

One example took place in our son's fifth-grade music class. One day at the end of the class the teacher instructed the students to meditate and practice relaxation. Joshua refused to participate, and he stood up alone. The teacher, somewhat frustrated, let it pass because none of the other students seemed to object. However, she had not counted on him sharing with other students why he did not join in. It seems the other students asked him to explain why he did not meditate. After Joshua told the students his views, other students began to join him in this quiet protest. Soon the teacher stopped the practice. This happened without any parental intervention. My wife later went to the teacher and shared the gospel with her. A Christian teacher also shared with the music teacher, and the music teacher began to attend church. In high school, the battles have become much more difficult. Indeed one recent battle involved a whole class angrily opposing Joshua with the instigation of the teacher.

Many times God has had us stand with our children in the battle. However, we had to fight and hate our urge to defend them so they could see God work. We want to make room for God to glorify His name and mature our children. After all, they will not always have Mommy and Daddy around. They will have only God, and we want them to trust in Him, for with Him all battles are won.

Hate your children and treasure the things God does in their lives that you cannot understand. Ask God to open your eyes when He starts to work in these situations. Learn this while they are young—you will gain strength from them later. We must come to have the attitude of the God who perfectly loves His children. For when He looks at His children He views them with an attitude of "slaughter." Until our minds are transformed to understand how love and slaughter can work together, hating for Jesus will all be a hidden treasure.

> Who shall separate us from the love of Christ? Shall trouble or hardship or persecution or famine or nakedness or danger or

> sword? As it is written: "For your sake we face death all day long; we are considered as sheep to be slaughtered." (Rom. 8:35–36)

Those who seek to shelter their children from the world apart from the inspiration of the Holy Spirit do their children a great injustice. For one day God will try to call them "outside the camp" to suffer "disgrace" for Christ.[8]

Surrendering our children helps us to guide them in God's will and yet allows them to be individuals in the Lord. Remember how Abraham and Isaac both set off for the mountain as God had directed? Isaac went willingly because he saw the fire of faith in his father. Isaac readily accepted the same fire into his life and offered himself fully to the Lord. Abraham "carried the fire and the knife" himself, and the Bible says that the "two of them went on together." No family seminar can ignite this kind of family fire; it comes only from years of hating one's life.

> Abraham took the wood for the burnt offering and placed it on his son Isaac, and he himself carried the fire and the knife. As the two of them went on together. (Gen. 22:6)

What a grand way for Isaac to begin his walk with God. Isaac could start where Abraham left off in the Lord. How I long for my sons to be twice as righteous as I am and to start from where I leave off. I am so wicked, and it has taken God so long to get me to a specific point that I do not want my sons to face the same delays. May God's name be glorified by my sons' readiness to run where I can only walk. The only hope I have for this is in hating my plans, dreams, and even religious ideas for them so that God may direct me to the place God has told me about.

> When they reached the place God had told him about, Abraham built an altar there and arranged the wood on it. He bound his son Isaac and laid him on the altar, on top of the wood. (Gen. 22:9)

A Rod of Comfort

As my two sons face manhood in the Lord, it becomes more and more clear what God has chosen for them. The place God has put on my heart is coming into focus, and I pray that I can walk there with my sons. If I am privileged to do so, then you know getting there will require that I hate their every wish and desire. So much of me wants to give them what they desire. Like any good father would, we love to see our children happy. With the hatred in place, God has shown me which desires to fulfill and which to deny. God can reveal to me how to teach them discernment in their desires, and He can reveal which desires to allow so that my sons can grow up in the Lord. While all of this is no promise that my sons will love God, it has allowed them a start in their walk with Him that I never had.

There is no greater joy for Christians than this kind of hatred. After all, Isaac's name means **laughter**. Abraham could laugh for joy at seeing God's promises fulfilled in his son. Can we see the promise of God fulfilled in our sons' and daughters' lives? May all our promises fall upon our children. Has the Holy Spirit been able to use you in fulfilling that promise? Are you walking with them to the place God has chosen for them? Do you hate your children enough to see their sins clearly and see how God wants you to deal with them? So many parents see their children as cuter than they really are. They show favoritism when they look at their child. Therefore, parents cannot hear from God how to deal with traits, weaknesses, and sins in their children. Usually by the time they do see their children's sins it is too late, and the sin too large to deal with easily. In order to see our children honestly, seeing both the good and bad, we must hate them. The Puritans sent their children to live with other godly families at around the age of thirteen because they knew it was too easy to show favoritism. While that is not advisable today, God has other ways to accomplish this in each family.

We must reject our favorable or negative viewpoints and let God speak the Truth to us. Hating our children will lead to careful consideration and discipline of them. In other words, this godly hatred allows us to see our children honestly and then to carefully act upon the truth—a truth that does not require books and magazines about family, but a wisdom that God works "powerfully" in all who surrender to Him. This is a power in which parents are not struggling with questions on how to raise their children, but instead are filled with "all wisdom" so that they can "present" their children "perfect in Christ." Are you filled with "all wisdom"? Can you feel Him working this "powerfully" in your life? Does this wisdom produce in you struggle and hard labor for your children? It will happen if you learn to hate for Jesus.

> We proclaim him, admonishing and teaching everyone with all wisdom, so that we may present everyone perfect in Christ. To this end I labor, struggling with all his energy, which so powerfully works in me. (Col. 1:28–29)

The rod in the Proverb below refers to interacting with your children in a physical way, in ways of measurement, guidance, and correction. In other words, do not spare the rod measuring up your children and do not be lax in being involved in their lives to guide, correct, and encourage. For as David says in Psalms 23:4, "your rod and staff, they comfort me." By the time you finish hearing from God on how to raise your children, the rod should be a thing of comfort.

It is amazing that parents who will not take the time to guide their children with the rod of God's Word actually hate their children in an ungodly way, while parents who hate their own lives and children by the Holy Spirit are filled with a love from heaven that is "careful" to guide them to the Lord.

> He who spares the rod hates his son, but he who loves him is careful to discipline him. (Prov. 13:24)

Let us be like Job, who not only sought to see his children clearly, but also went one step further and sought to make atonement for sins that they might have committed that he could not see. In Job 1:5 he rose early in the morning to deal with the sin that might be in their hearts. This is Jesus' admonition for us to pray so that we do not fall into temptation. Let us not only see our children's faults clearly, but also work to make atonement for ones they might have unknowingly committed. To such parents God gives great wisdom and love to know how to prepare their children for His loving arms.

On the surface, it sounds like this hatred would hinder your children's personal choices and autonomy, but nothing could be further from the truth. God can direct parents in such a way that allows the children to be who they are while the parents are still guiding them. Look at the children who have been given most of what they wanted. They are enslaved to their own whims and wants. Those children who have been diligently disciplined and loved can be at rest and think and plan a course of action for their lives. Their parents know that although the children may choose not to follow God, the children made such decisions honestly rather than by just going out with the tide to their destruction.

This reminds me of the warnings we were given while I lived on Guam. Sometimes individuals would fall asleep on their cheap rubber rafts, and the tide would carry them many miles out. When they woke up, they would be totally lost and surrounded by danger. There is nothing worse than unthinking children who do not realize spiritually what is happening to them. They came from Christian homes but were never taught to think for themselves in the Lord.

If your child does not want the Lord, you must hear from God how much freedom to allow them. For God does not want anyone forced to worship Him. On the other hand, He does not want you to let your children run wild into sin either.[9] Hate your ideas of forcing your religion on them; at the same time let God show you how to hem them in for their own good. While the vast majority of those in the church and the world make decisions in a spiritual fog, children raised by hating parents at least know exactly what they are doing.

Hating our children means some very simple and basic things. It means that no matter what they think, you will serve God in the way that He chooses. You will not bend to compromise in matters of personal holiness just to maintain a relationship with your children. It means you have no plans for them and will allow God to work what He has planned. You must hate your desire to send them to college, to see them be missionaries or workers at a specific occupation in order for God to use you to prepare them for Him.

Do this and your children will start their walks with God rich in faith. They will testify that as they watched you walk with the Lord, He provided for all your needs. They will have watched your wanderings in the desert and will say, "God provided for our family." They will be able to point to the mountain where God provided and revealed Himself.

> Abraham looked up and there in a thicket he saw a ram caught by its horns. He went over and took the ram and sacrificed it as a burnt offering instead of his son. So Abraham called that place The Lord Will Provide. And to this day it is said, "On the mountain of the Lord it will be provided." (Gen. 22:13–14)

Isaac witnessed the crowning achievement of faith in his father's life. What a privilege. He saw Abraham trust God, and Isaac soon trusted God to provide him with a wife. Indeed Isaac did not even have to waste time dating, for he knew that God would provide everything, even a wife.

Isaac saw firsthand that God helps those who wait upon Him.[10] He saw his father let the world go by and he grew in faith over the years. Isaac had been willing to wait at the tents for the call of God.

Isaac could point back and say, "I saw God in my father's life. I saw him hate his own life, deny himself, and follow the Lord." Isaac would also praise God for a father who hated his personal plans for his son and raised him according to the will of God. What blessed joy is theirs, for they have passed from being father and son to the everlasting joy of being brothers in the Lord.

Isaac was able to start his walk with God with the maturity it took Abraham a lifetime to achieve. It is noteworthy to see that God becomes silent after Abraham's test. This is because God had then blessed Abraham in "every way," and the fruit of righteousness for those who have been "trained" by it is "quietness and rest."[11] Abraham's flesh had been crucified, and he was at rest in the presence of God. In short, God and Abraham were just sitting and enjoying each other's company. It was with this rest and fellowship that Isaac began his walk with God. What a mighty blessing Abraham left to Isaac.

> After Abraham's death, God blessed his son Isaac, who then lived near Beer Lahai Roi. (Gen. 25:11)

9

Hating Brothers and Sisters

The Easy One

Certainly any related brother or sister who gets in your way of following Jesus must be ignored. Hating a brother or sister, however, means that we take action before such a situation occurs. Remember that we must learn to hate before we start to follow Jesus. Therefore, long before a brother or sister begins to interfere, we should be fully prepared in the Lord to deal with any discussion. If we are honest with ourselves, we will acknowledge the extent of our families' influences in our lives.

Our desire to remain close to a brother or sister is very strong and must be hated right from the start. If we fail to do this, God cannot use us in sharing the gospel with our brothers and sisters. In fact, as God puts you in a field to work, your desire to go back and see them will hinder you from hearing God's voice. We can only have one allegiance—to the Lord—and one voice to heed—the Lord's. In order to hear only His voice, we must hate all other calls with a hatred that feels repulsed at the demands, ideas, and wishes of our brothers or sisters.

In addition, our natural affection for our brothers and sisters must be hated. Otherwise we find ourselves continually trying to save them. We will be busy spinning our wheels in the mud because of a constant concern that a brother or sister comes to the Lord. We must hate these emotions so that we can trust God to deal with our brothers and sisters in His timing and in His way. We must open our hearts to the fact that God may not want us to evangelize them. He might have other work for us to do. If we are unwilling to hate them, we will always look back with unholy concern for them. Thus our work and labor for the Lord will never become what it should be.

This is what Jesus meant when He said that once we put our "hand to the plow," we can never look back. We should never be distracted by the demands of a brother or sister. We must hate the very thought that we might cave into their requests. Anyone willing to hate will be resolved never to let go of the plow. He who hates his brothers and sisters will work all the harder at fulfilling God's call. If we are plowing and we keep looking back, all our rows will be crooked. Our seeds (and the seeds others try to plant) will fall into ground hardened against the Word of God.

> Still another said, "I will follow you, Lord; but first let me go back and say good-by to my family." Jesus replied, "No one who puts his hand to the plow and looks back is fit for service in the kingdom of God." (Luke 9:61–62)

God will take care of our families, and we need to ask Him how much time in prayer and service we should devote concerning them. It is entirely possible that God does not want us to utter one single prayer for anyone in our families. He may have reserved that work for someone else. This is one aspect of praying in the Spirit—knowing how to pray for others. God may want us to devote ourselves to our families. However, if the hatred for them is not solid, we will fail at the work He calls us to.

Christian Brothers and Sisters

Let us understand that our family members are no more important to God than anyone else is. God has the same love for everyone, and if we are filled with His love, our love will be equal for everyone. As we have seen, a family member's salvation should be no more or less important to us than our next-door neighbor's. Prepare yourself for God's work by asking God how you are to hate your related brothers and sisters. Then turn your face toward the work God has for you and do not look back.

Now let us turn our attention to our brothers and sisters in the church. For if there is one place that hatred is missing, it is in the church. Pastors do not hate their congregations; therefore, godly hating never happens between brothers and sisters. This causes a slow and steady increase of favoritism and compromise in a church. Slowly more sin is allowed until only those on the outside of the church can see it. And we know that churches very seldom listen to those outside their congregation concerning hypocrisy.

Get Behind Me Satan

To find out if this happens in your church or in your immediate fellowship, answer one question. When was the last time you referred to another brother or sister as "Satan"? For that matter, name a time when you heard anyone in your church do this.

Sounds tough, doesn't it? Jesus, the perfect man of love, was a perfect man of hate. Jesus hated any fleshly nature in Him that wanted to show favoritism to those whom He loved. Jesus denied perfectly the subtle part of Him that would soften any comment God wanted Him to make. Since Jesus hated any thought of compromising the Word toward a person He loved, He could speak the truth as God directed at all times. For example, Jesus hated Peter and so God could lead Him to say whatever God wanted Him to say. Therefore, Jesus could refer to one of His most beloved apostles as "Satan." And Jesus was not talking to Satan himself, nor had Satan entered Peter. The only person that Satan actually entered into was Judas,[1] and Peter was no Judas. Don't let your religious flesh be so easily offended; Peter opposed the cross and that put him in league with Satan. Jesus merely rebuked Peter appropriately for the comment he made. The question we must ask is, is the Holy Spirit able to move such strong rebukes through us in love for our brothers and sisters?

> But when Jesus turned and looked at his disciples, he rebuked Peter. "Get behind me, Satan!" he said. "You do not have in mind the things of God, but the things of men." (Mark 8:33)

Paul was no stranger to hating brothers and sisters in the Lord. As a result, Paul could love all men deeply by the power of the Holy Spirit. He hated his love that might seek to please someone. Paul could later oppose Peter to "his face" in front of a whole crowd because it did not matter to Paul who Peter was in the Lord. Paul hated the status of Peter and of himself. It did not matter how long Peter had been in the Lord; if Peter was wrong, then he was wrong. In other words, Paul set out in the morning to fight against the urge to treat Peter with human respect.

> When Peter came to Antioch, I opposed him to his face, because he was clearly in the wrong. (Gal. 2:11)

How unlike Jesus we are, for the Holy Spirit cannot find men who hate enough to say, "How long shall I put up with you?" or to call someone "Satan." As we look at how Jesus spoke to those following Him, ask yourself why the Spirit of Christ cannot move this way in your church and life.

> "I brought him to your disciples, but they could not heal him." "O unbelieving and perverse generation," Jesus replied, "how long shall I stay with you? How long shall I put up with you? Bring the boy here to me." (Matt. 17:16-17)

> "Are you so dull?" he asked. "Don't you see that nothing that enters a man from the outside can make him 'unclean'?" (Mark 7:18)

Jesus calls the "disciples" an "unbelieving and perverse generation." Why can't the Spirit move us to speak this way? The answer: we want the approval of our brothers and sisters and would not even dare dream of making such a comment to them. If you hated enough, God's Spirit could move you to really love others by speaking the truth as clearly as He wants us to.

We remain so far from this teaching that we would think it utterly without love to call someone *dull*. We will not let the Spirit work this in us for one of two reasons. Either we love our sin too much and would not want anyone talking to us like this. Or we show favoritism and refuse to hate our brothers and sisters. When we show favoritism, one cannot trust our compliments either. For if godly hatred is not present, we may not be hearing from God but may be merely flattering. We can trust Jesus because He will always be honest. As He did to Peter, one minute Jesus will say you are "blessed" and then in the next He will call you "Satan." We can trust a brother or sister willing for God to move like this in his or her life. How sad that so much encouragement is just flattery because men refuse to hate for Jesus.

Many years ago a sister in our congregation continually showered my wife and children with gifts. She was a garage sale addict, buying clothing and toys at a bargain to please her flesh. Carla knew by the Spirit that the woman was in sin and that her gifts were a means to make herself feel good. The woman did not hate what she wanted to buy, and she tried to make her choices look good in the Lord. My wife mustered up the courage to tell this woman that such things were only flattery and did not meet the needs of Christ.

Think about someone who has a worldly hate; he could care less what others think of him. Indeed not only does he not care but also he goes out of his way to make his enemies upset. Dare I say that our attitude should be to make the flesh of our brothers and sisters angry with us when their sins must be dealt with? We should say we rejoice that God can bless us with brothers and sisters who hate us enough not to show us the slightest fleshly consideration or compromise. We need brothers and sisters dead enough to themselves that God can move them to perfect us in Christ. Should it not be our joy to keep up the festival of righteousness? Should it not make us happy to see God working in brothers and sisters a desire to really sharpen each other in the Lord?

Think of iron; it is one of the hardest metals man has ever made. In the same way, we have made ourselves hard over the years toward God. God tells us in Prov. 27:17, "As iron sharpens iron, so one man sharpens another." The only way to sharpen two pieces of iron is by rubbing them together with great force and speed. Heat comes from the friction, and both pieces of iron become red hot until an edge is formed. It is easy to see that when the Spirit can move mightily in men's lives, they become sharp in the Lord. The question is, are you willing to fellowship with someone who allows that much friction in the Lord?

As the Scripture below declares, we are talking about a "festival," a celebration in which everyone who does not repent of sin is kicked out of the church. You read that correctly; we should be happy when God moves us not to eat lunch with the hypocrites in the church. Read the following verses very carefully. We must not even eat lunch with anyone who calls him or herself a Christian yet will not repent of sin. If we value our brothers' and sisters' opinions of us, we will never let the Spirit work this festival. In order to really love a brother or sister who refuses to repent of sin, we must set out to hate them. We must say to ourselves, "I hate them and so I do not care anything about what they think of me. In fact, I hate them so much, I enjoy doing harm to their sin." He who hates like this is full of the love of heaven that longs for the person to repent; he is willing to pay the cost of disassociation. It is the deepest act of love to try and get someone to repent.

> Your boasting is not good. Don't you know that a little yeast works through the whole batch of dough? Get rid of the old yeast that you may be a new batch without yeast—as you really are. For Christ, our Passover lamb, has been sacrificed. Therefore let us keep the Festival, not with the old yeast, the yeast of malice and wickedness, but with bread without yeast, the bread of sincerity and truth. I have written you in my letter not to associate with sexually immoral people—not at all meaning the people of this world who are immoral, or the greedy

> and swindlers, or idolaters. In that case you would have to leave this world. But now I am writing you that you must not associate with anyone who calls himself a brother but is sexually immoral or greedy, an idolater or a slanderer, a drunkard or a swindler. With such a man do not even eat. What business is it of mine to judge those outside the church? Are you not to judge those inside? God will judge those outside. "Expel the wicked man from among you." (1 Cor. 5: 6–13)

A church that does not merely talk about righteousness is rare indeed. Blessed is the church filled with hating brothers and sisters who remain at peace with each other. It is true that this is no easy thing to live. The cross is not a comfortable place. Many mistakes will be made in correcting one another, but there is no other way to holiness in the church. This is why Jesus commands us to have this kind of "salt" and yet to be at "peace with each other." The effects of this salt deal so powerfully with sin that a church will have to strive to maintain the peace. Indeed the salt purifies so deeply that only the oil of the Holy Spirit can maintain unity and fellowship. No religious gimmicks or church socializing can hold a church together as the members begin to hate their brothers and sisters. It will take divine power to hold the body together; normal church fellowship will never cut it.

> Have salt in yourselves, and be at peace with each other. (Mark 9:50b)

Peter also hated his brothers and sisters and could hear from God what he needed to say and how to say it. Unlike those who constantly seek to "love" other Christians, Peter hated his love for his brothers and relied instead upon God's love to work what it willed through him. Thus Peter could see Simon's sin clearly and knew from the Lord what to say in order to deal with him.

> When Simon saw that the Spirit was given at the laying on of the apostles' hands, he offered them money and said, "Give me also this ability so that everyone on whom I lay my hands may

> receive the Holy Spirit." Peter answered: "May your money perish with you, because you thought you could buy the gift of God with money! You have no part or share in this ministry, because your heart is not right before God. Repent of this wickedness and pray to the Lord. Perhaps he will forgive you for having such a thought in your heart. For I see that you are full of bitterness and captive to sin." (Acts 8:18–23)

Sin and compromise keep growing in the church because we will not hate our brothers and sisters. It is preached constantly that we should not judge but must "love" each other. Unfortunately, the problem is that human emotion does the loving, and we refuse to hate the part of us that wants to please our brother or sisters. Since Peter hated any acceptance of others, he could see, by the power of the Holy Spirit, that Simon was "full of bitterness and captive to sin." Further, Peter was willing to say that only "perhaps" God would forgive him. Peter remained so dead to pleasing this man (who claimed to want God) that he was willing not to promise him forgiveness. Peter would not know if Simon were forgiven until God made it clear. Unlike so many of us, Peter would not presume to know God's heart on the issue. Peter did not read the Bible and then tell everyone that every promise was his or hers. Peter did not preach ink; he preached a living God. How many claim salvation for others when they have not heard from God! When they do, they sin grievously in the name of the Lord.

The church today would rebuke Peter. We would say, "Peter, be more loving. Didn't he ask for forgiveness?" Certainly Peter would be challenged for the sin of not loving if he said such a thing in our churches today. No doubt Peter would be run out as an ungodly man and never invited back to preach. You see, we do not want preachers who hate brothers and sisters in their church. We want preachers who preach tough but respect us. We, however, do not want preachers who speak strong words and hate us enough to demand we live it. We do not want preachers willing to use the "whip" on our sin. We want preachers who love us, not preachers who hate us enough to give us the true love of heaven.

> What do you prefer? Shall I come to you with a whip, or in love and with a gentle spirit? (1 Cor. 4:21)

If we expect to hear from the Holy Spirit on how we should love each other in the church, we must start by hating our Christian brothers and sisters. We must be willing to utterly oppose them in any way the Lord leads. What the church needs today are brothers and sisters striving to utterly abhor our desires to be liked by one another. Then we can love as God would want us to by His power and grace.

Broken Power

It must be pointed out again that we must hate long before we begin to follow Jesus. Our hearts must be purified of any fleshly acceptance of others. Such idolatry leads to what we see in the church today—a continual sliding away from the power of God. It is sad to observe that because the church has rejected this hatred, it slowly has lost its power and influence in the world. This is one of the things Daniel prophesied would happen in the last days.

> I heard him swear by him who lives forever, saying, "It will be for a time, times and half a time. *When the power of the holy people has been finally broken*, all these things will be completed." (Dan. 12:7*b*, emphasis added)

Toward the end of all things, God says that the "power of the holy people" will "finally" be "broken." How sad to see the church trying to regain its power by asserting its rights and by praying for revival when the answer lies right before them. For the church to regain its power or to hang onto what power is left, it must return to the basics of what Jesus taught. Now while everyone agrees to this, no one wants to hate his brothers and sisters enough to really let God work. No one is willing to hate enough to take the necessary steps to fully expose sin. Instead we play at purity through small murmurs of repentance but no one calls their brother "Satan." No disassociation or judging by the power of the Holy Spirit takes place.

We talk of repentance yet hold back because we want others to respect and like us. We are unwilling to lose our heads over doctrinal matters, as John the Baptist did on the issues of divorce and remarriage.[2] We want our brothers and sisters to respect and admire us and are unwilling to make enemies of our brothers and sisters. Peter understood all too well that such desires must be hated, and it showed in how the Holy Spirit could work in his life. As we look at the following example, ask yourself if God could work this in your church.

In the Bible we read about a man and woman who gave money to the church, but lied about the fact that they did not give all to the Lord. Like most in the church today, they said they had given everything over to the Lord, but they still held back much for self. This couple came into the church pretending to have surrendered all to the Lord. Through Peter, the Holy Spirit struck them dead. When was the last time anyone died in your church by the power of the Holy Spirit? Until we are ready to hate our brothers and sisters, we will be unwilling for the Holy Spirit to use us in this way.

> Now a man named Ananias, together with his wife Sapphira, also sold a piece of property. With his wife's full knowledge he kept back part of the money for himself, but brought the rest and put it at the apostles' feet. Then Peter said, "Ananias, how is it that Satan has so filled your heart that you have lied to the Holy Spirit and have kept for yourself some of the money you received for the land? Didn't it belong to you before it was sold? And after it was sold, wasn't the money at your disposal? What made you think of doing such a thing? You have not lied to men but to God." When Ananias heard this, he fell down and died. And great fear seized all who heard what had happened. (Acts 5:1–5)

Peter could judge Ananias' "heart" by the power of the Holy Spirit and proclaim that "Satan" had filled him. Peter did not care whether or not Ananias, or the church for that matter, liked him. He hated Ananias and the church enough to show no favoritism.

Can you imagine what would happen if such a movement of the Holy Spirit began to happen in the Christian music arena, the book market, or our churches? In today's spiritual climate we would whine to Peter that he ought to look at the good in Ananias. "After all," we would say, "Ananias did give a majority of the money away and did the best he could." The battle cry that "no one is perfect" is heard everywhere today. Peter would be thoroughly rebuked for being judgmental.

How much the first church when "seized" with "great fear" must have realized that this man Peter would show no favoritism to anyone. They understood in an instant what Jesus meant by "hating" one's brothers and sisters. Of course today the church fully rejects this teaching and would have run right out to warn Sapphira about what had happened to her husband. Just imagine the reaction in your church today during the three hours before Sapphira came to Peter to discuss her part in this money issue.

> About three hours later his wife came in, not knowing what had happened. (Acts 5:7)

During those three hours, there is little doubt that her phone would have rung off the hook with such messages as: "Hey listen, I can't believe what Peter did to good old Ananias. Peter set him up and played word games with him. He didn't show him any kindness, and he says the Holy Spirit killed him. Now you had better tell the truth about what you did with the money, or Peter will jump all over you."

This of course did not happen because the first church knew how to hate their brothers and sisters. They knew not to show any favoritism or kindness that did not come from the Holy Spirit. They had been taught well to start their days and to walk with the Lord by hating their brothers and sisters. The first Christians knew to hate their opinions about how spiritual or unspiritual they thought a brother or sister was. Today we pray for revival but certainly not this kind. Therefore, we experience the spirit of a football rally in the church rather than true revival.

Notice what Scripture records twice about this event.

> Then the *young men* came forward, wrapped up his body, and carried him out and buried him. (Acts 5:6, emphasis added)

> At that moment she fell down at his feet and died. Then the *young men* came in and, finding her dead, carried her out and buried her beside her husband. (Acts 5:10, emphasis added)

It says that the "young men" buried this couple. Why would God let us know this fact twice? Because every young person setting out to follow the Lord had better learn the seriousness of calling upon the name of the Lord. Every young person had better take to heart that Jesus is serious about this matter of hating our brothers and sisters. May every young man come in, look at the bodies, wrap them up, and slowly carry them off. Let every young man in the Lord dig the ditch, lower the body, and take a long hard look at the buried body of Ananias. For it was no idle comment Jesus made about the need to hate our brothers and sisters. Every young man must sit alone and consider both the kindness and the sternness of the Lord.[3] Let him plead with the Lord to open his eyes concerning this matter of hating for Jesus. Let him offer his cheek to be struck by those who understand and be "filled with disgrace" that he might also be filled with the mercy of God. Let him sit "quietly" while he waits for the Lord and ponders what Peter allowed the Holy Spirit to work through him.

> The Lord is good to those whose hope is in him, to the one who seeks him; it is good to wait quietly for the salvation of the Lord. It is good for a man to bear the yoke while he is young. Let him sit alone in silence, for the Lord has laid it on him. Let him bury his face in the dust—there may yet be hope. Let him offer his cheek to one who would strike him, and let him be filled with disgrace. (Lam. 3:25–30)

If real revival were truly happening in the church today, then we would hear prayers motivated by the Holy Spirit asking that everyone learn to hate as Jesus commands. As it is now, the revival taking place is nothing more than golden calf worship in the name of the Lord. The feasting, the partying mixed with tough talk about righteousness, is nothing more than the futile effort of man to avoid the cross that deals with sin in their lives. How we love the noise of revival that blocks out the Holy Spirit's voice of conviction.

Many years ago we visited a church where the preacher talked tough against sin. His message rang true with the words of repentance and self-denial. Our hearts were thrilled at the thought of finding someone living this message. But our hopes of revival were shattered when the preacher announced that church would be canceled the following week for the Super Bowl. He was not willing to hate his congregation enough to make them live what he taught.

What the church needs today is young men willing to hate each other in Christ. Everyone longing for righteousness must pray for young men willing to let God work and move in unprecedented ways. Ask God for holiness in brothers and sisters who couldn't care less what others think of them and who are willing to say whatever the Lord leads.

Levites

We each must be willing to be deserted by everyone else because of the cross in our lives. Like Paul, who found himself all alone several times because of Christ, so too there may be times when our brothers are against us.[4] Of course this cannot happen if we self-righteously hold onto some point we want to make.

We often speak, and rightly so, of the people of God being priests in the Lord. For that is what they are.[5] But have you ever considered what makes a man a priest in the Lord? Why did God consider certain individuals qualified to be priests? We need look no further than those who first became part of the royal priesthood. They were "set apart," they were "blessed" because they were "against" their "own sons and brothers."

> So he stood at the entrance to the camp and said, "Whoever is for the Lord, come to me." And all the Levites rallied to him. Then he

> said to them, "This is what the Lord, the God of Israel, says: 'Each man strap a sword to his side. Go back and forth through the camp from one end to the other, each killing his brother and friend and neighbor.'" The Levites did as Moses commanded, and that day about three thousand of the people died. Then Moses said, "You have been set apart to the Lord today, for you were against your own sons and brothers, and he has blessed you this day." The next day Moses said to the people, "You have committed a great sin. But now I will go up to the Lord; perhaps I can make atonement for your sin." (Exod. 32:26–30)

This reflects the hating of the New Testament. Each man straps a sword, the Word of God, to his side, and goes throughout the camp looking for sin. Certainly the Word should be used in a very loving way, but a love consumed first for the holiness of God that will not show any favoritism to friend or neighbor who claims to be a Christian. How holy and clean our churches would be if we had such loving (hating) men of God. We would be able to stand against our enemies and win many battles before the Lord comes back.

Today, however, we see obvious compromises taking place in the church. No one wants to offend or be offended by someone else in the church. Until we see repentance that brings this hating of our brothers and sisters, we have no hope, absolutely no hope, for revival in the church.

A Word of Caution

A very strong warning must be stated at this point. Unless the next hatred we look at is not fully in place in a man's life, then trying to live what we have looked at so far will result in total disaster. A man who will not hate himself will cause great harm if he tries to live any of this on his own power. If man cannot hate himself, he will not hate others.

Let every preacher and pastor take this to heart. For every teacher unwilling to hate the congregation could wind up becoming a false prophet. They must actively oppose the flesh that wants the approval of their congregation or depends on them for income. The very minute a teacher, because it might offend someone, changes the way the Spirit wants a message delivered, he steps into false prophet territory. Better to be poor, without a job or a congregation, than to change the way God wants a message preached.

How sad to watch many preach a "tough message" yet remove the offense of the cross. Only those willing to hate will not be taken in by this subtle temptation. Like the Levites, the priests of God, they must oppose their own brothers and sisters if they expect to preach Spirit-filled sermons.

10

Hating Your Own Life

Yes Even

"Yes, even his own life," Jesus said. Now we come to the really important aspect of the hating passages. If this particular hatred is not present, the rest of what we have looked at means nothing. As if it wasn't shocking enough for Jesus to mention all the other people we should hate, He goes on to emphasize, "yes, even his own life."

But most of us are too self-absorbed with our feelings to even get on with this. In the same passage where Paul tells us to live as if we did not have a wife, he also tells us to ignore a good portion of our feelings. We are so fleshly and emotional that most of our feelings will come and go with the same steadiness as the waves hitting the shore. Blessed is the man who can wait for the emotions of God to take hold of him; sweet rest from self will be his.

> Those who mourn, as if they did not; those who are happy, as if they were not. (1 Cor. 7:30)

Instead of finding a cross that will crucify us to every petty feeling we have, we separate and analyze ourselves to the point of total self-absorption. We like to declare that we are happy now or sad. We like to look at ourselves and spend time separating our emotions into categories. Peace and feelings of mercy then become the all-important goals, and we wind up using the blessings of God for our own selfish ends. When advice is given that says we are to hate our own lives, the arguments begin to burst forth.

> He who separates himself seeks his own desire; he quarrels against all sound wisdom. (Prov. 18:1 NASB)

We met a Christian woman who kicked her husband out after three weeks of marriage. He did not earn enough money or show her the affection she thought she deserved. She asked my wife and me, "Where did I go wrong? I lived by the commandments and did not fornicate or commit adultery. I thought God would bless me in this marriage." She did not understand that God's blessings come from hating her own life and laying it down for her husband.

People often ask me, "How are you doing?" My answer is that it does not matter; it will pass whether I am joyful or sad. In fact, the only thing that can be nailed down about how I feel is that my feelings are nailed on the cross. I hate my emotions and will not become subject to their whims. Those who analyze and separate their emotions seek to please those desires, and they are slaves to the flesh. Those who hate their emotions will have the peace of Christ overshadowing every feeling of sadness and joy.[1]

A Christian unwilling to hate his own life will not have eternal life. For Jesus says only those who hate their life in this world keep it for eternal life. It does not matter that you say you were saved on such and such a date; if you do not hate your own life, you do not have eternal life in you.

If someone tries to live all the other hates we have studied so far without hating his own life, then he will turn into a self-righteous demon of a man. He will feel justified in every rebuke he offers and will destroy everyone around him. He might speak boldly against sin and the sinner but will hear Jesus say, "I never knew you." He might even have his own circle of followers who agree with what he does, but inside will rage the haughtiness of hell. For if there is one thing that hating oneself brings, it is a destruction of self-esteem (pride) and self-effort (rebellion).

Let us deal with the self-esteem. Then we will look at the sin of self-assertion or self-effort. All of self is wicked and vile. Every aspect of ourselves, from the moment of conception, remains damaged and deadly.

> Surely I was sinful at birth, sinful from the time my mother conceived me. (Ps. 51:5)

For a true Christian, good self-esteem or proper self-esteem does not exist. The only self-esteem a Christian possesses reveals a true viewpoint of self. What is the true viewpoint of self? It is this one inescapable fact—worthlessness.

> As it is written: "There is no one righteous, not even one; there is no one who understands, no one who seeks God. All have turned away, they have together become worthless; there is no one who does good, not even one." (Rom. 3:10–12)

Even though God declared that we are "worthless," without any value, so many believe they are valuable enough because God died for them. Nothing could be further from the truth. Jesus did not die for us because He thought we were worth it. Jesus died for us because of who He is, not because of who we are.[2]

Until a man sees by the power of the Holy Spirit his worthlessness, he will never hate his life. He will always think he has some small piece of nobility in himself. When God looks at each of us, He regrets that He ever made us. Furthermore, He is filled with "pain" at the thought that He ever brought us into existence.

> The Lord was grieved that he had made man on the earth, and his heart was filled with pain. (Gen. 6:6)

Jesus died for us because He is a God of love. Jesus performed an unmerited act of mercy when He died. The more we grasp this and allow the Holy Spirit to work this conviction, the more we will praise God for His love. For how can a man be shown mercy if he is not convinced he is guilty?[3] A man who does not see his guilt will think himself falsely accused.

Paul knew that "nothing" good lived in him. Not one good thing lived in Paul as long as Paul, or his self, remained alive. Let us ask God to show us ourselves so that we can also say with true conviction that we "know" nothing good lives in us. In short, ask God to convince us of this fact so that we might thoroughly be blessed with humility.

> I know that nothing good lives in me, that is, in my sinful nature. (Rom. 7:18a)

Only when Paul put himself to death by the power of the Holy Spirit could Jesus come to live in him. Then of course the only good thing in Paul was Jesus. Only when a man is dead to his own life will he have life. This is not being a robot or a mindless human. Rather, in God we find life. For it is God that is life and gives life to all things. When we fell in the garden and decided to become a god, we died because we do not have the essence of life in us. Only Jesus has life in Him, and He can put life only in surrendered, emptied vessels.

> In him was life, and that life was the light of men. (John 1:4)

Until a man hates his own self, he will never be willing to let it be crucified. The man who hates his life can honestly say that he "no longer" lives. To have faith in Jesus means to hate ourselves and to allow Him to live in us.

> I have been crucified with Christ and I no longer live, but Christ lives in me. The life I live in the body, I live by faith in the Son of God, who loved me and gave himself for me. (Gal. 2:20)

If you still think that something good remains in you, then consider that even Jesus did not consider Himself good. He would not allow Himself to be called *good.*

> "Why do you call me good?" Jesus answered. "No one is good—except God alone." (Mark 10:18)

Now if the Son of God did not consider Himself to be good, why do you think of yourself as good? Please do not play the spiritual game so many do by saying, "Oh, I know I need God, and everything comes from Him." That game just will not work, and you really do not believe it anyway.

If we really hated our own lives, we would not be so surprised when someone pointed out our sin. If we really believed that nothing good lived in self, we would not be so defensive when confronted or say, "Well, no one is perfect." Instead we would claim 2 Cor. 13:11 and "aim for perfection" and be thankful for such a rebuke. If we arose every morning hating ourselves, we would eagerly agree with anything God graciously pointed out that we should change. This explains why those unwilling to hate themselves cannot become disciples of Jesus. They cannot become disciples because of their unwillingness to be taught, corrected, encouraged, and rebuked.

Sometime in your reading of Matthew, Mark, Luke, and John, notice how often Jesus rebuked and corrected the disciples. There wasn't anything they did right for over three years. Day after day Jesus would have to point out their mistakes and sins. Even to the last days of Jesus' life on earth they still stumbled all over each other. Up until the last moment the disciples did not understand who Jesus was or what He was about. A man unwilling to put up with that much conviction by God in his life had better learn to hate his own life.

Paul knew what it meant to be driven to total confusion concerning the will of God. Indeed Paul rejoiced in being confused because when he was weak, he was strong. The more he hated self, the more the power of God rested on his life. Therefore Paul could say when he felt confused and "perplexed" that he was not in "despair."[4] He did not despair because he knew that God wanted him to hate his own plans so that He might work His will. A man unwilling to hate his own plans will not tolerate this kind of despair working in his life.

How sad to see individuals who have just come to the Lord placed in charge of things or told that God has great plans for them. They become so puffed up that God cannot break them. This is why Scripture warns that no one "young" in the faith should be put in a position of leadership, for that would cause him or her to fall under the same judgment as the Devil.[5] To be sure, God has great plans ahead for them—the conviction of how wicked they are and how merciful He is. This produces the deepest of fellowship between man and God. And out of that fellowship flows the work of God through us.

Don't be surprised, young Christian, if for years you cannot do anything right in the Lord. God must work in you much humility and death. Just arise each day to hate your life, and you will be ready for Jesus to change you in any way He sees fit. A man who does not begin each day saying to himself, "I am worthless; I can't do anything right in God; I am downright stupid about what God wants to work," cannot be a disciple of Jesus. In other words, he remains unteachable about the grace, mercy, and power of God. So many stay entrenched in the exact spot where they first met Jesus. Like the Israelites who left Egypt, they wind up in the end just as wicked and sinful as when they first left. Of course these believers will never enter God's rest.

Listen to what Paul says about the frustration that resulted when he looked at himself and realized his weakness.

> Therefore, since through God's mercy we have this ministry, we do not lose heart. (2 Cor. 4:1)

Paul realizes fully that only God's mercy allows him to preach the gospel. If it were not for this mercy, he would "lose heart." When he looked at himself, he felt overwhelmed at his unworthiness to serve the Lord. The more we hate ourselves, realizing our unworthiness, the nearer God's mercy will come into focus. If you want to experience the mercy of God like you never have before, then begin today to ask the Holy Spirit to teach you to hate yourself.

After three years as houseparents in the group home, my wife and I were asked to leave. It seemed that the lives of the men who became Christians convicted the state administrators. At the time Carla was expecting our second child. We were spiritually and emotionally exhausted, homeless, jobless, and beyond despair. Yet, we picked up this cross and told God we would go wherever He desired.

Of course we hoped for a glorious ministry somewhere, but God had better plans. A man from my wife's home church offered us an old farmhouse to live in. During four hot summer months this city boy slopped pigs, pulled calves, and picked corn. I listened to the jeers of family and Christian friends telling me to get a "real job" and support my family. I wrestled with my own manhood as I watched my pregnant wife pick out the "good" bread from the pig slop and our four-year-old gather tomatoes from our measly little garden. Following the advice of church leadership, I enrolled in a theological correspondence course only to hear God tell me to toss it aside. Doubts raged in my own heart that maybe I was lazy as everyone said. Had I really heard from God? Was I going off the deep end? All of this waiting on God caused me to see sin and self that had to die.

As I look back, I know God was emptying me of self. He wanted me to literally hate my life so I would learn to hate for Him. He brought me to a point of despair and hopelessness so that I would see myself clearly and depend totally on Him.

Again, this despair of daily seeing self drives us to "lose heart" if it were not for the love of God. However, most want all the mercy without a daily despairing of self. But the mystery of the cross is this: a man can despair of self and still be full of life. If you want the abundant life of Jesus, then you will have to allow God to work both the sorrow and the joy of the cross in you at the same time. Paul says in 2 Cor. 6:10 that he is always "sorrowful, yet always rejoicing." If you refuse the sorrows of the cross, hating yourself, then you will never be given the joy of the resurrected life. For how can there be resurrected life without a crucifixion? Always carry around the death of Jesus and you will always rejoice in Him.

Always Carry

Paul said that every hour of every day he "always" carried the death of Jesus Christ in his life. When we have this death in our bodies, feeling its effect and suffering, then we also have the "life of Jesus . . . revealed in our" bodies. Dear believer, do you want the power to overcome sin in your life? Do you want others to see the life of Jesus in you? Then let His death be pressed in on your life. Yes, it will hurt, but at the same time you will be given His glorious life. Others will see that death in your life, yet they will also see His life. This is the only way to victory. Every other way leads to the wide-road Christianity that Jesus warned against.

> We always carry around in our body the death of Jesus, so that the life of Jesus may also be revealed in our body. (2 Cor. 4:10)

God cannot help us deal with our pride if we do not hate our own lives. A man who hates his life cannot wait for God to deal with his pride. Think again of the word *hate*. You utterly abhor, reject, vomit out, and despise something. A man who hates like that runs to the prayer closet and cannot wait for God to take his life. Like a man dying of cancer, he cannot wait to get rid of the tumor growing in him. He does not say to the doctor, "Gee, I would like to hang onto this tumor a little bit longer. I have grown attached to it, and it has grown attached to me." No, a thousand times no. The man hates the tumor that is destroying his life and eagerly desires to have it cut out.

You can see why those who hate their own lives can be taught by God. What keeps us from the wisdom of heaven is love for our tumors of opinions, church doctrine, and religious thoughts. Only a "fool . . . delights in airing his own opinions" (Prov. 18:2). Yet how many Sunday school classes spend the students' time sharing their "opinions" about what they think Scripture means. What fools we are when we agree to disagree. Thinking we can keep our religious opinions and still be taught by the Holy Spirit must cause God to shake His head in dismay. If you desire to follow Jesus, then begin now to hate every opinion you have about every biblical issue.

Our churches remain disunited because men refuse to hate their opinions and thoughts about God.[6] If each brother would go into the prayer closet hating their own opinions, God would give us His thoughts. Many years ago a brother wanted to join the church I served, but we differed on a key doctrinal issue. Normally I would have to exclude a brother because of this doctrine, but God impressed upon me to let him join. Without another word about the doctrine in question, we began to teach him about hating his own life. Some months later, he left his prayer closet excited because God had made clear to him the doctrine in question. He felt appalled that he had ever believed anything else and dumbfounded as to why he could not see it before. This is the way of the cross. It has the power to crucify a man to himself. What deep joy the young man had because he got his doctrine from God and not man. His faith rested on God's power instead of man's wisdom.

Every day I get up and hate my religion and spiritual concepts. I hate them because I could be utterly wrong or, worse yet, I might agree with the Lord doctrinally by the power of self. I must test everything daily before the Lord. For how can self, I, which is totally worthless, agree with God and be correct? This realization that self, even when correct about God, can lead to sheer death causes a man to willingly hate his thoughts. Remember well that Satan quoted Scripture in context, but did his words contain life? We are no better than Satan when we handle the Word of God without hating ourselves. For how can that which is worthless say and do anything good?[7]

Don't let an intellectual agreement to all this fool you. We are talking real despair and hatred here. A man can agree on the definition of hatred without feeling it himself. You can agree that we should hate our own lives without ever actually hating your own life. You must come to despair of self, which can only happen by the power of the Holy Spirit. Do a study of Proverbs 1–4 and note how often the words *rebuke*, *correction*, and *advice* appear. By rebuking a man, God makes him despair of self and be willing to hate his own life. The more willing we are to be wrong and rebuked by God, the more of His wisdom we gain. Prov. 1:23 puts it best: "If you had responded to my rebuke, I would have poured out my heart to you and made my thoughts known to you."

If you would have only "responded" to God's "rebuke," then He would have "poured" out His "heart" and made His "thoughts known to you." We have plenty of teachers, theologians, and preachers, but a man in whom the thoughts of God have been poured out who can find? As Proverbs says, "Gold there is, and rubies in abundance, but lips that speak knowledge are a rare jewel" (Prov. 20:15). They are rare because men refuse to hate their own lives and to allow the rebukes to come.

The more a man responds to godly rebukes, the wiser he will become. Too bad so many think they can gain wisdom by reading the ink on the pages of the Bible or by attending seminary or college. While those things are needed, only when a man willfully hates his own thoughts will he allow God to rebuke him. Indeed the man who hates self will long for God to bring the rebukes.

A man who hates his own thoughts and opinions about God's Word also hates his own actions before God. He hates when he wants to get up, when he wants to go to bed, when he eats, and what he eats; he hates every aspect of his life. This is why Jesus says those unwilling to hate their own lives cannot follow Him. A man who does not hate his plans will not go where the Holy Spirit leads but will try to conform the Holy Spirit to agree with his spiritual plans for the day. However, the man who arises and hates his plans for the day willingly hears from the Holy Spirit where to go and what to do. Let us look at one example. It seems that revival had broken out and the disciples were ready to settle down and open a church.

> Simon and his companions went to look for him, and when they found him, they exclaimed: "Everyone is looking for you!" (Mark 1:36–37)

The twelve had their plans and they were excited about what God did. They had spiritual, religious plans and were ready to walk in them all the way. They came to Jesus exclaiming that everyone wants to hear what He has to say. No doubt they were ready to pass the plate and put up the pulpit. But had the twelve learned to hate their own plans as Jesus hated His own, they would have first hated their ideas and asked God for His will. Jesus had spent the night in prayer and knew that just because revival broke out did not mean it was God's will to stay and preach. Very early in the morning Jesus went away from the pressure and demands of the religious world. Jesus hated His life. He hated when He slept and hated His ideas of the best way to serve God. Which of us as preachers are dead enough to self and hate our lives enough to leave a revival behind according to God's will?

> Very early in the morning, while it was still dark, Jesus got up, left the house and went off to a solitary place, where he prayed. Simon and his companions went to look for him, and when they found him, they exclaimed: "Everyone is looking for you!" Jesus replied, "Let us go somewhere else—to the nearby villages—so I can preach there also. That is why I have come." So he traveled throughout Galilee, preaching in their synagogues and driving out demons. (Mark 1:35–39)

Let us die to ourselves, and we too will know why we have come and where we must go to glorify God.

11

Disciples

The Word Disciple

Literally, the word *disciple* means "one who is a learner," but this learner must endeavor to apply what is taught. This is why Jesus says in Luke 6:40 that "A student is not above his teacher, but everyone who is *fully trained* will be like his teacher" (emphasis added). To accept Jesus Christ as Lord and Savior means that a man becomes a disciple of Jesus. Anyone unwilling to become a disciple of Jesus cannot rightly claim to be saved by Jesus. Scripture is clear that "whoever claims" to be in Jesus must "walk as Jesus did" (1 John 2:6). Without this quality of being a disciple, we become mockers very quickly. Mockers who read the Bible claim certain promises and obey specific Scriptures but do not know Jesus. A disciple can feel the Teacher pressing the teachings into his life and molding him into His image. Therefore studying the Bible without being disciplined by the Holy Spirit is a great deception many fall prey to. Jesus warned against the danger of Bible study without discipleship in John 5:39–40:

> You diligently study the scriptures because you think that by them you possess eternal life. These are the scriptures that testify about me, yet you refuse to come to me to have life.

So many people study Scripture and have a thorough knowledge of the Greek and Hebrew but refuse to go to Jesus in order to be disciplined. Their own knowledge of Scripture deceives them. They believe that because they have correct doctrine, they are saved. No man can have eternal life apart from being a disciple of Jesus. It is a very common delusion for men to think that because they read the Bible, they "possess eternal life." How can we keep ourselves from falling prey to the deception called *Bible study*? There is only one way; we must hate for Jesus.

Hating for the Lord allows us to move past the deception and to become disciples of Jesus. To measure the deception in your life, test yourself to see how much the Holy Spirit has taught you to hate for Jesus. I say the Holy Spirit because no man can commit suicide by crucifixion. No man can rid himself of self because the sheer act of dealing with self causes us to become self-righteous. Just try crucifying yourself. You might get one hand nailed to the board, and if you could endure the pain you might be able to nail your feet to the wood, but you would never be able to finish the job. You could never nail your other hand to the cross, and you certainly would not be able to lift the cross up in the air. But when someone else, like the Holy Spirit, crucifies us, a deep sense of helplessness sets in. You totally lose control of everything and are at the crucifier's mercy. You hang completely exposed, vulnerable, and dependent on God for everything. You will feel this as you begin to give the Holy Spirit permission to crucify you.

Jesus must first convince us of the hopelessness in dealing with self. The process of becoming a disciple begins with this feeling. Remember that Jesus spent three years convincing the disciples of how powerless they were to deal with the sin in their lives. This is the baptism of fire that Jesus promised would come in each person's life. Let us not stop that fire no matter how hot it becomes, and it can become very hot indeed. For when God sets

His sights on dealing with our pride, lust, greed, love of money, cowardliness, and many other impurities in our souls, He uses fire hot enough to bring dross to the top so that gold is left. Sadly most cannot speak of this fire because we will not permit God to make the fire hot enough to purge self. Like those in Jeremiah's day, we allow God to blow the fire to only a certain degree, and the dross is not purged.

> The bellows blow fiercely to burn away the lead with fire, but the refining goes on in vain; the wicked are not purged out. They are called rejected silver, because the Lord has rejected them. (Jer. 6:29–30)

We see the silver in us and ignore the dross. Therefore God says we will be called "rejected silver." When Jesus first called His disciples, they were broken and humbled but did not realize just how much more God had to do to break them. Look at Peter; when first called of the Lord he fell down on his knees and cried, "Go away from me, Lord; I am a sinful man!" (Luke 5:8b) How little we, like Peter, understand how much humility and self must be broken in us before Pentecost. It was not until Peter, years later and closer to the cross, finally went out and wept bitterly over the self that lived in him that he was ready to walk in the fullness of the Holy Spirit at Pentecost. This is the cost that a disciple must prepare himself for. Although we humbled ourselves when we first accepted the Lord, God must work much more brokenness in us.

Only a man willing to hate himself and everything around him will endure this kind of brokenness and revelation of sin that the Holy Spirit must work in each of our lives. This explains why we are encouraged in Hebrews not to give way to despair when God disciplines us. God's rod is swift, hard, and exact, but blessed are those who submit to its blows. When David prayed in Ps. 51:7, "Wash me, and I will be whiter than snow," he knew how clothes were cleaned in his day. Remember that dirty clothes were laid on a rock and beat with a large stick to get out the dirt. Let us too know that we will be laid on the rock, Jesus Christ, and the sin will be beat out of us. So, "do not lose heart when He rebukes you."[1]

As a result, our gospel calls must change to reflect the Lord's call to discipleship rather than our quick fixes to the problems in our lives. For Jesus did not come to fix *our* problems but to crucify the self living in us so that we are ready for His coming kingdom. You see, we were made for His pleasure, not our own. Sadly, everyone wants to clean up their lives, but no one wants to give up their lives.

We must present the cost of discipleship clearly and perfectly to every person thinking about becoming a Christian. If we do not, then we become false teachers and do the person great harm. They might think themselves saved and end up going to hell. More than that, when God does try to make them disciples, calling them to hate for Him, they think something strange is happening. They might even think Satan causes all the trouble rather than see the loving hand of God's discipline. Crucifixion of self is a very painful process, and naturally we want to avoid it. However, they must be warned in order not to refuse this work of the Holy Spirit.

Whether someone accepts salvation quickly or takes their time, one thing is certain: each man must sit down and estimate the cost. Estimating the cost happened in every case where someone in the Bible accepted salvation. For example, take the conversion of the jailer:

> They replied, "Believe in the Lord Jesus, and you will be saved—you and your household." Then they spoke the word of the Lord to him and to all the others in his house. At that hour of the night the jailer took them and washed their wounds; then immediately he and all his family were baptized. The jailer brought them into his house and set a meal before them; he was filled with joy because he had come to believe in God—he and his whole family. (Acts 16:31–34)

Verse 33 says that "at that hour of the night" the jailer and his whole family accepted the Lord by baptism. You might wonder how this man counted the cost. Remember, he was a jailer. He had put Paul and Silas in jail and had placed their feet in painful stocks. He washed their wounds and saw their pain.

The jailer experienced the cost in Paul's and Silas' lives. He understood all too well the cost of discipleship. He had seen the riot and watched the beatings and realized that to follow this Jesus meant he must hate himself and his family. It would have been foolish to sit down with the jailer and spend four days explaining to him the cost of discipleship. However, others may have to spend more time contemplating the cost. Recall the story of the young rich man, for example.[2] However, the important thing is that those with whom we share the gospel see our godly hatred. We must demonstrate the gospel by our lives long before we explain it with words.

Let each church examine before the Lord their salvation call. Let every church and Christian hate their doctrinally correct salvation plan so that God may work the truth in each person as He sees fit. This truth says, "Sit down and count the cost, for you must hate your father, mother, brother, sister, and yes even your own life."

The Essential Piece

As if hating were not enough, Jesus added the cross to His message. Jesus made it very clear that anyone who comes after Him must carry his cross. Anyone who accepts Jesus Christ as Lord and Savior will find a cross waiting for him—not just any cross but a cross that God has designed specifically for him. So many churches try to design crosses for their members and to apply the same cross to each person. Such crosses designed by the plans, seminars, and outlines of man will do nothing to create the new life. We must each come to Jesus and follow *Him*, not our outlines about Him. How sad to watch so many groups try all these things without truly following Jesus. This is how cults are born. Leaders seek to apply their cross to each person's life and wind up controlling everything. Men often want to avoid the cross Jesus has for them and therefore seek to design their own custom-made cross. This allows them to keep from dying to sin while feeling and looking holy. I am always amazed at how much energy Christians put into escaping the cross Jesus has for them. If they would submit to the Lord and follow Him, they would find the abundant life they claim to desire. However, most just do not want to give up their sin and self.

Hebrews tells us to run the course "marked out for us" by God. Do not try and pick your course or cross, and certainly do not let any man give you a cross to carry. Seek the brothers and sisters who can discern God's will in your life and encourage you to follow Jesus on the course chosen for you.

Take note that the cross Jesus said to carry daily is a painful thing. We must consider this cost before we start on the road with Jesus. In order to advance from being a mere traveler with Jesus, you must accept that the cross will be painful in your life. Peter understood this and wrote about the cross in our lives.

> Therefore, since Christ suffered in his body, arm yourselves also with the same attitude, because he who has suffered in his body is done with sin. As a result, he does not live the rest of his earthly life for evil human desires, but rather for the will of God. (1 Pet. 4:1–2)

When Jesus died on the cross, He suffered tremendous pain. Peter says that we must "arm" ourselves with the "same attitude." This attitude knows and understands fully that to carry a cross and follow Jesus will involve pain. Only those willing to suffer in their "body" with sin are "done with sin." You can feel this kind of Christianity. There have been many days when I felt like I had welts from the bruises the cross produced. Which of us cannot feel pain when God deals with our pride and sin? Which of us cannot feel wrenching in our stomachs when we wrestle with the sin around us?

It is a wondrous thing to watch a man carry a cross for Jesus. First God weakens him just as Jesus was mocked and beaten. Then God gives him a cross to carry through the public streets. The public carrying of our crosses leaves us humiliated. Then we hang naked on the cross for all to see. We become a people without pretense or pride as we carry that cross. We clearly see this cross in believers who honestly live 1 John 1:7:

> But if we walk in the light, as he is in the light, we have fellowship with one another, and the blood of Jesus, his Son, purifies us from all sin.

Carrying our cross puts everything in the light for all to see. Jesus carried His cross publicly, and so must we. But 1 John says that at this place the "blood of Jesus . . . purifies us from all sins." Do you want to be cleansed from all sin? If you do, then pick up your daily cross and carry it in the open for all to see. Of course it is humiliating and weakening, but, like Jesus, we will be given someone to help us carry the load.[3] As we "walk in the light," we have "fellowship with one another." Where you find this, you will see the deepest love that has all things in common, carries one another's burdens, and suffers and rejoices with the whole body. You will see a unity that the world may call "cultlike." This unity is a fellowship seldom seen and enjoyed today.

That is why James instructed all Christians to "confess your sins to each other and pray for each other so that you might be healed."[4] Anyone who says that their sins are just between them and God does not understand what it means to carry their cross and needs to wake up concerning the message of Jesus. For like Jesus, we will be given a crown of thorns to bruise our pride and intellect. Like Paul, we might even be given a "thorn in our flesh" to keep us from pride and conceit.[5] Each of us has a crown of thorns waiting to deal with our pride. God crowns our pride with thorns and pricks our thoughts so that we feel how far we are from Him. We will watch as the world takes advantage of us and gambles with our last bit of clothing. We will hear the world and the worldly Christians tell us to "come down off the cross." They will claim that this kind of Christianity misses the joy and peace of God. With one voice, they will declare that surely it cannot be the will of God for us to carry such a cross. The worldly will always insult this kind of Christianity because it looks foolish. We will continue to become weaker and weaker, losing more and more self, while they stand comfortably afar watching us suffer. They will shake their heads at our belief and trust in God as we carry our crosses daily. Yet pay them no attention; the joy will come. The resurrected life will be ours. God will come to comfort us in due time.[6]

> Those who passed by hurled insults at him, shaking their heads and saying, "So! You who are going to destroy the temple and build it in three days, come down from the cross and save yourself!" (Mark 15:29–30)

How sad to see so many wasting their time on religious self-help books when all they need to do is to suffer with sin in their body. We do not need more counselors in the church, but more brothers and sisters who can point someone to the cross. Indeed, look at what the abundance of counselors has brought. We do not need the psychology of the world with its ideas of how to cure the human soul. In other words, there is no such thing as a Christian psychologist because we have the power to change men through the cross of Christ.

> See to it that no one takes you captive through hollow and deceptive philosophy, which depends on human tradition and the basic principles of this world rather than on Christ. (Col. 2:8)

If there were more wrestling with sin in the church today, more people would find the resurrected life. Instead of settling for quick-fix prayers of deliverance, people would be delivered from all of self rather than from specific sins. Without carrying your cross, these kinds of prayers are just a quick housecleaning. As Jesus warned, such houses are swept clean, but the end condition of the person remains worse off than it was in the beginning. For a time they appear to have gotten well and their lives seem to move forward. Yet without daily carrying their crosses, they will come to a surprise destruction.[7]

The good news is that those willing to suffer like this find a grand "result." They discover that they can "live the rest" of their earthly lives for the "will of God." Only those who have suffered like this can rest assured that they are not deceived about the will of God in their lives. Many claim that God guides their lives, but they cannot speak of the pain of the cross. How can this be? You can easily tell those who have experienced this by the totality of the way they "Amen" this message.

If you want to overcome sin in your life, simply let Jesus Christ give you a cross that crucifies you. You don't have to jump up and down to get it, or cry a bunch of tears, or see a special speaker. Just simply say, "Yes, Lord," and you will wonder what hit you because those nails hurt. How many, although warned about the cost, seem surprised when God begins to take them at their word? They usually come back saying, "I thought I knew, but now I know. This is real stuff."

To many, this does not sound like good news, but to those who "hunger and thirst for righteousness" it is the grandest news of all. Let us go forth and pick up the cross God has for us. It is a perfect cross designed to make us fit for the holiness of God. It was fashioned with great care and wisdom by those hands that were pierced for our sins. I will not kid you; it is not a "pleasant" thing. It is, however, a grand thing. Let us "strengthen" our "feeble arms and weak knees" for the hope that we might share in God's "holiness"! "Later on" if you have been "trained" by the discipline, a "harvest of righteousness and peace" will be yours.

> Our fathers disciplined us for a little while as they thought best; but God disciplines us for our good, that we may share in his holiness. No discipline seems pleasant at the time, but painful. Later on, however, it produces a harvest of righteousness and peace for those who have been trained by it. Therefore, strengthen your feeble arms and weak knees. (Heb. 12:10–12)

The cross God gives you will leave you in the world but crucify you to the world. You will use the things in the world but not be absorbed by them. You might mourn but not as if it were the end of everything. You might rejoice but will not get caught up in your laughter.

> Those who mourn, as if they did not; those who are happy, as if they were not; those who buy something, as if it were not theirs to keep; those who use the things of the world, as if not engrossed in them. For this world in its present form is passing away. (1 Cor. 7:30–31)

Those who do not know this power of the cross are absorbed with their fleeting feelings. They become in tune with themselves every time they feel depressed or blue. They have to talk about it, pray about it, and seek to find some way to make themselves happy. They may read Scripture but are motivated by sad feelings. So with every session of sadness they become more and more self-absorbed. Jesus just becomes the means to the end of getting out of the depression.

Then there are those who fall in love with praising God when they are happy. And once the emotion of happiness begins to fade, they must pump themselves up again. They live for worship service after worship service. They only really care about their happiness in the Lord and therefore do not meet the needs of others. This is most often seen in those who talk about the freedom they have in Christ yet please their flesh.

Plenty of people are consumed with the things of the world. They have hobbies; they buy the current fads on the market. In short, there is work to be done for the Lord, yet they remain busy buying things. They buy a fancy luxury or sports car in the name of the Lord. They are "engrossed" in their homes, cars, or hobbies. Don't you just hate seeing a fish symbol on the back of luxury and sports cars?

The cross keeps Christians from being so self-absorbed that they cannot be led by the Spirit in all things. The cross allows a man to be in the world but not a part of the world.

> May I never boast except in the cross of our Lord Jesus Christ, through which the world has been crucified to me, and I to the world. (Gal. 6:14)

Denying Self

Christians lose something they can never find again: themselves. While people in the world constantly strive to "find themselves," Christians want to lose their lives. Every day I get up and say, "Where is Tim? I can't find him anywhere. I don't know what he likes or wants to do today." Of course I also say, "I don't want to find him either."

> Then he called the crowd to him along with his disciples and said: "If anyone would come after me, he must deny himself and take up his cross and follow me. For whoever wants to save his life will lose it, but whoever loses his life for me and for the gospel will save it." (Mark 8:34–35)

When we are willing to lose our lives for the sake of Jesus and the gospel, we will find eternal life. Yet what did Jesus mean by denying one's self?

Denying one's self means we deny all of self, not just specific areas now and then that trouble us, but *everything*. Even the world denies themselves of things that trouble them without really giving up self. All of this must happen by following Jesus, for without that, there is no victory in denying self or carrying a cross. Know that Jesus will want to meet you there and show you how and in what ways to deny yourself.

Think of a race. Everyone starts at the starting line. No one is permitted to start halfway up the course. Everyone must start the run from the same point and follow the rules of the race. In this race God has a track laid out for you. You can't take a short cut and you can't pick someone else's track to run in. For example, Anna, who prayed and fasted in the temple all the time, would have been in sin if she had left the temple to do other ministry work.[8] Likewise, if Simeon had stayed in the temple all the time praying and fasting, he would have been in sin and missed blessing Jesus.[9]

We each have a course that God has marked out for us. However, each course has one thing in common: denial of self. Whatever course God marks out for you will involve "strict training" and the beating of your body. Can others tell you are a Christian by how you beat your body and stay in strict training? Or do they see you running aimlessly from one worship service or seminar to the next? Do they see you reading one Christian novel after another but not really gaining any ground in the race to put self to death? Paul says that "everyone" who wants to be a Christian should do these things. Paul states that if he does not "beat" his body after he has shared the gospel with others, he will be "disqualified for the prize."

> Everyone who competes in the games goes into strict training. They do it to get a crown that will not last; but we do it to get a crown that will last forever. Therefore I do not run like a man running aimlessly; I do not fight like a man beating the air. No, I beat my body and make it my slave so that after I have preached to others, I myself will not be disqualified for the prize. (1 Cor. 9:25–27)

So the question begs itself. If someone were to ask how you beat your body, what would you say? Would your children testify that you deny yourself? In what ways could you tell others you are in strict training? Think of an athlete. Everything he does centers around his sport. It affects what he eats, whom he associates with, when he sleeps, what he reads, and how he uses his time. He will devote himself only to his sport and will deny himself much just to be able to play in the game. How long would your list be of denying self for the athletic game called *Christianity*? Do the worldly athletes put you to shame with their devotion and denial of self? If so, there is a very good chance you will be disqualified for the prize. Denying self is a specific quality, the organizing of your life to follow Jesus. May Jesus find you denying self so that you run in such a way as to get the prize.

Like so many in the church, we do not want to be just "running aimlessly" doing the Christian thing. How awful it is to watch people busy at being busy. With all their activity, they are never really going anywhere in the Christian life. They go to Bible study, they pray, fast, and serve in all kinds of ways, but the crucified life just is not there. Indeed they remain unwilling to accept a Jesus who goes up to Jerusalem to die and suffer. They do not want to follow Him there and are unwilling to deny themselves. Like the villagers in the following passage, they will not even tolerate a Jesus heading to Jerusalem to die on a cross. To them such messages feel cold, not loving, and not of God.

> And he sent messengers on ahead, who went into a Samaritan village to get things ready for him; but the people there did not welcome him, because he was heading for Jerusalem. (Luke 9:52–53)

Such individuals will not even receive those who preach and live a message that leads them to Jerusalem to die. Let us not be "astonished" disciples who find Jesus "leading" us this "way" to the cross and denial of self. As disciples, this should not catch us by surprise. As for the traveler, well, he will go along for the ride, but in total fear, because he has no clue as to what Jesus works.

> They were on their way up to Jerusalem, with Jesus leading the way, and the disciples were astonished, while those who followed were afraid. Again he took the twelve aside and told them what was going to happen to him. "We are going up to Jerusalem," he said, "and the Son of Man will be betrayed to the chief priests and teachers of the law. They will condemn him to death and will hand him over to the Gentiles, who will mock him and spit on him, flog him and kill him. Three days later he will rise." (Mark 10:32–34)

In verses 33–34 above Jesus speaks very specifically about what the cross means. He too will speak specifically with you if you will listen.

12

How?

Let's look at how we can hate for Jesus and add the essential puzzle piece of the cross into our lives.

How to Get This Surrender

How does one begin the process of crucifixion of self? By now it should be obvious that we cannot help it along or accomplish it on our own. Remember that you cannot commit suicide by crucifixion. Someone must crucify you. That someone, of course, is God, who has a cross perfectly tailored for each of us. Crucifixion of self is not a harsh treatment we put on ourselves. Indeed many churches preach about holiness and try all kinds of rules, guidelines, and concepts to keep sin in its place. All such effort is in vain and will do nothing to put self to death. Self will only resurface again in some other more wicked and hidden form. This is why so many Christians are blind to the plank in their own eyes. Individuals are never transformed or empowered because preachers do not really understand the power of the cross.

These kinds of churches always become controlling and fail at ridding others of self.

> Such regulations indeed have an appearance of wisdom, with their self-imposed worship, their false humility and their harsh treatment of the body, but they lack any value in restraining sensual indulgence. (Col. 2:23)

Everyone tries self-imposed rules sometime in their Christian walk. They commit a sin, resolve never to do it again, then begin to try and deny themselves whatever caused them to sin in the first place. For example, if they struggle with getting quiet times, they try to set their alarm early or attempt to apply some gimmick to get quality time with God. Well, even if you achieve your goal to get consistent, hour-long quiet times every day, it does not mean self is crucified.

So the question begs itself, how does one begin to get this cross from Jesus? It begins with Romans 12.

> Therefore, I urge you, brothers, in view of God's mercy, to *offer your bodies as living sacrifices*, holy and pleasing to God—this is your spiritual act of worship. Do not conform any longer to the pattern of this world, but be transformed by the renewing of your mind. Then you will be able to test and approve what God's will is—his good, pleasing and perfect will. For by the grace given me I say to every one of you: Do not think of yourself more highly than you ought, but rather think of yourself with sober judgment, in accordance with the measure of faith God has given you. (Rom. 12:1–3, emphasis added)

First, get before God and offer your body to Him every minute of every day. Tell God, "Here is my body to do with as you please." Surrender everything and all your plans and then totally forget them. Plead with God to take all you have and put it to His use. Ignore all pleas to come down off that painful cross. Humble yourself and fully realize that every defensive position against the sin living in you keeps you from fellowship and death to self. Offer your body to God for Him to direct as to when to pray, study, work, sleep, eat, and play. Tell the Lord that your mouth is His and to convict you whenever you say something not of His will. Ask Him to put a "guard over your mouth."[1]

Offer your whole body as a living sacrifice with no thought of gaining anything for yourself—no thought of reward, not one ounce of attention or anything else coming your way. You want to be so dead to self that you do not even realize you are not giving attention to it.

Do this with God's mercy in "view." In other words, because of His love for you, you offer everything about yourself to Him out of gratitude and joy. This is a joy that does not consider it a cost to sell everything so that one can have a treasure hidden in a field.

> In his joy went and sold all he had and bought that field. (Matt. 13:44*b*)

This, by the way, is true worship; "this is your spiritual act of worship" (Rom. 12:1). Tell God you will work where and when He wants you to. You will buy only what He directs—from the smallest to the largest of purchases. Let the despising of money become real in your life.[2] Explain to God that you will not go anywhere He does not guide you to, no matter how justified the reason. From work to family gatherings to sick friends to whatever circumstance, you will not go unless He directs. Be prepared for your flesh to rebel at even the thought of this surrender. After all, the flesh has had its way in all things, even religion, and will not submit easily. You must allow God to chase it down and put it to death.

Next, "Do not conform to the pattern of this world" (Rom. 12:2). The cross will work in you a pattern totally opposite of the world's pattern. While the world concerns itself with self and self-esteem, you will lose all of self. While the world and the worldly are only interested in themselves, you will lose any thought of self. Indeed you will not even know what your right hand is doing.[3] Let God take away the self that is aware of what self does.[4]

Be prepared for the Spirit of the Lord to separate you from the speech, dress, holidays, money, and things of the world. Although you live in the world, you come out and separate yourself in all you do both in motive and action.[5] This is really more exciting than it might sound at first. Every day I get up and ask the Lord what I should wear that day. From a suit to jeans, I never know what God has in mind for the day. All I do know is that I want to be found dressed and ready for His plans.

> That servant who knows his master's will and does not get ready or does not do what his master wants will be beaten with many blows. (Luke 12:47)

As you allow this, God will transform your mind. He will give you a transformed mind like you never had before—a new mind, a resurrected one—not your old one cleaned up a little. You will no longer think the empty religious thoughts or do things in the way and reason you did before. You will be able to say with joy, "Behold, all things are new."[6]

It is important to realize that *only* after this has been accomplished to a large degree in your life will you know the will of God. Until you sit in the dust waiting for the Lord to finish the work of crucifixion, you will not know His will. Self with its mixed motives must be dealt a deathblow. And even those who know this must be prepared for their lives to be trimmed back many times.

> He cuts off every branch in me that bears no fruit, while every branch that does bear fruit he prunes so that it will be even more fruitful. (John 15:2)

You can only hear the voice of the Lord by offering yourself to God to be crucified and by allowing your mind to be transformed and separated from the world. "Then" and only "then" will you be in a position to discern God's will. As Rom. 12:2 says, "*Then* you will be able to test and approve what God's will is—his good, pleasing and perfect will" (emphasis added). It is only after all these things are in place that we can "test and approve" God's will. Those who die to self will find God's will to be "pleasing and perfect" even if that means going to the cross to die. Until this happens, this teaching will appear to be only a painful message.

Why do you think Jesus had the abundant and victorious life? Why do you think Jesus' prayers were always answered? Simple: He only prayed according to God's will. Jesus always did what pleased the Father, and therefore He was given the Spirit "without limit."[7] If we want the same power in our lives, then we must "aim for perfection" in doing what pleases God at all times.[8] Surrender your willful prayers about your concerns and take on the concerns of Jesus,[9] then your prayers will be according to God's will and can be answered.[10] Jesus had the abundant life because He offered Himself as a "living sacrifice." Only with this kind of sacrifice will you know God's will, that is, His will concerning what to pray and how to pray it. What a truly abundant life this is because self is gone from your prayer life and the Holy Spirit can pray through you. This is what it really means to "pray in the Spirit."[11]

Because many have not surrendered this deeply, they do not find this a pleasing gospel call. Only after we do will we find the will of God pleasing and approving. Once Jesus had prayed with drops of blood, then, and not before, He found the cross to be pleasing and perfect. In the same way, with every step of the Christian life, you will at first not find His will to be pleasing. But after wrestling with your flesh and dying, the cross will become perfect. This is true with every commandment and every Scripture of God to one degree or another.

Because of this lack of death to self, most people simply tack on the name *Jesus* to whatever they do. Begin now to obey Rom. 12:3: Think and look at yourself with "sober judgment," not with your own mind and effort. Do this through dependence upon God and only with the "measure of faith" He has "given you," not the faith inspired by sermons or your own power. Remember; it is not you who lives to judge and deal with sin. It is not you who must come up with faith. You must die, and God will give you all you need, even the faith to judge yourself with sober judgment.

> Do not think of yourself more highly than you ought, but rather think of yourself with sober judgment, in accordance with the measure of faith God has given you. (Rom. 12:3)

Everything Said

With all of this said, I point you to the faith in Jesus that will work it out to His glory.

"To the obedience that comes from faith." (Rom. 1:5b)

ENDNOTES

CHAPTER ONE: THE TERM HATE

1. 1 Cor. 1:17
2. Acts 5:28 Contrast this with the attitude that is determined to make others guilty.
3. Ps. 119:27
4. John 4:14
5. John 15:12
6. 1 Tim. 6:16
7. John 15:2
8. Matt. 25:1–13

Chapter Two: Large Crowds

1. Rev. 3:2, 2 Kings 13:18–19
2. Rom 16:5, 1 Cor. 16:19, Philemon 1:2, 1 Cor 7:31
3. 1 Thess. 1:4–5
4. Matt. 24:12

Chapter Three: Following Jesus

1. Matt. 12:1, Luke 5:29
2. 1 Cor. 9:27
3. Gal. 5:25
4. Luke 10:21
5. Isa. 51:1
6. John 16:33
7. Heb. 4:6–11
8. Isa. 30:15
9. John 18:2
10. John 15:6
11. Luke 9:23
12. Heb. 9:28
13. Acts 26:14
14. John 21:18
15. Ps. 3:5
16. Isa. 53:3
17. Gal. 5:17
18. Jer. 12:1–3
19. Jer. 6:14
20. 2 Tim. 3:1–5
21. Matt. 6:23
22. 2 Cor. 6:1
23. John 13:34–35
24. John 6:63, 1 John 2:6
25. John 6:60
26. Rom. 14:23
27. Jer. 23:36
28. Matt. 8:21, Luke 14:20
29. John 3:8
30. 2 Tim. 3:4
31. Luke 4:26
32. John 11:5-6
33. Acts 17:28
34. Jude 1:6
35. 1 Sam. 15:20
36. 1 Sam. 15:24
37. Gal. 3:1
38. Mark 12:30–31

Chapter Four: Bible Knowledge

1. 2 Tim. 2:15
2. Col. 2:8
3. 2 Cor. 12:7
4. Mark 1:22
5. 1 Cor. 5:11
6. Luke 9:50
7. 2 Cor. 11:23
8. Matt. 23:26, John 4:11
9. John 2:15, 1 Cor. 4:21
10. 1 Cor. 2:16
11. Eccles. 5:1
12. Matt. 23:15
13. Matt. 15:13
14. 1 Cor. 10:11
15. Rom. 10:10, 2 Cor. 2:15, 1 Pet. 1:5, 1 Cor. 1:18, Eph. 2:5, Phil.1:28, 2 Tim. 1:9, Heb. 9:28, 1 Thess. 5:8, Rom. 8:24, Eph 1:13–14, Rom. 13:11, Eph. 1:4–5
16. Heb. 2:10

Chapter Five: Power, Grace, and Love

1. Matt. 5:4
2. Job 13:15
3. Ps. 6
4. Ps. 42:7
5. 1 Pet. 1:8–9
6. Gal. 4:19
7. 2 Cor. 11:30
8. Luke 11:25–26

Chapter Six: Hating Your Mother and Father

1. Isa. 55:8–9
2. When Jesus said, "Blessed are the peacemakers," He meant those who make peace between God and man. Jesus came to cause division between men (Matt. 10:34). Therefore our only goal is for men to make peace with God.
3. Luke 2:34–35
4. 1 Cor. 16:18
5. Luke 2:34
6. Prov. 25:15
7. Jer. 10:23

Chapter Seven: Hating Your Wife

1. 1 Tim. 4:3
2. Prov. 4:27
3. 1 Tim. 2:12
4. 1 Cor. 1:25
5. Prov. 27:15–16
6. Prov. 14:1
7. Heb. 11:8
8. Mark 13:32
9. 1 Tim. 2:14, Eccles. 7:28
10. Heb. 4:11
11. Prov. 16:9, Jer. 10:23

Chapter Eight: *Hating Your Children*

1. Phil. 2:14–15
2. 1 Sam. 3:13–14
3. 1 Pet. 3:6
4. Prov. 14:1, 27:15–16
5. 2 Tim. 3:12
6. 1 Cor. 7:28
7. Acts 7:22
8. Heb. 13:13
9. SOS 8:9–10
10. Isa. 64:4
11. Isa. 32:17, Heb. 12:11

Chapter Nine: Hating Brothers and Sisters

1. Luke 22:3
2. Mark 6:18
3. Rom. 11:22
4. 2 Tim. 1:15, 4:16
5. 1 Pet. 2:9

Chapter Ten: Hating Your Own Life

1. Ps. 42:11
2. 1 John 4:19
3. Luke 7:47
4. 2 Cor. 4:8
5. 1 Tim. 3:6
6. 1 Cor. 1:10
7. Matt. 12:34

CHAPTER ELEVEN: DISCIPLES

1. Heb. 12:5
2. Mark 10:22
3. Mark 15:21
4. James 5:16
5. 2 Cor. 12:7
6. 1 Pet. 5:6
7. Luke 11:24–26
8. Luke 2:36
9. Luke 2:28

Chapter Twelve: How?

1. Ps. 141:3
2. Matt. 6:24 A full explanation would take another book.
3. Matt. 6:3
4. Matt. 25:38
5. 2 Cor. 6:17
6. Lam. 3:23
7. John 3:34
8. 2 Cor. 13:11
9. Phil. 2:20–22
10. 1 John 5:14–15
11. Eph. 6:18

To order additional copies of

The Essential Piece
Living Out Luke 14:26 in Everyday Life

Have your credit card ready and call

(877)421-READ (7323)

or send $12.95 each, plus $3.95* S&H to

WinePress Publishing
PO Box 428
Enumclaw, WA 98022

*add $1.00 S&H for each additional book ordered

THE ART OF TRANSITION

A book in the series

Latin America Otherwise:

Languages, Empires, Nations

Series editors:

Walter D. Mignolo, Duke University

Irene Silverblatt, Duke University

Sonia Saldívar-Hull, University of

California at Los Angeles

THE ART OF TRANSITION

Latin American Culture and Neoliberal Crisis

Francine Masiello

DUKE UNIVERSITY PRESS Durham / London 2001

Printed in the United States of America on acid-free paper ∞

Typeset in Monotype Garamond by Wilsted & Taylor Publishing Services

Library of Congress Cataloging-in-Publication Data appear

on the last printed page of this book.

ABOUT THE SERIES

Latin America Otherwise: Languages, Empires, Nations is a critical series. It aims to explore the emergence and consequences of concepts used to define "Latin America" while at the same time exploring the broad interplay of political, economic, and cultural practices that have shaped Latin American worlds. Latin America, at the crossroads of competing imperial designs and local responses, has been construed as a geocultural and geopolitical entity since the nineteenth century. This series provides a starting point to redefine Latin America as a configuration of political, linguistic, cultural, and economic intersections that demands a continuous process of globalization and the relocation of people and cultures that have characterized Latin America's experience. *Latin America Otherwise: Languages, Empires, Nations* is a forum that confronts established geocultural constructions, that rethinks area studies and disciplinary boundaries, that assesses convictions of the academy and of public policy, and that, correspondingly, demands that the practices through which we produce knowledge and understanding about and from Latin America be subject to rigorous critical scrutiny.

Francine Masiello's title, *The Art of Transition*, embodies an ambiguity that defines the frame of her book. The "art" of transition refers simultaneously to artistic production after the dictatorships in Argentina and Chile and to the sociohistorical conditions and the search for democratic transformations that, in both countries, followed the end of dictatorial regimes. As in her previous book, *Civilization and Barabarism*, Masiello makes gender a pivotal category of her analysis. But also, as in her previous book, Masiello transcends the dichotomy between the Northern understanding subject and the Southern object to be understood. In fact, the cultural history of the Southern is the background for a critical reflection on gender "as a guiding trope to affirm the powers of the margin." Masiello's compelling argument directly and indirectly shows that "gender" is not a universal category and cannot be theorized and understood beyond the conditions in which "gender" becomes a category sociohistorically ingrained. Furthermore, Masiello constantly keeps in her analytical horizon the fact that regions geopolitically defined need to be linked to the neoliberal imaginary that nourishes globalization today.

CONTENTS

ILLUSTRATIONS

ACKNOWLEDGMENTS

This book engages an art of transition, tracing the scope of culture as it moves from conditions of dictatorship to democracy under neoliberal rule. At the same time, it tracks both the flow of intellectual projects that travel between North and South and the resistances offered by literature to the market economy, particularly in Argentina and Chile. In no minor way, this study gathers its momentum from the many conversations I sustained over time, drawing from the nourishing friendships that spanned the North/South horizon.

This project was stirred initially by a gracious invitation from Raquel Olea to visit Chile in 1994. The experience introduced me to a cultural polemic with which I had limited prior engagement and opened my eyes to the different possibilities for democracy and gendered politics on both sides of the *cordillera*. In the same year, Arcadio Díaz Quiñones and Jeremy Adelman organized a symposium at Princeton on Argentina after military rule, prompting me to begin writing seriously about the fate of culture under market domain. The late Susana Rotker then invited me to speak at Rutgers on the relationship between politics and art and inspired further thinking on the role of the aesthetic. Subsequent lectures at universities in the United States, Argentina, and Chile were significant in helping me to map out my research goals before diverse and demanding publics.

A grant from the Social Science Research Council and a University of California Presidential Research Fellowship afforded me time to define this project in its early stages. A good part of this book was written during a six-month residency at the University of California Humanities Research Institute at Irvine, where I participated in a seminar convened by Gwen Kirkpatrick on narratives of globalization. Gwen's constant good faith and her smart interventions were supremely valued as was the friendship built with other seminar fellows and colleagues whom I met at Irvine. Beth Marchant, Sergio de la Mora, David Luis Brown, Jacobo Sefamí, and Lucía Guerra were essential to this time of writing, but most important was the presence of my son, Joseph Manoleas. A fellow traveler in search of adventure, Joseph explored the culture of southern California with me when he wasn't engaged in homework or baseball. He also alerted seminar members to our proclivities toward "oversharing."

My students at Berkeley were particularly engaging during the years in which this text was written: Isabel Quintana was an exceptional reader of some of the draft material; Sergio Waisman and Chris Larkosh provided an ear for my arguments about translation; Marcelo Pellegrini was attentive to turns of phrase in the movement between Spanish and English; Pilar Alvárez and Amalia Pereira watched protectively as I pushed myself through the intellectual terrain of Chile; Regina West reminded me of my enthusiasm for the visual arts; Francine A'Ness and Ginny Bouvier raised questions that always made me think; Fabián Banga forwarded relevant materials from the arcane galaxies of cyberspace and repaired my computer on countless occasions with willingness and good cheer.

If this book depends on years of North/South dialogue, it above all announces a reawakening of my passions for poetry. Although I originally planned to focus on the narratives that accounted for this changing *fin de siglo* world, I found early on that the principal answers lay not only in fiction but also in the powers of poetic expression. For their inspiration, Diana Bellessi, Carmen Berenguer, Soledad Bianchi, Luisa Futoransky, Alicia Genovese, Mercedes Roffé, Lelé Santilli, and Mónica Sifrim claim an incalculable debt. As valued interlocutors, they generously shared their literary passions and knowledge with me and corrected my many misreadings. My immense gratitude to others who also read sections of the manuscript in its various stages and to those who volunteered energetic exchanges about literature and the arts: José Amícola, Diego Armus, Idelber Avelar, Dan Balderston, Tony Cascardi, Nora Domínguez, Beba Eguía, Diamela Eltit, Fabricio Forastelli, Jean Franco, Myrna García Calderón, Magdalena García Pinto, Tulio Halperín Donghi, Robert Kaufman, María Inés Lagos, Peter Manoleas, Ricardo Piglia, José Quiroga, Julio Ramos, Nelly Richard, Julia Romero, and Maryann Wolfe.

Diamela and Gwen deserve special recognition for their gifts of unfailing wisdom, boundless complicity, and humor. Maryann was a consummate reader of texts and minds during this intense period of writing and saw the fine points of my "art of transition" before I fully understood them myself. I dedicate this book to them with a spirit of unbridled affection.

¿Cómo nombrar en este mundo
con esta sola boca en este
mundo con esta sola boca?
[How to name in this world
with only this mouth in this
world with only this mouth?]
—Olga Orozco, *Eclipses y fulgores*

INTRODUCTION

The documentary film, *Fernando ha vuelto* (Fernando returns) (directed by Silvio Caiozzi, 1998), narrates the efforts of forensic scientists to identify a skeleton that had been exhumed years earlier from a common grave for Pinochet's victims. After examining photographs, dental x-rays, and comparative DNA chartings, the medical team was able to prove conclusively that the bones belonged to young Fernando, a MIR activist who disappeared in 1973. They then presented the reconstructed skeleton to the victim's spouse. This was a shocking, intensely dramatic scene, filmed from an angle that invited the viewer to recall Mantegna's Christ or the celebrated photo of Che Guevara's corpse. Here, the widow's flesh drew near to Fernando's bones, the couple's first encounter after more than twenty years. The materiality of the body (and what greater density could give expression to the body than its weight in bone?) was thus unmistakably claimed; bone and personal identity, past history and current moment were linked in a single image, joining the visual presence of the skeleton to the highly unrepresentable aspects of physical and emotional pain. Only family drama—inaugurated by the gendered gaze of Fernando's wife—offered a transition from fact to narration; it supplied a well-known arc of emplotment leading to the couple's reunion while also instigating a melodrama to veil spectators from the naked harshness of death.

I saw this documentary in Chile in November 1998 as part of the concluding program of a conference commemorating fifteen years of achievement of the Casa de la Mujer la Morada, a nongovernmental organization devoted to feminist activism from the time of the dictatorship period. La Morada had invited to the screening members of the Agrupación de Familiares de Detenidos-Desaparecidos (Organization of Relatives of the Detained and Disappeared) along with prominent Chilean intellectuals, all of whom were deeply moved by both the film and the historical circumstances in which it was shown—a time when the detention of Pinochet in London sparked heated debate throughout Chile. The fortuitous conjunction of these events tested many questions of memory and oblivion, injus-tice and rectification, and, not least among them, the relationship between truth and representation, private horror and public spectacle. But the gathering also stirred reminders of an intellectual issue: Could those of us committed to intellectual work and coming from geographic points far away share a common register of perception with family members of the disappeared as we together viewed a drama of unrelieved abjection? Are there artistic avenues of access through which a particular loss might help us make sense of a social whole? These questions prompt us to reflect on the interventions offered by practitioners of a formal aesthetic in monitoring the experiences of others.

I raise these points in order to address the relationships between experience and language, between image and notation, but also to reflect on the encounters sustained between intellectuals and their objects of study. These tensions are, of course, the basis of many approximations to society and culture, but in the Southern Cone, in the postdictatorship years, a number of peculiar issues emerge to sustain my attention here. First, a tug-of-war, which, in the representational field, amounts to a conflict between the mask and the face, between identity and its occlusion, often detonates a critical consciousness about the workings of democracy, its blindness and exclusions. Too, this crisis is often registered through metaphors of subalternity and gender. As in the film about Fernando's bones, the inquiry that leads to proof of his name reinserts questions of social class in the public eye; this tension is frequently mediated—although some might claim supplanted—by a highly gendered presence. As if to compensate the interest in subalternity that formerly preoccupied Southern Cone intellectuals, at least through the 1980s, gender enters as a guiding trope to affirm the powers of the margin. As such, the gendered field activates an anxiety about the shortcomings of representation; it introduces unevenness and double readings in a field where conflict once appeared settled. It resituates intellectuals in relationship to distant subjects and urges, however problematically, a linkage between worlds commonly divided by indifference.

The Art of Transition will try to come to terms with these issues in Chile and Argentina in the postdictatorship years by inquiring about cultural strategies to name and represent the "real" and by tracing the strategies of concealment and revelation that occur in politics and culture. Myriad examples herein serve to focus on the role that literature plays in managing these crucial issues. Faced with the numbing logic of neoliberal regimes, literature offers an intervention in order to consider identity and voice, to consider representation in both the political and artistic sense of the term. If neoliberalism, as a celebration of free-marketeering, paints a sheen of apparent neutrality on social contradiction, erasing strands of memory that bound individuals to their past and suppressing discussion of "value," literature and art instead cultivate tension, revealing the conflicts between an unresolved past and present, between invisibility and exposure, showing the dualities of face and mask that leave their trace on identitarian struggles today. In this way, cultural texts interrupt the comfortable "flow" of postdictatorship regimes, so easily given to the sale of "difference" yet so often indifferent to the depths of experience. They revel in many identities to push a point about society's blindness while also emphasizing in grander terms the shifting practices of a formal aesthetic in order to record one's conflicts with history. The art of transition thus evolves from duality and movement: a transition in political strategy from dictatorship to neoliberal democracy; a transition in cultural practices from focus on social class alone to matters of sexuality and gender; a transition in styles of representation that weave between modernist yearnings and postmodern pastiche.

In all of this the alignment of Argentina and Chile is, of course, not fortuitous; although habitually the two nations are not studied as a pair. Argentine culture, for its record of state authoritarian practice dating from the nineteenth century, has provoked countless intellectual meditations on the crisis of liberal thought and the failures of history; consequently it generates, as its dominant note, a peculiarly masculine narrative about one's quest for authenticity and subsequent intellectual disillusion, textual histories of the kind that Ricardo Piglia once described, citing Borges, as a test of the "prolixity of the real" (1980). More recently, the abuses by military governments and the corruption of neoliberal democracy have prompted desires among artists and writers to recuperate a totalizing story that might tell the fate of the nation in which even accounts of minor detail serve to allegorize the national dilemma. By contrast, Chile appears to have truncated any faith in the "grand narrations," those overarching fables that explain intellectual aspirations toward conquest and triumph or even of the intellectual's doubts with respect to the veracity of historical fact. Dismemberment and violence, instead, become the focus of Chile's national tale, truculent micronarratives observable from the nineteenth century, in the writings of Lastarria and Vicuña Mackenna or in countless legends about the notoriously vicious Quintrala.[1] In this tradition, Chilean fiction and history are littered with mutilated corpses and body fragments, grotesque metaphors for the decomposition of any desired social whole. It is perhaps the contrast between the Argentine anxiety for a *grand récit* and the Chilean cultivation of minor yet violent detail that separates, in a primary (and reductive) reading, the approaches of intellectuals of these two countries with respect to an appraisal of the real. Yet both might find common terrain in their cultural attraction to society's marginal or abandoned figures, those who cast a dilemma about the representation of otherness. As such, they announce the troubled plight of the "outsider," a figure who has become feminized in relation to the eye of the patriarchal state. Dual approaches to resolving the tension between universal and particular desires, the reemergence of subaltern figures is, this time under a postdictatoship gaze, marked by the unmistakable stripe of gender. The deliberate emergence of gendered drift as a metaphor for identitarian struggle bears uncanny fruition in the cultural texts of postdictatorship years and often supplies a dimension of representation that subalternity alone no longer affords. So when Chile inherited the "miracle" of economic reform and Argentina (despite its propitious start under Raúl Alfonsín) soon came to find itself mired in corruption and misgivings, popular subjects—now increasingly gendered and torn from their earlier, essentialized moorings in social class—absorbed the many issues produced from democracy's struggles, although their avenue of access to public space was often mediated by the market.

The Chilean "miracle," sociologists have told us, sparkles from the gloss of consensus, a concerted effort—until the recent detention and release of Pinochet—to "forgive and forget."[2] Argentine democracy, by contrast, has taken a more fitful path, with five aborted coups between 1987 and 1992 and a continued tradition of public protest, where citizens, ready to denounce government corruption, are answered by cover-ups and lies. Small wonder, then, that the metaphor of the mask represents neoliberal democracy's face, stressing a state-driven theatricality at a time when government has so much to hide and citizens are forced to dissemble in order to comply with the drive toward consensus. Whereas, in Chile, dissidents protest the scripts of state by recurring to cloaked identities and disguise that might protect them from surveillance, in Argentina, the state is described as the ultimate impostor. Both national cases remind us that the authoritarian past has not been dismantled and also signal that the basic cultural strategies for explaining this disjuncture remain intact: Argentines continue to refer to their national dilemma through a narrative desire for an all-encompassing history, while Chileans isolate small segments of local truth to disqualify larger versions of events. In both instances, however, they admit the impossibility of finding an authentic past that might settle once and for all their anxieties about misrepresentation. The centerpiece of their meditation often comes forth through a narrative tension sustained between truth and lies, between an array of dissident identities that circulate in civil society and the prescribed veils or cover-ups required of citizens by the fraudulent state. The discovery of Fernando's bones is but one element in a larger story about efforts to uncover a body and link it unmistakably to a name.

These tensions come to the surface in recent political events in both countries. The request for Pinochet's extradition, for example, incited a debate in Chile about the repressions of truth fostered by democratic rule. The hearings in London thus prompted a renewed interest in the ethics of representation, obliging individuals to ask about the connections between memory and justice and the burdens of accountability when public recollection of atrocity wanes. Ariel Dorfman addressed this issue in *La muerte y la doncella* (Death and the maiden) (1992), a dramatic work whose first staging in Chile coincided with the publication of the Rettig Commission Report on the horrors of military rule. Exposing the tenuous balance between civil order and the demands for justice, Dorfman pointed to the shifting boundaries between truth and fiction, between the experience of torture and the consequence of its representation, asking us if one person's truth might count more than another's, if one's story must be suppressed in order for the illusion of social harmony to thrive. The gap between truth and representation, so observable in this theatrical work, also depends upon stereotypes of gender and power that allow it to be detected easily through international venues. It touches upon the contradiction of all political representation in art that, in order to reach a global audience, must simplify complex positions. This is seen in recent debates about the Pinochet case and also in regard to those military officials responsible for the "Caravans of Death" of the dictatorship years and who today demand legal defense.

In Argentina, narratives of the "death flights" bring into alignment the mismatched quilt of truth and lies regarding the fate of disappeared persons. The revelations of retired navy captain Adolfo Scilingo in Argentina (1995) confirmed long-held public suspicions about the body drops from helicopters into the Atlantic Ocean. Practiced on a routine basis by members of the Navy School of Mechanics, these operations brought a horrendous finality to victims of the dirty wars but were not confirmed until the formal confessions of Scilingo followed by subsequent apologies from other military officials.[3] These admissions shocked public consciousness once again and also generated forceful reminders among cultural practitioners of the strategies of official cover-up and the feigned ignorance of the public. I am particularly interested in two responses to this undeniably painful aspect of the hidden past: the first obliging us to think about the *market* for social memory; and the second in which memory, surpassing the constraints of institutional politics, functions as an impetus for future social action. Both issues shift discussion, leading us to contemplate even more intricate issues regarding the ethics of representation.

In February 1999, Argentine rock star Charly García was scheduled to give an outdoor concert at a stadium near the River Plate. His plan was to stage a rock performance introduced by the arrival of helicopters, which were to dispatch life-size mannikins into the water below, a spectacle that was to evoke the "death flights" during the years of the dirty war. But observers such as Hebe de Bonafini, leader of the Mothers of Plaza de Mayo, perceived the gesture as a commercialization of pain and loss, a way to move the spectacle not toward rememberance, but mercantile gain. "You can't stage a show with death," she claimed.[4] Although cancellation of the simulated death drop allowed many well-known progressive figures to issue a sigh of relief, the episode nevertheless carries important elements pointing to the ambiguous relationship between art and one's profit from memory. Who is allowed to recall the past? Can the mediations of art ever respect the memory of horror? And, conversely, should one impose restraints on projects of avant-garde art? Our culture, both North and South, is densely marked by twofold inquiries of this kind, recalling the delicate line separating experimental innovation in art and potential abuse of the past as they also remind us of the stringent demands placed on individuals for narrations of firsthand experience, an insistence upon eyewitness accounts and testimonial values, usually to the exclusion of the aesthetic. In these circumstances in which personal pain confronts the test of art, art suddenly appears to be the enemy of truth, the violator of authenticity and singular experience, a traitor to the ethical values with which one might read the past.

On the underside of this model, the intervention of Argentine youth, who tag the doors of torturers' homes in order to remind the public of the cruelty of their neighbors, invites a different, although equally perplexing, reading of our relationship to the past. *Los escraches*, as this independent protest movement by children of the disappeared is known, have rallied hopes among the elders for a transgenerational pact, a way to find a place for youngsters within the broad spectrum of social movements devoted to human rights issues in Argentina. Yet the participants in this widespread activity claim, through graffiti-style "tagging," an autonomous voice of their own. Their random exposure of military agents responsible for human rights violations during the years of the dirty war carries an independent assertion of memory that refuses to be bound by political order. Against the usual strategies of citation that recognize a line of continuity with the past, los escraches leave random and unexpected marks in the scriptural politics of memory, bound as it has been by a clear genealogy and a disciplined political vision. Instead of relying upon traditional testimonial gestures to anchor a social movement, the taggers find an alternative citational system to register their opposition to the cover-ups that had prevented the circulation of truth. They thus produce a version of public memory with an independent course of its own and, in the process, surpass the inadequate efforts of politicians to rectify violations of human rights under the measures available by law.[5] Stretching the limits of the citational system, the names of former agents of murder appear in the public eye; as such, a youth-bound artistic movement comes to announce alternative forms of knowledge and rallies the public to action.

These initiatives remind us that while the dictatorships and even democratic regimes have tightly controlled our understanding of the real, cultural practices constantly subvert that discursive order, deregulating the seemingly fixed relationship between the real and its simulacra, reconstituting fields of identity and difference, testing the so-called authentic representations of "truth" against creative recastings. These interventions thus construct alternative communities of knowledge that override usual approaches to citation. Of course, conventional citation tends to deaden the possibilities of cultural critique, canceling free oppositional spaces so that they all appear to echo some earlier form, reinforcing the stability of temporal order, genealogy, and paths to the future. Traditional citation fixes the relationship between the state and its opponents, between North and South, East and West, city and country, men and women. It leads critics and philosophers to express a suspicion of these strategies as a dependency on imported ideas. Accordingly, when creative writers disrupt this expected transit, dismembering the reigning binarisms of social logic, they also question conventional alignments of truth. They disrupt the axis of intelligibility ordered by global and local cultural tensions. Scriptural shiftings erupt, new languages and encodings emerge such that cultural maps are rewritten, the cartography of the knowable is altered.

A final example helps to think about the disruptive practices of cultural texts in mediating the distance between truth and lies and altering the hierarchies of citation. *Un espacio al olvido* (A space from oblivion, 1997), an Argentine video directed by Sabrina Farji and filmed by Marcelo Brodsky and forming part of Brodsky's larger installation of photographs of the graduates of the Colegio Nacional, manipulates two forms of memory, two contrary citations of history.[6] The film tracks the experiences of a father whose son had been abducted by military forces during the dictatorship years and who here assembles images of the boy's life through old home movies and photographs. Superimposed upon this narrative, the filmmakers focus their camera on the turbulent ocean waters, presumably the tomb of the disappeared child; the ocean then becomes the background for traversing clips of super-8 film that show the boy, as a youngster, bathing at the sea. Saturating the viewers with reminders of redemption and death, the water commands dual orders of reflection: the super-8 film returns us to a nostalgia for childhood, the leisure-time activities of seaside fun, while the larger frame focuses on the silent ocean and points to the final resting place for victims of the dirty war. "The work of the father permits us to rescue the past; the work of the son permits the exercise of memory," reads a text superimposed on images of water, reminding us of the paradoxical reversal of time and the usual order of citation. Just as the River Plate is both the point of arrival and hope for immigrants new to America and also, in the case of the "death flights," a final destiny and tomb for youth, this dual system of citation opens alternative readings of history that challenge chronological flow. Not without its obvious ironies, the father, the elder of the set, constructs a future memory for a time of social justice, but it is the child who has tutored the parent, teaching the adult how to read the past and open to speculations on a possible future. More importantly, the collaboration between father and son wins a space against oblivion in order to defeat forgetfulness and loss, to interrupt the unquestioned advance of history and insist on the power of interpretation in restoring meaning to life.

Examples such as these point to the ways in which cultural texts intervene to alter the confidence of any *sensus communis*, to signal the contradictions between the "good sense" capability of citizens and the kind of common sense that flattens debate and critique just as it numbs our judgments and inhibits the power of voice.[7] The risk of art is staked here on exposing multiple truths and lies. It results in a struggle for social control over the symbolic field; it signals the importance of *representation* for ordering a social whole. One might say, of course, that the tension between truth and fiction, between one's absolute confidence in "fact" and the indeterminate nature of naming is the engine of the postmodern, the motor that propels our fin de siglo craft through often murky waters. But the Southern Cone experience with dictatorship makes this tension dramatically serious, taking away the frivolous aspects belonging to any sense of the global postmodern. Pastiche and parody, the playful exchange between original and copy, the exaltation of the regime of signs over the referents named are among the many techniques that lubricate the postmodern narrative machine; however, when applied to literature and culture that offer a reflection on authoritarian rule, the terms become laden with unsuspected meaning, the gratuitous free play of signs is lost and indicates other dimensions of experience. In a telling example belonging to Luisa Valenzuela's novel *Novela negra con argentinos* (Black novel with Argentines), a character acrimoniously comments on the pleasures offered by sadomasochistic sex parlors in New York: "How do you expect me to like sexual torture for pleasure when I come from a country where they tortured, let's say for political reasons, for the pure sake of horror, desperate victims who were under no circumstance compliant?" (1990, 151). While the representational free play of pleasure and pain travels beyond national borders, the example also reminds us of the ethical commitment that is found in Southern Cone literature and culture of the 1990s, a rejoinder to those poststructuralists who would dismiss the political potential of the literary text. It also restores an interest in gender that goes far beyond the visions and aspirations of first-wave feminist theory. Linked to issues of memory and market as well as the articulation of aesthetic value, gendered readings of postdictatorship culture deliberately take us to a critical scene where ethical issues cross with artistic choice.

In this arena of debate, a vexing question haunts all critical inquiry: Why is it so difficult to speak of the linkage between ethics and the texts of high culture? The sharp disjunction between the two has come to be regarded as uncontested fact, an axiom for that branch of cultural theory that equates the presence of imaginative texts as the last gasp of a once triumphant bourgeoisie, one that no longer carries weight in today's decentered economy of new technologies and mass-media practice. It has resulted in an *ars non grata* approach among those who would find art separate from social action and locate the political beyond high culture's reach.[8] From the aestheticist perspective, art and literature are said to evolve on their own ground, without any moral propellent; content, political interest, and the field of the "social" are separate from the purview of art.[9]

While, of course, literature cannot stand in for political activity in the manner assumed by nineteenth-century nation-building texts such as Harriet Beecher Stowe's *Uncle Tom's Cabin*, the poetry and chronicles of José Martí, or Domingo F. Sarmiento's *Facundo*, recent debates nonetheless remind us of the power that still lingers around the literary-ethical pairing. This discussion centers most forcefully around the capacity for aesthetic projects to bring us back to the larger project of linking universal and particular interests. Anthony Cascardi (1999), for example, premising his readings on Kant's third *Critique*, reminds us of the experience of critical thinking that emerges from one's surrender to the aesthetic aura. Arguing against the "autonomy of art" position, he draws us to the possibility of political claims formulated at the moment of aesthetic encounter. In this instance (and in accordance with Kant), our conceptual structure will not accommodate the unrepresentable nature of pleasure or pain; instead, we are left principally with an awareness of the distance between image and ethics. The seemingly unbridgeable gap is recuperated by the exercise of critical consciousness, which in turn stimulates questions of agency and then offers the conceptual possibility upon which to build future action (82).[10]

Provocative gaps of this kind remind us of the dislocations between the realm of "appearance" and one's claims for the real, the massive use of irony that expands its purview under the wing of postmodern influence, the constant and forced encounters in art between representations of the abject and allusion to the uncanny or absurd. All of these demand a reassessment of our avenues of access to knowledge, our constitution as readers and thinkers, the role of subjective agency in initiating a response to misalignments of reality and representation. In this respect, the aesthetic and ethical link invites us to move from particular self-interest to a grander logic of alliance and community, from visions of the dismembered past to a possible collective future.

Many defenders of cultural critique, weary of the tired exaltations of high culture, refuse this argument and lodge a major indictment against these literary-aesthetic claims, especially when they purport to bridge the gap between elite and popular sectors. Those who have engaged in debate about the phantom of authenticity generated by the *testimonio* of Rigoberta Menchú have especially considered this issue.[11] George Yúdice, for example, taking his cues from Terry Eagleton, argues that the aesthetic reinforces the illusion of individual freedom belonging to bourgeois necessity; moreover, he claims, contrary to the advances of the avant-garde, that art which is necessarily separate from life practices cannot be expected to represent the "other" save to reproduce strategies of repression (1996, 48–50). Observing the crisis of "high culture" models, Alberto Moreiras notes the reduction of the literary field in paradoxical conjunction with the "pretensions of the cultured literary elite to keep dictating taste" (1996, 192) as well as the illusions of progressive intellectuals to find in literature a bridge of identity linking social groups. The effect of literature cannot be one of alliance, he writes, since this pact is beyond the scope of possible representation; at best, the testimonio can only produce a "poetics of solidarity," a pact that leaves readers in the realm of complacency and self-indulgence (198). Responding to positions such as these, Santiago Colás asks with straightforward clarity: "What's wrong with representation?" (1996, 161–71). And from the realm of literature itself, poet Juan Gelman recently writes: "And what if we saw the novel not in its traditional configuration as a literary genre belonging to the spiritual climate of an emerging bourgeoisie, but as an expression of the ancient human need to tell of the disturbing aspects of social crisis, to learn from this experience, and to claim the crisis as our own?" (1999). The literary text thus becomes mobile, in subtle dialectic with the times. In other quarters, this is played out as a defense of the discursive, whereby a mobility between universal and particular interests is said to constitute the very activity of art. It is the engine of spectator cognition, the initiator of cultural critique; it leads to the repair of the gaps in the damaged social fabric.

In Latin America, Beatriz Sarlo and Nelly Richard have been the principal theorists of the aesthetic turn. After thirty years of constant engagement in the political and cultural debates of her native Argentina (and articulated most prominently through her journal, *Punto de Vista*), Sarlo has rightly earned the title of public intellectual. Her incursions into theory are prolific, but for my purposes here, I am especially interested in her understanding of the relationship between politics and art. Troubled by Argentine democratic traditions that failed to rally a common agenda, Sarlo frequently protests the shortcomings of any sensus communis; yet she often finds resolution to this quandary by seeking out the aesthetic values that link individual judgments (1997, 32–38). She thus turns to a sensibility founded on principles that might recall Eliot's defense of "individual talent," but also to restore faith in a Habermasian public sphere. Sarlo intervenes to stop the flow of a debased politics and halt the aura of "false" common sense by proposing an alternative mode of intelligibility, reclaiming ongoing difference as the basis with which to form "good" political and aesthetic judgment. Her viewpoint sustains a faith in democratic polis based on the impossibility of a truly universal consensus, although it enables an intersubjective space through which all parties might accept a compact of recognizable criteria and judgments. Although difference is the desired sign of democratic practice, Sarlo nevertheless distrusts the "particular" when it comes to threaten the more appreciated aspects of recognized social tradition emphasizing reconciliation and union.

Her theory poses a number of residual problems that have made her the target of recent criticism. Sarlo understands the role of art as a vehicle of the disruption, breaking up the kind of political authority that often extracts an unwillful and blind agreement from the public. For Sarlo, the *disruption* of mediocrity in political action is found, paradoxically, in a return to the *ordering principles* of the aesthetic, a value that celebrates internal differentiation among texts, hierarchies obeying a universally acknowledged code of merit, an almost ironic *nescio quid* regarding democratic thinking. Difference thus shows itself not necessarily by the pulsational forces within a given text, but surely by the comparative measurement and evaluation of one text against another. This position, of course, recalls the kind of Enlightenment pedagogy that utilized aesthetic identification to train the judgments of compliant, ethical citizens.[12] The basis of nation-building ideology, it aimed to establish a number of universal standards for the management of cultural and political life. In this respect, Sarlo cultivates similar ties between democracy and the manifestation of artistic difference insofar as both are premised on an understanding of what might be seen as the disordering effects of cultural process.

Another perspective on the aesthetic is offered by Nelly Richard (1998). A cultural critic of cutting-edge vitality who has achieved somewhat of a celebrity status among postmodern thinkers, a reputation assured by the journal she founded, the *Revista de Crítica Cultural,* Richard is a bridge figure among U.S., European, and Latin American critics although she has remained committed to specific debates originating in Chile. Despite what might appear to be a move in the direction of universalized, transnational discourse, Richard is inspired by a Deleuzian celebration of the "minor"; also echoing the arguments of radical democracy proponents Ernesto Laclau and Chantal Mouffe, she reaches for the power of disruption found in local resistance and social action. Translated to art and literature, a splintering of any totalizing vision stands as a form of rebellion against state power and its patterns of fixed representation. By extension, the local struggle shows the exclusions of postdictatorial democracy and neoliberal rule; its expression of choice in the realm of literature and art is found in the fragment.

Like Richard, other theorists, eager in recent years to flee macrohistorical accounts of history, have turned to the power of the fragment and celebrate the power of the local. In this way, they privilege the *microspace* (Deleuze, Foucault, Perlongher), the *entre-lugar,* or in-between (Bhabha, Silviano Santiago); they celebrate *interstitiality* and *disjuncture* (Achugar, Appadurai, Hopenhayn) or turn to the powers of *ungovernable subjects* (the subaltern studies group in India or Latin Americanists under the same rubric working in the United States). Through these images, critics seek to excavate the potential of counterhegemonic oppositional forces, to engage the prospect of revolt from below, to alter the monolithic discourses that dominate our times.

Yet is the fragment sufficient? My plan is to present the conditions for a reflection on alliance through critical thinking, to argue the ways in which art and literature do not cultivate the (gendered) margin simply for effects of scandal, but instead take these representations to reconsider our contemporary crisis, thereby leading one to the workings of a social whole. In this respect, the fragment or the microspace defended by certain voices of continental philosophy is not in itself forceful enough to recruit this desired insight; instead, what propels us is a constant longing for completion, a totalizing logic that links universal and particular forces both within the text and through the symbolic registers of a social whole. From the aporia or "dark hole," from the vortex of possible signifiers whose meaning has not been set, we are prompted to a practice of suture; we awaken to interpretation and the desire to travel *en route* to a conceptual whole, one which is not an allegorization of national quandary (as in the style of novels of the Boom), but more likely a response to the flattening gloss of the market, the so-called waning of affect that has been identified with the times. One might rightfully identify my faith in literature and art with modernist desire itself (or, for a faith in hermeneutics, with the foundations of what once was identified as the power of "reader response"), but I am here especially interested in the ways in which these strategies make themselves obvious at a time when individuals feel especially disabled in light of neoliberal rule. Art and literature thus force us to think of interpretative strategies of resistance, interrogating the past and leading to a politics of cognition with which to move toward the future. Against the marketed package of "ready-made" cultural products and ideas that neoliberalism places at our disposal, the cultural experiment provokes forms of thinking that move toward alternative frameworks for apprehending social forms. In this respect, mine is a course identified neither with those of Sarlo or Richard, although their different projects have a strong resonance in the chords of argumentation raised in the pages of this book. Rather, I am urged to track the linkages between order and difference, their overlaps and points of conjuncture in order to show how a critical sensibility is shaped from the realm of cultural texts and offers the potential of a political future. Literature and art open the way for readers and spectators to take the conceptual leaps necessary for the practice of politics; they also signal the monumental impasses that travelers find in their path.

The mechanism of translation also supplies another step toward this process of cognition. In the best instance, it constructs a desired bridge between individuals and the culture at large; minimally, it exposes the inadequacies of any claims to a universal language. Translation thereby places in evidence the multiple and irreducible languages belonging to the social whole; it enacts the performance of language on an international stage. By contrast, through the odysseys of North/South travelers who speak in many tongues, but without the security of comprehension, we are also reminded of a long-term practice that locks postdictatorial subjects from global inclusion, suppressing their particular symbolic registers and their local languages of self-definition. Translation, as the trope of interpretative practice, announces the limits of difference and the glaring gap between experience and language, between traditional order and flight. Starting from its condition of error, translation leads one to rethink the social whole.

These tensions, or "force fields," multiply paths for reconsidering art and social forms (amen Walter Benjamin, who once referred to the force fields that separate past and present[13]). Extending the metaphor here, I consider the force fields constructed by artistic pulsations of global and local desires, tensions between North and South, and the claims of fixed versus fluid identities that settle on the postdictatorial landscape. These tensions also map the uneven terrain of intellectual authority set against popular voices, the rhetorical constructions that separate "men" and "women," the ongoing pull between "authentic" expression and its supposed derivation or copy, and finally the market-run logic directing the "business" of literature versus the slow preponderance of ideas required by experimental texts. These polarities were announced during the dictatorship years, and, of course, one might claim that they are as old as literature itself, but I especially want to emphasize the way the cultural field is redefined in light of neoliberal regimes, where the dual faces of Janus are emblematic of a way of life. This doubleness marks the status of citizen-subjects under postdictatorial rule; not only an obligation of social life, doubleness becomes the guiding principle of a late-twentieth-century aesthetic. Nevertheless, from the tensions produced by these conflicts of articulation and action, a condition of possibility emerges with which to imagine a politics of alliance.

This book is organized under three principal headings: masks, maps, and markets. The first section points to the scripts that have been set in place in critical debate during the dictatorships and continue during democratic governance, most especially with respect to the representation of popular subjects. In a first instance, under the years of military rule, a yearning for democracy was articulated through the celebration of *lo popular* (a category that includes subalternity as well as a conceptualization of deviant figures, marginals, and delinquent subjects). Popular subjects thus entered cultural critique to give name to desired opposition to the state while often expressing a nostalgic longing for populism itself; in a second instance, however, and with the transition to democracy, critics come to regard the popular subject with suspicion. Although the appetite for lo popular responds globally to what might be likened to a postmodern fetish, allowing intellectuals to constitute a field of difference and facilitate the transit between canonical and emergent discourses or find a connection between the distinctions of "high" and "low," under democracy in Argentina and Chile, subalternity (albeit the product of an essentialist passion) becomes the focus of distrust; it stands for the disenfranchised groups who live on society's margins and is regarded as the disruptive element that fragments a social totality. Replacing this, gendered subjects have come to attract more recent interest and allow for a signifying field of popular and artistic difference that often substitutes for the draw offered by lo popular. In other words, the gendered field now fills in for the possibilities of political and aesthetic difference offered previously by popular subjects, allowing one to reexamine the critical distance between experience and representation in its various deployments. As an entry into discussions of literature and art, this first chapter makes a case for the political and social uses of gender that, framed in essays in critical inquiry, lead to unsuspected pacts and alliance, surprising negotiations of identity and desire. This sets the stage for discussion of the ways in which gender will create a critical consciousness about political and aesthetic formation.

In the second chapter, I focus on the question of *representation* taken in its double meaning—as a problem that addresses the theatrical illusion of representing some distant subject, as a promise of representation within the political sphere. Operating between the affirmation of individual identities and the consensual expectations placed on citizen-subjects by the larger social body, between theater as a metaphor for deception and as a strategic entry of individuals on the political stage, the metaphor of the mask enables a consideration of the gap between truth and lies, challenging the kinds of identities imposed by state and market. "The mask was the most costly face that each person gambled," writes Chilean novelist Guadalupe Santa Cruz (1997a, 182). The mask calls attention to our dual identities in the political sphere, but it also serves as a metaphor for sexual difference, articulating the struggles between masculine and feminine, between privileged and marginal identities. A principal argument connects the various sections of this chapter: if during dictatorship literary texts revealed a range of oppositional and "deviant" identities to challenge the patriarchal state, then under democracy an awareness of the market frequently drives these representations, tying sexual identities to the politics of commodification and sales. As the market becomes the new arena for the promotion and sale of "difference," alternative gendered identities lose their political thrust and are often considered commodities or tokens of exchange. I take into account the evolution of this problem through a number of Chilean and Argentine texts and settle on the writings of Manuel Puig and César Aira: the former, because he was far ahead of his time in unmasking the illusions of gender constructs and the vacuous proposals that sustain sexual normativity in language and social life, and the latter, as a formidable postmodern, possible heir to the projects of Manuel Puig, insofar as he incessantly meddles with the sexual economies regulating literature, thought, and markets.

Much of the identitarian debate is drawn not simply in the local arena, but through a reconceptualization of North/South axis and metaphors of translation. "Maps," the second section of this book, is devoted to these cartographies. In the film *Buenos Aires vice versa* (directed by Alejandro Agresti, 1996), a character affirms, "We have to end this crazy idea that claims North as North and South as South. We have to turn the map upside down." Chapter 3 first explores the way the Latin American gendered subject is often exoticized by both the northern academic lens and the phenomenon of the mass-market best-seller; I later turn to the ways in which Latin American critical theory and experimental literature answer those proposals. "Tell me, haven't you ever thought that the West might lie in the opposite direction?" (1994, 65), asks Diamela Eltit with a wry observation of the artificial frontiers separating cultures. By contrast, Diana Bellessi proposes a gesture of appropriation: "Is South an illusion? / By choice of the turning earth / a voice of faith rises . . . / South is / the continent whole" (1998, 122). *Feminaria* (Argentina) and *Revista de Crítica Cultural* (Chile), prestigious journals with reputations for theorizing these hemispheric divides through the lens of gender, set the groundwork for investigating the gloss of global theory that effaces local cultural production or rarifies its critical thought. Against ventriloquy of the kind that reinforces subservience, contributors to these venues propose local cultural answers to accommodate the realities of the South. This affirmation is played out, finally, in literature itself; here, South answers North through novels enjoying global "best-seller" status and through those that follow an avant-garde practice.

In chapter 4, these geopolitical anxieties are further considered by focusing on gender and translation. Instead of accepting the North/South cartography that has dominated Latin American culture, many writers redraw the map, shifting emphasis to an East/West axis. Equally important, they make apparent the ways in which culture is filtered—and changed—

through the lens of translation. The recuperation of "Orientalism" among contemporary Latin American writers paradoxically supplies a challenge to fixed ideations of Anglo-European modernism that have journeyed South just as it alters the mechanics of the "translating machine" that once achieved a certain prestige under the modernist brow. Gender is the principal token that moves on this gameboard of global meaning, showing the failures of naming, the arbitrariness of citation, while alerting readers to the dangers of arresting difference in order to transport it through geographic frontiers. These articulations in literature signal the sense of exclusion that Latin American writers—both men and women—experience in relationship to externally imposed discourses and distant aesthetic proposals, but they also indicate the possibility of an untested ethical and aesthetic pact that might be drawn by a community of intellectuals superseding national lines. The chapter thus dances through a mine field of imaginings about Asia as a way to open geographic containment, to alter the paths of citation that depend on a northern center, to show the points where gendered bodies fail to be accommodated by the languages of translation, but also—in its least complicated proposal—to point to the futility of monolingual expression.

Examining the distance between politics and representation necessitates a discussion of the ways in which the politics of the text resists the market. The aesthetic and ethical conflicts evoked by literary texts—among them, the *crónicas* of Pedro Lemebel, the recent novels of Ricardo Piglia and Diamela Eltit—structure the fifth chapter of this book. In particular, I focus on the representation of popular subjects in literature insofar as they help writers resist the homogenizing demands of the market, but paradoxically indulge the market's voracious appetite for novelty and "difference." The dilemma urges us to reconsider the concepts of culture we manage and the limited languages available to us for engaging in dialogue with others; it signals the ways in which literature articulates a crisis in our understanding of the "real." The project assumed by these writers is not to represent an allegory of neoliberalism, but rather to present the possibilities of alternative languages grounded in the materiality of popular voice. The subaltern subject these writers construct thus resists assimilation by the canonical values of realist fiction yet supplies an impetus to question the ethical values of literary and social projects in contemporary times. If chapter 5 manages these issues with respect to the conventions of prose, the final chapter delves into the politics of voice emerging principally from contemporary poetry by women. Here, in the strip of cultural production so isolated by the market—the margin of the margin, so to speak—the writings of Argentine and Chilean poets whose works began to circulate in the 1980s reconfigure the landscape of representation, revindicate place and language, and introduce a dynamic that resolves the ethics of alliance through the materiality of representation. A movement toward an all-encompassing ethics to join universal and particular meanings, experimental poetry foregrounds its function as a *bridge* over islands of noncorrespondence. Throughout this book, examples abound of writers who propose to explore the gap between experience and language, finding ways to sustain and reintegrate difference, to seek a common space for dialogue outside of neoliberal divide. This, then, is about their art of transition, moving *en route* to critical thinking and the imagined possibility of future alliance through a grasp of aesthetic form. They show us how the politics of culture vigorously asserts itself as the new millennium begins.

PART I. MASKS

In this island of time in which we live, it has to be possible to listen to the voices that come from the past. No one lacks responsibility and we know that responsibility is not exercised only upon future actions. We are as much responsible for the past as we are for the future.—Beatriz Sarlo, *Escenas de la vida posmoderna*

Critical thought from Latin America requires a theoretical-conceptual instrument that recuperates cultural resistance, mass political movements, heroic deeds, literary texts, essays, popular thought and disposition, testimonials, micro-histories, festivals, small or large accounts of human dignity, the full diversity of knowledge that lies on "the margins of science."—Alcira Argumedo, *Los silencios y las voces*

Even when global historicity appears frozen on the surface, moving below is a dark and slow work of reconstruction of the social fabric, a reconstitution of subjects.—Tomás Moulián, *Chile actual: Anatomía de un mito*

CHAPTER 1

In Search of a Subject: Latin American Intellectuals at Century's End

Among the more lucid figures on the international art scene, Argentine Guillermo Kuitca offers a valuable introductory lesson about conflicts between rootedness and displacement, memory and oblivion, experience and abstraction. In a well-known installation, Kuitca covered a number of small beds, all soiled to varying degrees, with enlarged paintings of highway maps representing different foreign locations. His juxtaposition of the shabby mattresses with the neat precision of the mappings hauntingly evokes an aching dilemma belonging to our time: How do we live out our local conditions under the weight of a global cartography? What is the dimension of experience and feeling set against the calculations of some distant eye? And how is the popular aspect of a scene recuperated by intellectuals and artists? Kuitca's work brings into alignment that most intimate space of our private lives—the sleeping quarter, the place where we rest body and soul, the site of eros and dream—but also the site that recalls our

1. Guillermo Kuitca. *Untitled,* 1993. (2 views) Acrylic on sixty mattresses, dimensions variable. Installation view: "Guillermo Kuitca, Burning Beds—A Survey 1982–1994." Whitechapel Art Gallery, London, 5 May–25 June 1995. Courtesy Sperone Westwater, New York. Permission to reproduce images granted by Guillermo Kuitca.

origins and announces our demise; he links this to the impersonal representation of a map, an abstraction of local meaning that simultaneously reminds us of the fiction of all charting and the illusion of our attachments to place. As a visual structure, the installation coordinates the eye and experience; but it also unites public and private codes, universal and particular meanings, allowing us all to navigate through the complexity of today's postmodern landscape. When map and bed are joined, space is defined anew; identity takes shape at the point where grand traditions and local differences cross. The cartography of the global plan literally covers intuitive knowledge; a figuration of *elsewhere* meets a diffused yet local sense of popular beginnings. At the same time, the range of experience belonging to the domestic sphere is far from transparent to the viewer. It reminds us that just as any map is a distortion, a falsification of reality that quickly turns hollow, so too the representation of what I just called "humble beginnings" awakens kindred suspicion.

Kuitca's work invites meditation on the dilemmas facing Latin American intellectuals around issues of authenticity and citation, especially as they conjugate imported and local knowledge, collective and individual choices, and determine ethical alternatives for democracy as well as a sense of the aesthetic. The confabulation of narratives emerging from these particular tensions depends in large part on the intellectual's fantasy of a popular subject who is inscribed in either a longing for home or an anxiety about modernization. In effect, the construction of this popular subject (*el sujeto popular*) serves as a pivotal point that allows us to approach different landscapes of critical discourse; it constructs a number of scenarios on the global and local axis; moreover, with the transition to democratic regimes, the popular subject becomes a site for debate about the course of political options available to Latin American thinkers, finding its way into cultural programs that articulate individuated or communitarian ideals; finally, the popular subject often determines the scope of an aesthetic.

This problematic figure intrudes in the scope of discussion as a token of international exchange: if, within the global context, the image of marginal figures permits Latin American intellectuals to assert a claim to original theory (that is, the originality of Latin America is marked by lo popular) in local contexts, and especially under the aegis of neoliberal regimes, the popular subject often comes to be named as an embarrassing archaism, a retrograde presence that impedes the course of modern progress. Consequently, the tie between intellectuals and the masses today appears irretrievably severed; replacing it in recent local scenarios is a discourse that defines equality in terms of a consumer-based civil sphere. In this resemanticized arena, the marginal figure is inimical to intellectual power; earlier utopian fantasies about the redemptive promise of lo popular now appears as a disembodied phantom. Lost is a plausible narrative about coalition and common rights; the material basis of communitarian ideals is dissolved. Instead, a vision of the future comes forth without a clear conception of alliance, space, or location.

Writing acerbically about the artificial constructs that govern this kind of utopian thinking, Chilean filmmaker Raúl Ruíz observed, "[Utopias] don't seem to exclude any body at all in general, though in fact they exclude everyone in particular" (1995, 25). Ruíz's remarks serve well to establish the staging of much contemporary intellectual debate regarding popular subjects. Indeed, with the disembodiment of specific grievances and the recent excitement provoked by technologies of the virtual real, the role of popular sectors is increasingly viewed with distance and suspicion; worse still, these groups lose the intellectual's trust insofar as they disturb illusions of public tranquility linked to an image of democracy itself. Caught in the thick of this quagmire, at a loss for a constructive discourse with which to alter the terms of debate, the liberal spokespersons who formerly defended projects of alterity now regard them with nervous distrust. These points notwithstanding, the popular sectors remain essential to an artistic imperative emerging on the dawn of the millennium; they are the necessary "other" on which much cultural representation is based. Moreover, as this concern for popular subjects is redefined, it is often translated in artistic and literary texts to focus on sexuality and gender. The reflections that follow track the evolution of these shifts in representation in both the critical and aesthetic landscapes of Latin American culture.

Thinking through Others

After the years of the dirty wars sustained by Southern Cone dictatorships, intellectuals faced the task of rebuilding a public sphere: they asked how to recuperate memory, how to bridge connections to the past, how to make sense of democratization as a market-run global enterprise. The postmodern inflections of this problem readily became apparent, prompting a crisis of universal knowledge that also called into question the status of intellectual work. In particular, in Latin America, because of a long history of activism among vanguard intellectuals, the recent move to democratization demanded that they rethink their relationship to popular traditions and to emerging social movements. Quite often, they felt removed, incapable of negotiating the different regimes of knowledge in circulation. Was cultural critique the space for emancipatory struggles, or, true to market-run logic, a means to advance one's privilege and individual prestige? When Beatriz

Sarlo asked in her journal *Punto de Vista* if the intellectual had become "archaic or marginal" (1993), she expressed the uneasiness of a generation of critics who felt orphaned from place and political function. No longer in the tradition of the founding fathers of nineteenth-century liberal thought, intellectuals of our times sustain a sharp identity crisis, provoked both within the borders of national landscapes and, far beyond, on the global horizon. A brief genealogy of the interface between intellectual and popular subject as it evolved in recent decades helps establish terms for discussion.

In its first phase, this was tied to the intellectual's perceived relationship with a popular subject who offered a redemptive narrative about Latin American creative power, a promise to restore dignity to a cultural project born in peripheral nations. This case was made with brutal cogency by Cuban critic Roberto Fernández Retamar who, thirty years ago and in his now classic essay about the relationship between metropolitan and third-world nations, reflected on a basic question often posed by foreigners: "Does Latin American culture exist?" (1971, 3). He went on to explore the assumptions underlying the nature of this query and suggested, ironically, that by negating their cultural component, one might ask just as well if Latin Americans existed at all. But he also noted that intellectuals, eager to prove an original contribution to this panorama, often staged a performance starring the marginal subject—the peasant, the subaltern, the racially different—in order to make Latin America visible on the global map. Far from resolving Latin America's quest for prestige, the strategy made apparent the great appeal of the exotic to the detriment of more urgently needed debate and critical exchange.

From the site of the metropolis, where avid readers elevate the writings of Isabel Allende and Laura Esquivel to the top of national best-seller book lists, where Rigoberta Menchú is a cause célèbre and her autobiography (although now under question for its claims to the veracity of horror) continues to be required reading in many university settings, North American academic critics also lament the poverty of intellectual reflection offered by their Latin American peers. As isolated raw materials—memoirs and magical realism—regularly spread their roots from southern soils to bear fruit in academic groves to the North, other finished products—theory and critical thought—rarely manage to travel, except to expose local failures or to corroborate a sense of the Latin penchant for the perverse or decidedly strange. From the North, then, Latin America is seen as a homogeneous block, unified by a mysterious and lush exoticism or a passion for political turbulence, or identified as a place where artists lack the capacity for abstract thought and "Western" logic. In the process, Latin American intellectuals are foreclosed from a hermeneutic circle of inquiry, while images of marginality are retained as signs of a rarified experience available routinely from southern exposures.[1] Like the infinite flow of a Moebius strip, the tag game between universal and local cultures as it persists in the imagination of critics reinforces the inferiority of Latin America, denigrating its impulses toward an independent conceptualization of theory.

Chilean critic José Joaquín Brunner (1991) has signaled the course by which certain thinkers of international prestige have confirmed this case against Latin American autonomy. Taking the writings of Octavio Paz as a key example, Brunner tracks the ways in which Latin American culture is represented as a "deficit," a tradition that, lacking the foundations of enlightenment philosophy, will never gain access to the platforms of continental thought. For its glaring omissions, Latin America can never rise above its self-portrait of turgid, inarticulate failure nor can it enter modernity except when it performs a belated and feeble mimesis of European achievement. The *novum* of Latin American modernization, writes Chilean philosopher Pablo Oyarzún, is seen in a close reproductive relation with metropolitan models; and if imitation is the rule of modernization, translation is its humble servant (1987–1988, 293). Seen in this way, Latin America is always one step behind Europe and the United States, asynchronically lost in a carnival of masks and cannibalistic perversions, uncloaking a feared perception of a dark and primitive self.

Curiously enough, it is the metaphor of the mask, so often synonymous with postmodern pursuits, that prevails in descriptions of the Latin American mind; it results in projecting a sense of basic identity, natural voice, or "origin" that suffers wrenching distortion. Years ago, Angel Rama signaled this irony when he referred to the "democratic masks" belonging to the modernization experience (1985); Rosalba Campra described the masked identity that all Latin Americans wear (1987). From a different perspective, Roberto Schwarz observed that cultural copying seems to dominate Brazilian intellectuals; moreover, this behavior is a fundamental part of national culture, compensating for a lack of a common bridge linking elite and popular sectors (1992). Mimicry, then, expresses the uneasiness of a dominant class caught up in the temporal and ideological tensions between modernity and tradition.[2] In a similar vein, Chilean critic Bernardo Subercaseaux noted that European conceptual paradigms have always been brought into Latin America for the purposes of sustaining the power of elites with respect to their local populations (1991, 223). Subercaseaux also insisted on the central role of the appropriative gesture as the essence of the nationalist project, a way to overcome the cultural dualism that wreaked havoc in the mind of elites.[3] Argentine Horacio González gives a different spin to this image when he locates this behavior as part of the trickster's mode of expression in Latin America, a strategy to bridge the gap between public common sense and private, unfulfilled needs (1992, 90). This representation of culture, which depends on translations and echoes for its principal tropes, appears purposefully improvisational (and hence, avant-garde?) by contrast to some "pure and folkloric" version of what we would imagine as local experience. As a form of critical thinking, it also places in opposition concepts of *genealogy* and *disguise*. In this way, although local markers of rootedness and remembrance continue to be identified with the archaic, no longer attainable in modern society and, quite possibly, no longer desired, they also acquire a contestatory force. By contrast, the realm of the possible copy, while it elicits a continuous yearning for the stable place of the other, situates one per force in the global postmodern. It produces a discursive movement between emphasized theatricality and a desire for an idealized "truth"; the theater even becomes a metaphor of politics today.

For all its confusions, the imitative paradigm has been ascribed, more recently, to the Latin American state itself, whose claims to considerable authority are drawn from media images and metaphors of the stage. Eduardo Rinesi, for example, emphasizes the theatricalized identities that define neoliberal regimes (1993). Here, the stage play that so dramatically indulges the frivolous side of postmodernism's pull toward ahistoricity and dissimulation is evoked to reflect all Latin American thinking as a game of mirror images, always leading to failure and always challenging any claim to authentic truth. In effect, the predominance of this mass-media environment has led Néstor García Canclini to situate all cultural practices in Latin America as acts of performance: "More than actions, cultural practices are forms of acting. They represent, they simulate social action, but only occasionally do they operate as action. . . . They are performances more comprehensible to the drama-lover's gaze than to the eye of the political 'purist'" (1992, 327).[4] Given the limited number of options in this *theatrum mundi*, Latin American contemporary history is often likened to melodrama, paradoxically limiting choices of movement and fixing roles for the actors.[5] It is no wonder, then, that Latin American intellectuals are always caught in a turmoil of contradictory demands. Like Kuitca's juxtaposition of the map and the bed, these images leave the intellectual hard put to affirm an original voice, to produce an alternative to metropolitan theory that does not fall into melodramatic excess or, worse, into a nostalgia for some harmonious yet unrecognizable past.

The quandary of the script and the mask, required of the global stage, is often addressed by intellectuals through an obligatory meditation on the value and originality of difference. But, although this struggle is seen as a contest between national and metropolitan centers, it also forms part of an *internal* debate about intellectual options at home; it resituates us in a theater of contention among local actors. Here, the myth of an authentic social pact to be regained through democratic process is seen as an innocent and forfeited moment of association between word and idea, a founding illusion about the purity of some original moment of unified social action and representation, a moment that has been lost to us and can never be regained. Latin American intellectuals have taken this idea through a full-scale debate, inserting themselves in two almost obsessive projects about matters of self-representation: one tied to a desired restoration of genealogical lines that might link them to a global elite, the other devoted to the marking of national difference through the figure of the popular subject. Although this figure offers an essentialist claim to Latin American originality (a claim for the authentic, often a cult of nostalgia), it may also insert a progressive agenda in cultural discussion.[6] The representation of the popular subject has produced a rich line of investigation that leads to our present day, although it is seldom free of conflicts.

Outlaws

With its emancipatory social movements and emerging reflections on the postmodern, the decade of the 1970s provides an especially ripe moment for the entrance of the popular subject in the critical imagination. From the time of the Popular Unity government in Chile, which took the indigenous legacy as central to its projects of agrarian reform and also brought media studies to focus on the value of popular culture, the popular subject became interpellated as a hegemonic state project and also stood as a sign of resistance to metropolitan centers.[7] These were years in which cultural studies (albeit *avant la lettre*) carried the imprimatur of the Allende regime and produced an emphasis on the manifestations of popular song, the workings of mass communications, and the emergence of alternative voices. This direction, of course, marks a paradoxical reversal of the disdain felt by Chilean intellectuals for the figure of the *roto*, the marginal figure who stood for the failure of local elites to ascend by European standards and to erase the class divisions that the Chilean nation had long wished to conceal. In large part, the Allende government had hoped to reconcile these oppositions, drawing popular sectors into the center of national consciousness. This project differs both historically and socially from the cultural situation in Argentina, where lo popular responded to other callings, notably the Peronist legacy, which had dominated a nationalist imaginary since the 1940s; against this tradition or in its favor, intellectuals saw popular resistance as a sign of revolutionary practice and nationalist fervor.

In the wider scheme of culture, the popular subject was designed to prove the heterogeneous originality of Latin America and to draw attention to the subversive role of the "outsider" who met the eye of the state. The figure of the subaltern thus provided an incentive to structure a counterhegemonic discourse. This work was also advanced in other regions of Latin America and was sustained in the cultural arena by Latin America's most significant critics. From the 1970s, and in the literary arena, intellectuals such as Angel Rama, Antonio Cornejo Polar, and David Viñas—to name the most prominent among them—set in motion a social and cultural agenda that lasted for a generation. Rama, for example, in *La transculturación narrativa de América Latina* (1982), a book whose first chapters were published in 1974, convinced us that the moment of conflict between popular and elite traditions produced a new model of culture; in *La ciudad letrada* (1984), he went on to show how the emergence of a lettered tradition, used to sustain the paternalist order and legitimize republican policy, was eventually challenged by the multiplicity of the *ciudad real*.[8]

Sharing Rama's vision, Antonio Cornejo Polar insisted on the heterogeneity of Andean culture as crucial to the construction of a vision of Latin America. In his last book, *Escribir en el aire: Ensayo sobre la heterogeneidad sociocultural en las literaturas andinas* (1994), Cornejo argued for the culture's debt to an indigenous and ethnic presence. In particular, he made a case for the constant intersections of oral and print traditions and the ways in which these steady borrowings and exchanges enlarged the creative process. For Cornejo, translation in particular became the sustaining metaphor to negotiate the distance between elite and popular cultures, bringing the marginal figure into the reign of canonical traditions. His important claims were directed in favor of proving an *exchange* among different social subjects, thus suppressing any tendency to construct narratives of victimization.

By now, it should be obvious that the representation of marginal figures, subalterns, or *malandragem* for many years offered symbolic capital to intellectuals and also allowed them to speak of their own dilemmas vis-à-vis the state. In the evolution of this project in particular in the Southern Cone, the popular subject indicates a wide arc of debate and polemic. It also poses some interesting solutions and some insurmountable problems. For here it is not simply a question of what Mabel Moraña recently described as "the 'boom' of the subaltern" (1997, 48), but a genuine struggle of intellectuals vis-à-vis left-wing or populist traditions; in other words, this is not just a surge of interest in the topic of alterity in general, but a planned interaction with a much-debated legacy of populism and, attendantly, a concern for the intellectual's status as one more "disappeared" among many. David Viñas, for example, repeatedly insists on the voice of the subaltern and asks, in the introduction to *Indios, ejército y fronteras*, "Where are the Indian women?" (1982, 8).[9] His argument is a strident attack on the classical liberalism belonging to the late nineteenth century, which effected the "disappearance" of indigenous groups in much the same way that the military regime of the 1970s created its own category of "disappeared." Not at all driven by a desire to prove the originality of Latin America through its marginal figures, Viñas insists instead on the state's constant need for a theory of difference; race theory provides the sustaining logic for a separation and domination of others. This founding binarism will consolidate for Viñas all official thinking about subalterns and will eventually prompt a national plan for their restriction or extermination. In other words, the state institutionalizes the binary thinking that creates the "outlaw" and eventually condemns him. Viñas, who is arguably one of Argentina's most formidable intellectuals (he trained generations of students, among them many of the thinkers cited in the pages of this book), set in place a reflection on marginality that continues to carry its weight upon those who seek to explain the social imaginary in terms of a critique of difference.

Usual Suspects

These visions are fundamental for signaling the importance of subalterns as the focus of intellectual theory. Yet in the closing years of the twentieth century, with neoliberal regimes everywhere affecting our sense of culture, the relationship between intellectuals and popular subjects, so basic to Latin American theory, shows signs of stress and wear.[10] The popular figures so celebrated earlier by liberal left thinkers become increasingly relegated to the margin; in some cases, in fact, they are seen as the source of irritation. Chilean sociologist Tomás Moulián observes, for example, the ways in which neoliberal regimes reinvent the category of the delinquent in an effort to split any general alliance between middle classes and marginal sectors; the latter are now identified with a lost populist imagining, with a realm of misguided passions linked to the successes of Allende and subsequent violence necessary for their suppression.[11] As part of a logic of forgetfulness that suppresses the atrocities of dictatorship, attention turns to the attractiveness of the market and focuses on the infractions committed by those who might stray from the rules of consumer culture. This invention of the popular subject as a modern-day delinquent belongs not only to the confabulations of state authorities; more importantly, as part of an apocalyptic discourse, it is also found in the texts of many progressive intellectuals, denoting a transition in ideological expression and a reformulation of critical choices. Perhaps, as Samuel Zaidman has put it, the democratic voyage of the man of letters who goes in search of the pueblo, can only wind up as a suicidal gesture (1999, 17). Announced a priori as a failure, the impossible meeting of intellectual and popular subject also signals a crisis in theory. It marks a decisive late-twentieth-century aporia between rootedness and difference, permanence and disorder, experience and representation. Attempting to negotiate these gaps, intellectual theory precariously wavers on edge.

To highlight this representational crisis, a brief exploration of several works by Beatriz Sarlo is helpful; not only do her turns of logic guide us through the preoccupations of one of Latin America's major intellectual figures, but also her shifting visions regarding the popular subject are instructive for reading a range of apprehensions belonging to an entire generation of cultural critics. Throughout her early work, Sarlo consistently expressed a concern for the fate of popular figures and attempted to bring them into debate as a *bridge* among different sectors within civil society; she later redefined this bridge by placing her confidence in the efficacy of political parties, which, for Sarlo, were the hallmark of democracy's success and proof of an active public sphere. This transition is expressed most succinctly in the move between several works, from her *La imaginación técnica* (1992) and *Escenas de la vida posmoderna* (1994) through *La máquina cultural* (1998). If the first book expresses a concern for what she calls "the poor man's know-how" (a term she borrows from Roberto Arlt), in the second work, she addresses the impoverished knowledge not of the lower classes, but of her generational cohorts in the intellectual field; the third book tracks the conflicts that emerge when one imposes, from an institutional apparatus, a violent yet homogenizing bridge between intellectuals and popular masses.

In *La imaginación técnica*, Sarlo reminds us that Latin America has claimed a position in the world order through its particular interest in projects of alterity; in particular, she signals how the ways of the poor are used by Latin American elites to transform their relationships to power. This becomes obvious, Sarlo observes, in the early decades of this century, when technology, as a tool of the dominant classes, was used to usher Latin America into modernity and captured the imagination of the working poor who were stimulated by its symbolic dimensions. The poor man's use of the technological imagination, his fascination for machinery and invention in the style of a *bricoleur*, becomes the focus of Sarlo's book. The grace of her logic here is sustained by a flexible definition of noninstitutional knowledge insofar as it circulates freely around a network of print sources and is distributed among the urban population regardless of social status. Technology, although distributed by elites, was soon absorbed by the masses; as such, it promised a democratic future, the basis for a common culture.

In *Escenas de la vida posmoderna*, however, Sarlo abandons this optimism. Now technology—in the form of the mass media and videos, along with flashes of ephemeral meaning produced by techniques such as zapping—is the culprit responsible for damaging the integrity of social life and for dismantling the quiet space of reflection demanded by intellectual endeavors. Sarlo delivers an invective to the media moguls who sustain this electronic republic through which simulacra eventually destroy our relationship to what we know as "real." Those who suffer most in this purview are intellectuals themselves, who are now rendered useless by the habits of postmodern life and by a general preference for the sound byte over sustained debate and analysis. Sarlo appears to tell us that if technology offered Latin Americans the fantasy of an *original* experience in the early decades of this century, in our current moment, it resoundingly announces loss and defeat. In other words, the intellectual has been marginalized owing to the state's indifference toward art and culture and to the growing powers of the media and the market.[12]

Sarlo's gloomy prognosis is founded not only on her suspicion of global technology but also on the changing structure of society itself. Although she seeks a common culture (1994, 136), she finds no basis for universal alliance. In this context, the poor who were celebrated in *La imaginación técnica* are now, in *Escenas de la vida posmoderna*, treated as independent of the intellectual's pull. The poor take their issues to public arenas, respecting neither the state nor conventional policy analysis performed by institutional voices. It is this feature, what Sarlo calls the "particularism" of special-interest groups, that offers the greatest challenge to intellectual work:

> Do we need intellectuals? . . . Is it necessary to have individuals speak beyond their limited range of self-interest? To speak of Vietnam as an Argentine; Jews or Arabs as a Christian; to speak of blacks though one is white; gays though one is straight; the poor though one lives in wealth; the rich though their profits never affect our well-being? Is it better if only Cubans speak of Cuba, if only Jews refer to the concentration camps, if only women speak of women? Does the specificity of one's discourse have greater resonance or greater claims to authenticity? Are ghettos, where each group speaks of its own dilemmas, pref-

> erable to those open spaces where each person speaks from his or her knowledge and interest, but also considers the knowledge and interests of others? (1994, 186)

Sarlo's intense reflection, of course, carries consequences for the intellectual's survival. The special-interest groups, the splintered languages of local experience—to a large degree, the products of neoliberalism itself—leave intellectuals in residual posts, either as "archaic or marginal" (1993). An irony of disproportionate scope given Sarlo's own success as a public intellectual in the years following Argentina's democratic reopening, the fear of intellectual marginality is marked in her subsequent works as well. Nevertheless, they carry the possibility of separating global possibilities of alliance away from popular initiatives and, instead, locate radical change within the province of an avant-garde.[13]

In our current fin de siglo, announcing a supposed end of history, critics tend to situate one another as fallen heroes expelled from paradise, exiled from the universe of modernist values that once had confirmed their voice and place. Some advocates of New Left critique have placed Sarlo among this band, accusing her of betraying the cause of popular missions because of her defense of aesthetic values.[14] Yet it would be too easy to cancel Sarlo's efforts, to charge her with abandoning faith in the possibility of a public sphere that included popular voices. To do so is to miss the aggrieved preoccupation of intellectuals in Latin America for seeking a restored sense of purpose in the postdictatorship years. Indeed, a recent avenue for Sarlo's inquiries reveals an underlying concern for uniting the multiple layers of voices belonging to democratic congregation and articulates the need for a plurality that often finds itself suppressed by the ploys of mass-media culture. In "Basuras culturales, simulacros políticos" (Cultural garbage, political simulacra, 1990), she first made this concern apparent by protesting the homogeneity imposed by the media on different sectors of the social whole; she reiterates this preoccupation in *La máquina cultural* (1998), where she shows how demands for a singular culture often have been extracted through forceful methods. In the first chapter of this book, she offers the testimonial of a schoolteacher who inaugurated her career in the early decades of the twentieth century. Eager to assimilate to national cultural values, the teacher seeks to achieve homogeneity and a single sense of citizenship and national duty among her students. Nevertheless, the desire for assimilation is so strong that she resorts to authoritarian tactics, provoking surprise among readers. And indeed, the teacher's desire to discipline her crop in the habits of confraternity leaves her, as Sarlo astutely observes, "insensitive to difference" (77). We remain, then, with the question about the limits of individual agency to realize goals of social integration and alliance, but the episode is also instructive for the quandary of intellectuals. Debating options of permanence and disorder, contemporary thinkers face a choice about the direction of focus: Do we work within the cultural projects of the state to achieve a plurality of voices? Or do we settle for the activities of the margin, far from the institutions and disciplinary tactics? The solution requires a balance between continuity and risk, a bridge that joins different cultures and that allows reconciliation between civil society and the state.

For Sarlo, this ambivalence was articulated not only in her scholarly writing but also in her approach and retreat from organized political parties; I refer to her commitment (since renounced) to the liberal Alianza Party, which succeeded in securing the election of Graciela Fernández Meijide (October 1997). Although the project originally announced a source of ethical coherence, linking at least for Sarlo intellectual and political practice, it later became the fount of her profound disillusion; "common sense" as the watchword of political action was simply insufficient to rally a calling for democratic change.[15] This alteration of ideas suggests a profound uneasiness with the current articulation of political society; it defines a hope for radical change yet a suspicion of extraparliamentary theory. Thus, utopian expectations once placed in electoral politics again meets frustration; at the same time, the alternatives proposed by civil society fail to engender sufficient support.

Civil Society Reviewed

The trajectory of concerns expressed by Beatriz Sarlo over the direction of civil society is echoed, although in less anguished ways, by many subscribers of cultural critique. More directly than she, they attribute today's misalignments to micropolitical groups. Their debates specifically focus on the easy deceptions of social movements along with a call to restrain the activities of popular sectors. Tomás Abraham, for example, director of the cultural review *La Caja*, supplies a suspicious view of civil sphere engagements and, although a former student of Foucault, discredits the value of local microresistance: "Anything can fill a vacuum or empty a cup that's full, not just local strategies. But there exists a certain difficulty in selling new versions of paradise, at least for intellectuals. Indeed, if the number of persons amassed by the evangelical movement is any indication, then it would appear that there's a great clientele eagerly awaiting paradise or at least its consolations" (1992, 75). The tendency to liken grass-roots activists to evangelical preachers is common enough, perpetrating suspicions about *all* local engagements. Chilean critic Martin Hopenhayn has even described this reaction as an "anti-secular retrenchment" (1994, 46), as if to indicate the military-like force with which opponents of social movements voice their claims.

Nevertheless, the current problem goes beyond an attack of the presumed fundamentalisms of these informal coalitions. Mario Wainfeld, from the UNIDOS group of progressive Argentine intellectuals, also rejects the role of NGOs in Argentine cultural life: "The NGOs have not been able to forge a viable 'macro' politics that might challenge the existing system with which they constantly interact. The only enduring and anti-statist NGOs in our history have been those tied to human rights movements; . . . Surely it was an exaggeration to 'demand' or think of them as initiators of any political response to existing models. The social movements which should assume responsibility [also] reflect a high degree of decomposition. They justify their presence by immediate objectives, not by a possible evolution toward a new overarching political plan" (1993, 10). Sociologists have devoted ample space to reflect upon the limits and failures of social movements in our current decade, frequently evoking fundamentalist imagery as part of their argumentation.[16] It is no surprise, then, that Emilio de Ipola explains current-day local struggles as a residual effect of earlier identitarian projects, all of which he claims were governed by responses to "fear and faith" (1997, 66).

These underminings of micropolitical groups, so central to liberal intellectual thought, can be understood in three principal ways. First, they correspond to a crisis of ideals, marking a moment when the "nation" is no longer a possible project; given the force of that disillusion, the popular sectors are also banished from the imagination.[17] Lacking a narrative of progress, intellectuals thus dismiss marginal subjects who engage in struggle for change. Second, a paradox emerges insofar as the refusal to acknowledge achievements of social movements comes at a time of democratic restitution, when faith is renewed in formal political parties and electoral representation; in the process, the identity debate is dismissed from the formation of late-capitalist culture.[18] No longer following a model in which civil society opposed the state (a paradigm prevalent in the minds of progressive intellectuals during years of authoritarian regimes), now a civil society project is considered by many as a bankrupt endeavor. Moreover, those groups lying outside of electoral politics (that is, mothers' movements, hunger marchers, gay and lesbian advocates) are seen as resisting those venues that would endorse democracy's triumph, failing to collaborate in a unified social whole. This line of thinking (which, please note, does not belong to Southern Cone intellectuals alone) also announces the problematic status of social movements principally because they lack a general strategy for producing a counterhegemonic discourse.[19] In the absence of any overarching plan, popular forces are dismissed and micropractices are viewed as divisive; they lack the authority of material analysis, separate Latin America from the metropolis, and, indeed, mark its difference. Finally, it is claimed that they intervene in a space demarcated as superficially cultural.[20] The tactic erases their political potential and the ability of the participants to enter in dialogue with others. But it also corresponds to a suspicion of identitarian politics in general. Within the Southern Cone political theater, it reveals the intellectual's fear of a native-run populism, a fear that evokes the early days of Perón or the failures of Allende. Another paradox emerges from this scenario: on the one hand, civil society depends on the illusion of "difference" as its constituting basis such that the existence of competing factions organizes the logic of political debate; on the other hand, the enactment of democracy cannot withstand excessive petitions lest it abandon its commitment to order.

Market Identities

The postdictatorship years create a kind of diglossia that separates the terms of intellectual debate from other less incorporated languages of social praxis. In this respect, the loss felt by contemporary critics, their melancholia and mourning for an imagined past, becomes a common thread holding together numerous essays on memory and recollection, oblivion and failure of community.[21] It also suggests a crisis in utopian thinking conditioned by the market itself.

The skepticism with respect to subaltern struggle has been cogently registered by Néstor García Canclini, who links social movements and a dream of popular action to a kind of folkloric nostalgia for some past moment of heroism. Referring to those sectors that support autonomous movements, Canclini observes with reservation, "But their political action is usually of short duration, with difficulties in building effective alternative choices owing to the fact that they fall into the error of folkloric and populist thinking. . . . They imagine a multiplication of actions at the micro level that will one day engender transformations of society as a whole without considering that the great constituents of popular thought and sensibility—the culture industries, the State—are the very spaces where one must force the issue of popular interests or fight directly for hegemony" (1992, 251). Pessimistic about the energies of social movements, disillusioned by the dream of popular struggle, Canclini emphasizes the contradictions of these utopias owing especially to the market economy (the first chapter of his *Culturas híbridas*, not surprisingly, bears the title, "From Utopias to the Market") and to an uneasy critical sense regarding modernity itself. Skepticism replaces faith; accommodation, political engagement. Lost, in his view, is the possible autonomy of popular action.

Canclini continues the argument of *Culturas híbridas* in *Consumidores y ciudadanos* (1995), where the definition of citizenship is now formed strictly by consumerism. A regulatory mechanism of identities and differences, this market-run economy displaces any sign of distinction that might have been acquired by subalterns or advanced by intellectuals. Even the concept of *hybridity* ceases to signify a possible convergence of popular and elites, but instead a redistribution of images in public zones of purchase. In other words, difference is now defined by degrees of conspicuous consumption; and while lo popular stands at the end of one line, representing the buyer and never the producer, similarly, the cultural capital of intellectuals is massified, ordered by the temporal and spatial vectors of the market. Canclini's reservations are decidedly beyond models of integration; instead, he advances a single system of intelligibility, erected by the market itself, to account for all differences and behaviors. In this context, it might even be claimed that the concept of hybridity is a fabrication administered by global enterprise and entirely within the logic of profit.

But is there no discourse that surpasses this pervasive lament? Is there no sense of a future that might recuperate the role of popular subjects? Most likely, this separation is the product of neoliberal thinking itself insofar as it places emphasis on an erotics of difference and announces pluralism as the primary condition for entering the market-run sphere. Here, consensus replaces strategies of confrontation and debate; and the marginal subject, allied in the past with populist forms of resistance, is eventually expelled from scenes of intellectual discussion for the disruption it poses.[22]

These texts appear to tell us that the emancipatory potential of popular social actors is destined to be absorbed in the market space as part of the effects of modernization; in fact, even the concept of diversity, like the fragments of residual social activism itself, avails itself for this kind of market subjection and, accordingly, finds a place in circuits of global distribution. What remains afloat, archaic and almost as a surplus of meaning, is a shifter in global discourse such that Latin American subalterns exist as symbolic currency *outside* their local environment—in foreign perspective, as exoticized victims or heroes, often with their images emblazoned on T-shirts or as subjects of Hollywood film. The task of mimicry, so often assigned to third world subjects, here becomes part of a first world utopian vision that casts its sights abroad.[23] Meanwhile, the emancipatory powers of popular leanings at home become habitually silenced, considered as residual forms of confrontational politics of the past.

"Becoming woman"

In this grim scenario, an overriding paradox emerges: democracy, which depends on the illusion of difference that civil society provides and, in fact, cannot survive without, condemns those very expressions of diversity that civil society supplies; its excess of representable identities is deemed unmanageable by the state. In *El poder de la identidad* Manuel Castells calls attention to forms of identity construction, observing three large formations: (1) *legitimizing identities* that allow the state to rationalize its project vis-à-vis certain social acts that lead to building an acceptable version of civil society; (2) *resistance identities* that foment coalition among marginalized groups; and (3) *project identities* wherein subject positions are reinvented to alter the overall social structure, leading us to question society as a whole (1997, 30). If the first two suggest strategies of containment, keeping the margins separate from the center, the third category proposes something new, altering both the codes for democracy and the possibility of an aesthetic. This practice goes far beyond the reproduction of social *roles*; in fact, it moves toward the reinvention of *meaning* on a symbolic plane. It thus produces the conditions for novel expressions of alliance through an expansion of the representational field.[24] In this way, the state and civil society can hardly be seen as dichotomous, but rather as mutually dependent.[25]

This desire for merger runs through some circuits of intellectual debate and artistic endeavors, where participants celebrate micropractices as a way to issue a challenge to existing values and fixed identitarian roles. Horacio González, for example, asks how to dissolve, through new social projects, patrimonial authority over knowledge. The contact, the pact, the conversation serve for this Argentine thinker as a way to reformulate identities and overcome the divisiveness enforced by administrators of neoliberal design (1992, 13).[26] Others echo this common longing. Eduardo Rinesi, in the wake of dictatorship years, seeks forms of collective coalition beyond the usual constraints of the law and the obligations often engendered by guilt (1993, 67).[27] Knowledge is produced not by *rules*, but by the dialectic of social forms that produce a theory of action. Tomás Moulián, borrowing from the concept of "molecular revolution" advanced by Guattari, urges us to look beyond neoliberal paradigms to discover alternative ways to comprehend historical process and change (1997). And in outlining a social project to recuperate a lost moral integrity, he proposes a "radical reform" outside of partisan politics (1998, 119–21). A critique of neoliberalism, this proposal favors popular social actors and foments critical consciousness. The emphasis here is on a desired *bridge*, not simply a counterhegemonic plan, a way to connect popular subjects with an intellectual field. In fact, Martín Hopenhayn, lamenting the loss of communitarian impulses, seeks what he calls an "intercultural utopia" that emerges from the heterodoxy of a *mestizaje* of culture and ideas (1994, 277). The goal in this instance is to extend concepts of solidarity over a broad span of subjects in order to reach a direct form of participatory democracy. For Hopenhayn, the project entails an equality or leveling in the field of representation through which his idealized model of mestizaje yields a social environment "capable of negating the negation of the Other" (280). Here, the move is against totalization theory, a defense of the "in-between." Yet Hopenhayn, like the other critics earlier cited, is at a loss for examples that might promote these desired collectivities; the social actors necessary for these reinvestments in democratic process are not within his reach.[28]

Perhaps it is Néstor Perlongher, a gay activist who died of AIDS and certainly one of Latin America's most engaging poets and thinkers, who best locates a social and political potential in what he calls a "devenir mujer" (becoming woman) (1991). Borrowing from Deleuze and Guattari, Perlongher rejects an essentializing definition of women and men, gay or heterosexual subjectivities and instead argues for a gendered reading of cultural conflict that allows some unanticipated possibilities for debate in the atmosphere of neoliberal regimes. He begins his account by observing the asceticism of Brazil during its early years of redemocratization. Here, Perlongher tries to comprehend the apparent absence of social action—a loss of dissident voices in the public plaza despite Brazil's political opening (71)—and to work toward some degree of analysis regarding future engagement. His solution rests on an antifoundationalist theory that leads him to read from the margins—from the interstices, from a radical privileging of the "in-between," from the borders of formally constituted discourses—and which, in lieu of reducing spatial dimensions to the confinements of a unified map, multiplies the possibilities of reading, enlarges a scene of action, and expands the number of force fields that challenge the integrity of any social center. The point is that the "minor" both alters and gives strength to collective alternatives to power. It is precisely from the often invisible margin—the site of the unincorporated, the irreducible, the constantly shifting and mobile—that a theory of democratic practice emerges to fill the blank horizon. Perlongher refers to this as a "devenir mujer"—becoming *woman* in opposition to the masculinity claimed by the authoritarian state, a feminine presence that is not necessarily fixed by one's biological identity or sexual preference, but which constantly asserts itself in terms of staging alternatives and, therefore, never forecloses possibilities of meanings that erupt in politics or discourse.[29] His reflection brings us to a topic often omitted from the general theory of social and democratic experience in Latin America: here, the question of gender (and specifically the condition of the feminine or sexualized "other") is more than a practice of difference; it finds insertion in an otherwise congealed discursive arena, it breaks up the frozen sediments of representation. More important still, the status of the "feminine" (that is, deviant, marginal, or other) allows us to begin to think of a range of issues from a realignment of the symbolic field to calls for coalition and alliance.

Two points of clarification are in order: first, some might claim that this proposal suffers from a lack of a concrete, theoretical structure (insofar as the micropractice of the "feminine" never really manages to muster sufficient force to overturn hegemonic projects). Second, it might also be said that attention to gender masks the popular gains that were made in earlier years usually in the name of social class; interest in gender shifts attention away from subalterns. But scrambling the foundational principles of an inefficient (and inadequate) democracy, gendered interventions open the path to needed debate; they demand a rearticulation of hegemonic reason and ethics and also test the delimitations of culture. More than the "in-between" advantage that Perlongher suggests, gender considerations are "en route" toward change, in transit to sites of anticipated, future practice; with this, they open to the theoretical possibilities that can link an analysis of normative sexuality with democratic performance. In this way, gender becomes a detonator of what has long been suppressed and offers crucial connections to a critical awareness in formation. Second, let us be clear of the metaphoric limitations of the gendered trope. It is not that a gendered presence or practice provides the *only* source of insertion in the logic to neoliberal regimes; indeed, one could take on the case of the Zapatistas, the protest marches against neoliberalism held in various countries, the food riots that drew middle-class sectors in alliance with the working poor, the indigenous demands for land restitution and citizenship rights, or the struggles of temporary agricultural workers throughout the length of the cordillera and Brazil. But by focusing on the ways in which gender and specifically sexualized bodies are inscribed in cultural debate, we locate a way to alter the difficult relationship between intellectuals and popular subjects. A consideration of gender and sexuality leads to a disruption of the totalizing practices of universal theory; it opens paths in comprehension leading to a different sense of the whole. Finally, gendered struggles bridge the gap between social analysis and the aesthetic. By tracking the position of gendered tropes, the activity of what Perlongher called the "devenir mujer," we can return again to the active politics of the text.

Intellectuals who have turned to gender representations for their work often articulate an overarching concern for the fate of the political field. They draw attention to the material specificity of what is understood as the "margin" and, in a wider focus, they question the distribution of allocated social spaces. Finally, through gendered bodies and tropes, some of today's most radical cultural theory grows, creating a space to articulate the conflicts and points of convergence shared by social actors and their spokespersons in the intellectual field. The gendered body is the prime metaphor of difference and likeness: it serves the debate about the self and other and tracks the tensions between elites and subalterns; it articulates the tension between North and South, between one's native language and its translation; it sustains a tension between genealogy and difference, between permanence and disorder; it represents ongoing movement. Gender clouds the straight line that grants us the comfort of identification.

In short, the unsettling presence of gendered bodies foreshadows the anxiety of intellectuals with respect to representation. But we also may find with this presence a cause for opening a renewed commitment to matters of public action.[30] It is not to suggest that gender issues can close an epistemological gap between intellectual subjects and subalterns and thus bring about a romantically charged illusion of solidarity between disinterested parties (I assume that this identification is, for some intellectuals, more self-valorizing than real and in this regard, it suggests genuine limitations); rather, groups of uneven power can often be united by a common petition for rights of representation. As such, gender as a public matter offers us a close-up view of processes of negotiation and dissent. It brings in play tensions between visibility and opaqueness that determine the logic of the social whole.

Fabricio Forastelli, historicizing the emergence of homosexual rights movements in Argentina from the decade of the 1970s, reminds us that the disguise of carnival can also be used as a tool of sabotage. Passing unrecognized allows one to establish connections with groups dissimilar from one's own; it disorders principles of state organization (1999, 117). It strikes at the basis of identity formation within the democratic state itself. Too, petitions for gendered rights enter any debate or discussion; they force the adjustment of matters of public interest to include the gendered margin. These protests function from a tension between discrimination (externally imposed) and exclusion (seen from within the marginal subject's camp), or as Forsastelli writes, "'Restitution' establishes in both the territory of the majority and the political arena the possibility of a demand for justice favoring minority sectors" (124). Yet the minority, once in the public sphere, destabilizes itself and the social whole; we find that the "ghetto" constituted by the illusion of specificity comes quickly apart. Earlier identificatory systems are thereby irremediably shaken. Seen in this way, gender issues in the public sphere alter the terms of democratic practice; they also upset the usual narratives of intellectuals in conflict with popular actors. Finally, the matter of gender leads us to rethink practices of representation.

Engendered Action

For the moment, let us undertake a double action, moving *toward* the margin, and taking the margin as a point of departure to move toward a different concept of a center. From that mobile practice, we can expand an inquiry that both alerts us to the major issues fundamental to democratic rule and signals its exclusions. Perhaps recalling the famous drawing of Uruguayan Torres García, who transformed the cartographic representation of the hemispheres so that Latin America occupied the conventional space of the North while the United States filled the place known as South, we can also manipulate an inverted picture of intellectual debate within the social whole if we begin with a focus on gender. In this way, starting from the gendered margin, we gain access to possible conversations (whether in the sense of Habermas or Rorty or in line with the more radical projects of thinkers such as Chantal Mouffe) that might elucidate the terms of democratic coalition and the power of an invigorated aesthetic. This presence carries us in the final analysis to a discussion of the rights and obligations claimed by citizens under democratic rule, but it also provides the basis of social interaction that bridges popular sectors and elites; it overcomes the separation stretched between critical speaker and object of study. By beginning with the presence of what Perlongher had called a "devenir mujer," we reconfigure the experience of "naming" within the projects of culture.

The tactics of neoliberal regimes and the strategies of appropriation they enact over alien space, property, and identity produce a number of concerns about naming. To cite, invoke, call forth, and delimit, to impose our identity on the social whole or fix the name of another, allows the illusion of a timeless, self-satisfying knowledge that expresses the province of our own interests. This was evident in the colonizer's gaze over the landscape of the New World and continues in our current times, as individuals capture the names of others both to attract a global market and to contain possible points of eruption. The electronic media further exploits this project by manipulating identities whose potential lability is explosive. Witness only the internationally televised forums that exploit the melodramas of family violence. Giving name to these dark passions, they feed upon audience desires to know the lives of others. At the same time, and despite the best-controlled plans, the effects of these mass-marketed images occasionally stitch webs of alliance and ventilate collective indignation among the public. Unanticipated conflicts emerge, various temporalities collide, irritations fester on the social fabric, overriding one's allegiance to class and place to dismantle the edifice of earlier reasoning. Gender is often the material limit against which the system is tested and produces, in this dark season of postpolitics, new terms of identification, new forms of recognition, as well as new expressions of doubt. Normative identities are disrupted, horizons for solidarity emerge, and the weight of authority, in the final instance, is shifted from one's place of origin to multiple locations on the map. Gender markers thus enact a redistribution of the various forms and dimensions of social agency. This experience at once becomes grounded and mobile; it restores to democracy a socially material component and also creates the possibility for another sense of the aesthetic.

A recent example draws together quite succinctly the points of discussion offered here: I refer to the case of María Soledad Morales, a high school student in rural Argentina who was raped and murdered in September 1990. The fate of María Soledad quickly drew national attention. Not only did the brutal story evoke outpourings of sympathy and an appeal to law, but the atrocities (and subsequent cover-ups, falsifications of autopsy reports, and extensive cases of perjury) implicated Ramon Saadi, the elected provincial leader of Catamarca and member of a traditional political family in power in the region since the 1940s. Saadi was forced to resign under the weight of public protest.

Here, questions of rights, corporeality, and justice were simultaneously drawn together to challenge Argentina's unreconstructed history of state terrorism and authoritarian rule and to protest the diminished role of ordinary citizens who, even with the return to democracy, still lacked access to power. These issues were articulated in public protest whereby the failures of respect in the gender system served to introduce the inequities reigning in the nation as a whole. Following the murder of María Soledad, Catamarca witnessed the beginning of a regular round of Marches of Silence, weekly protests first organized by a nun who was also director of María Soledad's school. The convocation, gathering thousands of protesters in the provincial city, and also inspiring similar assemblies through the length of the country, reminded citizens of their limited rights to protest injustice;

from the gendered perspective that originally gave impulse to these voiceless marches, matters of judicial corruption and state impunity then became a central issue. Moreover, at a later point, when the public was not allowed to view on television the proceedings of the investigation, and citizens felt once again that justice had been impeded, the marches of protest saw a resurgence. The right to *see* (a right deprived Argentines during years of dictatorship, yet curiously manipulated in the media explosion that came with the return to democratic rule) became a central demand by those wishing to observe the enactment of judicial process; citizens insisted that the workings of justice be "transparent" to all.[31] This was more than voyeurism; indeed, it rested on demands for ethics in representation. After seven years of investigation, extraordinary public demonstrations, and the fall of the Saadi government in the province of Catamarca, the murderers were judged guilty and condemned to prison in February 1998.

The case is exemplary of the ways in which the violation and cover-up of the gendered body precipitate public indignation, inspire a specific form of mass protest, evoke matters of corruption and abuse as a test of democratic rule, and place demands for corporeal respect on the national agenda for justice. From the tensions between spoken protest and silence, between evidence of crimes inflicted on a visible body and the cover-ups of nonrepresentation, the story reconnects a gendered presence to core issues of democratic rule. "After the sacrifice of María Soledad, history will be different," wrote poet María Elena Walsh.[32] With extensive public demonstrations, many of them charged with expressions of religious piety to demonstrate the immorality of the state, the matter of citizenship and demands for civil rights could hardly be overlooked. As in the case of the Mothers of Plaza de Mayo, who redefined the terms of public participation not to focus on partisan politics but on the ethical dimensions of democracy, those involved in the protests on behalf of María Soledad sought to occupy public spaces and put pressure upon the media for representation of their cause. In this way, the event forced a public deconstruction of a symbolic field of official images belonging to the democratic, paternalist state supposedly protecting childhood and youth; it exposed the vulnerability of representations that sustained the presence of female bodies in the images belonging to the domestic/private or filial/maternal fields; and, finally, at the center of these recent concerns was the specificity of a female body standing as both metaphor and direct representation of the absence of civil rights in general. This general "rereading" of democracy that engaged large sectors of the population also linked urban intellectuals such as Ernesto Sábato, David Viñas, and Pérez Esquivel to the interests of a provincial family; the pact enabled individuals over a broad geographical span to rechart together their readings of democracy from a perspective decidedly "off-center" and to break up a legacy of corruption that threatened civil expression.[33]

Democracy's Challenge

I do not want to celebrate too easily the success of gender debates under neoliberalism or the effect of their political focus. In fact, gender in Southern Cone countries often serves as a coin that trades at many tables: on the one hand, unplanned intrusions of feminized identity under the aegis of a masculine state have caused startling disruptions in democratic programs; on the other hand, the gender card has also served the purposes of legitimizing neoliberal regimes. Thus, in the wake of dictatorship years, newly democratic governments took gendered rights as a sign of modernization. In Argentina, for example, the return to democracy in 1983 brought many demands from the realm of partisan politics to modify family law and congressional representation: 30 percent of the parliamentary seats must now be filled by women; the *patria potestad* ruling was revised to allow women to share in the economic governance of the family; equality of rights of inheritance was allowed to both legal and natural offspring; divorce was formally recognized; and in Mendoza in 1998 a Court of Justice recognized the legal rights of a homosexual couple to establish and sustain a domestic partnership.[34] Regarding the scope of these advances, one columnist for *La Nación* wrote, "A century of women's demands had been condensed in scarcely eight years."[35]

Other narratives drawn from the gender debate further confirm the image of an inclusive democracy at work. Thus, while many have noted the mark of silence during the "lost decade" of the 1980s (aptly designated as such by the CEPAL), social scientists also tell of the increased numbers of women who participated actively in social formations, where they tried through micropolitical approaches to manage alternative political projects to meet the demands of life under structural adjustment. Often, this was translated through the length of the cordillera through soup kitchens in neighborhoods, unions of housewives and temporary agricultural workers in Chile, picketers blocking principal highways of Argentina, schoolteachers encamped in the Buenos Aires public square in order to protest wage freezes and degraded conditions of public education, international venues of debate (most recently in Beijing) connecting Southern Cone women globally, and the persistence of those NGOs that trained women for civic participation.[36] Some even claim that democracy itself was initiated by the thrust of the women's movements that were inaugurated with the presence of the Mothers of Plaza de Mayo. As a whole, they continue to alter any fixed sense of space and time set in place by the economy and the "official" memory of the state; they join local experience to the global and insist on the value of networks to continue gendered work.[37] In this way, and without arguing for the merits of neoliberalism as a whole, many point to the presence of women as agents of democracy; too, the neoliberal state expands its image and scope by taking gender as a token of exchange.

At the same time, critics of democracy point to the profound failures of achievement for women and sexual minorities: the sustained case against divorce in Chile (one of the only remaining nations in the world to prohibit divorce by law), the International Development Bank's alert to Latin America about the magnitude of domestic violence, affecting at least 40 percent of the female population; the continued prohibition of abortion from Mexico to the Southern Cone; and Carlos Menem's decree, signed in December 1998, declaring March 25 an Argentine national holiday to "celebrate the unborn," a clear defense of the Vatican's policies and a vindication for Menem who, in past years, sought to gain control of antiabortionist proponents even to point of silencing them through measures of constitutional reform.[38] Even the Chilean presidential campaign of 1999 and its subsequent runoff election in 2000, staged by conservative Lavín against the socialist Lagos, brought the question of reproductive rights to the center of discussion. "The Uterus of Estela," an ironic reference to Lavín's wife, who flaunted her eighth pregnancy as a sign of her husband's defense of family values, made obvious the desired restriction of women's rights in the Chilean political forum. By pointing to examples such as these, many correctly remind us of the failures of neoliberalism to advance the claims of women.

Feminist critic Raquel Olea (2000) refines this critique by explaining the ways in which Chilean democracy imposed disciplinary gestures on women that even dictatorship could not bring to fruition: consensus, models of "common sense," and values of consumerism as a sign of progress all serve to inhibit the advances of women and the expansion of popular voices under neoliberal rule. The church, political parties and the state, and appointed commissions on women and the poor have negotiated away gendered rights to the detriment of any constructive project while excluding the very women (subjects of state-run studies) from all deliberations and input.[39] More importantly, under neoliberal rule, women have lost what was their most powerful tool against authoritarianism itself: their capacity for anti-institutional subversion in the field of representation.

Not ironically, the promise of democracy has also been proven on the wounds of the gendered body. It may be said that when marginal movements are offered the opportunity to surface, to consolidate their ranks and formalize operations, the deepest conflicts surface, often polarizing constituent members joined in association.[40] Neoliberal economic policies are often the incentive for this crisis. On this point, although feminists have brought forward many cases instructive for contemporary democracy, they also underscore the failed relationships between intellectuals and those popular subjects they purport to represent under neoliberal rule. At the seventh meeting of Latin American and Caribbean feminists held in 1996 in Cartagena, Chile, participants raised a number of conflicts about strategies of negotiation and the representation of women's bodies, causing commentators to focus on a lesson that is central for our discussion: Which forces under democracy get to speak for women? And how, in the final analysis, can women speak for themselves? The debates in Cartagena signaled a crisis about the conflicts between autonomous and institutional feminism.[41] And here, participants asked, among the major questions, how feminist practice (in neighborhoods, urban districts, or agricultural areas) is compromised by an ongoing rapport with official venues. Put alternatively, they wondered how a once emancipatory impulse was domesticated and curbed by the draw of money.

As the Cartagena meeting brought these issues to light, an active polemic ensued about the viability of autonomous movements under neoliberal regimes. Equally important, the symposium raised a central question: Should debate be structured by a market-determined economics that separates "institutional" and "activist" feminism and thereby ignore questions of rights or the hardships of experience? Should local gender politics yield to the demands imposed by those financial institutions that set agendas from abroad?[42] The centerpiece of this debate focused on the situation in Chile following years of dictatorship when government organizations created for the study of women were accused of subduing critique, locking independent feminists outside the institutional fray. Despite its unpleasant disruption, the debate strikes at the heart of a negotiation characteristic of our times: Not only who speaks for whom, but what is lost in the process of absorption? Yet another issue emerges: If spaces are named in binary terms (that is, autonomous versus institutionally linked feminisms), what then is the possibility of alternative forms of alliance? Can we anticipate uncharted avenues of work for as yet uncharted actors? This brings to mind a caveat of the late Julieta Kirkwood, one of the strongest voices of Chilean and Latin American feminism during the dictatorship years: "Contemporary feminism reappears with strength in moments of tremendous ideological dislocation, when all perspective is disturbingly lost; where totality cannot be explained by reason and where one suspects the need for more subjective explanations by great masses of the population" (1982, 7). Kirkwood's defense of the inner lives of women has not been overruled nor has her respect for the convergence of minorities and intellectual figures.[43] Indeed, her idea was not to find a singular voice but to multiply internal projects, to avoid the threats of immobility and stasis as well as the folklore that often limit, even within the feminist camp, the possibility of movement.[44]

This was especially present in the Cartagena encounter, where women took stock of the economic realities set upon them by neoliberal markets. They perceived identity as a tool of trade in projects exterior to an individual's self-interest. Today we are still left wondering, in the line of many social scientists critical of institutional projects (Schild 1998), about the power of those who administer identity in order to justify international funding and, more broadly, about those intellectuals who utilize popular acts to screen their own desires.[45] Too, in an increasingly savage market, one questions how autonomous movements (both those of informal and funded stripe) might survive relying on sources that corrupt the integrity of social process and especially at a time when negotiation (as a concept) is submerged in looming chaos. Finally, one continues to wonder about the identity through which one must speak. These issues signal the conflicts unleashed by a market economy and also bring to mind the still unrealized and distant desire of Néstor Perlongher when he praised the concept of "devenir mujer" as an ongoing challenge to the state.

The Cartagena example is instructive. While the lesson of the meeting appears to be against complacency and stasis, it also takes us away from the foundationalist assertions that first gave meaning to the gender debate. Writing about the crisis that this Chilean encounter provoked, poet and feminist Diana Bellessi observed, "When *pacts* are broken, all codes are reinvented" (Bellessi et al. 1997, 28). This attends not only to a discursive concept of democracy but also to the irrepressible flow of gendered symbols in the cultural field. It urges a reconsideration of social relationships stretched over space, sites where different vectors of experience cross, and where, in their unbounded capacities, the possibility of cross-class alliance flowers despite the rigidity of the state.[46] These realignments of symbols promote ongoing revisions of politics; they make visible a gendered presence that surpasses national frontiers. Equally important, they demand a course of interaction among those who work with culture; they recall what Gayatri Spivak referred to as our sense of "responsibility" in the world (1998).[47]

Forcing a redefinition of semantics and syntax in the political arena as a whole, the gendered field begs a series of questions: What is democratic inclusion? What do we mean by "the people"? How is the discourse on the body implicated in the national symbolic imagination covering a range of matters from legal discourse to expressions of literature and art? Argentine critic Mabel Bellucci (1996) even asks if gendered identities can allow a reconceptualization of the market or eventually overcome its draw.[48] The questions are well worth asking. Moreover, they remind us that the interpretation of individual subjectivities and private experience, as interlocking concerns, is always linked to recognition in the sphere of representation. The problem, then, is not only one of sustaining "difference" for the sake of difference, nor is it a matter of reaching a common ethical ground only through impasse or a sense of defeat; it is one of tracking the places where different sets of expectations emerge, tracking the changing imperatives that determine a politics of representation against any "universal truth."[49] In this context, rather than enforcing the academic distance separating intellectual theory from its subaltern subjects, of the kind that preoccupied those cultural critics earlier discussed, we come to acknowledge our engagements as social actors as we happen in contact with each other.

In *Masculino/femenino* (1993), Nelly Richard insists that the micropractices and demands set by gendered representations test the Chilean government following years of dictatorial rule. Richard astutely manages to position gendered practices—and recognition of subjectivities marked by "difference"—as a way both to target the contradictory discourses of democracy and to challenge metropolitan practices. This observation leads to a way to stretch the given broth of postmodern theory beyond a specific context; it locates a place not only for women but for *all* Latin Americans as well. Together and in different ways, they test the rules of uniformity regulating cultural representations. From this, it follows that the gender issue instills a crisis in *all* epistemological certainties that stand on the global stage.

Many critics like Richard go so far as to claim that categories of both "*lo femenino*" and "*lo latinoamericano*" come to stand for emancipatory images within contrahegemonic paradigms for freedom (Richard 1994; Kirkwood 1983; Trevisán 1997).[50] These images function as a way to open closed definitions of identity that lie in sight of foreign eyes; they produce an alternative cultural model that is not strictly in response to market concerns or to the fragmentation of official power; they provoke the possibility of *alliance* not only among Latin Americans but on the North/South axis as well. In this respect, the interventions of women and sexual minorities unmoor our analytical constructions; they open the paradigms of the social sciences and dismantle the stock of images belonging to metropolitan centers. They test the limits of a modernizing project that affects Latin

Americans as a whole. In short, these counterutopian desires promise a realignment of power between cosmopolitan and local critics. At stake are the possibility of mobilizing a cultural project that challenges metropolitan hegemony, the chance to interrupt those well-known narratives that deny a space for alliance, and the challenge of rethinking projects of representation. In its most appealing aspect, a critique that takes into account gender and sexuality locates a point of contact between the critic's body and the body of an object of study; it refuses to isolate identitarian struggles from wider political objectives.

Southern Cone culture absorbs this problematic by expressing the multiple plays of gendered identities enacted on today's global map. Here, it is useful to remember the lessons of recent postmodern geographers who have argued that social relationships defined by gender are inscribed in spatial form.[51] These spaces are not necessarily to be read in terms of an origin or a home, but as sites where different vectors of experience cross. Read in this way, these sites of encounter are rarely fixed; in effect, their instability points to the flux of all relationships so that space and identity come unbounded.[52] In this context, what links individuals to a particular site is the temporary commonality of experience; often it is anchored in the experience that runs through the body. This corporeal presence overrides any stable reference of origin; for the abuses enacted upon it and for the needs that are registered upon its surface, the gendered body signifies in styles that go beyond the merely performative. Through its odysseys and reterritorializations, collisions and spontaneous encounters with others, it appeals to collective demands for rights and representation. Constitutive of the representational frame of the body is *movement*; hardly in return to primal definitions (that is, woman linked to a myth of origins), the body multiplies possibilities for discussion around rights of self-designation.[53] For its unavoidable materiality, it refuses stereotype and reduction, withdrawing also from what Nancy Fraser has called "the injustice of misrecognition" (1997). This anxiety is everywhere from the improvised laboratories of the streets to the parlors of high culture. In fact, as future chapters will lay bare, protean figures, double-voiced fakes, outrageous tricksters, and outlaws litter art and creative texts in order to acknowledge this misrecognition as an ongoing trope of our times. Announcing a great anxiety about cultural disjuncture, they point to gaps between universal theory and the particular actors it targets, the estrangement of high and popular culture, the schism between intellectuals and masses, and, of course, the irresolvable roles set in place for men and women. The gendered metaphor straddles these contradictions while imprinting discordance on the monochrome of history and narration.

Kuitca's representation of the mattresses, each covered with painted road maps, again brings these themes into focus. His work inspires at first glance a meditation on the relationship between home and some distant cartography, between local and global perceptions. But, rather than drawing attention to the maps of foreign countries, we might reflect on the network of absences signaled by the artist at home. By focusing on the many beds, one might speculate about the missing subjects, possibly absorbed by global maps or "disappeared" by politics in its local setting. The absence also brings to mind the possible experience of connection among those missing bodies and, in the personal lives of viewers, a sense of unfulfilled desire. It creates a longing not simply linked to a future erotics, but for the communal possibilities that still await in repose. *En route*, then, to a conversation between individuals of different spheres of experience, not only intellectuals and popular subjects but also men and women. Like the figures suppressed from the terms of so much of contemporary debate, Kuitca's empty beds provoke a nagging desire to render visible those lines of contact among missing social actors. As if to remind us that someone is lost in the contemporary landscape, they awaken a desire for bodies of action, for solidarities to come.

Desde la revolución cultural de mi impostura
[From the cultural revolution of my imposture]
—Gonzalo Muñoz, *La estrella negra*

El delirio resplandece en la copia
[Delirium shines on the copy]
—María Negroni, *La jaula bajo el trapo*

CHAPTER 2

The Spectacle of "Difference"

In August 1994, Chilean artist Juan Dávila caused an international scandal when he circulated postcard reproductions of his painting of Simón Bolívar. The "liberator" of Spanish America was portrayed with rouge and lipstick; beneath a flower-print cape and military uniform, he exposed the breasts of a woman. This camp representation of one of South America's most revered founding fathers drew immediate protests from Venezuelan and Colombian diplomats and irritated Chilean officials. And when FONDART, the sponsoring organization of fellowships for Chilean artists, rejected Dávila's petition for funding, the intellectual community of Santiago voiced harsh indignation, a debate recorded extensively in Nelly Richard's journal, *Revista de Crítica Cultural.*[1]

The episode recalls the ongoing discussion in the U.S. Congress about the NEA's censorial practice, but Dávila's project also brings to mind a number of contradictions about the reception and interpretation of "drag" in Latin American culture. Does the postmodern emphasis on gender drift

2. Juan Dávila. *The Liberator Simón Bolívar,* 1994. Oil on canvas on metal, 126 × 107 cm. Exhibited at Hayward Gallery, London, 1994. Permission to reproduce image granted by Juan Dávila.

always lead us to the same conclusions regarding the oppositional potential of art and literature? Is the transgression of "drag" encoded to universal symbols, or does it respond to a specifically local context? Finally, how does the intentionally gendered and cross-dressed body mark its presence in the political forum?

Dávila calls attention to the role that sexuality plays in defining Latin American subjects; he interrogates fixed notions of identity passed on from founding fathers as he obliges us to rethink our understanding of lo popular. If he asks about the corporeal grammar that organizes memory and history, he also inquires about the authorized voices that name national longings. On this, Pedro Lemebel writes, "Who can prevent someone queer from imagining these patriotic orgies, bringing us closer to the real and sexualized body of history?" (1996, 136).[2] Indeed, the cross-dressed Bolívar suggests to viewers that even marginal citizens have the right to interpret their national hero, thereby reversing the common symbolic legacies that have excluded considerations of gender.

This work of art leads us to both those with power to dictate the copy and the spectators who stand to judge it. Moreover, it raises a question about *who* in modern civil society has control over management of difference. In 1994, intellectuals made much of Dávila's painting and opened discussion to matters of state censorship and individual freedom. While I am guided by this critical strategy, I also want to elicit a second set of readings, which in the final analysis, may not at all prove secondary to the politics of gender that has emerged under neoliberal rule. In this way, the spectacle of difference is symptomatic of the market.

Beyond these primary readings, Dávila's painting also announces patriotism as a fabrication of commerce, based on the wholesale packaging and trade of poses, gestures, styles, and dress. In fact, if we resituate his portrait of Bolívar within the installation piece where it originally was placed, we reach a significantly different reading. In this larger work, entitled *Utopia* (1988), Dávila tests concepts of gender and nation on a canvas of images assembled from religious relics, tourist postcards, and mass-culture objects; by this juxtaposition, he underscores the ready-made tokens of popular exchange from which national symbols are born. The work thus evokes the excesses of commodity trade in general while mocking the traffic in national nostalgia. Finally, the cross-dressed Bolívar, inscribed within this larger scene, reminds us that aesthetic adventures are always part of a system of citation, forged by the tensions between foundational icons and their subsequent distortion, elite and popular readings of culture, one's genuine anxiety about identity and its wholesale appropriation for trade. In the hall of mirrors and echoes suggested by this model, a dominant masculinity is answered by transgressions in feminine form, but both gendered conventions are obviously subordinated to demands of the market.

The Dávila example reflects on the representational politics of neoliberal rule, its style of negotiating systems of difference for the interests of commerce and exchange. Through particular aberrations enacted on the gendered field, neoliberalism discovers a token of trade; it exploits the market value of scandal, it tantalizes by images of deviance. Moreover, when twists in normative gender patterns surface in the national arena, they acquire the quality of spectacle. Here, the accoutrements of gender—cosmetics, dress, and pose—are treated as commodities to be bought and sold in the image-making service of the nation. We can also turn this paradigm around and see dress from another perspective: dress—like culture itself—frequently covers up more crucial struggles in society. It can be seen as a discourse without fundamental meaning, only activated by the effects it produces in a particular context; it exposes both the power and the inadequacies of representation. The enigma of sexual identities that lies hidden beneath the garments of fashion finds a curious parallel as we come to inquire about the mysteries of state that hide behind the mask. It reminds us of a set of conflicts between elite and popular cultures, traditional and vanguard aesthetics; it pushes to the foreground a political and aesthetic awareness about the dynamics of "difference."

Sexual identity, as a principal trope of difference, is clearly manipulated by state and media; too, it is a form of identity that lends itself easily to tropes of masking. In relation to official discourse, the mask allows the state to manipulate its subjects and to activate a late-twentieth-century impulse to market "difference" on a global scale. From the side of civil society, the masquerade shields subjects from the intrusive eye of the state; it acts as a gesture of parody and freewheeling defiance. Imposturing, then, is dual-tinted: it serves both the state and its dissidents.

This is further complicated because the identity game varies according to ideological projects. If in a first stage, under authoritarian regimes, the mask leads to mobility for individuals who oppose the mandates of an unambiguously masculinist state, in its second phase, with the return to democracy, the struggle to control or conceal identity is frequently conditioned by expressly corporate desires. Facing both these extremes is the intransitive force of the aesthetic, which adopts the masquerade as a test of the limits of art. These contradictory positions map intellectual and political life in our fin de siglo, but they can be traced back to the inaugural moment of consolidation of the liberal republic.

Impostors and Double Agents

The presence of impostors and double agents is certainly not new to Latin American politics or to the projects of literature; in fact, it allows both intellectuals and popular sectors to rethink the face required for citizenship. The matter of dual identities was central to the debates of nineteenth-century republics and the foundation of liberal thought, testing the limits of rights and representation in politics and the exercise of authorship in the cultural field. It thus offered a record of conflicting political languages and incessant discord and revealed tremendous disagreement among founding fathers about concepts of the common good. Too, the nineteenth century registered a history of exchanges about the free flow of identities and voices in the republican milieu and, conversely, concerns about the duplicity and concealment of unchartable subjects. If this discussion inextricably depended on "difference" both for its construction of citizenship and for the practical operations of democratic rule, it also suggested the anxieties of a state that has recognized existing gaps between representation and expression and the inability to match particular interests to collective, universal ideals. This asynchrony was central to all discussion about the founding of the liberal republic; it was the basis for discrepancies between the state and civil society.

Ambiguity of this kind leads to what was perhaps the dominant, overarching question of nineteenth-century philosophy and continues today as a pressing topic: the formation of the "liberal republic." What, after all, is the liberal republic? For its liberal side, it suggests the autonomy of civil society, the flow of particular interests and the exercise of free will; for its republican aspect, it suggests a common and collective project, faith in consensus and the negotiation of a standard, universal ideal. As such, the liberal republic redirects the power of popular beliefs and sets patterns of national memory; paradoxically, it also constructs a semiotic field based on principles of exclusion. The project evokes a multitude of contradictions especially with respect to those who fall outside state authority. How, in effect, might they be included or represented?

Dualism, impersonation, a turn to the disguise or veil—even illness and self-mutilation—were central images for the nineteenth-century cultural imagination. Opera, melodrama, and cloak-and-dagger romances were born from the conjunction of mask and revelation, also inviting us to reconsider the grammar of male and female identities in the process of representation, to rethink the relation of sexualized subjects to the universalizing project of the liberal state. As the strictly literary realm enacted a tug-of-war around dramas of identity, the Latin American liberal republic also locked itself in irresolvable ambiguity. Instead of a cohesive, regulating language, Babel flourished in its multiple practices and defied a singular logic of identification. Moreover, the question of association (as a confederacy or federal state) was never resolved with absolute certainty.

The underlying transgressions of dress codes, an emphasis on bilingual speech, the astonishing attention to translated texts that had more to say about the inadequacies of a national project than any endorsement of homogeneity, managed to decenter the project of the liberal republic as they questioned simultaneously the nature of experience and the authority of representation. The history of state formation was dotted by these intrusions. Since the state would only recognize authorized voices, it thereby fell upon dissident citizens to assume alternative voice and dress in order to enter the public sphere. Often, the weight of this problem was felt in the area of gender and sexual identity.

Recall only Sarmiento's trangendered voice as it appeared in the pages of *El zonda* (1839) or Alberdi's feminine disguise in *La moda* (1837–1838) in the years when both were engaged in political struggle against Rosas. Women, too, assumed alternative identities when they entered the world of work or dared to approach the public arena, as the case of Argentine exile Juana Manuela Gorriti, who dressed as a man during her days in Lima, reminds us. Nor should we dismiss the renewed attentions in nineteenth-century Chile of Lastarria and Barros Arana to the colonial legends of the cross-dressed Spanish nun, Catalina de Erauso, a woman who dressed as a man and supposedly joined the Conquistadores in their march from Mexico to Chile.[3] The revival of her story in the nineteenth century accompanies an anxiety among liberals for the place and movement of citizen-subjects, not to mention the idea of deviant sexuality produced within the confines of the church.

As a whole, these examples draw attention to the faulty social contract that has accepted certain citizens in the public arena to the exclusion of others; they also open the door to different registers of experience not yet codified by law. At the same time, they announce a tension: these cases present both image and negative of the dual requirements of citizenship that insist on the singularity of a universal subject while also purporting to honor plurality within the nation. Too, by the requirements placed on citizens, through homogeneity of dress and rules for appearance, the state recognizes implicitly the need for a public mask. In this respect, the efforts at cross-dressing and impersonation, so richly suggested by the political figures and literary legends of the times, lead us to think that the ultimate theater is, in fact, upheld by the state.

David Lloyd and Paul Thomas (1998), referring to the period of the French Revolution, offer a different perspective on this problem when they claim that the state administers a kind of visual staging in order to control an audience of viewers; the theater generates a concept of public citizenry configured in a spectator's role. These authors argue that the spectator is central to the construction of an explicitly political subjectivity necessary for the modern state. The spectator facilitates the illusion of a disinterested citizen, one who defends universality and allows claims for competing interests.[4] In other words, through the theatrical metaphor, different practices of political representation emerge through which one sector manages the terms of inclusion and another learns to observe the process at a distance. But an interesting twist to the argument can also be made productive here. Lloyd and Thomas assert that the spectators like to feel themselves "capable of being represented" (33); indeed, it is their guarantee of entry to political life. Less a tactic of alienation, the theatrical metaphor allowed individuals to believe that they were part of civil society's extended dialogue: "Learning to be represented guaranteed, if not empowerment, at least enfranchisement" (33–34).

For nineteenth-century Latin Americans—especially for marginal groups that felt their interests were not adequately suited to the terms of official representation—history reveals their anxiety taking form as a set of explosive challenges to convening rules of decorum. Outlandish dress, carnival costume, the sartorial habits of cross-dressers or dandies were inscribed in the nineteenth-century imagination as a defiance of good taste and custom. More often than not, these images stood to protest one's exclusion from normative values.[5] In turn, the state responded with a counterinitiative of surveillance and increased control. Repeatedly, the metaphor of fashion gave form to these tensions of the late nineteenth century.[6] Public desire for inclusion was absorbed by a traffic in style.

Toward the century's close, "difference" had acquired a market and also served the liberal state as a vehicle to modernize culture. Dress and fashion created the illusion of choice. Nevertheless, these elections were offered within clearly marked boundaries of decorum; the mandates of dress brought individuals under a singular gaze. With this discourse in hand, Latin America was able to compete with European style and keep pace with trends from abroad. Fashion thus strengthened the projects of modernization; it also endorsed a mode of citizenship related to sales and commerce. How to act as a modern person in the nation was set out through prescribed behaviors and through standards of dress and speech, although individual differences were tolerated as a sign of innovation. Together, they created the illusion of plurality necessary for the image of a fledgling democracy.

This nineteenth-century legacy serves to establish terms for comparison with the recent and troubled Southern Cone history from the years of dictatorship to the period of market-run neoliberal rule.[7] Here, the transformational effects of dress and gendered identity (with its collateral found in acts of impersonation, copy, and disguise) allow a way to talk about the democratic transition, to track the course of altered identities as they first answer the authority of the state and later become compromised in a free-market spectacle that commodifies this "difference." In other words, under dictatorship, when the state posited a need for fixed subjectivities and stable positions of meaning as a way to control citizens' movement, writers and artists turned to the mask as part of a contestatory practice, a proposal for antiauthoritarian action. Nevertheless, with redemocratization, as configured under a neoliberal agenda, these tropes of identity now acquire another value, linking the experience of spectacle to commerce. With the globalization of capital, the constant movements of labor and markets, the advancement of a mass-media project that repositions our readings of local culture, fashion, sales, and the camera lens create a peculiar politics of identity; citizenship is defined as performance. This predominantly visual mode, which under dictatorship was initiated in response to the state's tactics of surveillance, belongs to the business of media flows. For its widespread influence, it orients our understanding of public and private dimensions of life; it shapes electoral campaigns and consumer preferences; it conditions us for immediate gratification. Dress and style count more than any program of collective well-being and needs. Beyond the independent aesthetic project that the mask and disguise often supply, one finds the social dilemma that dual identity—as a tension between some authentic model and its derivative or copy—produces for both critics and authors.

Copy and Citation

Consider two positions on the copy that have enjoyed wide readership in recent years as red flags within the burgeoning field of Latin American cultural studies: I have in mind the texts belonging to Nelly Richard and Roberto Schwarz. From the time of publication of her book *La estratificación de los márgenes* (1989), Nelly Richard has alerted us to the ironies implicit in the discourse on Latin American "otherness," which deprives Latin America of any sense of an authentic voice: "It deprives us of the chance to be actors—instead of tokens—in our own construction of discourse" (49). Otherness brings forth the relation between copy and model and reminds us of the secondary positioning of Latin America with respect to metropolitan theory.[8] Never destined to achieve equal status with Anglo-European critical production, Latin American intellectual legitimacy is always threatened, relegated to minor status. A retaliatory measure is often heard in the *style* of the imitation. In other words, derivative practices identified with Latin American cultural production carry an element of sabotage, a counterinitiative that undermines the validity of any "original" model. Argentine Germán García also claims that practices such as pastiche or cultural imitation constitute a form of "revenge" on the dominant metropolitan center; he reminds us that the word *parodiar*, or parody, revives the sense of the odious (*para odiar*).[9] In this vein, Richard finds that the copy devalues the foundational authenticity of metropolitan models; it pledges an act of sabotage initiated from peripheral locations.

By contrast, Roberto Schwarz, in "Misplaced Ideas" (1992), shows how the appropriation and transformation of European ideas (in nineteenth-century Brazil) obeys initiatives of a different order. Despite the fact that Latin American intellectuals insist on the rule of the copy in relationship to a European "original," the fit is always inadequate; like a set of borrowed clothing, the original is often several sizes too large. Nevertheless, the practice of cultural copying also responds to a separate project, quite local in its foundation: for Schwarz, it offers the privileged classes a way to avoid engagement with popular sectors at home. Cultural copying of the metropolis allows local elites to flee their environment of conflict and seek their identities elsewhere.

Schwarz's perspective alerts us to the dangers of using terms such as *inauthentic* and *secondariness* in identitarian debates. Rather than underscoring the relation of Latin American intellectuals to a foreign metropolitan source, he draws attention to the local context of struggles. Beyond his lucid commentary, I want to take the discussion of authenticity and its copy to marginal communities themselves and claim that the metaphor of the mask, the simulacra that confuse copy and model in our postmodern cultures, are part of an *internal* dynamic forged from the struggles *within* oppositional communities. In this context, gender also enters the narrative of cultural copying and evacuates the traditional masculine and feminine roles that have been formed as part of the identitarian practices belonging to the state; they dismantle authoritarian expressions of knowledge and refute the assuredness of naming and create a challenge to conventional forms of representation. Neither a parodic voice nor a slavish deference to a foreign model, gender reversals—along with the Bakhtinian carnival that is so much a part of our critical debate—emerge from the popular sectors as a direct resistance to reigning local politics and a closed circuitry in the management of literature and art.

This experience is synthesized with cogency and humor in the performance work of Pedro Lemebel and Francisco Casas, two gay social activists who assumed an identity as the "Yeguas del apocalípsis" (The mares of the apocalypse), presumably a pun on Blasco Ibáñez's novel or on the citation of masculine power that Tyrone Power made famous in the film adaptation. Their cross-dressed performances were especially significant in their work against the military regime in order to draw attention to the duplicities of the Chilean state and to warn of the control it exercised over the identities of citizens. Their later work, with the transition to democracy, signaled a critique of the flattening effects of the market.[10] Although their tableau vivant of "The Two Fridas" is perhaps best known to a critical public, a videotaped performance protest they staged at the door of an art theater, the Cine Normandie in Santiago, at the time of democratic return highlights relevant issues here.[11] *Lo que el Sida se llevó* (Gone with the wind of AIDS, 1991), directed by Francisco Casas and Pedro Lemebel, recreates an environment reminiscent of the Hollywood Academy Awards, with spotlights, racing camera men and fervid reporters, actors posing before the camera eye—all with the requisite sunglasses and smiles to greet the crowds—and Lemebel and Casas among them, dressed as the principal movieland divas; as a whole, they parody the glamor and excitement of Oscar night as televised to millions.[12] But the celebration is also an act of mourning for neoliberalism's disregard for art; in effect, the video celebrates the Normandie's final night. A small theater that hosted foreign films and one of the few sites of permissible congregation for intellectuals during the years of Pinochet's regime, Cine Normandie was to be closed in order to make way for a modern shopping complex.

Lemebel and Casas, along with a host of Chilean intellectuals and artists who attended the final show, articulate a crisis of market-run rule. Two phenomena deserve special mention: first, the video artists answer the Chilean government's leap to neoliberalism by highlighting the cultural dependency that informs the new economics. Chile, in order to succeed, must copy the neighbor to the north; locked in a prescribed role of imitative form, the simulacrum reigns. In this respect, the Hollywood copy captures the power of modernization. Nevertheless, this promotion can never find a comfortable match in Santiago de Chile; too large for local life, the Hollywood celebration announces the failure of a copy that will never compete with its model. Second, the video laments the end of a particular style of intellectual culture. Casas and Lemebel choose the Hollywood icon that disseminates fantasies of United States life throughout Chile in order to inquire about the impoverished future of dialogue and art. The price to be paid for introducing the Hollywood model in Chile is the reduction of an intellectual arena, the control of analysis and debate, the sacrifice of sustained critique in deference to the draw of glamor. Although it was limited during the dictatorship years, intellectual life under democracy also lacks a space for dissent.

The video offered by Lemebel and Casas reminds us of the losses sustained in favor of commercial, market-run imports; today, the Cine Normandie has been refashioned as an upscale theater for current blockbuster films. Ironically, the video is silent but for the background buzz of passersby; no conversation is heard, no voice in "off" narrates the proceedings. The spectacle blocks dialogue and debate; it paralyzes the flow of ideas. The community of speakers recorded on film lacks a name in the neoliberal order.

It should be obvious that the display of image and copy interfaces with a critique of ideology and media control. In effect, the tension between these extremes invites a powerful reflection of commodification in local and global arenas. At the same time, it overrides a modernist nostalgia for a fixed ontological closure. We should remember that the travesties of identitarian politics are not necessarily directed against the metropolis alone. Rather, the imposturing that we see moves within *internal* dynamics of state and community, sites where individuals are already committed to wearing multiple masks in order to elude the constraints of naming and classification. Paradoxically, this problem emerges at a time when civil society finds a maximum advantage in the exploitation of "difference."

The Trade of "Difference"

Following the lead of so many political philosophers, Norberto Lechner (1990) emphasizes the centrality of politics in forging collective and individual identities. While democracy takes as its primary charge the articulation of plurality and collective interest, it turns to three principal fictions: first, the fiction of the political arena as a determinant of national identity; second, the construction of a closed and limited historical identity that belongs to a specific nation; and third, the internal definition of national identity determined by contrast to a foreign threat. Despite these overarching efforts at control of a public imaginary, politics always falls short of satisfying the identificatory needs of its particular subjects. Failing to find representation, these excluded citizens lose faith in temporal continuum, in the stability of name and place. In this regard, Lechner writes, "The past is erased and, consequently, one also loses the historical distance that gave relief to the present. Condensing time in a singular present moment, social life becomes a flat surface, a collage. . . . Identity succumbs to vertigo" (1990, 115). The state refuses to incorporate individual interests and the historical components of its subjects. Instead, the public sphere is left open for market-run forces. "Everything falls under suspicion," Lechner observes. "Who is the *other* and who is oneself?" (121).

Ernesto Laclau offers another spin on this flattening of identities when he claims that the estrangement of universal and particular demands is permanently unresolved. This ongoing antagonism constitutes the precondition of what we know as democracy today (1996, 35). Meaning emerges from the need of particular groups to represent themselves symbolically, to gain *visibility* in the public arena. By contrast, the state seeks meaning through universal definitions; it cannot respect particular interests insofar as it always speaks beyond a specific body, content, or location. Nevertheless, the category of totality needs particularisms in order to thrive; the center needs its margins. Actualized to our current times, we can say that neoliberalism also allows the proliferation of difference in order to prove its legitimacy. A tolerance for difference creates the illusion of a noncoercive state. And insofar as the universal disembodied nature of state *depends* on the specific corporeality of particularist demands, we can claim that difference is, indeed, functional under democratic rule.[13]

Speaking directly to the question of gender, Monique Wittig offers a dire view of this problem when she writes, "The function of difference is to mask at every level the conflicts of interest, including ideological ones."[14] Any assertion of group autonomy is seen as a kind of subjection, serving a project that lies beyond purely emancipatory goals. Like the spectacle produced by Lemebel and Casas, the claim to difference is always embedded in a heavily structured platform of ideologies that enacts a tension between stasis and change. We thereby become trapped, as Judith Butler observes, in a "tropological quandary" (1997a, 4), an endless push-and-pull between universal and particular needs.

The enactment of this polemic depends on a metaphor of spatialization, a realignment of elite and popular cultures, attempts at territorial shiftings. Indeed, the tension between original and copy, between authenticity and disguise, between normative heterosexuality and its alternatives is really a matter of *movement between places*, enacted, as Néstor Perlongher has told us—with forceful Deleuzian resonance—usually outside the law, from the initiatives of the *malandro*, or rogue.[15] Through movement, bilingual signifiers surface to displace singular meanings; multiplicity escapes the single unit of trade needed for commodification. This kind of spatial expansion overrides the social boundaries usually assigned by the state.[16] In this respect, the state is the equivalent of an ever-vigilant "eye" from which we constantly flee.

The Eye of the State

Fredric Jameson (1992) has revisited the scopic regime, explaining a history of the gaze that corresponds to three distinct phases: in a first moment, belonging to the colonial encounter, sight functions as an instrument of domination; in a second phase, belonging to the bureaucratic phase of postcolonialism, the gaze suggests a form of oppression—here, the tactics of domination inherited from colonial rule are now transformed into an epistemology that links knowledge and power in a single visual instrument. The subject of power must be *seen* in order to prove the validity of the state. Finally, Jameson identifies a third phase in the scopic regime belonging to postmodernism, which transforms both spectator and image through the reign of simulacra. The copy diminishes any linkage to history and analysis; all experience is registered in a seemingly timeless present in which originality and memory count less than the spectacle of images observed.[17] The stages outlined by Jameson might easily find themselves condensed in Southern Cone practices occupying the years between dictatorship and neoliberal rule. In literature, these years were registered first by a fear of exposure by the vigilant eye of the state and then by an anxiety about the marketability of performance under the rules of a "media republic."[18] The gender system often set the stage to ventilate these ideological concerns in literature and art.

In *Máscaras* (1988), Ariel Dorfman supplies a political allegory about surveillance and identity that serves as an appropriate example to expand this discussion. Establishing a tension between a faceless narrator and a plastic surgeon, the novel locates a political fable in stories about subjection. Thus, the surgeon, whose physical features we never come to learn, is here an authoritarian figure who bears the power to alter the visage of others while protecting himself from public view. Tyrannically almost, this ability is accompanied by an equally sinister skill for erasing individual memory. Reminding us of the medical models promoted in concentration camp settings of the dictatorship years, surgeon and narrator are defined as villains who extirpate the histories of others while suppressing a truth of their own. Defined as chamaleonic, changing physical form to suit the environs, these characters link themselves to a project of commerce through which identities are bought and sold. Unable to imagine the dimensions that this second set of images would carry for Chile in the postdictatorship years, Dorfman remarkably signals a crucial point in the transition between dictatorship and neoliberal regime: he passes from a discussion of identity as an object of surveillance to the matter of identity as a token to be traded for profit.

Here, the scalpel, the photograph, and the camera lens are the technical props of the surgeon and narrator; they articulate ways to enact control and sell the faces of female characters. They also allow for the juxtaposition of competing discourses. If the surgeon transforms aesthetically the physical features of characters—altering their appearance under the scalpel—the roving eye of the narrator also transforms the subjects he views, reducing them to images in the camera lens; he threatens thereby to expose them in public or, alternatively, to blur their history. These are distinct approaches to domination that determine modes of revelation and disclosure, but they also point to modes of recognition set in place by the state. All history is thrown into visual mode, altering relations between observer and subjects and sustaining an environment that rehearses what Deleuze has called the creative "power of the false" (1989).

Sexualized subjects in particular fall prey to this authority, especially those who take a stand in opposition to conventional masculine roles. With reason, then, Carmen Berenguer, a prominent poet who emerged in the 1980s, opens her volume of poetry *A media asta* (a text devoted to the representation of Chile under dictatorial rule) with an observation about the all-powerful eye of the state: "El ojo vigila y comparte el conjuro / de las seminales trompas / esculpidas en la frontera. / La difama" [The eye watches and shares the spell / of the founding trumpets / sculpted on the horizon. / It defames her] (1987, 9). And literary critic Eugenia Brito, another Chilean poet who also began writing in the 1980s, describes herself in *Viá pública* in the following way: "Yo, la perdida/ la que generalmente surge/ como un recuerdo, un número/ siempre fracción de mí . . . Borrado de mí misma mi cuerpo está tendido" [I, lost / one who generally rises / like a memory, a number / always a fraction of myself . . . Erased from myself, my body lies extended] ("Obscuro" 1984, 72).[19]

In these works, the poets perceive themselves as subjects estranged from language, alienated from the state that has named them. Frequently, *shifts in gendered identity* appear as a condition for rebellion. This practice covers a multitude of styles and both men and women among a generation of writers. Recall only the staged public acts of poet Raúl Zurita, arguably Chile's most radical poet of the dictatorship years and today lauded as the nation's bard. Zurita mutilated his face in defiance of the norms of citizenship in Chile, thereby protesting the physical violations that had been enacted against individuals and national landscape. His *Purgatorio* (1979) is a testament to this experience of anguish. Deformed and mutilated, the skin of his body registers pain.[20] He is doubled into masculine and feminine, human and deified figure; he is both a totality and atomized parts. These metonymies are linked to a perceived fragmentation of his native Chile, which suffers similar violations under military rule. In this respect, the self-inflicted wound is an allegory for a nation in turmoil.

The mask is used to trick the presumed authority of the eye that exercises surveillance over individuals in a nation. Juan Luis Martínez, a poet much respected for his avant-garde innovations, also expresses an anxiety about skirting habitual patterns of meaning, severing the logical ties that construct coherent narratives of nation and preying upon the claims to veracity of experience claimed by the state. On the title page of his book *La nueva novela* (1985) he projects his name with a slash drawn through it as if to signal the mutilation of authorship. As Gwen Kirkpatrick has observed, his poetic text, while never referring directly to the military dictatorship, breaks down the categories of ownership that were propagated by authoritarian discourse. Names therefore lack history, things are different from what they appear. The resulting experience leads him to interrogate sexual identity (that is, "What is a girl?") and literary identities as well ("What is the function of the 'bateau ivre'?"). Martínez's writings destabilize faith in a primary representation of the "real" and work, as Eugenia Brito explains, to take away the sense of naturalness with which one approaches literary form (1990, 32). Displacement is the principle of his work.

Another poet of the same Chilean promotion, Gonzalo Muñoz turns to an androgynous project, alternating his lyric voice between masculine and feminine form. In *Exit* (1981), androgyny serves to test the limits of political choice as much as it interrogates the formal impositions of the Chilean regime on its individual subjects. Like the other poets discussed in these pages, Muñoz makes a case for decentered identity to interrupt institutional power. The state will always impose its own version of reality, he continues in *La estrella negra* (1987). Against such vast authority ("His portrait on every corner" [14]), our only response is our own effacement, if not a turn toward a monstrous mask that occludes as it protects us. With reason, he writes in the concluding section of one of his poems, "Somos nuestro propio Frankenstein" [We are our own Frankenstein] (21); we invent a phantom life in literature in order to resist external rule. Muñoz closes *La estrella negra* with a desired reconciliation with the masses: "El alma de Chile reside hoy en el espacio turbulento de las poblaciones" [The soul of Chile lies today in the turbulent space of its ghettos] (1987, 117). This project concerns many experimental poets—a legacy of Mistral and Neruda?—eager to draw ties between an avant-garde aesthetic and one's popular leanings. Oddly, when neoliberal designs banish from public debate the representation of dissidents and the poor, popular figures continue to survive in poetry as a stimulus for the imagination.

An anxiety for this representation takes form in visual modes of performance, as those subjects neglected by the state become actors on the poetic stage. Their presence seems to issue a fatal revelry, convening all citizens to pronounce their subjugation under military rule and, in a later phase, to forge a critique of the market. Diamela Eltit's *Lumpérica* (1983), written during the Pinochet years and arguably one of the most radically avant-garde texts to have emerged from Latin America, brings these issues together, addressing matters of representation as a crisis of the authoritarian gaze. She locates in the power of sight the basic epistemological privilege with which to control citizens and subalterns.[21] Furthermore, this is deployed in terms of a gendered tension. In *Lumpérica*, the light of a publicity billboard shines down upon a public plaza in a poor section of Santiago and, by accident, illuminates the body of a woman. This person acquires social meaning by the force of the electric sign; as a result, she exists as a fragmented image, not as a self-constituted whole. Even her name in the novel, "L. Iluminada," is a function of the mechanical lamp. The spotlight thus affects a symbolic economy of identity, value, and language; it is the source

of all discursive power and, despite its irrationality, it regulates all relations of exchange and the market value of those observed.

This gaze exercises a particular violence on human beings and their feelings, reducing individuals to object status and diminishing the weight of their interactions. More importantly, it isolates individuals, dissolving bonds among them. In this respect, Eltit's novel parallels the observations of Guy Debord when he writes, "Separation is the alpha and omega of spectacle" (1995, 20).[22] Eltit will attempt to reveal the tensions between isolation and association among individuals in the plaza, between the traffic of identities and the halting effects of commodification on persons and ideas.

The figures who cross the plaza are highlighted like commercial products: "Están aquí lamiendo la plaza como mercancías de valor incierto" [They are here licking the plaza, like commodities of uncertain value] (11). Specifically, the anonymous power of the spotlight focuses on the feminine features of L. Iluminada; the power of the gaze enforces itself around the materiality of her body. Eltit plays with the technological and ideological dominance of the spotlight insofar as it determines identity, manipulates appearance and meaning, and also creates the conditions for a commodification of form. Read in an allegorical mode, this spotlight represents the vigilant eye of the state, which in turn validates the kinds of persons and objects to be placed within public view. With this strategy, Eltit anticipates the market-run democracy that was to be installed in Chile seven years after the publication of her novel. The promotion of some products over others, the dismemberment and reconstruction of consumer desire, so apparent in this novel, later characterizes Chile under neoliberal rule. Nevertheless, regardless of regimes, Eltit's central question still holds: "¿Cuál es la utilidad de la plaza pública?" [What is the usefulness of the public plaza?] (45). Cleared of its original function as a site of festivity, the plaza is today at the mercy of an apparatus of representation. Nevertheless, there is slippage; chaos enters the scene of the plaza by chance intervention as when multiple permutations of light reveal unanticipated views of people and things. At the end of the novel, then, the narrative focalization shifts and, by haphazard luck, L. Iluminada even exceeds the power of the spotlight. As if to take charge of her body, she alters her physical appearance: with scissors and mirror in hand, she proposes an independent mode of self-perception beyond the focus of the billboard lamp. Too, the natural light of dawn intervenes to afford a different view, illuminating pedestrian traffic in the city: "La gente era ahora heterogénea, mujeres, hombres, estudiantes" [The people were now heterogeneous, women, men, students] (208). This is not to say that nature liberates its subjects—indeed, the train of workers also suggests regulation and order—but insofar as Eltit places in competition radically opposed strategies of focus, she announces the possibility of eluding a single, vigilant eye. Owing to the uneven power of these visual regimes, alternating between the dominant lamp and its dark spots, between mechanical dominance and nature, we also glimpse alternative forms of congregation, the possibility of gendered agency and the chance for political change. Finally, in Eltit's ever self-conscious style, she reminds us that the artistic eye (and *not* the eye of the state) has the power to alter history.

Disembodiment or Displacement?

Contemporary writers and artists insist on linking the experience of modernization to the visual mode. By showing that politics was never a disembodied process, but a series of maskings and disclosures, incisions and unfoldings over the taut surfaces of both text and human form, they insist on a *display* of difference as central to the discourse of our times. In particular, this spectacle of representation depends for its deployment on a reading of gender with its links to popular culture.

In *La prostitución masculina* (1993), Néstor Perlongher looks at Brazilian street culture in order to reflect on sexuality and difference. Masculine prostitution in São Paolo offers him the material to address the traffic of bodies that remap the space of the city; it also allows for an interesting conjunction of problems recalling those presented by Diamela Eltit. Both writers invite us to look at the spatialization of discourses, realigning elite and popular cultures over the materiality of human bodies, attempting a territorial shifting that tests both the authority of the state and the utopian desire of individuals for community resistance. More importantly, however, they both identify the specificity of identitarian politics through the urgent calling for a reterritorialization of physical space (in the Deleuzian sense) offered by the possibilities of art.

Perlongher's study allows us to approach this material in terms of the internal diversities created within a single community. The fetish of place (the plaza or the street), once broken down in its component parts, reveals a challenge to the public/private binarism; equally important, it multiplies those sites where different members of the community might convene. A disruption that refuses a set of specific loci belonging to fixed identities, movement through space unleashes flows in history as well as narration. This remapping is more significantly felt in Perlongher's poetic texts, where the full force of the aesthetic points us to the instability of names and historical referents and established fields of knowledge.

Perlongher in poetry cultivates the mask and disguise; he alters lines of signification that have sustained rigid hierarchies of meaning. It has been observed by many that this is the show of words on the surface of the page, a chain reaction of sounds and syllables that betrays the "deep" meanings of texts. Adornment, textures, cover-ups, and denuding, the fabric of language itself: some have adjudicated this practice to the frivolous aspect of language poetry of the 1980s whereas others have found in this initiative a challenge to *depth* that alters the basis of identity and knowledge, our claims to absolute truth. Pleasure, here, becomes the basis of knowledge, an ongoing reassessment of reality derived from one's engagement with auditory and visual realms: transgression is the sustaining trope in this sensorial excursus. Perlongher's work has been promoted among the "neobaroque" poets of the 1980s. A rejection of the solemn lyricism that was identified with romantic poets as well as a turn against the colloquial writers who privileged message over medium, the neobaroque (inspired by Lezama Lima) skips over clear referential connections, mixes registers and textures of speech, and emphasizes the artifice of telling; the accumulation of detail over linearity and "story," a fluid turn against permanence and inertia, words in play against each other become the neobaroque's central project such that language almost becomes physical to the detriment of meaning. Perlongher works to transcend conventional limits of linguistic authority; thus, all sense of origin is contested, the constructivist nature of truth is revealed. It may well be that this irruption of "the unspoken," as Raúl Zurita (1983, 14) has claimed as the underground force of contemporary poetry, brings the explosion of sexual ambiguity in texts, a disavowal of traditional roles, a way to reconnect "high" art with the interests of popular subjects. "It is not a poetry of the 'I,' but of its annihilation," Perlongher writes about this direction in contemporary writing (1997b, 94). Even beyond the dismemberment of a lyric "I" or an act of total destruction, Perlongher's poetic texts explore the relationship of original and copy that has governed Latin American discourse while they also reflect on the power of those institutional norms that set terms for representation. A consequence of this practice, subjectivity is threatened once and for all. This is less abstract than it seems for Perlongher takes the inquiry about mask and identity to the doorstep of the state, guiding his poetic critiques to cover both dictatorships and democratic regimes.

In his first book, *Austria-Hungría* (1980), Perlongher begins with the transgression of boundaries. Exceeding the limits of territories and maps, he debunks the normative inscription of bodies within the framework of nations. The first poem of that volume begins:

Es una murga, marcha en la noche de Varsovia, hace milagros
con las máscaras, confunde
a un público polaco
Los estudiantes de Cracovia miran desconcertados:
nunca han visto
nada igual en sus libros
No es carnaval, no es sábado
no es una murga
no se marcha, nadie ve
no hay niebla, es una murga

It is the *murga*,[23] the street band in the Warsaw night, miracle-maker
with masks, confusing
a Polish public
The students of Cracow watch disconcerted:
never have they seen
anything like it in their books
It's not carnival, not Saturday
Not murga
no one marches, no one sees
no fog to be seen, it is murga.
("La murga, los polacos" 1997a, 23)

Cracow, Warsaw, performance and observers, self-affirmation and denial: Perlongher brings the scene of a Bakhtinian carnival to this poem, confusing nationalities in a blend of heterogeneous desires. A possible allegory for a resistance to Argentine dictatorial rule? Perlongher displaces his political referent on alternative sites of meaning so that Warsaw and Buenos Aires are equally interchangeable in the poetic logic of his book. Too, in later poems of that volume, images of Nazis with swastikas, the cadaver of Eva Perón, the last march of nineteenth-century soldiers, and a salute to dying emperors all convey a sense of official authority. Nevertheless, one nation-state merges with others; present time crosses past eras in history. Their blurring of boundaries is effected through Perlongher's use of blended languages and in the changing identities of his poetic speakers, who move through different gendered poses throughout this and subsequent volumes. The shifting position of speakers, in fact, corresponds to the shifting of tongues in the poems. For their excess, Perlongher builds on chaotic enumeration and catalogues of sumptuous detail, he prevails upon the decorous surfaces of the text, leveling the differences between high and popular culture, between private and public speech. These multiple carnivals of language pry open standard expression, but they also guide a rebellion against authoritarian control. Perlongher's books also sit on the taut lines of geographic divides: *Austria-Hungía* as a nation internally confounded, but *Alambres* (1987) also refers to the wires that split nations in two, *Hule* (1989) as the tissue-thin fabric that conceals as it discloses, *Aguas Aéreas* (1990) as that paradoxical union of sky and sea that is the basis of poetry itself. "Invasión de pliegues" [Invasion of folds], Perlongher called it, trying to define the neobaroque (1997b, 93). These dualities, more often than not, begin with the carnival street band, or murga, and eventually find their way to the sexualized human body.

In this respect, as sexual identities are unleashed from the body of the text, they free themselves from national territories in which sexuality has been inscribed and determined. "An eschatology of the inside and outside and of the substances that flow in between," Nicolás Rosa observes as he celebrates the fluid movement of materials within the poetic texts of the neobaroque (1996, 30). Perlongher's poems become an homage to the mercurial powers of speech; they expand in range to include Portuguese and English citations and the most localized (hence, untranslatable) of *porteño* idiolects, mixed languages that destabilize a fixed sense of self as much as they prey upon the multiple talents and identities of the reader. A political assessment comes from this clash of subjectivities in which no group or individual finds adequate fit, no language is sufficient to define them. We are left, then, with the sumptuously decorative, an excess of style that has been claimed a summa of the neobaroque (and, in Perlongher's attempt at self-irony, "neo-barroso," or newly muddied), a refusal to be contained. Here, the matter of impostorship claims a life of its own; it asserts a linguistic and cultural autonomy free from institutional conventions. With reason then, Perlongher celebrates the untranslatable murga, the coda to the carnival march, the rebellious popular subjects that resist both name and place. He also confuses mothers and prostitutes, and Eva Perón as national heroine with the comic effects of pastiche.

This cultivation of excess that rubs ever so clearly against the popular body is a style of engendering poetry that is as old as antiquity itself; in the decades of the 1970s and 1980s under the influence of certain Argentine writers—Néstor Perlongher, Osvaldo Lamborghini, and Arturo Carrera are principals among them—this project linked literature to sexual ambiguity and defiance. Lamborghini is largely accredited for this violent breakthrough in form that depends strongly on a sexualized body to initiate a descent into excess, to ignite the fuse of language that explodes against the walls of the state. The abject is the basis of this literature, bodies deformed and quartered, bodies that invite us to reflect on the power of the gaze to subject and control the other. From *El fiord* (1969) to *Los Tadeys* (1994), Lamborghini—an obvious reader of Lacan—explores the visual exercises of power through which bodies become literature's spectacle. But Lamborghini also has a project to explore the surface of things: through the cultivation of excess, the flattening of depths, he forces the collision of languages and social classes, while drawing cartographies of the sordid and sublime together on a single page. With reason, then, César Aira refers to this gendered writing as political representation:

> For Osvaldo, reality culminated in women and in the working class. But at this apex, representation began. And that representation had a name: Argentina . . . Argentina was worth it for "its great power of representation." And he explained it in this way, "far away, a woman is just a woman; here, by contrast, she's a woman who's a worker walking en route to the factory." . . . Lamborghini's Argentina is the country of representation. Peronism was the historical emergence of representation. Peronist Argentina is literature. The worker is the man who is really real and who invents his own literature when he represents himself as a worker. . . . But at the moment a man represents himself as a worker, he becomes a woman. This is the extreme sign of transsexuality in Lamborghini. (1988, 12)

Aira's words remind us of the underlying connections between literature and sexuality, sexuality and social class, that underlie much literature of the 1980s. In this respect, Lamborghini, never free from the carnival, the deadly serious game that literature entertains, reworks political projects without glorifying the (subaltern) subject of representation. He reconsiders the arbitrary connections that leads from popular figures to nation, questioning whether the fabric of ideas might not lead from class to sexuality instead. Identity underlying nation is a matter of linguistic and philosophical leaps performed on the sexualized skin. Always erroneous, based on false analogy, and slippage in translation, the identity games that attract Lamborghini force the hand of those who would claim rights to absolute knowledge. A hide-and-seek or striptease show (to take the title of a Perlongher poem), Lamborghini's texts operate on dual rhythms in order to remind us of the perversions of gender and genre while also signaling the folds of representation that drape the body politic. Literality is no longer possible in this world; instead, high culture, artistic language, and especially politics of the state are subject to denaturalization.

The emphasis on maps and sexualities, the charting and reroutings of desire move in different directions in the writings of Arturo Carrera. "Mas mapas / sólo para atenuar la precisión de una / pulsión incierta, parecida al morir" [But maps / only to attenuate the precision of an / uncertain pulsation, like death], writes Arturo Carrera (1986a, 22). Maps orient his thinking, they lay out the groundwork for seeing, but they often track movements that challenge the precisions of form, transitions lacking destinations or points of origin. In "Splanch," he writes:

Recuerda que no hay contornos
(olvido de una posesión que
desposee);
sólo las transiciones oscilantes
de un enjambre
de colores, sombras,
vocecitas
planos de inconsistencia
donde nuestra palabra
se aísla.

Remember that there are no contours
(oblivion of possession that
dispossesses);
only shifting transitions
of a swarm
of colors, shadows,
tiny voices
planes of inconsistency
where our word
finds seclusion. (1986b, 13)

Carrera works self-consciously through his books to sustain movement; he uses the space between texts—the extended blankness on the page that emerges between the dark print of letters—to create a visual play as if between image and negative, a masking and unveiling of meaning. This is perhaps the secret to the poems that he manages within the structure of a book. Carrera repeatedly points to the mask to announce that we all have secrets; by extension, he doubles body and voice so that meaning proliferates from unsuspected places. If in his earliest work, *La partera canta* (1982) and *Mi padre* (1985), excess generates the text, in his later work he claims that imposture will be revealed in its form. For example, in *Animaciones suspendidas*, Carrera writes:

La impostura
la impronta;
el delicioso momento de

atisbar lo entintado;
y lo que caligráficamente apunta
a desnaturalizar lo escrito,
dormido en lo calcado.

Imposture
the model;
the delicious moment to
scrutinize ink;
and to show what points calligraphically
to unnatural writing
falling asleep in the traces. (1986a, 80)

Here, the sign on the page is material in form; if it announces a doubling and betrayal of any original meaning, it will be revealed in the texture of writing.

Identified in his inaugural moments with the sign of the literary neobaroque, Carrera travels through a geopolitical imaginary that leads him in his later poetry to the tranquility of place, genealogy, and family. In principle, this would suggest stability, on the surface a confidence in some fixed identity; nevertheless, Carrera takes us quickly to the brink of displacement, moving us through uneven cartographies that bring strange and familiar terrain into conflict. These landscapes are often seen from the perspective of the innocent child who observes crossovers of identities and names unconnected to persons. Carrera thus opens *La partera canta* (1982) with an ambiguous voice when a female persona begets the lyric text before us: "No soy la mujer indicada, soy la hombra voluptuosa, un breve pie que hace traspié en la ineficacia simbólica" [I am not the woman you think, I am the voluptuous he-she, a breve that stumbles over symbolic inefficacy] (13). The *partera*, or midwife, inaugurates the life of the poem, she at once gives life and delivers, transforming matter and nature; she is desire's expression. Birth and family relations are traditional metaphors for poetic creation, but here they stand in for matters of authority in the field of pleasures: "pero ningún museo ameniza nuestras fiestas, ningún ameno caminante aguijonea nuestro pie. Somos las mujeres bárbaras en vivaques a lo Rimbaud . . . todo juego" [But no museum enlivens our parties, no friendly traveler urges our foot. We are barbaric women in fatigues, Rimbaud style . . . all in play] (13). Traditional routes of meaning organized through the museum or the welcoming mentor are discarded in favor of an orgiastic celebration of what is savage and untamed. Displacement of reason guides the text.

In *Mi padre* (1985), Carrera continues with this theme when he writes with the voice of an androgynous child: "Hacé cualquier copia y rompé el original. Cualquier corrección, porque en la eternidad sólo las influencias hay que exaltar o deprimir. Yo, yo me llamaba Roldán. Ahora soy Fernández, Pérez, Macedonio; no los poderes de una Verdad" [Make any copy and destroy the master. Any correction, because in eternity you only have your antecedents to exalt or depress. Me, my name is Roland. Now I am Fernández, Pérez, Macedonio; not the powers of a single Truth] (49). Anxieties about literary paternity mask a restlessness for autonomous voice. But this restlessness is also the consequence of an identity struggle, an inquiry into the name that concedes genealogical ties. In this line, *Mi padre* looks for different linguistic forms that represent the paternal voice. Demanding yet gentle, forceful yet tender, the father evoked in Carrera's book is sketched on a canvas of varied emotions. Here, Carrera proposes another way of seeing, overriding the nostalgic potential that family life usually evokes in order to test the ways in which genealogy and feeling alter the linearity of text. For this reason, Carrera holds a longtime concern with dissimulation, evoking both identity and mask, the point of conjuncture where public voices meet private expression of speech. More frequently he finds, as in *Children's Corner* (1989), a "theater of emptiness." "¿Qué nos falta/ sino un conocimiento/ de lo discontinuo?" [What completes us/ but a knowledge/ of discontinuity?] (48), he asks in that volume, a question that leads Carrera to search out strands of identity intended to confirm genealogical lines. If in his early career this led to a sense of imposturing and irresolvable difference, in his later work it comes to represent faith in continuity *despite* elisions of form. The child, then, is a bridge, a mutable presence, subject to change and growth—a trope for the work of literature itself, for art about to emerge. A tie to past and present, the child so towering in Carrera's texts is the nexus between nostalgia and futurity, between dormant languages and those in formation. As a figure in the text, the child becomes the basis for a critical poetics about continuity and disruption. In a later book, *La banda oscura de Alejandro* (1994), this movement is traced in the space between trees, the point where wind touches blades of grass. The symbol of poetry and hope is achieved through a refusal of definite form:

> Frente a mí el agua corre desde lo indistinto
> y desembocará sin duda en placeres horrorosamente nuevos,
> y siempre dolorosos.
> Siempre desesperantes en su pasión esperanzada . . .
> "No hay placer en perfecta unión."
> "No hay goce en perfecto reposo."

Before me, water runs from indistinctiveness
and will empty no doubt into pleasures that are horridly new,
and always painful.
Always hopeless in their hopeful passion . . .
"There is no joy in perfect union."
"There is no pleasure in perfect repose." (14–15)

Even Carrera's most recent volume, *El vespertillo de las parcas* (1997), plays upon this ambivalence, as the opening refrain suggests: "No fue aquí, no fue en Sicilia" [It was not here, it was not in Sicily] (1997, 19). Place is rendered uncertain when the poet investigates inheritance and name. Joined with a preoccupation for literary sources, Carrera also confirms his uneasiness about home ("el exilio es también quedarse" [exile is also remaining] [31]). Caught between the knowable past and an uncertain present, the writer struggles to sustain a voice that flows between the history of literature and the private histories of family belonging. We may also read this allegorically as a nostalgic desire for popular roots set against the draw of artifice and mask, a return to the life of the pueblo that is never successfully reconciled with art.

Lo popular

The poetry of the 1980s and 1990s depends on a rare admixture of elite traditions combined with popular yearnings. This is sustained repeatedly in crossed identities and in carnivalesque celebrations. With reason, then, the murga occupies a central place in so many texts as if to announce a linkage between poets and the masses, a way to cut through the North/South axis that also holds intellectuals captive. "Haber sido unos grandes copiones / Fue lo nuestro" [A group of great copycats / we found what was truly ours], writes Chilean Diego Maquieira in *La tirana* (1983). His obsessions with original and copy, with elite and popular traditions, take form in a poetic text about impersonation and the flagrantly carnivalesque. This fête allows Maquieira's lyric "I" to recount a history of the conquest of America from different perspectives and also affords a way to surpass the fear of death. His focus falls on a popular folkloric festival held annually near Iquique that celebrates the legend of an Indian woman known as La Tirana. Combining pagan and Christian rituals, the feast of La Tirana is all spectacle; visual extremism, masks, and ventriloquies dominate the scene of representation. Maquieira's text, *La tirana*, begins, "Me sacaron por la cara" [They pulled me out by the face], signaling not only the corporeal vi-

olence that dominates poetry of these years, but also the power exercised by the state to control and sustain different identities. Official forces threaten to come to take him away, to remove him bodily, to remove his face. But this is also the initiation ritual for those desirous of the carnival march. Resistance, in both instances, is found in the multiple transformations that the lyric speaker might assume. Among the sources, Hollywood provides a stimulus for an alteration of name and visage. He writes in the first poem: "Yo, la Tirana rica y famosa, la Greta Garbo del cine chileno" [I, the Tirana, rich and famous, the Greta Garbo of Chilean film] (*La tirana* I, n.p.): but in a second text, he proclaims: "Yo soy Howard Hughes el estilita" [I am Howard Hughes the stylist] (*La tirana* II, n.p.). Through the transgendered, transnational pose, Maquieira also manages to denounce the history of the conquest, the Spanish Inquisition, and the fascist state, the military reign of terror maintained by the Pinochet regime. Dressed as Indians, Diego Velásquez and the conqueror Almagro, Mussolini and Derrida enter the poem to reverse the flow of history and death. The poet thus opens the possibility of telling "la vida privada de la historia de Chile" [the private life of the history of Chile], thus denouncing both official and foreign models of artistic practice. A crisis in identity is also spurred by the global condition of Chileans, who have been driven from their country as exiles: "El pianista norteamericano Arrau / Los franceses Matta y Raoul Ruíz / El neurocirujano panameño Asenjo / El autopoieta Humberto Maturana / El parisino Marqués de Cuevas" [The North American pianist Arrau / The Frenchmen Matta and Raoul Ruíz / The Panamanian neurosurgeon Asenjo / The poeta Humberto Maturana / The Parisian Marquis de Cuevas] ("Nuestra vida y arte i castrati," *La tirana*, n.p.). Chile, displaced over the globe owing to its diasporic fate, refuses a single voice and surpasses local boundaries of culture; against a return to some original form, it surrenders to imitation and copy. To remain at home, by contrast, is to accede to the demands of death. Allegorized in the poem, death is master of body and mask, language and physical features. In this instance, *la muerte* becomes a synonym for the state. This poem, celebrated during the dictatorship years by oppositional readers, recalls the street performances of Lemebel and Casas, who turn to the celebrity show to denounce the democratic regime. It also marked a contrast between rural and urban aesthetics.

Chilean poet Antonio Gil also questions this state-bound identity, exploring the faces of popular subjects drawn from rural areas of his nation. In *Los lugares habidos* (1980), identity is defined by the cloth that one wears; it also gives rise to one's occupation and name. "Yo el pañero digamos / la sola faz sobre el paño" [I the weaver let's say/ the only face upon the cloth]

(9). The lyric speaker can be a Christlike figure but also a buffoon; it all depends on one's interaction with the landscape observed and named: ("Transfiguración de mi faz en estos cerros./ Acres de silencio bajo estas ascensiones" [Transfiguration of my face upon these hills./ Acres of silence beneath these climbs] (11). This gesture subverts the glory of the Nerudian epic; instead of declaring the poet in charge of the world he views, the poet here is only an effect of his surroundings. He is not an agent of change. At the same time, he also investigates the human attachment to image; the realm of affections is articulated through a visual field in which photographs and video often play a role. These are the basis of memory, the source of remembrance and history: "Millones de videos y voces. Miles de rostros y marcos" [Millions of videos and voices. Thousands of faces and frames] (41). Gil's text is divided into four sections: Paños, Sintonías, Postales, Calcos [cloths, syntonies, postcards, tracings]. These are all figures that record or engrave an image, graphing the reception of ideas and reconfiguring national boundaries. "Al cuerno chilenito/ olvídate/ esto es sólo el campo de Arizona; reflejado por miles de espejos" [Forget/ the Chilean horn/ this is only the landscape of Arizona; reflected in thousands of mirrors], he writes in the same volume (65). The North/South paradigm enters again to confuse the groundings of names and places, to remind us of the tension between original form and copies and the mirrored hall of repetitions that all but weaken the effects of the real.

This obsession for multiple faces, for simulacra and "authenticity," is never separate from the aesthetic, from the anxiety that writers express about matters of authorship and inherited literary traditions; nor is it separate from their regard for marginal cultures. In effect, the poetic texts of the 1970s and 1980s closely link the relationship between identity and mask to popular voice. This is the point, then, where the formal aspects of the aesthetic anticipate conceptual thought of political critique. It structures the field of oppositions and exchanges that give shape to the intellectual field. More important, poetry absorbs the forgotten others of sociohistorical critique, not only though direct allusion but also through the formal structures of the debate. Accordingly, these inflections often rescue marginalized poets by linking them with popular subjects; they offer the possibility of bridging different cultures, joining "high" and "low" in a single location, drawing together the sober and festive for collective recognition.

In her poem, "Murga" (*Eroica* 1988), Diana Bellessi manages this problem aggressively as she integrates the representation of women with the murga. The popular culture of the streets, the marching of feet to drum beats, the public fanfare of costumed figures and unidentifiable voices, are confused with the rhythms of pleasure expressed by female bodies. Similarly, women's desire for each other also recalls ancient rituals of community. Throughout this volume, Bellessi urges us to locate the politics of the poem in the bridge between different constituencies and in the common gestures they share: faces and masks, virgins and lovers, naked and costumed dancers, the "cara y contracara" [heads and tails] of social experience. In this respect, the murga orchestrates the possibility of community staged by the poor of the earth, but it also allows alternative identities to be claimed; it is at once a celebration of merger and difference, a proclamation of festivity and fear. In Bellessi's poem, the street musicians are accompanied by a constituency of women who are the rearguard of the march:

el grupo
de danzantes sometidos
al terror del golpe
que invade el hueso
Sobre la testa
penachos de cortadera
alas
de la inmensa máscara
el cuerpo entero
una máscara
menear preciso
seguido apenas por la larga capa
leopardo rozando el polvo
de sudor rociado
Vírgenes intocables
travestis sobre el altar
la calle
Y sólo atrás
las muchachas
morenas de ceñidas piernas
pies caderas hombros tetas
derramar del brillo
en millones de lentejuelas
satén tafeta
la espalda tensa
el arco antiguo
carcaj cargado
fantasma
desnudas caras

altivas y violentas
cierran el cortejo
Abren el cortejo
al Pueblo entero
devorado
por el terror del golpe
el bombo
que invade el hueso
sagrado

the group
of dancers subjected
to the fear of the beat
that invades the bone
On their crowns
crests of wings
cut
from a giant mask
the whole body
a mask
precise movement
followed by a long leopard
cape grazing the dust
of beaded sweat
Untouchable virgins
drag queens on the altar
of the street
And only behind
the girls
with trim brown legs
feet hips shoulders breasts
spilling their brilliance in millions of sequins
sateen and taffeta
backs straight
the ancient arch
quiver poised
phantoms
naked faces
violent and proud
they close the march
They open the march

to the entire Pueblo
devoured
by fear of the beat
the drum
that invades the sacred
bone (28)

Together, the musicians of the poor man's band and women find a common ground against oppression in the public march. Joining forces through the festive rituals, the murga is a site to link popular inclinations with a gendered reading. Bellessi also finds a site for the aesthetic: the staccato beat that sets the rhythms of the march also sets the pace for an art of reading. In her poem, the unresolved ideological antagonisms that mark differences of gender, sexuality, and class are temporarily joined by the drum beats of poetry, the drum beats of different passions. Forward and back, first and last, order and chaos: the point is to expand the sober aspects of art, to emphasize travel and movement, to burst open the seams of language and reach polymorphous desires.

Recently, Bellessi wrote of her ongoing interest in the murga as the site for unlimited social possibilities, drawing a pact between women and the poor: "I consider myself part of the rearguard, because this position links me to the rearguard of the murga, where women habitually march, becoming the border zone between the murga and the masses. For me, this border is the authentic avant-garde."[24] Like Perlongher, who found in the street a challenge to social institutions, Bellessi also locates the possibilities for social rebellion through links among women and other marginal sectors. This multiplicity blends elite and popular knowledge; more specifically, it obliges us to think of the ways in which gendered interests constantly cut across the grain of aesthetic pleasure.

Puig and Aira: At Play in the Fields of "Difference"

The march of carnival, these authors remind us, is used to bring community in confrontation with hierarchies of power; it announces competing epistemologies that produce different routes of access to knowledge. It travels on a tightrope of transparency and opaqueness, between excess as defiance and camouflage as self-protection, a tension, as Guillermo Olivera tells us, that marks the politics of identity in our current times (1999, 143–44). But it also invites a reflection on concepts of stability and place that anchor social identity and literary art. Like the exercise of translation that transforms its source as it finds a voice, this Southern Cone spectacle of identity politics rethinks *connections* among dissimilar groups; instead of laying claim to any essentialized or original meaning, it alters the relationship between actors and spectators, between elite and popular traditions; finally, and most important, it alters the terms of aesthetic pleasure. This tour of contemporary texts with a focus on gendered relations is intended to show that these threads weave a tapestry of relentless concerns about sexual knowledge and aesthetic practice, inserted in the transition between authoritarian politics and neoliberal rule. In particular, Manuel Puig and César Aira bring forward these debates in fiction, taking matters of sexual identity to explain the consequences of the "turn of difference." I want to begin here to think about Puig's critique of an authoritarian agenda and move to Aira's novels in which he contemplates the spectacle of difference within the context of democracy and market.

Puig may seem anachronistic in a book devoted to postdictatorship culture, yet the value of his proposals still continues to inspire debate about the relationship between sexuality and literature, between authoritarian and neoliberal regimes, and, further, between a culture that once believed in "truth" and one that surrenders to the appeal of the market. A significant presence in Argentine literature from the late 1960s and 1970s, Puig brought the identitarian debate to the doorstep of literary culture, negotiating logical constructions of "truth" and the markers of "high" and "low" cultures far before they were to become the object of study by many recent postmoderns. Specifically, the framework of sexual politics that underlies all of Puig's novels sustains this field for discussion, bringing into contact exercises of abstract universality and the particularisms of desire. Here, Puig's work is followed by the novels of César Aira, whose literary trajectory begins much later and who is a direct heir to Puig. Aira offers an ongoing evaluation of the limits of knowledge, using the gendered trope as a way to understand the fallacies of our thinking about difference; he brings to ironic completion the masculine inquiry sustained throughout two decades in the Southern Cone insofar as he revisits the relationship between sexuality and politics, between sexuality and the avant-garde. As a whole, these writers allow us to track the way our identitarian projects are pinned to our desire for spectacle and in turn linked to an overarching motive of commerce and profit.

Puig is always suspicious of the weight assigned to identificatory labels; as a result, he turns to a set of vexing ironies to comment on our penchants for difference. Here, we come to learn that the symbolic realm controlled by the state fails to register the range of our fantasies; as such, Puig would insist that all of us share in deviant markers, which become normativized only when our desire encounters expression as a unit of commercial exchange. This problematic touches on the crucial yet inevitably failed relationship between desire and representation.

From *La traición de Rita Hayworth*, Puig insists that identity is implicated in a system of commerce. An exchange economy sets alternatives to the spatial distribution of public and private oppositions; it registers the contradictions between a closed domestic unit and a global flow of commodities that permeate the home through the visual media. "To seduce, narrate, and sell . . . these are the three faces of Puig," Alan Pauls reminded us in a still-compelling reading of Puig's first novel (1986, 27). Contracts, which can be read as the basis of a business or a social alliance, stipulate the course of conversation and movement between objects and people; they regulate an economy of exchange. Here, "difference"—as deviance from some universalized norm—becomes a master chip in a circuit board of exchanges, directing the terms of trade to become a driving force in narrative. Hence, Toto's appearance as a dwarf, with his potentially homosexualized body, initiates a series of pacts among characters, and sets the tenor of *La traición*; his stature assures his position as intermediary among the many characters of the novel. Juan Carlos's tuberculosis in *Boquitas pintadas*, Ana's cancer in *Pubis angelical*, Ramírez's confinement to a wheelchair and his bouts with amnesia in *Maldición*, the aging bodies of Luci and Nidia in *Cae la noche tropical* all contribute to the structuring of place and space in fiction as much as they provide the narrative logic and the basis for contractual agreements among characters. Puig emphasizes the *difference* of his characters as the crucial factor of narrativity; their exoticized *placement* in an otherwise normative field of events justifies their entry in fiction. This is where the postmodernity of Puig sheds light on the identity discussion.

Normative behavior lacks both the material for a story and the possibility of economic yield. Both require a corporeal noncomplicity (excess, deformation, transgression) in order to disturb the usual flow of a stable economy and uninterrupted narration. Particularly, when the erotics of difference brings in questions of sexuality, it affects the strategies of narrative and economic exchange. Much like the play of words suggested, in Spanish, by the cognates *invertido* and *inversión*, Puig links the interplay between "deviant" sexuality and money. Invertir: to turn outside in or to clothe or envelop. Inversión: an economic practice whereby one hopes that an original sum will expand to yield a greater return. Both turn reality around as if enacting a transformation of matter: an investment of libidinal energies engorges the normative channels of desire and fortunes, altering the course of savings and earnings, and normative desire and reproduction.

Nonconventional sexual affirmation always interrupts the economy of signs, disturbing our fixed understanding of experience and our perceptions of the real. It alters one's relationship to the market; it produces the ripe conditions to challenge the authority of the state; it opens a space for questioning the philosophical underpinnings of difference. The project of Puig is centered on this kind of proliferation of difference, the multiplication of identities that refuses fixed catalogs of beliefs. At the same time, the investment of these identities engenders a transformation of narrative economy. Thus, in response to the *managerial* style that often bureaucratizes identity and dialogue, Puig plots against universal systems of value; against restrictive social norms, he poses a flight of the imagination. The debate about sexual identities, then, is not focused only on the study of a minority, but is a disentangling of the cultural codes belonging to our fin de siglo. It disrupts presumptions about a unified community of citizens in order to generate a politics of knowledge based on visibility and opaqueness. As such, the play of *inverted* identities becomes Puig's *investment* in a form of social exchange.

Christian Ferrer notes the preponderance of the visual regime in contemporary culture: "The world shows itself *before* our eyes" (1996, 7). This claim to exteriority, supported by elaborate technological devices, puts different subjectivities on display; interiority is rendered visible in terms of a common cast of images drawn by analogy from the popular media or the lesser genres. In this respect, Puig reminds us, perhaps in a Heideggerian sense, that our knowledge of the world is based on the image. Spectacle dominates ideas, it sets the tone for community. It also leads to an anxiety of interpellation—one's fear of being intercepted in public and coerced to expectations of a norm. In the media, under the camera lens, in audio reproduction, identity is produced and transformed; it becomes a function of a visual market.

Puig was always sensitive to the attraction and repulsion of the media and the market, to the invidious squabbles for the public stage, and the power identified with the camera's eye. This results in what Octavio Getino has called "a dispute for the power of the image" (1995, 23), in a world where the production of images is in itself an act of control. Where in this broad panorama of culture can one find a place to record experiences of local activism or alternative identity politics? Can we reconstruct the cultural field without regard for the monumental? Can we peer beyond the surface? Here, in that most private sphere, is a call to interrogate identitarian logic through the eruptions of sexual desire. In this regard, it is no wonder that the metaphoric power of sexual identity exercises such domination over the visual field. It suggests a collision of subjective life and public record, a generalized urgency to "know" the secrets of the other, although it also threatens exposure.

In *Cat People* (directed by Jacques Tourneur, 1943), the first film that Molina evokes in *El beso de la mujer araña* (1976) and a guiding force for the logic of the novel as a whole, the architect, while admiring an attractive building in New York City, says, "I marvel about what lies beyond the front." This spatialization of desire is a way of imagining "essence"; it penetrates different fields of knowledge, it challenges representation. As one is propelled by a desire to peer beyond the surface, an alternative wisdom tells us that reality is without depth; our approach to this field of knowledge derives from a composite of visual data, at best to be registered in terms of proximity and distance. This contradiction between surface and depth organizes the inquiries of Puig's major novels in which even character and essence are explained as surface detail. In effect, the representational strategies of both Tourneur's film and Puig's novel return us to this unavoidable dualism. Here, ambiguity is both the center of art and its sustaining logic.

"She has the face of a woman, but also the face of cat" (*El beso*, 16), Molina says, referring to the Transylvanian woman who approaches Irena in *Cat People*. The ambiguity is indicative of Molina's ongoing attempts at description, whereby he positions dual interpretations of any given image. Metaphor and simile sustain this approximation, but remind us that, far from a single "truth," multiplicity abounds in all readings. Think also of the opening scene of Molina's narration of Irena, the woman as artist. Irena's art is doubly encoded: in the film image (suppressed by Puig), the actress draws a cat that resembles a devil; in the novel, the figure Molina describes for his cellmate looks like both cat and woman. Here, the film's ambiguity about the crossings of gender and evil are replaced in *El beso* by a narrative anxiety for the instability of representation. Moreover, while Irena introduces this instability and opens all readings to double interpretations, her acts are echoed by Molina's habits of dual narration. Molina's stories have double meanings and show signs of equivocation especially as he glides between movie screen images and his own fantasized reconstruction of what he believes he has seen. In effect, the novel is plotted on doubleness of this kind and supplies the marshy groundwork for allowing the reader to think about the organizing principles of identity. *Cat People* ends with the moralistic quotation: "We have whatever inner life we have or Black sin splits us in two." Essence or ambiguity: both Jacques Tourner and Manuel Puig repeatedly remind us that desire marks us as dual subjects, but if Tourner manages these dualities in terms of a moral promise, Puig uses the dualism of the linguistic turn to signal the gap between experience and naming. Far from turning to a moralistic call that might eschew sinister wisdom, Puig evokes these contradictions in order to question the founding principles of identitarian debate.

El beso de la mujer araña is formulated from this proposition, always moving us between the promise of some inaccessible core of dark identity and those designations that pretend to mark and delimit desire. Puig responds to the danger of stasis by playing in transient spaces, favoring a no-man's-land of uncharted wilderness in the field of representation. The novel records a history of these travels, convincing us time and again that the real danger for politics and art comes when the ambiguity of the "as if" is canceled, when absolute identity is named, when all mobility is halted.

With reason, then, Puig prefers to confuse a single story of origins that might link location and locution. For example, Irena is from Transylvania, Leni from Alsace: both are from zones of crossed identities, lands where hybridity reigns; both are alienated from the phallocentric control of a single language. Irena and Leni are bilingual speakers who turn to art (Irena) and music (Leni) to express a dual sense of self. Ironically, however, their voices escape Molina's ear for translation: Irena's vital exchange with her compatriot in "a very odd language" (16) eludes the linguistic skills of Molina as do the German songs that Leni offers in the cabaret (80). These different voices respond to the restrictions of national borders; nevertheless, when they escape the boundaries of Molina's linguistic map, they open the textual dynamics of the novel, thus refusing containment.

No ideal territory is defined as absolute in form, but as a site of conflict and collision. This encounter yields a partial reality, an approximation through metonymy, never a totalized representation. In this sense, the border conflict is paradoxically counterutopian, literally without any single individual's control over place; it provides for a questioning of limits and names, flowing, like a virus, through various bodies, regardless of point of origin.[25] Translation, in this instance, offers a possible bridge as much as one's inability to translate reminds us of our impartial knowledge.

Translation here conveys the perceived inadequacy of a single language, but it also serves to express a productive ambivalence in the management of representation. Whether treating a story of origins or a foreign film script, Puig reiterates a common anxiety regarding the inefficiency of one's hearth tongue to resolve matters of naming, identity, and difference. But the inefficiency also yields ambiguity and unleashes an imaginative leap. *El beso de la mujer araña* addresses this central issue, presenting translation as an opportune slippage between various discourses, a compensation for modes of self-representation that are offered in a single tongue. Note, then, the multiple languages that give the novel its force: Rumanian, German,

English, and French collide on the surface of the text, but are in fact never named. From their echoes and repetitions, these implicit languages in the novel also seem to diminish the importance of any original thought. Allusion to foreign language utterances become sites of investment for Puig insofar as they offer the possibility of transformation and expansion when they travel through secondary filters. But Puig also reminds us that foreign language texts resist proper translation and deliver a blow to the systematicity of codes belonging to majority expression. These languages provide a "zone of transition," as Deleuze and Guattari have observed (1987, 101); they are sites of indiscernibility that dissolve one's adherence to fixed systems of notation. As if to offer an ironic example of this proposal, Puig offers us the documents of prison police that announce the death of Molina. These papers proclaim triumphant confidence in the univocality of official discourse (not coincidentally, we are told that they have been reprinted in triplicate copy), announcing control over the "reality" staked by characters such as Molina. These claims notwithstanding, Puig seems to tell us that the circulation of government flyers holds little "truth" about the transit of different desires; they fail to harness the inner lives and passions of others nor can they engage with distinct systems of reference. Fantasy, in this instance, outlives the will of the state.

In the movement between languages, in the subterranean reaches of counterculture conversation, can we ever reach an agreement on meaning, or will we be hopelessly lost in our particular realms of self-referential privilege? Can we correctly interpret what the other speaks and agree on a center of ideas that is beyond our reach? Can we express communally those sources of desire that lack for a proper name? In chapter 2, Molina and Valentín enter into discussion about the nature of torture: "You *don't* know what it is," Valentín tells his cellmate. "But I can imagine," replies Molina. "No, you can't," Valentín retorts (33). Valentín manages a closed script, not allowing the possibility of a discursive pact with Molina, as he also signals the impossibility of entering the imaginative sphere of another. But, how, in fact do we agree about the field of representation? About questions of otherness, the common dreams of utopia, or the relevance of a historical past?

Puig's central obsession may be synthesized around these issues as he repeatedly invites us to speculate on the ways in which we come to agree on meaning. Not simply to describe, to look from a distance, but to reach a pact that acknowledges the contributing role that each speaker supplies through attempts at interpretation, attempts that often fail. This concern accompanied Puig throughout his literary career—recall only the early novels set in Coronel Vallejos where information shared between characters routinely misfires, the brokering of false information set in multiple discourses in *The Buenos Aires Affair*, the dialogue (in an unnamed language) sustained by Larry and Ramírez in *Maldición eterna* where amnesia collided with the construction of history, the conflicts of language and desire expressed in *Sangre de amor correspondido*, or the confusion of Nidia and Luci in *Cae la noche tropical* as they traveled between Buenos Aires and Rio (and also between Rio and Lucerne) and struggle with the veils of translation.[26] These equivocations between different languages, the repeated errors of agreement on meaning, inform all of Puig's novels, but they are especially evident in the pages of *El beso de la mujer araña*.

Perhaps as a way of resisting any universal signifying mechanism, Puig, during years of dictatorship, tested the discrepancies between experience and naming. In particular, he challenged the epistemological privileges assigned and endorsed by the state and questioned the effects of particularist interests on altering corporate state desire. Amid this discussion lies the question of common meaning and the ability to *reproduce and copy*. This activity often takes place in the novel through the vehicle of visualization.

Richard Sennett (1990, 238) reminds us that spectacle produces a way to remember. Referring to the sense of political community that is built by a *gemeinschaft*, he insists that we lose one form of memory in order to enter into the trace of another. Political reality is thus constructed from the miniature symbols belonging to communities; these are constructions that generate communal fantasies and promise incommensurable dimensions of belonging. This debate strikes at the center of all discussion about the community's contestatory representations issued against the state as it also allows for a communitarian agreement about the value of the spectacle in constructing an alternative language of identity and movement. Guy Debord also tells us that spectacle is "the very heart of society's real unreality" (1995, 13). The visual quality of discipline and control, as enacted during the dictatorship years, is recorded in *El beso de la mujer araña* as a competition for the technologies of telling, a struggle enacted within and against the commodification of dreams. Recall only the touching scene of the novel when Valentín, as he begins to adopt Molina's systems of reference, notices the forms of the shadows thrown by the heating mechanism of their cell. His leap to artistic fantasy is based on an ability to engage in a system of metaphor that belongs to Molina and is distinct from his usual claims to the "hard facts" of political analysis. Moreover, Puig consistently reminds us that the struggles for affirmation that are grounded in this visual thinking depend on a shared assessment of spatialization and *place*.

In turning away from the logic of many of Puig's critics who have claimed that Puig seeks to eliminate space from considerations of the novel, one can claim that space is central for the enactment of a discussion about shared access to representation. Identity is displayed on a landscape of difference, on geo-spatial coordinates (from the space of the cell to the space of the book); these are then negotiated in border zones that unleash alternative forms of signification and conflict (Alsace, Transylvania, the Caribbean plantation). In this way, Puig draws attention to the gap between local and universal coordinates for identity; he expands and shortens the distance between identificatory practices of the state and the more regionalized spaces for the affirmations of self. In addition, the spatial mode supplies the venue for disarming fixed meanings and forms; it is the lubricant, employed in so many compelling postmodern fictions, of the transformation of identities and the eruption of alternative voices.[27] These shifts, posted in alternative geo-spatial regions or in zones of transition, unmoor our sense of fixed subjectivities and the binary premises of conventional representation. They politicize location and bring into doubt the value of authenticity and essence. In the gap between these different spaces, an alternative proposal for subjectivity emerges.

Molina begins with a clear identification of individuals based on their physical appearance and his certainty about their race and gender. These allow him entrance into a system of simile and metaphor where the terms of comparison remain unquestioned: a woman who looks like a cat, a man who looks like a Jew, a man who looks like a homosexual. It is the surface detail that deserves Molina's attention, the fixed sites where the body can be made to corroborate public representations and generally accepted symbolic forms. Nevertheless, it is remarkable that so much of *El beso de la mujer araña* is also devoted to acts of bodily ingestion and expulsion: hunger, waste, and vomit are unavoidable elements of the book and as such *stretch* the body beyond the terms with which we normally see it. These images stand as examples of the ways in which the abject body exceeds its defining boundaries, surpassing the container of the flesh and universal coordinates of human form. Puig in this way presents a contestatory response, "a body outside the self," surpassing the conventional limits of corporeal representation. Sexuality too is implicated in these realities as a site of unbounded representation, as the ultimate experience of surpassing recognizable borders. For its incessant displacement, for its slippage between assignations, sexual representation becomes linked to movement and transformation, showing the failure of categorical logic and the limitations of systems of naming. As the greatest paradox, moreover, sexual representation, in the print tradition, is illegible; it cannot be seen or heard.

This becomes especially apparent in the scene of chapter 11 where Molina and Valentín make love. Here, Puig brings us to the scene of nonrepresentational experience of sex, a place where no one can broker its meaning through usual narration. Instead, Puig gives space to that voice that cannot name its subject, the body that speaks beyond language. Following the sexual encounter, Molina expresses bewilderment with the simplicity of the phrase, "Now I . . . was you" (222). In this scene, subjectivity is transformed, identities are confused, and Molina proceeds without recourse to a mask of representation.[28] Equally important, this compelling scene of *El beso* links the economy of the novel to a dual experience of discovery and concealment, as much as it details Puig's obsession with the relationship between representation and experience, distance and proximity, originality and its copy. In the process, it obliges us to reflect on the universal projects of language. Ironically, then, the scene of sexual encounter is almost devoid of words; the space of the text filled with ellipses and silence. Speech is thinned to the point of disappearance in order to express the paradoxical density and revelation of this dramatic encounter.

At this point in the text, we are not compelled to ask about the boundaries of the prison itself, but instead about the prison house of language that excludes noncompliant meaning and fails to admit deviant subjects. Puig therefore leaves us in stunning silence before the scene of love. Nonetheless, we face a paradox: although we cannot speak the love experienced between characters, we all the same enter a field of universal comprehension. In this regard, it suggests that as much as the merger of Molina and Valentín lies outside of a normative heterosexuality, the depth of experience is nonetheless clear to readers of that preference. For its commonality of sentiment, it is understood by all. Meaning, in this instance, surpasses the limitations of words. We also learn that it lacks a place in the world of commodities and trade; its irreducibility refuses investment for profit in normal systems of exchange. In this context, the unspeakable becomes the ultimate liberation.

Laclau has speculated abundantly on the utility of "difference" in contrast to universal desire. His thoughts are particularly apt for the workings of this central scene in Puig's novel, especially his concept of the "empty signifier" (1996, 36–46). Laclau refers to that expression that occupies a universal place in the hierarchical structures of meaning and value. It is a sign that everyone recognizes, not attached to any signified in particular, but that interrupts the conventional structures of signification itself. In other words, the empty signifier, as Laclau would put it, blocks the continuous expansion of the process of meaning; it temporarily brings the process to a halt (37). There are multiple consequences to this procedure. First, the empty signifier introduces an ambivalence within the system of differences in general; exclusions, fixed identities, even limits and boundaries are rendered problematic. Moreover, since all parties can lay claim to this signifier, "difference from" and "identification with" cancel each other as terms. Difference becomes equivalence; the empty signifier announces that all is different and yet the same. We momentarily reach pure presence; a communitarian fullness is achieved.

Similarly, the poignant scene of sexual encounter in *El beso de la mujer araña* reunites subjects who have been stretching themselves over the chasm separating representation and emancipation. This episode in *El beso* suspends hierarchies of knowledge; it levels distinctions and reformulates commonly held claims to totality. Here, Puig appears to tell us that epistemological confidence does not assist us in decoding categories of representation; thus, the grammar of "as if," the logic of substitution and copy is temporarily canceled, and our capacities for translation are halted. But absolute identity is not named; instead, contrary to all fears of stasis, we are thrust into a whirlwind of movement that will not allow a separation of universal and particular extremes. The sexual meeting brings a momentary suspension to the conflict over difference.

The central scene of sexual encounter between Molina and Valentín announces a crisis of paradigms, an aporia through which the novel leads us to forms of knowledge from a starting point of ellipsis. This gap, which has obsessed Argentine writers from Borges to Piglia, centers the crisis of naming, in this instance, on romantic passion. Sexuality is instrumental in establishing the grounds for reading the body and language, as it also supplies the basis for discussion of alternative social spaces. It simultaneously promotes and cancels the oppressive category of difference. Puig is devoted here to that unmasking, revealing the technologies that sustain difference and contribute to our misperceptions.[29] The process also sets the terms for a renegotiation of categories of masculine and feminine and the encounter between members of distinct social classes.

We have come to accept that the terms for identity are crystallized in the corporate board room or in the inner sanctums of the state, where belief systems take shape and are proposed for mass dissemination, often through the conventions of purchase. Against this oppressive system, alternatives for communitarian alliance and citizenship participation, indeed an alternative erotics, necessarily take place in settings unreachable by that master control. Puig's work evolves from *citations* of difference to *sitings* in the visual field that paradoxically dissolve identities into namelessness as in the scene of the characters' sexual encounter. For that reason, dress and disguise acquire significance in *El beso.*

Roberto Echavarren has looked at questions of dress and identity from a different perspective, riveting his attention on the points of intersection between personal style and the world of high fashion (1998a). In other words, if fashion determines the power of the fetish from the site of the corporate office, style is a uniquely personal experience and sets terms for fashion as seen from below. It offers the possibility of a local affirmation that can reach the transnational arena; it puts the know-how of the poor in contact with a global network. Departing from this initiative, the experience of dress can be seen as a deployment of power whereby the surface aspects of appearance (from the specificities of imposture to the broader areas of representation) allow for different conjunctions and exchanges in a social arena. Dress, in this instance, challenges the surveiling eye of the state yet also offers *sites* for the conjugation of individual experience within alternative political projects. Arrested from a social arena that claims authority in the field of knowledge, unmasking becomes the expression of alternative political expression. In this context, the sexual encounter between Molina and Valentín supplies a site of meaning to challenge official sitings and systems of citation; it is a form of undress as well as an unmasking of language.

Puig repeatedly insists on antiessentialist positions, on the queerness of all identity; he repudiates gayness and normative heterosexuality and even reflects on the social construction of gender as a way to question the general production of knowledge. In "El error gay" (1990), Puig writes, "Homosexuality does not exist. It is a projection of a reactionary mind . . . identity cannot be defined starting with sexual characteristics since we're dealing here with a justly banal activity." Puig looks for the production of identity based not on a ghetto mentality, but on a coalition drawn from our common sense of exclusion. It is a way in which the "I" that is under question permits us to understand a "We." In this respect, it is not surprising, as Julia Romero notes, that Puig's most significant works about the relations of sexuality are situated in the period between the *cordobazo* (*The Buenos Aires Affair*) and the dictatorial years (*El beso* and *Pubis*).[30] The sexual metaphor is designed to produce a short circuit in the usual networks of power insofar as no "official" language or text is ever adequate to universalize meanings. But it also allows one to consider the boundaries of one's exclusion and to form conditions of alliance with others who suffer different although related foreclosures. Neither origin nor essence, we are, in an anti-illuminationist way, produced both within a dialogue of voices and by movement through space.

With reason, then, so many travelers abound in Puig's novels; characters who leave place of origin to find their fortunes elsewhere, characters who learn to adapt to foreign tongues other than their own. From *La traición* to *Cae la noche tropical*, the characters are travelers and exiles situated in places from Buenos Aires and Hollywood to New York and Rio de Janeiro: they reinforce Puig's general concern with the placement of effects over the origins of meaning. As such, he also reveals the possibility of an ongoing negotiation about processes of signification that refute any claims to a preestablished authorized truth and link outsiders from different places so that they might feel—together—the effects of being "foreign." Consequently, we are left with the materiality of the location where these debates are staged; it is also the ways in which connections can be encountered and defined. This is the political work around questions of identity, a way to rally civil society through local and global encounters, beyond usual sites of encounter. It supplies a way to utilize difference without recurring to hierarchy, to maintain human relations without a predetermined economy of sameness. Here, the artistic project of Puig issues a challenge to narratives of origin and closure; it attacks our attraction to nostalgia and to rigid social convention. Nevertheless, an art of the possible is joined to an ethics of connectedness, starting from a common understanding of our condition of nonbelonging. This perhaps is Puig's *murga*, the thrust of his critical poetics.

Tricks of "Nun"-Recognition: Aira's Hare-Raising Adventure

Puig polemicizes the identity crisis produced by state and market by refusing to name experience; by contrast, César Aira exposes the fallacies of logic underlying the process of binary thought. Perhaps the most indebted of contemporary authors to Puig, he explores (and mocks) the structures of apprehension that are central to all interpretative experience. He thus begins with the grammatical aspects of this problem and goes on to play with our understanding of allegory, reminding us of our general analytical failures. In the process, he tests our faith in the illusions of similarity and difference on which binary thinking is founded. One could take this idea from his earliest novel to his most recent texts, but here I want to isolate only two of Aira's major works, *La liebre* (1991) and *Cómo me hice monja* (1993b). Although these novels are not precisely in the genre of the *conte philosophique*, one could make the assertion that Aira's writing appeals directly to our sense of reason and brings us into an arena of debate about universal claims of the aesthetic.

Both Puig and Aira test canonical literary culture from minor and popular genres; more importantly, they test the concepts of difference that enter the field of representation and register hierarchies of value. They know that a story, in order to sustain our attention, cannot survive without the pull of "difference." Yet Aira, unlike Puig, is determined to emphasize the pure artifice of telling, and more aggressively than his predecessor, he questions the philosophical underpinnings governing the logic of representation. This acquires the quality of a trompe l'oeil painting that promises verisimilitude and authenticity yet always reveals its source of fabrication. Most importantly, Aira ridicules our need to *believe* in the honesty of the copy as he also announces, ironically, the logical limits of simulation.

"I could never understand mimicry. It's a prohibitive language for me: I'm a polyglot, but mimicry is my insurmountable limit and it is the internal limit of all languages" (1997, 7), Aira writes in a recent text. Here, he strikes at the core of the identity problem that is placed in evidence when one tries to organize reality within the framework of mimetic reproduction: the copy is not logically possible because the tension between original and derivative forms is specious. In the process, he exposes the final emptiness—and, indeed, the aesthetic void—produced when one attempts to classify things and reproduce them in meaningful form. The truth—if there is one—lies less in the content than in the perceived *structure* of opposing forces. Binary thinking leads us astray. Chilean filmmaker Raúl Ruíz echoes Aira's opinions when he refutes the logic of oppositional thinking as the sustaining narrative of film: "To say that a story can only take place if it is connected to a central conflict forces us to eliminate all stories which do not include confrontation and to leave aside all those events which require only indifference or detached curiosity, like a landscape, a distant storm, or dinner with friends—unless such scenes punctuate two fights between the bad guys and the good guys" (1995, 11). *La liebre* becomes a testing ground for the full effect of this project. In its most elementary form, this novel is an adventure story modeled on nineteenth-century paradigms of loss and recovery and preys upon a central conflict, that of civilization versus barbarism. Clarke, the foreign explorer (a naturalist and geographer), finds his destiny linked to an encounter with a legendary Patagonian hare. He thus travels through the pampa on a mission of search and retrieval, a journey that is crossed with bouts of inebriation, delusions, and hallucinatory images—all sustaining a set of double visions in the minds of the characters of the novel. Other events of the text echo the ritualistic operations of doubling through a confusion of births and mismatched identities, and the reappearance of orphans who suddenly find themselves united with their long-lost twins. All autonomous characters are found to be part of a pair; all originality is inscribed within the logic of the copy. These doubling techniques, of course, serve as the staples of melodrama, whose logic Aira assaults by parody and exaggeration; nevertheless, as binary clusters drawn from absurd situations, they also offer the pretext to undermine all fictions of identity. In the process, Aira also plays with the *space* that supports these revelations: the Patagonia in particular is the terrain on which this work is deployed.

Aira tells us that these vast expanses must be filled with binary images in order to enter the symbolic realm; the Patagonia, in order to enter and exist in Argentine history and fiction, demands the form of melodrama with its dual identificatory tags assigned by a tourist's eye. Short of this, the geographic territory cannot acquire narrative status; in this regard, it is like the concept of *nation*. Both require a grammatical structure based on pairings of similarities and opposites in order to attain substance in the spectator's mind. Here, in contrast to Homi Bhabha's logic for narrating the nation, Aira exposes the *emptiness* of patriotic discourse that, in his fictions, only exists as a set of syntactic links, held together by analogical thought: good and evil, rich and poor, enemy and ally are the pairings found in the concept of nation. Even the idea of *brotherhood* is produced by terms of contrast: a logic of analogy links individuals in a family of words to the exclusion of others.

In *La liebre*, Aira addresses the question of philosophical analogy as a tool in fin de siglo logic that determines the maps and masquerades belonging to patriotism and identitarian politics as well as North/South paradigms. Analogical thought has been an obsession among Argentine writers from Borges, Macedonio, and Xul Solar to contemporary minimalists such as Alan Pauls and Sergio Chefjec. Like them, César Aira affords the insight into the futile logic of analogy, which structures identity in terms of oppositions of original form and copy. But his tone is one of festivity so that the identitarian game seems like a prolonged literary joke (and here, too, Aira plays with absurd oppositions of serious and light, the reverence expressed for Argentine intellectual traditions and the celebration of kitsch).

In the novel, the Patagonian hare initiates this critique and deconstruction. The animal is an elusive and mystical force, generating puzzles for urban travelers and native tribesmen alike. It is the center of a conundrum that tests law in any civil society; it becomes a block to inner reason and announces a gap between desire and language. The hare is thus Aira's way to reach a discussion of what he has called the problem of the "the law of the continuum." Aira has explained his project in the following way: "I myself, proposing me as an example of the singular experience that extends itself in time, climb upon the strip of continuity and I chase after the Monster that is dressed in the ridiculous trope of 'explanation.' In that way, I can choose between possible forms of the real, and I chose, without any real reason, only to force the rotation of that 'wheel of enigmatic factors' that is known as impressionist criticism" (1993a, 70).[31] The idea is not to *limit* experience, but to introduce the idea of an absurd experience that cannot be reduced or compared. But his goal is also to challenge our faith in the fixed reality of forms, to destabilize the logic that administers difference and thereby sets terms for any national project.

In this respect, Aira evacuates the potential of identity politics as a rationale for nation-state ideologies yet offers a plan that differs from that of Puig. If in *El beso* the scene of love between Molina and Valentín is the blind spot of the novel, recruiting universal meaning to make sense of a particular encounter, *La liebre* also offers a blind spot in the figure of the missing hare; characters compete to define it and long to give meaning to an otherwise invisible form. But the hare is clearly absurd—it lacks a basis in fact yet all the same marshals the attentions of disjunctive forces in the nation. Through the rodent, the process of naming is exposed as a joke, and even the concern for the materiality of its body is reduced, in the end, to slapstick and farce.

For Aira, the search for the hare strikes at the heart of our misguided beliefs about the "permanence" of essentialized cultures. Difference and likeness are explained as matters of (nationalist) susperstition. Aira tests this problem against the figures—both indigenous and European—who go in search of the hare. Defining them as prototypical figures of savagery and civilization, he describes each set in careful detail, drawn from positivist models. But to complete these descriptions, Aira alerts us to the need to speak in comparative terms. Here, the verb *parecer* (to appear) determines the logic of characters; it structures their interactions, it directs their dialogue and exchange; it determines all meaning in the novel: "He didn't appear to be English, but there were Englishmen like that who appeared to be Indians. They were even prototypical, as observed by Rosas, who appeared to be one more Englishman among many, blond and reddish in features. From the start, he found him ugly though he had the advantage of being small, like an Oriental" (17). Aira's trick is to remind us that all systems of comparison, which link national characteristics to physical features, can just as easily be sustained with false information or dissolved by an excess of detail. The construction of national character and, by extension, the similarities that appeal to a collective identity are always precarious and dependent on terms of contrasting opinion. This becomes especially apparent when one of the characters approaches the English traveler, Clarke: "Rosas's police force had determined the day before that Clarke was the man who he said he was, that the skipper from whose boat he had disembarked came from Valparaíso, and that beneath his disguise as a geographer and naturalist in the royal service, there was nothing worth remembering" (18). While state surveillance disrobes individuals of their costumes and seeks to uncover "real" identities beneath the masks, it also announces the limits of the search for life behind the veil. As a founding gesture of civil society, the mask confides the kind of representational doubling that encourages suspicions of treason, while, paradoxically, its disclosure promises a move against traitors and a defense of "true" patriots of the nation.

The catalog, the miniature, and the exercise of classification sustain the explorer's passion, but they also form the basis of unending superstition about the magical powers belonging to the moment when one might identify the representation of the *real.* Equally important, they invite us to consider the ways in which regroupings of images might sustain the mystification necessary for allegorical thought. Perhaps Jameson was right, in his often criticized although now classic essay "Third World Allegory" (1983), when he claimed that third world nations, so obsessed with the foundational motifs of individuation, could only produce literature that was an allegory for conquest and settlement. Aira too pokes fun at this illusion, rejecting the masculine heroics that celebrate discovery, but also turning against the formal philosophical grounding that embraces allegorical *structures* prevailing in collective thinking. Repetition and recycling, echoes and returns: allegory locks the text in a subordinate role with respect to some earlier level of meaning. It also prevails on mass agreement regarding the way in which meaning is structured. As in the stagnant aspect of the relationship between original image and its copy, it leaves us in a hall of dead repetitions without hope of conceptual advance. Nothing is ever accumulated, no profit is ever gained; at best, we are left with the trials of art and aesthetic experimentation.

For that reason, Aira ironically positions Clarke, the English explorer, as a collector and connoisseur. Clarke's catalog of miniatures is met by many sets of stunning repetitions and mirror-image doubling: experience is reproduced twofold, twinning all singular thought. Thus, we learn that there is no pure race or family, nor a single, dominant language. Genealogy is always crossed, and no language can claim to be adequate in the field of representation. Translation and interpretation set in motion these misunderstandings and unleash a plethora of languages with different laws for explaining territorial and spatial relationships and for arriving at the illusion of "truth." At the same time, the collection that Clarke hopes to amass opens to other considerations about the exchangability of products. Collection, after all, is sustained in a private space that removes goods from circulation; it breaks social continuity and challenges the process of exchange. In this respect it removes the products from practical reality of commodification. This opens the way for Aira to defend both the centrality of the aesthetic space, removed from matters of *useful* reproduction.

The culmination of this process is reinforced in Aira's more recent novel, *Cómo me hice monja* (1993b). Perhaps the most outrageous of Aira's works, this novel clearly indicts us for our faith in any hypothesis about difference, but most importantly challenges our fantasies about differences in the system of gender. Aira appears to tell us that gender exists as a category of knowledge that comes into being through our faith in the word. Along with the multiple fictions that propel us through daily life, gender is purely discursive, a confabulation that depends upon the language of difference and our faith in some essential "truth" to be reached through process of deduction. For that reason, the title of the novel, which suggests a future revelation, stands as an instructive false start. In effect, *Cómo me hice monja* will never lead us to the door of a convent; what's more, the text, dominated by the voice of a boy, will never incorporate any sign of religious or sexual conversion.[32] At best, as Daniel Link (1994) has suggested, *Cómo me hice monja* recalls the macarronic speech common to Argentine Spanish through which the word *monja* (nun) leads us, through inversion, to an alternative source, *jamón* (ham). An animal destined for slaughter, *fiambre* or *jamón*, suggests a story about the hero's impending death. But in the novel, the final death of the narrator is utterly unbelievable; it is the culmination of a string of absurdities sustained by a six-year-old boy named César, who refers to himself with a feminine pronoun and never gains our trust. *La monja* evacuates the linguistic codes that usually lead us to an understanding of gender; the female pronoun used by the child appears gratuitous. Aira thereby empties the language of the gender system that usually connects experience and meaning. It unleashes a chain of mistruths that breaks our faith in the story.

Referring to himself in the feminine voice, "la niña César" sets the reader's first stumbling block in the autobiographical pact.[33] Equally disturbing, the narration is also shaped as a bildungsroman, but it lacks any evidence of character growth or development; moreover, when the child is killed in the end, he still continues to speak. The story thus evolves from reiterated challenges to "truth," expressed in episodic form with little interior logic. In the process, Aira exposes the fallacies of a narrative genre that restricts our expectations of character, while also testing in general the institutions of literature and social convention.

"La niña César" sets his episodic adventure in the principal institutions of state: school, hospital, and penitentiary organize the major chapters, perhaps as a sign of the social machinery that thwarts our physical and psychological growth. These are sites that reproduce a particular nationalist logic and, at the same time, create the conditions for our collective understanding of the "real." They also draw us to the sites of conflict between personal experience and the state, announcing to each other their utter incompatibility.

Were Aira only engaged in an attack on institutions, his work would lack the complexity that it in fact offers; moreover, he would signal a retreat to allegorized modes of representation that his work, as a whole, seeks to suppress. Instead, the attention to institutional logic draws us to questions of language and taste. This topic is oversimplified by the inaugural anecdote of the novel through which the narrator tells of his loathing of ice cream, a revulsion sensed by the tongue. The tongue, which produces the pleasure of sound and speech as well as aphasia and misnaming, here creates terms for the evaluation of gustatory difference. Aira thus turns the banal experience of eating ice cream into the basis of philosophical decision; he tells us that difference is reinforced by habits of taste. At the same time, Aira uses this initial image to deliver a blow to the institution of letters and to our *taste* for reading.

One cannot help but associate this first chapter of *La monja*, in which César's father takes him to discover the wonders of ice cream, with the opening scene of *Cien años de soledad*, in which Aureliano Buendía recalls the day his father took him to discover ice. Aira's citation of this now classic scene is designed to derail us, to open a series of questions about identity and representation. If *Cien años de soledad* suggests a great modern epic of conquest and discovery, in which the father of the Buendía tribe unleashes his heterosexual passion as a model for generations to come, the father in Aira's novel suggests father-son incest, beginning with a description of his enforced "pleasures" of ice cream upon the son, a scene described with images of sexual assault and forced penetration. In this respect, we are doubly trapped: if Aira teases us with a reference to García Márquez's novel, he also teases our readerly inclinations to find sexualized references in literary texts through our experience with deductive logic. In the process, as he places the child's body at the center of his narrative project, it produces a dysfunctional language (perhaps to spite the reader's goal of comprehending the "secret" intentions of the author). More ironically still, César's body dissolves, it decomposes and shrinks, it refuses to obey scientific law. In fact, the body sits in opposition to the language that claims to represent it. If we accept Aira's invitation to find terms of comparison for the novel, we quickly enter a quagmire of nonsense.

Aira invites us to jump on the "wheel of enigmatic factors," to connect his list of gendered clues in order to interpret the stories. The feminized narrator living in a world of mothers (his biological parent, the school teacher, and nurse among them) leads to a prelinguistic world that should not, by logical consequence, find structure within the novel. Furthermore, a novel of multiple deaths should defy the stretch of representation. But Aira is obsessed with simulation, inventing a "reality" based on literary models. He is also obsessed with our narrative strategies of representation. What, in effect, should be the format of an appropriate story? What are the guidelines of a protagonist's movement? Aira preys upon our expectations of representation; he plays with concepts of likeness and identity, and the correlation between verisimilitude and literary form. When carried to their logical conclusion, these linkages are explained as acts of faith, similar to the draws of religion. In one scene of the novel, the child narrator is surprised when his parents return home and appear at his door: "They were exactly like my parents, even more real than reality" (29). The prolonged joke is against our presumptions of linear logic; of course, a child should recognize his parents, in both literature and life. Hardly a dramatic anagnorisis, the recognition scene is based on one's faith in the normative temporal and spatial order and on a sustained complicity between reader and author about the governing laws of nature. But Aira tells us that the great leap of faith is found in the match between representation and referent, in our expectation of continuity, and our faith in systems of identity and difference. Referring to a hospital nurse who was the driving force behind his medical care, César explains, "Having faith in the dwarf was coherence itself . . . through her ran the liquid of life, through tubes from arm to nose. But we had to maintain the faith. We had to pretend not to believe and in reality go on believing" (39). The statements lead to a reflection on the politics of knowledge and the organizing signifiers that lend coherence to normative beliefs and coherent systems of thought. In this comic pastiche Aira suggests inevitably that we will never possess sufficient knowledge to map all possible variants of bodies and thoughts. Personal identity, in this case, is never representable; it remains outside of the realm of logic and refuses coherence in language. As a result, in Aira's novel, difference proliferates without boundaries; it refuses categories of identity within the framework of history. Coherence, in the final analysis, depends on our willingness to *believe.*

But what happens if we cannot combine our talents into a universal language of identities? What if we sustain discreet experiences, autonomous in form and language? "La niña César," imagining that he is instructing his classmates in the art of writing fiction, observes the following:

> I didn't at all propose to correct the dyslexia of each student. I wanted to teach them to read and write on their own terms, each one with his particular hieroglyphic system; only within this system, could the student advance as in the case of the student who might write on the mir-

> ror the word "mama" and wind up writing, on a mirror, a thousand page book, dictionary and all . . .
>
> So I gave them a dictation (mental, imaginary, of course) and, after, I asked for their notebooks (also imaginary) to correct their work, and with this absolute honesty which you only see in children at play, I took conscious charge of forty-two hieroglyphic discourses which I corrected for each student according to his unique and intransferable rules. (78)

All systems of correspondence are broken. Identity finds no logic in repetition nor does it echo experience. At the same time, Aira would tell us, all sociability is lost.

Aira takes a radical positioning against our faith in the formal properties of naming. He places in question our trust in representation while he also attacks those institutions of learning that have taught us to have faith in the name. The school room, the hospital, the state penitentiary, as society's guarantors of truth, are undermined along with the founding principles of national identity and family. Aira especially rails against *families* of analogy as part of this larger protest. Even families of literary reference come under this author's assault. Thus Sarmiento's *Facundo* falls under suspicion as a foundational text of Argentine culture when César tries to reproduce an inscription scratched in chalk on the bathroom wall. Rather than announce heroically Sarmiento's citations of Diderot, in which he claimed (against the Rosas tyranny) that one cannot kill ideas, Aira's character cites an antifoundational vulgarity: "thecuntyoucameoutofthewhorewhoboreyou." In this respect, the preliterate narrator adds: "The letters looked like art" (49); by repeating letters of the inscription without knowing how to read, he inspires such rage in his teacher that her speech becomes aphasic. These breaks in syntax and structure, this colossal defiance of meaning are part of Aira's strategy to break the identificatory habits of the educational system and to interrupt the nexus between representation and signification, between past sets of apprehension and current assimilation of data, between inheritance based on respect for original models and the transitoriness of postmodern wisdom. Individuals, Aira appears to tell us, go consistently in search of coherence, seeking alignment between the spoken and printed word, between past and present narration as a way to constitute themselves as "authentic" subjects and establish continuity in history. Yet can we achieve a pure subjectivity without signs of prior modeling? Is absolute authenticity possible? Can we eradicate the past and still retain an identity in the present?

In a more recent text, *La serpiente* (1997), Aira invents a narrator who has earned his wealth from the business of imports and investments. Devoting a chapter to these exploits, Aira cites percentages of losses and gains and relates in detail his varied portfolios and accumulations, but the key to this gesture comes when he begins to speak of investment: "Self help is the best investment because it offers something like a world in reverse" (18). *Investment* and *reversal* once again bring us to a paradoxical world reminiscent of Puig's novels. The two words, in this instance, suggest an inversion of the usual form and appearance of things; but this shift is also based on the commercial values of identity that rides through neoliberal flow. Much like a miracle, belief in identity requires *faith* in difference.

Copy, mimicry, and parody, the reign of the impostor and fake: these practices dissolve models of identification as we know them. In the process, philosophical coherence dwindles and threatens the stability of knowledge. The spectacle of difference promoted by institutional forces in order to sustain the field of commerce blurs into a vortex of misrecognitions. In the style of Macedonio Fernández, who knew that the unfinished work was the one that most resisted the market, Aira leaves a sense of fragmented knowledge, which resists linear recuperation, and refuses a turn to nostalgia. As such, his texts remain outside the usual forms of best-seller commerce and sales and instead celebrate the dissolution of identity politics along with the dissolution of conventional narrative form.

Aira's example comes at a time in the media-driven republic when simulacra and theater organize social life. Whether we speak of the leaders of state who plead innocence while disseminating lies or the theater of mass representations that are sustained by commerce and market, the current age seems marked by ongoing performance. Aira intervenes in this practice of acting and impersonation and, accordingly, toys with the habits that govern contemporary politics and culture.[34] It is not surprising, therefore, that Aira's novels evoke a cast of fakes and double agents who betray the seriousness of literature, but who also allow the author to announce an uneasiness about the intellectual projects and destiny of an avant-garde. Their shifting identities reveal a preoccupation for the market-driven images that cross local and global circuits and, in the end run and despite commodity aesthetics, allow us to argue for the perseverance of literature. Equally important, they remind us that the gender system is heavily implicated in contemporary cultural projects, necessary as metaphor and form to articulate the quandaries of politics and art.

PART II. MAPS

Los vecinos proclaman que es indispensable custodiar el destino de Occidente. Dime ¿acaso no has pensado que Occidente podría estar en la dirección opuesta?
[The neighbors claim that it is necessary to take charge of the destiny of the West. Tell me, have you ever thought that the West might lie in the opposite direction?]—Diamela Eltit, *Los vigilantes*

CHAPTER 3

Gender Traffic on the North/South Horizon

In the paintings and collages of Liliana Porter, an Argentine visual artist residing in New York, one enters a world of tourist souvenirs and remnants of revolutionary kitsch, a world in which the relationships between original works and their copies, authenticity and forgery loom large. Her work relies on the icons of contemporary mass culture—Disney products, dime-store toys, cheap ceramic statues—all of which form a still life of our common, global experience. This is captured with particular eloquence in *Mutaciones con platito del Ché* [Mutations with little plate of Ché] (1994), a photographic collage and silkscreen. In this work, Porter invites us to speculate on the cross circuitry of postmodern culture by juxtaposing a plastic model of Mickey Mouse, a card drawn from the Mexican *lotería* deck, a bust of San Gregorio—a popular Venezuelan saint—and a postcard of a renaissance woman, taken from the Metropolitan Museum of Art holdings, alongside a ceramic dish bearing a decal of Che Guevara. These recycled images offer a glimpse of the contemporary cultural imaginations of North and South America. Formulated through factory reproductions, the copies

3. Liliana Porter. *Mutaciones con platito del Ché*, 1994. Acrylic, silk screen, and collage on paper, 102 × 153 cm. Courtesy Liliana Porter.

refuse to acknowledge any original moment of creativity. They thereby negate any hierarchical scale on a presumed mapping of Western values.

Nonetheless, the title of Porter's collage refers to Latin America's great revolutionary figure, Che Guevara, whose portrait is centered on a dessert plate and reflected in a vanity mirror. The double imaging of the hero suggests the way technology and memory dissolve any originary moment but more importantly, the mirror and plate evoke a domestic environment clearly identified with female consumerism. Che Guevara thus finds a place among bric-a-brac, as one more household trinket. In this world of simulacra, where high and popular culture cross, even domestic relationships are defined by mass production. The global market conditions us to regard difference for its exotic appeal, for the eclectic tastes of the consumer; in the process, all historical experience is lost, forgotten through the trade of kitsch.

Porter leaves us to contemplate the trappings of female domesticity that silently order these images drawn from global exchange. In this respect, we are led to ask about the missing female center in this assembly of objects. How does the female imagination move in global traffic? How do women negotiate between the habits of mass society and the values associated with high art and the aesthetic? And, finally, how does female invisibility surface—and become visible—in the syntax of North/South exchanges? Especially in the wake of cold war divisions, gender is traded freely across international borders as part of both a conceptual economy belonging to the academy, museums, and the media, and, more obviously, a market economy sustained by global capital. In the process, a gap is proclaimed between direct experience and representation, leading one to speculate about one's perception of the foreign and the effects of distance and upon gendered subjectivity, and the resonance of critical discourse and literary art.

As defined in the North, Latin American men and women are expected to perform according to regulated desires, to supply a particular narrative of identity that enters easily in the transnational flow. With our focus placed here, we might speak about forms of nostalgia that govern the North/South fantasy, a longing for an age of stability that predates the neoliberal project. This takes various expressions: in its conservative version, women continue to be identified with sentimentality and the realm of "feelings," which provide communities with an illusion of avoiding the gross inequities of the market. The rhetoric of family values sustains this perception and also links an image of well-behaved women and men to a desired ideal of citizenship. By contrast, within a progressive context, men and women are programmed for other responses: it might be expected, for example, that women issue a resistance to patriarchal nationalism, or that gendered interventions might upset conventional relations of family and state.

The hidden vehicle of transport for many narrative projects ranging from "best-sellers" to avant-garde aesthetics, gender shapes transnational consumers and tastes traveling north and south and also reminds us of the ways in which sexualized bodies are positioned in discourse, transforming original referents to produce unsuspected meaning. The gendered paradigm also allows us to look for shifts in the politics of *representation* as a question of both democratic inclusion and aesthetic form. Within the kinds of fictions that travel between North and South, one locates the inscriptions of gender first in the social sciences and then in literary culture. In both cases, the gender markings highlight particular narrative strategies in fiction and theory, but they also remind us of the crucial role of cultural brokering in the North/South flow.

Sights (Sites) on Theory

In the representation of gender in the Americas, cultural relativism determines hierarchies of knowledge, usually with Anglo-European theory perceived as a unitary source of ideas.[1] The North is not only perceived as a repository of theory, the presumed house of abstract, universal thinking, but also it imposes a mode of self-fashioning avidly copied elsewhere. A discussion offered by Carolyn Porter (1994) reminds us of the persistence of this course of critical thought. Porter has praised the merits of comparative North/South study, claiming that it might enlarge the focus of Americanist projects as organized within departments of English. Her strategy is to construct a larger framework to explain hemispheric cultures from the perspective of United States; despite the goodwilled intentions expressed in this project, her vision—like those of others who move toward the transamerican model—bespeaks an indulgence of a fantasized otherness, a nod of recognition to the South without any sustained commitment to the political or aesthetic projects that Latin America may offer. It also implies that intellectuals from the South had never considered this comparative problematic before.[2]

In the travel of ideas, a one-way route is often proposed. Years ago, Jean Franco alerted us to dangers of metropolitan dominance over theory and the devices it evokes: "1. *exclusion*—the Third World is irrelevant to theory; 2. *discrimination*—the Third World is irrational and thus its knowledge is subordinate to the rational knowledge produced by the metropolis; and 3. *recognition*—the Third World is only seen as the place of the instinctual" (1988, 504). The problem still awaits resolution; indeed, an insistence on Latin American inferiority in the field of theory continues to enter the imagination of critics on both sides of the border. Hence, discussions of Latin America's belated modernity have been installed on the North/South axis through the powers of theory produced in the North. Similarly, debates about Latin American postmodernism and even Latin American cultural studies have departed from an assumption that U.S. paradigms provide the necessary, initial stimulus toward opening debates in the South.[3]

From different points on the North/South axis, it is now considered that ideologies have failed Latin America, that the age of utopias has passed, that social movements have lost their imperative, owing to an absence of long-range theoretical visions. In these cases, Latin American thinkers are charged with a failure to theorize; their weakened ability to manage abstract thought inhibits the possibility of social action. Witness only the example of Jorge Castañeda's *Utopia Unarmed* (1993) in which the author ascribes Latin America's failures to the misdirected projects of the left. Figures such as Mario Firmenich, Cayetano Carpio, and Pascal Allende are seen as immature pranksters who forced the collapse of a "great man" theory of history in the decade of 1970s activism. Castañeda's later book on Che Guevara memorializes the epoch of failure. Yesterday's heroes are reduced to figures in an opera buffa, reminders of a misguided spirit that should finally be laid to rest.

With turns of logic such as these, Latin Americans would appear to depend on metropolitan guidance despite the neoliberal paradigm that claims equality under globalization. Here, a contradiction emerges: on the one hand, under global logic, the map doubles at the border like a sheet of folded paper, sustaining ink blots of identical ideas on both sides of the hemispheric divide. Some advocates of postmodernism see this impulse as a way to decenter all hegemonic thought, claiming that in this condition even marginal societies have the opportunity to correct the distinction between high and popular expression, between metropolitan theory and its peripheral translations. Through a global exchange of images—through media networks and technology—all minds are touched by a single system; the playing field is leveled. The historical past is abandoned to emphasize a ready-made world free of the burdens of polemic and debate. In this kind of analysis, the illusion of sameness prevails. On the other hand, it has been considered that difference, while it proliferates, is sustained from an imprint of postoriginal thought. In this way, the hierarchy of values is never completely flattened; rather, in this version of things, it is assumed, as Deleuze once put it (1994, 1–27), that resemblance never quite guarantees equality.

In *White Noise*, a popular novel about academic life by North American writer Don DeLillo, a character in the aftermath of a nuclear spill directs a question to the rescue crew: "Are you saying you saw a chance to use the real event in order to rehearse the simulation?" (1986, 139). Perhaps the representation of Latin America as seen from the North is also an attempt to build up simulations, to de-emphasize lived experience in order to cultivate abstract models. In *Donde van a morir los elefantes* (1995), another novel about U.S. academic life, this time by a Latin American, José Donoso's character asks about the image of the United States as seen by foreign eyes: "How will they see us? . . . How can they understand our vision of what is ridiculous or grotesque or admirable? I guess that for them we are only a reflection, a *virtual reality*" (79). For Donoso, one culture's real experience becomes a testing ground for the other's theory, which then acquires a life of its own; in turn, it is exported back to the home country to determine the lives of local inhabitants. As if to counteract the generalizations of a nationalist Yankee who appears in Donoso's novel, a Chilean protagonist observes, "It's the Yankees who demand that we be violent, sexual, and poor, that we be accusatory, always quick to finger the guilty party. And if we're not like this, they won't love us because then we cease to be objects in their policy about barbarians" (91).

From this muddle of critical issues, some intellectuals seeking to restore a sense of agency to Latin American subjects evoke alternative, if often insufficient, strategies of representation. The process yields salvation stories that announce Latin American triumphs; more than a new utopia, these narratives attempt to offer continually new categories of identity through instruments and research designs often overlapping with fiction.[4] In particular, a kind of narrative heroism emerges to counteract northern frameworks, to advance the agency of Latin American subjects, and activate alternative theoretical frameworks. The mimetic compulsion of Latin Americans to copy Anglo-American and European models is often claimed as a major condition of Latin American cultural life. But more than the mask, which structures the basis of a dependent culture, Latin America depends upon a number of fixed images that satisfy northern desire. Rosalba Campra has referred to these configurations as "archetypes of marginality" (1987, 27), Indians, gauchos, and immigrants who formed a celebrated cast of Latin American characters. In earlier times, these figures promoted a narrative melodrama of rebellion and healing, a romance of survival and triumph. Supplying an optimistic fantasy of resistance, marginal prototypes from Latin America continue to enjoy wide currency and override the sense of failure that has marked left-wing activism of recent years. In this context, Latin American women have recently moved to the center of this narrative heroics, promising hopes for redemption of society through a narrative discourse about social change as well as a new position urgent to the necessities of literature and art. This carries its own contingencies for theorization about the North/South divide and promotes certain forms of identity that celebrate society's margins whether in the "best-seller" texts that offer market appeal or in the projects of a select avant-garde.

Trading Women/Women Traded

Norma Alarcón has observed that Anglo-American feminist theory emphasizes individual triumph, while third world "natives" are theoretically linked together as collective subjects of colonialist or racist projects (1990, 357). In this regard, women outside the metropolis have no access to a story of their own; anonymous or collectively grouped together, they are obliged to speak for their communities but not for their individual achievements. Alarcón continues to argue that women of color are always *examples* of a particular cause. Recent books published by North American scholars give a different twist to this problem. They show us that Latin American women in fact exemplify *individual* values, but often in response to a narrative project whose laws of operation have been set down in the North. This is apparent, for example, in recent ethnography and literary studies that celebrate the triumphs of Latin American women as well as the good intentions of the cultural brokers who observe their course. The result is a new style of self-conscious narrative emerging in the 1990s that forces us to think of the power of mediation as a cultural discourse.

Consider, for example, Lynn Stephen's publication of the testimonio of a Salvadoran woman, María Teresa Tula. The editor explains that the experiences of her testimonial subject have "shaped her into a remarkable surveyor of political and economic events and thoughtful feminist theorist. . . . In the process, she also is awakened to her own oppression as a poor, Salvadoran woman and begins to see the world through gendered eyes" (1994, 1). By insisting on the feminist dimensions of her subject's experience over all others, Stephen comes to emphasize rape scenes, violations, domestic abuse, and abandonment as the key episodes of this book. Representing the abjection of woman becomes the narrative thread of her work. Stephen takes advantage of the discourse of testimonial, successful in the United States and abroad, to diffuse a message about organizing prostitutes, housewives, and single mothers and shaping a human rights agenda to coincide with a feminist platform. However, the narrative apparatus transforms the views of Tula into a story of consciousness awakening, made in the United States. Unlike Rigoberta Menchú, who guards the secrets of her nation and self, who masks the personal in defense of an unflinching commitment to her political mission, María Teresa Tula leaps all bounds of faith and adopts a North American perspective that is balanced against her role as "victim." Stephen explains, "What makes María's story different from other women's testimonials is that she directly reflects both on feminism and on the marginalization and oppression of women in Salvadoran society and in the popular movements of the left" (226). Among other things, we learn that the testimonial subject, on a trip to Europe on behalf of her organization, has come to accept the lesbianism of other women; she explains this insight as part of her general recognition of the full dimensions of female life. In this way, the editor moves from the grounds of local Central American struggle in order to coordinate Tula's discourse with political agendas set abroad. The editor then goes on to insist that testimonial must reveal the consciousness-raising experience of women in order to provide readers with "an important model for feminist analysis" (227). It is clear that the Latin American speaking voice volleys with North American theoretical demands, but in order to set the game in action, Stephen's narrative court is paved with the materials of rescue and conversion. When enacted upon a Latin American female subject, the strategy necessarily evokes scenes of abjection and also dismisses political concerns that lie beyond the purview of gender.

A more notable effort at cultural brokering and transformation is offered by Ruth Behar in her book *Translated Woman* (1993). Bordering on fiction and autobiography, Behar's project answers criticism lodged against those researchers who would undertake the transcription of a Latin American "life." Thus she accounts for the difficulties of transcribing the experiences of her subject and her own struggles as a writer who is located between two worlds. In this respect, the story of Esperanza becomes a pretext to tell the story of Behar. It also presents a number of issues in the construction of narratives about women.

Behar is well trained in the languages of criticism and is exceptionally attuned to the debates surrounding the "redemptive ethnographer." Her project, then, is to join the anthropologist and subject—the two are described throughout as *comadres*—as colleagues in a common process of recording *testimonio* and participating in the art of writing. Here, Behar proclaims her difference from more conventional ethnographers; her identity shifts, her status as a Latina in the academy, her travels north and south, and her bilingual skills in Spanish and English allow her to move among a range of postmodern identities; too, with a proven curriculum in literary study, Behar is more than competent to enmesh a narrative of private life within the structuring devices of fiction, thereby overriding the presumed objectivity demanded of anthropological record but also constructing an engaging tale. This unfolds as Behar links her subject's penchant for witchcraft to the fiction of "magical realism," drawing the text near to the fantasy narrative for which Latin American literature is best known abroad. In addition, the structures of fiction are sustained throughout the book, interrupted only when the author inserts her autobiographical reflections. Thus, for telling their story, Esperanza and the narrator are bound in a pact whereby they emphasize creative process. What remains is a "portrait of the artist" story in which the protagonist controls the naming of experience in order to absorb it in an optimistic plan for a new kind of North/South engagement.

In *Death Without Weeping* (1992), Nancy Sheper-Hughes actively considers the important questions of cultural relativism that have been raised from anthropological critique. Her study acts on the ethical concepts and dangers of "othering the other" as she questions whether morality can stand outside studies of culture. Her narrative style is devoted to exploring these issues while also developing a case for anthropology as a field of action, a subversion of existing relations of power and hierarchies of knowledge. Thus as cultural broker, she organizes a narrative about her personal engagement with her subject and tells her own experience as a central feature of the "story." In this way, the anthropological account approximates fiction, replete with narrative drama, high tensions, and denouement. Even the graphic descriptions of death and bodily destruction supply elements of suspense and, in a perverse way, details for pleasure. Here, the abject acquires its own place in the formation of an aesthetic.

Sheper-Hughes repeatedly warns us of the dangers of the overproduction of difference insofar as it annihilates any common ground for discussion among Latin American subjects and North American scholars. This observation notwithstanding, she wonders if this show of difference is not the basic quality that draws Latin America to the U.S. eye. The model constructs a surplus of eccentricities that begs for intervention and analysis by the North American scholar, who then assembles a narrative about community and the restitution of order. Sheper-Hughes's narrative sits precariously between these extremes as her book often assumes the tension of melodrama while she recounts stories of infant deaths and extols the survival skills of Brazilian women. It is this hunger for community, often a pursuit of a lost world that might restore an earlier way of being, that lies at the heart of many North American texts that regard Latin American culture. Indeed, it often extends to writers in the South who seek to enter the U.S. market and satisfy readers at home. Nostalgia and horror around family drama combined with a longing for community indulge the interests of a community of readers who seek to set history straight while also accommodating gender analysis in the course of study. This, of course, finds a parallel in texts unmistakably situated within the category of fiction; think only of the best-seller successes of Latin American women novelists who have chosen to interweave tales of family life with national history.

In the anthropological texts described, we witness a drama of a new kind of political representation through narrative form. They restore attention to the family and install the social scientist as "inspired producer." At the same time, they create a narrative romance around the role of the outsider or misfit who counters the current state hegemony. Narratives of this kind occupy a significant place in the cultural economy of North/South relations, reinforcing a particular perception of Latin American women. And while fixing patterns of female behavior and even offering prescriptions for agency, they produce a kind of storytelling that unmistakably carries the trappings of fiction. Under the guise of magical realism, portrait-of-the-artist tales, or narratives of loss and triumph, these accounts represent different dramas of victims oppressed by society. In this way and despite the postmodern scholars' claims for mobile identities, their subjects become resources once again for "authenticity" in Latin America. These projects serve to relate the ways in which Latin American gender issues are inscribed in a particular discourse in which researchers evoke a collaboration with their subjects to create something resembling a literary fiction. The "expert," so extolled by the neoconservative movement, now redefines authority in relation to the craft of telling and writing and to the celebration of the achievements of women joined in the North/South encounter. Balanced between a postmodern celebration of the carnivalesque and a nostalgia for lasting traditions of family and community, these stories express the anthropologist's self-critical reflection on gringa subjectivity while also valuing narrative art over the cold empiricism of data.

As if to continue the meditations of these social scientists named, Amy Kaminsky—from the field of literary criticism—writes that the deconstruction of gender experience is designed to "challenge the subordinate position of women vis-à-vis men" (1993, 18). This kind of criticism should take "as one of its goals the transformation of repressive cultural practice" (xiv), she explains. Like her colleagues cited above, Kaminsky also seeks alternative models for feminine identity and chooses to privilege a postmodern concept of a mobile female self. In the process, a curious paradox emerges: as the anthropologist moves toward a construction of fiction, the literary scholar looks for an objective reality. Kaminsky thus elevates feminist typologies as the basis of literary study: the exiled woman, the lesbian, the subject of testimonio become the basis for literary analysis.

Debra Castillo, in this respect, offers an interesting speculation when she shrewdly observes that from the perspective of the metropolis, "Latin American women do not write. From this statement depend other corollaries, other truisms of standard Latin American literary history. Latin American women certainly do not write narrative. What little they do write—poetry, mostly—deserves oblivion" (1992, 26). To correct this vision, Castillo sets out to prove the ways in which women writers question norms of authenticity and usability of texts, both as matters of theory and practice (33). Castillo wants to reject absolutes, to look beyond Western categories of analysis to find other theoretical criteria of evaluation. However, in a move that remarkably resembles the anthropological drive to locate gendered hierarchies, she chooses to name Latin American women in their positions as marginal subjects: housewives, Indians and saints, prostitutes and illiterates (293–94) are placed in a "series of temporary situations" (7) and not bound by a particular theory. Her strategy of analysis resembles a recipe for a stew: "A pinch of this, and a smidgeon of that" (36). In this way, ingredients added to a boiling cauldron are likened to a reading practice in which the parts cannot be separated from the whole; Derridian undecidability thus flavors the narrative stew of this book. Ironically, the stories of women are set, once again, in a domestic fiction.

The Pan-American highway of cultural brokers is lined by mad housewives and prostitutes, victims or steel-nerved survivors. Is there another way of imagining this voyage without siting these marginal subjects? How are we as cultural brokers to manage North/South relations? I signal the above examples not with a condemning voice, but as a point for introspection about our visions as North American scholars with a commitment to Latin America. To be sure, our positions have not passed unnoticed. The Argentine poet, Susana Thénon, wrote an acerbic poem commenting on the research interests of U.S. scholars presumably devoted to feminism. Her text mocks the plans of a literary critic who hopes to compile an anthology of Latin American women writers. It concludes with the following verses that parody the desire of a North American scholar who travels abroad in search of a feminist writing subject:

> porque tu sabes que en realidad
> lo que a mí me interesa es no sólo que escriban
> sino que sean feministas
> y si es posible alcohólicas
> y si es posible anoréxicas
> y si es posible violadas
> y si es posible lesbianas
> y si es posible muy muy desdichadas
> es una antología democrática
> pero por favor no me traiga
> ni sanas ni independientes

> because you know that in reality
> what interests me is not their writing
> but that they all be feminists
> and if possible alcoholics
> and if possible anorexics
> and if possible victims
> and if possible lesbians
> and if possible very, very unlucky
> it's a democratic anthology
> but please don't bring me
> any who are sane or independent ("La antología" 1987, 70)

Thénon's ironic meditation leads us to inquire about the reception of North American feminist ideas as they travel south. In her collection of essays, *Ciudad gótica* (1994), Argentine writer María Negroni dispenses with the strategies of double voicing and posits this problem more efficaciously. She observes the ways in which Latin American culture is expected to fulfill a promise of difference, leading to a ghetto of eccentric texts and behaviors: "On a literary plane, the 'ghetto' provokes startling confusion: 'Latin' writers are condemned to an implicit and ironclad obligation to behave in a certain way. Something like a Platonic archetype cast in the mold of a mandate that is explicitly political or exotic or folkloric. . . . Who is responsible for this suffocation? Those who produce it? The literary agents? The organizers? Who spreads the word? . . . I fear that as long as the symptoms of this ailment continue, we can hold few expectations. At least until Latin Americans win the only right which is refused them: the right to participate on an equal footing in the debate on aesthetic matters" (29–32). The projects of those women in Argentina and Chile who address the North/South transfer of ideas through the vehicle of the cultural review continue this interrogation and open new avenues for discussion of gendered identity and social practice.

The Culture Brokers: A View from the South

Following a tradition that is most fresh in our minds with the example of Margaret Randall, a North American who traveled to Mexico in the 1960s to found the journal *El corno emplumado* and opened a conversation among poets on both sides of the border, the intellectual projects of Lea Fletcher and Nelly Richard, foreigners currently living in Argentina and Chile, sustain a North/South dialogue through the medium of the cultural review. *Feminaria* and *Revista de Crítica Cultural* (directed, respectively, by Fletcher and Richard) are the most significant publications in the Southern Cone to examine a North/South feminist exchange, addressing questions of local politics, aesthetics, and gendered identity. Equally important, their cultural journals are dedicated to reversing the narratives of female heroics that are often sustained in the North. Not alone in this aspiration, however, these publications form part of a larger transnational endeavor that includes such reviews as the academically based *Mora* (Argentina), *Nomadías* (Chile), and *Estudos Feministas* (Brazil); the long-standing international feminist news brief *Fempress* (based in Chile); the independent and radical *Brujas* (Argentina); the feminist supplement of *Página 12* (Argentina); as well as *Debate Feminista* and *Fem* (both originating in Mexico).[5] Together, they contribute to a decisive project to put in circulation a full range of theoretical concerns about sexuality and gender and address the problems of identity politics from the vantage of Latin America.

The exchanges emanating from these publications (they share contributors and supporters) have created not only a lively dialogue but also an ongoing flow of ideas altering the configuration of the Latin American intellectual. At the same time, they seed the cultural field with fruitful reevaluation of North/South exchanges. Their contributors have investigated the organization of knowledge and the possible forms of gendered representation, understood both as an insertion in the symbolic field as well as a struggle for inclusion in agendas set by the state. Taking the subject in its minoritarian condition, the editors and contributors to these journals not only signal the limitations of the neoliberal endeavor but also point to the shortcomings of contemporary reflections on aesthetics and literature. Finally, just as this gendered subject of study allows intellectuals to argue against the illusory "unity" of the democratic state, it also allows one to argue against the illusion of a unified Latin American feminist subject that has been the focus of theory abroad. The proposals of these journals put us on alert, requiring that we rethink the relationship between body and representation, between lived experience and those cultural and political discourses that inscribe it. And indeed because they are independent journals, ephemeral publications usually beyond the purview of institutions or market, they allow approximation to *local* scenes of debate, immediate responses that often turn the table on those who might presume to speak with the confidence of universal authority.

Feminaria (1988–) is an endeavor designed to integrate northern feminist theory with Southern Cone intellectual production.[6] Its director, Lea Fletcher, has aligned two cycles of feminist reflection to focus both on culture and language and on the insertion of women within democratic process. Reflecting on the original impetus of the journal, Fletcher recently wrote:

> The return to democracy saw a renewal of women's activities: a greater incidence of social movements and unions, political parties, autonomous groups, research groups, and professional associations. Nevertheless, no publication accompanied this level of engagement, concentrating and allowing in its pages a mass circulation of national and international theory; the latter, in particular, was difficult to find in Argentina.
>
> Faced with this situation and the crucial need to establish stronger and more extensive networks of contact, we in *Feminaria* proposed to organize a pluralist space for feminist discussion, democratize information, and share high-level feminist theory produced both within and beyond the country. (1997, 62)

Not surprisingly, this call for democratic inclusion originated with a manifest faith in the possibility of dialogue among peers and a revision of language. In its earliest phase, *Feminaria* announced an agenda to study the weight of patriarchal values upon Argentine women and to expose the biases in language that excluded women's participation from civil society (Fletcher 1988). Evidence for this project was supported by articles drawn from Anglo-American and European feminists, which was then juxtaposed to the writings of Argentine women from the fields of literature and the social sciences. Equally important, the presentation of this material always has been anchored in a theory of conversation among women and a clearly expressed faith in the possibilities this dialogue might offer. It is this theory of conversation, produced repeatedly in the pages of *Feminaria*, that has structured a needed exchange about identity, aesthetics, and action. Rejecting the model of a women's "ghetto," *Feminaria* has argued for the construction of a community of interlocutors to orient feminist practices in contemporary Argentine culture (for example, Monzón 1992). Through community, conversation, and exchange through the world of ideas, a project was aligned to compensate the fragmentation of late-twentieth-century culture under neoliberal design. This restores a common memory (betrayed by years of military rule and currently by the homogenizing practices of neoliberalism itself) and opens the possibility of international conversation.

From the first issue, Fletcher published materials from Italian feminist Rossana Rossanda and Argentine women living abroad on the structure of female friendships and the discursive urgency that this relationship produces. Articles appeared on sites of feminist reunion, including the first (and now much lauded) meeting of Chilean and Argentine feminists convened in Santiago under dictatorship, and subsequent feminist conferences held elsewhere in Latin America with the publication of selected proceedings, announcements of bookstores for women in Buenos Aires and elsewhere, and commentary on women's studies programs in Argentine universities. Throughout, Fletcher continues to supply bibliographies of current materials on Argentine feminist topics. These entries organize a *record* of feminist intellectual practices in Argentina, providing an update on theories for social action and an overview of cultural production. Most interesting are the accounts provided of women's participation in society under neoliberal rule.

Reflecting on the current political climate provoked by the market economy, cultural critic Leonor Calvera remarked: "Internal disruption was fed by an unhealthy, external discontinuity. It is a proven fact that, openly or covertly, the manipulation of public opinion tends to break the strands of continuity in feminist experience. One thus speaks of survival or of failure. What is important is to separate the distinct moments of struggle for vindication or the transformational moments, to isolate them in order to deny them all coherence within a larger movement. In this way, each woman comes to feel as if she is a stranger to a common project. . . . Breaking the union of different temporalities and places, with an attendant eradication of memory, has become one of the main characteristics of terrorism exercised by dominant groups, especially the State" (1992, 6). To combat this isolation signaled by Calvera, *Feminaria* has sought continuity between women's movements of the contemporary period and earlier historical moments. In this respect, Fletcher provides the historical moorings of Argentine women's struggles: notes on Juana Manuela Gorriti, Eduarda Mansilla de García, and the Argentine generation of 1880s supply the nineteenth-century background of contemporary feminisms; studies of early Pan-American feminist conferences or literary gatherings convoked by women in the 1920s continue the inquiry this century. Meanwhile, a publishing house running in tandem with the journal is committed to archival recoveries. Through these projects, Fletcher maintains a *register* of women's intellectual practices, an active account of theories of social action and the evolution of a cultural field. Behind these gestures is a desire to preserve memory of a women's tradition in culture: to maintain an eye on a common past and to remind readers of repressive order under dictatorship that limited the voice of women. *Rights*—in the full span of political and legal claims as well as women's access to public culture—become the red thread of unity that weaves through the pages of Fletcher's review. Always aware of the conditions of social injustice, contributors work in the area of discourse and politics to call the question of rights to the surface.

In November 1996 (nos. 17–18), *Feminaria* recalled the participation of women during the years of military rule and the resistance they offered against state-originated terror. Other issues addressed the impact of neoliberal policies on women (no. 5, April 1990; no. 8, April 1992; no. 14, June 1995). Democratic reform, the free market, and policies of structural adjustment form part of the scope of interests of contributors to the journal insofar as these political problems show signs of disruption in the social and economic lives of women. The neglect of women and the repeated interruptions of equality signal, as contributor Patricia Gómez noted, "the paradoxes of democracy" (1995, 11).

Equally important, Argentine contributors to *Feminaria* interrogate the possibility of feminism in a dependent country whose model of ideas has consistently derived from the United States and Europe. Fletcher's contributors thus critiqued the categories of knowledge distributed in Anglo-

American circles. Notably brought under scrutiny is the binary logic used to mark sexual difference in U.S. theory: models of aggression/passivity (Brownmiller; Dworkin); nature/culture (Ortner; Griffin); or difference as a form of consciousness that advances the superiority of women (Chodorow; Gilligan). *Feminaria*'s local writers and philosophers extended this critical reflection in order to consider the politics of identity resulting from oppositional thinking.

Contemplating the imposition of Anglo-American theoretical premises, Argentine poet and critic Diana Bellessi observed that women of the Southern Cone are always working under the pressure of a "mortgaged imagination." To adopt the strategies of U.S. and European feminism in a doubly colonized culture already positions Argentine women precariously and threatens their epistemological certainties:

> To question a central culture internally colonized by Europe, from the instrumentality of a philosophy of resistance also founded in Europe, is one thing. To include the barbaric precariousness of a theoretical feminism born in the north, still infrequently read, hardly translated and not even questioned, demands a quick local production by women personally involved from their sites of domesticity. This is a phenomenon that is even more difficult to achieve. It means that one must confront a double cultural hegemony from the perspective of a kind of difference that we are barely beginning to understand. When one doesn't even have available the powerful arsenal of mythical thought founded in indigenous cultures in order to challenge the mainstream colonizing discourse, it's worse still. Then one has to work with a mortgaged imagination and put one's body on the line. It carries the danger of appearing Stupid. It means displacing an implicit interest in matters of prestige in order to move toward an interest in the erotic. It means scorning the applause of the kings in the palace for the loving praise of women. In an environment in which one doesn't risk too much in the personal arena, it means loosening one's undergarments and demanding to be seen and to see each other. (1990, 10)

As if to extend Bellessi's reflection on the need for local theoretical risks, philosopher Diana Maffia takes current Argentine political experiences as a basis for critical thought. Such is the case in her narration of the story of Marisela, a transsexual whose children were forcibly removed from her home on charges that she was an unfit mother (1994). This anecdote, published in the dailies of Buenos Aires and widely discussed in 1993, inspires Maffia to reflect first on "natural" categories of gender identity and then, more importantly, on the shifting relationships between sexuality and political power in Argentina. Similarly, the prohibition against abortion—a heated topic in Argentina—inspired an early issue of *Feminaria* on the limits of liberal philosophy as seen from the Southern Cone while later issues of the journal directly confronted the crisis of redemocratization and the situation of women. Seen as protagonic actors in market-driven society, women are positioned as the figures most severely affected by neoliberal rule, responsible for family survival and for economic defense of the household. Moreover, against the conservative perception of a general loss of values, the dominance of a market economy to the detriment of civil society, multiple possibilities emerge for the organization of women. They thus produce new expressions of social action and a challenge to traditional forms of authority (Maglie 1990).[7] The proliferation of new identities is celebrated as a positive response to the crisis of neoliberal rule. It is also a way to alter the North/South map.

A revised cartography emerges to destabilize the North/South crossing. Debates about the artificial nature of frontiers, the boundaries between self and other, the restrictions between public and private identities, between individual and collective endeavors are the repeated subject of interest in *Feminaria* and other reviews. As if to override the dominance of the North and move toward alternative configurations of the collective, attention frequently moves toward the value of feminist conventions. The Women's Forum in Beijing was the topic not only of *Feminaria* but also other journals. Inquiring about the possibility of alliance, rethinking the global and local paradigms, the North/South axis is displaced in order to interrogate the force of the global.

In this material, the sources for research are decidedly heterogeneous, drawing upon local intellectuals as well as public-policy scholars from the United States and Italy. Throughout, however, these critics continue to negotiate local conditions of women at home against the postmodern hypotheses so often sustained by metropolitan theory. In this respect, the journalistic production of Fletcher and her contemporaries first signals the failures of democratic culture at home to include questions of gender. The pages devoted to this critique lead us to inquire about the universal subject implicated in postdictatorial society and the relationship of intellectuals to that universal subject they prize. Included in these different issues and theoretical tasks is a reassessment of the role of the intellectual in our fin de siglo and particularly the role of women and sexual minorities. The gendered presence in these debates complicates the issue of democracy, but also brings forth a considerable reevaluation of the current direction of literature and art.

This critique surfaces most clearly in relation to aesthetics. In a particularly insightful essay, writer Tununa Mercado interrogated the voices of denunciation emerging from contemporary feminist movements in order to evaluate the impact of that discourse upon activities of women writers. Insisting on a position that echoes my own sentiments on this matter, Mercado wrote:

> Literature of protest was born in a mold: one thought that in order to reach the workers or the peasants or the secretaries, who are the persons one wants to reach—at least among socialist feminists—that one had to formulate a direct and unambiguous message. The project obliged us to make many cuts and, in the long run, had a repressive effect. In the world of the social sciences called "women's studies," texts followed traditional academic models and fit into an organized body of knowledge that was taxonomic, classifying the roles of women and their conditions in society. One had to write a science of woman, invent a theory, but without exposing the crisis of language. It wasn't even thought necessary to articulate this crisis: in the wide range of sociological literature, there are very few texts that show the complex elusiveness of language, as if one could never leave the field of description and interpretation in order to reach an epistemology that could make sense of the dense material about which one was speaking. . . . The theme or themes of the so-called feminine "problematic," I hate to say, little by little began to subjugate those texts, leading to a new oppression by the referent of the "real," placing demands of submission on narrative in order to make it illustrate with truth or verisimilitude what never happens to creatures in fiction. It left the story line and writing itself too tied to the dictates of representation, forcing a mimetic approximation of the text with the literal sense of the message. This narrative saw itself in the glow of the mirror, it never crossed the mirror itself. (1989, 22)

Although *Feminaria* has published articles drawn from postmodernist inspiration in the United States (Flax, De Lauretis, Benhabib), it is perhaps through an emphasis on literature where the confrontation of North/South cultures is most forcefully drawn. Here, "la crisis del lenguaje" [the crisis of language] signaled by Mercado becomes a target of sustained reflection. Starting with issue no. 7 (1991), *Feminaria* inaugurated a section entitled "Feminaria Literaria" to emphasize feminist cultural production in comparative historical focus. Joining the names of Elizabeth Bishop, Adrienne Rich, and Nicole Brossard with those of contemporary writers from Argentina and other Latin American countries, Fletcher managed to balance the urgency of a local political crisis, with emphasis on women's rights and engagement in national reforms, with literature while also keeping an ever-vigilant eye on North American culture.

In Chile, Nelly Richard supplies a radical intepretation of North/South relations in her *Revista de Crítica Cultural* (1990–). Although it is not her design to focus on feminist issues alone, she organizes a critique of postmodern debates and a search for Latin American identity as often seen through the lens of gender. Richard thus sustains a local inquiry about the advantage of micropolitics and celebrates the powers of literature and visual arts; in these areas, the gendered politics of the review gains its momentum and force.

In general, Richard views global theorization with a critical eye; she distrusts universalizing impulses, but also acknowledges the advantages of metropolitan concepts for engaging issues in Latin American culture. Richard accordingly rejects a narrow genealogy of the term *postmodern* insofar as it might interfere with real social action and insists repeatedly on the heterogeneous autonomy of local culture.[8] Above all, she claims, postmodernism, when expanded sufficiently, serves a Latin American interest of entering international debate. Consequently, Latin America should take advantage of this line of argumentation in order to enter global flow of discussion:

> It is possible to argue for a Latin American interest in postmodern debate by claiming that we are an interdependent part of a planetary network of influence that puts in telecommunicational contact the "here and now" of all those who receive cultural information disseminated in center and periphery. This globalization of culture in itself would oblige us to take a position in order not to lose a "situational consciousness." . . . Much of what dismantles the postmodern stance (from the breakup of social linkages to the loss of those guideposts and referents of mobilization and social struggle) is reflected in us, although darkened by the drama of historical convulsion (the dictatorships) which shake the grounding of any facile thesis about the "end of history" that is defended today by apocalyptic thinkers of the center. . . . All this reasoning, derived from the totality-centrist crisis, would argue in favor of a cultural revalorization of the periphery so that we would postulate [Latin America] as the main protagonist of the new postmodern narrative of decentering. (1991, 15–19)

Much in the way the Boom put Latin America on the map, the postmodern when anchored in the problematic of the South assures Latin Americans a central place in global discourse. It stretches the limits of theory, usually seen in the European and U.S. projects, and is a force that allows Latin Americans to rethink the asynchronies of culture and economic development, the pastiche of historical memory and forgetfulness that determines one's experience in modernization. Moreover, postmodernism at home in Latin America expands the range of its theoretical underpinnings that so often celebrate heterogeneity and thus emphasizes the crosses and unresolved blending of tradition and modernity. It is this relentlessly hybrid mixture, as an unstable collage, that creates an alternative to the usual projects of modernity in the so-called developed world; in fact, the suspension of heterogeneous materials opens the possibility of an alternative political voice and a way for Latin America to answer the United States and Europe on terms uniquely its own.

As a next step, Richard attempts to draw from the generalized crisis of totalizing discourses to show the ways in which different levels of development in Chile (also Argentina and Peru) break up ideals of history and progress and open the doors to micropolitics. The goal here is to discover what she describes as "the physionomy of ourselves" (1991, 15). As such, Richard is unwilling to relinquish ties to any local projects and thus finds a productive rationale for "peripheral" postmodernism in the culture of heterogeneity and mestizaje. The failures of neoliberal democracy, the detention of Pinochet, the protest marches of Mapuche Indians demanding rights and recognition are present in the *Revista de Crítica Cultural*, but the director is also attentive to the ways in which culture and politics, in both local and global conflict, are crossed by gender.

Richard strikes forth in favor of a peculiar Latin American alterity, ruling against hegemonic projects. Richard accords a privileged space to strategies of citation, to the productive tensions that she finds in the relationship between original and copy. The copy, when used in a local context, *answers* metropolitan culture, overturning the authority of its source. Gender is the field on which this theory is often deployed. And here, rather than offering the stock responses about women's resistance, Richard often shows the ways in which the gender platform is turned around to serve political interests. For example, when considering the Pinochet detention of 1998, Richard details the ways in which women in the streets were mobilized by pro-Pinochet forces. Capitalizing on the memory of women who had taken to the streets in 1973 to protest the government of Allende, conservative forces resuscitated the image of action in order to draw women's support for Pinochet (1999). The point is that all that is feminine is not gold: rather, the operations of memory produce rare associations that push women as subjects through the mediatic tracks of conservative and liberal agendas neither reaching a final determinant of truth nor breaking through the domestic stereotypes usually associated with women. It is here once again that the crisis of representation, so obvious in the way in which North American critics position Latin American subjects, becomes the object of study. Image over action, media concept over experience: the gap between these extremes reduces the agency of subjects to camera-ready copy.

The reinvention of sexualized subjects is a common topic of discussion in the pages of the review, often to show the limitations and advantages of individual agency in political critique. Arnaldo Cruz-Malavé inquires about the emergence of the homosexual subject in Cuba (1998); Jorge Salessi investigates the photographic representation of homosexuals by police agents in late-nineteenth-century Buenos Aires (1995a); Richard herself refers to the positioning of Bolívar as a desexualized historical icon (1994). These are attempts to discredit a single "authentic" truth about social culture, urging instead the proliferation of ethical questions about representations. Often when this travels through the North/South corridor and becomes subject to turns of language, the logic of singularity explodes and becomes unmoored from any national port.

Exercises in translation, which dominate Latin America, are thus seen as contestatory projects not bound by a single logic. Much in the way that Sarmiento had deformed European cultures when he translated from French to Spanish, thereby undermining the reigning traditions of international prestige, current Latin American practices of citation are not to be taken as a lack of originality, but show a determined resistance to metropolitan forms of expression. They are ways to claim Latin America's uniqueness, vindicating alterity and resisting domination. But there is a further turn to this exercise: the copy, while it announces a distance from some original model, also invites one to speculate about internal difference: differences internal to nation, a clan, or gender system; differences that mark temporal order. Far from locking Latin America in the shadow of the North, the models of citation offer a speculation on alterity and difference within the defined local conditions of Latin American meaning.[9]

Although the effects of the translator's turn are not central to Richard's conceptualizations in the journal, the strategies for interpretation this offers would coincide quite well with her projects insofar as translation celebrates the micropowers of cultural exchange, a way to insist on the volatility of representational practices as they cross global and local divides. In recent years, translation has been highlighted as a theoretical issue pertinent to the debates about gender and colonialism, identity and place. In the pages of the *Revista de Crítica Cultural*, contributors also translate public and private economies, regional and metropolitan meanings, and the gender question constantly announces its defiance of an original model of normative behavior or representation. A point of defiance emerges here. It is not incidental that Richard moves into the field of gender debate notably without the theoretical support that North American feminists have elsewhere supplied. A resistance, then, against translation in areas perceived as crucial to the journal's discursive field. Overriding strictly feminist theory, the *Revista de Crítica Cultural* draws instead from a mixture of continental philosophy and the practical grounding of Latin American cultural experience.

The contributions by Chileans Diamela Eltit, Olga Grau, Mabel Piccini, Raquel Olea, and Kemy Oyarzún on feminism and social identity significantly sustain these interventions, offering ways to consider the relationship between sexuality, institutions, and market. They remind the readers of *Revista de Crítica Cultural* of the inescapable importance of gender in the postmodern project, but also the ways in which the gender debate can be heard within the range of the Chilean political forum. They also remind readers of the weight of free-market concepts that is felt by Southern Cone scholars devoted to gender. As a result, subversions of market concepts are traced through acts of turmoil initiated by sexualized subjects.

In this respect, the Argentine poet, Néstor Perlongher, whose rereading of Deleuze is included in one issue of the *Revista*, observes how sexual and racial minorities stir the social body in an effort to recapture institutions or, in the final analysis, to destroy them (1991). But Perlongher is quick to note that minority cultures are not simply concerned with identity, but with the possibility of transforming themselves into points of alliance with others. Contacts especially among gendered minority groups—all identified under the rubric of the feminine—thus pose the opportunity for altering Latin American subjectivity as a whole; ultimately, they present a chance for a mutation of global order while undermining the fixed underpinnings of gender.

Kemy Oyarzún (1996), by contrast, is less confident when she considers the institutionalization of gender studies within the university. For the instability that circulates around the formalized study of gender, the academic institution is fortunately shaken; nevertheless, for its threatened absorption within the academy—for its visible legitimation—the field of gendered knowledge becomes endangered. A precarious discourse susceptible to institutional demands, gender studies are also vulnerable if left beyond academic walls where they might drift toward infinite dispersal. Thus, the academic market for gender studies is both an asset and a disadvantage.

Alternating currents of this kind circulate through the *Revista de Crítica Cultural*, echoing the ambivalence of Richard and a generation of critics regarding categories of identification. In effect, the pages of the journal show a consistent rejection of any absolute category of the Latin American subject yet warn of its constant susceptibility to institutional supervision and co-optations by the market. Insistently, the project of the *Revista de Crítica Cultural* returns readers to the complex realities of Latin America premised on an aesthetic and political avant-garde vision that has characterized a sector of Chilean culture since the dictatorship years.

An aesthetic tension between concealed identities and unmasking frequently draws the interests of the Southern Cone's most avant-garde artists and writers, with Nelly Richard as the dominant critical voice of that tendency within Chile. Quite apart from Anglo-American theoretical attentions to this matter, the staging of gender served in the Southern Cone as a challenge to the patriarchal state. As in the performance work of Casas and Lemebel or the art actions of Eltit and Zurita in the dictatorship years, social activism and aesthetic projects around gender have habitually been linked in acts of defiance. For example, a brief essay by Diamela Eltit (1991a), first published in *Debate Feminista*, describes the instrumentality of dress by taking the example of a Mexican hero of the revolution, a woman dressed as man. For Eltit, the transvestism is a spectacular example of the crossing of categories of citizenship, of the ways in which gender is bound in the services of patriotic ideals. As if in anticipation of the debate about Juan Dávila's portrait of a cross-dressed Simón Bolívar, which became a central topic of discussion in one issue of Richard's publication (no. 9, 1994), Eltit unravels the masculinist charge invested in heroic acts and presents as equally suspicious all attempts to fix identity under the law of the state. Finally, she proposes those social projects belonging to minority cultures as a way to override the commercial aesthetic forms promoted in the global market.

Given the emphasis on hybridization, the *Revista de Crítica Cultural* devotes ample attention to themes of shifting national and sexual identities in Latin America: mestizaje, the recycling of clothing and identity, the simulacra that organize modern cultural life all sustain a theory of ambivalence. The turns to identity drift and concealment are not simply installed as postmodern tropes; rather, these images are used to refute the authority of the metropolis just as they court the transnational theory they produce. The tropes of shifting identity, then, sustain yet another ambiguity: in transnational movements, they also expose the role-play of intellectuals under neoliberal regimes. Richard thus addresses the *effects* of the mask and the importance of unmoored gendered identities in the evolution of democracy. Anchored surely in the perspectives afforded by postmodern gender studies, she is also alert to the broad offerings of international culture that might facilitate debate in Chile. Her goal, then, is to find an adequate place for the seemingly revolutionary gestures that gender theory portends and to take advantage of metropolitan perspectives in order to advance local strategies of emancipation: "Latin American feminism also should direct attention to the crevices and interstitial spaces of metropolitan theory that can be twisted or rerouted in order to serve the advantage of the paradigms of the Other," she wrote in *Masculino/femenino* (1993, 80). This citation can serve as a summary of the gendered programs of Richard's journal, a way to enlarge the scope of postmodern theory in order to feed all participants at the North/South banquet. In the process, it allows a place for Latin American women and sexual minorities in metropolitan debates, where they might renegotiate their positions as "others."

Just as the cultural criticism assembled by Fletcher and Richard engages in an ongoing way the politics of international theory with local democratic practice, it also disrupts any uniform narrative about women and men and unmasks the heroic narratives belonging to a masculine, national state. It may well be, as María Moreno has claimed in *La Gandhi Argentina*, that the task of gender critics should be to maintain the presence of otherness: "to put in question that San Benito that makes us impervious to all difference, bringing us to oscillate between an ongoing and anguished translation of sameness while annihilating the other" (1997, 3). The duality of this enterprise is ironized by cultural critique. If, on the one hand, the slippage of identities is a challenge to hegemonic practice, on the other hand, the proliferation of differences that this practice evokes also satisfies the needs of the democratic state, which is eager to claim a reputation for inclusion and showcase its dissident figures. Gender critics from Latin America are aware of this double-edged sword through which public recognition of minority rights often benefits the interests of neoliberal regimes.[10] As if to answer this pressing issue, they insist on the power of Latin American feminism to articulate a crisis of representation in both metropolitan paradigms for postmodern theory and neoliberal projects for democracy. Identity politics in the gendered field shakes the realities of postdictatorship times just as it launches a forceful artistic project within wider metropolitan debates. Under the power of creative texts, this plan assumes yet another dimension: whether under the rubric of "best-seller" models or by the terms of an avant-garde, Latin American literature upsets the stability of the North/South horizon.

Answering "Occidente": Aesthetics and Representation

Both *Feminaria* and *Revista de Crítica Cultural* expand theoretical sources drawn from the North by drawing attention to a local gendered aesthetic that critiques the effects of globalization. In literary texts, this is deployed in two principal courses: one focuses the creative text on the United States itself, situating action and character conflicts within the metropolitan source that has defined the terms for the North/South encounter; a second configures the effects of northern hegemony as they reach the Southern Cone context. Crossing these divergent paths is yet another problem related to the venue of circulation: to speak against northern domination through the best-seller option or to locate a measure of protest through the strategies offered by a restricted, avant-garde aesthetic.

If we assume, with James Clifford (1997, 11), that travels through comparative cultures always result in imperfect equivalence and therefore free those sedimented meanings that have been firmly cultivated in a single place, we might claim that the movement of gendered issues also unleashes new meanings, enabling us to rethink concepts of North and South, of global signifiers of "men" and "women." An effect of this shuffling of cultural wares through the North/South corridor, Latin Americans imaginatively reconfigure the history of the North while North Americans often dream of an exoticized South. Of course, this phenomenon is hardly new. From Sarmiento's *Viajes* and Juana Manuela Gorriti's tales of the California gold rush to Herman Melville's dreams of island retreat in "The Encantadas," the imaginative possibilities of cultural difference have been the stuff of American literatures on both sides of the North/South border. In exploring the effects of the North on the South in the contemporary literary field, we discover the way in which the gender debate mediates the politics of hemispheric difference.

It would be odd not to commence this literary course through geography and gender without a look at the success of Isabel Allende in recruiting a mass audience of readers. In the United States, Allende's fiction has been received as a triumph of family values, a celebration of the survival of clan that parallels the struggles of the Chilean nation. From her first novel, *La casa de los espíritus* (1982), to her memoir, *Paula* (1994), Allende has achieved a secure reputation in the North/South exchange as a literary broker of sentiment and feelings. Although she usually writes from the autobiographical venue and thus explains Latin American events through narratives of family history, her novel *Hija de la fortuna* (1999) follows a different plan, creating a portrait of Anglo-Chilean migrations in the nineteenth century in order to alter the usual narratives of North American expansion. A significant challenge to a U.S. tradition that prides itself on the originality of the myth of Manifest Destiny, Allende tells of a young Chilean woman who travels from Valparaíso to San Francisco to join the gold rush fever in search of the man she loves; in the process, she manages to transform the emphasis of a well-known story belonging to North American lore and introduces the *foreign* as a significant force in the U.S. West.

Beyond the "slice of life" tale for which so much women's fiction is known, Allende in this novel seeks the *epic* mode as a counterbalance to the hegemony of North American narrative tradition. The story of the heroine's blurred origins and birth, her clandestine voyage north, her disguise as a man among the '49ers, her amorous pursuit of the notorious Joaquín Murieta, all announce a monumental adventure of potentially big-screen proportions that opens the archives of U.S. imaginings about its westward geographic expansion. Moreover, the multicultural framework—so privileged by the U.S. academy—becomes the soul of Allende's text insofar as it rewrites the minority discourses of much contemporary ethnic fiction. Hence, the novel encircles the figure of an Anglo-Chilean orphan, who is first enamored of the Chilean outlaw, Joaquín Murieta (a figure usually claimed in U.S. lore by the Chicano community), and later turns her romantic attentions to a Chinese immigrant healer. Not only do the romantic crossings flag the existence of a multicultural Chile, with its Spanish, Indian, and British heritage, but also they allow the author to claim a space for Chile in the multicultural debates of today's California, a place renowned for its minority politics although its fictions of identity usually exclude Southern Cone immigrants from sagas of struggle.

Within the realm of the ethnic narration, Allende tells the tale from the perspective of women. Her novel insists that women can be creative travelers, achieving a status equal to that of men: Rose writes erotic fiction to be sold in England; Paulina becomes an entrepreneur; and Eliza, the protagonist, is a free roamer and translator, bilingual in English and Spanish. The latter also takes on a final political project, freeing enslaved Chinese women from the brothels of San Francisco. Women in Allende's text thus become the upholders of a new world order, rescuing victims of racial conflict through wisdom and mediation. At the same time, and never missing a cue in the postmodern script that orchestrates our current debates, Allende traces the shifting identities of immigrants in relation to their pursuit of gold. The California described in this novel thus produces new bodies and subjects: Eliza dresses as a man, her Chilean lover changes his name to become Joaquín Murieta, and Jacob Todd, the writer, becomes Jacob Freemont, inventor of Murieta's legend. True to our contemporary multicultural debate, the novel shows the advantage of shifting names as it exploits the theatricality of performance; nevertheless, within the best-seller paradigm, the text simultaneously defends the essentialized values of women. In this way, although the novel relies on sites of difference to constitute a fiction, it also tracks the heroine's search to find an authentic female self: at the close of the novel, then, Eliza sheds her masculine garb to fulfill what she terms "a desire to become a woman again" (422).

These ingredients are formulaic within the conventions of the best-seller novel, especially the kind that has traveled the North/South route of cultural consumption.[11] Functioning from the clichés of social life that define both female behavior and the ethical values of immigrant culture, Allende preys upon global desires for stories of redemption. In this way, although the passion for gold is a theme of her book, the success of this novel in the market also begs a reading of North/South consumers. Sentimentality, Shirley Samuels has told us (1992), is an operation that teaches readers to be able purchasers of different bodies and cultures; it determines modes of identification and often allows affect to fill in for political responsibility. But it also announces literature's claim for a piece of the market despite the fact that many have relegated culture to a minor role in the global flow. Although it is convenient to condemn the facile readings that best-seller products often supply—an excessive sentimentality, predictable routes of narrative movement that flatten our critique of history, the illusion of success and triumph conducted by its melodramatic course—in this respect I find it remarkable that the best-seller text also serves as a contestation of U.S. market hegemony by drawing attention to women's participatory role in bridging the North/South divide.[12]

Writers from Julia Alvarez to Laura Esquivel often construct histories of the Americas from the threads of matriarchal culture, linking the continents through the efforts of women. Gender enters in these cases to play a significant role in joining metropolitan and peripheral sectors just as "women's writing" in recent decades comes to represent an entire field, a marketable commodity that circulates as proof of pluralism, supplying intimate connections among faraway lives. Here, Allende expands the paradigm by locating the activities of a Chilean heroine within a founding moment of U.S. territorial expansion. Although I do not wish to defend Allende, I find it nonetheless notable that she draws upon strategies of popular sentimentality in order to address this towering issue, intervening in a schema of values that traditionally have held Latin Americans as victims or minor figures. Moreover, with these strategies, she also establishes a fiction that will hold universal appeal among consumers, overriding the divisions of civilization versus savagery that have conventionally reduced the stature of Latin American subjects; in this line, she allows her Chilean heroine a free-willed and unchained autonomy. *Hija de la fortuna* offers the possibility to sustain the illusion of singular and universal appeal. The novel thus tantalizes by the exotic, but also lays claim to a needed Latin American presence in the North, crossing principles of market interest and nationalist desire.

Gender in literature becomes Latin America's bargaining chip to enter the game of global exchange, a legitimation of nonhegemonic voices and a point of entry to a resistant, yet globalized forum. What is "merely" bestseller is not to be "merely" dismissed; rather, through the presence of Latin American women in the North, it regulates "common sense." Other Latin American writers regard the North/South axis with a more forceful critique, pointing to the metropolitan culture that leaves women in alarming distress. Toward this end, they depend not on the resources of melodrama and sentimentality, but instead on the powers of disruption fostered by textual experimentation. In this regard, the question of "difference," which circulates for consumer pleasure, here serves as a critique of alienation and loss, prompting an alternative interpretation of the hazards of North/South divide; many authors thus remind us of the fetishization of difference that stimulates global flow, repatriating it once and for all in order to critique the market.

Lucía Guerra offers a brief although precise allegory of the grotesque nature of the operations of U.S. culture upon foreign women's lives. In "Travesías," a tale about the cultures of simulacra in Orange County, California, Guerra implicates the abuse of women in the manufacture of pleasure (1997, 25–45). A cautionary fable about the dangers that befall women who succumb to the fantasies offered by mass culture, Guerra's story addresses the plight of a provincial female subject, taken by the illusions of Disneyland and in particular the narratives constructed within the "Pirates of the Caribbean" unit of the theme park. Drawn to the dross of simulacra, the character herself is given to role-play presumably with the objective of gaining a role in modern life. Particularly attracted to excesses of costume and dress, she enters the studio of a sinister doll maker, who eventually takes her life. Beyond the obvious metaphor of women as dolls who become the playthings of men, Guerra takes us through a secondary level of horror when we realize that the murderer is also a simulacrum, one of the Pirates of the Caribbean manufactured by the world of Disney. While singing "It's a Small World After All," Disney's monotonous tribute to the homogenizing effects of globalization, the characters turn leisure culture into a tale of inescapable horror. To some extent, Guerra here recalls the defiance of writers such as Flannery O'Connor, who found in the U.S. South a realm of experiences that refused to be harnessed by northern law. But by situating a starstruck provincial woman in the world of fabricated pleasures, Guerra allows simulacra to absorb what might be considered as real. Women as victims of mass culture are also the victims of an alien narration, a story that they have not constructed but that envelopes them and takes their lives.

In a different style, novelist Luisa Valenzuela rewrites the noir tradition by situating narrative action in New York City where she tracks the adventures of detectives and writers.[13] *Novela negra con argentinos* (1990) thus becomes a modern perversion of the potboiler. Here, Valenzuela describes an Argentine character who penetrates the city in order to pursue an identity as a writer; he attempts to construct a story of his own from within the heart of the metropolis. Valenzuela also asks, not incidentally, about the subject matter available to the writer of a peripheral country especially at a moment of economic crisis and—to paraphrase Raymond Chandler—under "the smell of fear."[14] Indeed, an original claim to art or identity is not always within reach of the Latin American writer just as the romantic concept of "inspiration" suffers the debilitating effects of geographic displacements. Valenzuela's story is thus loaded with the trappings of cross-dressed figures who test the definitions of otherness, alienation, and exile as they emerge on the axis of North/South exchanges. These reworkings of tradition from the vantage of the neoliberal South are also ways to create a different heroics in narrative, a way to challenge a kind of fiction that would represent Latin Americans as complicit hostages, bound to metropolitan discourse of the North.[15] However, and although we are all spectators of a stage show of exile and transgression, it is not clear that we will necessarily feel inspired by performativity alone. Instead, what is required, Valenzuela appears to tell us, is to set new terms for identity, new forms of recognition of lived experience that might be transported to the world of words. In this way, the novel confronts the violence done to texts and bodies by consumerist practice; it exposes the glibness of postmodern devices that remove the inner life from writing. Too, the novel shows how women's bodies are implicated as victims in this game. In the transfer of individuals from the South to the North, such terms as torture and murder lose their political meaning; rather, they become part of a mass-culture discourse that would erase ethics and analysis in favor of the trade of pleasure.

Texts produced in opposition to consumer models yield stories of ambiguous exile, showing female bodies as tokens of North/South trade. This focus on hostage subjects within the United States also finds an equivalent in Southern Cone settings, wherein women are represented as victims of policies of the North; this becomes, in some instances, the focus of experimental projects of a literary avant-garde. In this regard, I want to attend briefly to a recent novel by Diamela Eltit, where she addresses the powers of the West as seen from the perspective of the southern periphery. Let me assert, first, that it is not the *plot* of this novel that resists the U.S. paradigm, but Eltit's focus on the *aesthetic*; art transforms our thinking about neoliberalism and the presence of the North in the South. It is indeed in the zone of aesthetic pleasure, with its codes uncracked by even the most rigorous practitioners of theory, that meaning flows uninterrupted and the language of repression is surpassed. It is the aesthetic, then, that offers a way to overturn the demands of a global market in order to reconsider questions of representation, both in politics and art. In other novels, Eltit focuses directly on the market itself, but most relevant here is the North/South engagement that she proposes. *Los vigilantes* (1994) is a story about a woman and the types of surveillance to which she is subjected by neighbors, relatives, and, most intensely, her son and an unnamed interlocutor, probably the father of the child. At the end, the woman is evicted from her home to live as an aimless vagrant. The novel is one of multiple exclusions: the child is expelled from school and the mother is cast from her home while the neighbors pursue any individual who refuses to comply with Western laws ("Las leyes de Occidente"). Institutions of family, school, and state thus reject the very individuals whom they were designed to contain.

Unlike Isabel Allende's best-selling memoir, *Paula* (1994), published contemporaneously with *Los vigilantes* and that celebrates "family values" and the sacredness of mother-child bonds, Eltit's novel is an inquiry into the way in which literary art resists and, finally, is undermined by neoliberal rule. Within this problematic, aesthetics belongs to the realm of the mother. Refusing to enter the market and the fashions of marginality with which feminist theory circulates globally, Eltit recounts the disintegration of family ties in the neoliberal age. There is no idealization of parenting, no special privilege accorded the child, no celebration of the Latin American family that satisfies the appetites of foreign readers. Instead, the child stands for an expression of otherness that threatens the art of the mother. Moreover, the state collaborates in this act of aggression.

Eltit observes that the state cannot articulate the interests of civil society; but owing to constant surveillance, it confuses the separation of public and private spheres and censors all expression. In this respect, Argentine journalist Mabel Bellucci also expresses concern for the interweaving of spaces: "Privacy in the domestic environment is invaded by an eruption of the *outside* and, worse still, the outside becomes the regulating mechanism—almost exclusively—of family functioning" (1992, 5). To an extent,

Los vigilantes corroborates this vision, but Eltit shows that there is no space for nostalgia while discussing the merits of family, no idyllic private or public space that respects adults and children. Instead, ruin is set on all thinking subjects; the Latin American family as myth is destroyed. The mask is finally removed.

Eltit begins by evacuating all symbolic markers belonging to women: images of house, maternity, the sacredness of writing, the intimacy of the epistolary novel are traded for the violence of the state. At the same time, she asks about the survival of art and the conditions of creativity in an age of surveillance. This is positioned as a problem in the dynamics between mother and child. It is clear from the start that the child resents his mother's engagement with texts; as "the only one who writes," she must be controlled. Set against the mother, who is pure discourse without physical description and—until the end of the novel—also without a name, the child is all corporeality, unrelenting physical need, and resents the abstractions of a writing system that would reduce him to a figure in print ("I exist only as a collection of papers," 16). His principal resistance to the writer is orality and a terse, simplified expression that contrasts to his mother's expansive epistolary meditations: "BAAM, BAAM, I laugh," he utters throughout. The book will also conclude with a similar "BAAM," when the child, controller of events in the novel, will enjoy the last laugh and bring writing systems to an end. Words are pure physicality in the world of the child, thwarting the dissolution of self, but enacting the destruction of others; they also devour all difference and annihilate the privacy of creative acts. In this respect, it is not surprising that the child's only talent is found in his penchant for numbers. Accordingly, the mother writes, "I intuit in the center of his brain a highly numeric talent that alters my moderate paces. A process that distracts his thought and unleashes his irritating outbursts of laughter" (36). The child is thus devoted to accumulation through which he is linked to "acts of universal value" (36); as such, he stands against the mother who is isolated in her regard for art. Numbers, corporeality, and oral expression prevail over writing: the child's presence dominates the mother's discourse and vision; even nature collaborates to suppress her desire for art and community. Even the cold freezes the homeless to death, it destroys culture as it had been known, pressing individuals to evacuate streets and public places. Similarly, the polluted waters promise certain death to local inhabitants; nature is contaminated, yet no one halts its flow. This conditions a preference for nomadic travel instead of social alliance, and rules against any attention to rootedness, community, and art. Ultimately, it produces a situation of surveillance, where difference is overdetermined by invisible, unspoken rules. The global population is divided accordingly by Eltit into irrational opposites of North and South, East and West, visible and invisible extremes, all determined arbitrarily by the monstrous hunger of the body, devoid of passion and spirit (112).

At the close of the novel, the mother partakes of the child's game of ordering empty cups and containers as he invents a new borderland of defenses that would separate friend and foe. "They will never be able to ruin the symmetry upon which we have managed to build our defenses," explains the mother as she turns the child's frontier game into an aesthetic project that challenges the artificial market symmetry of North and South (116). She finally breaks down the traditional binarisms to think of another form of community; art is evoked now in order to set terms for a different alliance. Nevertheless, in the final pages of the text, even the artist is crushed; expelled from her home, the mother becomes pure physicality (she bites, laughs, and copies the child's primitive language) whereas the child navigates through the frozen streets, thwarting those who watch them. Losing all concern for rationality, they surrender to the forces of nature, howling beneath the moon. As if responding to Jameson who claimed—in a much disputed essay—the importance of allegorical writing for third world intellectuals (1986), Diamela Eltit tests the limits of this literary mode: on the one hand, the novel represents the invasion of the neoliberal paradigm as set forth by the "West"; on the other hand, the literary model collapses, leaving unanalyzable subjects wandering on the edges of known narrative form. Only the sense of the *aesthetic* remains to undermine metropolitan theory.

In the able hands of Latin American women such as Eltit, the traffic of commodity culture comes to a temporary halt. A gendered aesthetic, a slow attention to language, a celebration of lettered culture cuts against the grain of mass society and the market-driven state. Nevertheless, Eltit and her colleagues do not defend the autonomy of the literary text, as was common in high-modernist mode; rather, they privilege local space, a voice forged from gendered traditions, always positioned to deflect the draw of the North/South market and reconstruct an arena for debate. Thus, under the aegis of neoliberalism, with its attempts to annihilate ambiguity and fix all categories of meaning on a tray of facile choices, the avant-garde literary text works to construct a space for slippage and uncertain meaning, to open a zone of experimentation that cannot be accommodated by the market or sales. The aesthetic, in the final analysis, reminds us of questions of ethics—generally omitted from the North/South neoliberal project. As in the example of Liliana Porter's photographic collage, feminine discourse enters here not only to arrange elements of North/South syntax but also to mock our preferences for mass culture and eliminate a space for nostalgia.

Finally, rather than offer absolute answers in the monumental style of neoliberalism itself, Latin American avant-garde writers of the late twentieth century return to ambiguity and debate; they offer a space for dialogue, they move against isolation. It is here that they refuse to occupy a single point on a hemispheric map and propose, instead, a long conversation that drifts over the North/South divide.

La geographie n'est que la forme apparente, toute de surface, de l'exil. . . .
Chaque langue nous fait mentir.
[Geography is only the apparent form, all on the surface, of exile. . . .
Each language makes us lie.]
—Héctor Bianciotti, *Sans la misericorde du Christ*

Mas mapas / sólo para atenuar la precisión de una /
pulsión incierta, parecida al morir.
[But maps / only to attenuate / the precision of an /
uncertain pulsation / like death.]
—Arturo Carrera, *Animaciones suspendidas*

CHAPTER 4

Bodies in Transit: On Travel, Translation, and Sexuality

In *Happy Together* (1997), a Chinese-language film directed by Wong Kar-Wai, two quarreling gay lovers on holiday travel from Hong Kong to Argentina. Following a frustrated visit to Iguazú Falls, they find themselves in Buenos Aires, marginally employed and lonely. The vision they supply of the capital city is one that Argentines rarely see on film: Wong Kar-Wai tours the daily life of Asians living in tenement housing, the desperation of barrio residents in La Boca, the squalid back rooms of restaurants and bars—all this alongside a decidedly postmodern landscape of plastic, neon, and gloss. *Happy Together* links concerns of sexuality and translation, history and exile, mapping and representation. Ironically, through the Hong Kong filmmaker's lens, we reach some fundamental contradictions about globalization and displacement as they are treated by Argentine writers.

The film begins with a citation of the "road" genre narrative, with the characters driving a failing automobile in search of Iguazú Falls. The monumentality of the landscape is set in color photography while other sections of the film, focusing on the bleakness of urban life, are recorded principally in black and white. In this way, the director establishes the terms for odyssey and redemption, offering reconciliation and hope for the squabbling partners should they arrive at the colorized "promised land." But these postmodern tourists fail to locate Iguazú: their car collapses, their funding is exhausted, and they forfeit the chance to see the natural wonder that might assure happiness and romantic fulfillment. This quest motif accompanies a considerable number of recent films set in Latin America that circulate on the international venue: think only of Fernando Solanas's *El Viaje* (1991) and, more recently, John Sayles's *Men with Guns* (1997). But if the films just named are motivated by the promise of social redemption, the Chinese filmmaker instead builds a story of frustrated romance with emphasis on postmodern displacement—of nation, language, sex, and labor—leading from rural terrain to the decadent city.[1]

Two languages structure the film, Chinese and Spanish, as if to suggest the verbal collisions tugging at all postmodern tourists, but also to attend to the global pull that confuses speech and sentiment. Ultimately, the bilingual environment betrays one's sense of place, national identity, and love. In this respect, it is strategic that one of the pair finds a post in Buenos Aires as doorman at a renowned tango night club, the Bar Sur, considered an obligatory stop for visitors to the city. His job is to usher the tourists (mostly Asian) into the atrium of nostalgia represented by tango itself; nevertheless, the doorman who guards the gate is, like any immigrant to America, forced to remain outside, exiled from the circulation of pleasures offered within the bar. Clearly, there exists a hierarchy among foreigners, through which the vacationing tourist benefits from the performative mode sustained by an alien culture while the migrant worker can only station himself at its door. As the film advances, the doorman loses his post at the club and goes to wash dishes in a Chinese restaurant in Buenos Aires. The other man continues as a hustler. It is obvious, then, that the immigrants' choices are relegated to physicality without language: through the sale of the body, the physical protection of others, or even the preparation of food, they are purveyors of the pleasures of others.

Only in the privacy of home can the doorman and his partner practice tango. This dance, so abundantly codified to express class and sexual desire, is here turned around to become a personal appropriation of a national longing, a redirection of an alien form. The private version of tango facilitates a possible amorous reconciliation between the two foreign men, but as a foreign language, its codes are entangled with unsynthesized meaning: bodies reorient speech and music compensates for dialogue, producing a language of representation that now includes homoerotic, Asian desire. In this respect, the tango exposes the contradictions between place and sentimentality. The foreign (in this case, Argentina) promises romantic fulfillment; but the foreign also signals isolation and loss and a language alien to the depths of the immigrants' feelings.[2]

As the film ends, a third character—a romantic interest of the restaurant worker—takes leave of Buenos Aires to travel south to Ushuaia. En route, he records the discrepancy between local landscape and his private language of sentiment. Here, where communication in Spanish fails, the actor resorts to photographs, listens to Chinese music, and carries tape recordings of his friend's voice as reminders of intimate experience. Kar-Wai exploits the paradox of technological intervention when used by actors in the film in order to preserve their sense of home and to retain a memory of each other. Nevertheless, these instruments are hardly adequate to relieve the travelers' pain, nor do they suffice to define the sexuality of immigrants that deviates from normative desires. In other words, the subjectivity of immigrants finds no suitable place in the foreign surrounding despite all efforts to record it. At the same time, the film begs other questions: Can we reroute desire through the experience of the foreign? How might a circuit of interlocutors be sustained in multiple tongues? And, finally, how can we empower our artistic gaze in order to preserve a past or to convey the experience of distance? The film ends with one of the characters remaining in Buenos Aires while the other returns to Hong Kong, recuperating the lost tracks of migration while enveloped by a sense of mourning.

This film highlights the surprising possibilities offered by the Asian perspective in order to enter the aesthetic and political debates engaging Argentine intellectuals as they work through postmodern geographies of identity, language, and voice. Although Wong Kar-Wai was primarily concerned with the plight of Hong Kong emigrants, his routing through Buenos Aires is paradoxically important insofar as local Argentine poets and novelists also struggle with this sense of the foreign even in that place they call home. I bring this material forward to show the ways in which intellectuals (globally) restructure the contemporary map, fostering novel geographic linkages in order to describe a pervasive uneasiness about origins, sexuality, and displacement. In Argentine poetry and fiction, this concern spills over the limits of the homeland and takes form in two principal narratives: first, directed toward the "Orient" as a promised alternative to the geopolitics of Western privilege; and second, a narrative that builds on the first, whereby the uses of the Orient open to a project on translation, allowing the writer to reflect on subjectivity and displacement, sexuality and language, history and literary form. In all of this, translation produces a countermapping, reversing the formal identifying tropes that limit name and movement; in the final instance, it yields an alternative epistemology for self-representation.

Contemporary literature conveys pervasive uprootedness, expressed through translations of the hearth language and increasingly bilingual inflections. At the same time, writers struggle with the verticality of domination set by the North/South axis and wrestle with a longing for a modernist moment that once upon a time promised a reintegration with communities at home. The presence of the Orient, brought into Argentine letters through the trope of translation, is used as a magnetic force field in the writer's imagined geography. This trope allows one to dismantle the authority of the North/South map; as a postmodern strategy, it also invites a critique of hierarchical, modernist desire. In the process, cartographies are redrawn. The borders that have separated East and West, North and South are tested through multiple languages.

The Postmodern "Orient"

Several things are to be noted as phenomena of Argentine literature today. In their move through the Orient (and I use this word with a decisive irony), Argentine writers pick up on a fascination for otherness and use the distance between cultures to explore the construction of local meaning, to explore their own conditions as "other" in the society in which they live. This, of course, is not a new phenomenon: recall only the case of Sarmiento and his fascination with the Middle East, his insistence on Turkish "barbarism" to explain the savagery of Argentina; the *modernista* preoccupation for the decorative aspects of chinoiserie; Borges's repeated attraction to the mysteries of Oriental culture—both Arab and Asian; or the derisive (and, indeed, racist) intrigues that Roberto Arlt set in Middle Eastern bazaars in his *Criador de gorilas.*[3] This project of representation accompanies moments of political crisis, shifts in public authority of the writer, and the arrival of immigrants to the national landscape. Today, the growth in Argentina of new Asian populations—mainly Korean and Chinese—is a source of preoccupation in a culture not especially tolerant of difference. While the Orient provides a field for fantasies of domination and control, it lays out the possibility of explaining multilingual complexities and internal nomadism of the Argentine nation. Moreover, the Orientalist paradigm is a metaphor for marginality; it signals the failures of an overarching national ethic to produce a language of communal expression. As such, it opens a critique of alterity while, at the same time, revising an earlier modernist plot in which the writer-hero exercised privilege and distinction, and still considered himself in control of the future. Finally, as an idealized locus, the literary representation of the Orient arrests the paradigm of North/South flows that traditionally have ordered the Argentine's imagined map. It permits double memories, a plurality of locations, and extends discussions of identity and voice as part of a landscape of translation.[4]

It is not surprising, therefore, that the Orient should occupy the site of so much contemporary Argentine writing. Witness only Diana Bellessi's *Tributo del mudo* (1982), dedicated in part to the image of an abandoned concubine and high priestess of Tao who was later put to her death; Mercedes Roffé's apocryphal book, *El tapiz* (1983), supposedly written by Ferdinand Oziel, a Sephardic Jew from Morocco, and translated into Spanish; the pages of *Tokonoma*, a contemporary Argentine journal directed by Amalia Sato and devoted to Japanese literature translated into Spanish; Ana María Shúa's *Casa de geishas* (1992), María del Carmen Colombo's *La familia china* (1999); or the success of Anna Kazumi Stahl, a North American writer of Asian descent writing in Spanish in Argentina.[5] In order not to allow us to think that the Oriental flame is only a femininst writer's passion, we should also remember Osvaldo Lamborghini's *La causa justa* (1983), César Aira's *Una novela china* (1987), Daniel Guebel's *La perla del emperador* (1990), Alberto Laiseca's texts from *Poemas chinos* (1987) to *La mujer en la muralla* (1990), the artistic works of Alberto Prior, and Juan Gelman's obsession for sephardic language and poetic traditions as witnessed in *Dibaxu* (1994). This is not a return to the modernista configuration of the Orient as in the works of Rubén Darío, but a call for a project in translation that resists official maps of meaning drawn on the North/South axis. In this respect, the Oriental trope is a challenge to modernismo itself, to the entrenched privilege accorded to Latin American writers of that last fin de siglo; indeed, it brings us to question the writer's authority as it had been configured in earlier times.

Julia Kushigian has spoken eloquently to the project of contemporary orientalism in Latin America as a way for writers to affirm and preserve their own sense of self vis-à-vis the construction of the "other." She also describes the "active polyglossia of the Orient" as a way to "overcome a fusion of opposites" (1991, 14). But the Orient is not only a site from which to enact a debate about the limits of the "real"; it offers a strategy that allows writers to emphasize voice over fixed written form, performance over established beliefs. The Orient brings together relations of translation and power, of translation and erotics.[6] As his male protagonist falls in love with a cross-dresser and double-agent posing as a diva in Chinese opera, David Hwang in *M. Butterfly* paradoxically observed that Asia was an ideal site to search for a "real man" (1988, 6). In the Latin American context, in the Argentine context in particular, the Orient also opens to a discussion of sexuality and the state, this time in the context of translation.

Contemporary literature devoted to this theme leads us to ask about the foreign challenges presented to the politics of gender. It invites us to reconstruct categories of masculine and feminine once removed from the North/South lens. It also allows us to think of the cross of languages that tests any global truth, to examine the secrets of state that foreclose dissident voices. In other words, the quest for identity so exhaustively announced by proponents of modernism is here described in constant change, mobile, and without fixed place.

Home and Exile

Juan Gelman and Luisa Futoransky, two exiled Argentine poets, both left Argentina during dictatorship, suffering the scars of displacement; both traveled the world in search of alternative expression, seeking to name their experience of dislocation. The Orient—in the first case, Sephardic culture, in the second, China and Japan—offered these writers a vehicle to express this loss, a grounding that established the terms for investigating relocation and difference, a way to struggle with the marginal situation of the nomadic, exiled writer. Masked under the anxiety of translation, their work creates a dialogue about the intersection between national and global traditions, between the boundaries of self and "other" in the field of representation, between the sound systems working in poetry. Nevertheless, each offers a different paradigm for these divergent ironies through a defense of either modernist values or postmodern fragmentation.

Juan Gelman is a master of the transformation. From the 1960s, Gelman has insisted on the role of ventriloquism in verse; he has relied on the practices of translation and bilingual expression in order to express the density of poetic process, to call attention to the artifice of lyric, but above all to remind himself of his permanent loss and exile from any original language. In "Exergue," Gelman observes, "To translate is inhuman—no language or face allows itself to be translated. We must leave this beauty intact and add yet another beauty to accompany it. Their lost unity lies ahead" (1997, xv; trans. Lindgren). Here, he assumes that translation is a task of betrayal, an appropriation of otherness that is at once aggressive and fiercely determined. But he also points to the eventual convergence of different tongues regardless of one's intervention; like the merger of rivers, the natural course of events leads to this supreme intralingual measure.

Gelman's uprootedness from Argentina is expressed through the vehicle of the foreign, through tropes and allusions to otherness within the context of world literature in general. I have in mind his *Traducciones* (1968–1969) and in particular those poems signed with the pseudonym of Sidney West. A great homage to the dead and to the foreign traditions that so ably capture a sense of the local, the doubled voicing suggests dialogue and ongoing displacement. Borrowing the style of Edgar Lee Masters's *Spoon River Anthology*, the Sidney West poems announce the prevalence of an anterior, translated language, a previous poetic moment located elsewhere, in another continent and foreign tradition; at the same time, Gelman tells us that the mourning and melancholia expressed for the dead are inevitably the same in any land. This conflict over desired originality and longing for what has been lost is echoed in other books. His *Citas y comentarios* (1982) is a tribute to the poets of the Spanish Renaissance (in particular, Santa Teresa) combined with a nostalgia for Argentina and the popular voiced poems belonging to the social realists of the 1920s and 1930s (principal among them, Raúl González Tuñón). This citational strategy (and deformation) is built upon bilingual flows and the merger of space and identities; it also depends on the oral preconstitution of subjects. Orality becomes a sign of authenticity and stands as an original voice that will later be transformed. Here, Gelman appears to inquire about the appropriate distance required of the poet in order to recast an accepted truth. In this respect, citation becomes a way to affix one's identity to some kind of tradition while also pretending to alter the scope of the intellectual field. Not merely parodic as some have claimed, Gelman's citational project simultaneously mixes the exile's fundamental longing for home and his suspicion of fixed cultural origins, although never relinquishing his Argentine roots, he also finds a home in the literatures of the Spanish Renaissance and the U.S. South.[7] His poetic projects in general emerge from dualities of this kind. Gelman, observes Miguel Dalmaroni (1993, 33), marks his poetic career with a conflict between lyric and narrative properties, placing in confrontation the diverging aesthetics of experimentalism in verse with social realist projects. But this tension between telling and describing, between narrating what is personal with a broader vision of politics and ideology, is also the conflicting terrain on which one inscribes foreign and local encounters. In this regard, the Orient comes to symbolize the world that is at once blocked by an inaccessible language and facilitated by the poem itself. Exile and longing, the assertion of one's place in literature as linked to a foreign tradition, the anxiety for self-representation coupled with an invention of the other: these points are crossed in translation projects that are scripted by the nomadic writer.

Dibaxu (1994) points to some of these conflicts while it also emphasizes a great search for lost agency belonging to the poet, a domination over language lost, a recuperation of origins that are not necessarily authentic. Gelman wrote the poems of *Dibaxu* in Sephardic Spanish. This is not a hearth language for Gelman; rather, he learned ladino through formal instruction and assumes it here as a foreign tongue. Equally important, Gelman chooses to write in the language of a nomadic people. Displacement marks its character and expression, a constant reminder of the conflict of relentless survivors who, over the centuries, have protected their language although they have lost a sense of place. *Dibaxu*, then, is an attempt to communicate within the flow of language preserved through orality itself. In this respect, it relies on the most forceful of national traditions—it recalls the epic forms that orality offers, but it also evokes the local expressions of romantic love. By writing in ladino, Gelman shows that no poem is free of the language of another, that a language is free for all to adopt, that it cannot belong exclusively to a single group. At the same time, he insists on disjunctures that the foreign language imposes on one's native tongue. He explains in his introduction to the volume, "It's as if searching for the substratum of that ancient Spanish, at the same time a substratum of our own tongue, had become my obsession. As if the extreme solitude of exile had pushed me to seek the roots of language, the most profound and exiled roots of language" ("Escolio," n.p.).

Gelman supplies us with translation in Spanish of his own texts written in ladino: poems of love, lost modernist yearning, reconciliation, and passion. He struggles with the limits of language in order to describe the experience of intimacy, to articulate the distance between word and sentiment, to reveal the gaps between traditions. Gelman shows through *Dibaxu/ Debajo/Below* the underlying currents of his tongue, the circulation and flows of the different voices that contribute to building a sense of self in poetic verse. Through dialogue with an earlier language, the Spanish tongue is expanded. This also comes as an effect of the representation of the other. The Orient—this time through Middle Eastern migrations of the Spanish Jews—provides a scenario through which the body of the lover finds alternative expression: "Qui avla ti dezirá? Qui nombri ti nombrará? (¿Qué palabra te dirá? ¿Qué nombre te nombrará?)" [What word will speak you? What name will name you?] (62–63). Through bilingual lyrics, Gelman signals the inexorable poetic search to name what is near but distant, to align word and figure in the same field of representation, or alternatively to announce the paradoxical futility of that linguistic pairing. Like language both near and distant, always announcing its possible equivocation in the field of enunciation, the strategy suggests the great quandary of the poet who can never possess the objects he names. Gelman closes his volume with a poem of loss and lament:

No stan muridus los paxarus
di nuestrus bezus/
stan muridus lus bezus/
lus pazarus volan nil verdi sulvidar/

pondri mi spantu londji/
dibaxu dil pasadu/
qui arde
cayadu co'il sol/

no están muertos los pájaros
de nuestros besos/
están muertos los besos/
los pájaros vuelan en el verde olvidar/

pondré mi espanto lejos/
debajo del pasado/
que arde
callado como el sol/

the birds of our kisses/
are not dead/
the kisses are dead/
the birds fly in green forgetfulness/

I will put my fear far away/
below the past/
that burns/
in silence
like the sun (64–65)

The meaning of experience, Gelman observes in these lines, is found in the *gap* between Sephardic and Spanish languages, between the speech of an ancient people and their reappropriation by modern-day exiles. In his search for poetic sources, Gelman shows his domination over a language nearly lost; he insists on his agency as a poet to sustain continuity in history and, in fact, to reclaim his Jewish roots that exhibit, in the Spanish-speaking world, a presence in language. Gelman dominates the utopian past through the space of a poetic text and opens a polemic about historical remembrance and representation.

Contrast this project, then, to the vision of Luisa Futoransky. Equally conditioned by the languages of exile, by the indignities and frustrations of displacement, Futoransky positions herself not as an *agent* of translation, but as a *subject who is constantly translated* and shows us the violent interpellations that have brought her through the world of speech. No person, she tells us, is free of the language of another. This insistence on subjugation as an effect of the exile's plight is clear from her earliest volumes. She writes in a volume of poetry:

> Un país es tu nombre
> y la ácida violencia con que acude una palabra
> a tu indefensa boca de viajero.
> Es un mapa con un río cuya desembocadura y nacimiento
> se únen, curiosamente, en el punto exacto de la tierra
> que desea abonar tu osario.
>
> A country is your name
> and the acid violence with which a word comes
> to your defenseless traveler's mouth.
> It's a map with a river whose source and outlet
> curiously unite at the exact spot on earth
> that your bones wish to fertilize.
> ("Vitraux de exilio" 1997, 18–19; trans. Weiss)

Futoransky refuses the turn to nostalgia; she rejects any containment or longing for a single place. One can be equally lonely, she also writes in this poem, in Samarkand or in the villages of the pampas. Instead, she turns her attention to the liquid borders of language and the flows of the imaginative realm. She studies the convergence of mythologies surrounding our illusions of nation, but ultimately rejects these assumptions in favor of hybrid modes of desire and a perception of the inadequacies of fixed place and form. This perspective, which corresponds to a late-twentieth-century disposition toward migrancy and dislocation, moves bodies and nations through a river of language, constructing an alternative global map from nomadic wisdom. One's name is the equivalent of a country: it is map and river, graveyard and air. Identity is carried on our shoulders like a shell on the spine of a snail; it is always susceptible to changes and movements within the terrain of words.

Futoransky has described this condition as the work of a "a contraband ant," a gesture not based on monumentality, but on the supplements of minor resistance. This illegal traffic mocks the power of official myth and attacks its subjugating forces. It also rejects the dominant, unified speech that serves the enterprise of any single nation. This condition belongs to all writers, as she recently explained: "Each writer in some way and in his own way is no more than a walking library, an atlas, which at once refers and sends us to other libraries where everything unwritten or uncharted proliferates."[8] For Futoransky, the contraband discourse of the writer is mounted by the practice of translation, an acknowledgment of the transformational magic of language.

Referring to the nomadic condition belonging to the writer, she evokes the tropes of misreading that occur when the foreigner attempts to negotiate difference. In this way, much of her poetry and prose is situated outside of Argentina; she congregates Africans, Asians, and Jews as examples of persons displaced, all tied together in a theater of linguistic errors prompted by acts of translation and reshaping of alien words. Here, identity is the result of erroneous social interactions and mistakes of verbal recognition. In the process, the human body is called into the literary text as the scene of this encounter.

In "Masatsugo," the poet recounts the travails of a Japanese man: his family relations, work, leisurely strolls, and idles. The poem closes with the observation, "Lo mejor que tiene es que aún dormido, se sonríe" [The best thing about him is that, even asleep, he smiles] (1997, 24–25); the silent body in repose is observed. Futoransky emphasizes the process through which poetry subjugates the foreigner and incorporates his customs, culminating in his sleeping hours when he is helpless against the writer's pen. But she is neither content with the power that this might bestow on the poet nor prepared to reify difference. Rather, she struggles with the multidimensionality of the foreign encounter insofar as it continually resists precise naming and authorial control. In "Tatoong," the precision claimed by the poet's gaze is undone by the "natives" once they are left alone. Neither interpreters, busloads of tourists, nor voyeuristic filmmakers are sufficiently capable of arresting a foreign reality and bringing it under control: "Y después nos vamos en nuestros buses a vaciarnos/ de más cenas, más templos, más compras/ ¿qué hacen estas decenas de miles de budas por la noche para estar tan compuestos y felices al amanecer?" [And after we go off in our buses to empty ourselves/ of more dinners, more temples, more bargains/ what do these tens of thousands of buddhas do at night/ to be so happy and composed the next morning?] (1997, 24–25). Searching for a subject to be fixed in language, Futoransky reiterates the irony of the quest while underscoring a persistent doubt about the efficacy of words to settle ambiguity and movement.

For this reason, Futoransky emphasizes the presence of the dictionary in her writings; she supplies stage directions for reading prose; she celebrates the cabalistic "abracadabra" that creates the illusion of magic through language; she plays with tongue twisters that both resist translation and integrate polyglot traditions. These are cues that help the foreigner to overcome the anxiety of displacement, to negotiate what Futoransky describes as "the untransferable humiliation that the language of others inspires, the sense of finding oneself even more distant and exiled—if that's possible—like a fish out of water" (1986, 105). In the process, she exposes the language of state that classifies immigrants and "others," prescribing rules of behavior and identity to fix the exile in a particular location in politics or history.

It is no surprise, then, that the author mixes prose and poetry, she trades citations and original thought, she offers multiple versions of a single phrase, and links translation to castration. In *De Pe a Pa*, she writes: "Thinking and thinking, she was struck many times by a word that she knows in English, pretty awful sounding and something with which she could identify: *pro-cas-tri-na-tion; Laura, enough procastrination*, which amounts to a castration for delay and hesitation. A stupid rhyme, huh?" (1986, 14). The flawed translation (an intentional slip in her move to English?) allows the author to uncover a submerged reading about the violations of language; the translation opens to facile rhyme, a castration of meaning in verse. These exercises are linked to a mutilation of form, they express the foreigner's loss in the absence of a linguistic pact, and they remind us that translated culture enacts a violence on sexualized bodies. This even has a reach in the travelogue account that the writer provides of her new surroundings. Futoransky, who spent the early years of the Argentine dictatorship first in Japan and then in China, reads Chinese culture, for example, through state medical services for women, in particular to practices of abortion, sterilization, and controlled sexual pleasure: "The State, after all, asks for your virility or femininity in exchange for a bowl of lentils," she writes (1991, 119). But the trade is not merely economic; it produces sexual knowledge. It is a way to acknowledge state repression over the possibility of desire.

Futoransky and Gelman are two established poets who take the trope of the Orient to express the exiled person's dilemma. They rely on the metaphors of translation and activate the movements between linguistic frontiers, attempting to cross the fixed circuitry of language and thus scramble the codes that separate local and foreign cultures. If Gelman turns to the Orientalist past and the safety of romantic love as a way to cover the anguish of loss, Futoransky sees the Orient (in her case, a code for the foreign) inscribed upon her body, marking a tortuous route to sexual knowledge that is both contradictory and unsettling. These are two different aesthetics that serve as an introduction to the contemporary writer's perception of an Orientalist otherness evoked through the experience of translation, a rewriting of the modernist past through the postmodern thrust of displacement. In Gelman's example, translation is claimed as a skill of the poet and is used by him to assert his authority while incidentally permitting his dominance over the erotics of translated romance. In Futoransky's case, however, the global experience of the translated woman restates an anxiety about endless fragmentation and the burden of an unresolved past, a cross-circuitry between assumed identity and signals of constant displacement.

Geography and Identity

These conflicting paradigms are repeated in the works of contemporary Argentine poets and novelists. If they prompt speculation on the violence of linguistic difference, they also propose cartographies of desire that often confuse our base understanding of home and nation. Within this, translation becomes a way to test the constraints of law, to put in doubt all original discourse and the authority of the writer; it carries the effect of masking, focusing relationships of sameness and difference; home is dramatically altered.

Take, for example, *El tapiz* (1983) by Mercedes Roffé. The text carries the pseudonym of Ferdinand de Oziel, a Sephardic author living in Morocco, who transcribes a story about a nun who pursues a life of erotic excess; at the same time, she weaves a cloth as a symbol of her artistry and a potential disguise. The body, the cloth, and the pseudonym are utilized as a resistance to authority, a challenge to censorial practice. They also suggest a need for alternative identifying tropes of authorship, a reversal of the commodity ideology that is linked to the circulation of letters. Although the disguise is celebrated for its transgressive possibilities, it also offers the opportunity to introduce an uncompromised lyric presence and celebrate the art of translation. Roffé appears to ask us how one might insert an autonomous voice in the controlled institution of literature, in the space of enunciation. Where might the chance interventions be opened that admit alternative texts, popular or submerged voices, or the kinds of lives—of Sephardim or women—that have been cloaked from public view? Interestingly, Roffé chooses to assign this impostored text to the inventions of Ferdinand de Oziel, a traveling Jew who carries the weight of exile as part of his past and present. Geographic distance, as set by the Orient and by Oziel's Jewishness in a Christian world, is further exoticized by the multiple disguises that proliferate in the craft of writing. Oziel thus offers a double disruption in space and identity. Clearly, one cannot trust the relationship between Roffé and Oziel, master and copy, writer and alter-ego, as one cannot trust the pact between Oziel and the weaving nun: all succumb to a fiction, authority falls by the wayside, leaving in the wake of the text a trompe l'oeil reminder about the tensions between eros and identification, subjectivity and translation. This seductive game is all the more forceful in a national community in which women writers metaphorically have been relegated to the space of a convent. Roffé's text is a playful investigation of a poetics of displacement that tests the weight of individual authorship while also questioning the authority of any originary language or a single writer's self-affirmation. In the final analysis, *El tapiz*, with its turn to the multilingual Orient, allows Roffé to reconsider the terms we accept for aesthetic contracts at home.

Writing from another perspective on the matter of exile, María Negroni in *Islandia* (1993) questions the condition of travel: "Primero se pone una máscara" [First one puts on a mask] (23), she explains. Principal to the texture of her poetry is the interrogation of doubleness; how to speak from the position of exile, how to speak through language belonging to others; how to collect minor experiences under the banner of epic poetry. For Negroni, writing is an act of impostorship tied to translation and exile from power. Her book is written in the halting language of one who is forced to speak a foreign tongue; she stammers in a voice of halting self affirmation. "En despoblados, en intervalos pulsa la travesti sus poemas" [In abandoned zones and intervals, the transvestite drums out her poems] (71). Negroni's project is to capture "Su Robinson narrar en femenino" [A Robinson Crusoe tale in feminine mode] (59) at the price of normal syntax and usual grammatical rule. Travel curtails the coherence of one's source language and produces a kind of aphasia. Surprising violations of linguistic norms call attention to the outsider's dilemma; they remind us of the price of estrangement from the language of home. But they also recall the kind of halting silence adopted by the foreigner lacking access to national stories belonging to one's native land. Julia Kristeva speaks of a similar phenomenon when she refers to the difficulties encountered by the foreigner: "According to the logic of exile, all aims should waste away and self-destruct in the wanderer's insane stride toward an elsewhere that is always pushed back, unfulfilled, out of reach" (1991, 6). Distance is always a condition of thinking, it is the space between languages in flux.

Catástrofes naturales (1997), a volume by Anna Kazumi Stahl, augments the density of this discussion both for the ideological dimensions of translation and the perceived (dis)locations of the author. Stahl is a North American writer of Japanese descent who resides in Argentina, where she works as a translator and teacher of English. Claiming various national belongings, Stahl engages the crisis of identity that besets a translator and marginal observer who is forced to wear the mask of immigrant identity and speak through the screen of several languages not readily her own. A number of the stories of her volume, some written directly in Spanish and others translated from English by Stahl herself, focus on the translator's mediating role between English, Japanese, and Spanish. They express her anxiety about a lost mother tongue (Japanese), her native dominance of English while living in a foreign land, and the author's tardy entrance into the Spanish-speaking world. While the collection as a whole is designed to complicate our sense of place of origin, it also tests the languages of self-identity and our preconceived assurances about national belonging. More importantly, this text about immigrants and labor is also about the workings of a migrant language. In this respect, Stahl calls attention to the immigrant's role as a *worker* in the field of language, a translator between two worlds who maneuvers words for compensation. To some extent, this turns around the exile's drama as perpetual outsider and as a subject peripheral to the organizing principles of the state. Almost in dialogue with Wong Kar-Wai's film about Hong Kong immigrants working in Buenos Aires, here Stahl insists on translation as labor and turns to questions of identity to explain one's travails with language. But she is also in potential disagreement with Gelman insofar as she refuses to claim her authority through translation, but structures translation as work. The conflicts of national identities—between North and South, East and West—here become a conflict of foreign languages and, with it, a test and revelation of the translator's engagement with an economy of words. In "La querida," for example, an unidentified man approaches the narrator, asking her for help in translating a text from Japanese to English. The narrator, untutored in this field of endeavor, stands in lieu of her mother, who until now had been the proper authority in matters of translation. For a minor sum, the innocent apprentice thus displaces the reign of the mother; more importantly, she discovers through the translator's trade certain truths about sentimental connection, the burden of mediation between culturally different worlds of feeling. As the narrator transforms and interprets, Stahl directs her concerns to the question of *responsibility* (and betrayal) that is held in the translator's purview. Too, she signals the capacity of the *foreign* language to alter the course of history and truth. Translation, in this instance, is also charged with revelation.

This strategy is not unusual in modernist canons set in place by writers such as Conrad and Joyce or by postmodern linguistic nomads under the tutelage of Borges, Bianciotti, or Puig (or more recently, Marcelo Cohen), but Stahl obliges the reader to posit the authority of the translator along the particulars of a North/South axis always disrupted by Asia. Translation from Japanese to English and then once again to Spanish is the entry point to alien lives. The experience of this process rests on multiplicity and movement; it offers power to the foreign eye and ear to alter the course of history.

Stahl does not insist on the magisterial agency of the translator. Rather, she selects for her literary focus the small lives that come to articulate the field of transnational exchanges. Furthermore, any dominant power is rebuked by the questionable location of the figure of the author both within and beyond the framework of fiction (is the writer an Argentine, a North American, a woman of Asian descent? for whom is this story told?). She leaves us with the overarching question of how to read an immigrant text in Argentina about a migration twice removed. Finally, Stahl draws attention to the multiple vectors of "authentic" truths that one can claim from the production of writing.

This global crossing and resistance to a single place for the enunciation of meanings opens alternative routes of exit and return to Argentina. As a process, migration and exile wrought through the translator's craft reorganize the *mapa mundi*, transforming relationships between North and South, East and West, familiar and distant landscapes. These experiences test the boundaries of home and foreign and chart courses for racialized bodies; they register bilingual and dissonant voices and cross the voyage of self-exploration with reflections on sexuality and translation. The following texts by Griselda Gambaro, Graciela Safranchik, and Diana Bellessi bring these issues under question, always reminding us of the alternatives that the "Orient" gives to the shaping of these problems in discourse. At the same time, they evoke the translator's craft to question the experience of representation and to challenge the standards of the modernist quest that promoted, in an earlier era, the authority of the writer. Finally, Ricardo Piglia and María Moreno draw upon the translator's cast of metaphors not to evaluate the eccentricities of Asia, but as a way to challenge the claims of modernist authority in the fields of history and writing.

Translation and Power

The convergence of rivers and tongues becomes the focus of Griselda Gambaro's attention in several of her dramatic works focusing on Asian culture. In "Es necesario entender un poco" (1996), she delves into the question of language by situating her dramatic action in a no-man's-land, on board a ship from China to France.[9] Here, she interrogates the linguistic relationship among men of unequal power. Basing herself on tales of Jesuit missionaries in eighteenth-century China, Gambaro explores the travelers' tolerance for difference and their capacity for recording this range of experience through measures of translation. The problem is enacted by the figure of Hue, a Chinese translator and scholar taken by a Jesuit to France and ultimately driven into bondage. Despite his skills at translation, his failure to understand the language of colonial rule relegates him to an asylum where he is forced to join in the theatrical projects of the Marquis de Sade. The Asian man is made victim for his linguistic and racial difference.

Hue inaugurates his commission on ship en route to France. The sustaining metaphor of translation practice, an agitated sea stirs bodies and tongues. For Hue, it creates the illusion of letters that dance on page as it also jostles the body, which cannot withstand waves of indefinite movement. Therefore, Hue cannot read or decipher once he begins his travel from home, despite the priest's assurance of the fixity of signs and the facile transparency of language. In this respect, the ocean voyage triggers a cultural conflict that will end with Hue's enslavement; when he arrives in France, the man of letters will become a *lacayo* (slave). Gambaro seems to tell us that colonial mastery determines meaning in language. Moreover, the struggle for interpretative rights, to borrow Jean Franco's phrase, becomes—in the seat of colonial command—a matter of physical force; the whip and the prison ultimately control our access to meaning. Translation is a matter of political power.

Nevertheless, when Hue returns home, after defeat and humiliation in France, he is received by his hostile mother. All along, it may be assumed that the mother, as a site of "truth," overrides corrupt paternal assumptions belonging to the priest and colonial power; Hue's return should signal logically a triumph of the maternal. Yet Gambaro quickly dismisses the nostalgic gaze, telling us that "the myth of origins" fails to offer redemption, just as the primary orality of the mother tongue promises no cohesion of meaning. Friedrich Kittler (1990) situates the reign of the mother decidedly within the romantic mode, claiming the maternal voice as the equivalent of desired unity; modernism, by contrast, produces attention to style and allows for plurality. Gambaro, here, moves away from both a romantic modality and modernist desire in order to produce conditions of rupture and nonrecuperation; her play introduces a postmodern nomadism whereby one relinquishes sentimental return in favor of the movements of language. As expressions of authorship and institutional power, neither the first language of the (mother-)nation nor the tongue imposed by colonial rule provides Hue an adequate solution to his enslavement. All categories of knowledge beg reevaluation, leaving him eternally migrant; he bears the curse of the translator who must swim through the infinite circulation of texts in which he finds himself immersed.

Literature devoted to this theme invites us to ask about the foreign challenges presented to the politics of gender and to the modernist certainties informing intellectual claims to truth. At the same time, the question of translation, when inserted in this panorama, also reconstructs categories of masculine and feminine and rearranges North/South alignments. It allows us to think of the cross of languages in any global vision, to examine the secrets of state that foreclose the marginalized person's voice. Finally, it forces us to put in doubt the guarantees of safety offered by maternal intervention.

In other words, the translational dilemma also allows us to speculate on representational form and eros. Like the other women writers to whom I have alluded, Graciela Safranchik cultivates this problem, this time, through Akinari, a Japanese translator in search of the ideal woman. Her novella *El cangrejo* (1995) is about Akinari's search for a woman called Miranda, whose name evokes that of Prospero's daughter and all the problems of colonial oppression through language that Shakespeare proposed in *The Tempest*. It is also a way to link the erotic to the dynamics of translation.

Safranchik's novel posits translation as a central metaphor of the book. It is not surprising, therefore, that this novel is focused on a Japanese figure removed from his native land; in an unnamed foreign country, he plays the role of the outsider who must make sense of difference. As in the original folio of *The Tempest* where Miranda (and not Prospero) teaches Caliban to speak, Miranda's presence in *El cangrejo* inspires Akinari to struggle with language and form.[10] These acts of translation and interpretation also offer the possibility of change in Akinari himself: "I am a chrysalis," he says early in the novel (8). Akinari assumes the names of the authors whom he translates. As if to negotiate between water and land, between different constructions of life and desire, between different temporal moments separating him from his writer of choice, he takes the name of "El Cangrejo," or "The Crab," as one of his writerly disguises. A convergence of form and text, of the beauty of image and one's comprehension of meaning, and—in a mythological sense—of the convergence of masculine and feminine as the basis of a rebirthing, *El cangrejo* engages the distances that separate and fuse image and name. At the same time, the novel explores the gap between culturally uneven subjects.

Safranchik mobilizes our wisdom about bilingual and translational divides. Akinari's father was a Japanese professor of languages; his mother, an "equilibrist of words" (68–69), and Akinari himself takes the title of "the joker, the great gabbler" (69). Yet Akinari's mother was a foreigner in Japan; her language skills derived from her role as an outsider in a distant country. The bilingual necessities of the parents are thus imposed on the hero; Akinari, an outsider himself, living in an unnamed country other than Japan, inherits a passion for translation, a different approach to intimate relationships and to the weaving of history and form. In the process, he studies the soul of "the other Akinari," a modern rendering of an ancient author dating from the age of the shogun (20), but he also teaches Japanese and corrects the written work of his students. Interlingual translation, Jakobson (1959) tells us, is the interpretation of linguistic signs in one language by means of other languages.[11] In other words, one's mastery of a foreign language sheds light on one's mother tongue; the field of difference also uses foreign experience for a closer inspection of and approximation to one's native terrain. This turn inward through translation is a path to self-knowledge; from an act of communication, it becomes an exposure of the gaps and silences within one's primary language. The economy of translation is founded on one's desire to designate this absence, to get closer to the opacities found in the source. Similarly, Akinari's work with language always reflects a translation sensibility that passes through time and nation, but it also allows him to construct different versions of self.

Does the translator give an exact dictionary account of experience? Or does he or she cultivate distortion in order to construct an object of love? The only clarity we have comes at the close of the novel, when Akinari embraces Miranda: this is not a simple love story, but a metaphor about the expression of desire. Akinari studies the ways in which aesthetic and erotic meanings are produced from the translational act, from the spatialization of oppositional values, from a conflict of cultural ideals. But he also tells us that the limits of sexual knowledge are produced from a crisis in language. Sexuality becomes the testing ground for the translator's exercise in self-representation. This is the silence that remains suppressed, only slightly scratched on the surface through the translator's act.

The late twentieth century may evoke the modernista's imagined voyage to the Orient in our last fin de siglo; but more importantly, it provides a way to raise the question of otherness from the perspective of the translator. Interestingly enough, Gambaro and Safranchik screen out the feminine voice and focus, instead, on a masculine figure as protagonist and writer. In a move toward impostorship of the kind noted earlier by María Negroni, the shift of gendered voice builds in the necessity for a sustaining mask in the act of literary translation.

Poet Diana Bellessi speculates on the effects of translation: "Translation is an attempt at alterity. Alterity of a body breathing the music of another language in the strict particularity of a voice that speaks it" (1996, 14). She repeats the words *double efforts, echo, love, mystery* throughout her text in order to prepare for her charge, a readiness to transform and create "something other than that rose full of meaning that the original sustains" (15). Bellessi notes the simultaneous efforts of mimetic respect and disavowal through translation. This text appears in the prologue to a remarkable collaborative endeavor, a bilingual edition of two sets of poems by Bellessi and Ursula K. LeGuin in which each author has translated the works of the other. *The Twins, the Dream/Las Gemelas, el Sueño* (1996) deserves serious attention both because it brings to light central issues of translation relevant here and because it provides one of the few contemporary examples of a convincing North/South alignment in the creative field.[12] Not only does the text rebuild alliance through the exercise of translation, but also its thematic focus on the landscape and language of the Americas opens radical alternatives for habitually nationalist readings of nature; it reveals the linguistic conflicts installed by competing visions. Again, Asia plays more than a minor role in anchoring these concerns, forming a locus outside the boundaries separating North and South.

Bellessi insists on the mediating role of the translator, attempting to bring the pieces of the Benjaminian "broken vessel" together once again.[13] Hardly adversarial or authoritative in voice and persona, the translator seeks reconciliation between cultures, urging an undisturbed respect in the relationship between original text and its foreign copy. But this complementary engagement nonetheless produces conflict, dismembering the original text and disrupting the unitary language of the translator. Translated language produces echoes and resonance, but also exposes a number of fault lines. In this respect, reading through translation redraws our horizons of intelligibility; not simply a betrayal, as some have advanced, the translator's effort builds simultaneous pacts among writers in which no participant is relieved of the presence of the other. In other words, the authoritative power of the translator yields to cooperation to bridge the gaps.

As a poet, Bellessi sets this vision of the translator's task upon the different representations of American landscape, rushing to unite different ideologies and cultures through the mediation of travel. More importantly, the mediation is sustained on an equal footing by poets as peers; Bellessi and LeGuin are reciprocal translators of the works of the other. Here, their mutual recognition of the poetic task temporarily unsettles the habitual dominance of the North/South axis. It upsets the concept of authority exercised with totalizing power. Both writers thus become migrants within foreign terrain. Uniting them is their recognition of the woman writer's role in reshaping the marshy fields of language; their temporary incursion into translating each other promises not a fixed conclusion, but points to future change.

LeGuin describes her project as compensatory; she links the role of the translator to the free will of the inventor. In this respect, translation becomes a supplementary act; through supplement, one announces the condition of temporary alliance and leaps the boundaries of nonrecognition as set in fixed time and place. But it also expands the world of the translator to include gestures of incorporation: "Translating is a way of making a foreign-language poem part of yourself," she writes (10). This is obvious in the prologue in which she sets up her project of translation and also in the poetic texts included in *The Twins.*

LeGuin's *Silk Days* (translated by Bellessi as *Días de seda* in the bilingual volume) conveys similar anxieties about translation and silence. "Give me back my language," LeGuin urges in her inaugural poem (160). Hers is not just a call to an originary voice, but a demand to overcome silence.[14] This petition is reiterated throughout her set of poems, alternating between a woman's right to speech and a forceful caveat to men about the dangers of usurping another's tongue ("To Saint George," 278). But LeGuin's volume, so appropriate for a dialogue about exchange through translation, is also about the transformational power of words: "You can read water. Now what? Walk on it? Drink, sweet lady" (162). Poetic language suggests an erasure of distance; moreover, it supplies the possibility of incorporation. She thus expands the commonplace to reach the materiality of language regardless of its structural encasement (164). "There was a word inside a stone," she writes, "I tried to pry it clear" (170). But if LeGuin works with these texts to reach the core of an Americanist landscape and to find the core of poetry itself, she is also especially clear about the objectives of the bilingual endeavor, designed to invade the dreams of the other, to be ensconced in the other poet's language and imagination. This becomes the maximum achievement that the translator might claim as her own. "I am in the dream of the puma, in the night of the huntress," LeGuin writes in a poem that refers to Bellessi (182). Is this the way to bridge the gaps between disparate languages, to fill the gaps in the North/South map, to override distance and longing? The collaborative endeavor certainly expands the range of possibilities in North/South representations.

The Argentine poet anchors a similar meditation on the possibility of transnational exchanges. Bellessi has always sustained an intimate relationship with North American lyric. A consummate translator, having rendered in Spanish a significant corpus of poetry by North American women, she addresses the encounters of translator with text, the transformations of sensibility required by one's entry into a foreign language and the lost legacy of women's voices that have been suppressed by modernist tradition.[15] These explorations also take fruit in her poetic explorations of the Americas, drawing the landscape into play as the substance and source of verse. The landscape in this instance always provides the soil of dialogue and alliance, a way to work marginal subjects, especially women, into projects of representation.

In this respect, it is significant that the texts offered for translation by Bellessi and LeGuin are texts of travel and exploration of feminine sensibility in writing. LeGuin assumes responsibility for translation of two of Bellessi's earlier volumes, *Crucero ecuatorial* (1981), a travelogue through the Americas, and *Tributo del mudo* (1982), a volume that begins with an evocation of Orientalist thematics about women and leads (again) to the American landscape. The axis then is established to move between North and South; secondarily, they evoke an Asian landscape to voice a protest about women's exclusion. In "Fragments from the Women's Writing," LeGuin tells of a group of elderly Chinese women who had written in an ancient script that was later suppressed by authorities. Although their texts explained the bonds among women, state interventions subsequently broke all tradition and memory of that alliance. LeGuin offers a set of poems that represents an imagined construction of what those exchanges might have been. In the first part of *Tributo del mudo*, Bellessi speaks of an abandoned concubine who became a Taoist priestess. For her talents as a poet, and for her authority in the literate world, she was later accused of crime and murdered. The poetry that accompanies this tale represents Bellessi's fantasy (and correction) of the life of that Chinese woman and a defense of women's access (in general) to literary culture. The Asian women named in poems of Bellessi and LeGuin call attention to a feminine lettered tradition that is suppressed even as it enters North/South terrain. As a paradoxical chiasmus in *The Twins*, this mapping of feminine presence disarms the reader's faith in a nation-centered project. In effect, the woman writer in this chain of global citations breaks conventional boundaries of territory and language.

Bellessi continues these explorations, investigating the ways in which a "foreign" subject enters poetic discourse. These inquiries are set in a zone of contact sustained by poet and American nature. From the first poem of *Crucero ecuatorial*, she sets this project in place: "Los tiempos verbales amarrados, como helechos a una misma piedra" [Tense of verbs / fastened like ferns to a single stone] (20–21). Nature generates language just as the landscape of America supplies the poet with material for verse. What appears passive, much like a stone, in fact orders temporality and life. Bellessi's lyrics included in *The Twins* announce the terms for quest: a search for meaning in unsuspected places and a celebration of the subjects and voices emerging from the American landscape. However, unlike the sitings named by writers such as Pablo Neruda, the landscape here is seen as a basis for meditation about the advantage of dialogue and exchange. Never denunciatory, it is a reach to the human subjects whose voices enter poetic texts through multiple vehicles of translation: Guayaquil, Tikal, and Tulum come alive with language. As in the poem that LeGuin will write to Bellessi, it is inebriation caused by desire for the other that transforms one's existence in language. Here, the project in translation is like a pact between lovers, poets allied in a common project, destined to transform the landscape into sites of communion.

But when—we might ask—does translation announce the inadequacy of language or even absence and loss? The acrid postmodern texts of Ricardo Piglia and María Moreno, writers skeptical of the uneasy relationships between minor and dominant traditions, address this darker aspect of translation.

Translating History and Desire

On issues of translation, Piglia is one of our most thoughtful and provocative critics, having explored this Argentine passion as a struggle to enter modernity that begins with the opening error in citation recorded in Sarmiento's *Facundo.*[16] More than any of the writers discussed earlier in this chapter, he brings the discussion of translated literature in confrontation with the objectives of state. Marginal literatures have their own possibility of irreverence, Piglia claims; herein lies their chance of transforming art from the periphery, a way to install different paradigms for reading that elude the demands of globalization as set from a metropolitan center. Greater issues are at risk: translation more than destabilizes, as Borges before Piglia might have told us; it obliges different relations to the world and, indeed, a different relation of individuals to experience. Here, the politics of representation, so avidly discussed during the initial years of democratic return, surfaces again as a politics of difference expressed through literary form.

Tejaswini Niranjana has written that translation in the colonial context produces its own conceptual economy. Unfortunately, she only sees translation as a way to produce "strategies of containment" (1992, 3). Through his critical texts and his novel *La ciudad ausente* (1992), Piglia reverses the terms of this problematic, opening sites for uncharted meaning and creating ambiguities of identity, style, and history. "To tell in lost words the history of all, to narrate in a foreign tongue," he proposes in that novel (17). Through the supplementariness of linguistic displacement, Piglia insists that the true identity of individuals is never completely confirmed; moreover, the fragile nature of bilingual texts sustains multiple versions of what one might accept as "real." Like Melville's character Bartleby, the scribe, who inverts his skill as a copyist to issue a voice of refusal, to say when asked to collaborate with authority, "I would prefer not to," Piglia turns to translation in order to dislocate the power of the state understood as a fixed repository of knowledge. Translation redirects information and shifts the terms for art and individual identity.[17] In this respect, Piglia brings into contact those private aspects of language (those that resist publicly accessible meanings) and those aspects of language that participate in an economy of regular exchange; alternative venues reroute the languages governed by state interests. In the tensions between these two is the possibility of creating a different version of history and social community. Translation signals those sites where languages collide, announcing a crisis of different systems for social meaning and value.

Piglia's great obsession alerts us to these problems in the narration of history; how to link language and emptiness, how to find a fictional strategy that explains a missing center of knowledge. Like *Respiración artificial, La ciudad ausente* also goes back to the Argentine past, but instead of accounting for the present in terms of a nineteenth-century vision, Piglia in *La ciudad ausente* depends on the particulars of translation such that a totalizing vision of history is impossible except by coordination of its parts. As if abandoning a search for narratable origins of individual development, Piglia now finds in the miniature another view of social evolution; metonymy and interconnectedness account for historical process.

It is not coincidental, then, that Junior, descendant of English explorers who reached Argentine shores in the nineteenth century, spends his life as a nomadic traveler, living in B-class hotels, having achieved neither distinction nor privilege nor even the possibility of continuing a family life. Yet it is Junior's task to inaugurate an investigative study of the museum, making connections between disparate images and episodes, balancing public and private lives, and linking past and present. In other words, Junior sets out to learn how to translate between two spheres of experience that presumably mirror each other despite the strange distance between them. His is an all-embracing task destined to fail insofar as the current times deprive him of access to a totalizing logic. In fact, in defining this search, even Junior is effaced from the novel, to be replaced by minor figures drawn from the technological imagination or from selections of literary tradition. Thus we are not only confronted with the principal question of *Respiración artificial*, "Is there a history?"; but in *La ciudad ausente*, Piglia also asks about the nature of inventiveness in an environment dominated by mechanical signs. In this situation, all subjects beg for a dialogue based on lived experience but are faced usually with fiction: fictions of daily experience, fictions of the state.

Throughout *La ciudad ausente*, characters search for momentary community, to make otherness legible within the realm of daily life. This is sustained by a preference for the nomadic, in which figures roam between objects and events in search of a common language gleaned from the exercise of translation. Deleuze and Guattari in *A Thousand Plateaus* (1987, 223) speak of the state machine that overcodes and compartmentalizes, of the binary structures that organize thought to the point of rigidity; against this state-defined apparatus, notably present in Argentina, Piglia—perhaps like Deleuze and Guattari—supplies another instrument, propelled by imitation and invention. "Imitation is the propagation of a flow; opposition is binarization, the making binary of flows; invention is a conjugation or connection of different flows," write the authors of *A Thousand Plateaus* (219); from this kind of invention, multiple "desiring machines" emerge that establish the possibility of dialogue and communal redemption. And insofar as the machines always translate from language to language, they facilitate a subversive communication that eludes the market-run state. Within this context, translation works to ponder aesthetic value and the relationships of individuals to community.

The strangers who inhabit Piglia's novel focus on the proliferation of texts and identities yielded by the exercise of translation. *La ciudad ausente* thus underscores the production of minor stories. Mediation and the process of creation count more than an originating text. From this experience, we learn that the strangers of the novel—as much as the Argentines themselves—are all invested in the cyclicity of translation, trying to make sense of their national histories and of each other through machines of language. Even Fuyita—the lone Asian character of the novel, one more "outsider" among many—carries significant information to Junior on ways of reading history. He produces an envelope that carries the clues to reading the "white knots," those marks found on turtle shells that are similar to the images found in Chinese oracular traditions for deciphering inscriptions on bones.[18] Asian antiquity here supplies an approach to alternative readings of contemporary history; like other foreign references, it opens a way for Argentine locals to translate the languages of home. The other meditations are found in women's voices (from the deranged surrogate daughter of Joyce and Macedonio's lamented Elena to the recording machine with female speech designed by Nolan to relieve his loneliness) which intervene and interpret the historical projects of men. As in the relationship of the authoritative original to the subservient copy (a pairing always described in highly gendered terms), the echoes supplied by women and the Asian man always announce a contradiction in the masculine heroes' search, leaving characters in solitude and without their desired insertion in history. Their presence calls into question any masculine approximation of the "real."

La ciudad ausente raises representational issues in a world in which an absolute, founding truth is no longer attainable despite our reach back in time. Moreover, this kind of activity is a way to surpass any model for literature described as national allegory, a resistance to any attempt to homogenize local culture. In it, Piglia invites us to see if "difference" can be analyzed in a more productive way that ultimately facilitates an infinite chain of variants on the themes of exile, isolation, and loss.

Piglia also situates this relationship between the original and its copy, between the source text and its translations in the heart of the mass-media age and the process of globalization. It is "the delirium of simulation" (15) that motivates characters of *La ciudad ausente.* The novel is composed through different copying machines: cassettes, walkmen, radios, television monitors, maps, and mirrors—even tattoos—reproduce in miniature the larger representations of life and feeling. Paradoxically, they promise a remedy for loneliness and isolation, but they also question the validity of any claims for an "authentic life." Nor is it surprising that reality is constantly altered by drugs, alcohol, hallucinations, and madness. These effects press characters toward places of eccentricity, socially without power, where they look for the possibility of writing a dissident kind of national history.

In this respect, Piglia evokes a modernist literary legacy that had promised to resolve these problems by making sense of some putative whole. Although Borges's "El Aleph" engulfs *La ciudad ausente* as an ur-text of sorts (for its lists and catalogs of objects that are designed to produce a "story," for the constant play between originals and copies, and an obsession for details of translation), the principal figures who inspire Piglia here are Macedonio Fernández and James Joyce, each supplying a paradigm for modernist translation and traditions of funerary mourning (Macedonio grieving the loss of Elena; Joyce grieving the madness of his daughter, Lucia) and terminating in a lament for loss of dialogue despite a proliferation of words.[19]

Equally important, Piglia evokes these writers to reflect on the disruptive practices of literature and the avant-garde role of the artist. Macedonio, by his refusal to publish a "completed work" or book, defied commercialization that would contain the possibilities of art. Here Macedonio is evoked as the master of the fragmented text, the episodic reading; he issues a disbelief in character and a refusal of fixed categories of being. Through his *Museo de la novela de la Eterna* (1967), an incomplete text that never qualified within the conventions of a genre, structured as it was by mirror images, by replicas without any original, Macedonio offered a profound reflection on our desire to capture individual identity and name it within a literary corpus. Too, his wake for Elena Obieta generated Macedonio's hope to find that point in space and time that would survive the passing of history. Piglia uses this constellation of materials to grieve the loss of conversation in the present, swept away by oblivion, politics, or mass-market trade.

Finnegans Wake (1939) also anticipates these anxieties. It is not simply that we should compare Dublin to Buenos Aires (a theme rich enough in itself); rather, the presence of Joyce in *La ciudad ausente* poses a number of questions about the interaction of national and foreign texts and the relationship between tradition and the avant-garde around questions of representation. Joyce's masterpiece, modeled in large part on the Egyptian Book of the Dead, can be linked of course to a metaphorical Argentine Book of the Dead, which is found in Piglia's museum, a space where a wake is maintained for the "disappeared" of both history and literature. Like Piglia or Macedonio, Joyce also sought to identify an original source of meaning and track its multiple reproductions, resulting in the constant dismemberment of discourse and text. And like Piglia, Joyce devoted himself to subterranean explorations of meaning and memory. It is worth bringing their two texts into conceptual alignment insofar as they share a cultural vocabulary that gives clues to the representation of history and loss. Joyce was concerned about the "Hole affair" (1967, 535)—how to represent memory and its lapses, how to reconcile life and dream and fill the blank spots of the mind, how to understand—and surpass—the common etymological roots that link the words "amnesia" and "man."[20] Perhaps anticipating the "white knots," which Grete Muller hoped to decipher in *La ciudad ausente*, the characters of Joyce's *Wake* were devoted to uncovering the ties between memory and experience in order to awaken from amnesia. For that reason, Joyce found inspiration in Vico's *Scienza Nova*, which sought a language to explain the concealed histories of the races and their interconnections. In a parallel way, Piglia investigates the chance of defining community through internal social history; language, here, is the key for this connection and a way to provide continuity and remembrance.

Like Joyce, Piglia studies the relationship between words and objects and emphasizes, above all, their mutability due to acts of translation, whether in the relationships of father and sons or directly in moving from one language to another. In the process, difference constantly proliferates, identities refuse reduction. One of the chapters of the *Wake* is entitled, "Who's who when Everybody is somebody else." Its message could also serve as a signal to read Piglia, whose book leaves us with simulations and copies, translations of archaic texts kept in secret museums, where the voices of unsettled figures echo and cross each other. It is interesting that Joyce acknowledges the *1001 Nights*, in translation by Sir Richard Burton, as an inspiration for the *Wake*; Piglia also evokes this classical text through his references to Scheherezade. This Arabic source allows us to think of art as transformation and the uses of a translating machine to postpone our meeting with fate. It allows a way to reconstruct the global and local encounter, a way to escape the market-driven economy that understands globalization as a trade of objects and bodies without soul. Here, Piglia decisively introduces concepts of *transformation* as if to say that Latin America is not just the repository of first world detritus, but an active site for the reinvention of literary forms and discourse. This optimism notwithstanding, Piglia reminds us through his citation of figures such as Macedonio and Joyce of the far more limited possibilities of today's avant-garde artist to violate codes of state and market. Trapped in a maze of echoes and repetitions, rerecordings of ancient songs that once promised teleological coherence, the contemporary writer is left alone and abandoned with only the outer trappings of a project that once promised redemption.

Where is the authentic text? Can any idea exist previous to the moment of writing? Can we return to the classics of high modernism and use those same forms of expression to narrate a different experience? In search of these connections, Piglia rivets his attention on Macedonio and Joyce. Just as he focused, in the magazine *Fierro*, on the classics of Argentine literature in order to disrupt the order of high and popular cultures and explore the multiple languages of national writing, Piglia in *La ciudad ausente* refers to enduring models drawn from different spheres of literary experience in the hope of finding alternative circuits of meaning, controlled neither by the duress of dictatorship nor the scarcity of neoliberal times.[21]

Piglia thus cross-circuits given fields of knowledge, but opens the gates to a reconstruction of the language of history and horror. It is not surprising, then, that madness, dreams, and unfinished invention occupy the space of narrative. Uttered by delegitimized figures, by outsiders and women, these delusions escape the image effects of the global market; at the same time, they test the order imposed by the state. Piglia inverts the market premium placed on image-effects and supplies another motive for invention, but he also acknowledges the impossibility of returning to modernist aspirations to teleological wholeness. These modernist desires, which are posited on the illusion (and failure) of romantic love between man and woman, on relationships between fathers and children, are all the same debunked by María Moreno, who announces, instead, the emergence of the reign of an autonomous (post) modern mother.

Strangers in Translation

In *El affair Skeffington* (1992), Cristina Forero, writing under the pseudonym of María Moreno, mocks the claims of the United States and Europe to any original culture; she toys with the projects of recuperating sources and of advancing an "authentic" voice. The vehicle for this irony is found in the exercise of translation set in the period of the frolicking avant-garde of Paris in the 1920s. A caveat should be issued here. Moreno has no pretensions of making sense of a totalizing history; unlike the anxieties expressed by Piglia for finding solutions in a modernist past, the concerns of María Moreno are directed against the institution of letters that excludes dissident voices. More important still, her turn toward modernism as the setting for her work allows her to explore a moment of upheaval in the formation of literary traditions, a moment when the discursive positionings of sexuality and the field of bilingual expression were the special targets of playful transformation in the cultural field.

El affair Skeffington tells of the discovery of a collection of poems written by Dolly Skeffington, described as a North American expatriate in the Parisian literary gatherings of the 1920s. The pretext of this anecdote allows Moreno to revisit what she calls the scene of Paris-Lesbos and the cast of characters and conventions that define high modernism as we know it. The scene also allows the author to explore questions of nation and exile, originality and translation, and the transformations of identity that are propellants of literary form.

We quickly realize that Dolly Skeffington wrote under pseudonym; for that, she is likened to Pauline Tarn who took the pen name of Renée Vivien or Judy Gerowitz who later became known as Judy Chicago. It is then an additional irony that author Cristina Forero takes the pen name of María Moreno. In the world of doubleness that becomes symbolic of writing itself, Moreno/Forero echoes the doubleness of "Paris-Lesbos," sustaining cloaked identities and secret liaisons, and an ambivalent regard of sexuality that was the hallmark of Paris in the 1920s. This doubleness is everywhere, at once fluid and defiant. It describes the group of lesbian and bisexual women nourished by modernist broth; it announces the screen or disguise that belongs to language, literature, and translation. This doubleness directs the reader to the pact between eros and writing, to the floating identities that contribute to the unstable idea of the "author." At the same time, Moreno makes clear that this unsettling and playful mobility affects all areas of social exchange except those that threaten to leap the social divide of class. In a world where Dolly is able to play with identities and flaunt her shifting sense of self, privilege and money are clearly announced as the lubricant of this public display. In this condition, "nomadic social classes" (39) are the only taboo. This class hierarchy, Moreno reminds us, has been set in place by the authority of the father.

"It's a matter of making fun of the father, occupying his place, seizing his role as pervert" (11), explains the narrator. On the one hand, Moreno's novel undermines the premises of modernist thinking that celebrated a communal brotherhood, foreclosing possibilities of alliances among women within the formally structured cultural field; on the other hand, the fatherly presence that is subject to Moreno's teasing also evokes quite deliberately the vast shadow cast by Freud not only on modernist terrain of the 1920s but also on questions of sexuality, language, and translation, on the representation of experience itself. What is experience, in effect, but the systems of substitution organized by that dominant "other" who chooses, writes, and records? Who is the subject of psychoanalysis, and who transcribes its representations? Who, in the final analysis, can claim privilege over an authentic citation? The discussion is centered on the paternal influence exercised over structures of family, identities formed by families of writers, canons that determine subjectivities and literary history, but also the logic of inclusion and expulsion that establishes norms of meaning.

Moreno turns the culture of psychoanalysis into the center of an absurd reflection on naming and representation in order to reach the unnamable of sexual alternatives for women. Not only is the description of Paris-Lesbos an assertion of the polyglot world of the exiles, it is also a matter of rebellion and perpetual movement around issues of sexual choice and one's authority to claim it in writing. In fact, same-sex love is always in movement in this book, at once source and actualization, a gesture against monumentality; it opens the possibility of an infinite flow of meaning. It allows a recodification of mythological tales from the perspective of women and reconstructs the symbolic field. However, as Moreno wrily notes, same-sex love, although it is everywhere, rarely finds a name.

In the early pages of her text, Moreno parodies the voice of the serious scholar who would pretend to identify sources and dates, bringing the tools of textual criticism to the service of modernist literature in English. She thus tracks the author's confused biography and the publication record of Dolly's twenty-eight poems, linking the texts to sources such as Margaret Anderson's *Little Review* or events in Greenwich Village. She also presents Dolly's poems about the outsiders of this distant culture: Chicanos in Los Angeles, gay men in World War II, and lesbians in love in Boston. The trick, of course, is as old as literature itself; what is worth our attention here is the linking of translational practice and sexual pleasure. For the unspeakable quality of lesbian love, Moreno explores what cannot be said, she devotes attention to sameness and difference, she takes her readers on an odyssey through prohibited territory and language, she tests asynchronicities against conventional literary order, she toys with traditional concepts of authorship and the genres that have excluded women. At the same time, she reminds us that the memory of all sexual pleasure is in itself an act of translation, a repositioning of discourses that creates an illusion of access to what is far out of reach or lost.

In the ambiguities of Paris-Lesbos, a woman's attraction to a man or a woman is the starting point for this endless quest. In the long run, it is joined to questions of authorship, identity, and nation. Dolly Skeffington as a character in a book opens questions about the constitution of literary form: What is character? What is an author? For the structure of the book at hand, atomistic and nonsequential (as much as the "life" described therein), one might also ask what a literary work is—if, indeed, it has a determined structure or is simply a recombination of forms without a necessary center. Finally, for the circulation of identities that Dolly's personage evokes, Moreno also brings into question one's allegiance to nation: "'I was also fascinated by feminine beauty, but lesbianism was an unknown temptation, an unknown territory for me. Man was my homeland,' roared Victoria Ocampo in another place (although she might have been there) and Nina Hamett sang in the bars of the *rive gauche*: 'We went off to Argentina / where all the men are queer.' Perhaps for the North American and English women who made Paris a revival of Lesbos, man was also their homeland. But it happened that they were in exile" (13). From the known maps of charted pleasure, we then move out of fixed terrain; lesbian sexuality in this instance is a condition of expatriation. It produces a need to speak beyond father and homeland, to announce the insufficiency of any single language, to celebrate the noncorrespondence of images emerging from flawed translation.

Moreno's book, of course, reminds us of the fiction of all writing authority. The false manuscript, the multiple languages, the shifts between Buenos Aires and Paris upset any stable idea of voice, sexual preference, and place. But hers is also a book that reminds us of the infinite flows of meaning set in motion by sexuality and language. Translation, in this context, shows us an economy of mismatched signs whose single truth is difference. It presupposes an unresolved conflict between source and copy in the same way that the image of Dolly is organized around the double: "In the life of Skeffington the number two persists: she was born in 1892, she arrived in Paris in 1922, she has two names, two objects of sexual desire, two forms of expression: writing—two styles, two genres—and a kind of conceptual art" (41). In addition, the text is made available in Spanish by the intervention of the translator Delia, who interprets the words of Lily Tate as she tells what she knows of Dolly. Delia translates from English to Spanish to explain the nature of Dolly's love for her girlfriend Gwen:

> When I was a girl, what struck me as the oddest thing about my grandmother and Gwen was the way they leaned on each other. It didn't seem like a way that sisters touched each other nor the style shared by mother and child, it was . . . a . . .
>
> There was a silence and then Lily Tate and Delia spoke rapidly in English. It was pretty boring until Delia, who didn't seem to be translating said "that's it!", but Lily was absolutely still, looking for the missing word. Her silence—and not her error—was anguish for the others. She seemed to have all the time in the world. As if she were dealing with a didactic proposal. Pilar, Lola, Marga, Marisa, and Mary Murci began to throw out words, each taking turns, but all at great speed: "embrace," "crossing," "mounting," "Siamese twinning," "coupling," "buttoning," "soldering," "zipping up." Lily Tate spoke up and Delia translated "fit." "You could've said it," said Lola, but Marga kept looking at the stone and Lily kept speaking through Delia. (51)

Following this, the narrator admits that the intense love of the pair eludes the precision of language. In this encounter, which in so many ways recalls the love scene in *El beso de la mujer araña*, individuals lose their constitutive identities; no longer separate, they enter a zone that is marked by the impossibility of complete translation into the observer's field of vision.

Elusive, lost, or transformed once again, translation fails to coordinate identity and desire, to breech the gap between representation and the intensity of female passion. In effect, *El affair Skeffington* signals our blind faith in the communicational truths of language; equally important, it signals the failure of translation to move tongues between different forms of experience. As a result, then, the inability to name passion between women unhinges our critical knowledge; it reminds us of the grave omissions of language and cultural history. More aggressively still, Moreno makes fun of the pretentious categories that govern the academic mind; she puts to test the translational process that fails to link language and sex. She also reminds us that what one suppresses or forgets in one language can be a starting point for discussion in another.

Traditional descriptions of the translation experience explain the dialogue between self and other, the transformations of a source text, the recollection of genealogies, the links between past and present. But these Argentine writers suggest that translation also evokes constant disruption, leading in the final instance to a reassessment of identity and power. Here, even the failures of translation are a liberating force since they free all individuals from the conceptual grasp of a single dominant language. Rather than subordinate a text or voice to the sphere of another, these reflections emphasize constant flow, an assertion of risk and mutability that urges future dialogue and exchange. These creative endeavors draw attention to the undefined edges of words that still fail to define us, the geographic boundaries that are always surpassed. They refer us to the sound of language, the basic human breath in the air that opens endless meaning to readers and invites unbounded translation. "Como una compuerta que cede espacios, respiración" [Like a floodgate that opens spaces, breathing] (1), writes Alicia Genovese in a book of poetry, significantly titled for our purposes here, *El borde es un río* (The border is a river) (1997). Writers like Genovese will constantly look to the flow of the margins rather than the river itself. They remind us that slippage and displacement lie at the soul of language; these gestures render one's condition as eternally "foreign," even within national frontiers, but they also leave writers unbound by rules of correspondence belonging to a sense of home. In turn, they upset the conceptual maps of North and South, East and West, modernist and postmodern assessments of knowledge. They bring into view the power of a gendered field to alter the politics of geography and the illusion of a global wholeness.

PART III. MARKETS

¿De quién era esa voz?
[To whom does that voice belong?]
—Ricardo Piglia, *Plata quemada*

CHAPTER 5

The Politics of the Text: Experience, Representation, and the Return of *lo popular*

In *Quadrivium (Ad usum Delphini)*, an installation presented in Santiago (November 1998), Chilean artist Gonzalo Díaz asks us to ponder the illusion of movement. His work suggests an enigma about noncorrespondence between image and language. Organized in a large room that is of purposefully difficult access to the viewer, the installation consists of fourteen displays, each of tripartite division and set flush against the gallery walls. Díaz positions these dioramas slightly above our line of sight, repeating the same landscape in each. A tunnel carved through a small plaster mountain protrudes from the left side of each scene, a painting of the sea stands on the right; connecting both is a miniature track that sustains a tiny metal boat, positioned in various stages of movement in each of the different displays. In the first, the boat protrudes from the tunnel until, in the final scene, it merges with the seascape, leaving visible only its stern. Above these settings, each of fourteen projectors flashes the name of a

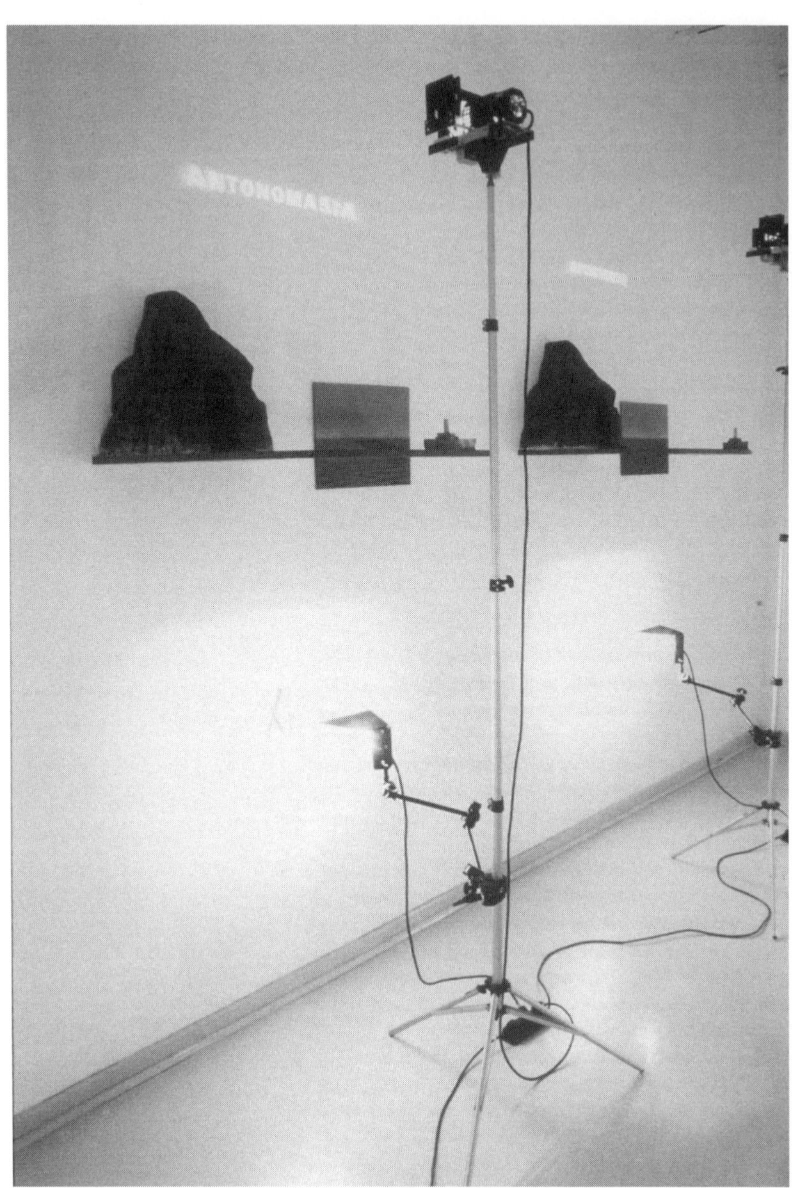

4. Gonzalo Díaz. *Quadrivium*, 1998. (2 views) Installation (XIV stations of the *via crucis*), oil on wood, plaster, and metal, tripod with projector and lamp, dimensions variable. From gallery catalog, *Quadrivium*. Introduction by Pablo Oyarzún. Galería Gabriela Mistral, Santiago de Chile, 1998. Photograph by Jorge Brantmeyer. Permission to reproduce images granted by Gonzalo Díaz.

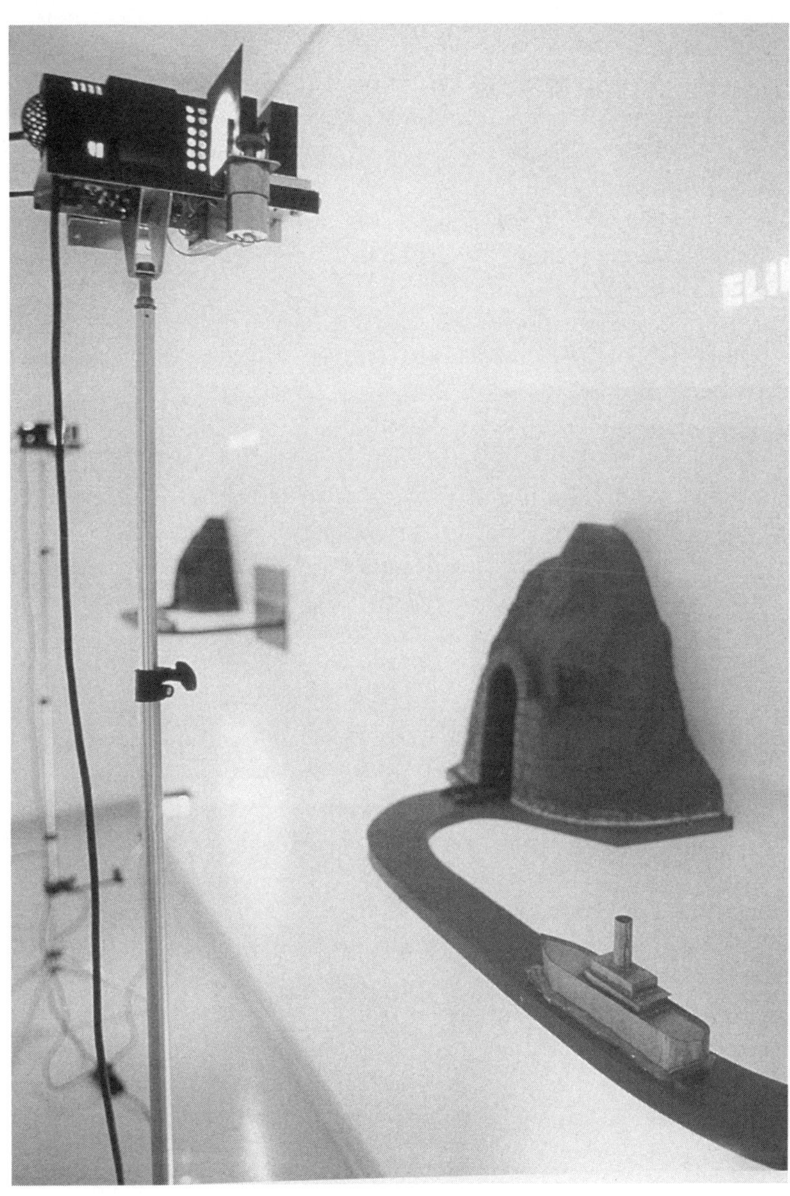

different rhetorical figure; words such as metaphor, catachresis, oxymoron, and metonymy blink in isolation although the significance or purpose of these poetic terms is not immediately obvious to the viewer. In a tier of images below the dioramas, fourteen slide projectors illuminate a sequence of roman numerals, indicating a proposed order of apprehension for the scenes above them, although they may also recall the stations of the cross. Meanwhile, the unending clicking of these machines creates a disturbing buzz in the air as if to urge viewers to resolve the perplexing mystery of the sequential vistas set before us.

Díaz calls our attention to the ways in which we infer movement and meaning from static pictorial scenes. Images flashing above and below these minimalist landscapes should supply a conceptual apparatus to link language and visual experience while also evoking an inheritance of artistic practices in the field of representation, yet in this instance we don't quite know how to put these images to use. The artist thus invites us to reflect on our verbal understanding of space and our construction of movement in history. He asks for the visitors' intellect and gaze to reconstitute disconnected signs such that *local* referents of the installation be connected with some *global* framework of meaning. In other words, the string of apparently simple scenes begs us to complete the historical continuum with knowledge from our previous experience, filling all temporal and spatial gaps with supplements drawn from our imagination and an inherited critical language. Although Díaz directs us to the workings of interstitial logic, a phantom yet obligatory "in-between" with which we link fragmented images, in the end, he also provokes our need to complete a story.

Is the scene an allegory for Chile? A citation of its narrow terrain? A comment on modernization or the vastness of a national project designed to link mountain and sea? Paradoxically, the countryside of Chile (signaled by the expanse from mountain to sea) is recuperated in the language of cities (the rhetorical tropes and guiding sequence of numbers). Framed in the metropolis, our aesthetic judgments must brook elliptical forms stationed *elsewhere* in order to resolve the enigmas of landscape and national history. In the process, we cannot help but remember that historical continuity is of our making, drawn together by taking our conceptual leaps over obvious gaps in time and space, bringing unfinished narratable movements to a satisfying close. Here, the enigma to be resolved is a matter of narrative construction itself; it becomes our own *via crucis.*[1]

Although not concerned here with the genre of "interactive" art, Díaz nonetheless insists on collaborative exercises to be performed by the viewer. His installation reminds us that the nature of narrative, indeed the retelling of history, functions from the supplementary knowledge that readers and spectators bring to the scene of perception, filling the crevices of broken narration in order to render it whole; moreover, completion of the frame depends on an outsider's vision. Like the medieval *quadrivium* that gives this installation its name, we are obliged to think of the paths of learning that guide us toward eventual knowledge. This work of art also serves as an introductory move for our thinking about literature, specifically for entering in discussion about the textual politics confronting authors and readers in our current times.

While neoliberalism attempts to render complete and totalizing narratives about culture under globalization, covering the unevenness of our different stories with a homogenizing gloss, avant-garde art and literature work from a contrary assumption, often revealing those sites of suture where fragments are weakly united, uncovering the point where art, on the verge of collapse, "magically" becomes whole through the intervention of spectators or readers engaged with narrative process. This does not mean, however, that avant-garde art rejects a "story." Exposing the margins, the "in-between," the unresolvable contradictions of contemporary times, or the contrasting impulses of commerce and art, of course, have been part of the festive and revolutionary aspects of the postmodern turn; but the symbolic realm also maps alternatives for our perceptions of social life. It responds to our pressing desire to reconstruct, from fragmentary or partial form, a sense of the whole. Whether we insist on a unit of completeness that takes us nostalgically to archaic legend or exalt irruptions of incomplete thought as a challenge to institutional law, we are revisited constantly by an obsessive pull between metonymy and wholeness, possibly the guiding tropes of our culture.

These strategies also remind us of the dilemmas of *responsibility* that still lie at the center of literature and art. Indeed, in an aesthetic project that signals the crises and fissures in the existing social mold, a pathway opens to reflection, a bridge of communal comprehension. Therein, the reconstruction of linear narrative, the revisited search for origins and meaning, the invitation extended to the outsider to build alternative versions of a given story. Although our times are marked by a great passion for melodrama and for the completeness that biography and memoir supply to mass consumers, avant-garde texts forge another type of engagement with the ideal of completeness. Exposing the stitches that seam the fabric of narration, revealing the illusion of totalizing logic that often governs mass-marketed writing, the avant-garde text posits other demands for the apprehension of art.

In today's literature, this cultural project is often directed to the cities where neoliberalism has taken hold. It obliges us to rethink our traditional ideas of a unified polis or, as in Díaz's work, the unified sense of a nation. Breaking urban scenarios into fiercely contestatory sites, testing the integrity of official narrative and the imagined coherence of a public sphere discourse that no longer fulfills our needs, disrupting the models for consumerism that promise totalizing form, avant-garde literature under neoliberal regimes answers with tactics of displacement in order to construct a wholeness of its own creation. Often, the inscription of lo popular, banished from intellectual debate for its delinquent status, returns in literature as a way to sustain this tension. The popular subject thus propels us toward movement while elsewhere stability is vaunted; it disrupts a previously uniform calm informed by the workings of nostalgia or the neat resolution of melodrama. The presence of popular subjects reminds us of the gap between experience and language, the dislocated idioms that beg for reintegration in local history. It sustains a realm akin to the Deleuzian "intermezzo" (1987, 25) while also directing us toward a desire for completion of narrative in an age where one assumes commonly that there is no tale to be told.

"I want to write a true history of what is really happening," asserts Ricardo Piglia's character Renzi in *Plata quemada* (1997, 199). To supply the narrative glue that will bind all fragments, to draw attention to the artist's hand as bricoleur in constructing the illusion of the real: this project engages writers at century's end, but not without their casting an ironic wink at readers who share both a desire for convincing narration and a knowledge of the narrative tricks of the trade. Especially in this age of skepticism and infinite disturbances of truth, these narrative projects invite us to rearrange geopolitical landscapes insofar as they disturb accepted temporal sequences and expose the gaps in standard knowledge. Narrative thus claims its rebellion against the common order of things in order to sustain alternative trackings of reference. This operation takes place in uncontrollable venues and through literary subjects who express themselves through equally uncontrollable languages. "Santiago is dislocated," observes Diamela Eltit in a fitting close to *Los trabajadores de la muerte* (1998, 205). The panoply of voices and visions, which consistently breaks apart, tests audience desire to maintain the narrative as an intractable whole. Often lo popular services this project of disruption.

When writers turn to popular roots as subject matter for fiction, they expose the flows of darkened meaning that underlie official discourse; they return us to an unauthorized rendition of the social whole. The impulse allows us to reflect on the different languages of civil society, to expand the basis for common experience, and to rethink the place where art and literature invent their spectators and readers. Although often accused of brokering the interests of elites as so many cultural critics have recently claimed, literature that returns to popular beginnings exposes the mutilations of the social corpus; it explores the inadequate sutures that pretend to align the fragments. Finally, it allows one to meditate about the interventions of knowledge that fill the gaps of the "in-between" and invites one to think about the movement that directs textual politics and form.

These texts structure space to suggest alternatives for community and art; they propose modes of intelligibility that stimulate collective reflection; they produce and defend different subjectivities that the state no longer cares to address. Although the implications of this project arise from literature principally from Argentina and Chile, the discussion can be extended to the problematic of cultural production anywhere in the Americas. The point of departure here is the city and its margins, the meeting of popular and elite traditions, the conflict of voices that enter in competition to reveal the politics of the literary text.

Cities of the Lost Millennium

In the era of high-modernist culture, the city was a central protagonist; the dark spaces of Dublin or Paris, Santiago or Buenos Aires were the focus of passionate writings, occupying the center of divagations about the expansion of metropolitan cultures and the labyrinthine spread of alienation and despair. Novelists and poets tested the limits of urban realities and explored the emergent voices of marginal figures: Borges's wanderings through the periphery, the *orilla* or the tree-lined neighborhoods of a growing porteño metropolis; Juan Emar's celebration of humble lives in the city; or the explorations of Roberto Arlt and Manuel Rojas, who drew upon the metropolis to foreground a world of delinquents. They all test the fragile borders that organize urban maps to express both a sense of marvel as well as a growing fear. One kind of postmodern excursus in particular produced in recent years uncovers versions of the city marked, on the one hand, by abandon and loss and, on the other, by hope for repopulation. The city devoid of its former inhabitants, an evacuation of its public plaza, the city that exists as an echo of previously spoken languages is the *site* of exploration. But this is a city that shelters simulacra, where translated experience and deformed citations compensate lost voices of the past. This is also a city taken by a chorus of unidentifiable popular voices, allowing readers to resemanticize old obsessions about the politics of alliance and movement. As if to run in conflict with postmodern attentions to the fragment, representation of this *other* city often reaches back to an archaic structure that promises a secure totality. To follow the metaphor of Gonzalo Díaz, while much contemporary narrative appears to leave us stalled on train tracks somewhere between mountain and sea, it often creates an anxious desire to recuperate an absent city. This fiction manages to propel the reader toward a scene of integration, toward a city that claims a resource of voices to speak about the linkage between politics and culture. In other words, this fiction works from an impulse to name yet unrecognized social formations and, in the final analysis, to set comprehensive tales drawn from the power of marginal speech.

Gonzalo Contreras constructs a sense of this longing in his novel *La ciudad anterior* (1991), an investigation of the blankness of an abandoned urban center that leaves individuals in an ethical vacuum regarding a course for social action. An important text that captured the alienation of Chile under dictatorship, it supplied an understanding of national fragmentation that was to be reiterated by other writers in both Chile and Argentina. The novel begins and ends with the narrator standing alongside the Pan-American highway, outside of a provincial city that will later occupy the focus of narrative action. Faced with regret for his misguided choices, for his alienation from a distant metropolis, Contreras's narrator inaugurates an odyssey that cannot be halted, a constant withdrawal from the dilemmas presented by ethical and affective conflict. And just as the highway connects distant points on a political map, it also reveals sites of disjuncture and uninterpretable actions whose significance the narrator repeatedly chooses to ignore.

In the unnamed city, the empty central plaza situates all events; surrounding it are neon signs, electronic devices, telephone lines, and a huge television satellite, technological markers that compensate for any personal illumination or real dialogue in the public square. A resemanticization of the kind of plaza that was central to Diamela Eltit's *Lumpérica*, the plaza of Contreras's novel invites a reflection on the absence of coherent conversation among individuals in public places. Instead, the narrator observes, "Everyone in this city has something to sell" (22). All that remains are suggestions of an "anterior city" that has since been evacuated of the possibility of political meaning, a center now dominated by a logic of sales and opportunistic exchange, where citizens lacking in habits of coalition or common cause ignore the chance for mass mobilization that surrounds them. In this novel, no one is capable of "reading" political unrest; thus, the elusive labor strikers, named occasionally in the course of the novel as a Greek chorus of collective memory, are largely ignored by the principal characters. The workers pass as a minor annoyance until the moment when their marches of resistance occupy the central plaza and interrupt the security of the town. In this way, Contreras appears to tell us that political activity is present despite our refusal to view it.

Set during the Pinochet years yet anticipating the market-run climate of neoliberal democracy, the novel hosts a cast of suspicious and itinerant figures: a traveling salesman who trades in arms, a corrupt airplane pilot allied with the military regime, and a disabled man in a wheelchair who is a supporter of Pinochet. Their itinerancy orchestrates an interrogation about the politics of movement and one's responsibility for making sense of the whole. They invite the reader to reflect on available venues of knowledge for incorporating social action. Above all, the protagonists elicit a reflection on displaced ethics and the weight of contradictory experiences that cannot be fully absorbed. Carlos Feria, the narrator, wanders through a country in ruins in order to trade in arms. Paradoxically, he promotes a product that promises individual security but leads potentially to the eradication of those who might have promised him dialogue and hope. Also within the space of paradox, Araujo, a pilot responsible for having thrown dissidents from airplanes in 1973, devotes himself to seeding clouds in order to make rain for profit; like others, he gains from the manipulation of nature and human life. The double conflict emerging from the conjugation of visible and hidden realms of experience, through the contact between nature and murder, is of course a code for the horrors of disappearance under years of military rule, but it points to the logic of a neoliberal market that would suppress all historical thought. Finally, it begs us to bring order to experience, to connect the space between ethics and action.

Contreras utilizes his characters as place markers in fiction. As silent figures, they offer fragments of evidence pointing to damaged social relations; through their movements, they also signal the illegal workings of individuals in an illegal state. In effect, the mobility of characters through and beyond the provincial town leaves a sea of contradictions about the ethical pact and the nature of a "national" space that joins them. Finally, as Contreras allows readers to grasp only fleeting moments of the many fragmented lives circulating in the novel, he calls into question the possibility of a totalizing yet ethical fable that might exist beyond the province of law.

An immensely successful book whose publication coincided with the return of democracy to Chile, this novel proposes, as some have claimed, to investigate the recuperation of possible meaning among a disaffected and lost population (Cánovas 1997, 87). It also propels a critique of a fragmented culture that other writers of the decade will embrace as well. Readers are asked to suture the mobile fragments that Contreras leaves in view, knitting distances, linking characters, rendering coherent a series of conflictive actions. In this way, the novelist places in opposition one's need for a plenitude of form against the unevenness of ethical content and asks us to take stock of the failed measures of knowledge with which one subject can engage in dialogue with another. He thereby forces us as readers to account for the distances that distort the nature of affective relations. What is required of us to bridge the gap in this dislocated logic? How might we recuperate a sense of integrity in action and experience? How do we construct a city?

Contreras's novel prompts us to ask a series of questions about aesthetic intervention in the field of reference and leads us to inquire about the "real referent" of fictional narration in general. In other words, departing from this text, we might ask about the nature of material that slips between bodies and social events named in fiction. *La ciudad anterior* speaks of relationships, proximities, and movements, connecting bodies to sites of social conflict and to the deadly effects of market-run culture. In general, movements in this textual space oblige us to contrast knowledge and imagination, memory and creative force against the deterministic anchor of an unyielding neoliberal project. Through the mobility of bodies touching upon different urban crises, this kind of fiction recognizes a contradiction between specific individual experience and larger political projects of state. It forces us to contemplate the space "in-between," that which has not been spoken, and to consider—from the effects of movement and naming—the possibility ad interim for dialogue and exchange.

Recent thinkers have meditated upon these tropistic movements in literature to link bodies and political events, to define what has no name. Benedict Anderson, for example, locates a structure of simultaneity in the novel that allows us to imagine the nation. Like the mortar that holds together the disparate elements of a text, our common understanding of nation links characters, place, and action (1991, 25). The interstitial glue that binds different representations evokes more than a retrospective vision of our shared national heritage; indeed, it offers the possibility of a social meditation of the future. In this respect, I have drawn clearer inspiration from the suggestive essays of Slavoj Žižek and Judith Butler when they speak of the "rock of the real" (Žižek 1992, 11; Butler 1993, 198). For these writers, the overarching question is not so much a nominalist matter of finding an exact correspondence between name and object, but a problem of locating the social content in discourse in the spaces between language and referent and between subjects and their objects of desire; from here, one might track the "effects" of language in shaping a political vision. This assertion rests upon a fundamental faith in language as an activator of change. Žižek organizes this discussion to say that language is a history of norms that functions through exclusion; it works through a set of repressions with its limits and boundaries. And when a subject is excluded from normative discourse, it becomes the basis of identity; a defining negativity emerges through acts of foreclosure. In other words, I am defined by what you won't allow me to be; my "true" identity is therefore postponed for some moment in the future.

At the same time, the discursive act inaugurates a trauma regarding the unbreachable distance between language and our understanding of the real. As there always exists an unattainable meaning that eludes our grasp, we fail in our efforts to speak a coherent version of reality. The real is unfigurable, always displaced, always postponed for some future time; for the present, we are left only with the *effects* of that struggle to signify and make meaning. So it is not that language fails us because it teaches the obvious; rather, because it can never recuperate a full sense of real experience, we are pressed into anxious reflection.

How do we overcome this trauma of not being able to say or mean? How do we recuperate the distance between bodies and representation? What, for instance, does it mean to speak about history, democracy, or loss? It is this great dance around naming the "real"—the "rock real" as Žižek puts it—that conditions our own self-definitions as subjects and our experiences in space and time. In postdictatorship Latin America, where a taboo is placed on community and where values outside of market sales are suppressed, the possible alignment of language with that "rock of real experience" is all the more elusive, postponed for some future moment of reckoning.

Žižek's ideas help us to talk about the aesthetic possibility of Latin American prose and poetry to activate our memory of the past and provide a collective sense of the future. By the highly mediated situation of the languages and "scenes" of a text—and the dynamics of difference produced therein—we can move toward recognition, suggesting far wider truths about our political existence in the world. The space between different representations is laden with unsuspected meaning; it allows a realization of a spatial "in-between" from which subjectivities are drawn. These figurations lead, in turn, to future political imaginings, instituting a mode of performance and a collective common sense not regulated by the state. In this way, the aesthetics of reference does not replace the rational hypothesis (Jameson 1992b), but supplies a different formulation of reason altogether; it inaugurates a collective inquiry about politics and reminds us of the failures of history to include the "disappeared": women, popular sectors, victims of political violence, workers—like those figures in Contreras's novel—whose actions pass unnoticed or persist as a social annoyance.

Inciting Representation

Bridging the gaps between dislocated experience and meaning has been the task of writers and artists. In *Cita capital* (1992), Chilean Guadalupe Santa Cruz charts this project on female subjects who travel through urban spaces. She draws a map of the city of Santiago, crossing traditional lines of demarcation in order to bestow a name to unstructured, unformed feeling. As the title of her novel suggests, her project is to secure a *cita*, in the double sense of citation and meeting, a point of convergence between name and object, between past and present enunciations. Is there an existing language capable of naming the dense cartography of bodies that populate the urban maze? Or must one always begin anew with a reinvention of syntax and sound? Santa Cruz gives identity to her protagonist through a number of devices ranging from the focus on a camera lens to the miniature as a souvenir. Too, the trained eye of the surgeon and the gaze of the torturer contribute different approximations to the female body. In one scene, the protagonist of *Cita capital* says wryly to the doctor, "You know where the body begins and ends" (74). She thus concedes that medical science has a closer hold on the manipulation of truth than the world of intuition or feelings. But do these points in fact cross? Can we locate with precision the sites where subjectivity and science converge? Or are we so embedded in binary thought that we fail to give voice to alternative tongues, to recognize alternative sources of meaning? Fighting the oblivion that has been imposed by the market-run state or unraveling fixed systems of citation, Santa Cruz's characters turn to interstitial rhythms and whispers. The power of suggestion counts more than direct affirmation and declarative statements. As if to close the gap between subject and object, between name and referent, the narrator hopes for the reproduction of objects in their organic rhythms ("The reproduction of things in their organic rhythm," [192]).

In *La letra de lo mínimo*, Tununa Mercado praises the power of the female whisper as a way to build community and structure an alternative narration (1994, 43). Mercado locates the whisper in its pure physicality, in its material representation; it fills the space between already existing discourses, it announces certain transgression. It is, in other words, an unexpected, invasive presence constructed with an eye toward disruption. For its subversive possibilities, it also allows the basis of an aesthetic project. The goal here is not to identify the interlinking webs of human experience founded on nostalgia. Rather, Mercado's remarks on the whisper point to the inadequate fit between language and form, the need for an alternative voice. Similarly, Santa Cruz turns to the organic presence of the voice that links past and future representations in language, the semiotic movements of speech capable of naming bodies that have eluded the appeal of a universal aesthetic. In *El contagio* (1997a), for example, Santa Cruz proposes a revised linguistic field that concedes authority to new bodies and voices. She writes in one section of this novel:

> Me brotaban por la boca letras hasta la frente, oscuriendo la visión del mí a mundo, echando hacia adentro la sangre, palabras pulsadas, tictac líquido repetido en venas. En vano rostro se distampaba un canto orfebre, epifanía que por coro llevaba el son *humanido*. Refregado, repercutido, mientras yo cocineaba canturrando.
>
> Es corpe humanido cariñaban partías de un de mío. Ser. Fragaban en disconcierto, fregatas, friegando alanzas de nochizo jurare: tambala mandibuleo y el simiento. Ne timoro ni agano, alindámesos del foresto más cureado, solicio antro, esnuda pátula dos fertiente, avor es manos, arcaïcio.

> Letters sprouted from my mouth to my brow, darking the vision of the my to world, pouring blood toward the innards, pulsated words, liquid tic-tac repeated in the veins. In vain, face unstamped a silversmith's chant, epiphany which by chorus carried the *humanite* sound. Rubbing, reverberating as I hummed and cookened.
>
> It is a humanite corpus, de-parting of my whole endearing. Being. They brambled in dis-concert, oaths of rubbing, frugging filings of filberts: staggering punch to the jaw and base. Neither fearly nor arousish, let's embellish the forest most drunkish, solicitous sinus, sneezy hustle but vlowing, to aver is aving hands, arkaic. (1997a, 141)

Familiar language disintegrates here into scarcely recognizable form. Based on the structures of an earlier understandable tongue, speech now becomes pulsational; other rhythms take over. This practice indicates an uncharted space of desire not controlled by the rules of science or by those doctors who, in the novel, are linked to prison camps and torture in Chile. In this way, Santa Cruz begs us to look at different rules for making meaning. The fragment and dismembered phrase are the basis for reconstruction of a whole.

Latin American intellectuals have been obsessed with these formal matters of naming and location in order to reverse the unreliable markers of historical signification and reach for expanses of meaning. In the process, they offer challenges to existing modes of citation and produce an inquiry into the aesthetics of space and location. This proposal is not dissimilar from the critique offered by Žižek insofar as all potentiate the fragment.

The interstitial form, the space of the "in-between," has become the basis of a radical textual politics that unsettles the comfort of narrative tradition, but it also signals a desire for reconstruction. Eugenia Brito, for example, celebrates the hybrid creations drawn from interstitiality: "It is the hollow . . . that casts light on the darkness from which 'plot' emerges" (1990, 181). Emptiness loans meaning to story; it illuminates recognition.

Many have written in defense of the fragment as a resistance to completeness (Richard 1994; Richard 1998) and celebrate discontinuous forms of expression as an alternative technology to linear memory. The pastiche, the uneven fragment, and hybrid forms of representation give voice to unplanned messages; they open to a culture of the margin. In the process, they override any totalizing efforts identified with official power and suggest an alternative to historical memory as a concept complete in itself. Even in their partiality—better stated, especially due to their incomplete form—these shards of experience document a possible subjectivity not endorsed by the state or market. Nelly Richard argues that this fragmented perspective also requires a *leap* (Richard 1994, 15). In the *leap* is the breakdown of order and linear logic; it inserts disorder in linear memory and disfigures the patrimony of the state and the market. Instead of disjuncture, however, the fragment elicits a desire for a reintegrated whole. Not simply the leap into chaos, then, but a move toward reconceptualization. *En route* to aesthetic possibilities, to new social configurations.

Thinking about this problem from the perspective of the lyric, Argentine poet Arturo Carrera seeks the mystery of separation and correspondences offered by a literary text (1993, 13). Fragments of images and dislocated sites of experience are juxtaposed in poetic process much like tropistic movement: "Tropisms . . . are movements that disconcert the will, passions, and desires. They are so secretive that they stir a game of sensations that even alters content; something always new and resistant to the profane: mystery. And a band of continuous beauty emanates from here, a commotion that is slow yet instantaneous" (56–57). This tropism is not random movement, but an initiation toward knowledge. Carrera expands this image in his poetry. In *La banda oscura de Alejandro* (1994), the poet insists on a splintered image of the world as the basis of a modern poetics: "Un ser no se afirma todavia en su ser/ Un ser se afirma todaviá en el terror de su música discontínua" [A being finds no affirmation in being/ A being still finds affirmation in the fear of discontinuous music] ("Siesta," 10). Discontinuity and excess are then reason for celebration. He writes in "El color índigo": "¿Qué nos une/ sino su esponjoso exceso de voluptuosidades?" [What joins us/ but the spongy excess of voluptuosity?] (20). This refractory sense of the aesthetic object is translated to a world of possible community; the parceled image invents a possible audience of readers. From the poetic stance, beauty lies in the multiple factions, in the band of darkness that separates the different colors of the rainbow. This space, which gives title to Carrera's book, promises a milieu for the crossing of references of stability and excess. It is both a source of aesthetic pleasure and a site for the reworking of knowledge.

These strategic deployments of spatial discontinuity prevail throughout modern Latin American criticism. Beyond the much vaunted discussion on this topic offered by Homi Bhabha (1994), they reflect a writer's uneasiness with a totality that might pass for official history; more important still, they suggest a way of managing past and present with an alternative sense of the whole. Uruguayan poet and critic Hugo Achugar is helpful here when he emphasizes the random multiplicity of art as a way to enact a leveling of social spaces (1992, 1994). But what is the relationship of this postmodern aesthetic to the past? For Richard, the very partiality of the fragment allows us to overcome nostalgia (insofar as nostalgia is formed from a totalizing effect of memory); it permits us to enter a relationship with the past that is critical and uneasy, never comfortably finished. Achugar, however, finds historical meaning in the crossing of boundaries, at the point when public and private, popular and high art cross, where the world of simulacra touches the sublime. From this decentered art, seemingly without transcendence, an art that only allows us to note the act of representation and not the ideological coherence between things, the political comes forth in the gesture of interpretation and analysis, in the space opened in the imagination of the reader, where a conflict simmers between a totalizing view of history and the specificity of one's personal past. Achugar locates the political reading in the residual, in that which cannot be locked in categories or contained (1992, 94). It is what remains of a national culture after the stereotypes have been stripped away. "What remains, that which we can't account for. That which we can't or don't wish to explain. What is there, before our very eyes, but we don't know how to see, what they haven't taught us to see. . . . That which others, instead, have been able to see. The unexplainable, that which the macro- or micro-theories have ignored, displaced, marginalized, because it complicates or contradicts what has been understood as fundamental" (1992, 95). Literature works from the residue to provoke surprises in our normal associative connections between historical events, to provoke alternative views of citizenry and action. The residue, I want to argue here, is significantly marked by deviations in the narrative field of sexuality and gender, and in the emergence of a suppressed popular subject who, in recent years, appears to have lost a place in political theory. But it is also a redirection of culture from global to local focus. This local rootedness, as Renato Ortiz (1996) reminds us, returns us to popular subjects.

Popular Excitations

The work of Pedro Lemebel, one of the most interesting writers in contemporary Chile, brings forward a number of these contentions between fragmented and total knowledge, using the recourses of gay subjectivity to enunciate the local rootedness so often desired by cultural critics but which seems to escape their view. A totalizing logic emerges in Lemebel's writing from a decided attention to popular *voice. La esquina es mi corazón* (1995), Lemebel's first book, follows the style of the crónica in describing the city of Santiago from a decidedly gay perspective. It is this gay vision of the city that supplies a model for micropolitics against the power of the state. Lemebel acknowledges the tensions between the market-driven paradigm and a vision of what he calls the "South American rubbish" (18); he chooses to represent this as a spatial issue, as a geography of those, internally exiled (20), who remain marginal in Chile despite a return to democratic rule. The result is a social utopia unraveled, compensated by what the author terms a "loca geografía" (85), a geography that is, in the double sense that *loca* lends, both queer and crazy.[2] A burgeoning chorus of unauthorized voices fills the city. These emerge from the beauty parlor, the baths, the street corners, the main public park; as sites for the potential political exchanges of bodies, they simultaneously disrupt all maps of urban planning that identify uniform, homogeneous spaces. In these places, Soledad Bianchi writes (forthcoming), no prohibitions hold, nothing is censured or limited to a single vision.

Lemebel begins from principles of antiorder, pulling together elements from the residues of the city. He gives privilege to objects, figures, and events that fall outside the market; he names sexualized subjects who refuse to be cataloged in the economy of the democratic state. Accordingly, he resists the tendency toward oblivion that characterizes contemporary politics in Chile: "It seems at this point in the century that memory of pain is a video clip that can make you dance with a bag of French fries in your hand. It seems in this same film that we see disappeared persons, Jews, women, blacks, and fags—all together—trampled by the thick undulating soles of army boots, Adidas sneakers, and tanks. It seems with each turn of the helmets that the scorn toward democracy is repeated. It seems, at right angle to the steps of the parade, that the rows of marching testicles are grenades in reserve about to explode once again on La Moneda" (42). The transition to democratic rule is here countered by an irresolvable violence. Against the neutral sheen of democratic order, a potentially explosive disorder challenges society's margins.

Lemebel's obsessions for the oblique perspective on cultural politics, for the vision that extends from the margin to cover the radical events of Chilean politics from the time of the transition to democracy, are an integral part of his writing project, essential to the crónica as form. A hybrid genre to endorse the hybrid nature of the city, to express the permeable nature of cultural exchange that prevails despite neoliberal regimes, Lemebel's chronicles permit one to travel through a force field of cultural artifacts drawn from the United States and Europe, from politics to mass-media culture, to forge an alternative global quilt of patchwork patterns to blanket the North/South map.

In *Loco afán* (1996), the AIDS virus becomes symptomatic of a general illness spreading throughout Chile: social communities broken down, the disaggregated conditions of the city, the presence of a globalization model that only serves to inflict harm on local subjects, alienating them from work and pleasure. While directly concerned about the virus that has plagued the gay community of Santiago, Lemebel also uses the AIDS trauma to speak of the plague of democracy and the crisis of culture. In "La noche de los visones" (11–23), for example, he tracks the changes of the gay male body from the time of Allende's Popular Unity government to today's market-run democracy. From the festive celebrations of impoverished drag queens on New Year's Eve 1973, captured in a still photograph, to the solemn rituals performed on the neoliberal landscape, Lemebel wryly observes the changing bodies of a community victimized by globalized models: "The photo bids adieu to the century with the threadbare plumage of the most broken-down queens, still folkloric in their illegal gestures. They seem assembled in an archaic frieze where the intrusion of the gay patron has not yet left his mark. Where the native land is still untouched by the plague's contagion, something of a recolonization through the medium of bodily fluids. . . . The 'homosexual man' or 'mister gay' was a construction of a kind of narcissist power that could not yet find a place in the famished mirrors of our local queens" (22). A paradox of inversion is apparent here: if dictatorship insisted on the virility of the state, it nonetheless permitted the social presence of the loca, or cross-dressed queen; neoliberalism, with its supposed tolerance for difference, imposes a masculine imaginary even upon its most deviant subjects. Now the masculinized image of gayness, copied from U.S. models, supplants the earlier aesthetic, although Lemebel will seek out the uncommon places where the loca continues to prevail. Thus, Madonna's style is absorbed by a cross-dresser of Mapuche origin who mimics his northern idol with catch phrases in English; the image of a transvestite in a public museum brings us to question the practice of censorship under democratic rule ("La muerte de Madonna," 33–40). Indeed, this crisscrossing of semantic fields dominates *Loco afán* such that the global language of the market, inflecting Chile in the 1990s, enters unavoidably to inflect (and infect) the body of Lemebel's work.

Like Gonzalo Díaz's installation, Lemebel's texts focus on fixed scenes of recognition (the photograph, the televised image) in order to ignite an uncontrollable movement of bodies and voices. Nevertheless, whether focusing on marginal figures in *Loco afán* or the well-known political celebrities in *De perlas y cicatrices* (1998), he repeatedly obliges the reader to draw a *connection* between elites and popular subjects. From media personalities who achieved fame during the Pinochet years to ironic representations of popular figures from the barrio, Lemebel's topics lead to a plenitude of meanings; interstitial references erupt on the flanks of monumental discourse. Thus the tranquil landscape of the cordillera is a pretext to speak about criminality and drugs, the wealth of the new bourgeoisie is juxtaposed to a representation of the impoverished *rotos*, or the fallen social classes; Lemebel's preferred subjects thus announce the instability of Chile before the law. They remind us, as one critic has noted, of the provisionality of the present (Bhabha 1994, 216). The cast of oddly matched characters who range from privileged corporate executives to personifications of subalternity itself allows us to see the yawning gap sustained by discontinuous historical realities in Chile. They show us the differences between private life and the mediatic version of global culture, but they also show us the power of the *voice* as the unifying factor that lends coherence to this rebellious version of history and structures Lemebel's texts. Many texts cultivate orality as a way to challenge official discourse (compare the writings of Carmen Berenguer, Hernán Rivera Letelier, and Lucía Guerra who borrow from popular sources; Alberto Fuguet who drew upon the voices of middle-class youth in his earliest works and now cultivates popular voices), but the crónica, for its unauthorized literary form, depends especially on popular speech to cut against the urban grain. In this context, it is especially telling that Lemebel's evolution as a writer moves from the silent *staging* of marginal culture (in his early performances with Francisco Casas) to the recuperation of *orality* drawn from the speech of the city's poor inhabitants. The fact that his texts are written for presentation on the air waves of Radio Tierra further confirms the increased appeal of this auditory aspect of lo popular.[3]

Style may be a resistance from below to the institutions of fashion (an idea advanced by Roberto Echavarren [1998a]), but it may also be said that style of *voice* is a challenge to the fashion of language. What captures the imagination is deviance from the linguistic norm; and in Lemebel's case, the marginal figure of the barrios, whose language has not yet been incorporated by high fashion or official discourse, initiates a contestatory voice, a defiance of institutional order. In this respect, the crónica, as an exchange of voices, works from a seething challenge to consecrated narrative fashion and the authority of "serious" literature. In other words, it depends on the kind of subaltern language that upsets the dominant tongue.

In the first chronicle of *Perlas y cicatrices* ("Las joyas del golpe," 11–13), elite sectors supporting the dictatorship donate jewels to support Pinochet. When a society matron later sees her donated brooch on the dress of another woman, she loses all control of speech, she becomes inept and aphasic. At this point, Lemebel likens her to the roto when her voice of indignation cracks and removes her from the world of elites. He thus uses the trivial episode, a miniature scene of conflict within the scope of a single social class, in order to reach for the places that elite culture rarely touches. Roto and elite both speak of injustice in a language incomprehensible to those who claim to uphold the law.

As an ensemble of creative interventions, these texts reverse canonical narrative form; they destabilize the accepted cartographies of meaning that shape cities and nations; they challenge the presumably fixed relationships between popular voices and elite traditions. Moreover, these crónicas question the rapport between local and global forces, between dominant and subaltern languages that have been aligned in relationships of hierarchical power. Years ago, Brazilian critic and novelist Silviano Santiago (1975) shaped this problem to speak of the "entre lugar," or in-between, opened by strategies of translation. Preoccupied with local and global considerations, Santiago argues that the goal of translation is not to highlight the tension between the original text and its copy, but to break up the authority of the model and show the value of micropractices. Through lexical gaps, pauses, and the traffic between cultures, translation opens the dimensions of experience and places all images in movement; it breaks any strategy of containment and destroys concepts of essentialist unity. This mobile exercise is also another way of widening the gap between the stable image of a fixed historical past and the volatility of an undetermined present, an effort in elasticity that shows the span of urban cultures, a translation exercise that opens an intermezzo (in the Deleuzian sense) to test one's perceptions of reference. Finally, the translational movement between elite and popular voices allows us to examine the construction of dominant myths that control our times. In this respect, it leads to a critique of the social whole.

Latin America's most interesting texts are devoted to these metaphors of translation, seeking out the "entre lugar," investigating the fracture and recomposition of historical and cultural discourses. From the resulting languages of Babel, a plea for community often emerges; the absent city is filled with a chorus of voices in search of a common project. This style of writing sustains a micropolitics of representation, minor stories that elude universal law and corrupt traditional meaning. Ricardo Piglia and Diamela Eltit, two major Southern Cone writers, draw on this kind of material to critique the neoliberal market and state. In their writings, they refer to minor voices as a first step toward imagining alternative social units, but they also engage the power of popular voices to indict the failures of society and the limits of narratable history.

Piglia's novel *Plata quemada* (1997) presses the contradictions sustained by hoodlums in conflict with the law. Elaborating on a widely reported shoot-out between cops and robbers, Piglia sets his story in 1965, a period predating the horrors of military rule and the subsequent celebration of free-market logic. He signals a moment in history when both common delinquents and men of the law begin to share a common ethos and vision within the space of the city. The story tracks a planned bank robbery in Buenos Aires followed by the criminals' flight and subsequent confrontation with police in Montevideo. Written with an ear to the sordid language of those who inhabit the underworld of drug culture and prisons, Piglia's novel tests the relationship between orality and fiction, between the fiction created by telling a tale and its bizarre resemblance to historical process. Piglia deploys this project in a metropolitan center soon to experience radical change.

One of Argentina's best readers of nineteenth-century cultural politics, Piglia does not allow us to miss the obvious connection between the criminals' flight to Montevideo and the flight of exiles from Rosas's regime more than one hundred years before, a founding gesture that inaugurated a new style of making history, containing both the promise of liberalism and an invitation to modernity. But unlike the towering presence of Mármol and Echeverría, those Argentine men of letters and politics who sought refuge in Uruguay, Piglia's exiles are a hoodlum crop who follow a passion for money; criminality thus dislocates any previously held platform of utopian ideals. This dual vision, what Piglia once described with reference to Sarmiento as a case of Argentine strabismus, a bipolar desire placed at once on the grandeur of European civilization and the seductions of savagery at home (1994), here preys on the reader's memory of a double Argentine literary history—the foundational and the transgressive—but it is also played out as a crossover between state corruption, at the official level, and the roaming delinquency of subaltern figures in the belly of urban culture. In the process, Piglia tests the distance between performativity and value, between the spectacle of crime (as covered by media) and the deeply set symbolic attributes of consumerism and purchase generated by the availability of *money.* Piglia reminds us not simply of the purchasing power of money but also of our voracious desire for the bills themselves, our desire for possession. Far from a "virtual real" of computer-generated exchanges, of markets that trade in abstract symbols without reckoning with the weight or consequences of neoliberal measures, Piglia allows us in *Plata quemada* to maneuver among the raw form of money that exists less as a symbolic medium of exchange than as paper bills to be robbed, transported, incinerated, and eventually destroyed. This process thus stands in contrast to the usual disembodiment of labor and dollars that belongs to current economic theory. And in defiance of the universal law registered in brokerage houses in cities from New York to Tokyo, Piglia sustains a debate about the materiality of money through the popular voices of subaltern figures who test the limits of the law.

Piglia is not alone in this reading of contemporary culture. The conflict sustained between cops and robbers is also the stuff of contemporary potboilers and also much recent film. Gustavo Graef Merino's *Johnny cien pesos* (1993) or Marcelo Piñeyro's *Caballos salvajes* (1995) are among the many feature-length films that use the tropes of media spectacles and the run on banks in order to examine the greed of neoliberal society. At the center of these operations is the question of desire and the creation of concepts of value. Rich and poor occupy the concerns of the directors of these recent popular films, reminding us of the voracious appetites of the media and the neoliberal state, which both exploit and then dismiss the popular subjects who enter their purview. These films thus focus indirectly on what is lost from spectacles of looting when they are covered by mass-media endeavors; they point to the need to *experience* desire directly—giving it form and name—and to the efforts to create *value* from abstract symbols, to build an ethical pact. Nevertheless, Piglia goes beyond these film projects, seeking to explore the ways in which the passion for money and drugs acquires material form in language. He brings forward the complexity of narrative at the point when popular voices contribute to the density of experience and representation.

The *distance* between intellectual theory and popular subjects is ever increasing, or so it appears, as the new millennium begins. But while Southern Cone critics tend to estrange themselves from popular subjects, repudiating social movements and retreating from the interests of marginal sectors, writers turn to popular voices in order to construct a field of "difference" that functions as both aesthetic challenge and social critique. Of course, "difference" derived from a contrast between dominant and subaltern subjects has always been the basis of literature. From medieval times through the romantic impulses offered by *costumbrismo*, it stimulates both an aesthetic project of contrast and a social debate, making accessible what some have called "the vision of the vanquished" in high-culture texts.[4] In Argentina, in particular, this phenomenon extends from the ninteenth-century *gauchesca* literature to the aestheticized treatments of creole and immigrant voices of the 1920s and 1930s (here, I have in mind the early poetry of Borges, the fictions of Arlt, or the *teatro criollo* of Discépolo). Orality continues to be sustained through evocation of popular speech, whether in the disembodied style of Puig, who erased bodies in order to let his middle-class voices serve as the basis of characterization, or the code switchings of César Aira, who teases the linguistic pretensions of different social classes; even the nostalgia-based novels of writers such as Roberto Raschella and Antonio Dal Massetto recuperate Italian idiolects to call attention to alternative visions of law and social community. Piglia is also an heir to these hybrid traditions, but in *Plata quemada* he brings forth a conversation among marginal figures in order to highlight drugs and crime. Written in the slang of the modern porteño underworld, the novel is densely enshrouded in violence. Moreover, Piglia will not let the reader escape this fundamental component of style; indeed, even the most resisting audience cannot read around this thick celebration of delinquency and oral expression. The foregrounded verbal exchange among thieves becomes Piglia's major project as he joins aberrant style with a social critique of the nature of money and narration.

Style, Deleuze and Guattari once wrote, offers the possibility to create an alternative language of memory. In *A Thousand Plateaus*, for example, they explain, "What is called a style can be the most natural thing in the world; it is nothing other than the procedure of a continuous variation . . . an assemblage of enunciations that unavoidably produces a language within a language" (1987, 97–98). Indeed, as these writers add in a different section of their text, style constitutes the basis of a minor language, one that sends the "major language racing" (105). Here, style exposes the conflicts between different strategies of representation; it announces the intrusion of something new, a traumatic distance between languages belonging to a social whole. To exacerbate that conflict, writers often turn to the representation of lower classes, marginal or immigrant voices.

Piglia goes one step further and deliberately inquires about the effects of one's struggle to make meaning, seeking in subaltern speech a way to foreground both the power of marginality and the corruption of the state. "Malito understood the assault as a military operation" (20), writes Piglia, suggesting early in the novel the overlappings between criminals and state officials, who share a similar arsensal of metaphors and images related to their desire for power. This is also linked by an effort to reconstruct links between past and present. In *Plata quemada* the seemingly linear aspect of narration, which recounts the criminals' plans to rob a bank, their flight, and subsequent entrapment, is repeatedly interrupted by a distorted temporal syntax; *antes* and *después* (before and after) are so commonly foregrounded in style that we cannot help but confront the contrivances of all linear narration. Too, Piglia reminds us of embellishments by the media that contribute to this debate on style. Augmented by the pretensions of newspaper accounts, television broadcasts, and wiretap transmissions set by police, the novel as a whole confuses the order of events, but also constructs an odd sequential logic in order to justify the authority of telling. Renzi, for example, a figure in all of Piglia's fictions, makes a reappearance in this novel as a newspaper reporter; he follows the events of the crime, structuring a before and after, until he becomes, in the final chapters, a figure with a voice of his own. Renzi tells us of his dream of reaching the uncontested truth of fact, but more important still, by observing the incendiary activities of the lumpen protagonists of the novel, he gains the verbal courage to confront the chief of police and expose the inadequacies of this man's stories. His reward for persistent reporting, then, is to challenge the claims of the state.

Plata quemada leaves us with a series of questions about the authority of narration: Who has the power of access to information, who controls retrospection, who directs the ear of the state and usurps the readers' trust, who controls the art of telling? In this context, the registry of voices is always suspect. As Piglia tells us, even the transcriptions are open to multiple readings. However, these paths of reading, which belong to all strategies of constructing a fiction, here create startling echoes that remind us of the distance between experience and recording. Malito, for example, reads about his colleagues in crime in the daily newspaper and is surprised to see the velocity of reportage and the image of his friends in print; the characters also watch the television news to learn of their own war on the city such that the virtual reality supplants all the trappings of direct experience: "Also (as the chronicles show) the gun slingers watched on the TV in their room the events that they were actually living" (163). The gap between real death and the reported murders seen on the evening news, the temporal delay between direct actions and habitual replays of video paradoxically signal a distance and convergence of generational cultures, separating 1965 from the decade of the 1990s yet ironically drawing them together as one; simultaneously, they proclaim a necessary distance between any "original" action and its repetition in media form. Does the intermediary space between the two extremes beg us to reflect on a lost country and foregone ethics, in the style of nostalgic narration? Piglia does not permit this; rather, he reminds us of a culture in which bodies no longer matter. In effect, the gaps he structures in the pages of *Plata quemada* point to a noncorrespondence between experience and naming, a misalignment of the symbolic field between what we might sense as the "real" and its representation in words. The gap signals the loss of direct engagement in the construction of value.

Can we ever recuperate a totality? Can we know the subject of discourse? "So many thoughts and such little real experience," comments Nene Brignone as he reflects on the quality of time he spent in prison (96). But he could also be speaking of the dreams of wealth that allow the lumpen to desire a life in New York or the utopian fictions that propel the characters through various phases of addictive desire. From another angle, he also suggests that we are left with virtual form without access to the possibility of meaning. As the narrator explains about Roque Pérez, a character who devotes himself to wiretaps and interpretation: "He didn't want to capture the meaning . . . but the sound, the difference between voices, the tones, the breathing, in order to identify each one" (182). Form overrides content and style displaces meaning, but more importantly, Roque Pérez attempts to reassign materiality to voice despite the state's mandate against it.

Although it is certain that the state wins out in the end (after all, the criminals are killed or captured), what is lost upon the state are the symbolic codes, the personae behind the voices, the agency of those individuals who are the subject of surveillance. In a similar example, the psychiatrist Bunge tries to make his patient Dorda "equal to everyone else" (224), normativizing his speech so that his differences are suppressed, so that deviance will cease to pose a threat to existing social order. The density of speech is such, its dangers of revelation so severe, that the narrator, speaking from police chief Silva's point of view, declares, "They had to be killed so they wouldn't talk" (195): twin versions of truth, which refer to both the need to kill the delinquents in order to stop their idle chatter and the menace that their confession might pose to the reputation of police. This double voicing or double entendre comments on the corrupt publicity tactics of the state as well as the inadequacy of univocal interpretation.

Insisting on the multiple technologies that produce sound and voice,

Plata quemada, like *La ciudad ausente* before it, refers to recording devices that bring the contradictions of true and false experience into alignment. Not only does the schizophrenic Dorda hear voices in his mind, likening them to tape recordings or cinematic tracks, but also the media produce such an abundance of images, all at war with each other, that the reader is left in doubt about the veracity of all narration:

> Some witnesses claim to have seen Malito in the hotel with a woman. But others say that they only saw two guys and there was no woman. One of the two was a skinny guy who shot up every so often, the Crooked Bazán, who really was with Malito that afternoon, in the hotel room on San Fernando, watching the movement in the bank from the window that looked onto the street. After the robbery, the police raided the place and, in the bathroom, they found syringes and a spoon and the abandoned crystal. The police figured that Crooked Bazán was the young guy who went down to the bar and asked for an alcohol warmer. The witnesses contradicted each other, as always happens, but everyone agreed that the young guy looked like an actor and that he had a distracted look. From this, they concluded that he was the one who did heroin before the assault and that he had asked for the little burner to heat up the drug. (15–16)

Piglia provides a discursive screen that separates the reader from action. Reminding us of the veil of language that always imposes itself on direct experience, he uses indirect discourse to narrate events; he emphasizes the infinite expansion of oral exchange as the basis of reporting. Stories thus circulate beyond prescribed modes of telling, rumor sustains the "truth" of the day, and through inference and deduction, shared by media, the state, and the masses, the fiction before us takes life. In the process, Piglia underscores the increased monetary value attached to the reproduction and sale of stories that deal with crime or scandal. Not only is the story about a conflict between bank robbers and police, but also the text itself becomes a story to be appropriated by the media and sold for profit. We learn that all fiction is private property to be sold, exchanged, and moved from hand to profitable hand often without respect for the human subject caught in the mesh of the tale. Like Puig's *Maldición eterna* (1980), where a tale about one man's amnesia is eventually stolen for another man's gain, *Plata quemada* reminds us that the story itself engenders profit in the world of exchange. Fiction, drugs, and money are thus placed in alignment. As signs that interfere with direct experience (in fact, they create a delirious supplement to one's engagement with the real), their value is determined ultimately by market demands and by one's habits of addiction. A paradox enters, however, when the money is set on fire, thereby curtailing circulation and the possibility of future trade.

Money is, of course, at the center of this novel; it produces language and plot, it finds itself at the center of a symbolic system that creates tokens of exchange, linking the delinquents who are presented in the text as well as middle-class readers. In short, the body of money brings meaning to all involved; it is a key instrument in the war for symbolic dominance over desire. Piglia links this to cultures of addiction: in the world of *Plata quemada*, the drug of choice is *la plata*. In perhaps the most memorable scene of the novel, the criminals, realizing their losing cause, set fire to the money in their possession and send the bills, in flames, through the windows to awaiting crowds in the streets:

> If money is the only thing that justified the deaths and, if they did it, they did it for the cash and now they're burning it up; this means that they have no morality or motives and they act and kill without reason, just for the pleasure of evil, simply for evil intent. They're natural-born killers, insensitive criminals, inhuman. Indignant, the citizens who watched the scene let out shrieks of horror and hate, like a witches' sabbath from medieval times (according to the newspapers). They couldn't bear that fact that right before their eyes five hundred thousand dollars were burning up in an operation that froze the city and country in horror. . . . The people, indignant, remembered immediately the needy, the poor, the squatters in the Uruguayan countryside who live in precarious conditions, and the orphaned children for whom all that money would have been the guarantee of a future . . .
>
> "Burning innocent money is an act of cannibalism . . . "
>
> But they all understood that this act was a declaration of war, a direct war and in due form against all of society. . . . From this, the idea emerged that money in itself was innocent; even though it produced death and crimes, it couldn't be considered guilty. It was neutral, a sign that changed according to the use that each person cared to give it. (191–92)

Just as heroin achieves its maximum effect under the transformational heat of fire, the stolen bills when set aflame trigger hallucinatory pleasures; they remind us of the ways in which money flows in the veins of culture, deadening direct experience and producing secondary forms of mediation among people, language, and objects. In this way, the fire also produces a debate about signification, allowing us to ask whether money—as a pure, abstract symbol—can only produce intoxication or fulfill a need for the directness of corporeal feeling. In the same way, Piglia puts into play the construction of social value as if to allude to deadening of experience produced by the discourse of the neoliberal state.

In effect, when the criminals set fire to dollars, their act is regarded as an attempt to burn the ethos of modern culture: "And after those countless minutes in which they saw the bills burn like birds on fire, a pile of ashes remained, a funeral pyre of social values" (193). Their actions force the collapse of a system of signs that sustains normative behavior; no longer criminals, the perpetrators are now called cannibals and nihilists (193). Ironically, the burning of money points to the perverse inversions that continue to define social mores.

Once again, investment and sexual deviance surface together as a form of critique. In chapter two, I referred to a curious linkage in Spanish between the terms *invertido* and *inversión*, which both form a paradoxical unit of meaning in Puig's *El beso de la mujer araña*, whereby investments of money and sexual deviance exceeded a totalizing whole. Piglia's novel also exploits these two terms by pointing to *inversion* as the opposite of *investment*. Here, the homosexuality of Dorda and Nene Brignone comes to signify irrecuperable extravagance, a cult of irrepressible excess. Like the burning of money, it undermines the prudence of a symbolic universe that depends on consistency and order and reminds us that any investment in stable identities is always subject to inversion.

Since doubleness begets this disorder, Piglia leads us to a twin path for all readings: hallucinatory fantasy versus direct action, original voices against echoes, material presence versus a universe of abstract symbols. This bipolarity is everywhere to be seen: in the cross-eyed character Dorda, whose strabismus is an indication of the cross-circuitry of images that dominate in the novel as well as the echo of voices that he hears in his mind as a "translating machine"; in the double voicing of lies perpetrated by the state and the underworld figures; in the value assigned to *hybrid* qualities of courage and theft, in the *hubris* of criminality itself. Too, the replication of all events by the media contests the veracity of original accounts while repeated use of verbs of resemblance, the repeated grammatical structure of the *como si* (as if), and the strategic placement of the duplicating mirrors in the novel all confirm the double effects engendered in readers.

Finally, this doubleness is manifested in a tension between masculine and feminine identity that informs the homosexual figures of the novel and by the threats they issue to the masculine state. For example, the cross-eyed Dorda, who constantly hears radios and voices, at times thinks that he is a woman. Piglia centers him in a great play of resemblance and doubling, leading eventually to a paradoxical linking of opposites such that the criminal mind is compared to behaviors of state. Both produce parallel stories of violence and endless lies. Thus the narrator tells us (copying the thoughts of Renzi), "The police and the ruffians . . . are the only ones who know how to make live objects from words, needles that bury themselves in your skin and destroy your soul like an egg that is cracked on the edge of a pan" (186). The contest between delinquents and the state is here a battle for authority in speech, a contest for an oral domain over logic and discourse; at the same time, it undermines the very premises of binary logic that separates good and evil, masculine and feminine, intellectual and popular subject.[5] All investment in logical pairings meets a potential inversion.

This interweaving sheds light on the ways in which truth and fiction merge when literature sets out to measure (albeit indirectly) the faults of neoliberalism today. In *Plata quemada* the intellectual as witness over the actions and crimes of subalterns is considered an unreliable source of knowledge, in fact a producer of fiction. This is further accentuated when Piglia supplies a cast of characters who also compete for the right to narrate the central truths about the crime. From this chorus of voices, Piglia points to a story in which all individuals are suspect, both those with a criminal past and those who stand for the law. Not only are good and evil crossed, but also one's investment in a given economy of signs is similarly turned on its head.

Piglia organizes this inquiry through a syntax of telling that not only structures a before and after of robbery and shoot out but also instructs us about the cartographies of greed and desire that define the modern city. Just as Guadalupe Santa Cruz tracked a map of the capital of Santiago, Lemebel the marginal barrio, Contreras the rural enclave that he termed an "anterior" city, Piglia supplies a map of criminal longing that motivates assault and escape, a cinematic run through the urban maze that implicates all figures in illegal actions that sabotage the state. For all, however, the final object of desire is found in New York City. As if to anticipate the dream-world utopia of petty gangsters that has been promoted by television and film, the site from which today's global economy pumps it first daily breath, New York is central to the imagination of the Argentine criminal mind of this novel, the architectonic space that permits a fantasy of power for the poor. "We have to reach New York; there's a road that goes from Tierra del Fuego to Alaska" (146), one of the gangsters urgently reminds the others, despite his misguided directions. Replacing the nostalgic appeal of the South (a topic prevalent in Argentine culture from the fictions of Borges to the cinema of Solanas), the North exercises a claim on one's vision of the future.[6] Under it, all Argentine subjects—criminals and authorities alike—remain helpless; the power of its symbolic draw, the seduction of its fiction, are irresistible to the imagination.

The language of the text brings us to this seduction. Just as we look at the fiction of money that populates local minds, we also see a tension between a *here* and *there* that reinforces a story of difference, pressures for building an economic tall tale whose images are set, remotely, abroad. To echo this concern, direct and indirect discourse compete for space in the text, past and present literary histories enter into debate. Thus while the conversations of criminals are recorded by police surveillance or the inner thoughts of outlaws return to past moments in time, Piglia returns to a literary past to show the contradictions of history.

The power of criminals in *Plata quemada* may be contrasted to the limpid heroism of Borges's character in "Sur," but it more surely recalls *Los siete locos* of Roberto Arlt, a writer who shares with Piglia a desire to link the fiction of telling to the fictions of economics and finance. I refer not simply to the focus of both writers on a set of criminal characters who gather in enclaves outside the city and are driven by florid fantasy for rapid wealth and planned rebellion against the law (with the ultimate fantasy of liberation to be found in the United States), but more significantly to the strange effects of temporal crossing that Piglia produces as if in homage to the visionary capacity of Arlt. If in 1929 Arlt anticipated through his novel the coup d'etat of 1930, *Plata quemada*'s events situated in 1965 also pretend to announce, before their time, future crises in the Argentine nation: the rise of Onganía and the military dictatorship of the 1970s followed by the imposition of a neoliberal market economy that emphasizes the triumph of a virtual real. The book hints at a society on the verge of change in the 1960s, a heroism soon to assume a different face; it bespeaks a messianic desire to change the flow of history despite the nation's retrograde past. No longer possible to return to Temperley (the town of Arlt's Astrologer), we are left in *Plata quemada* only with Dorda's recollection of his rural past, described as a site of abuse and violation, a site of homoerotic initiation and desire. The first violence, then, is begotten not in the city but the country, reminding us of a long historical tradition of national violence that comes from endemic woes of an agricultural society that has moved its interests to the city. It also recalls a rural discourse that has homoerotic delirium as its subtext and basic component. Evoking the Generation of 1837, a founding pact among men, the homosocial allegiance among the delinquents of *Plata quemada* serves as a reminder of the pacts that organize the criminal state. Moreover, Piglia's tale is carried by the authority of the popular voice that will sustain the power of narration, telling us how to see city and country through a history of violence and greed. "To whom does that voice belong?" (179), asks the surveillance crew representing officials who surround the criminals' hideout. The uncertainty of voice is, like money, generated by indeterminacy of ownership and belonging. Money produces language and plot; it generates a fiction of its own, yet its terms for circulation are always elusive.

In this respect, two peculiar images organize the logic of his text: the drug-addicted bodies of criminals and the addicted social whole that depends on the materiality of money to sustain it. Here, we learn of the addictive needs of the social body, for all of the double meaning that this term conveys. Piglia tells us of the tics of characters, the markings on their bodies, the food they eat, the details of their hands and faces. As if to restore the corporeality to the literary characters, whose physical and erotic deficit in Argentine literature had once been lamented by writers such as Cortázar, Piglia gives a notable turn to his own earlier fiction (where bodies were notably absent), linking the representation of physicality to the addictive demand for money and drugs: "Money is like a drug; the main thing is to have it, know that it's there, touch it, look for it in your closet, between your clothes, in your bag; see that you have the half kilo, the hundred thousand bucks, stay calm" (44), claims a character in the novel. A form of addiction, the dependency on drugs and money is relentlessly described as a paradox of corporeality; an irrational need becomes the substance and focus of bodily urges. And just as addiction might be seen as an irrational appetite for accumulation and possession, so too by analogy, the addiction to money is described as a compulsion, an act without justification in reason. Narration, addiction, and financial gain are linked as the same process of art; they are the basis of this novel, of course, but also a speculation on the fiction of money itself.

This points to what is perhaps the significant difference between Argentine and Chilean narration. If Argentine writers such as Piglia are devoted generally to macroprojects exposing the failures of state or reviewing the nation's history in order to track an authoritarian legacy and practices of resistances and deviation, producing what in the final analysis may be read as an allegory of national history, the Chilean model has emphasized the smaller tale, the practice of micronarration, attention to the consequences of the state on the daily lives of citizens and travelers. Less a reference to a historical past, the fiction evokes the materiality of cities and the violence issued to bodies, it draws upon popular subjects competing for the space of narration. Piglia, in *Plata quemada*, appears to cross lines of national aesthetics, if one can speak in this way. In a story devoted to the foregrounding of voice, he focuses on the ways to read a city, to tell a story of competing representations about money, market, and spending, to track a moment in Argentine history when an interstitial logic of state corruption seeps into public view, to read the state from the representation of the *body.*

In this way, Piglia appears, at first glance to work in a territory that avoids the grand themes of Argentine literary history. Nevertheless, Piglia is also deeply historical in his vision, tracing the movement of Argentine society from one form of social organization to another. The difference here, however, is that the metonymy fills in for the whole. Departing from the fragment, one can speak of an allegory for the Argentine state.

While the *style* of this narration privileges orality and popular voice, it also points to an age that is about to suffer the decomposition of direct experience, to announce the emergence of a logic that reduces the tie between language and feeling. Here, Piglia cultivates the *gap*, the in-between that separates forms of representation and bodies, in order to restore a debate about the hope of naming experience beyond the numbness of our addiction to money. His novel points to a dispute about the ethos of money and representation through which bodies rapidly vanish as material signs and are later recuperated in the literary text. It is the human body (not the body of money) that brings us to question all representation; it is the basis of material experience, a way to challenge the abstraction of today's market economy; it is the center of exchange.

The Market of Re-citations

The aestheticization of subaltern bodies and voices is also a concern of Diamela Eltit. In *Los trabajadores de la muerte* (1998), she offers not quite an indictment of the criminal state in the style of Ricardo Piglia, but a challenge to the domain of the "market." Here, Eltit revisits public sites of congregation ranging from local tavern to town plaza. Working from fragments of myth and folklore, the detritus of the city, and images of violence exercised upon female bodies, she shows the aggressions cast against subaltern subjects who compete for a space of their own. They are assaulted, in particular, for their will toward narration. This situation will allow Eltit to question the *style* of engendering stories, especially one's quest for origins, a search that rests upon fixing a place and name within the discourse of history. Her investigation is grounded in the bodies and voices of popular subjects, whose expressions carry different theories for realist reflection and prophecy for agency and action. The poor and the abandoned thus redirect a wide range of artistic experience; they command the power of the aesthetic; they transform the rules of language. These minor figures are the guiding principles of Eltit's narrative law and will expose the fiction of the *market*.

Eltit has founded her literary projects on the representation of popular subjects who have become the compelling force and trademark of her creative and critical writing. From the marginal figures represented in *Lumpérica* (1983) and *Por la patria* (1986) to the testimonials of abject figures in *El padre mío* (1989) and *El infarto del alma* (1994a), the protagonists of Eltit's oeuvre form part of a coherent project to give voice to marginal sectors, to announce the possibility of ethical and artistic reconfigurations outside of the all-embracing social totality defined by the state. The presence of an aestheticized popular subject is the source of creative interruption and social critique. For example, in *Lumpérica* (1983), when the penetrating eye of the spotlight focuses dispassionately on subaltern bodies that occupy the center of the city, their presence opens to another language and vehicle of social debate. Too, from the voice of "El Padre Mío," a vagrant whose testimonial is the basis of Eltit's eponymous book, the writer issues a stinging criticism of social life in Chile. His irrational although utopian demand for an end to hardship is not, in Eltit's words, to be curative ("it doesn't claim to change anything, to cure anything" [16]); rather, it is designed to bring us to interrogate the order to telling. In *El cuarto mundo* (1988), she foregrounds the literary characters represented by the derogatory term *sudaca*, or "south-shit," as Spaniards have sometimes referred to Latin Americans, in order to focus on the condition of the marginalized poor who live outside the social center and resemanticize the language of violence. And in *El infarto del alma* (1994a), written in collaboration with photographer Paz Errázuriz, Eltit organizes the fictionalized testimonials of the mentally ill who have been relegated to an institutional facility.[7] In each work, she emphasizes the aesthetic capability of popular subjects, not simply the aesthetic possibilities that these subjects might offer to a highbrow author who wishes to represent them in fiction.

Eltit's subjects serve to recall the ways in which individuals create totalizing stories from systems of citation, drawing their original tales from a collage of images supplied through the diffusion of mass culture. Repetition and re-citation (with its double meaning of quotation both as copy and performativity) are central to this operation and, as such, remind the reader of the intersection of popular culture with the circulation of other products on a more massive scale. Thus, the performances cited in Eltit's texts often lead the reader to think of the conceptual framework and symbols associated with the condition of the market.

Equally important, *Los trabajadores de la muerte* takes a new turn from Eltit's earlier work by allowing us to see the construction of fiction drawn from ready-made sources. She shows the power of the popular voice to undo the banality of the ready-made, to challenge the flatness of a neoliberal economy that, by presupposing no uneven edges, would make a pretense to a totalized social whole, disembodied and lacking in rebellious human subjects to take under its wing. Eltit repopulates the absent city, reminds us that the human center still holds, and brings back to life the movement and inventiveness of popular masses, that—according to recent legend and political fiction—have relinquished their place in civil society. Finally, she focuses on the presence of popular voices vis-à-vis the market.

The market has been the center of neoliberal reform and the driving force of democratic governments globally; it is also the staple and obsession of contemporary cultural critique. In this novel, Eltit brings us to the literal sense of the market—not the disembodied virtual market of transnational brokerage firms and on-line computerized trading, but the market in its originary and local sense, whereby the central plaza is the site for exchange of goods offered by impoverished peddlers, participating members of the polis as it had been defined in classical antiquity. With this strategy, Eltit works on paradox: if today's neoliberal market (in the economic sphere) is cast from the illusion of fiction, Eltit returns in her novel to a primitive sense of the market, which restores immediacy to the term. From fragmentary tales of marginal social actors, from the interstitial experiences of characters, the market emerges as a totalizing story rooted in everyone's direct experience. Not founded upon nostalgia or melodrama, without begging for the reader's compassion for the poor, the market emerging from *Los trabajadores de la muerte* signals a triumph for the representational power of the popular imagination. The narrative voice of women is central here.

Los trabajadores de la muerte could well be explained as a novel about characters in search of a story, marginal figures who take themes of murder and revenge from legends of classical antiquity and expand this material in order to create stories of their own. Above all, the novel leads to an unmistakable defense of the resilience of oral tradition. Storytelling, Walter Benjamin has told us, is an art that is coming to an end (1978, 83). Formerly the assignment of the leader of the tribe, storytelling was originally linked to the narration of personal experience; with the passing of time and as experience lost its privilege and value, perceived as incommunicable to another person, this linkage was eventually broken. Thus, in antiquity if an individual vested with communal authority were charged with the transmission of the congregation's significant legends—stories about local habits or tales of voyage and adventure—this individual was also charged with securing the bonds between direct experience and narration, thereby creating narrative grounds for solidarity within the tribe. In our contemporary moment, however, this power is all but weakened, surrendering to more mediated types of narration and other forms of abstraction; we relinquish hope of establishing a communal linkage among listeners of tales. Eltit appears to struggle against this common slippage, restoring the original power of telling as way to claim the power of the margin, using the novel as a vehicle to highlight the agency of popular actors. From the province of local secularism, the sacredness of experience and tradition, the popular voices of Eltit's fiction thus defy those versions of contemporary cultural politics that would undermine the value of social participation. She cultivates this proposition in two significant ways: first, by insisting on the centrality of corporeal experience in the construction and telling of tales and claiming the survival of this dimension of culture against official odds; and second, by citing canonical myths to give this experience a narrative framework. She uses tales from antiquity to evoke and construct a story from the "givens" of legends and to resemanticize those words in contemporary parlance that have been emptied of their political sense. By returning to myth, Eltit concentrates the energy of enduring legends about family competition, about parenting and abandon, betrayal and eventual murder. This corpus is dramatically unlike the material of much of the so-called light fiction of Chile and Argentina, which emphasizes a unified assembly of voices orchestrated by the privileged classes and focuses on the facile exchange that settles many debates without conflict. By contrast, Eltit reaches back to the lasting elements of mythical narration, situating the experience of popular actors squarely within the framework of archaic longing. Far from stabilizing the flow of narration, however, she focuses on the conflicts and competition set among those who purport to tell their stories.

Eltit's popular figures express a commitment to both craftsmanship in narration and voicing those experiences that derive from timeless needs and desires; they eventually weave the disparate threads of their stories in the *memory* of listeners. Again, I take my cues directly from Benjamin, who contrasts the task of the novelist to that of the storyteller, claiming that the former insists on remembrance of a single hero, whereas the storyteller is dedicated to "*many* diffuse occurrences" (98). Eltit, as will become apparent, also obliges us to remember many embedded stories as part of one great epic. The nearly anonymous actors give voice to the anxieties of every man and woman; from their partial visions, we reach the overarching drama of our times. Hardly an indictment of any failed narrations, Eltit emphasizes the power of narrative construction that, here, is a tool of affirmation used by marginal women and the poor. Their residual texts surpass any originary tale.

Los trabajadores de la muerte draws attention to the contrivance of art. She presents the competition between different aesthetic options, turning to the popular roots of legend and representation. This is celebrated as the carnivalesque depiction of the popular masses, joined at a ritualized scene of storytelling or in congregation at the public plaza. The novel thus opens with an episode that takes place in a tavern, a site of reunion for travelers that, although situated in modern Santiago, surely recalls the popular gathering spots described in *Don Quijote* or the inns of the *Lazarillo de Tormes* or *El buscón*. The tavern joins individuals in rituals of communal festivity; they congregate not for obligations of work or remuneration, but for shared imbibing and pleasure. Here, a storyteller captivates the crowd by narrating his dreams to an audience of eager listeners. Ironically deprived of a proper name, but assured a title that bestows prestige and confirms his craft as a teller of tales, "el hombre que sueña"—the man who dreams—offers his oral renditions of dreams, all of which deal with matters of authority: a rebellion of soldiers against their commanding officer, surreal mutations of animals and phantoms that threaten the leader's power. Deciphering his own narration, "the man who dreams" admits that the dream content reflects his apprehension about those popular subjects who now claim control of the city streets. Interrupting the man's art of telling are a girl with a mutilated arm accompanied by two disabled persons, who take a seat at the bar. Their physical incapacity creates sufficient distraction among the audience such that they come to interrupt the narrative control of the man who dreams; in turn, he accuses them of disturbing the dreams of patrons of the tavern. Indeed, the armless girl manages to rival the man's narrative authority (a horrifying actualization of his dreams of persecution?) to the point where she finally begins to narrate a dream of her own. Responding to him, she claims that her story will allow her to take control of the streets and assert her authority over lineage, history, and urban space. She thus prophetically announces a tale of hate and revenge that will occupy later chapters of the book.

Eltit obsessively insists upon a grammar of telling. Distancing the characters from readers, reducing all compassion from the text, she imposes the structure of indirect discourse to call attention to the practice of speaking:

> The man, flattened, begins to tell an epic dream inhabited by metallic soldiers absorbed by hopes of resurrection. He says that the leader . . . comes forward with clean hands and calls his troops together in order to get them to muster the valor required for battle. He says that the war scene happens on uncultivated land, covered only by weeds. . . . He says that while the leader delivers his epic oration, the troops quickly desert, he says that the soldiers take sudden flight through the field and then the leader has no choice but to pick up the weapons that have been scattered in the course of their flight. He says

> that a dog runs by with one of the weapons in its snout and the leader goes in pursuit of the dog. . . . He says, finally, that the dog drops the weapon from its snout and with fury bites the bully, who cannot stop crying and feeling sorry for himself. (15–16)

The act of telling is foregrounded by repetition of the phrase "dice que" (he says): it reminds the readers of the artistry of oral composition and the power of popular voice that, in turn, inspires Eltit's work. Here, narration is clearly explained as a force that restores the power of the streets, the hegemony of the poor over the city's center. And the armless girl, who lacks a corporeal instrument for writing, insists on orality to control the culture of narration.

From this introductory section, set in chiaroscuro frames often evocative of Renaissance painting, Eltit then situates three evenly structured chapters (a triptych that echoes in structure the three sections of the man's final dream), designated as "acts," a nod to the theatricality of all representation. This staging features a mother and her children, and a man who has an incestuous relationship with his half-sister in Concepción. The stasis of the introductory scene is thus lifted in these chapters: if the tavern suggested a site of repose for itinerant travelers and focused on the crisis of authority pursuing the teller of tales, the story told by the girl recuperates an element of voyage. Against the densely populated spaces of the city, the girl, in describing the voyage to Concepción, reaches for the plenitude of the South. A return to origins, to a mythical space that predates the rise of a central city, the South intensifies the primitive violence of the novel and sustains the enigma of narration.

Although they at first appear isolated, the different tales woven by the girl are in fact connected, centering on the aggressions of domestic life, the burden of unmet desires, and the virulent passions of a man toward his lover and a mother toward her firstborn son. "Eight years he remained at home and of those eight years—tell me, someone—how many days or even minutes were worth it? But were they worth it at all?" (41): eight years without pleasure, under the tyranny of a dominant man, this image enters as an unfailing allegory for eight years of social deprivation experienced by Chile under democratic rule. As the mother laments her exclusion from all feelings of pleasure, she plans to conquer her abnegation by killing her firstborn child and, like the man who dreams, from the introductory pages, she also sharpens a knife as she proceeds to tell her tale. In the end, the knife will emerge as protagonist, used by the woman to kill her child and, in different chapters, also evoked by the male voice as he makes plans to kill his lover. What is uncertain is the order of events, which rage begets which order: if the cruelty of the gods, an intervention by the father or a disturbance by the firstborn child inspires the ire of the mother or if aggressions by the woman anticipate the masculine domination and violence of the concluding third act. Eltit returns not only to the power of orality but also to legends of antiquity—and here both the cycles of Oedipus and Medea loom large—to insist on the panhistoric tragedy of family violence and human thirst for revenge. This regression to premodern traditions also assures the recuperation of the original meaning of the polis, the public plaza, and the market.

The rivalry between the man who dreams and the girl with the mutilated arm is rearticulated as a story of incest and revenge. If, on the one hand, *Los trabajadores de la muerte* is about one narrative tradition set against another, a story of return to archaic ritual and a prophecy for the future ("destiny is what calls the archaic figure," [109]), on the other hand, the novel entwines different experiences of history through incest and repetition. "Your lover is nothing less than your half sister. Of course, the copy of the Oracle now winds up merging with the bridge that sustains it," Eltit writes regarding the man who travels to Concepción and realizes that he is the sibling of his lover (112).

Drawing on the mythical taboo of incest, Eltit is able to offer a narrative frame for repetition and convergence, a structural device that orders the use of images in the novel and also reminds the reader of the tragic prohibitions that often are launched against these encounters. She insists on two points of contact: one, drawn from the incest taboo (and murder) that organizes the story of the girl with the mutilated arm; two, a "narrative incest," what we might describe as a merger of images that are known to us, available and familiar, forming part of a postmodern strategy through which we repeat the "ready-made" past, evoked however frequently without regard for the tragic consequences that await those who indulge in practices of repetition and copy. In the process, Eltit reminds us that we have come to disrespect principles of originality that were so central for storytelling and experience, at least through the dominant years of a modernist aesthetics; instead, the repetition of ready-made images is, in itself, a guiding illusion of our times. It is the main operation of a market economy that relies on simulacra to organize serial logic and sales; it is the operation that cancels linear time and weakens all claims to individual triumph. This practice also breaks the boundary around isolated bodies and discreet units of knowledge; it links images through space and time, it reveals a circularity of violence that sustains patriarchal order and, ironically, points to human forgetfulness of an original moment of physical violation, revenge, and betrayal. The repetitions point to our shortsighted memory of the past, our inability to correct past errors, our failure to negotiate actions on a transformation of inherited experience.

Too, these repetitions announce a relentless struggle with the material of death (hence, the title of the novel), which is enacted in countless versions on the bodies of women and children. Art allows this transformation and gives the inventor a name. Hence, at the end of the novel, when the man kills his lover and sister, both enter the symbolic order and achieve proper names (Patricio and Mónica), proving that crime, when it is retold, still assures one a place in history. In an attempt to override paternal authority (both the masculine power of the man who dreams and the murderer in the girl's story), these tales will be revealed, thereby allowing women to achieve recognition in the symbolic order. At the end of the description of this crime, saturated with mythic and biblical content, the assassin remarks, "And up there, between the rafters, the shadow of my mother, nailed to a digital cross, spies down upon me" (186). The gender transformation of the Christ figure along with an electronic image that modernizes the scene of piety and crucifixion moves the static material from its timeless domain and feminizes the final authority. It thus becomes a crucifixion in the double sense of the term, evoking both the suffering of Christ and a *cruci-fiction*, or crossing of fictions, that redirects the power of narration.

Eltit presents these intertwined stories as "actos," three acts that underscore the theatricality unfolding in the girl's narration. Following this tripartite structure, she appends an epilogue bearing the title, "Los príncipes de las calles" [The princes of the streets] suggesting the popular triumph of the girl's version of history over that of the authoritarian man who dreams. This final section finds the girl with the mutilated arm in the hubbub of a public market where vendors hawk their wares and beggars clamor for donations, where minor theft is the rule of the day and the police circulate to thwart infractions. This is not the public plaza of debate that was, in its Enlightenment model, central to the nation and defined by a culture of elites; rather, Eltit takes us to a more archaic sense of the public space when the market was the center of the polis. Here, the market as a space inhabited by bodies in close vicinity—persons trading wares and giving voice to their needs—is defined as the social center, a clear reminder of a conjuncture of identities whose linkage has long been dismissed, yet a prophecy for a still vital version of an urban public sphere.

Peter Stallybrass and Allon White remind us that the marketplace is the epitome of local identities as well as a place where categories of identities intersect, lying at the heart of the polis (1986, 27). Criticizing the oversimplifications offered by Bakhtin, who located the marketplace *outside* of the business of governance, they look to the original sense of the festive market as a site for a politics of negotiation, crucial to the order of state. Eltit's market, described in the epilogue of *Los trabajadores de la muerte*, is likewise an intense scene of mobility, focusing on the exchange of bodies and voices, the sale and theft of goods. It brings political meaning to an observation conceded earlier in the novel by the potential assassin when he claimed, "I understood that the only thing that we can admit as victory travels first through the spoils" (70). Here, plunder in the market and the quick trade of objects generate their own fiction, announcing the triumph of a popular voice competent in the economy of minor details. Thus the girl with the mutilated arm enters a plaza in which everything is for sale, where exchange is ferocious and the rules of competition savage. In this respect, it recalls the final scene of *El cuarto mundo*, where Eltit concludes dramatically that all bodies have a destiny in common, much like that of the sudaca who eventually will be put up for sale (1988, 128). Here, Eltit tells us that all culture is available for purchase under a neoliberal economy, but in *Los trabajadores de la muerte* she also offers a congregation of popular subjects leading to a critique of political action from the perspective of their imaginative field. In particular, the novel insists on a radical rethinking of our own power of purchase and our use of "ready-made" objects in a visually based culture where decals reduce complex ideas and brand-name products promise value.

The marketplace is the site for public debate but also for an economy of trade, a site where merchandise of a minor scale is peddled by popular actors. The many perspiring traders are described by the images on the T-shirts they wear: one carries an image of a monetary sign; another, the image of an unnamed Asian hero, his face encircled by stars; another, an image of an African nationalist leading a rebellion of masses. Ironically, political revolution finds itself alive only as an image in mass production. And the poor, who were said to be the beneficiaries of the revolutionary figures whose emblems they wear, are here represented as subjects without any history at all, engaged in a carnival of present-bound exchanges, unincorporated and beyond the law. In this way, the political struggles that were so central to liberation projects of earlier times, and are here reduced to decals on T-shirts, stand as icons without clear meaning in the present. They serve as tags that distinguish one vendor from another; they identify mass produced objects; they remind us that our culture is assembled as a sea of signs. More simply, they cover otherwise naked bodies. A residual effect of policies of neoliberal planning, the decals on T-shirts remind us of the evacuated power of images that everywhere abound in market-run centers. But Eltit also allows us to see competing fictions in all public places, images that beg for incorporation as stories and that, in their cyclicity, once again beg to be told. In this respect, the narrative work of the girl is an alternative form of heroism, a different kind of political action not captured in the circuits of serialized fabrication. It is the triumph of art.

Beyond the decals on T-shirts, Eltit turns in significant ways to the narrative value of the serialized copy. Here, she works from paradox: repetition is not only the guiding principle of mythical story, orchestrated in the girl's story of love and revenge but also the guiding principle of a market-driven aesthetic in which originality is dismissed as a value. In the epilogue, these issues surface with respect to the circulation of images in the plaza. Eltit thus refers to mechanical mice and birds, knives, hair combs and mirrors, cosmetics, and souvenirs: the popular trinkets that circulate in any popular market. The girl wanders through this densely populated field of peddlers and objects, passing by an eight-year-old child and an elderly woman who looks at herself in a mirror, adjusting her hair. These images described in the epilogue are nevertheless strangely familiar: Eltit signals objects that we have all seen in shops, sold under regulated terms of sale (190); in the public marketplace, however, they acquire a pulsation not controlled by formalized business. More important still, Eltit creates the illusion of a déjà vu or a second-order simulacrum when, as readers, we recognize images that had made an appearance in the preceding chapters of this book. For example, the knife sold in the market recalls the instrument of murder in Concepción and also reminds us of the knife brandished by the man who dreams; the live rats that scurried through the prologue and were embraced by the mutilated girl are now represented as electronic toys that dance on the ground through remote control; the eight-year-old child who walks through the market evokes the child who so exasperated his mother in earlier chapters. Since these images are unrelated, bearing no internal connection within the structure of the novel, we find ourselves as readers torn on a temporal sequence, not certain of the order of events or the sequence of narration. Did the earlier stories inspire the images of the market? Does the marketplace of the epilogue supply the girl with images for her inaugural fiction in the prologue, thus suggesting a disrupted chronological sequence in which the final chapter precedes the first? Or does Eltit mean to tell us that all these images circulate constantly in the popular imagination regardless of the order of events or the spatial limitations that enclose them? Eltit, in effect, reminds us that the elements of fiction have no respect for the rules that govern the logic of seriality or the copy. Were chronology and sequence the only focus of narrative disturbance, the novel's vertiginous force would be triumphant, but these images, at the same time, also elicit Eltit's earlier novels: the plaza of *Lumpérica* and *Por la patria* returns as a central scene; L. Iluminada, who in Eltit's first novel combed her hair in the plaza and verified her image in a mirror, now appears in the epilogue of this text as a nameless elderly woman, available to tell her fantasies to all while she relentlessly scratches her head. The incest and sudaca culture of *El cuarto mundo* also dominate this recent text; the violence of the couple in *Vaca sagrada* anticipates the planned murders of *Los trabajadores de la muerte* as does their travel to the south; the oppressive relationship between mother and child so central to *Los vigilantes* emerges once again; and, finally, the girl with the mutilated arm recalls the self-representation of Diamela Eltit, who mutilated her arms as part of an art action staged in Chile during the Pinochet years. *Before* and *after* are effectively crossed in this project of constructing a fiction; too, by systems of self-referentiality, Eltit eliminates the distance between the original model and its copy, between authenticity and its simulacrum. In effect, the test of authenticity to which so many simulacra are submitted loses all meaning and, in this instance, yields to an operation that, much like a Moebius strip, sustains principles of continuity and self-citation. In this way, the hall of mirrors that upholds so much of *Los trabajadores de la muerte* creates a heightened awareness of the conditions of production and materials available to those who pursue the art of narration. Instead of inserting itself in the interstitial openings between dominant discourses, the novel works from the totality of Eltit's previous body of literature and the body of the author herself. The "in-between" and the "simulacrum"—as staples of the postmodern project—here surrender to a totalizing vision that sustains the integrity of female agency in the production of culture.

Like the girl with the mutilated arm who insists on her right to narrate a story, who reconstitutes her story from ready-made tokens of culture, Eltit insists on a project to recuperate fragments of meaning that lead to a unified whole. Like myth and dream, her fiction fills the space of the city; it finds in a popular voice an answer to the censorial state and restores the creative aspect of invention by contrast to the dull and aseptic seriality sustained by neoliberal markets. Eltit here tells us that the public plaza offers a wealth of images for future tales, a way to structure the narratives of an alternative history. Instead of turning to the tyranny of theater as orchestrated by the market-run state, Eltit thus defends the theater of popular traditions, celebrating the original sense of the market qua polis as a source of inventiveness and art.

I opened this chapter with reference to an installation by Gonzalo Díaz, in which the unresolved threads of fragmented meaning brought on a crisis of interpretation, urging viewers to reconstruct the totality of narration.

Similarly, the fiction of Ricardo Piglia and Diamela Eltit is driven by an enigma, which begs both the elaboration of story and resolution by the reader. The enigma here, however, is found in the power of popular imagination and the resilient culture of the streets; it serves as the impetus of narration while it also inaugurates a creative field. This enigma accordingly demands a resemanticization of the public sphere, obliging us to think of the spaces where citizens and subalterns meet, to track the crossroads where aesthetics and politics are born, the site for a revision of history. If cultural criticism today is hestitant to defend popular spaces, claiming that they are infused by nostalgia and a turn toward the lost heroic past, literature answers by sustaining the vitality of popular imagination and form. From an assembly of fragments, the literary text conveys a hope for reconstruction.

Altera el orden: la creación empieza
[Order is altered: creation begins]
—Diana Bellessi, *Eroica*

las grietas hablan / y golosas las palabras dicen más
[the fissures speak / and impatient words say more]
—Carmen Berenguer, *A media asta*

CHAPTER 6

From Museum to Street: Poetry for the New Millennium

Within avant-garde possibilities of montage, Chilean artist Catalina Parra stitches bold, uneven yarns on a canvas of photographs and newsprint. The threads run through headlines and popular slogans, drawn from advertisements or government mandates, all of which display the banal imperatives of our modern world. "Alive with Pleasure," "Let's Talk Dirty," and "The Human Touch" are among the many English-language clips laced on Parra's frames; these are juxtaposed with photographs of familiar political events and desecrated bodies. This suturing allows the artist to patch random textual forms on historical experience and memory. It also incites us to draw connections between local and global powers, between present and past times. In this context, it is not surprising that Parra's collages are often international in focus. The debt crisis, religious fundamentalism, torture, and ecological ruin guide the themes of her work as if to articulate a globalized indifference to horror and suggest our common immunity to media overload and manipulation.

Parra defamiliarizes our relationship to local context, testing the absur-

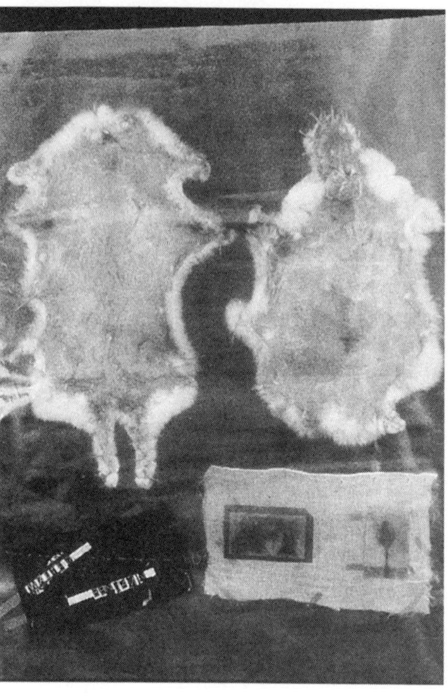

5. Catalina Parra. *Diariamente*, 1977. Newspaper, thread, transparent paper, thread, 28 × 22 inches. Courtesy of Catalina Parra. Permission to reproduce image granted by Catalina Parra. 6. *Walter Benjamin*, 1977. Mixed media wall piece, 70 × 53 inches. From gallery catalog, *Catalina Parra in Retrospect*. Curator Julia P. Herzberg. Lehman College Art Gallery, Bronx, New York, 6 February–4 April 1992. Permission to reproduce image granted by Catalina Parra. 7. *The Human Touch: The Final Edge II*, 1989. Newspapers, magazines, thread, red tape, photographic material, 28 × 22 inches. From gallery catalog, *Catalina Parra in Retrospect*. Curator Julia P. Herzberg. Lehman College Art Gallery, Bronx, New York, 6 February–4 April 1992. Permission to reproduce image granted by Catalina Parra. 8. *What's It To You?*, 1982. Newspapers, gauze, thread, tape, 17 × 25 inches. Courtesy of Catalina Parra. Permission to reproduce image granted by Catalina Parra.

dities of language that shape our modern lives and censor our voices and protests. She works, as Ronald Christ has described it, from "an aesthetic inquest into modes of silencing" (1987, 22). For that reason, in addition to yarn, Parra uses animal skins, wool, and spools of barbed wire as archaic residues of rural experience; they challenge mass-media domination and slice through our indifference to horror. These material implements also

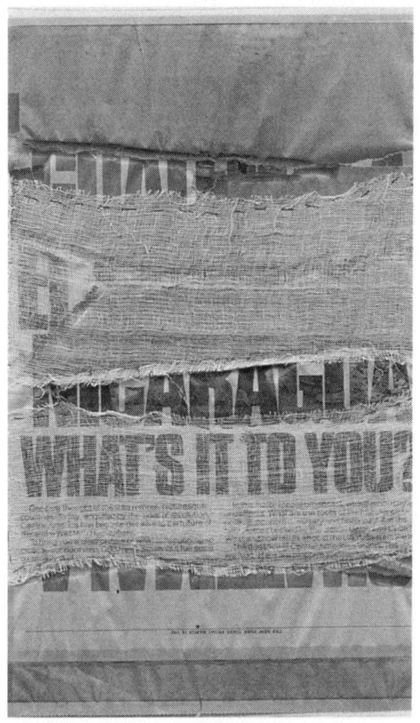

test the presumed neutrality belonging to official rhetoric, the censorship of popular origins. In an introduction to a 1987 gallery exposition, Parra explained that the ordinary materials used in her work—gauze, animal hides, thread—were laden with social meaning for Chile: "The gauze spoke of hospitals, wounds, the dead; the animal hides and plastic bags spoke of corpses, and the stitching and thread I was using invoked a Chilean legend, that of the *imbunche*, . . . those who consulted captive witches and sorcerers . . . or the person who has all the body orifices sewn shut, all the holes blocked so that the evil spirits can't get out of his body, so it's a kind of censoring of release" (1987, n.p.). The visible presence of thread on canvas is both a silencing and a denial of pleasure, but because of the loosely stitched yarn we also have the possibility of unsuspected readings. In other words, despite the scene of repression identified with the imbunche, this ritual practice allows access to new ways of seeing. Parra's canvas teaches us to learn to read between the lines of official history, to override the ill effects of the media, and to challenge the banality of consumer culture. From the stitching of fragments to forge a different sense of the whole, she reconsiders the language we use and the global sale of media and art. More than the messages printed directly on canvas, the fragments beg recomposition. Art directs the needle of weaving, it is the segue to cognitive potential.

I prevail on the inaugural example supplied by Parra's work to embark on a discussion of contemporary poetry. This connection is not to be made through the normally expected circuit, tracing the artist to her illustrious family of poets and singers, but through the expressed anxieties shared by women about the status of knowledge and the authority of their voices. At a time when the consequences of representation are especially important in the political and artistic arenas, poetry—for its mediation and transformation of the contemporary world—offers theoretical stances about language and repression that we can hardly afford to dismiss. Yet, what form can poetic language take at the start of the millennium? What can poetry be allowed to say? And what happens to the course of experimental poetry when claimed by writers whose lives are defined beyond institutions and canons, most specifically by contemporary women? Women's poetry returns to history and identity, to experience and representation. Far beyond the speculations offered by some proponents of critical theory, poetic discourse in the hands of women opens to a different critique, tracing memory as it is etched in sound and speech, linking popular and elite traditions, reminding us of the somatic effects of geography and politics on the fin de siglo gendered body. Above all, their poetic inquiry draws attention to an ongoing struggle for authority through language and, ultimately, reminds us of the theoretical capacities of art to come to terms with political issues that critics can scarcely begin to name.

If we address the question of representation in neoliberal times, we evoke a number of tensions: the circulation of mass-media reproductions versus particular claims to originality and defiance, market demands for normativized "difference" versus the circulation of unincorporated, heterogeneous expressions, the orchestration by state institutions of determined cultural projects versus the expressions of individual artists and writers who fail to conform to a general mandate for homogenized style. The issue of representation is often about giving free reign to alternative voices, challenging dominant paradigms (or, at the very least, writing *through* them), and finally tracking individual agency among those who speak from unauthorized places. Contemporary poetry goes about addressing these questions in a more oblique way as it brings to the surface a number of issues about sound and meaning, the ties between memory and voice, the problematic relationship between sameness and difference. In the process, it closes in on audience responsibility and engagement. Far beyond current critical debate, of the kind described in chapter one, poetry places forceful and immediate demands on readers: it transforms the connotations of writing and provokes conditions for dialogue; it announces a crisis of language and society's failures to address it; and, finally, it produces a kind of wisdom not usually charted in public discussion.

In order to move toward the depths of this project, we might first inquire about the spaces from which poetry speaks. In the United States, we are experiencing a vital renewal of interest in poetry. Through widely popularized poetry "slams," lyrical excerpts posted on subways and public buses, televised programs on writers and a general mass-mediatization of verse, poetry has reached a general audience appeal unachieved in earlier years. Under the rubric of a "restricted aestheticism," manifested through the vehicles of small-press distribution, writers' workshops, and independent recitals, poetry enjoys an unparalleled moment of enthusiastic attention. Clearly, the power of experimental writing, from the neoformalists to hip-hop, is alive and well.

In Latin America, where the novel has offered a master narrative for explaining history, poetic production has been overshadowed by critical attention to fiction especially in the years of the so-called Boom. But it might also be claimed, against these narratives of national foundation and collapse, that another saga has been simultaneously constructed through the vehicle of poetry. This has become especially apparent in Argentina and Chile in the years since redemocratization, although it is wrong to suggest that the poetic genre was invisible during years of dictatorship. Witness in Argentina the intense rhythm of publication belonging to Ediciones de Tierra Firme under the stewardship of José Luis Mangieri in the early 1980s; in Chile, the forceful texts of Parra, Rojas, and Lihn or under different banners, the endeavors of J. L. Martínez, Millán, and Zurita, all of whom published during the Pinochet years. Although some have preferred to describe poets under dictatorship as the "generación N. N."—signifying the poets' status as anonymous or among the disappeared—their texts nonetheless had a commanding resonance among vanguard intellectuals in Chile and abroad.[1] Poetry under military rule set alternative visions of social alliance, revising the status of language and form. As such, from the decade of the 1970s to the years of redemocratization, and as a countervalence to market-based culture—with its emphasis on "light," easily engageable texts that enter circulation without provoking conflict or radical signs of dissent—poetry continues to act, unsettling a late-fin de siglo preference for totalizing narratives of comfort. It speaks from places unauthorized by the state and, in defiance of massification, it exacerbates uneasiness and disorder.

On both sides of the cordillera—in Argentina and Chile—the expansion of poetic texts has been nothing short of impressive, witnessed in the increased production of books and journals devoted to poetry, web sites on the Internet, recitals, and workshops (*talleres*). The poetry workshop or the bookstore reading—taken, during the years of dictatorship, as a resistance in public spaces—continues to offer an alternative to systems of promotion. Now, for example, the prestigious cultural center Centro Cultural San Martín in Buenos Aires sustains a cycle of poetry readings for the general public, and the Casa de la Poesía and the Centro Cultural Ricardo Rojas regularly sponsor the most exciting congregation of experimental poets in the country. Daniel Freidemberg (1993, 141) noted the publication of two hundred books of poetry a year in Argentina (although few actually reach bookstore distribution). He has also observed under redemocratization a raw energy, a "surge in poetry," heterogeneous, multiple, uncoordinated, lacking a fixed center. Is this the expression of disaffected intellectuals who retreat to the sanctum of their homes, devoting themselves to an archaic proposal of measuring rhymes and meters as they await millennial disaster? Or does poetry express a degree of instability with respect to the current, market-run order, where memory is recycled as mass-produced kitsch and the experience of human loss is often reduced to media entertainment or televised melodrama? Indeed, in this environment of sales and promotions—of the kind that Catalina Parra ironically exposes in her canvas—poetry counters with a denunciation of inauthenticity in language and announces a crisis of authority and voice.

Adrienne Rich has spoken eloquently of the gaps that poetry fills as individuals are expelled from the public realm and remain with a disquieting turbulence about the present state of language (1993, 78). In this context and with the supposed end of ideologies, we are left with no structures of intelligibility on which to express our discomfort. As if to compensate for this vacuum, poetry offers a broad investigation into the legitimacy of language practices, testing the veil of words that cloaks the imagination. Moreover, in an age of discontinuities, it promises alternative paths of investigation, releasing itself from the instrumentality of culture so often required by the managerial state.

With the return to democracy in the South, Freidemberg again observes that poetry experienced an extraordinary rise; but more than democracy itself, poetry went hand in hand with a general "crisis of paradigms" that marks the postmodern mode (1993, 141). Although some have referred to the successes of neobaroque poets in stimulating poetic reform, one senses, more importantly, a generational project belonging to poets of all persuasions designed to decentralize public language and its triumphalist voice. Poetry after dictatorship has rebelled against *useful* language, against confessionalism and heroic legends. Moreover, this activity emerges as a vigorous engagement with the premises of theory. Poets of the 1980s and 1990s thus investigate the challenges of surfaces and depths, masks and identity, artifice and order, taking a step against the fixed assumptions about the functional uses of everyday speech. In short, the projects initiated with the return to democracy reflect the energies of a dispersed and heterogeneous range of experimental writers eager to forge a theoretical reflection on language, society, and culture and to test the endurance of North/South relationships through poetic discourse rather than focusing on politics alone. On both sides of the cordillera and in the broadest range of styles, poets offer radical possibilities for rethinking recent culture and drawing alternative directions for theory. For their marginality from centralizing critical recognition, for the gaps and fissures they open in poetic practice, these writers insert a chord of protest in the airtight managerial logic belonging to our times.

In a national tradition devoted to the novel and intellectual essay, the expanse of Argentine poetry in the past decade can be considered nothing less than astounding. Supported in part by such publications as *Diario de Poesía* (1986–), a newspaper format that reaches a quarterly circulation of 5,000, or the enthusiastic although ephemeral little reviews such as *Último Reino* (1979–), *Xul* (1980–), *La Danza del Ratón* (1981–), and most recently *El Desierto* (1994–), *El Jabalí* (1994–), and *Tokonoma* (1993–), not to mention Internet projects like *Poesía.com*, these outlets distribute a new consciousness about literary craft and authority as they also call into question the interventionist possibilities of poetry within a global context. Speaking for the Argentine Nusud group, which publishes *El Desierto*, poet Ana Lia Schifis explained: "The desert as a site for perception of minimalist detail. From here, the members of the editorial group begin their work, from dialogue inspired by evocation, and not from positions defined by political debate. . . . We also think of the desert as a a site where cultural discussion is stifled, where the lack of incentives and institutional support for culture leads to discouragement and silence among those who, lacking economic means for wide circulation, still try to keep it alive" (1994, 3). In this context, where can the project of poetry be found? Some link local poetic discourse to the musical inspiration of rock and blues; others speak of poetry as an intermediary among different worlds of radio, video, performance art, and photography; still others track the interrelationship of local poetry within an international context. These paths, of course, are the most predictable among possible choices especially given our historical memory of government intervention in the cultural world, the factors of exile and displacement that restructure global understandings, the interdisciplinary alliances that intellectuals naturally find through collaborative work. For our purposes here, these are useful preliminary considerations in order to think about the convergence of private spaces of writing with a public authority secured by poetic voice.

Regarding Chilean poetry of the 1980s, critic Soledad Bianchi observes (1990, 162) the circulation of poetry in mimeograph copy, the volatile nature of literary societies, the shrinkage of outlets for publication, the weakening of academic institutions.[2] Despite this problem, poetry managed to find an opening in alternative sites, through what Jorge Montealegre called a "writing between the lines" (1998, 18) or directly through new public space: in this regard, think only of Raúl Zurita's sky-writing in New York in 1982 or his inscriptions in the Atacama desert or the performances of younger poets held in underground venues.[3] Even today publication venues such as Cuarto Propio and LOM are responsible for the circulation of poetic texts in innovative places as are a number of cultural magazines such as *Posdata, El Espíritu del Valle, 101 y matadero,* and *Aérea*, publications that integrate discussions of poetry with the other arts. These are projects that certainly emphasize the performative aspects of poetry, but they also call attention to the need for alternative sites that the state must concede to experimental writing.

But what, then, of community? Lucien Goldmann had observed that "the most important consequence of the development of a market economy is that the *individual* . . . becomes . . . an independent element, a sort of monad, a *point of departure*."[4] Poetic activity often reverses this individualist priority, creating other forms of complicity, other opportunities for dialogue and debate. It is especially in the talleres where this alternative gains potential. The private workshops held in writers' homes were a unique phenomenon of Argentina and have since extended throughout Latin America. Begun as a practice in the 1930s under the auspices of the Hogar Obrero, the workshops became a common source of reunion and, of course, provided income to writers who were otherwise excluded from institutional support. Exempted from university posts, usually because of political dissidence, leading figures of intellectual life forged their identities from workshops based in homes. This especially became apparent during the years of dictatorship when universities were under surveillance, when public intellectual production had diminished considerably, and when the status of literature was under duress owing to censorship and economic sanctions; in this context, literature was often kept alive, eliciting theoretical proposals and dialogue, from the space of the writer's home where many of the talleres convened. Many took this practice into exile, sustaining the workshop tradition in other countries, notably Mexico and Spain. Today, even after the exiles' return, the practice still prevails. In Argentina and Chile, some talleres have produced publications of student writing in the form of periodicals or book-length anthologies, a possible testimony to the project of reorganizing public spaces from the site of the private sphere.[5] Liliana Heker (1993, 188) observes the taller as the space from which style is created and sustained, the place for invention and experimentation with language. In Chile, certain workshops even took to the airwaves. This was the case of the Casa de la Mujer la Morada, a nongovernmental agency devoted to feminist culture, which inaugurated a number of talleres that eventually took voice through Radio Tierra, an outlet that continues to sustain its commitment to programming on poetry and the arts. These projects undoubtedly succeed as an academy without walls; these are sites where group identity is constructed outside of traditional institutions. They also allow the possibility that literary activity might recognize a more complex interaction among its proponents, bringing into relief the kinds of questions ignored in the more conventional forum for public debate.

In the creation of alternative intellectual spheres, late-twentieth-century poetry proposes to go beyond the negative aspects of a universalizing aesthetic. It thus pluralizes the possibilities of expression and multiplies languages in circulation; it disrupts the "natural" relationship of speech sustained between a nation and its subjects. Departing from a partial vision, it sustains a possibility for the emergence of local voices. In this context, it obliges us necessarily to direct our attentions to questions of gender.

The consolidation of women's poetry marks a special feature of the recent decades. Gwen Kirkpatrick observes a veritable "explosion" of women's poetry starting in the late 1970s, in which women rewrite myths and transform expressions of collective memory (1989, 132); Diana Bellessi insists on the rise of women's poetry as the decisive mark of Argentine literary culture of the 1980s when she claims that women offered the literary establishment a "mixture of erudition and savage originality" (1986, 149). Ironically, she adds that women constitute a *lobby* as if to parody the way in which the neobaroque poets had announced a lobby of their own. Writing about Chile, Raquel Olea observes that until the later years of the dictatorship, the poetry of men and women was basically undifferentiated insofar as *all* authors—regardless of gender—perceived their common marginality from state-imposed discourses about arts and letters (1994b, 1998). Hence, the emphasis on the fragment, on the residues of a failed society, the multifaceted critiques of social life and oppressive, inherited traditions. However, in following years, gender analysis enters to account for alternative readings of patriarchal tradition, to conceptualize writing as it is rooted in corporeality and sexual difference, to open a dialogue within the intellectual community about exclusions of theory.[6] Eugenia Brito, poet and critic, while acknowledging codified gender roles as a legacy of a questionable culture, also makes a case for the study of women's poetry insofar as it allows us to reach the underside of a national patrimony; it touches a reserve of signifiers that have been overlooked by a singular vision of political and literary history (1998b, 7–19). Alicia Genovese explains this multiplicity in a different way by describing the advantages of women's writing as an irreducible double voice: "a second voice attuned to writing, which gives a different meaning to the first, which organizes the texture of the text, like a contralto voice that refuses to follow the notes of the principal melody, of the mainstream or central thrust . . . a voice that gives body, a strange body leaving markers from its biological base (understood as a complex corporeal and libidinal structure) and from its positionality within a given culture" (1998, 16). From doubling or excess, women's poetry also supplies an act of irreverent disruption, an intervention in the canonical traditions of national writing, a way to rethink one's access to the kind of verbal authority that has defined intellectuals in Argentina and Chile.

Contemporary women's poetry is most importantly an attempt to interrogate the status of knowledge and history with the compositional space and sound of the poem; to utilize the literary page in order to show the instability and contradictions of multiple languages in convergence; and to register, from the margins of a debilitated public sphere, an anxiety about one's role in cultural production and interpretation. Not content with the fragment, the poets voice a new approach *en route* to alternative social and cultural visions. Poetry thus maintains a tension between *permanence* and *disorder.*

These uneasy relationships may well explain the history of poetry from the time of the troubadours, but if we start here with a contemporary anxiety for representation as a specifically gendered inflection, then we produce a vision of language and form that moves to the unauthorized margins of contemporary culture. In this respect, as women poets alter the more conventional spaces of representation, their work bears on the order of language, the cruel impact of the marketplace, and the traditions of nature and urban realities that structure the political imagination. I am not arguing, however, for a direct representation of the political, but instead for a focus on the ways in which form and sound emerge on the page, producing a translation of imaginative schema that bears on our conceptualizations of public life. The cultural work developed in the talleres, the enclosed spaces of the home, or other ex-centric sites beyond formal institutions are thus introduced into poetry in unsuspected ways, producing forms of reading, alternative voices, and conflicts. To this effect, Chilean poet Cecilia Vicuña refers to the necessity of "spatial metaphors," altering the urban construction of space in order to redraw the representation of cities (Bianchi 1990, 111). Poetry today has taken another dimension, not relinquishing the first proposal of restructuring urban spaces, but adding to it another kind of territorial struggle over the nature of language that informs any community of speakers. By drawing on the tensions between competing styles and expressions, poetry obliges another look at the hidden languages of the tribe; it draws the eye and ear to the words and syntax occluded by discourses of state. This is more than heteroglossia used for practices of disruption; it is a bid for establishing one's authority in the process of representation, albeit through the production of a highly conflicted speaking self.

Although I have chosen to address the contemporary poetic production of Chilean and Argentine women, combining here their different achievements, it may be argued that the national traditions of each country require separate treatments insofar as a vertical axis of historical influence shapes radically different intellectual quests and communities.[7] It may be claimed, for example, that in Chile—"a country of poets," as many have told us—the poet has assumed an authority unparalleled in Latin America.[8] Yet in her first book, Malú Urriola unsurprisingly writes: "La mistral ha muerto/ neruda ha muerto/ lihn ha muerto / sólo quedamos los necios" [Mistral has died/ neruda has died/ lihn has died/ only we idiots remain] (1988, 49). Inescapably, the weight of tradition rests heavily on the shoulders of writers today. But it also leads to fear of defeat. Urriola's comments encapsulate a sense held by many Chilean writers that the ghosts of a national past haunt—and perhaps inhibit?—contemporary cultural production. In the Argentine tradition, by contrast, where the novel and critical essay usually set the tone for political debate, registering powerful intellectual critiques that have been crucial to defining the nation, poetic discourse often has been reserved for a more limited group, a scattered counterpoint to the narrative hegemony that dominates the literary field.[9]

Poetic traditions in Argentina and Chile are also separated by a different public recognition of writers who speak for affairs of nation. In Chile, women poets insist on the geography and history of their country as their rightful thematic terrain. In this respect, they follow a pattern of authority set in place by Gabriela Mistral as they continue to write about landscape and politics as proper topics of their inquiry. Yet their vision is always oblique. Mary Pratt (1990) has observed how the Chilean landscape absorbed by Pablo Neruda was transformed in the able hands of Gabriela

Mistral. Instead of looking from the Andean promontory at the native landscape below, in the style of Neruda in *Canto general*, Mistral looked up from the valleys and rivers, shifting the perspective of poetic influence from mountain top to nature's floor. This contested terrain becomes a metaphor for one's right to speak for the nation, although the angle of vision varies according to the authority claimed by the speaker. Undoubtedly affected by the Mistralian legacy, today's women writers in Chile also sense themselves as poets endowed with the legacy of public speaking, although often from unexpected points of departure.[10] They answer the force of neoliberal rule by reclaiming the power of lyric; therein, they address the exclusions and silences wrought by the postdictatorship years, the marginalization of popular sectors, and the tensions between global culture and local experience that determine poetic voice. Carmen Berenguer, Eugenia Brito, Soledad Fariña, and Elvira Hernández are among the prominent contemporary poets to have posed these questions, answering the voice of the masters as they speak from minor detail, from the uneven textures of a national landscape, or from the stains of blemished meaning imprinted by marginal subjects on the fabric of civil society. Their most recent work sustains this direction while also recuperating the legacies of an indigenous past.

In Argentina, by contrast, female poetic authority was never sufficiently assured, especially from the decade of the 1920s when Norah Lange and Alfonsina Storni were marked for a secondary role in the literary activities of their day. Even now, despite frequent evocations of local precursors, Argentine women still doubt their rights to interpretation and knowledge. Not surprisingly, then, a stinging irony is often expressed by their bilingual texts, by an unrelenting emphasis on divided allegiances to both international and local visions, by poetic accounts of travel and flight, evocations of masks and disguises. These are also accompanied by frequent challenges and reversals of canonical masculine traditions. Not uncommon here is the use of pseudonym used by women in their odyssey through poetic form, a way to account for the split subjectivity of the woman who writes. While it might be both misguided and facile to claim that the Argentine tradition defines itself for its connections to Europe and a cosmopolitan avant-garde, what is clear is that the poet finds herself lost in the language she speaks, seeking a voice that often leads to travels beyond national borders. In this respect, Alicia Genovese aptly observes the writer as "a stranger in her own tongue" (1992, 71). With this problematic in mind, even the relation of Argentine women poets to landscape differs quite sharply from that of their Chilean sisters. With few exceptions, the Argentine poets rarely turn to the national terrain as a site for an inquiry about history, but use landscape to test ethical premises within the poetic work. Diana Bellessi is a principal example of a poet devoted to this kind of inquiry; for her emphasis on landscape and an archaic American past, she most closely approaches the thematics of Chilean writers, but her poetic rendition of local terrain more importantly leads to questions about the evolution of knowledge and the consolidation of poetic form. This investigation of the relationship between epistemology and poetic language is also common to the projects of María Negroni, Mirta Rosenberg, Mercedes Roffé, and Mónica Sifrim whose poetry recomposes memory and place through deliberately heightened attention to form. Rhyme, sound, internal meters, alterations of classical Spanish verse, and an acknowledged respect for the strategies of English-language women poets are evoked in their various projects. These resources allow the Argentine poets to signal the artifice of both language and ordered knowledge within their national tradition.

The Chileans take the linguistic inquiry in a different direction, emphasizing the many popular languages that fill the poetic text. Carmen Berenguer, whose writing offers the most convincing example of this kind of experimentation, has drawn attention to the "mancha," or stain, on the canvas of normally ordered speech; she claims that women's writing draws attention to the hybrid quality of language and not to its homogeneity: "Voices, grafted materials, are reproduced through acts of violence, through aphasia. A racial praxis is concealed through the cosmetics of story and its correlative, what is told from common places" (Berenguer et al. 1994, 11). A multiplicity of tongues rushes through the span of popular cultures; like underground streams, they feed the wells of national language. Moreover, they work violently against the centrality of a single voice; they challenge standard reference and shake one's faith in a unified narrative about nation and homeland. While this aggressive plurality shatters the unity of a nation's heroic past, it also reminds the poet of her constant presence as both intruder and marginal figure. Chilean Eugenia Brito writes: "Yo, la residuo, la pura perdida/ Mi mente no puede soportarme / Pues soy su espasmo / su traicionado y solitario espasmo" [I, the residue, wholly lost / My mind cannot bear me / I am its spasm / its betrayed and solitary spasm] (1984, 72). If language creates an awareness of this residual condition, it also allows the poet to move away from any essentialized concept of self. Brito thus draws attention to the somatic effects of language on all writing subjects.

Part of a poetic recomposition placed in early evidence by Mistral and Storni, it acquires forceful resonance in the hands of poets like Marina Arrate, as she restructures fragments and residual forms, often using theory as the surgical needle of her endeavor. In particular, she draws close attention to the outlines and borders of bodies, rooms, and landscapes that have met the human eye but have been neglected by history. These isolated particles, scenes of decomposition, are reunited under a larger umbrella plan of moving *en route* to a new perspective on Chilean culture as seen from the vantage of the less empowered.

Space becomes an important feature of this poetry—not simply the landscape of the nation, but the space of houses, containers, and surfaces that enter the compositional realm. It may be claimed, of course, that writing of the late twentieth century yields to the scopic regime. Fredric Jameson, as an example, had offered a strenuous argument for the contemporary movement away from psychological depth in art and literature and toward a gliding of surface forms, moving in collision with each other (1993, 15). However, a celebration of visual spheres no longer figures as playful activity of the kind belonging to early avant-gardism of the 1920s (recall the experiments of Vicente Huidobro or Oliverio Girondo); rather, a return to aesthetic spatial pleasure is now a challenge uttered *against* the state, an antiauthoritarian gesture that replaces the rational hypothesis.

This possibility is constructed in women's poetry through deformation of domestic space. Oddly enough, the realm of the home, the metaphor that avails itself most obviously to female writing, is not often evoked with confessional seriousness; rather, it draws attention to certain formal components of pastiche or spatial collage that disrupt the presumed unity of a protected space within the home. The domestic environment, a traditional site of feminine creativity, a metaphor that many critics may still want to use, is thus open to debate. As an example of this unfolding, Argentine poet Tamara Kamenszain in *El texto silencioso* insists that the basis of writing is maternal in nature: the maternal as the site of infant speech, a female emphasis on orality, and later the pedagogical role assumed by women as teachers all contribute to what the poet calls a "domestic vanguard" (1983, 81) in literature. Throughout the ages, the author also reminds us, sewing, weaving, and embroidery have supplied a wealth of metaphors to describe the art of writing (76–77). Kamenszain signals this artisan's work as the basis of poetry itself, a useful feminine image to remind us of poetry's resistance to the streamlined efficiency of the market.

Paradoxically, however, even Kamenszain, in her poetry, refuses to evoke the home as a site of focus for confessional poetry; instead, she takes it as a pretext for an investigation of poetic process, using domesticity to voice a biting irony about inhibitions placed on female voice. In *La casa grande* (1986) and *Vida de living* (1991), books where domesticity is projected even from the titles, Kamenszain supplies some approximations toward alternative meanings of house and family. *La casa grande* begins with an evocation of the eye and the ear. The poetic house is thus constructed from a legacy of spatial boundaries and rhythms, delimited by observing subjects in the act of watching and listening:

> Vitral es el ojo dibujado, un
> cuadro de interiores con ventana
> que por la vista filtra lo que pasa
> en el dibujo, afuera, de la casa.
>
> The eye portrayed is vitreous, a
> picture of interiors with window
> that filters through sight events in the
> portrait, drawn from the outside, of home. (1986, 13)

This house is not a space for reflection on sentiment, but for realignment of those spatial parameters basic to our vision. The home is a medium for the art of seeing.

More acerbically still, writers such as Argentine María Negroni and Chilean Carmen Berenguer reject the received wisdom of domestic models. They represent the miseries of the household as a first step toward rewriting history; the house is cage and cell, a condition of internal exile. Nor is it shocking to read the household rendered grotesque. In the poetry of Argentine María del Carmen Colombo, for example, the paintings of Brueghel and Bosch are elicited to represent the family. A decided foreignness defines the home she constructs and, more recently, she pokes fun at its almost exotic rareness, outside of the canon of national fantasy. Chilean poet Nadia Prado brings the domestic into view through ruins and urban waste: "Corres a casa / a tu gran casa caja de piedra jaula loca/ cárcel hecha de tus propias tripas" [You run home / to your big house box of stone maddened cage / prison built from your stringy guts] (1992, 17). More often than not, the home as dissolute enclave offers a cast of aggressive images. It also lacks the intimate resonance that others might wish to assign it. Carmen Berenguer addresses this in *Naciste pintada* (1999), where the home is at once the house of poetry, the house of imprisonment and torture, the house of memory without consolation. Berenguer's house is also a "casa de citas"—in popular speech, a brothel, but literally, a house of citations—a place of reunion of different texts joined under the roof of writing. For others, traditional domesticity is reversed by a lesbian poetics: Argentines Diana Bellessi, Mercedes Roffé, and Mirta Rosenberg offer versions of household obsessions where men as interlocutors are rarely present. They take the home in poetry as the pretext for epistemology, for a philosophy of form. This alternative household is hardly of the tame variety; rather, it serves as a spatial field to draw attention to the different linguistic and visual regimes at work in the poetic process. The "domestic vanguard" cited by Kamenszain seems to collapse within the walls of the versified house.

In this context, what becomes of the female body so celebrated by recent critics? Is it so commonplace to speak of corporeality as the basis of feminine literature that we fall into banality and tedium? Or is it a mistake to assume that poetic production can ever originate elsewhere? Eugenia Brito, Carmen Berenguer, Mirta Rosenberg, and María Negroni all attempt to situate the relationship between mother and daughter as the initiating gesture of intellectual life and language, a bond that will generate a stinging critique of society and its values. The poetic bodies of mother and child thus register conflicts between different subcultures belonging to society. In Chile, these relations are pretexts for narrating different histories of the nation; in Argentina, the attempts to situate the corporeal self on the page are a gesture toward understanding the postmodern pose, but they also bridge the gap between private lives and community.

These paths of women's poetic inquiry are rarely divided neatly according to national lines. Instead, we find an overlapping of problems, a sharing of similar visions as poets pry open the structures of knowledge that shape language and subjectivity. They lead us to theories of symbolic value that register the voices and identities of national subjects in the contemporary world.

Of Museums and "Savage Whispers"

In order to address the legacies of inherited wisdom that have structured historical memory as well as actions drawn in the present, poets frequently turn to the image and function of the museum. A repository of high culture and an institution that orders the gaze, the museum evoked in poetry allows the writer to question the production of categories of knowledge as well as the languages of inclusion and exclusion that regulate its order. The museum thus constructs a relation of paternal domination over objects represented therein; and, for those artists excluded from its range, it simultaneously creates an "anxiety of influence" with respect to individuals and tradition. Speaking to the construction of the museum, Néstor García Canclini writes: "The museum is the ceremonial seat of national patrimony, the place where it is guarded and celebrated, where the semiotic regime of hegemonic groups who organized it is reproduced. To be in the museum is not simply to enter a building and view its works, but to enter a ritualized system of social actions" (1992, 158). Beyond Canclini's observations, the museum also brings nature and artifice into contact, showing the transformation of popular culture under the lens of formally constituted disciplines. In this instance, the museum draws into collision the famed oppositions of civilization and barbarism, translating the languages of the latter for the advantages of the former.

Diana Bellessi builds on the image of the museum as a site where official culture dominates marginal subjects; more importantly, she considers the power of marginal voices to alter the meaning and status of art. In "Manhattan Revisited," a poem in *El jardín* (1992), Bellessi speaks of the anthropological objects on display in New York's Metropolitan Museum of Art. Seen from the periphery, the museum's treasures bring into contradiction the presence of living, active subjects and the sterile encasement of their artifacts guarded in the urban archive. For Bellessi, this is also the powerful tension that joins the North/South encounter.

Gano las calles
por la basura. Pasión
de cazar de no
terminar de más
de servidumbre
La vida tranquila no es
para el puma. Le lleva
a muerte y siempre
recuerda ¿qué? la jungla
Singular
estado presente
donde se es, nadie
Partida en dos
por el verde
tierno de los parques
tienden un lecho
para ambos
lados del horror. País
hambriento
de servidumbre
coloreada. Como los
Asmat
de Nueva Guinea. "Están
hambrientos" dijo
la guardiana del Metropolitan
"se comieron al antropólogo

—un tal Rockefeller—mire
sus caras, usted puede
verlas, gente desagradable" dijo

nosotros los comimos
a ellos dije
y todo lo que poseen—sus naves
maravillosas de veinte
metros de largo hechas de una
sola pieza con gárgolas de
niños en las proas
abrazados, sus tótem
de falos erectos
convirtiéndose en
pequeños equilibristas
en la cîma . . .

Reino
inestable del puma
los barrios abigarrados como frutas
ácidas que calman la sed:
"Pepe se está culiando en el rufito"
—he is taking cool on the roof—
está tomando fresco en la terraza dijo
la vecina puertorriqueña. Castellano
disolviéndose en la ciénaga. "Today
I walked into the sunset"
Es nuestra esta ciudad
en la negra vasija
ritual comimos
su espíritu

I take to the streets
through the rubbish. Passion
for the hunt not
to finish last
in servitude.
A tranquil life is not
the puma's course. It leads
to death and always
recalls—what?—the jungle.

Singular
present state
where one is, no one
Split in two
by the green
sweetness of parks
spreading a mantle
on both sides of horror. A land
hungry
for servants
of color. Like the Asmat
of New Guinea. "They're
hungry," said the guard in the
Metropolitan
"They ate an anthropologist
—someone named Rockefeller—see
their faces, you can
tell, unpleasant people," she said
we ate
them I said
and everything they own—their boats
splendid single keel
sixty-foot boats
with gargoyles of
children embracing the bow, totems
of erect phalluses
turned into tiny high-wire artists . . .
From the black ritual vessel,
we even ate
their spirit

Unstable
kingdom of the puma,
neighborhoods speckled like fruits
gone sour to quench our thirst.
"Pepe se está culiando en el rufito"
—He is taking cool on the roof—
said the Puerto Rican neighbor. Spanish
runs liquid in the mire. "Today
I walked into the sunset"
This city is ours

Observed from the perspective of the Asmat, the tribe accused of having murdered a member of the Rockefeller family, the cannibalism performed by high culture far exceeds the ritual gestures of survival enacted by indigenous groups. The poet goes on to link those populations whose cultural artifacts lie in museums with New York's underclass, the homeless, and Spanish-speaking barrio inhabitants. She concludes her Spanish-language text with an act of bilingual appropriation and a citation from Georgia O'Keeffe: "Today I walked into the sunset." While a dominant language—English—is used to define the culture of cities, another more subversive tongue will open spaces for a marginal population and alter all conversation. Translation and bilingual practice are thus used as a sign of defiance; they belong to the experience of the poet, the puma, the people of the street. From this juxtaposition, a voice of subalternity is heard, the poem takes form around subjects not controlled by the edifice of the museum. It even transforms English and Spanish.

For other poets like Bellessi—the writings of Genovese and Roffé come to mind—the museum supplies an inaugural image from which to generate a critique of organized knowledge. It limits the space where individuals might speak; it imposes constraints on memory. It also harnesses debate about the encounters of mainstream culture and periphery, of elite and popular voices. In this way, as the museum appropriates and isolates social identities from their usual environment, putting artifacts on display without taking stock of history, it also freezes all social movement and ritualizes legend and myth. Instead of dialogue and futurity, the museum leaves us with trinkets or weak reminders designed to "authenticate" past tradition. Accordingly, its presence brings all speech practices to a halt; it resembles the weight of literary tradition as it rests on the writer's shoulders. Nevertheless, in this poem, languages flourish and proliferate all the same. Neighbors, the guard, the poetic speaker all offer a colloquial counternarrative to stand against institutional authority.

Bellessi's signal text, which appears in the final section of *El jardín*, is designed to find an inroad into the discourses of institutional order, bringing the voices of popular encounter to the site of traditional authority and learning. Indeed, the entirety of Bellessi's volume takes on this inquiry about lost popular voices, testing the rigid structures of knowledge that inhibit a more fluid understanding of history, language, and form. Nevertheless, she refuses to sustain a facile binarism of a cultivated yet inhuman "civilized" society against a popular "savage" world of feelings. Thus, the poet mixes contemporary and past cultures, she listens to the heroic myths of martial conquests in antiquity as they bear on modern poetic traditions, she tests the value of scientific knowledge against one's sense of justice, and she reflects on the loss of an unstructured barbaric past that has been devoured by an equally aggressive contemporary culture. She deliberately confuses the boundaries of North and South: "Es sur / el continente entero" [South is / the entire continent] (1998, 122), she writes in *Sur*, a book that covers the length of the cordillera from Argentina to Arizona in search of common landscape and language. This is not didactic poetry; instead, Bellessi insists on the ear and eye to alter official traditions, thereby locating cultural value both within and beyond the museum and the map. Her project emphasizes the exchange of languages and tongues, the encounters of form and formlessness, the convergence of fissures and totalities. As she writes in an early poem of *El jardín*:

> Tras la anécdota
> el vacío se revela:
> datos visibles que componen
> una imagen
> que compone
> la metáfora completa
>
> Behind the anecdote
> the void is revealed
> visible data that compose
> an image
> that composes
> a complete metaphor (11)

The circle is defined, in this instance, by both revelation and a will to secrecy. Visible and hidden spheres of meaning converge to define the poetic image, a feature emphasized both in the sound system of the poem and selected repetition of words. Thus the */v/* of *vacío* (void) also surfaces through adjacent words of plenitude such as *visible* and *reveal*. At the same time, the poet offers twice the verb *componer* (compose) followed by *completa* (complete); this is not a faulty repetition, but the poet's way of emphasizing the ongoing act of composition: *com* + *pose*, a compound word, draws attention to the inseparable linkage of visible images and hidden meanings; in turn, they yield what is "complete" through a chain of adjoined images. The connection among disparate elements is, for Bellessi, what counts.

Metaphor depends for its success on these opposing yet entwined signifying systems as much as the museum depends on the crossings of enlaced cultural voices. It is this tension, then, that drives *El jardín*, a tension that Bellessi repeatedly identifies in the space between garden and wilderness, roots and air, form and formlessness. In the process, one encounters a simultaneous struggle for intellectual domination over matter albeit with a paradoxical surrender to the elusiveness of form:

A punto de apresar una certeza
se vuelven ceniza
imagen e idea. La pregunta apela
en aquello que la origina
hallar respuesta
El mundo entero de las formas
expresa
un plan y gloria
aciertos en la fuente donde
chopos de la vida y
la muerte
tejen agua

About to capture a certainty
image and idea
become ash. The question calls
in what found it
to find an answer
The world full of forms
expresses
a plan and glory
grounded in the source where
poplars of life and
death
weave water (49)

Bellessi proposes a quest for knowledge drawn upon a utopian hope of reconciling opposites; she seeks the roots of experience in an infinite circularity of forms. This is expressed as an antidote to the rigorous structure of a conservative world, dominated by paternal discourse.

atiendo
ahora al reino del padre
El sintagma claro, el sentido
salvador en un mundo que se disgrega.

I attend
to the reign of the father
Syntax clear, saving
sense in a world that falls apart. (23)

Despite its flagrant irony, this is neither a defense nor a facile denunciation of patriarchy; rather, the text offers a proposal for a recombination of traditions and forms, a dissolution and realignment of categories of knowledge and systems of identification.

I refer to Bellessi's lyrics to open a meditation on the languages of poetry that collide, change, and reemerge against a background of inherited traditions. Her example is instructive insofar as she prompts us to think of the genealogies of literary style that, here in the hands of women poets, are recombined and presented anew, always recalling age-old traditions, yet obsessively always in flux, owing this movement to the aesthetic possibilities of body, language, and sound.

Embodied Texts and Landscapes

Women writers offer various solutions to the weight of influence and order, whether through irony, parody, or a serious investigation of the formation of historical memory. Here, both sound and image challenge the languages of traditions past. Chilean Malú Urriola transforms the motif of Jakobson's celebrated analyses of Baudelaire's poem "Les Chats" to write about alley cats and street urchins, untamed ferals leaping from roof to roof. In *Piedras rodantes* (1988), she makes the point that Jakobson, in a seizure of high structuralist devotion, forgot the corporeality that defines urban adventure; yet it is this fundamental attention to the body that underlies Baudelaire's verse. Urriola returns to these representational obsessions, devoting the entirety of her book to Jakobson's misreadings of "Les Chats," which in turn allows her to evoke the rhythms of the street and the violence of all verbal exchanges. How does one negotiate the abstraction of the word with the realities of daily existence? In the same book, she writes:

> La malú no existe, como la casullística [*sic*], sucede; pero es sólo una proyección inanimada más en esta gran pantalla indefinible y abstracto logos: VIDA. Donde cada elemento y secuencia está fotografiada, a punto de verbalizarla y transformarla así en movimiento, que no es otra cosa que representar la palabra y ni siquiera ya la palabra, sino el maldito enjambre del código alfabético u otro aún más carajo . . . ¿cómo también tragarse esta necesidad de lenguaje anexo al habla normal?

> Malú doesn't exist, as casuistry would have it; she is only one more inanimate projection in this great undefined screen of abstract logos: LIFE. Where each element and sequence is captured, to the point of verbalizing it and transforming it in movement, which is no more

> than the process of representing words and then not even; and words, the damned swarm of the alphabet or maybe something more, fuckit . . . how can you swallow this need for language appended to normal speech? (25)

Urriola deliberates over projects of representation, the mismatched pairing of sounds and words that pretend to give form to life yet overlook the expressions of marginal subjects, in particular women's writing. This concern continues in her latest volume, *Hija de perra*: "Estoy sola y las palabras terminan consumiéndome, promoviendo en mí un estado de total decriptud" [I am alone and words consume me, pushing me to a state of total decrepitude] (1998, 13). Despite the alienation provoked by this verbal environment, she adds an uneasy acknowledgment to her need to overcome silence.

But what of the material of poetry? And what of our analytical capabilities to make sense of poetic discourse in an age of commodification? The Argentine Irene Gruss focuses on the nature of the poetic object from a different perspective by isolating a plastic container as a topic of study for a poem. In what is largely a narrative text, Gruss speaks of a pastoral setting of a public park—a lake, ducks, children. A discarded plastic container of bleach floats on the water and becomes a topic for reflection: "Para algunos filósofos y poetas/ esto fue/ una imagen de lo real miserable" [For some philosophers and poets / this was / an image of miserable reality], she writes ("Pesca en el lago" 1991, 11). But the poet refuses to discard the value of this commercial object; instead, floating gracefully on the lake, attracting birds and children, the vessel acquires its own sense of beauty, registered in the spectators's response with which Gruss concludes the poem:

> Los chicos veían como se alejaba su botella
> hacia el centro del lago,
> maldijeron al viento
> y sólo atinaron a sufrir
> y a sonreír.
>
> The children saw how the bottle drifted
> toward the center of the lake,
> they cursed the wind
> and only guessed how to suffer
> and smile. (11)

Bathos and sublime are inspired by the mass-produced bottle, causing children to smile and suffer. Clearly, the terms for poetry have been altered at the century's close. Yet Gruss shows no signs of ironic disenchantment; instead, she proposes that we receive this event as a measure of our capacity to enlarge the aesthetic field. The return to common events in poetry is in part a continuation of the project of conversational poets of the 1960s and 1970s, but it also registers a concerted effort to redesign aesthetic objects, admitting not only prosaic details, popular languages, and banal phrases, but also the utterances of a female voice that might reverse or expand literary traditions. Susana Thénon and Susana Villalba in Argentina and Marina Arrate and Carmen Berenguer in Chile turn repeatedly to the pedestrian, often common qualities of urban life, to find topics and languages for poetry that escape the usual parameters of art.

Huellas de siglo (1986) represents Berenguer's investigation into popular culture, the scraps of urban street life, the punk traditions brought from abroad that configure Chilean language and poetry. Her verses resonate rock music, film clips, jet-set dress, and high-tech automobiles, creating the sounds and visions of an urban culture about to explode. The first poem of that volume, "Santiago Punk," evokes the staccato rhythms of late-twentieth-century global culture:

> Punk, Punk
> War, war. Der Krieg, Der Krieg
> Bailecito color obispo
> La libertad pechitos al aire
> Jeans, sweaters de cachemira
> Punk artesanal made in Chile
> Punk de paz
> La democracia de pelito corto
>
> Punk, Punk
> War, war. Der Krieg, Der Krieg
> Little dance in purple
> Freedom breasts bobbing in air
> Jeans and cashmere sweaters
> Punk of artisans made-in-Chile
> Peace punk
> Democracy with short-cropped hair (11)

The postmodern youth culture to which Berenguer's verses allude also strikes paradoxically at the core of another semiotic system that organizes popular hopes for democracy: peace, freedom, and popular participation intersect as desires within the youth music culture, but in this case they also annihilate traditional compositions of meaning. Berenguer crosses oppositional sound systems to draw attention to the paradoxes of democratic practice (nonexistent in Chile of 1986, neoliberalized in the 1990s), deformed under the weight of a banalized, consumer culture. Her poetry thus confronts historical referents with the materiality of sound. In this way, she does not denounce military rule directly except by alluding to the staccato rhythms of a train (symbolic of unending power?), splintered visions of a dissolute city, or the beats of alternative youth culture with its gruff enunciations juxtaposed to casual evocations of army, police, and cadavers. The reader is invited to link the fragments and make sense of the rhythms of horror.

In *Sayal de pieles* (1993), Berenguer takes this project in a different direction and expresses what might be considered an *ars poetica* as she refers to the elements that enter in arbitrary alignment in her text:

> Esto podría ser la telaraña de una carretera
> un tendón o un llamado a cruzar, un pendón,
> una basurita en el ojo, un insecto; ahí mismo.
> Pero es un batir de olores, perfumes, no,
> pescado, rayas, rémoras que hacen pic-nic.
>
> This could be the crossroads of a highway
> a tendon or a signal to go, a banner,
> a flick of dust in the eye, an insect; right there.
> But it's a flash of odors, perfumes, no,
> fish, rays, remoras on a picnic. (11)

The trivial elements of daily life—even a particle of dust in the eye—form the basis of her poetic style; they offer incentives for poetic sight and sound, all partial and incomplete; they even recall the verses of earlier poets (Mistral is an obvious reference here) to structure new ways of seeing. How we choose to arrange these images is entirely within our control. This is a principle for alternative art; it demands participation. This strategy does not belong exclusively to women, of course, but insofar as women writers register this aggressive speech, they often restore the auditory quality of poetry in relationship to the female body. The nexus between the two gives rise to an unusual subjectivity in verse.

Sayal de pieles, in this respect, is a magisterial realization of the social possibilities of poetry as they emerge from the thematics of flesh. The title already suggests a canvas of skin that doubles as a writing tablet, but Berenguer goes one step further to discuss the textures, resonances, and odors of skin, and the multiple sounds that record them, linking body to landscape and nation. "Sudales" is the title that introduces the first section of the book, connoting both bodily perspiration (from *sudar*) exuding on the page and the southern landscape (*Sur*) of America that slips into Berenguer's verses. The poet will proceed to map the openings of the body/land and discover the sounds yielded by both:

En un cruce vórtice fijeza
allí en un abrir
Encerrar el fulgor su estambre.

Roce que al rozar se aciaga
deslizando brote
Abrir apenas terso la rodilla
crujir tramado damasco ciérrase
ábrase rocíese.

In a cross steady vortex
there in an open
enclosed stamen's brilliance.

Friction which when rubbed is fated
sliding shoot
Barely terse knees opened
Crackling twisted damask silk close
open rub. (19)

Movement and sexuality are mapped as vortex and hinge, taut with the open/shut opposition that responds to desire. This is also supported by a crossing of sounds: */s/* (*vórtice, fijeza, encerrar, roce, rozar, deslizado*) and */o/* (*vórtice, fulgor, roce, rozar, brote, terso, rodilla, damasco*), one sound literally tripped by the other in a friction of quick rapid movements.

Sayal de pieles is a project of alliteration and inversion in which the author outlines the sounds produced and registered by tissues and organs. The first section closes: "El clic del oído es un clic en el piélago / basurita en la fijeza" [The click of the ear is a click on the skin / a flick of dust on fixity] (14); Berenguer draws together images evoked in earlier pages of the volume, yet here she links the "click" to the ear and the skin; even minor sound resonates, gliding like flotsam on water. More importantly, the "click" is a point of conjugation and synthesis, a reference to a poetic process that joins sound and logic in a single beat. She also inquires, from this schema, about collisions of material and abstract forms, their continuity on the flesh of the page. "Piele(s)" introduces the second section, eliciting with greater emphasis both skin (*piel*) and sea (*piélago*) as surfaces that gather sound. Again, Berenguer pursues the trivial detail, *grano, piojo* (grain, lice), as it sits upon the skin, first described as *cuero* and *tajo* (reminiscent less of human membrane than of the leathered epidermis of animals) and later as *hoja* (eliciting petals, silks, and sheets of paper).

The multiple surfaces named in this book produce their corresponding fruits in sound, repeated from poem to poem in order to provide continuity in the auditory realm. This expands in "Sura(L)," the third section of Berenguer's volume, suggestive of yet other limbs and voices: the calf of a leg; the southern extremes of the land that sweat minerals just as the body sweats fluids; the "Sura" lessons imparted by the holy book, the Koran. The "L," omnipresent in the book as addendum and marker, what Berenguer has called, "the letter of infamy in Chile," refers to the government's designation for citizens who left their country and sought refuge in exile during the Pinochet years.[11] Together, body, voice, and landscape are conjugated in a single image; together, they transpire sound. For that reason, this section hisses alliterations with the letter */s/*, combined with hypercorrections in Spanish (*quedoses*) that remind us of the stickiness of remaining in place (*quedar*) and also thickness of cheeses (*quesos*).

Alli quedoses sudando
Oh fragorosos tumbados
enhierbados suda
leprosos de hierba suda
volcanos de piedra suda
sulfur de hierba letosos
escalpados de suda sodados

turbados y sudales
salar quedose la turba
salares los paisajes quedos
Quedose de jugo los carnos jugos
De piedra jugos

o todo o nada,
o azar.
de quesos.
del.

There they were stuck sweating sweat
Oh obstreperous and arched
threads breathing and sweating
lepers of grass sweating

volcanos of stone sweating
lethal and swarming in herbage of sulfur
scalped by sodas of sweat

massified and sweatified
salty sticky rabble
salty landscapes stuck
Stuck in the juice of fleshy juices
juices of stone

all or nothing
or fate.
of cheeses.
of the. (24)

Berenguer manages to link flesh, landscape, and sound as if songs on a string. The repeated sounds of salt and sweat (*sal* and *sudar* in Spanish), bodies and masses (*turba*) are used to describe a scene recalling sexual engagement, but the poem closes with the contracted preposition "del," as if to suggest tired bodies. Here, language has also reached its point of exhaustion. There is no more blood to run from meat, no liquid to drain from cheese, no breath to exhale from the spirit. All recourses for the production of sound from flesh are finally spent. The poem must therefore come to an end, closing with an isolated preposition without meaning. Residue or waste, Berenguer seems to tell us, is both a founding resource and the final destination of art.

The poet takes this project through a topographical exploration of surfaces, all linked to the human body and its production of sounds and forms. Even the medical model enters the text to stain the flesh with alternative staccato systems. AIDS and its symptoms are linked to alphabetic speech; its laboratory cures are seated in the orality of poetic diction itself: "Zeda papiloma intraoral/ por ceda y suda en ceta. / ZETA ORAL" [Zeta papilloma zidovudine / for ceding and sweating in semen / ORAL ZEE] (37). Ironically, of course, the only remedy available here is poetic diction itself especially in an age of market-run cures that commercialize all relationships between bodies and voices. Following a trek through a body of illness, emblematic of late-twentieth-century culture, Berenguer brings her volume to a close with a clearly autobiographical reference and by allusion to the factory-stamped identities cast on women. They yield a poet of split subjectivity ("Beren Guer"), a woman of ruined flesh. Above all, she draws attention to the cosmetic transformation that alters the female body just as poetic rhythm alters the body of text:

blanqueadas nalgas sajada, rapen la nariza
y suban los ojos con tirantes por las orejas
tejidas; pelos de silicona.
Manos revoladas estiran la estética
y hormonas pegadas en el culo harpan,
doblando los recortes de sobras;
hierben, hierban
acidos y engasten los pómulos más arriba,
por la piel, piren la rastra facial;
papiro de pielas, peldefebre sin escote
manga, mangan
porcelana hendida en las grietas mapas
mapean pieses flacas, flecan.

whitened buttocks scarified, nose peeled and skinned
eyes raised by wires through woven
ears; silicon hairs in abundance.
Fluttering hands stretch this art
scratching hormones to stick on the ass
doubling the trimmings of excess;
acids
boil, soil
and set cheekbones up high
burning tracks on facial flesh;
papyrus of skins, camlet sans neck
sleeves, sleazing along
porcelain cracked on creviced maps
mapping flimsy feet as they flounce. (56–58)

A cosmetic surgery takes place in this poem, reshaping appearance and desire, refashioning women's bodies, reinventing poetic form. Berenguer also reminds us that the surgical transformation is in fact a struggle for the writer's autonomy, a project designed to emphasize the malleability of ear and the flesh before both scalpel and pen.

Marjorie Perloff observes, "How is it that in the late 20th century we are once again foregrounding the *sound* of poetry?" (1990, 14). Of course, poetic language is speech-based, but in current times, the attention to sound is a way to heighten our awareness of the false messages that contemporary language announces, and in so doing offers detours and inversions of the banalities of our age. Nevertheless, poetry does not enter in relationship exclusively with the languages of mass media or with the languages of landscape, but more importantly with poetry itself, with earlier texts in the traditions of the genre. In this context, language—and not just styles of representation—is the proclaimed arena of struggle. In the hands of women writers who wrestle with tradition, this intertextuality at times becomes overtly aggressive, often parodic in the extreme, as the poetry they write asks how language can be used and read by opposing forces.

Marina Arrate, for example, links the historical traditions of verse form to the representation of fabrics and textures and the adornment of human bodies. Her volume *Tatuaje* (1992) recalls the archaic traditions of marking the flesh of people: "Y desde el siglo diez y seis/ se taracean los soldados, los marinos, los mineros/ las prostitutas, los obreros y los criminales / sobre la espléndida epidermis" [And from the sixteenth century / soldiers, sailors, miners / whores, workers, and hoodlums / have carved upon their splendid skin] (12). Like the traditions of poetry itself, Arrate's verse is produced from a history of corporeal markings; sounds, dress, and textures inscribe themselves on the body of verse. Thus, she traces the sounds of satin and velvet that open to histories of both adornment and lyric expression (15–16); she also reconstructs the roars of predatory animals whose onomatopoetic movements are likened to the human voice. At the same time, classical metrics, popular ballads, and myth evoke the human forms that drive the aesthetic. Arrate's totalizing poetic project is devoted to this investigation.

In *Este lujo de ser* (1986; republished in *Máscara negra*, 1990), Arrate offers a series of eight interrelated poems that explore the cosmetic alteration of a woman who stands before a mirror. A facile reading of these verses would suggest simply that women write to see their reflections in the textual mirror. But Arrate's pages—all colloquial in tone—inform us of the complex, often intensive task of assessing one's bodily image and correcting its natural imperfections. This series of poems thus brings forth another dimension related to the formal disposition of space and the transformation of planes of vision. "Writing from the body"—a watchword so common in our current critical language that it threatens to foreclose our interest—acquires here the value of a highly charged aesthetic. The human eye that the female sees in a mirror is Arrate's pretext for studying line and vortex, reflection, doubling, and ritual. Approaching the body with cosmetic trappings is similar to the ritualistic traditions of a writing practice that produces and transforms its object of attention. In the final instance, it produces pleasure. The poem thus concludes as the female observer, pleased with the transformation enacted, responds with her satisfaction:

> Al igual que con el izquierdo
> se desliza algunos milímetros más

alargando la comisura exterior del ojo
y simulando una extraña oblicuidad
penetra en el espejo el simil soñado
de una idea figurada.
La boca emite guturales sonidos placenteros,
una boca mojada y untuosa
desde ese ojo y medio semeja.

As with the left one,
the hand glides a few millimeters more
stretching the exterior edge of the eye
and, faking a strange obliquity,
one drills the mirror with a phantom simulacrum
of an imagined ideal.
The mouth emits guttural sounds of pleasure,
a wet and glossy mouth
as seen from that eye, which it halfway resembles. (1986, 12)

Here, the poet struggles with forms, taking human countenance as the basis of inquiry: What is the human face, but the surface from which meaning emerges, the specific site that awakens dispute over formal order, subjectivity and change? Arrate devotes herself to the pressing theme of these formal transmutations whether writing of cosmetics or dress. Much of her poetry thus recalls early cubist painting in which small actions (a nude descending a staircase, in the example of Duchamp; a man ascending the same, in one poem by Arrate) are the pretext for juxtaposing formal planes and investigating the relationship between the eye and canvas. The statuesque female figures who emerge in Arrate's texts are a source for the study of formal properties, a point of reflection on the transformational possibilities of an aesthetic object. This leads to a vertiginous condition in which all landscape, animals, and human subjects are exchangeable: "Seré gato, mula, elefante, paloma, jirafa, araña . . . , aceituna, calambre, rayo" [I may be cat, mule, elephant, dove, giraffe, spider . . . , olive, cramp, ray] (15).

But there is another element at work in Arrate's poems, signaled also by Gruss and Bellessi: the power of *emotion* capable of altering one's perception of matter. In *Tatuaje*, Arrate again raises the question of bodily markings: "Se taracea / por punción / con aguja o punzón/ . . . o con pincel de fibra de coco,/ o con pluma de la cola del Trópicas,/ o con ascuas" [One marks the self / by puncture / with needle or pick / . . . or with the fiber brush of coconuts / or with the tail feathers of a tropical bird / or with red-hot coals] (9). The pun about transformation lies in the double entendre of the final verse in which "ascuas" refers to both burning coal and the erotic restlessness of human subjects. Does change occur from physical mutilation alone, or does passion also mark the body?

In *Uranio* (1999), the human body is cadaverous material in decay, described by Arrate in phases of decomposition in order to challenge our assumptions about beauty. Also in the vein of strangeness, Arrate constructs a world of ghosts that haunt us, rendering language dense and excessive, not at all transparent; in this, she supplies an x-ray of city and family, love and its phantasms, asking a propos of these ghosts if they are not "vestiges of dead illusions" (1999, 14). The cross between inscription and feeling leads to reflection on the poetic task insofar as it stirs the emotions and often generates an unsettling distress. The markers that tattoo the body and mind are often past reminders. In a concluding text to *Carnal*, Chilean Nadia Prado gives a twist to this logic: "Mi letra es invisible, pero las palabras me pertenecen. / Y aunque mi mano no tenga fuerzas para levantarse, sé que estoy completamente escrita por dentro" [My letter is invisible, but the words are mine. / And though my hand has no strength to rise, I know that I am fully written from within] (1998, 92). Prado inquires about a longstanding theme in poetic discourse regarding the relationship between the materiality of text and the invisible threads of emotion that generate inscription. Hers is an interrogation about the underside of writing, the subjectivity that refuses to be named, and the irreconcilable distance between desire and representation.

(Re)sounding Verses

How does one write through tradition? Where are the resources for constructing an object of study in the poem? And how, at this turn-of-century, when intellectual authority of earlier years increasingly has come under fire, does the experimental writer manage to sustain any faith in an artistic avant-garde? It may be true, as Beatriz Sarlo (1994) has claimed, that the leadership of yesteryear's intellectuals is now irretrievably lost, surrendering to mass-media commercialization of Latin America under free-market rule. But how does this affect women who in fact never attained the position of avant-garde leadership that is now supposedly behind them? And how do they resolve this through poetry? For women writers, the project is still one of opening tradition, of reconstructing lines of inheritance dominated not by nostalgia, but by one's rootedness in alternative sources of identity and imagination. Gerda Lerner (1986) has insisted on the need to recuperate a feminist past in order to supply sufficient intellectual ware for women in the present moment. The idea, hardly new, is consonant with feminist inquiries in the Americas, retrieving a sense of identity from the international past and at the same time reactivating one's critique of local traditions. In Chile, the current indebtedness to Mistral is everywhere to be seen; in Argentina, the turn to Lange and Storni and, greater still, the reverence expressed to more recent senior figures such as Olga Orozco or Alejandra Pizarnik are widespread. Moreover, a devotion to North American modernists is notable for its vibrant intensity. It is no surprise, in these traditions, to encounter persistent attention to the writings of Djuna Barnes, Mina Loy, Hilda Doolittle, and Gertrude Stein, proponents of an avant-garde project not easily recuperated in the Southern Cone. These precursors inspire both a thematic revision of practices of disruption, but they also allow contemporary writers to trace a history of collisions between feminist literary practices and the dominance of a masculine avant-garde that has misauthenticated women's voices. At the same time, they prompt today's writers to valorize another style of speaking and writing. In organizing this perspective, a productive first step is often taken by poets by unraveling the inherited literary sources that have relegated women to silence.

María del Carmen Colombo's *La muda encarnación* (1993) gives strong evidence of the woman writer's will to resist and overturn a dominant poetic voice that has defined female subjectivity. Colombo enters in playful dialogue with the Argentine tradition of avant-garde verse, overturning its past exclusions of women and reclaiming the free play of *écriture* so characteristically belonging to men. *La muda encarnación* is thus a forceful acknowledgment of the pleasures of the text, a construction of a sound system that calls attention to the feast of language. It is also a direct but unnamed engagement with the works of masculine poets of the Argentine tradition: Lamborghini, Gelman, and, most forcefully, Oliverio Girondo, the consummate practitioner of experimental avant-garde verse of the 1920s and also the writer whose notorious denigration of women could scarcely be ignored by a contemporary author such as Colombo.

The epigraph of *La muda encarnación* is taken from Nietzsche: "Woman still resembles a cat or bird. Or in the best case, a cow." Indirectly, it also recalls Girondo for his well-known text, "Interlunio," which features a cow ("the mother cow") as maternal inspiration for the poet's work. Colombo will attempt to turn around the telluric impulses defining much of Argentine poetry, takng the cow, the horse, and the chicken to speak for rhythms of feminine writing. There is nothing nostalgic here, no sentimentality for a rural past; rather, the forceful aggression of sounds emanating from the poetic texts drills at the basis of poetry itself while, secondarily, supplying a vindictive critique of the misogyny of avant-garde traditions.

She thus heralds the death of the "ancestral cow" (25) and indulges a free flight of logos (31). Parodying Girondo to the most incisive consequences, she will even assume the role of his "triste yovaca" [sad mecow] replete with neologisms styled on his works, moving the site of poetic reference from house to pampas and wincing at the sacrificial tone with which this metaphor has always been evoked (21).

In this way, Colombo aims to insert herself in the canonical tradition of men who have evoked the national landscape in order to speak of their condition as poets, but she also exposes the uses of animal imagery that sustain the identification of women with nature. Girondo, in "Campo nuestro," took the land as a pretext for writing, reconstructing the galloping horses on the plains as the basis for poetic meter.[12] She will also use the images of horse and cow to organize an ars poetica:

un caballo
en la pampa
de papel
nervioso inquieto
movimiento
del sonido
sin parar en la noche
en el desierto pozo oscuro
el eterno

a horse
in the plain
of paper
nervous restless
movement
of sound
unstopped in the night
in the desert dark hole
eternal (13)

In a style that is clearly indebted to Girondo (for its short staccato verses, the debt to *En la masmédula* is clear, although the animal imagery from which she draws recalls his "Campo nuestro"), Colombo will take the gallop of the horse to develop a reflection of the writing impulse. In a subsequent poem, she writes: "Un caballo/ de luz/ un espejismo/ fluyendo /sin parar/ llama de coces voces/ ese torrente/ ese sonoro/ llamado / caballo" [A horse / of light / a mirage / flowing / endlessly / flame of boiling voices / that rush / that sound / called / horse] (15). Again, the horse orders the text, but in its condition of fleeting form and producer of sound, it allows Colombo to stress the business of poetry as an act that relates auditory system and image. This strategy is clear even in her odes in which she situates the creative process as a merger with a creative object. Writing then is "un modo de montar/ cuando fundo la palabra/ confundo caballo con jinete" [a way of riding / when I found the word / I confound the horse with rider] (17). Referent and sound are interchanged for the purpose of writing; unsettled movement enters the text. In the process, Colombo draws in the philosophical implications of influence and continuity, origin and reproduction; she intertwines incubation and creation as part of the writer's environment without falling prey to the facile trompe l'oeil of postmodern copy. The author of these poems thus acknowledges her debts, but surpasses the traditions that bind her.

There is an irony, then, in the discussions organized by today's women poets with respect to the relationship between body and word: on the one hand, their work invites a correspondence between the materiality of flesh and the concreteness of language; on the other hand, poetic speech is often severed from carnal presence. It enters, then, in dialogue with literary tradition. But in *Matar un animal*, Susana Villalba writes, "Aunque el cuerpo no olvida / no encontrás el argumento" [Though the body will not forget / you can't find the plot of the story] (1997, 47). Language and theme fail the poet, but the body prevails in its experience of recording; to produce a direct correspondence between body and language, the poet must resort to violence. *Matar un animal* thus reproduces the tensions between a poet in search of language and the aggressive struggles for appropriation and control that often yield a cadaver. Her volume is littered with bodies, victims of assault and violence; nevertheless, the cadavers are the basis of a literary corpus. They promise the poet an entrance into the world of language, authority in representation: "Se despedaza para unir / una voz / que no te pertenece" [You destroy in order to unite / a voice / that is not yours to claim] (1997, 119). In this way, it appears that the order of literature is based on absorption of a common past that is always fraught with suspicion.

Traveled Women, Translated Cultures

Regarding these intertextual relationships and the formation of subjectivity, Derrida in *The Ear of the Other* (1985) asks a preliminary question about the relation of the ear that links speaker and listener; he links this to a founding principle of autobiography, what he calls "otobiography." The contested auditory terrain between listener and speaker creates the terms for an alternative subjectivity. Moreover, it allows one to think of the ear as a basis for the creation of meaning. What the ear captures reorders our sense of what passes for authenticity or falseness. Recent poetry by Argentine and Chilean women shows the tentative quality of traditional meanings and often seeks a more "authenticated root" of signification in the formation of sound. This is not a defense of undecidability in the construction of meaning, but a way to let the auditory path serve as a route of access to subjectivity.

This conflict of sounds is often expressed as a contest between different languages, a negotiation of poetic space through the foregrounding of auditory practice. Eugenia Brito identifies this negotiation with tradition as the opening of a corporeal wound, a way to challenge the "mother tongue" and at the same time to absorb its traditions: "This work with syntax dismounts the very pillars of support belonging to the maternal voice in order to produce, paragrammatically, yet 'another' language capable of confronting the first, clouding it, and stimulating a game of multiple meanings whose major characteristic is the signifier's insistence on revealing a wound; from there, to call attention to the crevice that generates a vacuum from within the fractured body. This provokes a fascination with borders: not to see the cut or incision, but to go instead toward the margins, disabling the dominant system from within" (1990, 173). Brito will insist on the value of the margins, the residual effects of the "real," the power of peripheral discourses from which to enact a challenge to tradition and reconceptualize language and inheritance. As she writes in the same book, "Melody, punctuation, silence will become alternatives to official language" (72). For Brito, the demarcations of "other" languages or silences will produce an open sore on the flesh of the text; they will cultivate alternative routes of resistance and prompt a flight to the margins. Different linguistic systems thus enter the text, notably through the use of citation and the challenge to the literary past. Here, in particular, poetry draws on the art of bilingual expression and shows the inadequacy of any primary language to render full account of sentiment or wisdom. For that reason, Kamenzsain writes with allusion to Yiddish; Arrate and Sifrim rely on wordplay in English; Hernández turns to German; Roffé cites from Latin and Greek; Negroni draws from Italian; Bellessi and Rosenberg establish their skills as translators of literature in English, expanding those skills in their poems; and Brito, Berenguer, and Vicuña listen to popular voices. These global crossings remind us that the translator's craft lies at the basis of poetic practice, a way to reorganize the mapa mundi, to transform familiar and distant landscapes, to alter the certainty of voice. They also remind us that a new tongue is likely to erupt from the old. As Kamenszain writes, "Un lenguaje antiguo que ató el cordón al cinturón del habla . . . se descarga"

[An ancient tongue that tied its cord to the waist of speech . . . is unraveled] (1991, 29). Poetry is cause for protean movement, for the unleashing of unanticipated meaning and form.

Argentine poet Lelé Santilli observes that when an infant is born into the world, it is bathed in a sea of languages; among them, one, the mother tongue, will emerge to prevail over others. But residually, other sounds and tongues will also flow occasionally to erupt and collide with others. Poetry can be a repository of this swell of difference, to be both a condition of universal possibility and a marker of individual experience. "We poets try to join heaven and earth. That's why it is said that writing—and poetry in particular—acts like a point of suture," she explains (1998). The cross of universal and private languages in literature draws past and present into contact, but it also provides a curious undercurrent to political globalization, a counterinflection to issues of mixture and sameness.

In a section of her book *Anónima* (1992), Alicia Genovese notes the asynchronicity of this experience, drawing attention to the uneven process of translation that poetic texts sustain. She insists on the distance that always mediates between memory and referent: "Quiere escribir su realidad / reescribe ficciones" [She wants to write her reality / she rewrites fictions] (57). The poet points to the balancing acts of past and present, truth and distortion that run through the craft of writing: "Dice que era / un camino de robles / que el otoño enrojecía / un mar con peces amarillos / y algas púrpuras / es decir / escribe en pasado / sobre las cosas inmediatas / marca sobre el papel / un tiempo que clausura el paisaje" [She says it was / a road of oaks / that autumn blushed / a sea with yellow fish / and purple algae / that means / she writes in the past tense / about details now before her / she marks on paper / a time that closes off all landscape] (58). In this poem, immediacy of vision is delayed by the introduction of the expression, "es decir" (that means). Reinterpretation and translation defer all meaning; they recall a history of misalignments, disturbances of time and perception. They also stir the broth of languages and temporalities to produce unsuspected combinations. This situation yields an irrepressible flow of meaning: *El borde es un río* (The border is a river), she notes in a recent title (1997), as if to signal the ongoing movement of language and form.

Latin American poets often return to this theme, expressing anxiety and awe about the polyglot environment that sustains a slippery relationship between word and referent. In particular, they reveal the tentative quality of traditional meanings, the disjunction between words and things, the arbitrary linkages between sound and signification, the violent disturbances of orality by the force of print conventions. Of course, all writing is predicated on this linguistic drama, but the exclusion of Latin American women from the literary canon further emphasizes this conflict and engagement, bringing into question—once again—the status of knowledge and tradition.

Owing to the recent experience of exile, political displacement, and loss, the motif of the journey has allowed poets to explore the frontiers of this problem, particularly their bilingual condition. Like Luisa Futoransky drawn through exile to Asian culture, Elvira Hernández in *Carta de viaje* (1989), Diana Bellessi in *Crucero ecuatorial* (1981), and Alicia Genovese in *Anónima* (1992) insist on the voyage in order to interrogate new languages and poetic forms; the voyage also allows them to test the concept of any fixed subjectivity or voice and to ponder a sense of *home*. Hernández, for example, reconstructs the tensions between Huidobro's poetry of flight and Valery's ocean graveyard (implicit references in the book) as the basis for a textual composition in her *Carta de viaje*. Here, she joins heights and valleys, air and sea, east and west, in order to lead her readers to the vertiginous, hybrid experiences of the South American mestiza. The voyage is thus a pretext to explore the movement of identities, to allow her to take a name: "Yo herma . . . / india sudamericana" [I, labile pillar . . . / South American Indian woman] (10), she writes in a poem dated October 12, recalling the significance of the day of discovery in order to affirm, paradoxically, her South American self. She also evokes this date to inaugurate a voyage to European shores, initiating a counter-Conquest. The travel motif thus restores the question of race to poetry as it also registers its somatic effects on the body (22): she is at once mutilated, described with severed arms ("busto sin brazos" [armless bust]); as an effect of the Nordic snow, she becomes a passive golem (20). Equally important, she is transformed by the whiteness of the page, by the calling of literary tradition (*Die kunst zu reisen*, hermano / el acto y el arte de partir / de confundirse con el blanco" [*Die kunst zu reisen*, brother / the act and art of leaving / of confusing oneself with whiteness] (19). In this respect, travel allows the expansion of language, the mutation of tongues. "Soy lengua ampollada por la electricidad" [I am a tongue blistered by electric currents] (11), she writes, as if to signal the technological markers that affect her speech and production of language. Travel allows the accumulation of the materials of art and self-construction: pillars, sculptures, electricity, and paper contribute to a sense of self. The voyage thus reconstructs poetic diction; it allows the displacement of desire; it accommodates the uneasiness of a speaking subject anxious about expression.

The relationship of travel to language is often repeated although for different ends. In *Viaje de la noche* (1994b), Negroni announces the poetic odyssey as a way to collect nomadic experiences and reconstruct discourse and memory: "Es un riesgo. Se parte, sin entender por qué. O más bien, en su vagar inmóvil, de cautiverio en cautiverio, extraviado en el rostro oscilante de la noche, el viajero busca signos, como quien busca su figura en la figura de la ausencia, sin reconocer su propio hogar" [It's a risk. One leaves without knowing why. Or better, in wandering stillness, from prison to prison, lost in the roaming face of night, the traveler looks for signs, like a person who seeks his image in the figure of absence, without knowing that he's home] (82). The travel to which Negroni alludes is based on a tension between nation and global traditions, between visual arts and writing, between the different languages of literature that allow one to construct a self. She seeks what she calls "the cursive city" (82), a paradoxical counterpart to Angel Rama's "lettered city" that allows her to construct alternative versions of the metropolis through available writing systems. Negroni's writing begs for the inflections of medieval Spanish, Petrarchan conceits, Nordic legends, and English-language citations, along with frequent reference to film and painting. Venice, Sweden, Paris, and the United States are also evoked in her work in order to map the detail necessary for poetic discourse and self-affirmation. Her heightened emphasis on spatiality in representation allows a tension between observer and object.

In an earlier text, *Islandia* (1993), an epic account of exile, migration, and loss, Negroni refers to the question of travel by reconstructing Nordic sagas, presumably the Icelandic legends made famous in Argentina by Borges although, for the speaker's gelid abandon among skyscrapers and airports, the book reminds the reader of Negroni's time spent in New York. Were this merely a parodic intent at literary reconstruction, Negroni's text would lack any remarkable attraction. However, she uses the very masculine premises of migration and conquest, settlement and expansion as the basis for an inquiry into the effects of displacement upon individual identity and human community. Recalling H. D.'s famous trilogy, which corrects masculine versions of history through secret languages and meanings, Negroni's book is similarly an epic archaeology in which foundational tales of travel and conquest serve a female counterpart's lament about the dilemmas of exile.

Negroni communicates this material largely through a series of prose segments, narrating from a presumably gender-neutral voice the triumphs of masculine heroism; however, the interspersal of occasional poetic texts announces a preoccupation for a female speaking subject, herself a nomadic figure. Questions emerge about the gendering of experience, the ways in which feelings and perceptions traverse the official sagas of male domination. How is nature perceived? And how is the orphaned universe inhabited? By the juxtaposition of prose and lyrical texts and through the merger of different languages, Negroni shows the inefficacy of quick, telegraphic synopsis of events. Instead, she shows how poetry clears space for an intervention in history that simple prose narrative fails to supply.

Aside from these gendered aspects of their work, it is unmistakably clear that the poet juxtaposes reason and distant narration to the intimacy of the female voice, a project that rehearses uncommon forms of telling. Thus, if the first prose text of *Islandia* describes the arrival of migrants, their betrayals and ambitions, the second text—in verse form—focuses on different modes of representation, an alternative to the chronicles of conquest, a different experience of departure and discovery:

En el teatro lírico de Islandia
—naturaleza muerta en primer plano—
su propio autorretrato la sosías,
de trazo en gramática releva,
en retazos. En lullaby que dice:
sabidurías no fueron hechas para mí.

A Islandia no se llega atravesando
fiordos sino membranas de espacio:
dalias, lamés en demasía
y una fanfarria de aeropuertos
cuyas luces, con franjas de espuma
pudieran confundirse o vanagloria.
¿Laborioso derroche de soportes
o escritura flagrante
de lágrimas cansadas?

In the lyric theater of Islandia
—still life close up—
the sosias completes her portrait
from pen stroke to polished grammar,
in pieces. It is a lullaby that claims:
philosophy was not my calling.

Islandia is reached not by crossing
fjords but by leaping membranes of space:
dahlias, lamés in excess,
and a bluster of airports
whose lights, with bands of foam
can be missed for praise.

Labored waste of bearings
or flagrant text
of tired tears? (14)

A first-person voice assumes control of the text in order to express an alternative to the logic of conquest, crossing not simply fjords, but also postmodern "membranes of space." In the process, this speaker raises doubt about her exclusion from a historical project and thus brings herself centrally into the field of representation. Here, Negroni calls upon the *sosias*, the comic figure from antiquity who represents the inverse figure of another, the second of a pair manqué. This image will prevail in *Islandia* through evocations of masks and travesties and theatrical voices that remind the readers of omissions from history. Female performance on center stage alters the terms of travel and its representation.

This masked presence is central in undermining the authority of any master narrative; it supplements the epic vision with a meditation on memory and loss. In this respect, the sosias even transforms nature so that "Islandia" is less a country of fjords than a suspension of spatial membranes; the island is less a place defined by physical extension than a composite of its tenuous borders. In the process, literary genre is also transformed: against philosophy's foundational epic, Negroni refers to lyric theater, still life, portraiture, even lullaby. These supplementary genres constantly move through the text, as if to avoid any "strategies of containment" that high literary tradition affords.[13] In this regard, it may be said that major genres are put into question by subversive desire. Is the power of genre once again confused with the power of gender?

Negroni's book allows the reader to meditate on the power of women's poetry to reshape our past. It is no surprise that each of the sections of *Islandia* is accompanied by citations from a pantheon of canonical poets—from Borges to Elizabeth Bishop—travelers who often reconstructed the experience of home and migration. Their presence reminds us that the founding myths of nationhood are verse inspired; poetry is the first gesture, the first affirmation of conquest, but it also offers a mark of doubt and hesitation about society's progress. Poetry contains the rumor of an alternative language that undercuts the spirit of triumphalism belonging to any master tale of origins, but it also suggests that lyric writing is an avenue to memory and recall:

De su isla, la fugitiva per se
enciclopedia aprende de memoria.
Despistes y estrategia que en sintaxis,
en descripción meticulosa, su juego

al contrincante han de ocultarle.
Maliciosa tarea, adelantarse
hacer de la alusión un recuerdo.

From her island, the fugitive on her own
learns the encyclopedia from memory.
Deviations and planning, which in syntax,
in meticulous form, will hide her
game from her rival.
Malicious task, leaping ahead
to draw memory from allusion. (46)

Here, the female thinker featured in the poem reverses the grammars of memory that the encyclopedia holds. Too, Negroni's alteration of syntax foregrounds language in its archaic roots, allowing a paradoxical movement simultaneously forward and backward in time. Later in the same volume, Negroni will write the nation from sources belonging to Fray Luis de León, Lope de Vega, *La Celestina*, and the medieval troubadours. Equally important, she will disrupt the authority of tradition by crossing literary history with the power exercised by gender.

Structures of Memory, Families of Images

The relationship of poet to tradition is informed by a convergence of language systems and translation practices between cultures. This is superimposed on a prolonged meditation on the uses and function of memory in describing exile and return, in outlining the contours of family. Mercedes Roffé introduces this problem in a style that differs from Negroni's as she refers to traditions from antiquity through the Golden Age of Spanish letters. In the process, she reconstructs a relationship to an idealized site of origin: "Se dibuja un paisaje de retorno / Voces / Idioma nacional la música de las esferas" [One sketches a landscape of return / Voices / National tongue the music of the spheres] (1987, 9). In *La noche y las palabras*, Roffé links memory to the work of enchantment, a way to capture time and distance through the transformational effects of language. "Cómo retomar el hilo" [How to find the path again] (1996, 8) will become her great obsession. She thus approaches minor images that prevail in memory and that—in their literary expansion—explode like drops of water to form sand castles or submerged cities:

como un tick
como un hipo

como un bajo continuo
gotas hay que horadan
aguas hay que corren
ciudades sumergidas
y castillos de arena
castillos en el aire
fosos hay que aislan y aseguran
y torres de homenaje—como ésta
y puentes levadizos
y hay cadenas.

like a tick
like a hiccup
like a drone bass
there are drops that burrow
waters that run
submerged cities
sand castles
castles in air
moats that isolate and assure
and towers of praise—like this one
and drawbridges
and then there are chains. (8)

Roffé opens her text to a retinue of images drawn from ordinary experience and diverse literary traditions, as if to seek links and connections between past and present, summer and winter, North and South. Throughout the book, this concern is ordered through the evocation of staccato rhythms alternating with long, extended verses and occasional poems in prose. This juxtaposition has the effect of confronting contemporaneity with metrical conventions of the past, a sonorous approach to the linkages between historical times and geographical locations.

In the poems of *La noche y las palabras*, Roffé evokes the cultures of the Middle East and Asia, Christian and Jewish religions, the roles of daughter and mother. Family genealogy finds its articulation in the conflict of traditions, but all genealogy is ultimately explained as the transformation of languages through historical progression. Thus, archaic forms of Spanish construct another form of lineage, drawing on a pagan literary past that is mixed with current speech and conversation. Nevertheless, the encounter of styles that sustains a tension between temporal moments eventually surrenders to the poet's insistence on an authentic voice that recalls the language of home: "Recordad que en mí cualquier vosotros no es más que una ironía / el tú un resabio y vos la única voz verdadera" [Remember that in me any 'you' is only ironic / the 'tú' is all too learned, verity alone in the voice of 'vos'] (10).[14] Roffé repeatedly inquires about the paradoxical rootedness of words that transport us from familiar shores to unknown destinations and still concede an enduring sense of self. This double function of language as both movement and root is reiterated throughout Roffé's work and is expressed through the double entendre of the chain, as cited in the poem above, that simultaneously offers a connecting link to the past as it also represses and restrains the poet.

Roffé exploits the double movements of these images in order to pursue the limits of memory, explained as one's idealized construction of the past. In effect, is there a chaste ethnicity, a purity belonging to the discourse of origins? Is it possible, in the final analysis, to possess an original language? To return to the concept of home? Or to overcome it? As if to answer these rhetorical queries, she reminds us that the linguistic pact is always fragile, based on delicate consensus, reflecting the tenuous balance of present and past, of dialogues between national traditions. The second section of Roffé's volume is thus organized in two dimensions, with prose poems juxtaposed to facing citations from poets of international repute. "Se escribe en contra" [One writes against] (17), she insists, acknowledging the necessary presence of an unnamed adversarial other, representative of one's cultural heritage or a fateful past. Throughout her book, she makes a claim for this tactic of differentiation (27), although she reminds us in the final poem of the limits of her project. In the poem "La noche y las palabras," like the eponymous title of the volume, Roffé returns to the fragile capacities of words to find their corresponding referents: "A la luz de las velas / las palabras / iban perdiendo toda realidad / ese poco de peso que arrastran en sus ruedos / como cuelgan de las eses / de hierro las reses y sus moscas" [By candlelight / words / went losing all reality / the slight anchor that they dragged on their heels / much the way cows and their flies / hang from iron yokes] (51). Here, Roffé reminds us of the inaugural poem of her volume in which she stipulated the need for linkages between different literary traditions despite the burden of weight that they impose upon the poet; now, however, although the linkages are affirmed, she observes that the work of words continues regardless of the reality behind them.

Argentine poet Mirta Rosenberg approaches this from a different perspective and inquires if poetry can theorize the workings of memory. However, she is suspicious of the elevated attentions given to the current topic of historic remembrance. Memory, as the theme of so many intellectual inquiries in postdictatorship countries, where forgetfulness and loss are actively debated among writers and public figures, is valorized differently by

Rosenberg, who insists on the primacy of the imagination over recall and order. As she writes in *Teoría sentimental* (1994), "La imaginación, decía, plantea más problemas que la memoria/ que podría ir de Sofocles a Auschwitz, sobrevivir a su historia / y no decir palabra" [Imagination, I was saying, proposes more problems than memory / that might extend from Sophocles to Auschwitz, outliving its history / without saying a word] (15). This return to a more archaic, less structured form of thinking is designed to give privilege to the flows and rhythms of alternative constructions of daily life, to separate public and private spaces of reflection, to override any need for consensus. Rosenberg thus directs her attentions to the unlimited freedom of the imagination:

> Pero la imaginación no tiene tema sino la varia
> materia de la noria personal: no se memoriza una araña,
> se la sueña o se la ve en la hebra. Yo trabajo con sobras
> y con saña.
>
> But imagination has no theme except for the varied
> material of one's draw-well: one cannot memorize a spider,
> but dream it or see it in the web. I work with fibers
> and with fury. (15)

In *Teoría sentimental*, Rosenberg retraces this course by addressing family tradition, genealogy, and the history of an object of desire; she also engages with lyric tradition through a determined play with sound and metrics. In the above-cited verses, for example, the constant repetition of a final "ia" (*varia, materia, noria*, and echoed in the words *araña, sueña, saña*) is akin to the expansion of the imagination evolving from sound and not simply from theme. Moreover, as she works from *sobras*, or the residual, uncharted effects of memory, her labor resembles that of the spider named in the previous verse. Imagination inspires the work, it weaves a web of its own. This plan illustrates Rosenberg's system for the expansion of poetic form. She thus takes epigrammatic statements as generators of her poetic texts; haiku extends to prose poems; verses of *arte mayor* often reach eighteen syllables. Rosenberg regularly exceeds the metric traditions most common to Hispanic verse, organizing her lyrics with appropriate internal repetitions of sound and constant attention to caesura. As a neoformalist, she extends the reach of language yet returns inevitably to its literary sources, recalling the precisions of metrical form and the resonant circularity of sounds belonging to classic versification in Spanish.

The thematic equivalent here is drawn from Rosenberg's emphasis on a search for origins, in particular in relationship to family. The scriptural legacy of the family organizes points of reference as it consolidates past and present:

> Me quedo aquí, te vas de viaje. En lo que a mí respecta,
> no me has abandonado: es tan solo el dolor del padre en su certero
> viaje solitario, como semilla-lápida y así, en mí,
> los restos de Europa se terminan como punta de un lápiz agotado
> por fatiga del grafito, debilidad del leñador o el carpintero.
>
> I remain, you leave for travel. From my view,
> it's not a case of abandon: the pain of the father is so lonely in his
> certain
> solitary voyage, like a lapidary-seed and so, in me,
> the remains of Europe end, like the point of a pencil spent
> by graphite's fatigue, a weakness of the carpenter or the woodsman.
> (47)

Rosenberg's poetic constructions emphasize the formal convergence of genealogies that meet at the point of writing; they link disparate traditions, life and death, past and future. For this reason, family line is useful to the construction of an ars poetica, a possible theory of writing:

> Aquí llegué, lo sé, para escalar esta altura consecuente,
> este *lingam* de blindada superficie, este monte de las rosas,
> arrasado, que en mi padre es punto de partida y en mí,
> punto de caída. Te amo: sólo el vacío es exacto,
> punto de giro.
>
> I reached here, I know, to scale this expected height,
> this *lingam* of iron-clad surfaces, this satin mount of roses,
> which in my father is a point of departure and in me,
> a point of languor. I love you: only the void is precise,
> a point of rotation. (33–34)

Clearly, the "monte de las rosas" [mount of roses] draws upon the poet's surname, common to the style of bilingual punning that characterizes much of Rosenberg's work, but more importantly, her return to origins is drawn on a map of countercurrent movements, heights and valleys, emptiness and plenitude. And in her most recent volume, *El arte de perder* (1998), an evocation of the mother brings tensions of revelation and occlusion to the center of the poetic text: "Ahora soy la fotografía / y vos el líquido revelador. Tu muerte / me convierte en yo: como una ciencia aplicada / soy la causa y el efecto, / el ensayo y el error, este vacío / de la nada que golpea el corazón / como una cáscara vacía" [Now I am the photograph / and you the revealing solution. Your death / renders me whole: like applied science / I am cause and effect, / trial and error, this void / of nothingness that beats on the heart / like a hollow shell] (1998, 51–52). The writing subject is once again moved through time and space, order and origins are reversed, plenitude and absence inverted. This poetic current is also sustained through reminders of relationships in nature: seed and fruit, leaf and tree, larva and flower are balanced. Like Bellessi to some extent for her persistent attention to relationships between formal expression and epistemology, she evokes these images in order to recall the desired symmetries of the imagination and also to deliberate on the nature of the poetic craft so often linked to memory and myths of return.

> Y me excuso de tener oficio, sudo, porque cualquier cuerpo
> me da pena y ejercicio, casi siempre fortaleza.
> Sacudida-sístole, insegura, por tener todo anotado
> en los márgenes de una historia mayor, por más vieja
> o por más grande.
>
> And I excuse myself for having a craft, I sweat, because any body
> inspires my sorrow and labor, almost always valor.
> Shaken-systole, still uncertain, eager to have it written down
> on the margins of a larger story, larger for age
> or grandeur. (47)

Rosenberg's synthetic will, expressed both in metrics and thematic material, forces a convergence of different forms, noted, as she says, "on the margins of a larger story." Nevertheless, she is hesitant to trust the stable efficacy of the word (although, as a poet, she ironically notes her limited alternatives to verbal expression):

> Un sol exprimido para mi tesoro, y sin embargo estoy cansada
> de la apariencia de las cosas y los nombres que les damos.
> Cada sol, un don, y su tesoro, sinónimos calculados para acopio del
>   vacío.
> Semilla-tornasol, morir como reflejo y es verdad.
>
> A sun squeezed for my thesaurus, and still I am tired
> by the appearance of things and the names we give them.
> Each sun, a gift, and its treasure, synonyms calculated to fill the void.
> Color wheel-seed, death as reflection and truth. (44)

A philosophical problem is at risk in this poem regarding the relationship between object and meanings: Are words inspired by things that we see, or do the words bestow first meaning to objects? In our search for precision in representation, can words exhaust the beauty of the fragile things that they name? Here, by positing the sun as seed and inspiration, Rosenberg leads us to wonder how we eventually come to deaden its magic by linguistic excess, by turning the treasure of an image into a matter of words, a "thesaurus" of synonyms and substitutions that darkens the natural source that first gave illumination. In the final analysis, only emotion remains firm while the lexicon arouses suspicion.

Searching for the many facets of poetic meaning, the women writers considered here engage in a restructuring of surfaces and depths, masks and genealogies; they question the authority of inherited history that brings signification to language. With reason, then, memory of the family is much more than a cult of nostalgia; it constructs an alternative poetic space to test the conflicts of authenticity and falseness, to probe the line between reality and illusion, the signifying chains we manage. Mónica Sifrim draws this forth in *Laguna* (1999), a volume whose title already suggests a gap between different worlds, a play between those ponds of meaning found in nature as well as the hiatus between thought and expression drifting on the textual page. In both senses, she marks interruptions in the flow of language and history. For Sifrim, the laguna gives form to the experience of memory itself, eclipsing sites of fixed meaning in favor of those different worlds that float free of original form. The site for this exploration, initially, is drawn upon an image of the father whose empty memory challenges both linguistic structure and the usual grammar of family. In a manner reminiscent of Wordsworth's epigraph to the "Ode on Immortality" ("The child is the father of the man"), Sifrim inaugurates her volume by describing the reversal of history that the child as poet enacts. "*Hoy lo llevo de la mano por primera vez.* / Un anciano pequeño con los ojos azules . . . Todo lo olvidará" [*Today for the first time I take him by the hand.* / A tiny elder with blue eyes . . . He will forget it all] (9). Who can translate the memory of the other? Who is authorized to give meaning to form? These questions are at the root of Sifrim's project, although, on the surface, the pretext is family.

If the father's lost memory is the inaugural anecdote that opens this volume of poems, it is clear that Sifrim takes this crisis to articulate a drama of noncorrespondence between language and image. Water and blankness, the two terms derived from "laguna," are the metaphorical bases for establishing the terms of crisis. "Una laguna nos enlaza / un hueco recatado en la ilación. / Escenas pantanosas nos completan / con agua / lo que no se recuerda" [A laguna enjoins us / a modest hollow in illation. / Mired scenes gloss / with water / what we can't recall] (11). The struggle to remember, while basic to genealogy and life, is central to the poet's task: it resituates the drama of aligning experience and meaning in each poetic text. It also produces a stunning irony that wavers between ignorance and adroitness as Sifrim observes in the concluding poem of her volume: "Qué desatino / sujetar con tizas / lo fluído" [What a craft / to fasten fluid / with chalk] (67). The challenge of poetry is to sustain this clever balancing act between word and evasive meaning, to pry open the comfort of clear-running logic and disturb it with poetic form, to provoke a new sensus communis based not on logic alone, but on one's experience of art.

Disguise, Doubt, and Artifice

Charles Bernstein has referred to the power of "official verse culture" in describing the way in which hegemonic structures determine the language of poetry (1990). Women poets respond to these coordinates by a constant subversion of images, cutting away at expectations belonging to both gender and genre. Hence, their rewriting of history, their reinscription of the domestic sphere, their repudiation of confessional verse, their satires of canonical authors identified with earlier national traditions. Refusing the norms of any single language belonging to poetic diction, Argentine and Chilean writers resist the impositions of inheritance and open their texts to a wide spectrum of alternative expressions of knowledge, often challenging accepted wisdom and the rationality of state and market. Here, the feminine in its various forms explodes upon any fixed order of discourse, opening the possibilities of knowledge and subjectivity in the fin de siglo climate. Nevertheless, for the struggle, the poet often defines herself as an impostor.

Against a background of immigration and the polyglot traditions of the Argentine experience, Tamara Kamenszain insists on dual visions, a "doubling of language" (1991, 23), necessary for the writer but also misleading. It leads one to ask about the status of the relentless impostor-poet in relation to experience. Where is the line dividing an original speaking voice and the artistic copy? Where is the "true" female body in a text about family matters? In *Tango bar* (1998), Kamenszain continues to express these doubts as she opens the volume with the following lines: "Decime quién sos vos. No me falle mascarita" [Tell me who you are / Don't fail me little mask] (11). A reworking of the lyric tradition that claims its roots in tango, a world in which women are decidedly reduced to silent objects of desire, the poet seeks an originating point for self that might challenge the ideologies of popular verse. In this way, she ventures beyond the family home, to travel to a more precarious dwelling—national cultural tradition. Like Colombo who challenges the pastoral traditions of the Argentine rural past or Bellessi who looks suspiciously at the legacy of the archive and museum, Kamenszain reminds us of the false persona the woman writer assumes when she engages with the legacy of a national culture.

Mirta Rosenberg also balances doubt with self-consolidation when she describes herself as a masked writer carrying forged credentials. The strange voice of inauthenticity is especially obvious in *Madam* (1988), a book that allows Rosenberg to speculate on the range of expressions that the woman writer might claim as her own. In "Madam," the first poem of that volume, she focuses on the question of an authorized writing subject constituted by and within language:

> En el momento de nacer, poco más tarde,
> no hubo sentidos revelados. Lo auspicioso
> de ese día fue una luz de neón, perecedera,
> incandescente, enrarecida, dibujando el signo
> de la palindromía—Madam, I'm Adam—más perfecta
> en otro idioma y más sombría
> que dominar los sentidos. El reflejo
> intermitente tornó inútil el espejo; demorado, ¡ay!
> el círculo callado, sorprendido
> de los cuerpos que buscándose se evitan
> en el calor de lo íntimo. ¡Haber nacido
> bajo ese signo! haber nacido. A diario
> el tedio vuelve del revés el derecho natural,
> y el asedio es del sitio de lo mismo:
> Al no desear, me muero. Quiero a ese pájaro
> de mal agüero, al que amenaza *Mad am I*
> con énfasis vital y tanto élan . . . Madam, ¡ay!,
> perdamos tiempo si todo está perdido, hablemos
> trivialmente del paso, del abismo.
>
> At the moment of birth, a while later,
> there were no revelations. The auspicious event
> of that day was a rarefied neon light,
> incandescent, flickering, depicting a palindrome
> sign—**Madam, I'm Adam**—more perfect
> in another tongue and darker
> than mastering meanings. Intermittent

glow made the mirror minor; the silent circle
halted oh!, surprised
by bodies, which seeking each other, ran away
from intimate passion. To have been born under
that sign! to have been born. Every day
tedium returns from the reverse of natural law
and at siege is the site of sameness:
When I don't desire, I die. I want that bird
of bad omen, the one that threatens "Mad am I"
with so much life and élan . . . Madam, oh!
let's lose time if everything is lost, let's speak
trivia of the crossroad, of the abyss. (11)

The writing subject is present as both origin and copy, constructed as androgynous palindrome—she is both Madam and Adam—an expression of both reason and madness ("Mad am I"). In its polysemiotic breadth, "madam" lends itself to further ambivalence in the larger text as a whole. In the poem, one first passes from the natural light of day to the glow of neon signs as alternating currents of meaning. Reversals then fill the textual arena; like the trivium, evoked in the final line, all creation is set at a crossroads between future promise and collapse in abyss. The full volume of *Madam* addresses this linguistic challenge and, like a hinge, allows a pivotal opening and closing of meanings. Just as the "Madam" recalls the originating force of the biblical Adam, she also points to a future. Reversals yield to advances. The sound system of this unnamed poem reveals a zigzag movement between words, indicating different states of mind and different directions of meaning despite the affinities of sounds that link them (for example, "tedio/asedio," "reflejo/espejo," "me muero/mal agüero," "demorado/callado," "élan/Madam"). Meaning also rests on a chiasmus of internal rhythms ("énfasis vital y tanto élan"; "perdamos tiempo si todo está perdido"), often betraying the irregularity of Rosenberg's free verses and uneven external line breaks. In other words, the poem is driven by carefully controlled rhythms, contributing to a wavering sense of self expressed by the stretch of a poetic voice.

Speech and thought are constantly split, constructing a dual subjectivity: one who writes is pitted against one who survives the routines of daily life. But it is indignation that inserts a double-edged sword into the flesh of speaking subject as Rosenberg writes in another text of the same volume:

la voz que habla
no es sedante pero arrecia, pues es ella
y es aquélla de su propia madre invitándose

a sí misma a una conversación que cuadre
a esta ocasión tan íntima en que en una
se han juntado dos en sumo grado separadas
por la vida, perpetuada como estigma
que somete lo que prende, consumida
en fertilidad que enciende muerte, sumándose
a la suerte de decir, de dirimir, de ser
la indigna.

the speaking voice
is not sedated but strengthened, for it is she
and the other of a single mother inviting herself
in conversation that fulfills
such intimate occasion in which in one
two are joined in sum, separated
through life, perpetuated like a stigma
that subjects what it emblazons, consumed
in a fertility that fires death, adding to that
the chance of denoting, dissolving, being
herself indignant. (1988, 13)

The poem works from wordplay, untranslatable into English, which depends on the links between sound and meaning: *decir, dirimir, indigna* each contains the cloaked marker of doubleness signaled by the prefix *di-*. One speaks from the dualities of indignation and, in the process, splits the self in two and recomposes the sum; the writer thus begets a second subject, twin offspring from the language of anger. The play on duality is the operating principle of the poem, the condition for poetic writing in which two voices, each the challenge and sustenance of the other, beget a single text. Similarly, Mónica Sifrim writes, "Poesía—te dije—arma de doble filo. Mientras te cicatriza te desdice" [Poetry—I told you—double-edged sword. As it scars you, it undoes you] (1999, 68). By contrary gestures that both mark and erase, that separate as they elicit oneness, the writer takes the conflict of identity and difference to be the source of poetry itself.

The convincing irony of texts such as these is tied to an ars poetica of never fully sutured identities. Oblivion and presence, emptiness and plenitude, the contrast of water and stone are the basis of these works: they all lead to a reflection on the tension between authenticity and falseness. Equally important, they are connected to the identity of the woman poet: Is the impostor one who speaks or one who retreats to silence? Moreover, they introduce a second question: Can a woman poet speak through the taboos of nation and tradition?

Identities and Popular Subject

In their search for an original language capable of reconstructing memory, in using artifice to express the formal boundaries between what is prohibited and accessible to readers, Argentine and Chilean women repeatedly bring the question of authenticity to bear on their relationship to recent history. This problem, of course, is densely shadowed by contradictory inclinations: on the one hand, in lyric traditions of the Southern Cone, where figures such as Neruda dominate the literary field, how can a woman feel entitled to record the national past? On the other hand, what wider field for this exploration, what greater advantage for poetic diction than the broad expanse of subalternities comprising language and landscapes of the South? These investigations are central to tropes of female identity and support a poetics based on the multiple possibilities of language, artifice, and voice. In this respect, a gendered aesthetic represents much more than a frontal challenge to conventional lyric; it grafts fragments of diverse experiences onto the branches of South American tradition, producing a hybrid fruit marked by its difference, one that is uneven and irregularly named, not easily classifiable by encyclopedic knowledge. By evoking prohibited landscapes, by focusing on the marginal events of a nation's consciousness, by drawing attention to the lesser elements of life that fail to enter the national canon, this poetry alters categories of information, it produces other forms of wisdom, it allows other tongues to speak.For that reason, the poetry of recent decades often exposes the underside of a coherent national project; its edges are raw and uneven, the topics often sordid and base. But as a project, these texts expose the ambiguities of language as a contested terrain between the state and its various marginal constituencies; they forge a different vision of an *authentic* community.

Elvira Hernández's *La bandera de Chile* (1991) is instructive in this respect. Written during the dictatorship, at a time when other poets like Raúl Zurita were also experimenting with the radical possibilities of mixed genres to destabilize any center of official truth in form, Hernández evoked the Chilean flag, a symbol of patriotism and national unity, deformed through its different uses in Chile by supporters of Pinochet. Full negation thus opens the poem:

> Nadie ha dicho una palabra sobre la Bandera de Chile
> en el porte en la tela
> en todo su desierto cuadrilongo

no la han nombrado
La Bandera de Chile
ausente.

No one has said a word about the Flag of Chile
in the port in the cloth
in the whole quadrilateral desert
no one has named
The Flag of Chile
absent. (1991, 9)

The Chilean flag is absent because its traditional symbolic content has been evacuated. Nevertheless, the lyric speaker goes on to observe the flag draped on walls and windows, displayed on television programs, and elevated over the National Stadium; in each instance, the flag is literally a "cover-up" of hidden meanings, protecting the sinister wisdom of the state and devoid of ethical value. The poem thus points to the multiple deceptions of a symbolic process in which citizenship has been sold, twisted, and perversely distorted in concept as well as form. In this respect, the woman poet enters to signal a need to transform tradition, to interpret variations of the patriotic symbol, and to denounce the violence engendered by the state. This results in a poem of mixed genres, multiple voices, and with spectacles of destruction that register the semiotic breadth of corruption set against the powers of popular knowledge.

Under democracy, Chilean and Argentine poets continue to register their concerns for the gap between state-conferred identity and alternative symbolic expressions. For this reason, the question of popular voices so frequently surfaces as a theme; issues of mestizaje and rootedness in the nation accompany the multivoiced eruptions that resonate in women's texts.[15] Soledad Fariña absorbs indigenous traditions in her work by referring to the Popol Vuh in *El primer libro* (1985) and to a common Andean cultural past in her volume *En amarillo oscuro* (1994). Searching for the precision of the poetic word—a direct connection between the language of representation and the breadth of Latin American experience—Fariña goes in quest of popular speech, pagan rituals, and the landscapes of a specifically Andean experience that might reach the poem in print. If women's bodies were clearly present in her first books, equally important in later texts are the bodies of speech that give us definition. *En amarillo oscuro* corrects an inquiry begun in *El primer libro,* where the poet tested the limits of her representational power:

> Había que pintar el primer libro pero cuál pintar
> cuál primer tomar todos los ocres también
> el amarillo oscuro de la tierra.
>
> We had to paint the first book, but which should we paint
> which comes first taking all the ochres also
> the darkened yellow of the earth. (1985, 9)

With her more recent volume, Fariña investigates the deep hues of nature as a pretext to turn to the multiple languages circulating in Chile, the glyphs with which writing systems are formed, the cadences that link sounds to words, the light that brings meaning to color. Clearly on a search for origins, fueled by a desire to seek the roots of a language system that confers identity to self and others, she comes to describe in minimalist tones the landscape of a people and nation. For this reason, Fariña's poetry recuperates ancient rituals and gestures laden with multiple meanings. In the process, she shows that urban readers must learn to enter the scriptural system with a different order of demands, a new system of correspondences between referents and signs. *En amarillo oscuro* addresses this problematic to signal the inadequacies of the writer: "Cómo voy a nombrarla / pregunta en espiral el aire de la boca" [How will I name it / asks the spiraled air of the mouth] (1994, 11). What, after all, is a name but an assembly of sounds through air? Again, she asks regarding the articulation of name: "¿En qué hueco en los dientes / se alojaba la lengua / cuando nombraba el rojo?" [In which hollow between the teeth / was the tongue housed / when it named the color red?] (14). We are woefully inadequate to speak about meaning, especially in the Andean landscape, where a rich indigenous heritage escapes the talents of a city poet; instead, that writer is left only with air: "Paradeando el sonido (Pac Pac / Pec Pec) llena de filigranas / el aire de mi boca" [Parading the sound (Pac Pac / Pec Pec) full of filigranes / the air of my mouth] (17).

Robert Pinsky once asked how newness enters the world of the text (1988, 4), but here Fariña proposes a question of a different order when she asks how the smallest detail of nature or the trace of an archaic practice can be grasped by the breath. This question serves as a segue to the theme of mestizaje, a central concern of her book. The hybrid traditions of Chile, its multiple languages and cultures, are set in movement as a river of tongues that eludes recuperation. Gushing streams, birds, and stones—the ostensible subject matter of *En amarillo oscuro*—enter this schema of meaning when Fariña dismantles them in component parts of color, fragrance, density, and sound. These elements are hardly open to universal representation, Fariña repeatedly warns us; in fact, they belong to divergent traditions that elude our standard language. Of course, Fariña traces in poetry the inadequate naming of all desire, but situated in the natural world, she also demands a recognition of the rich mixture of Andean traditions, the mestizaje that underlies all representational experience in Chile, the difference from which speech emerges.

Cecilia Vicuña has also devoted her career to this investigation. A poet and visual artist who has adamantly refused to respect disciplinary categorizations—in this sense, her cross of cultural passions has a hybridity of its own—she tests the limits of word and image on a canvas of indigenous Andean culture. The cordillera is her avenue of access to enter the North/South landscape and to remind her listeners and viewers of the mestizaje of cultural expression throughout the Americas. Despite the broad expanse of terrain covered in her personal travels (her departure from Chile took her first to London and, eventually, to New York), she roots the question of signification in the *local* power of tradition, in the precarious words that lead to larger meaning. *Precario* (1983), in fact, is the title of one of Vicuña's more significant books and the basis of an art installation. The project introduces minor details of local Chilean landscape into a poetic text in order to find the transformative sound and verbal power of objects. The miniature, then, is a metaphor for the small dramas of popular life that disturb familiar terrain and lead one to construct new understandings of the social whole. "Palabra es pala y abra / para que entre la luz" [Word is a shovel, an opening for light to come in] (1992, 40; trans. Weinberger and Levine), she writes on another occasion, signaling the violent destabilization that the word engenders on conventional meaning.

Visual poems, spatial metaphors, and weavings from scraps of nature create their own language of defiance, they expose the drama of representation, the conflict of poet and marginal culture and the weaving that is possible between them. In her visual art, Vicuña works with textiles and threads (ways to register and systematize knowledge in Andean culture), weaving signification from minimalist elements of indigenous cloth; the yarn also offers ties between cultures and allows her to work through the possibility of joining strands of meaning into a larger whole. From minor detail, then, she posits a challenge to the authority of universal language and the power of official discourse. She reclaims the voice and traditions of the Aymara Indians and unsettles the comfort of signifying practices offered in a dominant tongue; in this regard, her poetry performs almost like a shamanistic ritual of healing.

The mestizaje of Vicuña's texts recalls the border crossings of Gloria Anzaldúa; designed to disturb our safe structures of knowledge, the security of our language, they invade global registers that emphasize sameness and thereby raise an alternative consciousness about meaning and form. As she investigates the ancient indigenous past and its hybrid legacy in the field of language, the poet repeatedly celebrates the crossings of marginal subjects into dominant language spheres, testing the porosity of rhetorical tropes and figures of speech. In one text of *Precario*, she writes:

> La metáfora lleva a otro espacio de contemplación:
> Contemplar nos templa juntos
> O templa simultáneamente lo interior y exterior.
>
> Metaphor takes us to another space of contemplation:
> Contemplation calms us both
> Or it calms at once within and beyond. (1983)

The hybrid project, resonant with indigenous voices, stands as an agent of transformation, collapsing categories of thought and perception within the verbal corpus. For that reason, Vicuña, in subsequent volumes (1990, 1992), insists on Quechua and Guaraní words incorporated in the Spanish-language poem as she saturates an English-language text with words and visual images from the Andes (1997). Not only do they destabilize a dominant language, but also they infuse new collective life into familiar patterns of sounds. In this bilingual vein, she writes:

> Undísono magma
> Curvó manantial
> Pacha pacarina
> Esfera y turbión
> Una sola eres
> Aguaá
> Meandro
> Tu kenko
> Gozo espiral
>
> Curving soundulating
> magmatic stream
> Pacha Pacarina
> flashflood sphere
> You are one
> Waterrr
> Zigzag meander
> Spiraling joy (1992, 104–5)

The collision of tongues creates a new source of meaning, fusing indigenous rhythms with Spanish. Here, the aesthetics of local rootedness invigorates conventional reason.

Evocations of local traditions circulate restlessly in women's poetry. Rosabetty Muñoz, writing from Chiloé, revises the identitarian challenge in terms of Mapuche culture; Delia Domínguez writes epic poetry of the South and also attends to common events drawn from regional specificities of Osorno. Elvira Hernández structures *Santiago waria* (1992) around the origins of the Santiago settlement, referring to the indigenous word "waria," literally city of "others." I want to focus briefly on Hernández's text because of her attention to the role of the outsider, which is tied to both the indigenous past and the place of the poet. Her story, then, is about the exclusion of others, the exclusion of the poet from society, and the masks that must be worn in order to speak in public. She is the marginal figure, the rejected voice, the outsider beyond the settlement's gates. *Santiago waria* offers a cast of marginal positionings, with twenty-nine poems whose first words are organized in alphabetical sequence, from A to Z, as if to remind us of the tyranny of the colonizer's language superimposed upon all Chilean subjects. In one of the final texts of the volume, the writer inquires about her identity as an author:

> Yo, Elvira Hernández, la del bardo estertor, la
> que no tiene lugar ni contactos en la Corte, la
> que se rompe la piel para salir de sí misma, la
> que se droga con el veneno *pasado,* la
> que tendría que desaparecer
>   pronto
> se hace humo con un pitillo de sueños
>
> ______________________
>
>   cabeza vendada
>   ojos cerrados
>   peregrina
> un rincón de "A Brasileira"
> un pessoa bloody mary doble
> un brindis solitario en el boulevard
>   del Chiado
>   autora de sí misma
> camina por la Coquillé de San Sebastián
> repitiendo a media lengua: *aitor, aitor*
> como si dijera: "Padre, por qué me has abandonado"
>   otro brindis.

I, Elvira Hernández, the one with the bard's throaty rattle, the one
who has no place nor contacts in Court, the one
who breaks her skin to jump out of herself, the one
who is drugged with the poison of the *past*, the one
who should disappear
soon
becomes smoke with a cigarette of dreams.

---

head bandaged
eyes closed
pilgrim
a corner of "A Brasileira"
a Pessoa's double bloody Mary
a solitary toast on the boulevard
of Chiado
author of herself
walking through the Coquille de San Sebastián
repeating with half a voice: *aitor, aitor*
as if she said: "Father, why have you abandoned me"
another toast. (1992, 46)

This poem is at once an exploration of female authority and rights of linguistic citizenship. The woman poet refuses credentials or honors and instead describes her abjection; a subject of broken form, inebriated, destined to disappear, she is a split in two, the product of colonial intrusion. The poet draws a line that divides the text, indicative of a recomposition of voice. The rattling "I" of the early part of the poem, removed from a centralizing culture, reappears as a third-person speaker, blindfolded and nomadic, yet assuming control of creation ("autora de sí misma" / "author of herself"). Mumbling in the Basque tongue ("*aitor, aitor*") to signify the first man, Adam, she admits to loss of the father but, at same time, claims rights to her craft; Hernández cannot imagine the coexistence of both. This is an ironic twist to the parricidal ferocity with which writers are said to bury their literary elders: here, as the woman poet seizes an independent voice, she assumes a condition of doubleness—she becomes both tradition's orphan and the father's twin.

Mestizaje is the inaugural voice of this poetry, with its shifts between tongues, alternations between prose and verse, colloquial parlance and formal rhetoric. Mestizaje also reminds us of the confusing order of history. To found a city, Hernández seems to tell us, is synonymous with the founding of language, a way to bring order to sounds and expression, to account for history, citizenry, and speech; but this is not the privilege of the mestizo subject. The poet as orphan thus works from a double order of history, from Spanish and indigenous encounters, from the traces of alien tongues. An exile from the tribe, lost and without proper access to citizenship and speech, the poet wanders in the hybrid doubleness of cultures.

In *Danzante de doble máscara* (1985), whose title already points to a split subjectivity in celebratory mode, Diana Bellessi explores the double-speaking self in relation to national landscape, through different pieces about the history of colonization, drawing from Schmidl's diaries telling of the expedition of Pedro de Mendoza ("Ulrico") to an autobiographical text describing the arrival of Italian immigrants to work the Argentine fields ("Detrás de los fragmentos"). Interspersed are the voices of indigenous figures who observe the violation of the land, who withstand a constant assault on identity first by early colonizers and later by the threat of disappearance under years of military rule. Bellessi's texts in this volume emphasize the hybridity of conquest and integration, the crossing of forms and languages that configure the basis of mestiza American subjectivity and a plurality of voices. Indigenous and immigrant pasts are thus conjugated in this book, drawn together over the landscape of the living and dead, masks and crossed lineage and destiny. In this context, Bellessi inquires about the location of an authentic American self and asks with which authority one might dance through the minefields of the nation. This rhizomatic advance of alternative identities is designed to emphasize fluid and shifting frontiers, a grafting and transformation of any fixed definition of self as it emerges from Argentine history; it also restores poetry to its popular roots, allowing a cultural opening to those who have been abandoned under neoliberal rule.

Latin American women writers are usually attentive to the possibilities of historical transformation and often question their authority to absorb the national terrain in verse. The contradictions of this project are forcefully felt in the writing of Eugenia Brito. In *Emplazamientos* (1993), she claims in the opening text, "América duerme enteramente recostada en mi lengua" [America sleeps entirely recumbent on my tongue] (11). Evoking the lyric of Gabriela Mistral insofar as the book is a large meditation on the relation of the poet to landscape, she allows for the spatial investigation of the relationship between landscape and writing, nature and corporeality. "Andes adentro" [Andes within me] she repeats through the volume, structuring an ars poetica in which the poet seeks sustenance from the land, a land inscribed within the self.

But the totalizing span of this project is quickly betrayed by the poet's doubts with respect to her authority to speak. She thus seeks her place as a poet through the crevices of national discourse; she is summoned by her own incompleteness: "Debo escribir esos huecos malditos" [I should write these cursed hollows] (32), she writes in the first section of *Emplazamientos.* Brito looks through the American landscape for interstitial forms, residues, and hidden caverns that promise to unlock the secrets of self, nation, and poetry. "Sólo el trazo me salva" [Only the trace will save me] (12), she claims, grafting an alternative version of self from the scraps of memory and residues of landscape. The residual markings, the grooves in the stone offer another version of reality, a latent whisper that carries the possibility of the aesthetic:

> Estrías grises las latinoamericanas,
> fallas de un muro
> criptas de un rito:
> Es la heredad que nos habla
> Gimen
> arrodilladas
> chispas nacidas en otra historia
> casi casi un murmullo
> casi casi un lamento
> por el que claman las grietas encendidas
> tras el pavor de la rosa y el peso de la carne.
>
> Stone markings are Latin America's claims
> faults in a wall
> crypts of ritual:
> It is country land that speaks to us
> Kneeling
> embers moan
> born of a different history
> almost almost a ripple
> almost almost a lament
> for the one whom the ardent fissures claim
> beyond their dread of roses and the weight of flesh. (16)

Brito's poetic oeuvre is devoted to tracing the fissures and the recomposition of American landscape; but it also structures a female voice, defined in fragmented form and anxious for realignment. In an earlier book, she wrote:

> abro mi cabellera oscura y me reescribo.
> En espacios diseñados mejor
> que una fiesta de gala

mi propio día de gloria desde la
medida universal de mis fragmentos.
Yo, partida de mí misma
como un quejido vertical agotado en el puro acto de nombrarme.
Perpendicular paradigma recostado en la nada
de su lenguaje: un cuerpo dormido
. . .
en ese espejo se me devuelve
se me retira
se me disecta

I unfurl my dark hair and rewrite myself.
In spaces better crafted
than a full-dressed ball
my own day of glory from the
universal measure of my fragments.
I, departing myself
like a vertical moan exhausted by the very act of naming.
Perpendicular paradigm reclined on the void
of language: a sleeping body
. . .
I am returned to myself in that mirror
I am retired
I am dissected (1984, 73)

In *Filiaciones* (1986), she expresses doubt about the efficacy of writing: "Me temblo el sonoro final de los desbordes / transeúnte travesti marginal mi palabra" [I quiver the sonorous conclusion of excess / my transient marginal transvestite word] (121). Even in *Emplazamientos* (1993), she continues to write about her fear of failure as a writer:

he dejado mi máscara mítica
no soy reina ni tampoco diosa
soy solo una veta
que quiso ser palabra
y fue gesto.

I have abandoned my mythical mask
I am neither queen nor goddess
I am only a gash
that hoped to be a word
and was a sign. (79)

Writing as a woman always implies a parceling of identities, a tear in subjectivity that separates private language of the speaker from the performative role of poet. As such, it evokes physical violence, mutilation, and other forms of inevitable harm. This is more than the kind of castration anxiety often traced in writing by men; here, female violation is an inextricable part of the writing subject *in potentia*. For the woman poet, entry into the scene of writing can only be described as a bid for self-deformation; it is confusion, hybridity, the mestizaje of American culture.

It is no surprise that in *Dónde vas* (1998a), Brito's recent volume, she ponders the dilemma of Chilean rural women whose wisdom has been called into question. Another language, another representation of self is needed in order to restore their reputation and to bring forward the archaic traditions that constitute and value marginal voices. This is produced through a primary repudiation of the betrayed knowledge and inadequate tongues originating in city and nation: "Loca fue la historia que las cerca, loca su resistencia, cruel la domesticación" [Mad was the story that enclosed them, mad their resistance, cruel their enslavement] (1998a, 124). Alternative voicings can only emerge by recuperating a tradition anchored in Chile's rural past. "Mi guerra ha sido brindar / un nombre al deseo voraz de la memoria / a su obstinación que quiebra los sentidos / al milenario goce" [My war has been to toast / a name in honor of their voracious desire of memory / for their persistence that fractures all senses / for millennial pleasures] (1998a, 57). Like Soledad Fariña and Cecilia Vicuña, who return to the landscape of the cordillera, Brito seeks a poetic language from what she describes as "las materias carnales" [carnal materials] (91). The goal is to override the language of cities, to seek a space and verb that predate nations.

Forcefully corporeal representations of the conflict between languages and traditions are but one of a series of metaphors to give form to multivoiced texts, characteristic of the fin de siglo discourse and of special importance to women. Carmen Berenguer positions this inquiry differently, suggesting that all sound and speech find their origins not in the land, but in the somaticized body. Moreover, it is the violated female body that provides the material of the text, the foundation of speech and vision, with which to denounce state violence. Berenguer's poetics offers constant attention to the interplay of sight and sound, and the languages of abuse, exclusion, and victimization. In *A media asta* (1988), she brings these thematics under the shadow of the nation's flag, flown—as the title of her book suggests—at half mast in mourning for Chile. Mother and daughter tell the story of the embattled nation, joining their voices with those of indigenous women who issue a shared lament about state violation and abuse. The eye dominates much of this text: eyes that have watched atrocities performed on women, eyes that have been blinded by torture, eyes that observe Oedipal crimes committed against the mother. Oral tradition sustains these visions, linking popular speech to poetry, disordering the syntax of Spanish grammar to preserve a communal reality. ("Sangrantecercadalasangran" [Bleedingbesiegedtheybleedher], she writes [8]). Specific voices speak as well: thus, the first section narrates a woman's lament about rape; the second section of the volume is devoted to the expatriate Raimunda (taken from a figure described in the poetry of Pablo de Rokha), as she tells of loss and grieving; the third section allows madwomen to speak the ills of Chile as part of a dialogue between mother and daughter; the fourth section resembles a cinematic frame capturing women frozen in action, posed under a camera lens.

Berenguer's women speakers are exiled from their land, deprived of authority and voice. They are decidedly linked to popular voices that have been foreclosed from contemporary Chile. Accordingly, they speak through fragments and unincorporated syntax; their marginal discourse is shaped from taboo: "Esto que te escribo chiiit, no se lo digas a nadie caladita porque / si me escuchan me cuelgan: chiiit, son las ventajas de la escritura" [This thing that I'm writing shhhh, don't tell anyone quiet because / if they hear me they'll hang me: shhhh, these are the gains of writing] (33). In the same section, the poet adds: "La patria querida es una boquiabierta muralla donde se puede pin- / tar en las periféricas zonas no soñadas por labio alguno no men- /cionada por voz alguna pulsada por cuerdas que nadie mueve al / interior" [The beloved country is an openmouthed wall where you can pain- / t on the edge never dreamed by any lips nor men- / tioned by any voice beating to strings that no one moves / within] (34). The flag of Chile incorporates words without respect for syntax, spread on the page of the book in graphic form, letters and words conforming the visual image of the flag. Popular songs from the streets cut into words of the text; even an ugly toothless woman will find her way through the passage of words. The text ends: "lloranportiquetelopasasmenstruandopasa" [theycryforyouwhoarealwaysbleedingby] (36). Written on the Chilean flag, indeed forming the basis of its visual composition, is the narrative of a woman fleeing victimization. Jaime Lizama López (1994, 175–83) has noted the progression of the four sections of the poem to emphasize a totalizing endeavor in which the poet desmystifies history and decolonizes language. But the poetry also reorganizes a fin de siglo project anchored in the voices of the marginal, the underclass, the dispossessed.

A media asta insists on the eye and the pose as the basis of this poetic inquiry. The eye becomes the authority of the state, fixing the identity of citizens, invading female bodies, altering language with threats of violation and destruction. Similarly, the eye of the state erases all sense of self, leaving a face without identifiable features:

> Marcial lamento de las horas
> transito por un rostro
> sin marcas ni pliegues
> simulando tus labios
> ese gesto.
>
> Martial lament of hours
> I travel through a face
> without signs or traces
> simulating your lips
> with that grimace. (8)

The tyranny of the eye over the feminine subject are nowhere more forcefully joined than in the final section of the book, "Cuatro tomas para un cuerpo azul" [Four takes for a blue body] (61–68). Here, the female body is detained under a camera lens, halted as a still frame of action. The effect of the pose is to kill body and speech, bringing both to a halt in a gesture that links domination over woman to the violence enacted on Chile during years of military rule. In the concluding pages, desire is supervised, action is halted, and a chorus of elderly women sings without voices ("Las viejas cantan sin voces" [The old women sing without voices] [62]). The paradoxical surveillance by the eye of the state yields a caricature of female form, a grotesque, expressionist portrait of women emitting only nonverbal signs, howling without end in their primitive desire for language. This emphasis on marginalization brings us full circle, back to where we began: the drama of women and popular subjects finds its way into literature as a protest against impoverishment and loss. It is the basis of a powerful aesthetic for our times.

By Way of a Conclusion: A Subject Found?

These anxieties are like red threads running through the history of any national literature, but they carry special weight in Southern Cone culture in the years since military rule. Not only because of the state's relationship to cultural practices during and after dictatorship, but also because of the apparent duplicity required by the act of writing, authorship is like a double-edged sword, severing the identity of the person who writes from the implicit body of an author. Borges addressed this years ago in his essay

"Borges y yo," but the dilemma of writers—and women poets in particular—is still far from resolved. The crisis of authorship finds its way into literature through a tension between muteness and voice, the abundant use of pseudonym (Teresa Adriazola as Elvira Hernández; Cristina Forero as María Moreno; Mercedes Roffé as Ferdinand Oziel), an ironic appropriation of masculine voice that allows a writing woman to pass as a man (not to mention those men such as César Aira who write with the feminized first-person in fiction). This is more than a market strategy to call attention to one's trade; rather, it settles on the disputed rights of the author to lay claim to literary tradition, to speak a discomfort about the uncertainties of representation, and finally to cast into question the social categories that divide us. The gap between experience and language is never clearly bridged; instead, the dual faces of Janus continue to cast a shadow over the landscape of society and culture.

The mask, the disguise, the disabled self are also expressions of a contemporary conflict, a noncorrespondence between the writer's wisdom and the contemporary gloss of indifference that flattens debate and meaning, an ethical drama created by the misalignments of truth and promise. The persistent inadequacy of this match is absorbed by literature and art. With reason, then, Marina Arrate's poetic voices appear as acts of ventriloquy; Alicia Genovese asks if the poet is not always a stranger to herself; Eugenia Brito observes the cosmetic transformation engendered upon the body by language: "Mírame detrás de todo el maquillaje que me alquila esta lengua" [Look at me behind all the cosmetics rented to me by language] (1993, 123). But Néstor Perlongher and Arturo Carrera are also given to multiple voices. And Juan Gelman and Ricardo Piglia, ensconced in a literary and cultural tradition to which they are generally considered rightful heirs, inquire about the generations of orphans seeking the consolation of art. Literary maskings offer impossible solace for the diminshed authority of writers; toward that point, even the crisis of gendered power found in Piglia's *Plata quemada* suggests that conventional poses of masculinity demand serious revision. Through double voicings and translations, odysseys crossing north and south or east and west, a turn toward mestizo traditions to juxtapose intellectual and popular subjects, writers challenge the certainties that have governed modernist desire. But the postmodern fragment hardly suffices as an alternative to this pressing need for wholeness. Just as the play between original and copy, between authenticity and simulacra conveys the false passes of global logic, it also reveals the doubleness required of those who pursue the cultural craft. A sign of anxiety or incompleteness? Perhaps. But it is also a measure of one's uncertainty about the fate of cultural critique and literary art.

There is no escape from these quandaries that govern the poetic self. It may be claimed, as one era comes to a close and a new millennium begins, that we are all devoted to a prolonged dispute over the rights to manage difference: market, media, the state, and academic canons demand a positioning of "otherness" that many wish to control. And, of course, this signals the impostoring required of the cultural critic: How does the critic bridge the gaps between responsibility and practice? With which identity do intellectuals approach their objects of study? And in the process, how is the divide of North and South expressed without resorting to tactics leading to individual gain? Beyond questions about vested interest, writers also register the disturbances of internal difference and the unsettled multiplicity of voices that fill the imagination; the doubleness bespeaks unresolved crisis in the field of politics and art. In turn, it yields to an ongoing search for meaning, a longing for a utopian wholeness that need not sustain nostalgia. This desire is cast over the yawning chasm between intellectuals and marginal subjects, between men and women, and between communities North and South. Like the yarn that Catalina Parra stitches on canvas, literature offers threads of conscience to both sustain and suture this disorder.

NOTES

Introduction

1 This reverses the public legend of Chile's political success and its reputation as a land of stability; under this gaze, the 1973 coup came as a surprise especially for those willing to dismiss the turbulent underworld of Chilean history. Nevertheless, and against those stabilizing legends that endorse a single, propitious version of the Chilean past, fragmented stories of dissection and dismemberment are ever-present as a challenge to state authority.

2 See, most notably, the analysis of Tomás Moulián (1997).

3 On the Scilingo case, see the general analysis of Marguerite Feitlowitz (1998) and Horacio Verbitsky's account (1995) when Scilingo's confessions were first made known.

4 Cited in Mariano del Mazo (1999).

5 Paradoxically, los escraches recall the gestures of Sarmiento, Argentina's first "tagger," who claims to have left his graffiti on public walls during the years of the Rosas regime. Among those who have commented on this youth movement, Hugo Vezzetti (1998) emphasizes the discrepancy between memory and direct involvement and criticizes the absence of an autonomous political movement to incorporate the protests by youths.

6 Marcelo Brodsky's "Buena memoria" [Good memory] (1997), an installation of photography and film, includes the video by Sabrina Farji. The catalog of the exhibition, with commentary by Martin Caparrós, Jose Pablo Feinmann, and Juan Gelman gives a good overview of the debate about memory.

7 It is here that I want to move beyond the Kantian *sensus communis logicus,* which defends the reign of political debate derived from carefully posited building blocks in the exer-

cise of logic, and instead turn to Adorno's *sensus communis aestheticus*, which admits a momentary constellation of future possibilities, a provisional imagining of political change.

8 For this perspective, see especially John Beverley (1993).

9 On the evolution of the "art for art's sake" ideology as well as the history of a disengaged aesthetic in Europe and Latin America, see Gene H. Bell-Villada (1996).

10 Here, I differ from Cascardi, who sees the political in the aesthetic event itself; by contrast, I am arguing that the aesthetic problem creates the conflicts that lead eventually to a conceptualization for political action.

11 The recent collection of essays of Georg M. Gugelberger (1996) devoted to the testimonio debate is especially instructive regarding current critiques of representation.

12 On this, see David Lloyd and Paul Thomas (1998).

13 On this, see Martin Jay's collection of essays, which begins with a tribute to Benjamin (1993).

1 In Search of a Subject

1 George Yúdice astutely notes the limits of the postmodern paradigm, which sustains a new kind of cultural capital dependent on marginality; in this instance, the marketing of "marginal" products—indeed, the concept of subalternity protects the estate of the metropolitan intellectual and continues to colonize intellectual activities abroad. Yúdice, perhaps postmodernism's most sensitive reader of this dilemma, also alerts his readers to dangers of celebrating "difference" such that, when seen from abroad, foreign differences become homogenized and flattened (1994, 44–50). From a different perspective, Arjin Appadurai refers to the "constructed primordialism," which identifies marginal subjects from the vantage of "Western" discourse (1996, 28).

2 Roberto Schwarz writes, "These [the original and the imitative] are unreal oppositions which do not allow us to see the share of the foreign in the nationally specific of the imitative in the original, and of the original in the imitative" (1992, 16).

3 Subercaseaux describes cultural appropriation as the result of a dual vision inherent in Latin American culture (1991, 231). See also Ricardo Piglia, who refers to Sarmiento's strasbismic gaze as a way to define a dual temporality created by one's awareness of the contradictions of European and Argentine cultures (1994, 130).

4 García Canclini also moves this theatrical image to a quest for origins when he writes, "The staging of patrimony is an attempt to simulate a point of origin" (1992, 152).

5 On the importance of melodrama in Latin America, see Barbero (1987), Bartra (1987), and Monsivais (1986). From a more radical perspective, however, the staging itself becomes a gesture to repudiate traditions and custom.

6 William Rowe and Vivian Schelling (1991) make different claims when they say that the state's role is shaped by popular culture; they argue that the violent encounters between the state functionaries and popular figures shape state agenda and control.

7 Recall, for example, the work of Dorfman and Mattelart, the forceful dialogues sustained in *Comunicación y cultura*, the attentions given to mass communication, television and the press, the critiques of the disciplinary influence of imperialist "hard sciences" on Latin American education. With the dictatorship, when popular culture became oppositional to the state, lo popular as a category of analysis served as a way to open a critique of the Pinochet regime. This was enacted through CENECA, founded in 1978 and also through the FLACSO. On this, see Subercaseaux (1991, 205).

8 Compare this to the perspective of Jesús Martín Barbero (1993), who explains that the

status of writing is the same as that of the nation insofar as both are traversed by local or regional identities; Julio Ramos, by contrast, insists on the margin as the fundamental ordering principle of nation (1996).

9 With a discussion quite different from mine, but with proposals that nonetheless traverse this critique, see William Rowe on the critical discourses engendered by Viñas and later Josefina Ludmer (1991, 28–29).

10 See Carlos Altamirano, who observes the separation of cultural elites and pueblo not simply as symptomatic of current neoliberal regimes, but as a dominant topic of debate in twentieth-century Argentina (1999). For an overview of this evolution from the nineteenth century, see Graciela Montaldo (1999).

11 Tomás Moulián brings to light a convincing discussion regarding neoliberalism's relationship to the delinquent, explaining that Santiago de Chile, a city with relatively low rates of homicides and aggressive crime and with a geographic area in excess of 15,000 square kilometers, becomes redefined since democracy's return as a "city besieged." In other words, a myth is invented about the invasive threat of the popular sectors and is sustained by the manipulation of statistical evidence and the construction of a discourse on fear (1997, 129–43).

12 Taking issue with Sarlo, some claim the positive effects of the media in drawing a connection with the masses. On this, see Silviano Santiago (1993) and Jesús Martín Barbero (1987).

13 As an example, see Sarlo's discussion (1997) in which she returns to questions of aesthetic value and a defense of "high culture," undermining the projects of cultural studies insofar as they have sought to recuperate symbolic importance from popular or mass expression and place in question the cultural relativism that now dominates the intellectual field. Above all, Sarlo laments the loss of social impact that literary criticism exercised in earlier decades in shaping a common forum for a larger social community. In this respect, Sarlo continues the preoccupations expressed in *Escenas de la vida postmoderna.*

14 For critiques of Sarlo's positions, see, for example, Horacio González (1997) and Alberto Moreiras (1999), and Judith Podlubne's reflection on the polemics sustained between González and Sarlo (1998).

15 See various authors, "Debate sobre política e ideas," *Punto de Vista* no. 61 (Aug. 1998): 18–30. Here, Sarlo and the frequent contributors to *Punto de Vista* express their profound disillusion with the Alianza program.

16 On this, see, for example, Marcos Novaro (1997), who raises questions about the political potential of popular sectors in the future.

17 On this, see, for example, the ideas of Renato Ortiz (1996, 37).

18 In this respect, see Oscar Landi who laments, "The entrance into the democratic regime occurred necessarily through political parties" (1987, 40).

19 For a critique of social movements as archaic or residual, see, for example, Alberto Moreiras, who insists on the libidinal impasse of intellectuals in postdictatorship culture and on the failures of social movements to provide any reasonable possibility for the future. This is due, Moreiras claims, to the absence of theoretical focus found in social movements and their regressive insistence on identity and social agency in an attempt to defend their roles as subjects of social history; Moreiras identifies this as a "neurosis of representation" (1993, 34). See also Neil Larsen for a similar skepticism about social movements (1995). From a Marxist although not Latin Americanist perspective, Todd Gitlin sees social movements as especially destructive to revolutionary causes (1995).

20 Judith Butler has observed the dangers of taking minority protests as the zone of the "merely cultural," relegating material analysis to the terrain of traditional Marxism (1997b, 265–77).

21 On this aspect of melancholia and mourning, see the compelling arguments of Idelber Avelar (1997, 1999) and Eduardo Rinesi (1994b).

22 I want to issue a cautionary sign about the dangers of generalization in the Latin American context. If the phenomena I have been describing pertain to the Southern Cone, the Mexican case has been premised on a different scenario. See, for example, the defense of social movements offered by Carlos Monsivais (1987).

23 I am reminded here of an experience during past visits to Santiago de Chile, where I happened upon the Santa Lucía open-air market, a venue for artisans from the Andean regions. In the stalls one can find weavings from Ecuador, flutes from Peru, wood carvings from the north of Chile. Most impressive, however, are the T-shirts carrying the images of Che Guevara and Allende, presumably an attraction for foreign tourists in search of trinkets of local culture. Political images thus circulate in the tourist bazaar whereas, until the Pinochet detention in London in 1998, this kind of iconography had disappeared from all other sites in the city of Santiago.

24 Castells (1997) shows the structure of domination in the information age is, indeed, marked by the emergence of identity politics and a formation of networks. Beyond that, I also want to claim that this debate is about *representation*, in both the political and the aesthetic spheres.

25 Those who endorse this commonality seek from the overlapping spheres a common project of representation, thus repudiating the schism between state and civil society. On overcoming this schism, see Evelina Dagnino (1998).

26 See also the various debates in *El Ojo Mocho*, a cultural review directed by González and Rinesi.

27 His project obviously responds to a Habermasian schema for interaction. See especially his *Seducidos y abandonados* (1993).

28 The urgency of Hopenhayn's search is articulated most clearly when he asks: "How can solidarity movements respond to this new vision of a secularized world, if they can even respond? Or better said, *which images and strategies* can redesign the terms for an eventual impulse toward solidarity in order to provide satisfaction in this emerging world? Where can we see the clear impetus for solidarity *within the discursive arc of secularization*; which collective images try tentatively to synthesize a poetic affinity (aesthetic and productive) with ethical choice?" (1994, 79). Hopenhayn's plan for democracy, although not articulated with specific cases, revolves around a dialogic exchange (Habermasian in its model) and the revalorization of social movements in order to challenge hegemonic control (148–49).

29 Perlongher writes, "Becoming is not to transform oneself in another, but to enter in (aberrant) alliance, in contagion, immersed in what is different. 'Becoming' doesn't travel from one extreme to another, but enters in the 'between' of the middle; it is this 'in between' " (1997, 68).

30 Here, I cannot help but recall the inspirational prose of Adrienne Rich, who wrote, "I am really asking whether women cannot begin, at last, to think through the body, to connect what has been so cruelly disorganized" (1976, 284). Also fundamental for my thinking about these issues are the works of Zillah Eisenstein (1994), Anne Phillips (1991), and Carole Pateman (1989), who address the field of U.S. political theory; Eisenstein thus situates the abortion debate as a central test of democracy insofar as it

raises issues of corporeal rights and privacy, while Phillips and Pateman use gender as a way to radicalize the practices of democracy.

31 See, for example, "La justicia cuestionada," *Clarín* (2 Mar. 1998).

32 María Elena Walsh, cited in "El crimen de María Soledad," *Clarín* (28 Feb. 1998).

33 One might claim that these issues are also thick with contradiction insofar as many competing forces are interested in sustaining media-generated scandal over sex and gender to the detriment of advancing the cause of justice in the legal arena. This point notwithstanding, the media focus reminds us all the same of the ways in which neoliberalism produces new forms of opposition through convergence of technological and corporeally based petitions. In spite of the climate of conservatism that directs the televised media, the gendered violation surfaces as a term of alliance to test the limits of democracy and justice.

34 *Patria potestad* refers to the nineteenth-century regulation, as part of the Argentine civil code, in effect until recent years, which stipulated that the male head of household was entitled to oversee and control all aspects of female labor, commerce, income, and wealth.

35 Gabriel Pasquini (1998, 1), along with others (among them, Beatriz Sarlo and Hilda Sábato), recognizes that politics in Argentina continues to be an affair of men despite the legal gains for women.

36 For an excellent discussion of the effects of the Beijing conference for Latin American feminism and the continuation of NGOs, see the report of the Comité de América Latina y el Caribe para la Defensa de los Derechos de la Mujer (1996).

37 See, for example, the recommendations of independent feminist organizations and NGOs in the Andean regions where structural adjustment as a topic was the principal focus of interest. As a way to raise a critique and resistance to global crisis, the workshops of "Grupo Mujer y Ajuste" (a group founded in Lima in 1992 to respond to the "fujishock" of neoliberal impositions, but later extended to analyze the situation of women in Latin America as a whole) insisted on the importance of Latin American network: "Generally, working groups move at a local level. But we have to think globally and act globally. We have to think of new forms of cooperation. . . . Create an autonomous network of women in light of the contradiction of productive work/daily work. We have to think of a transformation of economic theory that takes into account the necessities and, above all, the contributions of women." The encounter of feminists in Lima insisted on international network to organize a response to neoliberal models. This was a principal focus of the Latin American contribution in Beijing and continued in subsequent reunions of Latin American feminists. See unsigned, *Ajuste estructural: Debate y Propuestas* (1996).

38 Editorial, "Mujer y violencia, problema social," *Clarín* (30 Oct. 1997). See also the extensive work by Eva Giberti and Ana María Fernández (1989) on Argentina, and on Chile, Olga Grau et al. (1991) for Casa de la Mujer la Morada, and Guadalupe Santa Cruz (1997b) for the Instituto de la Mujer. See, for example, the writings of Marta Lamas who records in her journal, *Debate Feminista*, the local and national campaigns of the Catholic Church and "family values" in Mexico as an offensive that launched a new round of activism around sexual rights for women and gays. She also offers a recent history of these struggles in "Scenes from a Mexican Battlefield" (1998).

39 Olea (2000) notes, in the Chilean example, the major cases that resulted in setbacks in the cause of women: the collaboration of SERNAM (Servicio nacional de la mujer) with neoliberal policies; the declarations of the bishop of Santiago against abortion and di-

vorce; and the events anticipating the International Women's Conference in Beijing through which the Chilean Senate publicly claimed that gender was a sociological construction and not biological, thereby obviating further discussion about reproductive rights for women.

40 See, for example, the concessions made by women in electoral politics in the October 1997 contest between Alianza Party candidate Graciela de Fernández Meijide and Hilda de Duhalde as reported by María del Carmen Feijóo (1997, 3).

41 I am grateful to Mercedes Roffé for informational pamphlets she made available from the proceedings of the Cartagena conference. See also the special dossier on the Cartagena conflicts by Diana Bellessi et al. (1997).

42 On the claims of autonomous feminism in Chile, see Sandra Lidid and Kira Maldonado (1997).

43 This theme is often echoed by Southern Cone activists. For example, Marta Fontenla and Magui Bellotti, directors of *Brujas*, an Argentine feminist journal, wrote, "To make sense of the different forms of oppression that cross the lives of women and to find the points of contact among them would help us to elaborate feminist strategies and politics that have implications for all. Beyond questions of diversity, pluralism, and difference, the point is to emphasize the links that join us" (1996, 9). Like Kirkwood, they remind us of the need to speak not just of diversity but also of the material grounds for common practice. Nevertheless, in the move toward new alliances, a caveat is required, as Gayatri Spivak notes, "No amount of raised fieldwork can ever approach the painstaking labor to establish ethical singularity with the subaltern" (cited in Buell 1999, 10). In this respect, the gendered project moves less toward finding the deep chemistry of bonding between subject and object than toward identifying the sites from which to renew a debate about justice and rights, to force questions of moral representation, to reactivate sensibilities for ongoing political engagement.

44 Warning of these dangers, Diamela Eltit and Sonia Montecino, advising the Oficina Nacional de las Mujeres soon after Chilean redemocratization, alerted constituents to avoid a folkloric celebration of art by women. At the same time, however, they signaled the need to pluralize the core of feminist work while not occluding the cultural specificities of social order: "The project takes as it main focus the concept of difference, pluralizing from the interior of women the specificities of the social and cultural order, with the goal of avoiding universal statements that do not correspond to reality. This concept of difference, on the first level, alludes to the woman from the popular sectors (peasants, indigenous women, squatters, etc.) in relation to the woman of the middle sectors, given that in both sectors there are different ways to see and act in a social environment; moreover, from the interior of each group, one can establish differences according to each member's social and historical emergence" (1990, 101).

45 In the shuffle for foundation or governmental support, NGOs often force female subjects into categories of identity that lack basis in daily life. Veronica Schild (1998), for example, notes the way in which the categories of "entrepreneur" or "head of household" are manipulated in statistical evidence of the success of job placement activities in NGO reports. In turn, these categories set new expectations—indeed, they cast new subjectivities—among the community served. Too, with the obligations of NGOs to deliver a "final product" (often set by categories invented abroad), new definitions emerge about the success of negotiations around gender.

46 Geographers and cultural anthropologists have produced a rich corpus on this topic. See, for example, Massey (1994) on space and social relationships, or Radcliffe and West-

wood who claim that affiliation emerges from place as a structure of feeling and produces what they call a "geography of identity" (1996, 108). See also Eugenia Hola and Gabriela Pischedda (n.d., 56), who insist on reterritorialization as a significant strategy of prompting new alliances under democracy. Similarly, William Rowe and Vivian Schelling remind us that "memory does not survive without a social space where it can be articulated" (1991, 18). From a more skeptical perspective, Raquel Olea (1991, 29–30) inquires whether postmodernism affords sufficient *critical space* to Latin American women or whether the question of postmodern inclusivity is even legitimate. Furthering this discussion of the relationship of postmodernism and feminism, see Jane Flax (1990) and Seyla Benhabib (1995).

47 See also Jean Franco, who offers a meditation on the implementation of responsible practice in Latin America (1998).

48 It may also be claimed that the fragmentation characteristic of our time allows a provisional and emancipatory opening of unanticipated political spaces. On this Mabel Bellucci writes: "In effect, what's at play is not only a questioning of a determined model of political leadership, with its own characteristics (populist in its treatment of people, personalist in behavior, fractured between its rhetoric and practice), but basically a whole style of organizing the relationship of State-Civil Society-Market. The offensive of neoliberal politics breaks the nineteenth-century model and then these three units become disarticulated, collapsing one on top of the other. Therefore, we should ask, what are the places that politics fills if only in a provisional way at this historical moment of tensions?" (1996, 13). Gender, I am arguing here, enters as one of these sites.

49 On the dangers of defending difference without critical and political thought, see Marta Lamas's forceful attack on what she calls "mujerismo" [womanism], that vision which claims the exclusivist authority of feminist discourse (1998). Laclau and Mouffe offer a valid reflection of the need to sustain multiple interests simultaneously: "A radical and non-plural democracy would be one which constituted *one* single space of equality on the basis of the unlimited operation of the logic of equivalence, and did not recognize the irreducible moment of the plurality of spaces. . . . It is never possible for individual rights to be defined in isolation, but only in the context of social relations which define determinate subject positions. As a consequence, it will always be a question of rights which involve other subjects who participate in the same social relation" (1985, 184). It should be noted that this intersubjective impasse is a place from which critics such as Jeffrey Nealon (1998), borrowing from Levinas and Žižek, seek to resolve the ethical dilemma.

50 Liliana Trevisán, for example, links Latin American "difference" to the specific range of "differences" generated by a feminine presence in universal terms. The stigmatized margins of both foment an uncomfortable and conflictive sense for managing the category of Latin America as a whole (1997, xv).

51 Regarding home and radical consciousness, bell hooks writes: "The very meaning of 'home' changes with experience of decolonization, of radicalization. At times, home is nowhere. At times, one knows only extreme estrangement and alienation. Then home is no longer just one place. It is locations. Home is that place which enables and promotes varied and ever changing perspectives, a place where one discovers new ways of seeing reality, frontiers of difference" (1990, 148).

52 It should be noted that this unboundedness is not cause for universal celebration. Leonor Calvera, for example, looks at late-twentieth-century fragmentation of space with a certain suspicion: "The break in unity of time and place, and the attendant era-

sure of the capacity to evoke, are among the main features of terrorism exercised by dominant groups, especially the State" (1992, 6).

53 See, for example, Isabel Barranco Lagunas, writing on the Cartagena experience: "The body is the synthesis and point of departure for all existential and political behavior. . . . Our legitimacy is proven in our work, not in the occasional recognition given by the State" (1997, 35). This perspective clearly alters the arguments of those who would defend feminism from the perspective of "rights" alone and works against the legitimating role of the state with its claims toward a universalizing truth.

2 *The Spectacle of "Difference"*

1 Nelly Richard in both the *Revista de Crítica Cultural* ("El 'caso' Simón Bolívar" 1994) and her book *Residuos y metáforas* (1998) traces the significance of the Dávila episode in great detail, noting the emphasis on mobility supplied by the postcard format, which escapes institutional control and thereby repoliticizes art in unanticipated locations. Differing from Richard's reading of this cultural scandal, I start with the anecdote about Dávila in order to reach the question of the commercial duplication of identities. I have also referred to the Dávila episode in an earlier work (1997a).

2 Cited in Lemebel's essay devoted to the Dávila episode: "Juan Dávila (la silicona del libertador)" (1996, 135–36). See also Raquel Olea (1994a).

3 See Masiello (1997a, 1997b) on the "monja alférez" as well as the question of double agency and masquerade as a feminine strategy to oppose the state.

4 For a different view, see Eduardo Rinesi, who claims that the theatrical mode set in place by the state requires the passivity of the audience; the balcony is for isolation and submission. "The masks were not bridges, but veils," he writes (1994b, 140).

5 On the question of dress and good taste, see my essays (1997a, 1997b). See also Jorge Salessi (1995a, 1995b).

6 On the tension between fashion and style, Roberto Echavarren (1998a) offers a valuable discussion. See also Masiello (1994a).

7 The nineteenth century is also the fertile terrain on which so many contemporary literary texts about crossed identities are set: think only of Perlongher's poems devoted to the age of Rosas, Juan José Saer's novels set in the last century, Griselda Gambaro's "El campo," and César Aira's *La liebre*, not to mention the current enthusiasm for historical novels written by women that are set in that century.

8 See especially the chapter, "Latinoamérica y la postmodernidad: la crisis de los originales y la revancha de la copia" included in *La estratificación de los márgenes* (1994).

9 García here was referring to the writings of Osvaldo Lamborghini. Cited in Perlongher (1993, 12).

10 See, for example, the videos prepared by Pedro Lemebel in collaboration with Carmen Berenguer entitled "Postales Norte/Sur" (1990), which display the effects of a market-run economy on individual subjectivity. In one video in this series, subtitled "MU," the artists create a sense of Chilean citizens being herded to the marketplace, much like cattle put up for sale and slaughter. Lemebel's commentary on neoliberalism is also recorded in two books, *La esquina es mi corazón* (1994) and *Loco afán* (1996).

11 On "The Two Fridas," see Jean Franco (1996, 1998).

12 In *Loco afán*, Lemebel tells the story of a transvestite named Madonna who modeled herself, of course, on the North American music star and challenged the presumptions of

both dictatorship and democracy by her publicly staged performances. Her AIDS-awareness protests elicited the visual images of Hollywood as part of the necessary background effects. The staging Lemebel describes for these performances is similar to the Cine Normandie act; together, they remind us of the symbolic weight of Hollywood not only for an affirmation of the cross-dresser's identity through style but also for addressing the North/South divide. To this effect, Lemebel writes: "Surely back then in the 80s, when body art was the boom of Chilean culture. When the unveiled body could represent and denounce the atrocities of the dictatorship. Maybe in that cultural framework no one would have imagined that the metaphor, 'Gone with the Wind of AIDS', would coagulate on many of the people who participated in that art action on San Camilo Street. . . . The intervention staged an homage, a star-filled night unfolded on the dirty cement. A parody of Broadway in the mud of Latin American sodomy. . . . The stars, painted in positive and negative, reaffirmed the poetic title of the action, 'Gone with the Wind of AIDS.' The Hollywood montage of spotlights and cameras, the drag queens more beautiful than ever, dolled up for the premier, posing for the alternative press, showing the brand new silicon of their breasts. The whole neighborhood ablaze from the instant light of the flashes. And all the cultural resistance during dictatorship—politicians, artists, art critics, photographers, and camera men—enjoying the performance of the 'Mares of the Apocalypsis,' who loaded the commercial alley of transvestite sex with stars" ("La muerte de Madonna" 1996, 35–36).

13 Etienne Balibar's reading of the production of difference is far less generous. Claiming that the identity of actors depends directly on the maintenance of hegemony (1991, 4), he argues that dominant ideology *needs* to sustain a language of universality, which spreads itself over a world constituted by different agents always in conflict. In other words, the divisions of society—by race, gender, or class—are far from receding; indeed, they are accentuated by programs of the liberal state.

14 Cited in Bersani (1995, 39).

15 Note, however, that Deleuze's sense of territory is defined not so much by physical space but by the linguistic code, the place where a flow is interrupted by a knot of unsuspected meanings. Perlongher in this essay was actually interested in the physical aspect of place, although his poetry, of course, transforms this discussion to the linguistic registers of place and movement (1993, 72).

16 In this respect, Perlongher explains that the proliferation of gendered categories has to do with a collision of different classificatory models: a hierarchicial structure (marica/macho) and one that tends toward egalitarian relations (gay/gay) (1993, 71).

17 Baudrillard has a different understanding of this problem, emphasizing various phases of simulation, ranging from adherence to some original image to the "copy of the copy" paradigm through which any "original" is banished from our comprehension (1983).

18 Eduardo Rinesi (1993, 1994) offers a compelling reading of the neoliberal state as a game of representations. If we think about the emerging prominence of talk shows, the repeated references to a "media republic," the televised performances of elected officials, and the cost of a mediatized society, we can reach an accord about Rinesi's perceptions. Once again, the spectacle serves as the basis of the democratic state.

19 Brito's critical discussions of Chilean literature during the dictatorship years stands, in my mind, unrivaled. She notes with acumen, "During the first years of the dictatorship, a barricade zone—until then, unthinkable—emerged in Chile: it was the body as a scene of protest or as a histrionic action. The body as a double of thought, taken from

neurosis or broken up into fragmentary pulsations, many of them lethal, or in other cases, motivated by a desire for restoration and wholeness. In any case, the body as a signifier of transgression against the system" (1990, 11).

20 On Zurita's self-mutilation, see Nelly Richard (1986).

21 Laclau and Mouffe (1985, 59) have referred to this process of representation as the basic political mechanism of the state. Eltit's text here seems to parallel their lines of critical thinking.

22 Christian Ferrer also notes that spectacle goes against the movements of an activist community that desires to retain memory of historical past (1996, 48).

23 Murga refers to the popular street musicians who join the festivities of carnival. Disorganized, spontaneous, usually beating upon homemade drums, the murga represents the expression of popular neighborhoods, the maximum example of the uncontrollable impulses that resist the state. The murga has a strong popular resonance and is often identified with the congregation of street bands that joined the protest marches of the first Peronist movement.

24 Cited in Moreno (1999, 5).

25 On utopian yearnings and counterutopian projects in Puig, see Santiago Colás (1994).

26 On the translation conflicts surfacing in Puig's writing, see Paula Siganevich (1998) and Christopher Larkosh (unpublished).

27 On the Latin American contemporary interest in travel as tied to questions of sexual identity in particular, see for example, Manuel Ramos Otero, *El cuento de la mujer del mar* (1979), Silviano Santiago's *Stella Manhattan* (1985), Cristina Peri Rossi's *La nave de los locos* (1984), and César Aira's *Una novela china* (1987).

28 Roberto Echavarren, in a brilliant exegesis of *El beso* as related to ideologies of simulation and sexual affirmation, reminds us that the novel "vaporizes" all concepts of identity (1998b). Regarding this scene, he writes, "The I is another, is the other, isn't any one, has no identity, is vapor" (255). He uses this image to elaborate a theory of anteriority through which the character reverses to a previous model of subjectivity that has been obfuscated through temporal distance. Although my reading of this crucial scene in the novel is different from Echavarren's, it is my sense all the same that his point is extremely well taken.

29 At the risk of repeating what has been already adequately discussed, the footnotes in the novel track Puig's sense of these misperceptions; see especially the commentary of the apocryphal Dra. Anneli Taube (Puig's voice in the footnotes) against fixed identities and the danger of essentialism in both the gay and the mainstream communities. On the footnotes in *El beso*, see Daniel Balderston (1998).

30 Julia Romero (forthcoming) notes that Puig's novels from *La traición* to *Sangre de amor correspondido* can be read as a history of representations of gender in counterpoint to national politics and also as the center of ideological persecution by the authoritarian state.

31 See also Judith Podlubne (1996), who reflects in detail on this concept.

32 However, a figure of a nun appears in his recent book, *El sueño* (1998).

33 In an interview published in *El Universal* (Mexico), Aira, when asked about the feminine voice of the the child narrator, replied: "It's a boy because it's me, but the thing about seeing himself as a girl has to do with that problem in the Spanish language of making the adjectives or any other word end with an 'a' instead of an 'o.' And I liked the idea that so simple a recourse such as changing the letters, whereby instead of putting an 'o'

at the end of a word, you'd put an 'a,' would change everything; it would change the atmosphere and all the metaphysics of the story" (Velásquez Yebra 1996).

34 Aira's texts strangely coexist with those of contemporary writers who turn to the trick of impersonating female voices in order to sustain a literary fiction. Many prominent authors have experimented with gendered voices in narration to see the world from a different perspective, although at times they turn to these strategies in order to poke fun at the feminist critical theater that has often left these male writers excluded from participation. For examples of female impostoring in recent fiction, see David Viñas, *Claudia conversa* (1995); Sergio Chefjec, *El llamado de la especie* (1997); Charlie Feiling, *El mal menor* (1996); and Juana Caballero (Hugo Achugar), *Cañas de la India* (1995).

3 Gender Traffic on the North/South Horizon

1 Ferman (1993) and Mohanty (1989) have addressed in depth the issue of cultural relativism, and I am indebted to them in these pages. See also Edward Said (1983), whose term of expression, "traveling theory," has influenced my thought.

2 Since the early years of independence, Latin American intellectuals have always taken serious stock of the North/South divide and sought to find theoretical models that might include them as active subjects. Witness only the towering case of Sarmiento in this regard.

3 George Yúdice (1994) has written an attractive critique of the process by which paradigms of minority culture, formulated in the U.S. academy under the rubric of cultural studies, have met a cool reception in Latin America.

4 Although her understanding of this phenomenon differs from mine, Gwen Kirkpatrick provides a lucid analysis of the utopian fictions produced by feminism; in particular, she remarks on the recent interest in marginality: "Women in the public sphere catch our attention because of their deviance: it is not their heroism, their capability, or simply their will for survival that draws us" (1995, 47).

5 LAS/*12*, a supplement belonging to the Argentine daily, *Página 12*, has been directed by María Moreno since 1998. It represents among the sharpest critiques of North/South exchanges currently in circulation, taking as its premise the representation of gender in mass culture, literature, and art. As a strategy, the supplement playfully engages the projects of a market-run culture that at once pegs the identity of consumers to the spectacle of difference. Equally important, LAS/*12* exposes the fraudulent linkage of gendered identities that are marketed through global order and reveals the fault lines on supposedly solid North/South map. For a detailed examination of LAS/*12*, see Masiello 2001.

6 I do not wish to suggest that *Feminaria* is the first project of this kind. In an earlier study, I showed the ways in which Argentina has been privileged in the field of women's journalism from the early decades of the nineteenth century (Masiello 1994b). Since the return to democracy, Argentina has also witnessed an explosion of small reviews devoted to questions of sexuality and identity. On this recent evolution, see Marcela Nari (1997).

7 On women in the neoliberal economy, see the special groupings of articles in *Feminaria*: "Mujer y crisis" (1990, 29–35) and "El feminismo en estos tiempos neoliberales" (1992, 3–14).

8 On the reception of metropolitan theory, see especially the issue of *Revista de Crítica Cultural* devoted to Baudrillard's visit to Chile (1993, vol. 7).

9 Deleuze (1994) has offered a lengthy argument about the local effects of simulation and copy, which clearly are applicable here.

10 For the uses of feminism to uphold the democratic state, see the commentary of Raquel Olea (2000).

11 I am certainly aware of the dangers of assuming that mass-culture works are to be understood by all readers in an identical way. Janice Radway (1984) has alerted us to the multiplicity of possible readings and the particular gaps that separates consumers of mass fiction from academic critics. Rather than allowing Allende's work to speak for the whole field of mass-marketed fiction, I wish to use it more modestly as an example of the complexity of literature circulating in the North/South venue and the strategic importance of a Chilean text that works well among popular audiences in both continents.

12 It is not that the best-seller phenomenon is especially new, although it seems to be registered nowadays as a primary cultural feature belonging to globalization. Think backward, for example, to the international success of Martínez Zuviría (Hugo Wast), a best-selling author of the 1920s, whose novels sold hundreds of thousands of copies in Latin America and Spain. His was the *interamerican* melodrama that allowed for reverberations of jingoist nationalism, adventure novels that promised a future of progress by controlling the actions of women. This, perhaps, is a model of the early best-seller as conservative force. Think, too, to the decade of the 1960s and the success of the Latin American Boom under the stewardship of publishing firms such as Seix Barral and Joaquin Mórtiz. In these past eras, a masculine faith in diffusing Latin American reality directed literary projects in contrast to an astounding female presence in today's best-seller arena.

13 I am not claiming that Latin American literature situated in New York is unique to Valenzuela (see only the novels of Alberto Laiseca, Manuel Puig, and Silviano Santiago or the poetry of María Negroni and Mercedes Roffé to expand this discussion).

14 The parallelisms between *roman noir* and recent attempts by Latin American novelists to write under the shadow of neoliberalism is certainly worth exploring. A starting point worth noting is the essay by Jayne Walker and David Reid (1993).

15 It is not surprising that so much of Argentine and Chilean literature devoted to gendered projects seeks to skirt the effects of the market by drawing, instead, upon the resources of *earlier* texts from Anglo-American traditions; partly in homage to modernism, but also as a way to short-circuit the antiaesthetic claims apparent in the current transnational flow, a series of linkages are forged that reconstruct the North/South alliance through the pleasures of the literary text. Curiously, just as the advocates of neoliberalism also propose to turn the clock backward, looking to a more stable and conventional moment of untampered "truth," the aesthetic gaze also looks toward the past, but to fulfill another mission, to travel a less common route linking North/South cultures. This is not a feeble recycling but another way to stretch a dialogue, to engage in conversation without surrendering principles of identity through art. Hence, Guerra's citation of a Flannery O'Connor grotesque or Valenzuela's evocation of noir, but also the devoted reappraisal, apparent in recent women writers, of the modernists of the 1920s. See, for example, Graciela Safranchik, in her novel *Kadish* (1993), where she not only evokes the title of Allen Ginsberg's celebrated poem, but more significantly pays a tribute to Vita Sackville-West for her novel *All Passion Spent.* Similarly, Argentine poet and publisher Mirta Rosenberg has assumed responsiblity to bring into Spanish translation the writings of Anglo-American high modernists through her press, Bajo la luna nueva.

These are efforts to reach back in historical time to an earlier version of Anglo-American exchanges, where modernity was less invasive, less offensive to aesthetic temperaments.

4 *Bodies in Transit*

1 In an interview with Charlotte O'Sullivan (1998), the director admits his indebtedness to Manuel Puig's *The Buenos Aires Affair* (1973), although, paradoxically enough, the themes of exile, displacement, and translation, which concern the filmmaker, would better be matched to Puig's fiction produced in a later period.

2 See also *The Tango Lesson* (directed by Sally Potter, 1997), which grapples with themes of foreign alienation and identity, domination and submission as expressed through the medium of dance.

3 For a meditation on the representation of the Arab world in Argentine literature, see Christina Civantos (1999).

4 The "meanwhile" of national discourse signaled by Benedict Anderson (1991) here assumes a transnational scope when we consider questions of translation.

5 See also *Teoría del cielo* (1992), a volume edited by Arturo Carrera and Teresa Arijón, in which Sarduy's reading of "Tokonoma" is featured prominently along with Alberto Prior's discussion of Japan. Alberto Prior has advanced an "Orientalist" aesthetic in the visual arts and music, most recently with an installation and libretto inspired by the Chinese Opera (*Operas chinas completas*, 1999). María del Carmen Colombo, by contrast, writes of Asian immigrants to Buenos Aires in her *La familia china* (1999) in order to propose Argentina itself as the site of exotic.

6 This trope was developed most clearly by the Cuban Severo Sarduy, beginning with his novel *De dónde son los cantantes*, but it circulated effectively with later writers. For a useful discussion on the relationship between translation and erotics in the context of Sarduy in particular, see Suzanne Jill Levine (1991). Christopher Larkosh refers to a "migrant sexuality" to describe the practices of foreigners such as Gombrowicz in Argentina and their interchanges with Argentine writers who devoted themselves to translation (1996).

7 From a different perspective, deliberately parodic, Leónidas Lamborghini continues to mock traditional verse in order to expose the fallacies of authoritative literary traditions.

8 Cited from "De dónde son las palabras" (1998).

9 See also Griselda Gambaro's "Del sol naciente" (1984), which focuses on power relations among women situated in Japan.

10 For a splendid discussion of Miranda's voice in *The Tempest* and the problem this poses for feminist literary theory, see Joanna O'Connell (1995).

11 See also Lydia Liu's work on interlingual process relating to Asian literatures and their exchange with Western influence (1995).

12 The North/South desire for merger has been thematized through translation, but beyond the venue of the cultural journal, it rarely results in an actual collaborative enterprise between authors. When the translation enters literature as a topic of North/South exchange, it often resonates through matters of sexuality. See, for example, Manuel Ramos Otero's short fiction *Cuentos de la mujer del mar* (1979), in which a love relation is negotiated through common effort at translation, and Manuel Puig's *Maldición eterna a quien lea estas páginas* (1980), a novel set in New York and dealing with exchanges between

an Argentine invalid and his North American assistant. Deeply anchored in the discourse of the voyeur, Puig's novel is, on one level, about the gap between representation and experience and, on another level, an exploration of questions of sexual desire and translation.

13 Bellessi acknowledges the influence of Benjamin, most probably his essay, "The Task of the Translator."

14 Again, as Benjamin might remind us, orality restores the experience of community.

15 See, for example, Bellessi's translation of North American women poets (1996).

16 On Piglia's discussion of the role of translation in *Facundo*, see his fundamental essay, "Sarmiento the Writer" (1994). In an earlier essay, while reflecting on Borges and Gombrowicz, Piglia identified what he considers as a principal problematic of Argentine letters: "How can we achieve universality from this remote outpost of the world?" (1986, 81). This anxiety, in Piglia's view, drives a national sensibility toward translation.

17 On this, see Jacques Derrida, *Positions* (1981, 39).

18 See Nicolas Bratosevich, who refers in detail to this Chinese source (1997, 139).

19 Compare this strategy to Piglia's most recent novel, *Plata quemada* (1997), an evocation, at least initially, of Roberto Arlt; accused by many of inadequate writing style, Arlt has always been defended by Piglia for his disruptive presence in Argentine literary history. He is celebrated again in *Plata quemada* through the violence of Piglia's language and, by allusion, for the delinquent characters who organize the action of the novel. The language of subaltern groups is recodified by Piglia to express the antiheroism of modern times; Arlt's project, "to write poorly," is expressed through Piglia's language of delinquents.

20 John Bishop observes the proto-European roots that link these terms and others in Joyce's *Wake* (61).

21 These essays have been compiled in Piglia's *La Argentina en pedazos* (1993).

5 The Politics of the Text

1 Not ancillary to the artist's purpose, a perception of the fourteen scenes also requires our strenuous physical movement insofar as we must adjust ourselves to the awkward height of the display, stretching to see the dioramas and the elevated rhetorical figures flashing on the walls above them. Too, the fourteen slide projectors intrude in the gallery space and, like lanky spectators, they often block our visual access to the artistic scene. We even bend and contort our bodies to gain entry to the gallery itself, passing with difficulty through an artificial portal, too narrow and low for the average adult. The corporeal challenge that viewers accept only confirms our desire to be included among the "insiders" who bear witness to the work of art; in other words, we must first acknowledge our exclusion from place as a first step toward interacting with the avant-garde installation. On this, see the catalog notes of Pablo Oyarzún (1998).

2 The reference to Chile as a place of "loca geografía" owes its source to Benjamín Subercaseaux's positivist construction of Chilean archetypal figures, published in 1943. See his *Chile o una loca geografía* (1989).

3 In effect, the chronicles in his *De perlas y cicatrices* (1998) attest to this draw. Here Lemebel works from popular subjects to create a sense of style. His readings of these texts on Radio Tierra become a testimony to the power of the oral-aural exchange, a seduction through the ear of the anonymous other.

4 Here I am running against the grain insofar as critics such as Martin Lienhard and Antonio Cornejo Polar exclude nations with smaller indigenous populations from the debate about orality and literature. On this topic, I would coincide more closely with Markus Klaus Schaffauer (1998), who explores and defends the significance of orality in River Plate letters.

5 The state will not accept the feminine role, yet paradoxically, women are its accomplices; in *Plata quemada*, they betray the principal characters and lead police to the criminals' hideouts, thus instigating their capture and fall.

6 It is symptomatic of the times that New York replaces Hollywood as the city of Latin American desire. Thus, if Barsut, the protagonist of Roberto Arlt's *Los siete locos* and *Los lanzallamas*, expressed a desire to flee to Hollywood, the city that controls the fantasy of the cinematic image, that dream is now replaced by a fantasy of New York as the center of global capital and crime. Of course, as Tulio Halperín-Donghi and Isabel Quintana observe, New York today may simply be a mecca for intellectuals—and Piglia, among them—while Miami draws the imagination of the vast majority of Latin Americans (from personal correspondence with the author, June 2000).

7 On *El infarto del alma*, see the excellent readings of Mary Beth Tierney-Tello (1999) and Julio Ramos (forthcoming).

6 *From Museum to Street*

1 The term belongs to Jorge Montealegre, who in 1983 described a lost generation of poets (cited by Tomás Harris 1998, 92).

2 For a forceful indictment of today's market policies that have limited the circulation of poetry, also see Bianchi (1998).

3 Ironically, despite his transgressive stance—or perhaps owing to the very success of his earlier position on the margins—Zurita is now regarded as Chile's most prominent poet since redemocratization and is actively supported by the government. *La vida nueva* (1994), his monumental epic of Latin American landscape and in particular Chile and its people, was celebrated as the representative text of a new, democratic Chile.

4 Cited in Robert McDowell (1991, 41).

5 The taller is a prominent feature of intellectual life as evidenced by the group publications emanating from such encounters. Think, for example, of the anthologies produced from the studio of Pía Barros in Chile.

6 On the relationship between gender and poetry in Chile, see Olea (1998) and the anthologies of Brito (1998b), Koski (1998), and Villegas (1985, 1993).

7 For an ironic observation about the different traditions separating Argentina and Chile, see the commentary of Jorge Fondebrider (1992) regarding the first Biennial of Latin American Poetry held in Valparaíso. He notes that the Chilean poetic tradition, unlike that of Argentina, is structured around great figures who create an exclusivist and localized corpus of readings; he also observes with some degree of acrimony that in Chile, "There exists a tradition of confusing the figure of the poet with poetry itself." In Argentina, by contrast, Fondebrider notes that the cosmopolitan influence in poetry is due to a less canonical local tradition (33).

8 For an interesting critique of the circulation of this term, especially under the conditions of the current market economy, see Soledad Bianchi (1997, 36).

9 Note, however, the traditions of the politicized national poet as in the case of Lugones

in the first part of the twentieth century, or recently, the role occupied by Juan Gelman, first as Argentine poet in exile and opposed to the dictatorship and now celebrated with accolades as Argentina's national poet.

10 The influence of Mistral is rightfully unrelieved. See, for example, the tribute to Mistral offered by writers and whose proceedings have been published by Olea and Fariña (1997).

11 "*L* is also the sign of infamy, *L* is the letter of exile, imposed on Chilean citizens to prohibit them from entering the country; . . . it is the establishment of instability, in a trembling landscape where reason is imposed by force" (from personal correspondence with the author, 6 June 2000).

12 On Girondo's "Campo nuestro," see Masiello (1999).

13 The term belongs to Niranjana (1992) in her discussion of colonialism and translation.

14 In Argentine Spanish, the familiar form is expressed through "vos," although in the rest of the Spanish-speaking world, "tú" is more common; the "vosotros" form is the plural and, although used in Spain, it is scarce in Spanish America.

15 I do not wish to make the case that the incorporation of popular voices in poetry is a project belonging only to women (witness only the contemporary efforts of Zurita in *La vida nueva* and, in a different style, José Angel Cuevas in his *Diario de la ciudad ardiente*); rather, what emerges uniquely from women's poetry in their attention to popular subjects is a social alliance that links diverse groups—women of all social classes—through a politics of corporeality and feminine subjectivity.

WORKS CITED

Abraham, Tomás. 1992. Entre el sarcasmo y la pedrada. In *Rebeldes y domesticados: Los intelectuales frente al poder*, ed. Raquel Angel, 67–86. Buenos Aires: El Cielo por Asalto.

Achugar, Hugo. 1992. *La balsa de la Medusa: Ensayo sobre identidad, cultura y fin de siglo en Uruguay.* Montevideo: Ediciones Trilce.

———. 1994. Fin de siglo: Reflexiones desde la periferia. In *Posmodernidad en la periferia: Enfoques latinoamericanos de la nueva teoría cultural*, ed. Hermann Herlinghaus and Monika Walter, 233–55. Berlin: Langer Verlag.

Aira, César. 1987. *Una novela china.* Buenos Aires: Javier Vergara.

———. 1988. Prólogo. In Osvaldo Lamborghini, *Novelas y cuentos*, 7–16. Barcelona: Serbal.

———. 1991. *La liebre.* Buenos Aires: Emecé.

———. 1993a. Arlt. *Paradoxa* 7: 55–71.

———. 1993b. *Cómo me hice monja.* Rosario: Beatriz Viterbo.

———. 1997. *La serpiente.* Rosario: Beatriz Viterbo.

———. 1998. *El sueño.* Buenos Aires: Emecé.

Alarcón, Norma. 1990. The theoretical subject(s) of *This Bridge Called My Back* and Anglo-American feminism. In *Making face, making soul: Haciendo caras*, ed. Gloria Anzaldúa, 356–69. San Francisco: Aunt Lute.

Allende, Isabel. 1994. *Paula.* New York: Harper Libros.

———. 1999. *Hija de la fortuna.* Barcelona: Plaza y Jarnés.

Altamirano, Carlos. 1999. Intelectuales y pueblo. In *La Argentina en el siglo XX*, ed. Carlos Altamirano, 314–24. Buenos Aires: Ariel.

Alvarez, Sonia, Evelina Dagnino, and Arturo Escobar, eds. 1998. *Culture of politics, politics of cultures: Re-visioning Latin American social movements.* Boulder, Col.: Westview Press.

Amícola, José, and Graciela Speranza, eds. 1998. *Encuentro internacional Manuel Puig.* Rosario: Beatriz Viterbo.

Anderson, Benedict. 1991. *Imagined communities: Reflections on the rise and spread of nationalism.* London: Verso.

Appadurai, Arjin. 1996. *Modernity at large: Cultural dimensions of globalization.* Minneapolis: University of Minnesota Press.

Argumedo, Alcira. 1993. *Los silencios y las voces: Notas sobre el pensamiento nacional y popular.* Buenos Aires: Colihué.

Arijón, Teresa, and Arturo Carrera, eds. 1992. *Teoría del cielo.* Buenos Aires: Planeta.

Arlt, Roberto. 1951. *El criador de gorilas.* Buenos Aires: Futuro.

Arrate, Marina. 1986. *Este lujo de ser.* Santiago de Chile: Mirador.

———. 1990. *Máscara negra.* Santiago de Chile: Mirador.

———. 1992. *Tatuaje.* Santiago de Chile: Mirador.

———. 1999. *Uranio.* Santiago de Chile: LOM.

Avelar, Idelber. 1997. Alegoría y postdictadura: Notas sobre la memoria del mercado. *Revista de Crítica Cultural*, no. 14 (June): 22–27.

———. 1999. *The untimely present: Postdictatorial Latin American fiction and the task of mourning.* Durham, N.C.: Duke University Press.

Balderston, Daniel. 1998. Los progresos de la doctora Anneli Taube. In *Encuentro internacional Manuel Puig*, ed. José Amícola and Graciela Speranza, 271–77. Rosario: Beatriz Viterbo.

Balibar, Etienne, and Immanuel Wallerstein. 1991. *Race, nation, class: Ambiguous identities.* Trans. Chris Turner. New York: Verso.

Barbero, Jesús Martín. 1987. *De los medios a las mediaciones: Comunicación, cultura y hegemonía.* Mexico: Gustavo Gili.

———. 1993. Nuevos modos de leer. *Revista de Crítica Cultural*, no. 7 (Nov.): 19–23.

Bartra, Roger. 1987. *La jaula de la melancolía: Identidad y metamorfosis del mexicano.* Mexico: Grijalbo.

Barranco Lagunas, Isabel. 1997. ¿Qué pasó en Cartagena, Chile? *Fem*, no. 167 (Feb.): 34–36.

Baudrillard, Jean. 1983. *Simulations.* Trans. Paul Foss. New York: Semiotexte.

Behar, Ruth. 1993. *Translated woman.* Boston: Beacon Press.

Bell-Villada, Gene H. 1996. *Art for art's sake and literary life: How politics and markets helped shape the ideology and culture of aestheticism, 1790–1990.* Lincoln: University of Nebraska Press.

Bellessi, Diana. 1981. *Crucero ecuatorial.* Buenos Aires: Sirirí.

———. 1982. *Tributo del mudo.* Buenos Aires: Sirirí.

———. 1985. *Danzante de doble máscara.* Buenos Aires: Ultimo Reino.

———. 1986. La abdicación de la reina y del maestro. In *Literatura y crítica: Primer encuentro*, 147–56. Santa Fe, Argentina: Universidad del Litoral.

———. 1988. *Eroica.* Buenos Aires: Tierra Firme/Ultimo Reino.

———. 1990. Contra una retórica feminista. *Feminaria*, no. 6 (Nov.): 10–11.

———. 1992. *El jardín.* Buenos Aires-Rosario: Bajo la luna nueva.

———. 1995. *Diez poetas norteamericanas.* Caracas: Pequeña Venecia.

———. 1996. *Lo propio y lo ajeno.* Buenos Aires: Feminaria.

———. 1998. *Sur.* Buenos Aires: Tierra Firme.

Bellessi, Diana et al. 1997. VII Encuentro feminista latinoamericano y del Caribe. *Feminaria* 19 (June): 28–36.

Bellucci, Mabel. 1992. El feminismo en estos tiempos neoliberales. *Feminaria*, no. 8 (Apr.): 3–5.

———. 1996. Crisis de legitimidad: Los avatares de la ciudadanía. *Brujas* 15, no. 23 (June): 13–19.

Benhabib, Seyla. 1995. Feminism and postmodernism. In *Feminist contentions: A philosophical exchange*, ed. Linda Nicholson, 17–34. New York: Routledge.

Benjamin, Walter. 1978. *Illuminations*. Trans. Harry Zohn. New York: Harcourt Brace.

Berenguer, Carmen. 1986. *Huellas de siglo*. Santiago de Chile: Manieristas.

———. 1988. *A media asta*. Santiago de Chile: Cuarto Propio.

———. 1993. *Sayal de pieles*. Santiago de Chile: Francisco Zegers.

———. 1999. *Naciste pintada*. Santiago de Chile: Cuarto Propio.

Berenguer, Carmen et al. 1994. *Escribir en los bordes: Congreso internacional de literatura femenina latinoamericana*. Santiago de Chile: Cuarto Propio.

Bernstein, Charles. 1990. *The politics of poetic form: Poetry and public policy*. New York: Roof.

Bersani, Leo. 1995. *Homos*. Cambridge, Mass.: Harvard University Press.

Beverley, John. 1993. *Against literature*. Minneapolis: University of Minnesota Press.

———. 1994. How newness enters the world: Postmodern space, postcolonial times, and the trials of cultural translation. In *The location of culture*, 212–35. New York: Routledge.

Bianchi, Soledad. 1990. *Poesía chilena (miradas, enfoques, apuntes)*. Santiago de Chile: CESOC.

———. 1997. "¿La insoportable levedad . . . ? (imágenes y textos, postdictadura y modernidad en Chile). *Documentos de trabajo: Universidad Arcis, Centro de investigaciones sociales*, no. 21 (Oct.).

———. 1998. Cabos sueltos. *Posdata* 1, nos. 1–2: 6–9.

———. (Forthcoming). Paisajes (ciudad presente/ciudad distante). *Revista Chilena de Literatura*, no. 44.

Bianciotti, Hector. 1985. *Sans la misericorde du Christ*. Paris: Gallimard.

Bishop, John. 1986. *Joyce's book of the dark*: Finnegans Wake. Madison: University of Wisconsin Press.

Bratosevich, Nicolás et al. 1997. *Ricardo Piglia y la cultura de la contravención*. Buenos Aires: Atuel.

Brito, Eugenia. 1984. *Vía pública*. Santiago de Chile: Editorial Universitaria.

———. 1986. *Filiaciones*. Santiago de Chile: VAN.

———. 1990. *Campos minados (Literatura post-golpe en Chile)*. Santiago de Chile: Cuarto Propio.

———. 1993. *Emplazamientos*. Santiago de Chile: Cuarto Propio.

———. 1998a. *Dónde vas*. Santiago de Chile: Cuarto Propio.

———, ed. 1998b. *Antología de poetas chilenas*. Santiago de Chile: Dolmen.

Brodsky, Marcelo. 1997. *Buena memoria [Good memory]*. Buenos Aires: Ed. La Marca.

Brunner, José Joaquín. 1991. *Modernidad y cultura en America Latina: Una discusion con J. J. Brunner*. Ed. Enrique Gomariz. Documento no. 7. Santiago de Chile: FLACSO.

Buell, Lawrence. 1999. In pursuit of ethics. PMLA 114, no. 1 (Jan.): 7–19.

Butler, Judith. 1993. *Bodies that matter: On the discursive limits of sex*. New York: Routledge.

———. 1997a. *Excitable speech: A politics of the performative*. New York: Routledge.

———. 1997b. Merely cultural. *Social Text* 52–53 (fall/winter): 265–77.

———. 1997c. *The psychic life of power*. Stanford, Calif.: Stanford University Press.

Caballero, Juana (Hugo Achugar). 1995. *Cañas de la India*. Montevideo: Trilce.

Calvera, Leonor. 1992. La cosmovisión feminista. *Feminaria* 5, no. 8 (Apr.): 6–8.

Campra, Rosalba. 1987. *América Latina: La identidad y la máscara*. Mexico: Siglo XXI.

Cánovas, Rodrigo. 1997. *Novela chilena, nuevas generaciones: El abordaje de los huérfanos*. Santiago de Chile: Universidad Católica de Chile.

Carrera, Arturo. 1982. *La partera canta.* Buenos Aires: Sudamericana.
———. 1985. *Mi padre.* Buenos Aires: Ediciones de la flor.
———. 1986a. *Animaciones suspendidas.* Buenos Aires: Losada.
———. 1986b. *Ticket para Edgardo Russo.* Buenos Aires: Ultimo Reino.
———. 1989. *Children's corner.* Buenos Aires: Ultimo Reino.
———. 1993. *Nacen los otros.* Rosario: Beatriz Viterbo.
———. 1994. *La banda oscura de Alejandro.* Buenos Aires-Rosario: Bajo la luna nueva.
———. 1997. *El vespertillo de las parcas.* Barcelona: Tusquets.
Cascardi, Anthony J. 1999. *Consequences of enlightenment.* Cambridge, Mass.: Cambridge University Press.
Castañeda, Jorge. 1993. *Utopia unarmed: The Latin American left after the cold war.* New York: Alfred A. Knopf.
———. 1997. *Compañero: The life and death of Che Guevara.* Trans. Marina Castañeda. New York: Alfred A. Knopf.
Castells, Manuel. 1997. *El poder de la identidad.* Madrid: Alianza.
Castillo, Debra. 1992. *Talking back: Toward a Latin American feminist literary criticism.* Ithaca, N.Y.: Cornell University Press.
Chefjec, Sergio. 1997. *El llamado de la especie.* Rosario-Buenos Aires: Beatriz Viterbo.
Christ, Ronald. 1987. Catalina Parra. *Arts Magazine* (Feb.): 22.
Civantos, Christina. 1999. Between Argentines and Arabs: Nation formation and immigrant culture. Unpublished diss. University of California at Berkeley.
Clifford, James. 1997. *Routes: Travel and translation in the late twentieth century.* Cambridge, Mass.: Harvard University Press.
Colás, Santiago. 1994. *Postmodernity in Latin America: The Argentine paradigm.* Durham, N.C.: Duke University Press.
———. 1996. What's wrong with representation? In *The real thing,* ed. G. M. Gugelberger, 161–71. Durham, N.C.: Duke University Press.
Colombo, María del Carmen. 1993. *La muda encarnación.* Buenos Aires: Ultimo Reino.
———. 1999. *La familia china.* Buenos Aires: Tierra Firme.
Comité de América Latina y el Caribe para la defensa de los derechos de la mujer. 1996. *La muralla y el laberinto: Huellas de las mujeres en la conferencia de Beijing.* Lima: CLADEM.
Contreras, Gonzalo. 1991. *La ciudad anterior.* Santiago de Chile: Planeta.
Cornejo Polar, Antonio. 1994. *Escribir en el aire: Ensayo sobre la heterogeneidad socio-cultural en las literaturas andinas.* Lima: Horizonte.
Cruz-Malavé, Arnaldo. 1998. Lecciones de cubanía. *Revista de Crítica Cultural,* no. 17: 58–67.
Cuevas, José Angel. 1998. *Diario de la ciudad ardiente.* Santiago: LOM.
Dagnino, Evelina. 1998. Culture, citizenship, and democracy: Changing discourses and practices of the Latin American left. In *Cultures of politics, politics of cultures,* ed. Sonia Alvarez et al., 33–63. Boulder, Col.: Westview Press.
Dalmaroni, Miguel. 1993. *Juan Gelman: Contra las fabulaciones del mundo.* Buenos Aires: Almagesto.
Debord, Guy. 1995. *The society of the spectacle.* New York: Zone Books.
Del Mazo, Mariano. 1999. Entrevista a Charly Garcia. *Clarín* (Feb. 16).
Deleuze, Gilles, and Felix Guattari. 1987. *A thousand plateaus: Capitalism and schizophrenia.* Trans. Brian Massumi. Minneapolis: University of Minnesota Press.
———. 1989. *Cinema 2: The time image.* Trans. Hugh Tomlinson and Robert Galeta. Minneapolis: University of Minnesota Press.

———. 1994. *Difference and repetition.* Trans. Paul Patton. New York: Columbia University Press.

DeLillo, Don. 1986. *White noise.* New York: Penguin.

Derrida, Jacques. 1981. *Positions.* Trans. Alan Bass. Chicago: University of Chicago Press.

———. 1985. *The ear of the other: Otobiography, transference, and translation.* Eds. Claude Levesque and Christie V. McDonald. Trans. Peggy Kamuf. New York: Schocken.

Donoso, José. 1995. *Donde van a morir los elefantes.* Buenos Aires: Alfaguara.

Dorfman, Ariel. 1988. *Máscaras.* Buenos Aires: Sudamericana.

———. 1992. La muerte y la doncella. In *Teatro 1.* Buenos Aires: Ediciones de la Flor.

Echavarren, Roberto. 1998a. *El arte andrógino: estilo versus moda en un siglo corto.* Buenos Aires: Colihue.

———. 1998b. Identidad *versus* vapor. In *Encuentro internacional Manuel Puig,* ed. J. Amícola and G. Speranza, 245–58. Rosario: Beatriz Viterbo.

Echavarren, Roberto, José Kozer, and Jacobo Sefamí. 1996. *Medusario: Muestra de poesiá latinoamericana.* Mexico: Fondo de cultura económica.

Eisenstein, Zillah R. 1994. *The color of gender: Reimaging democracy.* Berkeley: University of California Press.

Eltit, Diamela. 1986. *Por la patria.* Santiago de Chile: Ornitorrinco.

———. 1988. *El cuarto mundo.* Santiago de Chile: Planeta.

———. 1989. *El padre mio.* Santiago de Chile: Francisco Zegers.

———. 1991a. Las batallas del coronel Robles. *Revista de Crítica Cultural,* no. 4: 19–21.

———. [1983] 1991b. *Lumpérica.* Santiago de Chile: Planeta.

———. 1991c. *Vaca sagrada.* Santiago de Chile: Planeta.

———. 1994. *Los vigilantes.* Santiago de Chile: Sudamericana.

———. 1998. *Los trabajadores de la muerte.* Santiago de Chile: Seix Barral.

Eltit, Diamela, and Paz Errázuriz. 1994. *El infarto del alma.* Santiago de Chile: Francisco Zegers.

Eltit, Diamela, and Sonia Montecino. 1990. Arte y cultura. In *Tramas para un nuevo destino: Propuestas de la concertación de mujeres por la democracia,* eds. Sonia Montecino and Josefina Rosetti, 95–113. Santiago de Chile: Arancibia Editores.

Fariña, Soledad. 1985. *El primer libro.* Santiago de Chile: Amaranto.

———. 1994. *En amarillo oscuro.* Santiago de Chile: Surada.

Feijóo, Maria del Carmen. 1997. Ellas no bailan solas. *Clarín* (Oct. 16): 3.

Feiling, C. E. 1996. *El mal menor.* Buenos Aires: Planeta.

Feitlowitz, Marguerite. 1998. *A lexicon of terror.* New York: Oxford.

Ferman, Claudia. 1993. *Política y posmodernidad: Hacia una lectura de la anti-modernidad en Latinoamérica.* Miami: Iberian Studies Institute.

Fernández, Macedonio. 1967. *Museo de la novela de la Eterna.* Buenos Aires: Centro Editor.

Fernández Retamar, Roberto. 1971. *Calibán.* Mexico: Diógenes.

Ferrer, Christian. 1996. *El mal de ojo: El drama de la mirada.* Buenos Aires: Colihué.

Flax, Jane. 1990. *Thinking in fragments: Psychoanalysis, feminism, and postmodernism.* Berkeley: University of California Press.

Fletcher, Lea. 1988. El sexismo lingüístico y su uso acerca de la mujer. *Feminaria,* no. 1 (June): 29–32.

———. 1997. *Feminaria* festeja su primer aniversario. *El Desierto* 4, no. 4 (Nov.): 62.

Fondebrider, Jorge. 1992. Del otro lado de la cordillera. *Diario de Poesía,* no. 22 (fall): 33.

Fontenla, Marta, and Magui Bellotti. 1996. Políticas feministas. *Brujas* 15, no. 23 (June): 9–12.

Forastelli, Fabricio. 1999. Políticas de la restitución: Identidades y luchas homosexuales en Argentina. In *Las marcas del género*, ed. Fabricio Forastelli and Ximena Triquell, 117–41. Córdoba: Centro de Estudios Avanzados.

Franco, Jean. 1988. Beyond ethnocentrism: Gender, power, and the third world intelligentsia. In *Marxism and the interpretation of culture*, eds. Cary Nelson and Lawrence Grossberg, 503–15. Urbana: University of Illinois Press.

———. 1996. *Marcar diferencias, cruzar fronteras*. Santiago de Chile: Cuarto Propio.

———. 1998. The long march of feminism. *NACLA, Report on the Americas* 31, no. 4 (Jan.–Feb.): 10–15.

Franz, Carlos. 1999. Crónicas del postboom: Novelas del fin del mundo. *La Jornada Semanal* (27 June).

Fraser, Nancy. 1997. *Justice interruptus*. New York: Routledge.

Freidemberg, Daniel. 1993. Poesía argentina de los años 70 y 80. *Cuadernos Hispanoamericanos* 517–19 (July–Sept.): 139–60.

Futoransky, Luisa. 1982. *Partir, digo*. Valencia: Editorial Prometeo.

———. [1983] 1991. *Son cuentos chinos*. 2d ed. Buenos Aires: Planeta.

———. 1986. *De Pe a Pa (o de Pekín a París)*. Barcelona: Anagrama.

———. 1997. *The duration of the voyage/La duración del viaje*. Trans. Jacob Weiss. San Diego: Junction Press.

———. 1998. De donde son las palabras. In *De donde son las palabras*. Barcelona: Plaza y Jarnés.

Gambaro, Griselda. [1984] 1992. Del sol naciente. In *Teatro 1*. 2d ed. Buenos Aires: Ediciones de la Flor.

———. 1996. Es necesario entender un poco. In *Teatro 6*. Buenos Aires: Ediciones de la Flor.

García Canclini, Néstor. 1992. *Culturas híbridas: Estrategias para entrar y salir de la modernidad*. Buenos Aires: Sudamericana.

———. 1995. *Consumidores y ciudadanos: Conflictos multiculturales de la globalización*. Mexico: Grijalbo.

Gelman, Juan. 1982. *Citas y comentarios*. Madrid: Visor.

———. 1994a. *Dibaxu*. Barcelona: Seix Barral.

———. 1994b. *Los poemas de Sidney West: Traducciones III (1968–1969)*. Buenos Aires: Seix Barral.

———. 1997. *Unthinkable tenderness*. Trans. Joan Lindgren. Berkeley: University of California Press.

———. 1999. Temas. *Página 12* (13 May).

Genovese, Alicia. 1992. *Anónima*. Buenos Aires: Ultimo Reino.

———. 1997. *El borde es un río*. Buenos Aires: Tierra Firme.

———. 1998. *La doble voz: Poetas argentinas contemporáneas*. Buenos Aires: Biblos.

Getino, Octavio. 1995. *La tercera mirada*. Buenos Aires: Paidós.

Giberti, Eva, and Ana Maria Fernández. 1989. *La mujer y la violencia invisible*. Buenos Aires: Sudamericana.

Gil, Antonio. 1980. *Los lugares habidos*. Santiago de Chile: Ornitorrico, Germinal.

Gitlin, Todd. 1995. *The twilight of common dreams: Why America is wracked by culture wars*. New York: Metropolitan Press.

Gómez, Patricia. 1995. Mujeres y política en la Argentina de fin de siglo. *Feminaria*, no. 14 (June): 11–14.

González, Horacio. 1992. *La ética picaresca*. Buenos Aires: Altamira.

———. 1997. Nuevos relativismos culturales. *El Ojo Mocho* 9/10: 135–38.

Grau, Olga et al. n.d. *Discurso, género y poder, discursos públicos: Chile 1978–1993*. Santiago de Chile: LOM-Arcis.

Gruss, Irene. 1991. *La calma*. Buenos Aires: Tierra Firme.

Guebel, Daniel. 1990. *La perla del emperador*. Buenos Aires: Emecé.

Guerra, Lucia. 1997. *Frutos extraños*. Santiago de Chile: Cuarto Propio.

Gugelberger, Georg M., ed. 1996. *The real thing*. Durham, N.C.: Duke University Press.

Harris, Tomás. 1998. Desarrollo de la poesia chilena: 1960–1990. *Posdata* 1, no. 1–2: 92–115.

Heker, Liliana. 1993. Los talleres literarios. *Cuadernos Hispanoamericanos*, no. 517–19 (July–Sept.): 187–94.

Hernández, Elvira. 1989. *Carta de viaje*. Buenos Aires: Ultimo Reino.

———. 1991. *Bandera de Chile*. Buenos Aires: Tierra Firme.

———. 1992. *Santiago waria*. Santiago de Chile: Cuarto Propio.

Hola, Eugenia, and Gabriela Pischedda. n.d. *Mujeres, poder y política: Nuevas tensiones para viejas estructuras*. Santiago de Chile: CEM.

hooks, bell. 1990. *Yearning: Race, gender, and cultural politics*. Boston: South End Press.

Hopenhayn, Martin. 1994. *Ni apocalípticos ni integrados: Aventuras de la modernidad en America Latina*. Mexico: Fondo de cultura económica.

Hwang, David. 1988. *M. Butterfly*. New York: Penguin-Plume.

Ipola, Emilio de. 1997. *Las cosas de creer*. Buenos Aires: Ariel.

Jakobson, Roman. 1959. Linguistic aspects of translation. In *On translation*, ed. Reuben Brower, 232–38. Cambridge, Mass.: Harvard University Press.

Jameson, Fredric. 1986. Third world literature as allegory. *Social Text* 15 (fall): 65–88.

———. 1992a. *The geopolitical aesthetic: Cinema and space in the world system*. Bloomington: Indiana University Press.

———. 1992b. *Postmodernism or, the cultural logic of late capitalism*. Durham, N.C.: Duke University Press.

———. 1993. Transformaciones de la imagen en la posmodernidad. *Revista de Crítica Cultural*, no. 6: 12–25.

Jay, Martin. 1993. *Force fields*. New York: Routledge.

Joyce, James. [1939] 1967. *Finnegans wake*. New York: Viking.

Kamenszain, Tamara. 1983. *El texto silencioso: Tradición y vanguardia en la poesía sudamericana*. Mexico: UNAM.

———. 1986. *La casa grande*. Buenos Aires: Sudamericana.

———. 1991. *Vida de living*. Buenos Aires: Sudamericana.

———. 1998. *Tango bar*. Buenos Aires: Sudamericana.

Kaminsky, Amy. 1993. *Reading the body politic: Feminist criticism and Latin American women writers*. Minneapolis: University of Minnesota Press.

Kirkpatrick, Gwen. 1989. La poesía de las argentinas frente al patriarcado. *Nuevo Texto Crítico* II, no. 4: 129–35.

———. 1995. El feminismo en tiempos de cólera. *Revista de Crítica Literaria Latinoamericana* 21, no. 42: 45–55.

———. (Forthcoming.) Desapariciones y ausencias: "La Nueva Novela" de Juan Luis Martínez. *Revista de Crítica Literaria Latinoamericana*.

Kirkwood, Julieta. 1982. Feminismo y participación política en Chile. Santiago de Chile: FLACSO.

———. 1983. La política del feminismo en Chile. *Revista Internacional de Ciencias Sociales* (Paris) 35, no. 4: 671–83.

Kittler, Friedrich A. 1990. *Discourse networks, 1800/1900.* Stanford, Calif.: Stanford University Press.

Koski, Linda. 1998. *Mujeres poetas de Chile: Muestra antológica, 1980–1995.* Santiago de Chile: Cuarto Propio.

Kristeva, Julia. 1991. *Strangers to ourselves.* Trans. Leon Roudiez. New York: Columbia University Press.

Kushigian, Julia. 1991. *Orientalism in the Hispanic literary tradition: In dialogue with Borges, Paz, and Sarduy.* Albuquerque: University of New Mexico Press.

Laclau, Ernesto. 1996. *Emancipation(s).* New York: Verso.

Laclau, Ernesto, and Chantal Mouffe. 1985. *Hegemony and socialist strategy: Towards a radical democratic politics.* London: Verso.

Laiseca, Alberto. 1987. *Poemas chinos.* Buenos Aires: Tierra Firme.

———. 1990. *La mujer en la muralla.* Buenos Aires: Planeta.

Lamas, Marta. 1998. Scenes from a Mexican battlefield. *NACLA: Report on the Americas* XXXI, no. 4 (Jan.–Feb.): 17–21.

Lamborghini, Osvaldo. 1988a [1983]. *La causa justa.* In *Novelas y cuentos.* Barcelona: Serbal.

———. 1988. El fiord. In *Novelas y cuentos.* Barcelona: Serbal.

———. 1994. *Tadeys.* Ed. César Aira. Barcelona: Serbal.

Landi, Oscar. 1987. La trama cultural de la política. In *Cultura política y democratización*, ed. Norberto Lechner, 39–64. Buenos Aires: CLACSO.

Larkosh, Christopher. 1996. Migrant voices: Translation and sexuality in modern Argentine literature. Ph.D. diss., University of California, Berkeley.

———. Manuel multilingüe: Traducción, tránsito intercultural y entrelugares literarios. Unpublished essay.

Larsen, Neil. 1995. *Reading north by south: On Latin American literature, culture, and politics.* Minneapolis: University of Minnesota Press.

Lechner, Norberto. 1990. *Los patios interiores de la democracia: Subjetividad y política.* Santiago de Chile: Fondo de Cultura Económica.

LeGuin, Ursula K., and Diana Bellessi. 1996. *The twins, the dream: las gemelas, el sueño.* Houston, TX: Arte Publico Press.

Lemebel, Pedro. 1995. *La esquina es mi corazón.* Santiago de Chile: Cuarto Propio.

———. 1996. *Loco afán (crónicas de sidario).* Santiago de Chile: LOM.

———. 1998. *De perlas y cicatrices.* Santiago de Chile: LOM.

Lerner, Gerda. 1986. *The creation of patriarchy.* New York: Oxford University Press.

Levine, Suzanne Jill. 1991. *The subversive scribe.* St. Paul, Minn.: Greywolf.

Lidid, Sandra, and Kira Maldonado, eds. 1997. *Movimiento feminista autónomo, 1993–1997.* Santiago de Chile: Ediciones Tierra Mía.

Link, Daniel. 1994. *La chancha con cadenas: Doce ensayos de literatura argentina.* Buenos Aires: Ediciones del Eclipse.

Liu, Lydia. 1995. *Translingual practice: Literature, national culture and translated modernity, China 1900–1937.* Stanford, Calif.: Stanford University Press.

Lizama López, Jaime. 1994. "A media asta" o "la lengua maldita" (Poema de Carmen Berenguer). In Berenguer et al. *Escribir en los bordes.* 175–84.

Lloyd, David, and Paul Thomas. 1998. *Culture and the state.* New York: Routledge.

Maffia, Diana. 1994. Lógica, sexualidad y política. *Feminaria*, no. 12 (May): 10–11.

Maglie, Graciela. 1990. Bajo sospecha. *Feminaria*, no. 5 (Apr.): 29–31.

Maquieira, Diego. 1983. *La tirana.* Santiago de Chile: Edición Tempus Tacendi.

Martínez, Juan Luis. 1985 [1977]. *La nueva novela.* Santiago de Chile: Archivo.

Masiello, Francine. 1994a. Estado, género y sexualidad en la cultura del fin de siglo. *Las culturas de fin de siglo en América Latina*, ed. Josefina Ludmer, 139–49. Buenos Aires: Beatriz Viterbo.

———. 1994b. *La mujer y el espacio público: El periodismo femenino en la Argentina en el siglo XIX.* Buenos Aires: Feminaria.

———. 1997a. Gender, dress, and market: The commerce of citizenship in Latin America. In *Sex and sexuality in Latin America*, ed. Daniel Balderston and Donna Guy, 219–33. New York: New York University Press.

———. 1997b. Las mujeres como agentes dobles en la historia. *Debate Feminista* 8, no. 16 (Oct.): 251–71.

———. 1999. Oliverio Girondo: Naturaleza y artificio. In *Oliverio Girondo: Obra completa*, ed. Raúl Antelo, 404–16. Nanterre: Colección Archivos.

———. 2001. The travels of theory: Queering the North/South axis. *Estudos Feministas* (Rio de Janeiro).

Massey, Doreen. 1994. *Space, place, and gender.* Minneapolis: University of Minnesota Press.

McDowell, Robert, ed. 1991. *Poetry after modernism.* Brownsville, Ore.: Story Line Press.

Mercado, Tununa. 1989. Atravesar el espejo. *Feminaria*, no. 3 (Apr.): 21–22.

———. 1994. *La letra de lo mínimo.* Rosario-Buenos Aires: Beatriz Viterbo.

Mohanty, S. P. 1989. Us and them: On the philosophical bases of political criticism. *Yale Journal of Criticism* 2, nos. 21–31.

Monsivais, Carlos. 1986. *Amor perdido.* Mexico: SEP, Consejo Nacional de Fomento Educativo.

———. 1987. *Entrada libre: Crónicas de la sociedad que se organiza.* Mexico: Era.

Montaldo, Graciela. 1999. Intelectuales y artistas en la sociedad civil argentina en el fin de siglo. *Latin American Studies Center* (University of Maryland), Working Paper No. 4.

Montealegre, Jorge. 1998. Poesía en transición. *Posdata* 1, nos. 1–2: 18–20.

Monzón, Isabel. 1992. Una mujer en el pozo de la soledad. *Feminaria*, no. 8 (Apr.): 3–5.

Moraña, Mabel. 1997. El boom del subalterno. *Revista de Crítica Cultural*, no. 15 (Nov.): 48–53.

Moreiras, Alberto. 1993. Posdictadura y reforma del pensamiento. *Revista de Crítica Cultural*, no. 7 (Nov.): 27–35.

———. 1996. The aura of *Testimonio.* In *The real thing*, G. M. Gugelberger, 192–223. Durham, N.C.: Duke University Press.

———. 1999. The order of order: On the reluctant culturalism of anti-subalternist critiques. *Journal of Latin American Cultural Studies* 8, no. 1: 125–45.

Moreno, María (Cristina Forero). 1992. *El affair Skeffington.* Rosario-Buenos Aires: Bajo la luna nueva.

———. 1997. Editorial. *La Gandhi Argentina* 1, no. 1 (Apr.): 3.

———. 1999. Lolas y besos. LAS/12 (Nov. 12): 1–5.

Moulián, Tomás. 1997. *Chile actual: Anatomía de un mito.* Santiago de Chile: Lom-Arcis.

———. 1998. *Conversaciones con Allende.* Santiago de Chile: Lom-Arcis.

Muñoz, Gonzalo. 1981. *Exit.* Santiago: Archivos.

———. 1987. *La estrella negra.* Santiago de Chile: F. Zegers.

Nari, Marcela. 1997. En busca de un pasado: Revistas, feminismo y memoria: Una historia de las revistas feministas, 1982–1997. *Feminaria* 10, no. 20 (Oct.): 32–40.

Nealon, Jeffrey. 1998. *Alterity politics: Ethics and performance subjectivity.* Durham, N.C.: Duke University Press.

Negroni, María. 1991. *La jaula bajo el trapo.* Buenos Aires: Tierra Firme.

———. 1993. *Islandia.* Murcia, Spain: Carabelas.

———. 1994a. *Ciudad gótica.* Rosario-Buenos Aires: Bajo la luna nueva.

———. 1994b. *El viaje de la noche.* Barcelona: Lumen.

Niranjana, Tejaswini. 1992. *Siting translation: History, post-strucuralism, the colonial context.* Berkeley: University of California Press.

Novaro, Marcos. 1997. El liberalismo político y la cultura política popular. *Nueva Sociedad* 149 (May–June): 114–29.

O'Connell, Joanna. 1995. *Prospero's daughter: The prose of Rosario Castellanos.* Austin: University of Texas Press.

Olea, Raquel. 1991. El feminismo, ¿Moderno o posmoderno? *Mujeres en Acción* (Santiago de Chile) 1: 29–36.

———. 1994a. Libertad de arte y otros imaginarios. *La época* (Santiago de Chile) Aug. 19.

———. 1994b. Recitales de poesia femenina: Un escenario por construir. In *Escribir en los bordes,* ed. Carmen Berenguer et al., 229–32. Santiago de Chile: Cuarto Propio.

———. 1998. *Lengua víbora: Producciones de lo femenino en la escritura de mujeres chilenas.* Santiago de Chile: Cuarto Propio.

———. 2000. Femenino y feminismo en transición. In *Escritura de la diferencia sexual,* ed. Raquel Olea, 53–64. Santiago de Chile: Lom-La Morada.

Olea, Raquel, and Soledad Fariña, eds. [1990] 1997. *Una palabra cómplice: Encuentro con Gabriela Mistral.* 2d ed. Santiago de Chile: Isis-Cuarto Propio.

Olivera, Guillermo. 1999. Políticas de la representación homosexual en la Argentina. In *Las marcas del género,* ed. Fabricio Forastelli and Ximena Triquell, 143–58. Córdoba: Centro de Estudios Avanzados.

Orozco, Olga. 1998. *Eclipses y fulgores.* Barcelona: Lumen.

Ortiz, Renato. 1996. *Otro territorio: Ensayos sobre el mundo contemporáneo.* Buenos Aires: Universidad Nacional de Quilmes.

O'Sullivan, Charlotte. 1998. Happy Together. *Sight and Sound* 8, no. 5 (May): 49.

Oyarzún, Kemy. 1996. Estudios de género: Saberes, políticas, dominios. *Revista de Crítica Cultural,* no. 12: 24–29.

Oyarzún, Pablo. 1987–1988. Arte en Chile de veinte, treinta años. *Chile 1968–1988.* Special volume of *Georgia Series on Hispanic Thought* 22, no. 5: 291–324.

———. 1998. La cuna del Delfín: Sobre *Quadrivium* de Gonzalo Díaz. *Quadrivium* (Gallery notes). Santiago de Chile: Galería Gabriela Mistral.

Parra, Catalina. 1987. Plaquette for Terne Gallery exposition. Trans. Kevin Mathewson. New York, Terne Gallery.

Pasquini, Gabriel. 1998. El poder no tiene cara de mujer. *La Nación,* 8 Mar. 1.

Pateman, Carole. 1989. *The disorder of women.* Oxford: Polity Press.

Pauls, Alan. 1986. *Manuel Puig: La traición de Rita Hayworth.* Buenos Aires: Hachette.

Peri Rossi, Cristina. 1984. *La nave de los locos.* Barcelona: Seix Barral.

Perloff, Marjorie. 1990. *Poetic license: Essays on modern and postmodern lyric.* Evanston, Ill.: Northwestern University Press.

Perlongher, Néstor. 1991. Los devenires minoritarios. *Revista de Crítica Cultural,* no. 4: 13–18.

———. 1993 [1987]. *La prostitución masculina.* Buenos Aires: Ediciones de la Urraca.

———. 1997a. *Poemas completos.* Ed. Roberto Echavarren. Barcelona: Seix Barral.

———. 1997b. *Prosa plebeya: Ensayos 1980–1992.* Buenos Aires: Colihué.

Phillips, Anne. 1991. *Engendering democracy.* Oxford: Polity Press.

Piglia, Ricardo. 1980. *Respiración artificial.* Buenos Aires: Pomaire.

———. 1986. *Crítica y ficción.* Santa Fe, Argentina: Universidad Nacional del Litoral.

———. 1992. *La ciudad ausente.* Buenos Aires: Sudamericana.

———. 1993. *La Argentina en pedazos.* Buenos Aires: Ediciones de la Urraca.

———. 1994. Sarmiento the Writer. In *Sarmiento, author of a nation* ed. Tulio Halperín Donghi, I. Jaksic, G. Kirkpatrick, and F. Masiello, 127–44. Berkeley: University of California Press.

———. 1997. *Plata quemada*. Buenos Aires: Planeta.

Pinsky, Robert. 1988. *Poetry and the world*. New York: Ecco Press.

Podlubne, Judith. 1996. César Aira: La lógica del continuo. *Paradoxa* 10, no. 8: 59–71.

———. 1998. El pensamiento de la crítica (Beatriz Sarlo y Horacio González). *Boletín* (Rosario) 6 (Oct.).

Porter, Carolyn. 1994. What we know that we don't know: Remapping American literary studies. *American Literary History* 6, no. 3: 467–526.

Prado, Nadia. 1992. *Simples placeres*. Santiago de Chile: Cuarto Propio.

———. 1998. *Carnal*. Santiago de Chile: Cuarto Propio.

Pratt, Mary Louise. 1990. Women, literature, and national brotherhood. In Seminar on Feminism and Culture in Latin America, *Women, culture, and politics in Latin America*, 48–73. Berkeley: University of California Press.

Prior, Alberto. 1999. *Operas chinas completas* (installation with libretto).

Puig, Manuel. 1976. *El beso de la mujer araña*. Barcelona: Seix Barral.

———. 1980. *Maldición eterna a quién lea estas páginas*. Barcelona: Seix Barral.

———. 1995. El error gay. *El Porteño*. IX (Sept).

Radcliffe, Sarah, and Sallie Westwood. 1996. *Remaking the nation: Place, identity and politics in Latin America*. New York: Routledge.

Radway, Janice. 1984. *Reading the romance: Women, patriarchy, and popular literature*. Chapel Hill: University of North Carolina Press.

Rama, Angel. 1982. *La transculturación narrativa en América Latina*. Mexico: Siglo XXI.

———. 1984. *La ciudad letrada*. Hanover: Ediciones del Norte.

———. 1985. *Las máscaras democráticas del modernismo*. Montevideo: Arca-Fundación Angel Rama.

Ramos, Julio. 1996. El proceso de Alberto Mendoza: Poesía y subjetivación. *Revista de Crítica Cultural*, no. 13 (Nov.): 34–41.

———. (Forthcoming). Dispositivos del amor y la locura. *Nomadías*.

Ramos Otero, Manuel. 1979. *Cuentos de la mujer del mar*. Rio Piedras: Huracán.

Rich, Adrienne. 1976. *Of woman born*. New York: W. W. Norton.

———. 1993. *What is found there: Notebooks on poetry and politics*. New York: W. W. Norton.

Richard, Nelly. 1986. *Margins and institutions*. Melbourne: Art and Text.

———. 1989. *La estratificación de los márgenes*. Santiago de Chile: F. Zegers.

———. 1991. Latinoamérica y la posmodernidad. *Revista de Crítica Cultural*, no. 3: 15–19.

———. 1993. *Masculino/femenino*. Santiago de Chile: Francisco Zegers.

———. 1994. *La insubordinación de los signos*. Santiago de Chile: Cuarto Propio.

———. 1996. Chile, women, and dissidence. In *Beyond the fantastic: Contemporary art criticism from Latin America*, ed. Gerardo Mosquera. Cambridge, Mass: MIT Press.

———. 1998. *Residuos y metáforas (ensayo de crítica cultural sobre el Chile de la transición)*. Santiago de Chile: Cuarto Propio.

———. 1999. Reescrituras, sobreimpresiones: Las protestas de mujeres en la calle. *Revista de Crítica Cultural*, no. 18: 16–20.

Richard, Nelly et al. 1994. El "caso" Simón Bolívar. *Revista de Crítica Cultural*, no. 9 (Nov.): 5–36.

Rinesi, Eduardo. 1993. *Seducidos y abandonados: Carisma y traición en la 'transición democrática' argentina*. Buenos Aires: Manuel Suarez.

———. 1994a. *Buenos Aires salvaje.* Buenos Aires: America Libre.

———. 1994b. *Ciudades, teatros, balcones: Un ensayo sobre la representación política.* Buenos Aires: Paradiso.

Roffé, Mercedes. 1983. *El tapiz, de Ferdinand de Oziel.* Buenos Aires: Tierra Baldía.

———. 1987. *Cámara baja.* Buenos Aires: Ultimo Reino.

———. 1996. *La noche y las palabras.* Rosario-Buenos Aires: Bajo la luna nueva.

Romero, Julia. (forthcoming.) Manuel Puig: Del delito de la escritura al error gay. *Revista Iberoamericana.*

Rosa, Nicolás. 1996. Una ortofonía abyecta. In *Lúmpenes peregrinaciones: Ensayos sobre Néstor Perlongher,* eds Adrián Cangi and Paula Siganevich, 29–43. Rosario-Buenos Aires: Beatriz Viterbo.

Rosenberg, Mirta. 1988. *Madam.* Buenos Aires: Tierra Firme.

———. 1994. *Teoría sentimental.* Buenos Aires: Tierra Firme.

———. 1998. *El arte de perder.* Rosario-Buenos Aires: Bajo la luna nueva.

Rowe, William, and Vivian Schelling. 1991. *Memory and modernity: Popular culture in Latin America.* London: Verso.

———. 1992. War and cultural studies: Reflections on recent work in Peru and Argentina. *Travesía* 1, no. 1: 18–37.

Ruíz, Raúl. 1995. *Poetics of cinema I.* Trans. Brian Holmes. Paris: Dis Voir.

Said, Edward. 1983. *The world, the text, and the critic.* Cambridge: Harvard University Press.

Safranchick, Graciela. 1993. *Kadish.* Rosario-Buenos Aires: Bajo la luna nueva.

———. 1995. *El cangrejo.* Rosario–Buenos Aires: Bajo la luna nueva.

Salessi, Jorge. 1995a. "Carlos: Devolvéme mis fotos, Esteban" (simulación y travestismo). *Revista de Crítica Cultural,* no. 10: 36–43.

———. 1995b. *Médicos, maleantes, maricas.* Rosario–Buenos Aires: Beatriz Viterbo.

Samuels, Shirley. 1992. *The culture of sentiment: Race, gender, and sentimentality in nineteeth-century America.* New York: Oxford.

Santa Cruz, Guadalupe. 1992. *Cita capital.* Santiago de Chile: Cuarto Propio.

———. 1997a. *El contagio.* Santiago de Chile: Cuarto Propio.

———, ed. 1997b. *Veredas por cruzar.* Santiago de Chile: Instituto de la mujer.

Santiago, Silviano. 1975. O Entre-Lugar do discurso latino-americano. In *Uma literatura nos trópicos,* 11–28. Rio de Janeiro: Editora Perspectiva.

———. 1985. *Stella Manhattan: Romance.* Rio de Janeiro: Nova Fronteira.

———. 1993. Reading and discursive intensities: On the situation of postmodern reception in Brazil. *The Postmodernism Debate in Latin America: Boundary 2* 20, no. 3 (fall): 194–202.

Santilli, Lelé. 1998. La poesía en el mundo. Unpublished lecture, University of California at Berkeley.

Sarduy, Severo. 1967. *De dónde son los cantantes.* Mexico: Joaquin Mortiz.

Sarlo, Beatriz. 1990. Basuras culturales, simulacros políticos. *Punto de Vista* 37 (July).

———. 1992. *La imaginación técnica: Sueños modernos de la cultura argentina.* Buenos Aires: Nueva Visión.

———. 1993. ¿Arcaicos o marginales? Situación de los intelectuales en el fin de siglo. *Punto de Vista,* no. 47 (Dec.): 1–5.

———. 1994. *Escenas de la vida posmoderna: Intelectuales, arte y videocultura en la Argentina.* Buenos Aires: Ariel.

———. 1997. Los estudios culturales y la crítica literaria en la encrucijada valorativa. *Revista de Crítica Cultural,* no. 15 (Nov.): 32–38.

———. 1998. *La máquina cultural: Maestras, traductores y vanguardistas.* Buenos Aires: Ariel.

Sarlo, Beatriz et al. 1998. Debate sobre política e ideas. *Punto de Vista*, no. 61 (Aug.): 18–30.

Schaffauer, Markus Klaus. 1998. La "farmacia" del diálogo criollo: La innovación de un género a través de la oralidad. *Cuadernos de Recienvenido* (Universidade de Sao Paulo), 9.

Schifis, Ana Lía. 1994. Editorial. *El Desierto* 1, no. 1.

Schild, Verónica. 1998. New subjects of rights? Women's movements and the construction of citizenship in the new democracies. In *Culture of politics*, ed. Sonia Alvarez et al., 93–117. Boulder, Col.: Westview Press.

Schwarz, Roberto. 1992. Brazilian culture: Nationalism by elimination. In *Misplaced Ideas*, 1–18. London: Verso.

Sennett, Richard. 1990. *The conscience of the eye: The design and social life of cities.* New York: Alfred A. Knopf.

Sheper-Hughes, Nancy. 1992. *Death without weeping.* Berkeley: University of California Press.

Shúa, Ana María. 1992. *Casa de geishas.* Buenos Aires: Sudamericana.

Sifrim, Mónica. 1999. *Laguna.* Rosario: Bajo la luna nueva.

Siganevich, Paula. 1998. Brasileridad, traducción y género en la escritura de Manuel Puig. In *Encuentro internacional Manuel Puig*, J. Amícola and G. Speranza, 237–42.

Spivak, Gayatri. 1998. Responsibility. In *Gendered agents: Women and institutional knowledge*, ed. Silvestra Mariniello and Paul A. Bové, 19–66. Durham, N.C.: Duke University Press.

Stahl, Anna Kazumi. 1997. *Catástrofes naturales.* Buenos Aires: Sudamericana.

Stallybrass, Peter, and Allon White. 1986. *The politics and poetics of transgression.* Ithaca, N.Y.: Cornell University Press.

Stephen, Lynn, ed. 1994. *María Teresa Tula: Hear my testimony.* Boston: South End Press.

Subercaseaux, Benjamín. [1943] 1989. *Chile o una loca geografía.* Santiago: Editorial Universitaria.

———. 1991. *Historia, literatura, sociedad: Ensayos de hermeneútica cultural.* Santiago de Chile: CESOC/CENECA.

Taylor, Diana. 1997. *Disappearing acts: Spectacles of gender and nationalism in Argentina's 'dirty war.'* Durham, N.C.: Duke University Press.

Thénon, Susana. 1987. *Ova completa.* Buenos Aires: Sudamericana.

Tierney-Tello, Mary Beth. 1999. Testimony, ethics, and the aesthetic in Diamela Eltit. *PMLA*, 114, no. 1 (Jan.): 78–96.

Trevisán, Liliana. 1997. *Política/sexualidad: Nudo en la escritura de mujeres latinoamericanas.* Lantham, Md.: University Press of America.

Urriola, Malú. 1988. *Piedras rodantes.* Santiago de Chile: Cuarto Propio.

———. 1998. *Hija de perra.* Santiago de Chile: Cuarto Propio.

Valenzuela, Luisa. 1990. *Novela negra con argentinos.* Buenos Aires: Sudamericana.

Velásquez Yebra, Patricia. 1996. César Aira: Soy un escritor circunstancial. *El Universal* (Mexico). Nov. 30.

Verbitsky, Horacio. 1995. *El vuelo.* Buenos Aires: Planeta.

Vezzetti, Hugo. 1998. Activismos de la memoria: El "escrache." *Punto de Vista*, 62 (Dec.): 1–7.

Vicuña, Cecilia. 1983. *Precario/precarious.* Trans. Anne Twitty. New York: Tanam Press.

———. 1990. *La wik'uña.* Santiago de Chile: Francisco Zegers.

———. 1992. *Unravelling words and the weaving of water.* Trans. Eliot Weinberger and Suzanne Jill Levine. St. Paul, Minn.: Greywolf.

———. 1997. Quipoem. In *The precarious: The art and poetry of Cecilia Vicuña*, ed. M. Catherine de Zegher. Hanover, N.H.: Wesleyan University Press.

Villalba, Susana. 1997. *Matar un animal.* Rosario-Buenos Aires: Bajo la luna nueva.

Villegas, Juan. 1985. *Antología de la nueva poesía femenina chilena.* Santiago de Chile: La Noria.

———. 1993. *El discurso lírico de la mujer en Chile: 1975–1990.* Santiago de Chile: Mosquito.

Viñas, David. 1982. *Indios, ejército y fronteras.* México: Siglo XXI.

———. 1995. *Claudia conversa.* Buenos Aires: Planeta.

Wainfeld, Mario. 1993. *Los que quedaron afuera.* Buenos Aires: Ediciones Unidos.

Walker, Jayne, and David Reid. 1993. Cornell Woolrich and the abandoned city. In *Shades of noir*, ed. Joan Copec, 57–96. London: Verso.

Yúdice, George. 1994. Estudios culturales y sociedad civil. *Revista de Crítica Cultural*, no. 8 (May): 44–53.

———. 1996. *Testimonio* and postmodernism. In *The real thing*, ed. G. M. Gugelberger, 42–57. Durham, N.C.: Duke University Press.

Zaidman, Samuel. 1999. La interrogación. In *Letrados iletrados*, ed. Ana Maria Zubieta, 17–26. Buenos Aires: EUDEBA.

Žižek, Slavoj. 1992. *The sublime object of ideology.* London: Verso.

Zurita, Raúl. 1979. *Purgatorio.* Santiago de Chile: Editorial Universitaria.

———. 1983. *Literatura, lenguaje y sociedad (1973–1983).* Santiago de Chile: CENECA.

———. 1994. *La vida nueva.* Santiago de Chile: Editorial Universitaria.

Unsigned. 1996. *Ajuste estructural: Debate y propuestas*, 2. Lima: Ediciones Mujer y Ajuste.

Unsigned. 1997. Mujer y violencia, problema social. *Clarín*, 30 Oct.

Unsigned. 1998. El crimen de María Soledad. *Clarín*, 28 Feb.

Unsigned. 1998. La justicia cuestionada. *Clarín*, 2 Mar.

INDEX

Francine Masiello is Professor of Spanish and Comparative Literature at the University of California, Berkeley. She is the author of *Between Civilization and Barbarism: Women, Nation, and Literary Culture in Modern Argentina* (Nebraska, 1992) and *Lenguaje e ideología: Las escuelas argentinas de vanguardia* (Hachette, 1986). She is the editor of *La mujer y el espacio público: El periodismo femenino en la Argentina del siglo* XIX (1994) and coeditor of several works.

Library of Congress Cataloging-in-Publication Data
Masiello, Francine.
The art of transition : Latin American culture and neoliberal crisis / Francine Masiello.
p. cm.—(Latin America otherwise)
Includes bibliographical references and index.
ISBN 0-8223-2806-2 (cloth : alk. paper)
ISBN 0-8223-2818-6 (pbk. : alk. paper)
I. Spanish American literature—Southern Cone of South America—History and criticism. 2. Spanish American literature—20th century—History and criticism. 3. Literature and society—Southern Cone of South America. 4. Art—Political aspects—Southern Cone of South America. 5. Southern Cone of South America—Intellectual life. I. Title. II. Series.
PQ7551 .M37 2001 860.9'98—dc21 2001040217